Dine Like a Dragon:

The Complete Chinese Cookbook

Master Chinese Cooking with 999 Legendary Recipes

Ziyi Cheng

Comprehensive Table With Recipe Names On Next Page

MAIN TABLE OF CONTENTS

INTRODUCTION

Chinese food requires no introduction. It is some of the most popular and commonly available food, regardless of where you live. Chinese food is diverse, and tastes absolutely amazing. All you need is fire and a stove to cook most of the recipes, and they don't take much time either. Delicious, easy, and quick- Chinese food is a must-have in the arsenal of any cook.

Although any stovetop will get the job done in a pinch, if you're really serious about cooking Chinese dishes the Chinese way, you should go get a "wok". If you want to try out the recipes in this book before you invest in a wok, that is fine too.

KNOW YOUR MEASUREMENTS

American cooks use standard containers, the 8-ounce cup and a tablespoon that takes exactly 16 level fillings to fill that cup level. Measuring by cup makes it very difficult to give weight equivalents, as the density plays an important role when it comes to weight. The easiest way therefore to deal with cup measurements in recipes is to take the amount by volume rather than by weight. Thus, the equation reads:

1 cup = 240ml = 8 fluid Ounces

½ cup = 120ml = 4 fluid ounces

It is possible to buy a set of American cup measures in major stores around the world.

In the States, butter is sometimes measured in sticks. One stick is the equivalent of 8 tablespoons. One tablespoon of butter is therefore the equivalent to ½ ounce/15 grams.

Liquid Measures

1 Teaspoon= 5 Millilitres

1 Tablespoon = 14 millilitres

2 Tablespoons= 1 Fluid Ounce

Solid Measures

1 Ounce= 28 Grams

16 Ounces= 1 Pound

GENERAL GUIDELINES

- Approximation is fine. Feel free to increase or decrease the amount of ingredients to suit your taste. It helps to have measuring equipment in the kitchen.
- Quite a few recipes in this book call for eggs. The eggs used are size 3 unless mentioned otherwise. Size 3 eggs are the most common medium sized eggs available.
- It is usually a good idea to clean all the fresh ingredients before using them in recipes.
- Even if it is not mentioned in the recipe, onions used are always peeled, and carrots are washed and then scrubbed or peeled.
- It is usually a good idea to taste the food during the cook to reach your desired amount of seasoning. Therefore, it is usually a good idea to use less seasoning at the start of the cook. More seasoning can always be added later, but it is impossible to extract, so keep that in mind.
- Freshly ground pepper if best. If you wish to use pepper readily available in the market, use Szechuan peppercorns. If you don't have anything on hand, conventional black pepper will do in a pinch.
- Chinese recipes commonly call for herbs. Both fresh and dried herbs will get the job done, but it goes without saying that fresh herbs are always better if you can get your hands on them. However when it comes to garnishing, fresh herbs are your only option.
- Experimentation is good. Think of the recipes in this book as a bland canvas. Once you get a hang of these Chinese recipes, feel free to play around, and add ingredients that you personally like.
- There are quite a few fried recipes in this book. Oils that can he heated to high temperatures are best for this purpose. I personally like groundnut oil, but any other oil will do too, as long as it can withstand high temperatures.
- If you really want to get the Chinese feel while cooking these Chinese recipes, you might want to invest into a large cleaver to do all the chopping, slicing, and cutting. If you do not with to invest, any sharp old knife will do the job.
- A wok really will make cooking easier when it comes to Chinese recipes, as it can be used to cook food quickly at high temperature, and can also be used for streaming and braising. If you do not with to invest in one at the moment, feel free to improvise with what you have on hand.

ONWARD, TO THE RECIPES!

I'm going to keep the introduction section of this book short, as Chinese cooking is quite easy and I don't really have any tips and tricks for you. Practice really is the best thing you can do for your Chinese cooking skills. So, without much ado, lets jump straight into the recipes!

MARINADES AND CONDIMENTS

A significant share of all Chinese recipes are cooked quickly over high heat. It is usually a good idea to marinate the ingredients of such recipes before throwing them into the frying pan, as doing so can add delicious flavours to the final recipe.

While a lot of the recipes in this book recommend a marinade in the recipe itself, feel free to play around and experiment with different marinades and condiments. You'll find some of the most common Chinese marinade and condiment recipes below.

BARBECUE MARINADE

Yield: 375 ml/13 fl oz/½ cup

Ingredients:

- 1 slice ginger root, minced
- 15 ml/1 tbsp brown sugar
- 15 ml/1 tbsp rice wine or dry sherry
- 2 cloves garlic, crushed
- 250 ml/8 fl oz/1 cup soy sauce

Directions:

1. Combine all the ingredients and pour over spare ribs.
2. Allow to stand for one hour, basting intermittently, then eliminate the excess liquid and cook.
3. Baste with the marinade while cooking or use as the base for a sauce.

CANTONESE SALT

Yield: about 75 ml/5 tbsp

Ingredients:

- 10 ml/2 tsp Szechuan peppercorns
- 60 ml/4 tbsp salt

Directions:

1. Heat the salt and peppercorns using a dry pan over a low heat, shaking constantly, for approximately five minutes until slightly browned.
2. Crush the peppercorns then store the mixture in a screw-top jar.
3. Serve with fried or roasted foods.

CHICKEN STOCK MARINADE

Yield: 350 ml/13 fl oz/1½ cups

Ingredients:

- 1 slice ginger root, minced
- 15 ml/1 tbsp brown sugar
- 250 ml/8 fl oz/1 cup chicken stock
- 3 cloves garlic, crushed
- 30 ml/2 tbsp rice wine or dry sherry
- 60 ml/4 tbsp soy sauce

Directions:

1. Combine all the ingredients and pour over spare ribs.
2. Allow to stand for one hour, basting intermittently, then eliminate the excess liquid and cook.
3. Baste with the marinade while cooking, or use as the base for a sauce.

CHILLI OIL

Yield: about 250 ml/8 fl oz/1 cup

Ingredients:

- 250 ml/8 fl oz/1 cup groundnut (peanut) oil
- 4 fresh red chilli peppers

Directions:

1. Heat the oil and chilli peppers over low heat until the oil becomes dark.
2. Strain and store ready for use.

3. Feel free to alter the strength of the oil according to your taste by adding more or fewer chilli peppers.

CINNAMON SPICE

Yield: about 75 ml/5 tbsp

Ingredients:

- 15 ml/1 tbsp ground ginger
- 2½ ml/½ tsp freshly ground pepper
- 30 ml/2 tbsp ground cinnamon

Directions:

1. Heat all the ingredients using a dry pan over a low heat, shaking constantly, for a few minutes until the mixture is hot.
2. Store in a screw-top jar and serve with chicken dishes.

FIVE-SPICE MARINADE

Yield: 120 ml/4 fl oz/½ cup

Ingredients:

- 2 cloves garlic, crushed
- 30 ml/2 tbsp groundnut (peanut) oil
- 5 ml/1 tsp five-spice powder
- 5 ml/1 tsp salt
- 5 ml/1 tsp sugar
- 60 ml/4 tbsp soy sauce
- freshly ground pepper

Directions:

1. Combine the ingredients and rub the mixture over chicken, inside and out.
2. Allow to stand for one hour, basting intermittently, then eliminate the excess liquid and cook.
3. Baste with the marinade while cooking.

FIVE-SPICE MARINADE FOR PORK

Yield: 60 ml/4 tbsp

Ingredients:

- 15 ml/1 tbsp rice wine or dry sherry
- 2½ ml/½ tsp five-spice powder
- 2½ ml/½ tsp salt
- 30 ml/2 tbsp soy sauce
- 5 ml/1 tsp sugar
- pinch of freshly ground pepper

Directions:

1. Combine the sugar, five-spice powder, salt and pepper and rub the mixture over pork strips.
2. Allow to stand for 2 hours.
3. Put in the soy sauce and wine or sherry and allow to stand for another 30 minutes.

FIVE-SPICE MIX

Yield: about 75 ml/5 tbsp

Ingredients:

- 5 ml/1 tsp cinnamon
- 5 ml/1 tsp five-spice powder
- 5 ml/1 tsp sugar
- 60 ml/4 tbsp salt

Directions:

1. Heat the salt using a dry pan over a low heat, shaking constantly, for approximately five minutes until slightly browned.
2. Add the rest of the ingredients then store the mixture in a screw-top jar.
3. Serve with chicken dishes.

GARLIC MARINADE

Yield: 250 ml/8 fl oz/1 cup

Ingredients:

- 120 ml/4 fl oz/½ cup soy sauce
- 2 slices ginger root, minced
- 2 spring onions (scallions), chopped
- 2½ ml/½ tsp sesame oil
- 3 cloves garlic, crushed
- 45 ml/3 tbsp sugar

Directions:

1. Combine all the ingredients and rub over pork strips.
2. Allow to marinate for 2 hours, then eliminate the excess liquid and cook.

HOISIN AND CHILLI MARINADE

Yield: 120 ml/4 fl oz/½ cup

Ingredients:

- 1 spring onion (scallion), finely chopped
- 15 ml/1 tbsp hoisin sauce
- 15 ml/1 tbsp honey
- 2 cloves garlic, crushed
- 2½ cm/1 in garlic root, minced
- 2½ ml/½ tsp salt
- 30 ml/2 tbsp soy sauce
- 5 ml/1 tsp chilli sauce
- 60 ml/4 tbsp rice wine or dry sherry

Directions:

1. Combine all the ingredients and rub over pork.
2. Allow to stand for 2 hours, then eliminate the excess liquid and cook.

3. Baste with the marinade while cooking.

HOISIN AND SHERRY MARINADE

Yield: 120 ml/4 fl oz/½ cup

- 2½ ml/½ tsp five-spice powder
- 30 ml/2 tbsp brown sugar
- 30 ml/2 tbsp rice wine or dry sherry
- 45 ml/3 tbsp soy sauce
- 75 ml/5 tbsp hoisin sauce

Directions:

1. Combine all the ingredients together and rub over spare ribs.
2. Allow to stand for 2 hours, basting intermittently, then eliminate the excess liquid and cook.
3. Baste with the marinade while cooking.

HOISIN SAUCE MARINADE

Yield: 250 ml/8 fl oz/1 cup

Ingredients:

- 120 ml/4 fl oz/½ cup hoisin sauce
- 120 ml/4 fl oz/½ cup water

Directions:

1. Combine the hoisin sauce and water and brush over chicken.
2. Allow to stand for 2 hours, basting intermittently, then eliminate the excess liquid and cook.
3. Baste with the marinade while cooking.

HONEY MARINADE

Yield: 120 ml/4 fl oz/½ cup

Ingredients:

- 15 ml/1 tbsp brown sugar
- 2 cloves garlic, crushed
- 30 ml/2 tbsp honey
- 30 ml/2 tbsp rice wine or dry sherry
- 5 ml/1 tsp salt
- 60 ml/4 tbsp soy sauce

Directions:

1. Rub strips of pork with salt and allow to stand for 2 hours.
2. Mix the rest of the ingredients and pour over the pork.
3. Allow to stand for one hour, basting often, then eliminate the excess liquid and cook.

ORANGE MARINADE

Yield: 450 ml/¾ pt/2 cups

Ingredients:

- 1 clove garlic, crushed
- 1 strip orange peel
- 120 ml/4 fl oz/½ cup soy sauce
- 15 ml/1 tbsp sugar
- 2½ ml/½ tsp sesame oil
- 375 ml/13 fl oz/1½ cups chicken stock
- 5 ml/1 tsp salt
- freshly ground pepper

Directions:

1. Soak the orange peel in warm water until slightly softened then mince and mix with the garlic.
2. Bring the stock almost to the boil, then blend in the rest of the ingredients.
3. Pour over chicken and allow to stand for 2 hours, basting intermittently, then eliminate the excess liquid and cook.
4. Baste with the marinade while cooking.

PINEAPPLE MARINADE

Yield: 400 ml/14 fl oz/¾ cup

Ingredients:

- 1 clove garlic, crushed
- 120 ml/4 fl oz/½ cup pineapple juice
- 250 ml/8 fl oz/1 cup soy sauce
- 30 ml/2 tbsp brown sugar
- 60 ml/4 tbsp rice wine or dry sherry

Directions:

1. Combine all the ingredients and pour over spare ribs.
2. Allow to stand for one hour, basting intermittently, then eliminate the excess liquid and cook.
3. Baste with the marinade while cooking, or use as the base for a sauce.

RICE WINE MARINADE

Yield: 250 ml/8 fl oz/1 cup

Ingredients:

- 1 slice ginger root, minced
- 10 ml/2 tsp honey
- 120 ml/4 fl oz/½ cup
- 2 spring onions (scallions), chopped
- 2½ ml/½ tsp salt
- 30 ml/2 tbsp brown sugar
- 30 ml/2 tbsp chicken stock
- 60 ml/4 tbsp rice wine or dry sherry
- pinch of freshly ground pepper

Directions:

1. Combine all the ingredients and pour over pork.

2. Allow to marinate for 2 hours, then eliminate the excess liquid and cook.
3. Baste with the marinade while cooking, or use as the base for a sauce.

SOY AND GINGER MARINADE

Yield: 120 ml/4 fl oz/½ cup

Ingredients:

- 1 slice ginger root, minced
- 15 ml/1 tbsp brown sugar
- 2 cloves garlic, crushed
- 5 ml/1 tsp salt
- 60 ml/4 tbsp soy sauce
- pinch of freshly ground pepper

Directions:

1. Combine all the ingredients together and rub over spare ribs.
2. Allow to stand for one hour, basting intermittently, then eliminate the excess liquid and cook.
3. Baste with the marinade while cooking.

SOY AND WINE MARINADE

Yield: 250 ml/8 fl oz/1 cup

Ingredients:

- 1 spring onion (scallion), chopped
- 120 ml/4 fl oz/½ cup soy sauce
- 15 ml/1 tbsp honey
- 15 ml/1 tbsp sugar
- 2 cloves garlic, crushed
- 5 ml/1 tsp salt
- 60 ml/4 tbsp rice wine or dry sherry

Directions:

1. Combine the salt and sugar and rub over pork strips.
2. Allow to stand for half an hour.
3. Mix the rest of the ingredients and pour over the pork.
4. Allow to stand for one hour, then eliminate the excess liquid and cook.

SOY SAUCE MARINADE

Yield: 250 ml/8 fl oz/1 cup

Ingredients:

- 120 ml/4 fl oz/½ cup water
- 30 ml/2 tbsp sugar
- 5 ml/1 tsp salt
- 60 ml/4 tbsp soy sauce

Directions:

1. Heat the water then blend in the rest of the ingredients and pour over pork strips.
2. Allow to stand for 2 hours, basting often, then eliminate the excess liquid and cook.

SPICY MARINADE

Yield: 60 ml/4 tbsp

Ingredients:

- 1 clove garlic, crushed
- 15 ml/1 tbsp rice wine or dry sherry
- 2½ ml/½ tsp cinnamon
- 30 ml/2 tbsp soy sauce
- 5 ml/1 tsp salt
- 5 ml/1 tsp sugar
- pinch of freshly ground pepper
- pinch of ground cloves

Directions:

1. Combine all the ingredients and rub over pork strips.

2. Allow to stand for approximately an hour and a half, then grill or fry as directed in the recipe.

SPRING ONION MARINADE

Yield: 375 ml/13 fl oz/1½ cups

Ingredients:

- 1 slice ginger root, minced
- 15 ml/1 tbsp honey
- 2 cloves garlic, minced
- 250 ml/8 fl oz/1 cup soy sauce
- 30 ml/2 tbsp rice wine or dry sherry
- 4 spring onions (scallions), chopped
- 5 ml/1 tsp salt

Directions:

1. Combine all the ingredients, blending well.
2. Rub the marinade over chicken, inside and out, and allow to stand for one hour, basting intermittently, then eliminate the excess liquid and cook.
3. Baste with the marinade while cooking.

SUGAR MARINADE

Yield: 120 ml/4 fl oz/½ cup

Ingredients:

- 1 slice ginger root, minced
- 2½ ml/½ tsp five-spice powder
- 45 ml/3 tbsp soy sauce
- 5 ml/1 tsp rice wine or dry sherry
- 60 ml/4 tbsp brown sugar

Directions:

1. Combine all the ingredients together and rub over spare ribs.

2. Allow to stand for one hour, basting intermittently, then eliminate the excess liquid and cook.
3. Baste with the marinade while cooking.

APPETISERS

Chinese appetizers are scrumptious, and light. They are perfect to tickle the appetite before the main course. Feel free to adjust the quantities of ingredients used depending on how many people you are cooking for.

BAKED HAM TURNOVERS

Yield: 4 Servings

Ingredients:

- 100 g/4 oz bamboo shoots, chopped
- 120 ml/4 fl oz/ ½ cup water
- 15 ml/1 tbsp soy sauce
- 175 g/6 oz cup butter
- 2 spring onions (scallions), chopped
- 225 g/8 oz ham, chopped
- 30 ml/2 tbsp sesame seeds
- 350 g/12 oz/3 cups plain (all-purpose) flour

Directions:

1. Put the flour into a container and rub in the butter.
2. Mix in the water to form a dough. Roll out the dough and chop into 5 cm/2 in circles.
3. Combine all the rest of the ingredients except the sesame seeds and place a spoonful on each circle.
4. Brush the edges of the pastry with water and seal together.
5. Brush the outsides with water and drizzle with sesame seeds. Bake in a preheated oven at 180 degree Celsius or gas mark 4 for half an hour.

BRAISED BAMBOO SHOOTS

Yield: 4 Servings

Ingredients:

- 15 ml/1 tbsp soy sauce
- 225 g/8 oz bamboo shoots, chopped into strips

- 5 ml/1 tsp rice wine or dry sherry
- 5 ml/1 tsp sugar
- 60 ml/4 tbsp chicken stock
- 60 ml/4 tbsp groundnut (peanut) oil

Directions:

1. Heat the oil and stir-fry the bamboo shoots for approximately three minutes.
2. Combine the stock, soy sauce, sugar and wine or sherry and put it into the pan.
3. Cover and simmer for approximately 20 minutes.
4. Allow it to cool and chill and serve.

BUTTERFLY PRAWNS

Yield: 4 Servings

Ingredients:

- 15 ml/1 tbsp plain (all-purpose) flour
- 15 ml/1 tbsp soy sauce
- 2 eggs, beaten
- 2½ ml/ ½ tsp salt
- 30 ml/2 tbsp cornflour (cornstarch)
- 450 g/1 lb large peeled prawns
- 5 ml/1 tsp minced ginger root
- 5 ml/1 tsp rice wine or dry sherry
- oil for deep-frying

Directions:

1. Slice the prawns halfway through the back and spread them out to form a butterfly shape.
2. Combine the soy sauce, wine or sherry, ginger and salt. Pour over the prawns and allow to marinate for half an hour.
3. Take out of the marinade and pat dry.
4. Beat the egg with the cornflour and flour to a batter and immerse the prawns in the batter.
5. Heat the oil and deep-fry the prawns until a golden-brown colour is achieved. Drain thoroughly and serve.

CHICKEN AND BANANA FRIES

Yield: 4 Servings

Ingredients:

- 120 ml/4 fl oz/ ½ cup milk
- 2 cooked chicken breasts
- 2 firm bananas
- 225 g/8 oz/4 cups fresh breadcrumbs
- 4 eggs
- 50 g/2 oz/ ½ cup plain (all-purpose) flour
- 6 slices bread
- oil for deep-frying

Directions:

1. Chop the chicken into 24 pieces. Peel the bananas and chop lengthways into quarters.
2. Cut each quarter into thirds to give 24 pieces. Chop the crusts off the bread and chop it into quarters.
3. Beat the eggs and milk and brush over one side of the bread.
4. Put one piece of chicken and one piece of banana on the egg-coated side of each piece of bread.
5. Coat the squares slightly in flour then immerse in egg and coat with breadcrumbs.
6. Immerse again into the egg and breadcrumbs.
7. Heat the oil and fry a few squares at a time until a golden-brown colour is achieved.
8. Drain using kitchen paper and serve.

CHICKEN AND HAM

Yield: 4 Servings

Ingredients:

- 1 clove garlic, crushed
- 15 ml/1 tbsp brown sugar
- 15 ml/1 tbsp rice wine or dry sherry
- 225 g/8 oz chicken, very thinly sliced

- 225 g/8 oz cooked ham, cubed
- 30 ml/2 tbsp honey
- 5 ml/1 tsp minced ginger root
- 75 ml/5 tbsp soy sauce

Directions:

1. Put the chicken into a container with 45 ml/3 tbsp of soy sauce, the wine or sherry, sugar, ginger and garlic.
2. Allow to marinate for approximately three hours.
3. Thread the chicken and ham on to kebab skewers.
4. Mix the rest of the soy sauce with the honey and brush over the kebabs. Grill (broil) using a hot grill for approximately ten minutes, turning often and brushing with the glaze as they cook.

CHICKEN SESAME

Yield: 4 Servings

Ingredients:

- ½ head lettuce, shredded
- 120 ml/4 fl oz/ ½ cup water
- 15 ml/1 tbsp sesame seeds
- 2½ ml/ ½ tsp salt
- 350 g/12 oz cooked chicken
- 45 ml/3 tbsp chopped fresh coriander
- 5 ml/1 tsp mustard powder
- 5 spring onions (scallions), chopped
- pinch of sugar

Directions:

1. Thoroughly shred the chicken until you obtain fine shreds.
2. Pour just enough water into the mustard to make a smooth paste and mix it into the chicken.
3. Heat the sesame seeds using a dry pan until slightly golden then put them into the chicken and drizzle with salt and sugar.
4. Put in half the parsley and the spring onions and toss comprehensively.

5. Put the lettuce on a serving plate, put the chicken mixture on top and garnish with the rest of the parsley.

CHICKEN WITH BACON

Yield: 4 Servings

Ingredients:

- 1 clove garlic, crushed
- 100 g/4 oz water chestnuts, very thinly sliced
- 15 ml/1 tbsp brown sugar
- 15 ml/1 tbsp rice wine or dry sherry
- 225 g/8 oz chicken, very thinly sliced
- 225 g/8 oz lean bacon, cubed
- 30 ml/2 tbsp honey
- 5 ml/1 tsp minced ginger root
- 5 ml/1 tsp salt
- 75 ml/5 tbsp soy sauce

Directions:

1. Put the chicken into a container. Mix 45 ml/3 tbsp of soy sauce with the wine or sherry, garlic, sugar, salt and ginger, pour over the chicken and marinate for approximately three hours.
2. Thread the chicken, bacon and chestnuts on to kebab skewers.
3. Mix the rest of the soy sauce with the honey and brush over the kebabs.
4. Grill (broil) using a hot grill for approximately ten minutes until cooked, turning often and brushing with more glaze as they cook.

CHICKEN WITH CUCUMBER

Yield: 4 Servings

Ingredients:

- 1 cucumber, peeled and seeded
- 2.5 ml/ ½ tsp salt

- 225 g/8 oz cooked chicken, torn into shreds
- 30 ml/2 tbsp wine vinegar
- 5 ml/1 tsp mustard powder

Directions:

1. Chop the cucumber into strips and lay out on a flat serving plate. Put the chicken on top.
2. Combine the mustard, salt and wine vinegar and spoon over the chicken immediately before serving.

CHICKEN WITH GINGER AND MUSHROOMS

Yield: 4 Servings

Ingredients:

- 1 clove garlic, sliced
- 1 slice ginger root, chopped
- 100 g/4 oz mushrooms, quartered
- 120 ml/4 fl oz/ ½ cup groundnut (peanut) oil
- 15 ml/1 tbsp plain (all-purpose) flour
- 15 ml/1 tbsp rice flour
- 2½ ml/ ½ tsp turmeric
- 225 g/8 oz chicken breast fillets
- 25 g/1 oz cup cashew nuts
- 4 crisp lettuce leaves
- 4 shallots, halved
- 5 ml/1 tsp five-spice powder
- 5 ml/1 tsp honey
- 5 ml/1 tsp soy sauce
- 6 yellow chilli peppers, halved
- 75 ml/5 tbsp rice wine or dry sherry
- juice of ½ lime
- salt and pepper

Directions:

1. Chop the chicken breast diagonally across the grain into fine strips. Drizzle with five-spice powder and coat slightly with flour.

2. Heat 15 ml/1 tbsp oil and stir-fry the chicken until a golden-brown colour is achieved. Take out of the pan.
3. Heat some more oil and stir-fry the shallots, garlic, ginger and cashew nuts for approximately one minute.
4. Put in the honey and mix by stirring until the vegetables are coated.
5. Drizzle with flour then mix in the wine or sherry.
6. Put in the mushrooms, turmeric and chilli peppers and cook for approximately one minute. Put in the chicken, soy sauce, half the lime juice, salt and pepper and heat through.
7. Take out of the pan and keep warm. Heat some more oil, add the lettuce leaves and fry quickly, sprinkling with salt and pepper and the rest of the lime juice.
8. Put the lettuce leaves on a heated serving dish, spread the meat and vegetables on top and serve.

CHINESE PRAWNS

Yield: 4 Servings

Ingredients:

- 15 ml/1 tbsp brown sugar
- 15 ml/1 tbsp rice wine or dry sherry
- 15 ml/1 tbsp soy sauce
- 30 ml/2 tbsp Worcestershire sauce
- 450 g/1 lb unpeeled prawns

Directions:

1. Put the prawns into a container.
2. Combine the rest of the ingredients, pour over the prawns and allow to marinate for half an hour.
3. Move to a baking tin and bake in a preheated oven at 150 degrees C or gas mark 2 for 25 minutes.
4. Serve hot or cold in the shells.

COLD TOFU

Yield: 4 Servings

Ingredients:

- 45 ml/3 tbsp groundnut (peanut) oil
- 45 ml/3 tbsp soy sauce
- 450 g/1 lb tofu, sliced
- freshly ground pepper

Directions:

1. Put the tofu, a few slices at a time, in a sieve and immerse into boiling water for approximately forty seconds then eliminate the excess liquid and lay out on a serving plate.
2. Allow it to cool. Combine the soy sauce and oil, drizzle over the tofu and serve sprinkled with pepper.

CRAB BALLS WITH WATER CHESTNUTS

Yield: 4 Servings

Ingredients:

- 1 clove garlic, crushed
- 1 cm/ ½ in slice ginger root, minced
- 100 g/4 oz water chestnuts, chopped
- 15 ml/1 tbsp rice wine or dry sherry
- 3 eggs, beaten
- 30 ml/2 tbsp soy sauce
- 45 ml/3 tbsp cornflour (cornstarch)
- 450 g/1 lb crab meat, minced
- 5 ml/1 tsp salt
- 5 ml/1 tsp sugar
- oil for deep-frying

Directions:

1. Combine all the ingredients except the oil and shape into small balls.
2. Heat the oil and deep-fry the crab balls until a golden-brown colour is achieved.
3. Drain thoroughly and serve.

CRAB MEAT WITH CUCUMBER

Yield: 4 Servings

Ingredients:

- 1 slice ginger root, minced
- 100 g/4 oz crab meat, flaked
- 15 ml/1 tbsp soy sauce
- 2 cucumbers, peeled and shredded
- 30 ml/2 tbsp wine vinegar
- 5 ml/1 tsp sugar
- few drops of sesame oil

Directions:

1. Put the crab meat and cucumbers into a container.
2. Combine the rest of the ingredients, pour over the crab meat mixture and toss together well.
3. Cover and place in the refrigerator for half an hour and serve.

CRISPY PRAWNS

Yield: 4 Servings

Ingredients:

- 10 ml/2 tsp soy sauce
- 100 g/4 oz breadcrumbs
- 15 ml/1 tbsp rice wine or dry sherry
- 2 eggs, beaten
- 450 g/1 lb peeled tiger prawns
- 5 ml/1 tsp five-spice powder
- 90 ml/6 tbsp cornflour (cornstarch)
- groundnut oil for deep-frying
- salt and pepper

Directions:

1. Combine the prawns with the wine or sherry, soy sauce and five-spice powder and season with salt and pepper.
2. Toss them in the cornflour then cover with beaten egg and breadcrumbs.
3. Deep-fry in hot oil for a few minutes until slightly browned then eliminate the excess liquid and serve instantly.

DIM SUM

Yield: 4 Servings

Ingredients:

- 1 egg, beaten
- 10 ml/2 tsp soy sauce
- 100 g/4 oz peeled prawns, chopped
- 225 g/8 oz lean pork, finely chopped
- 24 wonton skins
- 3 spring onions (scallions), chopped
- 30 ml/2 tbsp cornflour (cornstarch)
- 5 ml/1 tsp oyster sauce
- 5 ml/1 tsp sesame oil
- 50 g/2 oz Chinese cabbage, finely chopped
- oil for deep-frying

Directions:

1. Combine the prawns, pork, cabbage and spring onions.
2. Mix in the egg, cornflour, soy sauce, sesame oil and oyster sauce.
3. Put spoonfuls of the mixture on to the centre of each wonton skin.
4. Softly press the wrappers around the filling, tucking the edges together but leaving the tops open.
5. Heat the oil and fry the dim sums a few at a time until a golden-brown colour is achieved.
6. Drain thoroughly and serve hot.

GRILLED CHICKEN LIVERS

Yield: 4 Servings

Ingredients:

- 1 clove garlic, crushed
- 15 ml/1 tbsp brown sugar
- 15 ml/1 tbsp rice wine or dry sherry
- 45 ml/3 tbsp soy sauce
- 450 g/1 lb chicken livers
- 5 ml/1 tsp minced ginger root
- 5 ml/1 tsp salt

Directions:

1. Parboil the chicken livers in boiling water for approximately two minutes then eliminate the excess liquid well.
2. Put into a container with all the rest of the ingredients except the oil and marinate for approximately three hours.
3. Thread the chicken livers on to kebab skewers and grill (broil) using a hot grill for approximately eight minutes until a golden-brown colour is achieved.

HAM AND CHICKEN ROLLS

Yield: 4 Servings

Ingredients:

- 1 clove garlic, crushed
- 1 egg, beaten
- 2 chicken breasts
- 2½ ml/ ½ tsp five-spice powder
- 2½ ml/ ½ tsp salt
- 25 g/1 oz plain (all-purpose) flour
- 30 ml/2 tbsp milk
- 4 egg roll skins
- 4 slices cooked ham
- oil for deep-frying

Directions:

1. Slice the chicken breasts in half. Pound them until very thin.
2. Combine the garlic, salt and five-spice powder and drizzle over the chicken.

3. Put a slice of ham on top of each piece of chicken and roll them up tightly.
4. Combine the egg and milk. Coat the chicken pieces slightly with flour then immerse in the egg mixture.
5. Put each piece on an egg roll skin and brush the edges with beaten egg. Fold in the sides then roll together, pinching the edges to seal.
6. Heat the oil and fry the rolls for approximately five minutes until a golden-brown colour is achieved and cooked through.
7. Drain using kitchen paper then chop into thick diagonal slices to serve.

LYCHEES WITH GINGER

Yield: 4 Servings

Ingredients:

- 1 large watermelon, halved and seeded
- 450 g/1 lb canned lychees, drained
- 5 cm/2 in stem ginger, sliced
- few mint leaves

Directions:

1. Pack the melon halves with lychees and ginger, garnish with mint leaves.
2. Chill and serve.

MARINATED ABALONE

Yield: 4 Servings

Ingredients:

- 30 ml/2 tbsp wine vinegar
- 45 ml/3 tbsp soy sauce
- 450 g/1 lb canned abalone
- 5 ml/1 tsp sugar
- few drops of sesame oil

Directions:

1. Eliminate the excess liquid from the abalone and slice it finely or chop it into strips.
2. Combine the rest of the ingredients, pour over the abalone and toss comprehensively..
3. Cover and place in the refrigerator for one hour.

MARINATED GARLIC MUSHROOMS

Yield: 4 Servings

Ingredients:

- 15 ml/1 tbsp sesame oil
- 225 g/8 oz button mushrooms
- 3 cloves garlic, crushed
- 30 ml/2 tbsp rice wine or dry sherry
- 30 ml/2 tbsp soy sauce
- pinch of salt

Directions:

1. Put the mushrooms and garlic in a colander, pour over boiling water and allow to stand for approximately three minutes.
2. Drain and pat dry comprehensively..
3. Combine the rest of the ingredients, pour the marinade over the mushrooms and allow to marinate for one hour.

MARINATED MUSHROOMS

Yield: 4 Servings

Ingredients:

- 15 ml/1 tbsp rice wine or dry sherry
- 225 g/8 oz button mushrooms
- 30 ml/2 tbsp soy sauce
- few drops of sesame oil
- few drops of tabasco sauce
- pinch of salt

Directions:

1. Briefly boil the mushrooms in boiling water for approximately two minutes then eliminate the excess liquid and pat dry.
2. Put into a container and pour over the rest of the ingredients.
3. Toss together well and chill and serve.

OYSTER SAUCE MUSHROOMS

Yield: 4 Servings

Ingredients:

- 10 dried Chinese mushrooms
- 15 ml/1 tbsp cornflour (cornstarch)
- 250 ml/8 fl oz/1 cup beef stock
- 30 ml/2 tbsp oyster sauce
- 5 ml/1 tsp rice wine or dry sherry

Directions:

1. Soak the mushrooms in warm water for half an hour then drain, reserving 250 ml/8 fl oz/1 cup of soaking liquid. Discard the stalks.
2. Mix 60 ml/4 tbsp of the beef stock with the cornflour to a paste.
3. Bring the rest of the beef stock to the boil with the mushrooms and mushroom liquid, cover and simmer for approximately 20 minutes.
4. Take the mushrooms out of the liquid using a slotted spoon and lay out on a warm serving plate.
5. Put in the oyster sauce and sherry to the pan and simmer, stirring for approximately two minutes.
6. Mix in the cornflour paste and simmer, stir until the sauce becomes thick. Pour over the mushrooms and serve instantly.

PORK AND CHESTNUT MEATBALLS

Yield: 4 Servings

Ingredients:

- 1 clove garlic, crushed
- 1 egg, beaten
- 15 ml/1 tbsp rice wine or dry sherry
- 30 ml/2 tbsp cornflour (cornstarch)
- 30 ml/2 tbsp soy sauce
- 450 g/1 lb minced (ground) pork
- 5 ml/1 tsp minced ginger root
- 5 ml/1 tsp sugar
- 50 g/2 oz mushrooms, finely chopped
- 50 g/2 oz water chestnuts, finely chopped
- oil for deep-frying
- salt to taste

Directions:

1. Combine all the ingredients except the cornflour and shape the mixture into small balls. Roll in the cornflour.
2. Heat the oil and deep-fry the meatballs for approximately ten minutes until a golden-brown colour is achieved.
3. Drain thoroughly and serve.

PORK AND LETTUCE ROLLS

Yield: 4 Servings

Ingredients:

- 10 ml/2 tsp oyster sauce
- 10 ml/2 tsp sesame oil
- 100 g/4 oz bamboo shoots, chopped
- 100 g/4 oz water chestnuts, chopped
- 15 ml/1 tbsp groundnut (peanut) oil
- 15 ml/1 tbsp soy sauce
- 175 g/6 oz crab meat, flaked
- 225 g/8 oz lean pork, chopped
- 30 ml/2 tbsp rice wine or dry sherry
- 4 dried Chinese mushrooms
- 4 spring onions (scallions), chopped
- 9 Chinese leaves

Directions:

1. Soak the mushrooms in warm water for half an hour then drain.
2. Discard the stalks and chop the caps. Heat the oil and stir-fry the pork for 5 minutes.
3. Put in the mushrooms, bamboo shoots, water chestnuts, spring onions and crab meat and stir-fry for approximately two minutes.
4. Combine the wine or sherry, soy sauce, oyster sauce and sesame oil and mix it into the pan. Turn off the heat.
5. In the meantime, briefly boil the Chinese leaves in boiling water for approximately one minute then drain.
6. Put spoonfuls of the pork mixture on the centre of each leaf, fold over the sides then roll up to serve.

PORK AND PRAWN WONTONS WITH SWEET AND SOUR SAUCE

Yield: 4 Servings

Ingredients:

- 1 clove garlic, crushed
- 10 ml/2 tsp cornflour (cornstarch)
- 120 ml/4 fl oz/ ½ cup water
- 2 spring onions (scallions), chopped
- 2½ ml/ ½ tsp grated ginger root
- 24 wonton skins
- 25 g/1 oz mushrooms, chopped
- 25 g/1 oz peeled prawns, chopped
- 30 ml/2 tbsp tomato purV©e (paste)
- 5 ml/1 tsp soy sauce
- 50 g/2 oz lean pork, chopped
- 60 ml/4 tbsp brown sugar
- 60 ml/4 tbsp wine vinegar
- oil for deep-frying

Directions:

1. Combine the water, wine vinegar, sugar, tomato puree and cornflour in a small saucepan. Bring to the boil, stirring constantly, then simmer for approximately one minute. Turn off the heat and keep warm.
2. Combine the mushrooms, prawns, pork, spring onions, soy sauce, ginger and garlic.
3. Put spoonfuls of the filling on each skin, brush the edges with water and press together to seal.
4. Heat the oil and deep-fry the wontons a few at a time until a golden-brown colour is achieved. Drain using kitchen paper and serve hot with sweet and sour sauce.

PORK AND VEAL RISSOLES

Yield: 4 Servings

Ingredients:

- 1 egg, beaten
- 1 slice streaky bacon, minced (ground)
- 100 g/4 oz minced (ground) pork
- 100 g/4 oz minced (ground) veal
- 15 ml/1 tbsp soy sauce
- 30 ml/2 tbsp cornflour (cornstarch)
- oil for deep-frying
- salt and pepper

Directions:

1. Combine the minced meats and bacon and season with salt and pepper.
2. Bind together using the egg, shape into walnut-sized balls and dust with cornflour.
3. Heat the oil and deep-fry until a golden-brown colour is achieved. Drain thoroughly and serve.

PORK DUMPLINGS

Yield: 4 Servings

Ingredients:

- 1 slice ginger root, minced
- 15 ml/1 tbsp rice wine or dry sherry
- 15 ml/1 tbsp sesame oil
- 15 ml/1 tbsp soy sauce
- 2 cloves garlic, crushed
- 2 spring onions (scallions), finely chopped
- 225 g/8 oz peeled prawns, chopped
- 4 stalks celery, chopped
- 450 g/1 lb cooked pork, minced
- 450 g/1 lb plain (all-purpose) flour
- 5 ml/1 tsp salt
- 500 ml/17 fl oz/2 cups water

Directions:

1. Combine the flour and water to a soft dough and knead well. Cover and allow to stand for 10 minutes.
2. Roll out the dough as thinly as possible and chop into 5 cm/2 in circles.
3. Combine all the rest of the ingredients.
4. Put spoonfuls of the mixture on each circle, dampen the edges and seal into a semi-circle. Bring a saucepan of water to the boil then gently place the dumplings in the water.
5. When the dumplings rise to the top add 150 ml cup cold water then return the water to the boil. When the dumplings rise again, they are cooked.

PRAWN AND NOODLE ROLLS

Yield: 4 Servings

Ingredients:

- 1 egg, beaten
- 100 g/4 oz mushrooms, chopped
- 100 g/4 oz peeled prawns, chopped
- 15 ml/1 tbsp groundnut (peanut) oil
- 15 ml/1 tbsp rice wine or dry sherry
- 24 wonton skins
- 3 spring onions (scallions), chopped
- 50 g/2 oz egg noodles, broken into pieces

- 50 g/2 oz lean pork, finely chopped
- oil for deep-frying
- salt and pepper

Directions:

1. Cook the noodles in boiling water for 5 minutes then eliminate the excess liquid and chop.
2. Heat the oil and stir-fry the pork for 4 minutes.
3. Put in the mushrooms and onions and stir-fry for approximately two minutes then remove from the heat.
4. Mix in the prawns, wine or sherry and noodles and season to taste with salt and pepper.
5. Put spoonfuls of the mixture on the centre of each wonton skin and brush the edges with beaten egg.
6. Fold over the edges then roll up the wrappers, sealing the edges together.
7. Heat the oil and deep-fry the rolls a few at a time for approximately five minutes until golden.
8. Drain using kitchen paper and serve.

PRAWN CRACKERS

Yield: 4 Servings

Ingredients:

- 100 g/4 oz prawn crackers
- oil for deep-frying

Directions:

Heat the oil until scalding hot. Put a handful of prawn crackers into the frying pan a time and fry for a few seconds until they have puffed up. Take out of the oil and eliminate the excess liquid using kitchen paper while you carry on frying the crackers.

PRAWN TOASTS

Yield: 4 Servings

Ingredients:

- 1 onion, finely chopped
- 15 ml/1 tbsp cornflour (cornstarch)
- 15 ml/1 tbsp rice wine or dry sherry
- 2 eggs 450 g/1 lb peeled prawns, minced
- 30 ml/2 tbsp soy sauce
- 5 ml/1 tsp minced ginger root
- 5 ml/1 tsp salt
- 8 slices bread, chopped into triangles
- oil for deep-frying

Directions:

1. Combine 1 egg with all the rest of the ingredients except the bread and oil.
2. Spoon the mixture on to the bread triangles and press into a dome. Brush with the rest of the egg.
3. Heat about 5 cm/2 in of oil and deep-fry the bread triangles until a golden-brown colour is achieved.
4. Drain thoroughly and serve.

PRAWNS AND CAULIFLOWER

Yield: 4 Servings

Ingredients:

- 100 g/ 4 oz peeled prawns
- 15 ml/1 tbsp soy sauce
- 225 g/8 oz cauliflower florets
- 5 ml/1 tsp sesame oil

Directions:

1. Part boil the cauliflower for approximately five minutes until tender but still crispy.
2. Mix with the prawns, drizzle with soy sauce and sesame oil and toss together. Chill and serve.

PRAWNS WITH GINGER SAUCE

Yield: 4 Servings

Ingredients:

- 15 ml/1 tbsp soy sauce
- 15 ml/1 tbsp wine vinegar
- 30 ml/2 tbsp chopped fresh parsley
- 450 g/1 lb peeled prawns
- 5 ml/1 tsp chopped ginger root
- 5 ml/1 tsp rice wine or dry sherry
- 5 ml/1 tsp sesame oil

Directions:

1. Combine the soy sauce, wine or sherry and sesame oil. Pour over the prawns, cover and allow to marinate for half an hour.
2. Grill the prawns for a few minutes until just cooked, basting with the marinade.
3. In the meantime, mix together the parsley, wine vinegar and ginger to serve with the prawns.

PSEUDO SMOKED FISH

Yield: 4 Servings

Ingredients:

- 1 clove garlic, crushed
- 1 sea bass
- 1 spring onion (scallion), thickly sliced
- 10 ml/2 tsp sugar
- 120 ml/4 fl oz/ ½ cup stock
- 2½ ml/ ½ tsp ground anise
- 2½ ml/ ½ tsp sesame oil
- 3 slices ginger root, sliced
- 30 ml/2 tbsp rice wine or dry sherry
- 5 ml/1 tsp cornflour (cornstarch)
- 75 ml/5 tbsp soy sauce
- oil for deep-frying

Directions:

1. Trim the fish and chop it into 5 mm (¬º in) slices against the grain. Combine the ginger, garlic, spring onion, 60 ml/4 tbsp of soy sauce, the sherry, anise and sesame oil. Pour over the fish and toss gently. Leave to stand for 2 hours, turning occasionally.
2. Eliminate the excess liquid from the marinade into a pan and pat the fish dry on kitchen paper. Put in the sugar, stock and remaining soy sauce to the marinade, bring to the boil and simmer for approximately one minute. If the sauce needs to be thickened, mix the cornflour with a little cold water, mix it into the sauce and simmer, stirring, until the sauce becomes thick.
3. In the meantime, heat the oil and deep-fry the fish until a golden-brown colour is achieved. Drain well. Immerse the pieces of fish in the marinade then arrange them on a warmed serving plate. Serve hot or cold.

RED-COOKED CHICKEN WINGS

Yield: 4 Servings

Ingredients:

- 120 ml/4 fl oz/ ½ cup water
- 2 spring onions (scallions), chopped
- 30 ml/2 tbsp brown sugar
- 75 ml/5 tbsp soy sauce
- 8 chicken wings

Directions:

1. Slice off and throw away the bony tips of the chicken wings and chop them in half.
2. Pur inside the pan with the rest of the ingredients, bring to the boil, cover and simmer for half an hour.
3. Take the lid off and carry on simmering for another 15 minutes, basting often.
4. Allow it to cool then chill and serve.

SESAME HAM STICKS

Yield: 4 Servings

Ingredients:

- 10 ml/2 tsp soy sauce
- 2½ ml/ ½ tsp sesame oil
- 225 g/8 oz ham, chopped into strips

Directions:

1. Put the ham on a serving plate.
2. Combine the soy sauce and sesame oil, drizzle over the ham and serve.

STUFFED MUSHROOMS

Yield: 4 Servings

Ingredients:

- 1 egg white
- 12 large dried mushroom caps
- 15 ml/1 tbsp cornflour (cornstarch)
- 15 ml/1 tbsp rice wine or dry sherry
- 15 ml/1 tbsp soy sauce
- 2 spring onions (scallions), finely chopped
- 225 g/8 oz crab meat
- 3 water chestnuts, minced

Directions:

1. Soak the mushrooms in warm water overnight. Squeeze dry.
2. Combine the rest of the ingredients and use to fill the mushroom caps.
3. Lay out on a steamer rack and steam for 40 minutes. Serve hot.

SOUPS

Chicken stock is a staple in the Chinese kitchen, especially when it comes to soups. If you don't know how to make it, you will find the recipe below. We Chinese cooks prepare chicken stock in bulk and freeze it in smaller portions, to use it as needed.

Homemade stock is best, but if you aren't in the mood to make your own, feel free to buy stock cubes from a nearby market. Store-bought leave you with little to no control over the amount of salt and other ingredients you put in there, and the final recipes don't taste as good as those made with homemade stock, but it does get the job done.

The wok is my personal favourite utensil to make these soups in, but if you don't have one on hand, any old pan will do.

Enough talk. Let's dive into the recipes!

CHICKEN STOCK

Yield: 2 litres/3½ pts/8½ cups

Ingredients:

- 1 clove garlic, crushed
- 1 cm/½ in piece ginger root
- 1.5 kg/2 lb cooked or raw bones of chicken
- 2.25 litres/4 pts/10 cups water
- 3 spring onions (scallions), sliced
- 450 g/1 lb pork bones
- 5 ml/1 tsp salt

Directions:

1. Bring all the ingredients to the boil, cover and simmer for approximately fifteen minutes.
2. Remove all excess fat. Cover and simmer for approximately an hour and a half. Strain, cool and skim.
3. Freeze in small quantities or place in the fridge and use within 2 days.

ABALONE AND MUSHROOM SOUP

Yield: 4 Servings

Ingredients:

- 1.5 l/2½ pts/6 cups water
- 100 g/4 oz lean pork, chopped into strips
- 100 g/4 oz mushrooms, sliced
- 15 ml/1 tbsp cornflour (cornstarch)
- 2 onions, sliced
- 2 slices ginger root, chopped
- 2 stalks celery, sliced
- 225 g/8 oz canned abalone, chopped into strips
- 30 ml/2 tbsp wine vinegar
- 45 ml/3 tbsp soy sauce
- 45 ml/3 tbsp water
- 50 g/2 oz ham, chopped into strips
- 60 ml/4 tbsp groundnut (peanut) oil
- salt and freshly ground pepper

Directions:

1. Heat the oil and fry the pork, abalone, mushrooms, celery, ham and onions for 8 minutes.
2. Put in the water and wine vinegar, bring to the boil, cover and simmer for approximately 20 minutes.
3. Put in the soy sauce, ginger, salt and pepper. Blend the cornflour to a paste with the water, mix it into the soup and simmer, stirring, for approximately five minutes until the soup clears and becomes thick.

BEAN SPROUT AND PORK SOUP

Yield: 4 Servings

Ingredients:

- 1.5 l/2½ pts/6 cups chicken stock
- 15 ml/1 tbsp salt
- 350 g/12 oz bean sprouts

- 450 g/1 lb pork, cubed
- 5 slices ginger root

Directions:

1. Briefly boil the pork in boiling water for approximately ten minutes then drain.
2. Bring the stock to the boil and add the pork and ginger.
3. Cover and simmer for approximately fifty minutes.
4. Put in the bean sprouts and salt and simmer for approximately 20 minutes.

BEEF AND CHINESE LEAVES SOUP

Yield: 4 Servings

Ingredients:

- ½ head Chinese leaves, chopped into chunks
- 1.5 l/2½ pts/6 cups beef stock
- 15 ml/1 tbsp groundnut (peanut) oil
- 15 ml/1 tbsp soy sauce
- 2.5 ml/½ tsp sugar
- 200 g/7 oz lean beef, chopped into strips
- 5 ml/1 tsp salt

Directions:

1. Combine the beef with the soy sauce and oil and allow to marinate for half an hour, stirring intermittently.
2. Bring the stock to the boil with the salt and sugar, add the Chinese leaves and simmer for approximately ten minutes until almost cooked.
3. Put in the beef and simmer for another 5 minutes.

BEEF SOUP

Yield: 4 Servings

Ingredients:

- 1.2 l/2 pts/5 cups chicken stock

- 15 ml/1 tbsp cornflour (cornstarch)
- 15 ml/1 tbsp rice wine or dry sherry
- 15 ml/1 tbsp soy sauce
- 2 eggs, beaten
- 225 g/8 oz minced (ground) beef
- 5 ml/1 tsp chilli bean sauce
- 6 spring onions (scallions), chopped
- salt and pepper

Directions:

1. Combine the beef with the soy sauce, wine or sherry and cornflour.
2. Put into the stock and progressively bring to the boil, stirring.
3. Put in the chilli bean sauce and season to taste with salt and pepper, cover and simmer for approximately ten minutes, stirring intermittently.
4. Mix in the eggs and serve sprinkled with the spring onions.

CABBAGE SOUP

Yield: 4 Servings

Ingredients:

- 1.2 l/2 pts/5 cups chicken stock
- 10 ml/2 tsp sugar
- 100 g/4 oz lean pork, chopped into strips
- 15 ml/1 tbsp cornflour (cornstarch)
- 2 onions, chopped
- 225 g/8 oz Chinese cabbage, shredded
- 45 ml/3 tbsp soy sauce
- 60 ml/4 tbsp groundnut (peanut) oil
- salt and pepper

Directions:

1. Heat the oil and fry the onions and pork until slightly browned. Put in the cabbage and sugar and stir-fry for approximately five minutes.
2. Put in the stock and soy sauce and season to taste with salt and pepper.
3. Bring to the boil, cover and simmer gently for approximately 20 minutes.

4. Combine the cornflour with a little water, mix it into the soup and simmer, stirring, until the soup becomes thick and clears.

CELESTIAL SOUP

Yield: 4 Servings

Ingredients:

- 1 clove garlic, crushed
- 1.5 l/2½ pts/6 cups water
- 15 ml/1 tbsp groundnut (peanut) oil
- 2 spring onions (scallions), minced
- 30 ml/2 tbsp chopped fresh parsley
- 30 ml/2 tbsp soy sauce
- 5 ml/1 tsp salt

Directions:

1. Combine the spring onions, garlic, parsley, salt, oil and soy sauce.
2. Bring to the water to the boil, pour over the spring onion mixture and allow to stand for approximately three minutes.

CHICKEN AND ASPARAGUS SOUP

Yield: 4 Servings

Ingredients:

- 1.5 l/2½ pts/6 cups chicken stock
- 100 g/4 oz bean sprouts
- 100 g/4 oz button mushrooms
- 100 g/4 oz chicken, shredded
- 2.5 ml/½ tsp salt
- 2 egg whites
- 225 g/8 oz asparagus, chopped into 5 cm/2 in chunks
- 30 ml/2 tbsp cornflour (cornstarch)

Directions:

1. Combine the chicken with the egg whites, salt and cornflour and allow to stand for half an hour.
2. Cook the chicken in boiling water for approximately ten minutes until cooked through then eliminate the excess liquid well.
3. Briefly boil the asparagus in boiling water for approximately two minutes then drain.
4. Briefly boil the bean sprouts in boiling water for approximately three minutes then drain.
5. Pour the stock into a large pan and add the chicken, asparagus, mushrooms and bean sprouts.
6. Bring to the boil and season to taste with salt.
7. Simmer for a few minutes to let the flavours develop and until the vegetables are soft but still crisp.

CHICKEN AND BAMBOO SHOOT SOUP

Yield: 4 Servings

Ingredients:

- 1.5 l/2½ pts/6 cups chicken stock
- 100 g/4 oz bamboo shoots, chopped into chunks
- 2 chicken legs
- 3 spring onions, sliced
- 30 ml/2 tbsp groundnut (peanut) oil
- 5 ml/1 tsp minced ginger root
- 5 ml/1 tsp rice wine or dry sherry
- salt

Directions:

1. Bone the chicken and chop the flesh into chunks.
2. Heat the oil and fry the chicken until sealed on all sides. Put in the stock, spring onions, bamboo shoots and ginger, bring to the boil and simmer for about 20 minutes until the chicken is soft.
3. Season to taste with salt and serve.

CHICKEN AND COCONUT SOUP

Yield: 4 Servings

Ingredients:

- 1 green chilli pepper, chopped
- 1 l/1¾ pts/4¼ cups coconut milk
- 10 ml/2 tsp cornflour (cornstarch)
- 12 lychees
- 2 lemon balm leaves
- 30 ml/2 tbsp groundnut (peanut) oil
- 350 g/12 oz chicken breast
- 5 ml/1 tsp grated lemon rind
- pinch of grated nutmeg
- salt
- salt and freshly ground pepper

Directions:

1. Chop the chicken breast diagonally across the grain into strips.
2. Drizzle with salt and coat with cornflour. Heat 10 ml/2 tsp of oil in a wok, swirl round and pour it out. Repeat once more.
3. Heat the rest of the oil and stir-fry the chicken and chilli pepper for approximately one minute.
4. Put in the coconut milk and bring to the boil.
5. Put in the lemon rind and simmer for approximately five minutes.
6. Put in the lychees, season with nutmeg, salt and pepper and serve garnished with lemon balm.

CHICKEN AND CORN SOUP

Yield: 4 Servings

Ingredients:

- 1 l/1¾ pts/4¼ cups chicken stock
- 100 g/4 oz chicken, minced
- 15 ml/1 tbsp rice wine or dry sherry
- 200 g/7 oz creamed sweetcorn

- eggs, beaten
- slice ham, chopped

Directions:

1. Bring the stock and chicken to the boil, cover and simmer for approximately fifteen minutes.
2. Put in the sweetcorn and ham, cover and simmer for approximately five minutes.
3. Put in the eggs and sherry, stirring slowly with a chopstick so that the eggs form into threads.
4. Turn off the heat, cover and allow to stand for approximately three minutes and serve.

CHICKEN AND GINGER SOUP

Yield: 4 Servings

Ingredients:

- 1.5 l/2½ pts/6 cups water or chicken stock
- 10 slices ginger root
- 225 g/8 oz chicken meat, cubed
- 4 dried Chinese mushrooms
- 5 ml/1 tsp rice wine or dry sherry
- salt

Directions:

1. Soak the mushrooms in warm water for half an hour then drain. Discard the stalks.
2. Bring the water or stock to the boil with the rest of the ingredients and simmer gently for about 20 minutes until the chicken is cooked.

CHICKEN AND RICE SOUP

Yield: 4 Servings

Ingredients:

- 1 l/1¾ pts/4¼ cups chicken stock
- 1 onion, chopped into wedges

- 100 g/4 oz cooked chicken, chopped into strips
- 225 g/8 oz/1 cup cooked long-grain rice
- 5 ml/1 tsp soy sauce

Directions:

1. Heat all the ingredients together gently until hot without letting the soup boil.

CHICKEN SOUP WITH CHINESE MUSHROOMS

Yield: 4 Servings

Ingredients:

- 1.2 l/2 pts/5 cups chicken stock
- 100 g/4 oz chicken, shredded
- 25 g/1 oz dried Chinese mushrooms
- 30 ml/2 tbsp rice wine or dry sherry
- 30 ml/2 tbsp soy sauce
- 50 g/2 oz bamboo shoots, shredded

Directions:

1. Soak the mushrooms in warm water for half an hour then drain. Discard the stems and slice the caps.
2. Briefly boil the mushrooms, chicken and bamboo shoots in boiling water for 30 seconds then drain.
3. Put them into a container and mix in the soy sauce and wine or sherry.
4. Allow to marinate for one hour. Bring the stock to the boil add the chicken mixture and the marinade.
5. Stir thoroughly and simmer for a few minutes until the chicken is comprehensively cooked.

CLAM SOUP

Yield: 4 Servings

Ingredients:

- 1.5 l/2½ pts/6 cups chicken stock
- 12 clams, soaked and scrubbed
- 15 ml/1 tbsp rice wine or dry sherry
- 2 dried Chinese mushrooms
- 2 spring onions (scallions), chopped into rings
- 50 g/2 oz bamboo shoots, shredded
- 50 g/2 oz mangetout (snow peas),halved
- pinch of freshly ground pepper

Directions:

1. Soak the mushrooms in warm water for half an hour then drain.
2. Discard the stalks and halve the caps.
3. Steam the clams for approximately five minutes until they open; discard any that remain closed. Remove the clams from their shells.
4. Bring the stock to the boil and add the mushrooms, bamboo shoots, mangetout and spring onions.
5. Simmer, uncovered, for approximately two minutes.
6. Put in the clams, wine or sherry and pepper and simmer until heated through.

CRAB AND SCALLOP SOUP

Yield: 4 Servings

Ingredients:

- 1.5 l/2½ pts/6 cups chicken stock
- 1 egg, beaten
- 1 slice ginger root, minced
- 100 g/4 oz bamboo shoots, sliced
- 100 g/4 oz shelled scallops, sliced
- 15 ml/1 tbsp groundnut (peanut) oil
- 175 g/6 oz crab meat, flaked
- 2 egg whites
- 2 spring onions (scallions), chopped
- 20 ml/4 tsp soy sauce
- 30 ml/2 tbsp rice wine or dry sherry
- 4 dried Chinese mushrooms
- 45 ml/3 tbsp cornflour (cornstarch)

- 90 ml/6 tbsp water
- a few cooked, peeled prawns (optional)

Directions:

1. Soak the mushrooms in warm water for half an hour then drain.
2. Discard the stalks and slice the caps finely.
3. Heat the oil, add the egg and tilt the pan so that the egg covers the bottom.
4. Cook until set then turn and cook the other side. Take out of the pan, roll up and chop into thin strips.
5. Bring the stock to the boil, add the mushrooms, egg strips, crab meat, scallops, bamboo shoots, spring onions, ginger and prawns, if using. Bring back to the boil.
6. Combine the cornflour with 60 ml/4 tbsp of water, the wine or sherry and soy sauce and stir into soup.
7. Simmer, stirring until the soup becomes thick.
8. Beat the egg whites with the rest of the water and drizzle the mixture slowly into the soup, stirring vigorously.

CRAB SOUP

Yield: 4 Servings

Ingredients:

- 1.2 l/2 pts/5 cups chicken stock
- 1 slice ginger root, minced
- 150 ml/¼pt/ cup rice wine or dry sherry
- 225 g/8 oz white and brown crab meat
- 3 onions, chopped
- 45 ml/3 tbsp soy sauce
- 90 ml/6 tbsp groundnut (peanut) oil
- salt and freshly ground pepper

Directions:

1. Heat the oil and fry the onions until soft but not browned.
2. Put in the crab meat and ginger and stir-fry for approximately five minutes.
3. Put in the stock, wine or sherry and soy sauce, season with salt and pepper.
4. Bring to the boil then simmer for approximately five minutes.

EGG SOUP

Yield: 4 Servings

Ingredients:

- 1.2 l/2 pts/5 cups chicken stock
- 3 eggs, beaten
- 4 spring onions (scallions), sliced
- 45 ml/3 tbsp soy sauce
- salt and freshly ground pepper

Directions:

1. Bring the stock to the boil.
2. Progressively whisk in the beaten eggs so that they split into strands.
3. Mix in the soy sauce and season to taste with salt and pepper.
4. Serve garnished with spring onions.

FISH AND LETTUCE SOUP

Yield: 4 Servings

Ingredients:

- 1.2 l/2 pts/5 cups water
- 10 ml/2 tsp finely chopped ginger root
- 10 ml/2 tsp lemon juice
- 100 g/4 oz lettuce, shredded
- 150 ml/¼ pt/generous ½ cup rice wine or dry sherry
- 225 g/8 oz white fish fillets
- 30 ml/2 tbsp chopped fresh parsley
- 30 ml/2 tbsp cornflour (cornstarch)
- 30 ml/2 tbsp plain (all-purpose) flour
- 30 ml/2 tbsp soy sauce
- 6 spring onions (scallions), sliced
- 90 ml/6 tbsp groundnut (peanut) oil
- salt and freshly ground pepper

Directions:

1. Chop the fish into thin strips then toss in seasoned flour. Heat the oil and fry the spring onions until soft.
2. Put in the lettuce and fry for approximately two minutes.
3. Put in the fish and cook for 4 minutes.
4. Put in the water, ginger and wine or sherry, bring to the boil, cover and simmer for approximately five minutes.
5. Combine the cornflour with a little water then mix it into the soup. Simmer, stirring for another 4 minutes until the soup clears then season with salt and pepper.
6. Serve sprinkled with parsley, lemon juice and soy sauce.

FISH SOUP

Yield: 4 Servings

Ingredients:

- 1.5 l/2½ pts/6 cups fish stock
- 1 slice ginger root, minced
- 15 ml/1 tbsp rice wine or dry sherry
- 225 g/8 oz fish fillets
- 30 ml/2 tbsp groundnut (peanut) oil

Directions:

1. Chop the fish into thin strips against the grain.
2. Combine the ginger, wine or sherry and oil, add the fish and toss gently.
3. Allow to marinate for half an hour, turning occasionally.
4. Bring the stock to the boil, add the fish and simmer gently for approximately three minutes.

GINGER SOUP WITH DUMPLINGS

Yield: 4 Servings

Ingredients:

- 1.5 l/2½ pts/7 cups water

- 2.5 ml/½ tsp salt
- 225 g/8 oz/2 cups rice flour
- 350 g/12 oz brown sugar
- 5 cm/2 in piece ginger root, grated
- 60 ml/4 tbsp water

Directions:

1. Put the ginger, sugar and water in a pan and bring to the boil, stirring. Cover and simmer for about 20 minutes.
2. Strain the soup and pout it back into the pan.
3. In the meantime, place the flour and salt into a container and progressively knead in just enough water to make a thick dough.
4. Roll it into small balls and drop the dumplings into the soup.
5. Return the soup to the boil, cover and simmer for another 6 minutes until the dumplings are cooked.

HOT AND SOUR SOUP

Yield: 4 Servings

Ingredients:

- 1 l/1¾ pts/4¼ cups chicken stock
- 100 g/4 oz bamboo shoots, chopped into strips
- 100 g/4 oz chicken, chopped into strips
- 100 g/4 oz tofu, chopped into strips
- 15 ml/1 tbsp soy sauce
- 2 eggs, beaten
- 30 ml/2 tbsp cornflour (cornstarch)
- 30 ml/2 tbsp wine vinegar
- 8 dried Chinese mushrooms
- a few drops sesame oil

Directions:

1. Soak the mushrooms in warm water for half an hour then drain. Discard the stems and chop the caps into strips.
2. Bring the mushrooms, stock, chicken, bamboo shoots and tofu to the boil, cover and simmer for 10 minutes.

3. Combine the soy sauce, wine vinegar and cornflour to a smooth paste, mix it into the soup and simmer for approximately two minutes until the soup is translucent.
4. Slowly add the eggs and sesame oil, stirring with a chopstick.
5. Cover and allow to stand for approximately two minutes and serve.

MUSHROOM AND CABBAGE SOUP

Yield: 4 Servings

Ingredients:

- 1.2 l/2 pts/5 cups chicken or vegetable stock
- 15 ml/1 tbsp groundnut (peanut) oil
- 15 ml/1 tbsp rice wine or dry sherry
- 15 ml/1 tbsp soy sauce
- 25 g/1 oz dried Chinese mushrooms
- 5 ml/1 tsp sesame oil
- 50 g/2 oz Chinese leaves, shredded
- salt and freshly ground pepper

Directions:

1. Soak the mushrooms in warm water for half an hour then drain. Discard the stems and slice the caps.
2. Heat the oil and stir-fry the mushrooms and Chinese leaves for approximately two minutes until well coated.
3. Mix in the wine or sherry and soy sauce then add the stock.
4. Bring to the boil, season to taste with salt and pepper then simmer for approximately five minutes.
5. Drizzle with sesame oil and serve.

MUSHROOM AND WATER CHESTNUT SOUP

Yield: 4 Servings

Ingredients:

- 1 l/1¾ pts/4¼ cups vegetable stock or water

- 100 g/4 oz bamboo shoots, sliced
- 100 g/4 oz water chestnuts, sliced
- 2 lettuce leaves, chopped into pieces
- 2 onions, finely chopped
- 2 spring onions (scallions), chopped into pieces
- 225 g/8 oz button mushrooms
- 30 ml/2 tbsp soy sauce
- 5 ml/1 tsp rice wine or dry sherry
- few drops of sesame oil

Directions:

1. Bring the water, onions, wine or sherry and soy sauce to the boil, cover and simmer for 10 minutes.
2. Put in the mushrooms, water chestnuts and bamboo shoots, cover and simmer for approximately five minutes.
3. Mix in the sesame oil, lettuce leaves and spring onions, remove from the heat, cover and allow to stand for approximately one minute and serve.

MUSHROOM EGG DROP SOUP

Yield: 4 Servings

Ingredients:

- 1 egg, beaten
- 1 l/1¾ pts/4¼ cups chicken stock
- 1 slice onion, finely chopped
- 100 g/4 oz mushrooms, sliced
- 2.5 ml/½ tsp soy sauce
- 3 drops sesame oil
- 30 ml/2 tbsp cornflour (cornstarch)
- pinch of salt

Directions:

1. Mix a little stock with the cornflour then blend together all the ingredients except the egg.
2. Bring to the boil, cover and simmer for approximately five minutes.
3. Put in the egg, stirring with a chopstick so that the egg forms into threads.

4. Turn off the heat and allow to stand for approximately two minutes and serve.

MUSHROOM SOUP

Yield: 4 Servings

Ingredients:

- 1.5 l/2½ pts/6 cups chicken stock
- 15 dried Chinese mushrooms
- 5 ml/1 tsp salt

Directions:

1. Soak the mushrooms in warm water for half an hour then drain, reserving the liquid.
2. Discard the stalks and chop the caps in half if large and place in a large heatproof bowl.
3. Stand the bowl on a rack in a steamer.
4. Bring the stock to the boil, pour over the mushrooms then cover and steam for one hour over gently simmering water.
5. Season to taste with salt and serve.

PIQUANT BEEF SOUP

Yield: 4 Servings

Ingredients:

- 1 clove garlic, crushed
- 1 green pepper, chopped into strips
- 1 l/1¾ pts/4¼ cups beef stock
- 1 red pepper, chopped into strips
- 2 eggs
- 2 pieces stem ginger, chopped
- 225 g/8 oz cabbage, shredded
- 225 g/8 oz minced (ground) beef
- 225 g/8 oz transparent noodles, soaked
- 30 ml/2 tbsp hoisin sauce
- 30 ml/2 tbsp plum sauce

- 45 ml/3 tbsp groundnut (peanut) oil
- 45 ml/3 tbsp soy sauce
- 5 ml/1 tsp salt
- 5 ml/1 tsp sesame oil
- 6 spring onions (scallions), chopped into strips

Directions:

1. Heat the oil and fry the garlic and salt until slightly browned.
2. Put in the beef and brown quickly. Put in the vegetables and stir-fry until translucent. Put in the stock, plum sauce, hoisin sauce, 30 ml/2 tbsp of soy sauce and the ginger, bring to the boil and simmer for 10 minutes.
3. Beat the eggs with the sesame oil and rest of the soy sauce.
4. Put into the soup with the noodles and cook, stirring, until the eggs form strands and the noodles are soft.

PORK AND CUCUMBER SOUP

Yield: 4 Servings

Ingredients:

- 1 .5 l/2½ pts/6 cups chicken stock
- 1 cucumber
- 100 g/4 oz lean pork, finely sliced
- 15 ml/1 tbsp rice wine or dry sherry
- 15 ml/1 tbsp soy sauce
- 5 ml/1 tsp cornflour (cornstarch)
- 5 ml/1 tsp salt

Directions:

1. Combine the pork, cornflour, soy sauce and wine or sherry. Toss to coat the pork. Peel the cucumber and chop it in half lengthways then scoop out the seeds.
2. Slice thickly. Bring the stock to the boil, add the pork, cover and simmer for 10 minutes.
3. Mix in the cucumber and simmer for a few minutes until translucent.
4. Mix in the salt and add a little more soy sauce, if liked.

PORK AND MUSHROOM SOUP

Yield: 4 Servings

Ingredients:

- 1.2 l/2 pts/5 cups beef stock
- 1 clove garlic, crushed
- 1 stick celery, chopped
- 15 ml/1 tbsp cornflour (cornstarch)
- 15 ml/1 tbsp soy sauce
- 2 carrots, sliced
- 2 onions, sliced
- 225 g/8 oz lean pork, chopped into strips
- 50 g/2 oz mushrooms, sliced
- 60 ml/4 tbsp groundnut (peanut) oil
- salt and freshly ground pepper

Directions:

1. Heat the oil and fry the garlic, onions and pork until the onions are soft and slightly browned.
2. Put in the celery, mushrooms and carrots, cover and simmer gently for 10 minutes.
3. Bring the stock to the boil then put it into the pan with the soy sauce and season to taste with salt and pepper.
4. Combine the cornflour with a little water then mix it into the pan and simmer, stirring, for about 5 minutes.

PORK AND WATERCRESS SOUP

Yield: 4 Servings

Ingredients:

- 1.5 l/2½ pts/6 cups chicken stock
- 1 bunch watercress
- 100 g/4 oz lean pork, chopped into strips
- 2 spring onions (scallions), sliced
- 3 stalks celery, diagonally sliced
- 5 ml/1 tsp salt

Directions:

1. Bring the stock to the boil, add the pork and celery, cover and simmer for approximately fifteen minutes.
2. Put in the spring onions, watercress and salt and simmer, uncovered, for about 4 minutes.

SOUP WITH PORKBALLS AND NOODLES

Yield: 4 Servings

Ingredients:

- 1.5 l/2½ pts/6 cups chicken stock
- 1 spring onion (scallion), finely chopped
- 2.5 ml/½ tsp salt
- 225 g/8 oz minced (ground) pork
- 30 ml/2 tbsp water
- 5 ml/1 tsp cornflour (cornstarch)
- 5 ml/1 tsp soy sauce
- 50 g/2 oz rice noodles

Directions:

1. Put the noodles in cold water to soak while you prepare the meatballs.
2. Combine the pork, cornflour, a little salt and the water and shape into walnut-sized balls.
3. Bring a saucepan of water to a rolling boil, drop in the pork balls, cover and simmer for approximately five minutes.
4. Drain thoroughly and eliminate the excess liquid the noodles. Bring the stock to the boil, add the pork balls and noodles, cover and simmer for approximately five minutes.
5. Put in the spring onion, soy sauce and rest of the salt and simmer for another 2 minutes.

SPINACH AND TOFU SOUP

Yield: 4 Servings

Ingredients:

- 1.2 l/2 pts/5 cups chicken stock
- 200 g/7 oz canned tomatoes, drained and chopped
- 225 g/8 oz spinach, chopped
- 225 g/8 oz tofu, cubed
- 30 ml/2 tbsp soy sauce
- 5 ml/1 tsp brown sugar
- salt and freshly ground pepper

Directions:

1. Bring the stock to the boil then add the tomatoes, tofu and spinach and stir gently.
2. Return to the boil and simmer for approximately five minutes.
3. Put in the soy sauce and sugar and season to taste with salt and pepper. Simmer for approximately one minute and serve.

SWEETCORN AND CRAB SOUP

Yield: 4 Servings

Ingredients:

- 1.2 l/2 pts/5 cups chicken stock
- 1 egg, beaten
- 200 g/7 oz crab meat, flaked
- 200 g/7 oz sweetcorn
- 3 shallots, chopped
- salt and freshly ground pepper

Directions:

1. Bring the stock to the boil, add the sweetcorn season with salt and pepper.
2. Simmer for approximately five minutes.
3. Just before serving, pour the eggs through a fork and swirl on top of the soup.
4. Serve sprinkled with crab meat and chopped shallots.

SZECHUAN SOUP

Yield: 4 Servings

Ingredients:

- 1 .5 l/2½ pts/6 cups chicken stock
- 1 egg, beaten
- 1 red pepper, chopped into strips
- 10 ml/2 tsp wine vinegar
- 100 g/4 oz lean pork, chopped into strips
- 100 g/4 oz peeled prawns
- 15 ml/1 tbsp soy sauce
- 175 g/6 oz tofu, cubed
- 2 .5 ml/½ tsp chilli sauce
- 30 ml/2 tbsp cornflour (cornstarch)
- 4 dried Chinese mushrooms
- 5 ml/1 tsp sesame oil
- 50 g/2 oz cooked ham, chopped into strips
- 50 g/2 oz water chestnuts, sliced
- 6 spring onions (scallions), chopped
- 60 ml/4 tbsp water
- 75 ml/5 tbsp dry white wine

Directions:

1. Soak the mushrooms in warm water for half an hour then drain.
2. Discard the stalks and slice the caps. Bring the stock, wine, soy sauce and chilli sauce to the boil, cover and simmer for approximately five minutes.
3. Blend the cornflour with half the water and mix it into the soup, stirring until the soup becomes thick.
4. Put in the mushrooms, pork, ham, pepper and water chestnuts and simmer for approximately five minutes.
5. Mix in the wine vinegar and sesame oil.
6. Beat the egg with the rest of the water and drizzle this into the soup, stirring vigorously.
7. Put in the prawns, spring onions and tofu and simmer for a few minutes to heat through.

TOFU AND FISH SOUP

Yield: 4 Servings

Ingredients:

- 1.2 l/2 pts/5 cups chicken stock
- 10 ml/2 tsp finely minced ginger root
- 100 g/4 oz mushrooms, sliced
- 100 g/4 oz tofu, cubed
- 150 ml/¼ pt/generous ½ cup rice wine or dry sherry
- 2.5 ml/½ tsp salt
- 2 onions, chopped
- 225 g/8 oz white fish fillets, chopped into strips
- 45 ml/3 tbsp soy sauce
- 60 ml/4 tbsp groundnut (peanut) oil
- salt and freshly ground pepper

Directions:

1. Put the fish into a container. Combine the wine or sherry, ginger, soy sauce and salt and pour over the fish.
2. Allow to marinate for half an hour. Heat the oil and fry the onion for approximately two minutes.
3. Put in the mushrooms and carry on frying until the onions are soft but not browned.
4. Put in the fish and marinade, bring to the boil, cover and simmer for approximately five minutes.
5. Put in the stock, bring back to the boil, cover and simmer for approximately fifteen minutes.
6. Put in the tofu and season to taste with salt and pepper. Simmer until the tofu is cooked.

TOFU SOUP

Yield: 4 Servings

Ingredients:

- 1 .5 l/2½ pts/6 cups chicken stock
- 225 g/8 oz tofu, cubed
- 5 ml/1 tsp salt
- 5 ml/1 tsp soy sauce

Directions:

1. Bring the stock to the boil and add the tofu, salt and soy sauce.
2. Simmer for a few minutes until the tofu is heated through.

TOMATO AND SPINACH SOUP

Yield: 4 Servings

Ingredients:

- 1 .2 l/2 pts/5 cups chicken stock
- 2.5 ml/½ tsp rice wine or dry sherry
- 2.5 ml/½ tsp sugar
- 225 g/8 oz canned chopped tomatoes
- 225 g/8 oz spinach
- 225 g/8 oz tofu, cubed
- 30 ml/2 tbsp soy sauce
- salt and freshly ground pepper

Directions:

1. Bring the stock to the boil then add the tomatoes, tofu and spinach and simmer for approximately two minutes.
2. Add the rest of the ingredients and simmer for approximately two minutes then stir well and serve.

TOMATO SOUP

Yield: 4 Servings

Ingredients:

- 1.2 l/2 pts/5 cups chicken stock
- 1 slice ginger root, minced
- 10 ml/2 tsp sugar
- 15 ml/1 tbsp chilli bean sauce
- 15 ml/1 tbsp soy sauce
- 400 g/14 oz canned tomatoes, drained and chopped

Directions:

1. Put all the ingredients in a pan and bring slowly to the boil, stirring intermittently.
2. Simmer for approximately ten minutes and serve.

TURNIP SOUP

Yield: 4 Servings

Ingredients:

- 1 l/1¾ pts/4¼ cups chicken stock
- 1 large turnip, finely sliced
- 15 ml/1 tbsp soy sauce
- 200 g/7 oz lean pork, finely sliced
- 4 shallots, finely chopped
- 60 ml/4 tbsp brandy
- salt and freshly ground pepper

Directions:

1. Bring the stock to the boil, add the turnip and pork, cover and simmer for approximately 20 minutes until the turnip is soft and the meat cooked.
2. Mix in the soy sauce and brandy season to taste.
3. Simmer until hot serve sprinkled with shallots.

VEGETABLE SOUP

Yield: 4 Servings

Ingredients:

- 1 l/1¾ pts/4¼ cups vegetable stock
- 5 ml/1 tsp soy sauce
- 50 g/2 oz bamboo shoots, chopped into strips
- 50 g/2 oz water chestnuts, sliced
- 6 dried Chinese mushrooms
- 8 mangetout (snow peas), sliced

Directions:

1. Soak the mushrooms in warm water for half an hour then drain. Discard the stems and chop the caps into strips.
2. Add them to the stock with the bamboo shoots and water chestnuts and bring to the boil, cover and simmer for 10 minutes.
3. Put in the mangetout and soy sauce, cover and simmer for approximately two minutes.
4. Leave to stand for approximately two minutes and serve.

VEGETARIAN SOUP

Yield: 4 Servings

Ingredients:

- ¼ white cabbage
- 1.5 l/2½ pts/6 cups water
- 15 ml/1 tbsp rice wine or dry sherry
- 15 ml/1 tbsp soy sauce
- 2 carrots
- 2 spring onions (scallions)
- 3 stalks celery
- 30 ml/2 tbsp groundnut (peanut) oil
- 5 ml/1 tsp salt
- freshly ground pepper

Directions:

1. Chop the vegetables into strips. Heat the oil and fry the vegetables for approximately two minutes until they begin to soften.
2. Add the rest of the ingredients, bring to the boil, cover and simmer for approximately fifteen minutes.

WATERCRESS SOUP

Yield: 4 Servings

Ingredients:

- 1 l/1¾ pts/4¼ cups chicken stock
- 1 onion, finely chopped
- 1 stick celery, finely chopped
- 225 g/8 oz watercress, roughly chopped
- salt and freshly ground pepper

Directions:

1. Bring the stock, onion and celery to the boil, cover and simmer for approximately fifteen minutes.
2. Put in the watercress, cover and simmer for approximately five minutes.
3. Season with salt and pepper.

SAUCES

If you're looking to add a little more "oomph" to your Chinese dishes, serve them with a fiery sauce on the side. Chinese sauces come in a wide variety of flavours and colours. Feel free to experiment, and find out ultimate combinations of sauces and dishes!

In the recipes that follow, you will find a suggestion about where to use the sauce in almost every recipe. Don't think too much about it, and feel free to try beef sauce with fish, or the other way around. The possibilities are endless!

BEEF SAUCE

Yield: 4 Servings

Ingredients:

- 1 clove garlic, crushed
- 1 onion, chopped
- 1 tomato, skinned and chop into wedges
- 100 g/4 oz minced (ground) beef
- 15 ml/1 tbsp chopped fresh parsley
- 15 ml/1 tbsp cornflour (cornstarch)
- 175 ml/6 fl oz/¾ cup beef stock
- 2½ ml/½ tsp salt
- 30 ml/2 tbsp groundnut (peanut) oil
- 45 ml/3 tbsp water
- 5 ml/1 tsp sugar

Directions:

1. Heat the oil and fry the salt, garlic and onion until slightly browned.
2. Put in the beef and stir-fry until slightly browned.
3. Put in the stock, sugar and tomato and bring to the boil, stirring.
4. Combine the cornflour and water to a paste then mix it into the pan and simmer, stirring, until the sauce becomes thick.
5. Pour over noodles and serve garnished with parsley.

BROWN SAUCE

Yield: 4 Servings

Ingredients:

- 1 spring onion (scallion), minced
- 10 ml/2 tsp brown sugar
- 15 ml/1 tbsp groundnut (peanut) oil
- 15 ml/1 tbsp soy sauce
- 30 ml/2 tbsp water

Directions:

1. Heat the oil and stir-fry the spring onion until slightly browned.
2. Put in the sugar, soy sauce and water and stir-fry for a few seconds until heated through.
3. Drizzle over fried eggs to serve.

CELERY SAUCE

Yield: 4 Servings

Ingredients:

- 15 ml/1 tbsp cornflour (cornstarch)
- 15 ml/1 tbsp rice wine or dry sherry
- 2 stalks celery, finely sliced
- 250 ml/8 fl oz/1 cup chicken stock
- 30 ml/2 tbsp groundnut (peanut) oil
- 30 ml/2 tbsp soy sauce
- 4 spring onions (scallions), minced
- 45 ml/3 tbsp water

Directions:

1. Combine all the ingredients except the cornflour and water in a pan and bring slowly to the boil.
2. Cover and simmer for approximately fifteen minutes.

3. Combine the cornflour and water to a paste, stir into the pan and simmer, stirring, until the sauce becomes thick.

CHICKEN SAUCE

Yield: 4 Servings

Ingredients:

- 15 ml/1 tbsp cornflour (cornstarch)
- 2½ ml/½ tsp salt
- 250 ml/8 fl oz /1 cup chicken stock
- 45 ml/3 tbsp water
- 5 ml/1 tsp soy sauce

Directions:

1. Bring the stock to the boil with the salt and soy sauce.
2. Combine the cornflour and water to paste, mix it into the pan and simmer, stirring, until the sauce becomes thick.
3. Pour over chicken or vegetables to serve.

CHICKEN STOCK SAUCE

Yield: 4 Servings

Ingredients:

- 15 ml/1 tbsp groundnut (peanut) oil
- 20 ml/1½ tbsp cornflour (cornstarch)
- 450 ml/¾ pt/2 cups chicken stock

Directions:

1. Heat the oil.
2. Blend together the cornflour and stock, add to the pan and simmer, stirring, until the sauce becomes thick.
3. Pour over noodles to serve.

COCONUT CREAM AND COCONUT MILK

Yield: 4 Servings

Ingredients:

- 225 g/8 oz desiccated coconut

Directions:

1. Put the coconut in a large bowl and pour on enough warm water to cover.
2. allow to stand for one hour.
3. Squeeze the coconut through a piece of muslin in a fine sieve to collect the coconut cream.
4. Mix the rest of the desiccated coconut with a further 500 ml/17 fl oz/ 2¼ cups of warm water and allow to stand for another 1 hour.
5. Squeeze out the liquor again to make coconut milk.

EGG FOO YUNG SAUCE

Yield: 4 Servings

Ingredients:

- 10 ml/2 tsp cornflour (cornstarch)
- 175 ml/6 fl oz/¾ cup chicken stock
- 5 ml/ 1 tsp soy sauce
- salt

Directions:

1. Heat the stock with the soy sauce.
2. Blend the cornflour to a paste with a little of the stock then mix it into the mixture and season with salt.
3. Heat, stirring, for approximately one minute then spoon over the egg foo yung.

EGG YOLK SAUCE

Yield: 4 Servings

Ingredients:

- 10 ml/2 tsp cornflour (cornstarch)
- 2 egg yolks
- 2½ ml/½ tsp salt
- 250 ml/8 fl oz/1 cup water
- 30 ml/2 tbsp groundnut (peanut) oil

Directions:

1. Beat the egg yolks with 60 ml/4 tbsp of water.
2. Heat the oil, mix in the cornflour and cook over a low heat until smooth.
3. Mix in the rest of the water and salt and heat gently, stirring, until the mixture is smooth and bubbling.
4. Progressively pour in the egg mixture in a thin stream, stirring constantly.
5. Simmer over a low heat, stirring, until the sauce is smooth and creamy.
6. Pour over chicken or vegetables to serve.

FISH SAUCE

Yield: 4 Servings

Ingredients:

- 1 slice ginger root, minced
- 100 g/4 oz lean pork, chopped into strips
- 15 ml/1 tbsp cornflour (cornstarch)
- 15 ml/1 tbsp rice wine or dry sherry
- 15 ml/1 tbsp soy sauce
- 2½ ml/½ tsp salt
- 2½ ml/½ tsp sugar
- 30 ml/2 tbsp groundnut (peanut) oil
- 375 ml/13 fl oz/1½ cups water
- 4 dried Chinese mushrooms
- 50 g/2 oz bamboo shoots, chopped into strips
- 50 g/2 oz Chinese leaves, shredded

- 6 dried lily buds

Directions:

1. Soak the mushrooms and lily buds separately in warm water for half an hour then drain.
2. Discard the mushroom stalks and slice the caps.
3. Halve the lily buds then mix then with the soy sauce, wine or sherry, salt and sugar.
4. Heat the oil and fry the ginger until slightly browned.
5. Put in the pork and stir-fry for approximately three minutes.
6. Put in the mushrooms, bamboo shoots and Chinese leaves and stir-fry for approximately two minutes.
7. Put in the water and bring to the boil, cover and simmer for approximately two minutes.
8. Mix in the lily bud mixture and heat through.
9. Blend the cornflour to a paste with a little water, stir into the pan and simmer, stirring, until the sauce becomes thick.
10. Pour over fried fish to serve.

HAM SAUCE

Yield: 4 Servings

Ingredients:

- 1 egg, beaten
- 1 onion, chopped
- 100 g/4 oz ham, chopped
- 2 stalks celery, chopped
- 250 ml/8 fl oz/1 cup chicken stock
- 30 ml/2 tbsp groundnut (peanut) oil
- 5 ml/1 tsp cornflour (cornstarch)
- 60 ml/4 tbsp water

Directions:

1. Heat the oil and fry the celery, onion and ham and stir-fry for approximately two minutes.
2. Put in the stock, bring to the boil, cover and simmer for approximately three minutes.
3. Combine the cornflour and water to a paste then blend in the egg.
4. Pour into the pan and simmer, stirring, until the sauce becomes thick.

5. Pour over the noodles to serve.

MILK SAUCE

Yield: 4 Servings

Ingredients:

- 15 ml/1 tbsp cornflour (cornstarch)
- 15 ml/1 tbsp rice wine or dry sherry
- 2½ ml/½ tsp salt
- 30 ml/2 tbsp butter
- 375 ml/13 fl oz/1½ cups milk
- 45 ml/3 tbsp water
- 5 ml/1 tsp sugar
- Heat the milk to just below boiling.

Directions:

1. Mix in the butter, wine or sherry, sugar and salt and heat through gently.
2. Combine the cornflour and water to a paste, mix it into the sauce and simmer, stirring, until the sauce becomes thick.
3. Pour over chicken or vegetables to serve.

MUSHROOM SAUCE

Yield: 4 Servings

Ingredients:

- 12 dried Chinese mushrooms
- 15 ml/1 tbsp cornflour (cornstarch)
- 15 ml/1 tbsp rice wine or dry sherry
- 15 ml/1 tbsp sugar
- 2½ ml/½ tsp salt
- 45 ml/3 tbsp groundnut (peanut) oil
- 60 ml/4 tbsp soy sauce

Directions:

1. Soak the mushrooms in warm water for half an hour then drain, reserving 120 ml/4 fl oz/½ cup of the liquid.
2. Discard the stalks and halve the caps.
3. Heat 30 ml/2 tbsp of oil and stir-fry the mushrooms for approximately two minutes.
4. Put in the soy sauce, wine or sherry and salt.
5. Mix in the rest of the oil, mushroom liquid and sugar, cover and simmer for half an hour, stirring intermittently.
6. Blend the cornflour to a paste with a little water then mix it into the pan and simmer, stirring, until the sauce becomes thick.
7. Pour over rice to serve.

MUSHROOM SAUCE WITH TOMATO

Yield: 4 Servings

Ingredients:

- 1 clove garlic, crushed
- 1 large tomato, skinned and chopped
- 3 spring onions (scallions), chopped
- 30 ml/2 tbsp butter
- 5 ml/1 tsp cornflour (cornstarch)
- 5 ml/1 tsp sugar
- 6 dried Chinese mushrooms
- salt

Directions:

1. Soak the mushrooms in warm water with the sugar for half an hour then drain, reserving the liquid.
2. Discard the stems and slice the caps.
3. Melt the butter and fry the spring onions and garlic until softened.
4. Put in the mushrooms and liquid, tomato and a pinch of salt.
5. Bring to the boil and simmer for approximately ten minutes until the vegetables are cooked.
6. Blend the cornflour with a little cold water, mix it into the sauce and simmer, stirring, until the sauce becomes thick.

OYSTER SAUCE

Yield: about 300 ml/½ pt/1¼ cups

Ingredients:

- 15 oysters
- 45 ml/3 tbsp soy sauce

Directions:

1. Shell the oysters, reserving the liquid.
2. Mince the oysters finely and place them and their liquid in a pan.
3. Bring to the boil, cover and simmer gently for half an hour.
4. Strain, discard the oysters, and stir the soy sauce into the liquid.
5. Store in a screw-top jar in the refrigerator.

PEANUT SAUCE

Yield: 4 Servings

Ingredients:

- 100 g/4 oz peanut butter
- 120 ml/4 fl oz/½ cup chicken stock
- 120 ml/4 fl oz/½ cup groundnut (peanut) oil
- 15 ml/1 tbsp lemon juice
- 15 ml/1 tbsp soy sauce
- 2½ ml/½ tsp chilli powder
- 2½ ml/½ tsp salt
- 2½ ml/½ tsp sugar

Directions:

1. Combine all the ingredients together comprehensively.
2. in a small saucepan over a low heat, stirring constantly.
3. When the ingredients have all mixed together, remove from the heat and allow to cool.
4. Store in the refrigerator in an air-tight jar and stir thoroughly before using.

PEKING SAUCE

Yield: 4 Servings

Ingredients:

- 100 g/4 oz lean minced (ground) pork
- 120 ml/4 fl oz/½ cup yellow bean paste
- 15 ml/1 tbsp hoisin sauce
- 30 ml/2 tbsp groundnut (peanut) oil
- 30 ml/2 tbsp soy sauce
- 375 ml/13 fl oz/1½ cups water
- 4 spring onions (scallions), finely chopped

Directions:

1. Heat the oil and fry the pork until slightly browned.
2. Mix in the spring onions and stir-fry for approximately one minute.
3. Mix in the bean paste, soy sauce, hoisin sauce and water and simmer, stirring, for approximately two minutes.
4. Pour over noodles to serve.

PINEAPPLE SAUCE

Yield: 4 Servings

Ingredients:

- 120 ml/4 fl oz/½ cup pineapple juice
- 15 ml/1 tbsp cornflour (cornstarch)
- 45 ml/3 tbsp sugar
- 45 ml/3 tbsp wine vinegar
- pinch of salt

Directions:

1. Combine all the ingredients and simmer, stirring, until the sauce becomes thick.
2. Pour over cooked carrots or cabbage to serve.

PLUM SAUCE

Yield: about 750 g/1½ lb

Ingredients:

- 120 ml/4 fl oz/½ cup wine vinegar
- 2 canned pimentos, drained and chopped
- 225 g/8 oz dried apricots, soaked and roughly chopped
- 225 g/8 oz plums, peeled, stoned and roughly chopped
- 225 g/8 oz/1 cup brown sugar
- 60 ml/4 tbsp apple purée

Directions:

1. Combine all the ingredients in a pan and bring slowly to the boil, stirring.
2. Cover and simmer gently for about 1 hour, stirring intermittently, and adding a little water if the sauce becomes too thick.
3. Pour into warm jars, seal, label and store in a cool place for a few weeks before using.

PORK SAUCE

Yield: 4 Servings

Ingredients:

- 10 ml/2 tsp brown sugar
- 15 ml/1 tbsp cornflour (cornstarch)
- 15 ml/1 tbsp rice wine or dry sherry
- 15 ml/1 tbsp soy sauce
- 2 cloves garlic, crushed
- 2 spring onions (scallions), chopped
- 225 g/8 oz minced (ground) pork
- 225 g/8 oz mixed vegetables, diced
- 30 ml/2 tbsp oil
- 450 ml/¾ pt/2 cups chicken stock
- 90 ml/6 tbsp tomato purée (paste)

Directions:

1. Heat the oil and fry the spring onions and garlic until slightly browned.
2. Put in the pork and stir-fry for approximately three minutes.
3. Put in the vegetables and stir-fry for approximately two minutes.
4. Put in the sugar, wine or sherry, soy sauce, tomato purée and stock, bring to the boil, cover and simmer for 4 minutes.
5. Combine the cornflour to a paste with a little water then mix it into the pan.
6. Simmer, stirring, until the sauce becomes thick.
7. Pour over noodles to serve.

SAUCE FOR FRIED FISH

Yield: 4 Servings

Ingredients:

- 1 slice ginger root, minced
- 15 ml/1 tbsp cornflour (cornstarch)
- 15 ml/1 tbsp groundnut (peanut) oil
- 30 ml/2 tbsp brown sugar
- 45 ml/3 tbsp water
- 60 ml/4 tbsp chicken stock

Directions:

1. Combine the ginger, sugar, oil and stock then bring to the boil, stirring.
2. Combine the cornflour and water, stir into the pan and simmer, stirring, until the sauce becomes thick.
3. Pour over fried fish to serve.

SAUCE FOR LOBSTER

Yield: 4 Servings

Ingredients:

- 1 clove garlic, crushed
- 100 g/4 oz minced (ground) pork

- 120 ml/4 fl oz/½ cup water
- 15 ml/1 tbsp black bean sauce
- 15 ml/1 tbsp cornflour (cornstarch)
- 15 ml/1 tbsp rice wine or dry sherry
- 15 ml/1 tbsp soy sauce
- 2 eggs, beaten
- 2 spring onions (scallions), chopped
- 30 ml/2 tbsp groundnut (peanut) oil
- 5 ml/1 tsp sugar

Directions:

1. Heat the oil and fry the garlic and black bean sauce for 30 seconds.
2. Mix in the pork and stir-fry for approximately two minutes.
3. Put in the spring onions, soy sauce, wine or sherry, sugar and water, bring to a simmer, cover and simmer for approximately three minutes.
4. Combine the cornflour with a little water then mix it into the pan.
5. Simmer, stirring, until the sauce becomes thick.
6. Stir the eggs into the pan then remove from the heat.
7. Pour over lobster or prawn dishes to serve.

SWEET AND SOUR EGG SAUCE

Yield: 4 Servings

Ingredients:

- 15 ml/1 tbsp sugar
- 15 ml/1 tbsp wine vinegar
- 30 ml/2 tbsp soy sauce

Directions:

1. Combine all the ingredients together and simmer, stirring, until well blended.
2. Pour over fried eggs to serve.

SWEET AND SOUR SAUCE

Yield: 4 Servings

Ingredients:

- 100 g/4 oz/½ cup sugar
- 120 ml/4 fl oz/½ cup wine vinegar
- 15 ml/1 tbsp cornflour (cornstarch)
- 15 ml/1 tbsp soy sauce
- 250 ml/8 fl oz/1 cup water
- 30 ml/2 tbsp tomato purée (paste)

Directions:

1. Bring three-quarters of the water to the boil.
2. Mix in the sugar and stir until the sugar dissolves.
3. Put in the wine vinegar and stir for approximately one minute.
4. Mix the rest of the water with the tomato purée, cornflour and soy sauce, stir into the pan and simmer, stirring, until the sauce becomes thick.

SWEET AND SPICY SAUCE

Yield: 4 Servings

Ingredients:

- 120 ml/4 fl oz/½ cup water
- 15 ml/1 tbsp cornflour (cornstarch)
- 45 ml/3 tbsp sugar
- 45 ml/3 tbsp wine vinegar
- pinch of salt

Directions:

1. Combine all the ingredients in a pan and simmer, stirring, until the sauce becomes thick.
2. Pour over cooked carrots or cabbage to serve.

DIPS AND DRESSINGS

Chinese dips and dressings go great with pretty much everything. However, you will like certain combinations over the others. It is upto you to find out the combos you like, so don't be afraid to play around and experiment! The dressings are especially good with the Chinese salad recipes that follow.

GARLIC DIP

Yield: about 250 ml/8 fl oz/1 cup

Ingredients:

- 120 ml/4 fl oz/½ cup soy sauce
- 15 ml/1 tbsp tabasco sauce
- 4 cloves garlic, crushed
- pinch of sugar

Directions:

Blend all the ingredients together well and serve with roast chicken.

GARLIC DIP WITH SOY SAUCE

Yield: about 120 ml/4 fl oz/½ cup

Ingredients:

- 10 ml/2 tsp brown sugar
- 10 ml/2 tsp chilli oil
- 4 cloves garlic, crushed
- 60 ml/4 tbsp soy sauce

Directions:

Blend all the ingredients together well and serve with fried or roast chicken dishes.

GINGER DIP

Yield: about 120 ml/4 fl oz/½ cup

Ingredients:

- 1 slice ginger root, minced
- 15 ml/1 tbsp brown sugar
- 30 ml/2 tbsp wine vinegar
- 90 ml/6 tbsp soy sauce

Directions:

Blend all the ingredients together well and serve with prawn or seafood dishes.

HOISIN DIP

Yield: about 90 ml/6 tbsp

Ingredients:

- 5 ml/1 tsp sesame oil
- 90 ml/6 tbsp hoisin sauce

Directions:

Blend the ingredients together well and serve with pork dishes.

HOT CHILLI DIP

Yield: about 120 ml/4 fl oz/½ cup

Ingredients:

- 2½ ml/½ tsp mustard powder
- 60 ml/4 tbsp soy sauce
- 90 ml/6 tbsp chilli sauce

Directions:

Blend all the ingredients together well and serve with pork or chicken dishes.

MUSTARD DIP

Yield: about 120 ml/4 fl oz/½ cup

Ingredients:

- 120 ml/4 fl oz/½ cup made mustard
- 2½ ml/½ tsp salt
- 60 ml/4 tbsp soy sauce

Directions:

Blend all the ingredients together well and serve with pork dishes.

MUSTARD DRESSING

Yield: about 90 ml/6 tbsp

Ingredients:

- 15 ml/1 tbsp mustard powder
- 2½ ml/½ tsp sesame oil
- 30 ml/2 tbsp soy sauce
- 30 ml/2 tbsp wine vinegar
- 5 ml/1 tsp brown sugar

Directions:

1. Combine all the ingredients until well blended.
2. Chill for several hours before using to dress cold chicken dishes.

OIL AND VINEGAR DRESSING

Yield: about 90 ml/6 tbsp

Ingredients:

- 30 ml/2 tbsp wine vinegar
- 5 ml/1 tsp brown sugar
- 60 ml/4 tbsp groundnut (peanut) oil
- few drops of sesame oil
- salt and freshly ground pepper

Directions:

Blend all the ingredients together well.

PEANUT DIP

Yield: about 75 ml/5 tbsp

Ingredients:

- 15 ml/1 tbsp peanut butter
- 15 ml/1 tbsp soy sauce
- 30 ml/2 tbsp groundnut (peanut) oil
- 5 ml/1 tsp chilli sauce
- 5 ml/1 tsp salt
- 5 ml/1 tsp sesame oil

Directions:

Blend all the ingredients together well and serve with tofu or chicken dishes.

PEANUT MAYONNAISE

Yield: about 250 ml/8 fl oz/1 cup

Ingredients:

- 2½ ml/½ tsp salt
- 2½ ml/½ tsp sesame oil
- 30 ml/2 tbsp wine vinegar
- 5 ml/1 tsp groundnut (peanut) oil

- 60 ml/4 tbsp peanut butter
- 75 ml/5 tbsp water
- freshly ground Szechuan pepper

Directions:

Progressively blend all the ingredients together, seasoning with pepper and extra salt to taste.

RICE WINE DIP

Yield: about 250 ml/8 fl oz/1 cup

Ingredients:

- 120 ml/4 fl oz/½ cup rice wine or dry sherry
- 5 ml/1 tsp brown sugar
- 60 ml/4 tbsp soy sauce

Directions:

Blend all the ingredients together well and serve with fried or roast chicken dishes.

SALAD DRESSING

Yield: 4 Servings

Ingredients:

- 15 ml/1 tbsp chopped garlic
- 15 ml/1 tbsp chopped ginger root
- 15 ml/1 tbsp sesame seeds
- 15 ml/1 tbsp sugar
- 45 ml/3 tbsp groundnut (peanut) oil 45 ml/3 tbsp soy sauce
- 45 ml/3 tbsp lemon juice
- 45 ml/3 tbsp orange juice
- 45 ml/3 tbsp rice wine or dry sherry
- 45 ml/3 tbsp wine vinegar
- salt and freshly ground pepper

Directions:

Blend all the ingredients together well and serve in a sauceboat with cold vegetables or green salads.

SEAFOOD DIP

Yield: about 120 ml/4 fl oz/½ cup

Ingredients:

- 1 slice ginger root, minced
- 120 ml/4 fl oz/½ cup wine vinegar

Directions:

Blend the ingredients together well and serve with fish or seafood dishes.

SESAME AND HOISIN DIP

Yield: about 75 ml/5 tbsp

Ingredients:

- 15 ml/1 tbsp brown sugar
- 15 ml/1 tbsp sesame oil
- 15 ml/1 tbsp water
- 30 ml/2 tbsp hoisin sauce

Directions:

Blend all the ingredients together well and serve with prawn or seafood dishes.

SESAME DIP

Yield: about 120 ml/4 fl oz/½ cup

Ingredients:

- 1 clove garlic, crushed
- 120 ml/4 fl oz/½ cup soy sauce
- 5 ml/1 tsp sesame oil

Directions:

Blend all the ingredients together well and serve with pork dishes.

SOY AND GROUNDNUT DRESSING

Yield: about 90 ml/6 tbsp

Ingredients:

- 30 ml/2 tbsp groundnut (peanut) oil
- 5 ml/1 tsp salt
- 5 ml/1 tsp sugar
- 60 ml/4 tbsp soy sauce

Directions:

1. Combine all the ingredients together well.
2. Pour over meat or fish.

SOY AND SESAME DRESSING

Yield: about 90 ml/6 tbsp

Ingredients:

- 5 ml/1 tsp sesame oil
- 90 ml/6 tbsp soy sauce

Directions:

Blend the ingredients together well and pour over cold meat or fish.

SOY AND VINEGAR DRESSING

Yield: about 120 ml/4 fl oz/½ cup

Ingredients:

- 15 ml/1 tbsp brown sugar
- 45 ml/3 tbsp groundnut (peanut) oil
- 45 ml/3 tbsp soy sauce
- 45 ml/3 tbsp wine vinegar

Directions:

Blend the ingredients together well and pour over cold vegetable dishes.

SOY SAUCE AND MUSTARD DIP

Yield: about 60 ml/4 tbsp

Ingredients:

- 10 ml/2 tsp mustard powder
- 45 ml/3 tbsp soy sauce
- 5 ml/1 tsp sesame oil

Directions:

Blend all the ingredients together well and serve with chicken or tofu.

SOY SAUCE DIP

Yield: about 250 ml/8 fl oz/1 cup

Ingredients:

- 120 ml/4 fl oz/½ cup soy sauce

- 90 ml/6 tbsp groundnut (peanut) oil

Directions:

1. Heat the oil to smoking point then remove from the heat.
2. Mix in the soy sauce and serve with chicken dishes.

TOMATO AND CHILLI DIP

Yield: about 120 ml/4 fl oz/½ cup

Ingredients:

- 30 ml/2 tbsp chilli sauce
- 5 ml/1 tsp hoisin sauce
- 60 ml/4 tbsp tomato ketchup (catsup)

Directions:

Combine all the ingredients together well and serve with prawn or seafood dishes.

SALADS

Chinese salads are delicious, nutritious, and easy to make. Make sure you have a few of these in your arsenal, and serve them with your favourite Chinese salad dressings!

ASPARAGUS SALAD

Yield: 4 Servings

Ingredients:

- 10 ml/2 tsp wine vinegar
- 30 ml/2 tbsp soy sauce
- 450 g/1 lb asparagus
- 5 ml/1 tsp sesame oil
- 5 ml/1 tsp sugar

Directions:

1. Parboil the asparagus in boiling water for approximately three minutes then rinse with cold water.
2. Drain thoroughly and allow to cool.
3. Combine the rest of the ingredients, pour over the asparagus and chill for approximately 20 minutes and serve.

AUBERGINE SALAD

Yield: 4 Servings

Ingredients:

- ½ lettuce, separated into leaves
- 1 aubergine (eggplant), halved
- 1 clove garlic, halved
- 15 ml/1 tbsp groundnut (peanut) oil
- 2½ ml/½ tsp salt
- 30 ml/2 tbsp wine vinegar

- pinch of freshly ground pepper

Directions:

1. Put the aubergine in a dish on a steaming rack and steam for about 30 minutes until soft.
2. Allow it to cool slightly then peel.
3. Rub the chop side of the garlic across the inside of a bowl.
4. Combine the rest of the ingredients, pour over the aubergine and toss together.
5. Cover and place in the refrigerator overnight.
6. Put the lettuce on a serving plate and spoon the aubergine on top.

BEAN AND PEPPER SALAD

Yield: 4 Servings

Ingredients:

- 10 ml/2 tsp sesame oil
- 2 red peppers, chopped into strips
- 225 g/8 oz green beans
- 5 ml/1 tsp minced ginger root
- 5 ml/1 tsp sugar
- salt

Directions:

1. Briefly boil the beans and peppers in boiling water for 30 seconds then eliminate the excess liquid well.
2. Combine the sesame oil, ginger, sugar and a pinch of salt and pour over the vegetables.
3. Toss together well and serve.

BEAN SPROUT SALAD

Yield: 4 Servings

Ingredients:

- 30 ml/2 tbsp soy sauce

- 450 g/1 lb bean sprouts
- 5 ml/1 tsp sesame oil
- 5 ml/1 tsp sugar

Directions:

1. Briefly boil the bean sprouts in boiling water for 20 seconds.
2. Drain and allow to cool.
3. Combine all the rest of the ingredients, pour them over the bean sprouts, toss comprehensively. and chill for approximately 20 minutes and serve.

CARROT AND CELERY SALAD

Yield: 4 Servings

Ingredients:

- 10 ml/2 tsp salt
- 2 carrots, shredded
- 2 slices ginger root, shredded
- 2½ ml/½ tsp sesame oil
- 30 ml/2 tbsp soy sauce
- 4 stalks celery, shredded
- 600 ml/1 pt/2½ cups iced water

Directions:

1. Combine the celery, carrots and ginger into a container.
2. Dissolve the salt in the water, pour over the vegetables and allow to stand for one hour.
3. Drain thoroughly and arrange in a serving bowl.
4. Drizzle with soy sauce and toss together well then drizzle with sesame oil and serve instantly.

CELERY SALAD

Yield: 4 Servings

Ingredients:

- ½ head celery, chopped into chunks
- 1 slice ginger root, minced
- 10 ml/2 tsp sesame oil
- 10 ml/2 tsp wine vinegar
- 30 ml/2 tbsp soy sauce
- 5 ml/1 tsp salt
- 50 g/2 oz peeled prawns

Directions:

1. Briefly boil the celery in boiling water for 30 seconds.
2. Drain and pat dry then mix with the prawns.
3. Combine the rest of the ingredients, pour over the celery and toss together well.

CHICKEN SALAD

Yield: 4 Servings

Ingredients:

- 15 ml/1 tbsp sesame oil
- 15 ml/1 tbsp soy sauce
- 2 cloves garlic, crushed
- 2½ ml/½ tsp freshly ground pepper
- 3 stalks celery, diagonally sliced
- 350 g/12 oz cooked chicken, chopped into strips
- 5 ml/1 tsp salt
- 5 ml/1 tsp wine vinegar

Directions:

Combine all the ingredients together well and chill and serve.

CHILLED TOMATO SALAD

Yield: 4 Servings

Ingredients:

- 8 ripe tomatoes, skinned and quartered
- 45 ml/3 tbsp sugar
- 10 ml/2 tsp Worcestershire sauce

Directions:

1. Put the tomatoes into a container and drizzle with sugar and Worcestershire sauce.
2. Chill comprehensively.
3. and serve.

CHINESE LEAF SALAD

Yield: 4 Servings

Ingredients:

- 1 head Chinese leaves, shredded
- 15 ml/1 tbsp sesame oil
- 30 ml/2 tbsp soy sauce
- 5 ml/1 tsp sugar
- salt

Directions:

1. Briefly boil the Chinese leaves in boiling water for 30 seconds then eliminate the excess liquid well.
2. Combine the soy sauce, sesame oil, sugar and a pinch of salt.
3. Pour over the Chinese leaves and toss comprehensively. and serve.

CRAB MEAT AND CUCUMBER RINGS

Yield: 4 Servings

Ingredients:

- 1 clove garlic, crushed
- 1 large cucumber, thickly sliced
- 15 ml/1 tbsp chilli sauce
- 15 ml/1 tbsp chopped fresh chives

- 200 g/7 oz canned crab meat, flaked
- 5 ml/1 tsp horseradish sauce
- 5 ml/1 tsp soy sauce
- 5 olives, chopped
- 50 g/2 oz cottage cheese
- salt

Directions:

1. Combine all the ingredients except the cucumber.
2. Put the cucumber slices on a flat platter and drizzle slightly with salt.
3. Spoon the crab meat mixture on top of the cucumber and serve as a salad or cocktail snack.

CRAB MEAT SALAD

Yield: 4 Servings

Ingredients:

- 1 cos lettuce
- 100 g/4 oz bean sprouts
- 100 g/4 oz Chinese leaves, shredded
- 100 g/4 oz water chestnuts, chopped into strips
- 15 ml/1 tbsp chopped cucumber
- 15 ml/1 tbsp chopped green pepper
- 15 ml/1 tbsp tarragon vinegar
- 225 g/8 oz crab meat
- 30 ml/2 tbsp cider vinegar
- 4 sprigs watercress
- 5 ml/1 tsp chopped fresh chives
- 5 ml/1 tsp chopped fresh parsley
- 5 ml/1 tsp soy sauce
- 90 ml/6 tbsp olive oil
- For the dressing:

Directions:

1. Put the salad ingredients into a container.
2. Combine all the dressing ingredients, pour over the salad and toss together gently.

3. Garnish with the watercress.

CUCUMBER SALAD

Yield: 4 Servings

Ingredients:

- ½ small onion, finely chopped
- 1 clove garlic, crushed
- 1 red chilli pepper, seeded and finely chopped
- 10 ml/2 tsp salt
- 10 ml/2 tsp soy sauce
- 10 ml/2 tsp sugar
- 15 ml/1 tbsp sesame oil
- 2 cucumbers, peeled and seeded
- 30 ml/2 tbsp wine vinegar

Directions:

- Combine the rest of the ingredients and pour over the cucumbers into a container.
- Chop the cucumbers roughly then place them in a colander and drizzle with salt.
- Cover and allow to stand for half an hour and serve.
- Leave for half an hour.
- Rinse the cucumber and pat dry.

CUCUMBER SALAD WITH SPRING ONION DRESSING

Yield: 4 Servings

Ingredients:

- 1 cucumber, sliced
- 4 spring onions (scallions), chopped
- 5 ml/1 tsp sugar
- 60 ml/4 tbsp groundnut (peanut) oil
- salt

Directions:

1. Put the cucumber in a colander and drizzle generously with salt.
2. Mix well then allow to stand for half an hour.
3. Rinse slightly in cold water and eliminate the excess liquid off the excess.
4. Put into a container and mix in the sugar.
5. Heat the oil until moderately hot then remove from the heat and mix in the spring onions.
6. Pour over the cucumber and toss comprehensively. and serve.

GREEN PEPPER SALAD

Yield: 4 Servings

Ingredients:

- 10 ml/2 tsp brown sugar
- 15 ml/1 tbsp sesame oil
- 2 green peppers, chopped into strips
- 2½ ml/½ tsp salt

Directions:

1. Briefly boil the peppers in boiling water for 30 seconds then eliminate the excess liquid well.
2. Combine the sesame oil, sugar and salt, pour over the peppers and toss together well and serve.

MARINATED CUCUMBER

Yield: 4 Servings

Ingredients:

- 1 cucumber, finely sliced
- 120 ml/4 fl oz/½ cup wine vinegar
- 45 ml/3 tbsp sugar
- 5 ml/1 tsp salt

- 75 ml/5 tbsp water

Directions:

1. Drizzle the cucumber with salt and allow to stand for half an hour.
2. Heat the vinegar then mix in the sugar and water, stirring until the sugar dissolves.
3. Bring to the boil and boil for approximately two minutes.
4. Turn off the heat and allow to cool.
5. Put in the cucumbers and allow to stand for several hours and serve.

PORK SALAD

Yield: 4 Servings

Ingredients:

- 10 ml/2 tsp salt
- 120 ml/4 fl oz/½ cup mild mustard
- 250 ml/8 fl oz/1 cup wine vinegar
- 30 ml/2 tbsp chopped flat-leaved parsley
- 450 g/1 lb cooked pork, finely sliced
- 450 g/1 lb green beans

Directions:

1. Briefly boil the beans in boiling water for approximately ten minutes until just soft but still crisp.
2. Drain well.
3. Mix with half the salt and half the wine vinegar and allow to marinate for 2 hours.
4. In the meantime, mix the rest of the salt and wine vinegar with the pork and mustard and leave to marinate.
5. Combine the pork with the beans and serve garnished with parsley.

RICE SALAD

Yield: 4 Servings

Ingredients:

- 1 head lettuce
- 100 g/4 oz canned sardines, drained
- 100 g/4 oz peeled prawns
- 15 ml/1 tbsp capers
- 2 hard-boiled (hard-cooked) eggs, chopped
- 2½ ml/½ tsp mustard powder
- 2½ ml/½ tsp paprika
- 225 g/8 oz cooked long-grain rice
- 250 ml/8 fl oz/1 cup wine vinegar
- 30 ml/2 tbsp chilli sauce
- 30 ml/2 tbsp groundnut (peanut) oil
- 4 small Chinese pickles, chopped
- 4 spring onion (scallions), chopped
- 5 ml/1 tsp chopped fresh parsley
- 5 ml/1 tsp sesame oil
- 5 ml/1 tsp sugar

Directions:

1. Combine the rice and spring onions.
2. Combine the oil, sesame oil, 45 ml/3 tbsp of wine vinegar, sugar, mustard and paprika.
3. Pour half the dressing over the rice and mix well.
4. Put the sardines and prawns into a container, pour over the rest of the wine vinegar and allow to stand for approximately ten minutes then drain.
5. Put the lettuce leaves on a serving plate and mound the rice on top.
6. Put the sardine mixture on top and drizzle with eggs and pickles.
7. Combine the chilli sauce, eggs and capers into the rest of the dressing and serve with the salad.

SESAME CHICKEN SALAD

Yield: 4 Servings

Ingredients:

- 1.5 l/2½ pts/6 cups water
- 15 ml/1 tbsp groundnut (peanut) oil
- 15 ml/1 tbsp sesame oil
- 15 ml/1 tbsp sesame seeds

- 2½ ml/½ tsp five-spice powder
- 2½ ml/½ tsp salt
- 3 chicken breasts
- 3 stalks celery, sliced
- 30 ml/2 tbsp soy sauce
- pinch of freshly ground pepper
- pinch of ground ginger

Directions:

1. Heat the sesame seeds using a dry pan until a golden-brown colour is achieved.
2. Put the chicken, water, 15 ml/1 tbsp soy sauce, salt and five-spice powder in a large saucepan.
3. Bring to the boil, cover and simmer for approximately 20 minutes.
4. Turn off the heat and leave the chicken to stand in the water for one hour.
5. Remove the chicken, reserving the stock and drain.
6. Remove and discard the bones and chop the meat into thick slices.
7. Bring the stock back to the boil, add the celery and cook for about 3 minutes until it is soft but still crisp.
8. Drain well.
9. Combine the rest of the soy sauce with the oils, ginger and pepper and add the chicken and celery.
10. Toss well, transfer to a serving dish and serve sprinkled with sesame seeds.

SHANGHAI SALAD

Yield: 4 Servings

Ingredients:

- 1 onion, finely sliced
- 100 g/4 oz bean sprouts
- 175 ml/6 fl oz/¾ cup mayonnaise
- 450 g/1 lb cooked veal, diced
- 5 ml/1 tsp soy sauce
- 50 g/2 oz Chinese mixed pickles, chopped into strips
- 60 ml/4 tbsp French dressing
- salt and freshly ground pepper

Directions:

1. Put the veal into a container.
2. Combine the French dressing and soy sauce, toss with the veal, cover and leave in the refrigerator overnight.
3. Combine the rest of the ingredients and stir them carefully into the veal.

SHREDDED CUCUMBER SALAD

Yield: 4 Servings

Ingredients:

- 1 clove garlic, crushed
- 1 cucumber, peeled and grated
- 15 ml/1 tbsp groundnut (peanut) oil
- 15 ml/1 tbsp soy sauce
- 2½ ml/½ tsp sugar
- salt

Directions:

1. Drizzle the cucumber with salt and allow to stand for one hour.
2. Rinse and eliminate the excess liquid well.
3. Combine the rest of the ingredients, pour over the cucumber and toss together well.
4. Serve Immediately.

SMASHED CUCUMBER

Yield: 4 Servings

Ingredients:

- 1 cucumber
- 1 slice ginger root, minced
- 30 ml/2 tbsp brown sugar
- 60 ml/4 tbsp wine vinegar

Directions:

1. Peel and slice the cucumber, then smash the slices with a mallet or the bottom of a mug, leaving the slices just intact.
2. Lay out in a serving bowl and refrigerate.
3. Mix the rest of the ingredients in a pan over a low heat and stir until the sugar dissolves.
4. Spoon over the cucumber and serve instantly.

SMASHED CUCUMBER WITH SPRING ONIONS

Yield: 4 Servings

Ingredients:

- 1 cucumber
- 120 ml/4 fl oz/½ cup wine vinegar
- 2 spring onions (scallions), minced
- salt and freshly ground pepper

Directions:

1. Peel and slice the cucumber then smash the slices with a mallet or the bottom of a mug, leaving the slices just intact.
2. Lay out in a serving bowl and refrigerate.
3. Combine the spring onions with the wine vinegar and allow to stand for half an hour.
4. Pour over the cucumber and season with salt and pepper.

SPINACH SALAD

Yield: 4 Servings

Ingredients:

- 450 g/1 lb spinach, chopped into strips
- 30 ml/2 tbsp soy sauce
- 15 ml/1 tbsp wine vinegar
- 5 ml/1 tsp sugar
- 10 ml/2 tsp sesame oil
- 5 ml/1 tsp peanut butter

Directions:

1. Briefly boil the spinach in boiling water for approximately two minutes then eliminate the excess liquid and rinse in cold water.
2. Combine the dressing ingredients, pour over the spinach and toss together well.
3. Chill for approximately 20 minutes and serve.

TOMATO AND ONION SALAD

Yield: 4 Servings

Ingredients:

- 10 ml/2 tsp wine vinegar
- 2 onions, finely sliced
- 30 ml/2 tbsp soy sauce
- 450 g/1 lb tomatoes, finely sliced
- 5 ml/1 tsp sesame oil
- 5 ml/1 tsp sugar

Directions:

1. Layer the tomatoes and onions into a container.
2. Mix the rest of the ingredients and pour them over the tomatoes and onions.
3. Chill for approximately 20 minutes and serve.

TUNA SALAD

Yield: 4 Servings

Ingredients:

- 1 green pepper, chopped
- 1 stalk celery, diagonally sliced
- 100 g/4 oz bean sprouts
- 2 spring onions (scallions), chopped
- 200 g/7 oz canned tuna, drained and flaked
- 300 ml/½ pt/1¼ cups mayonnaise

- 5 ml/1 tsp salt

Directions:

Combine all the ingredients carefully and chill well and serve.

POULTRY AND GAME

Chicken is ultra-popular in china, and goes perfectly with the Chinese way of cooking. Chinese chicken recipes are great for people on a budget, or in a hurry.

Chicken Is cheap, cooks fast, and tastes absolutely amazing!

ALMOND CHICKEN

Yield: 4 Servings

Ingredients:

- 1 egg white
- 1 large carrot, diced
- 100 g/4 oz bamboo shoots, sliced
- 100 g/4 oz mushrooms, sliced
- 15 ml/1 tbsp soy sauce
- 2½ ml/½ tsp salt
- 3 stalks celery, sliced
- 375 ml/13 fl oz/1½ cups chicken stock
- 4 chicken breasts
- 45 ml/3 tbsp cornflour (cornstarch)
- 5 ml/1 tsp grated ginger root
- 6 spring onions (scallions), sliced
- 60 ml/4 tbsp rice wine or dry sherry
- 75 g/3 oz/½ cup briefly boiled almonds
- oil for deep-frying

Directions:

1. Combine the stock, half the wine or sherry, 30 ml/2 tbsp of cornflour, and the soy sauce in a saucepan.
2. Bring to the boil, stirring, then simmer for approximately five minutes until the mixture becomes thick.
3. Turn off the heat and keep warm.
4. Remove the skin and bones from the chicken and chop it into 2½ cm/1 in pieces.

5. Mix the rest of the wine or sherry and cornflour, the egg white and salt, add the chicken pieces and stir thoroughly.
6. Heat the oil and fry the chicken pieces a few at a time for approximately five minutes until a golden-brown colour is achieved.
7. Drain thoroughly.
8. Remove all but 30 ml/ 2 tbsp of oil from the pan and stir-fry the almonds for approximately two minutes until golden.
9. Drain thoroughly.
10. Put in the carrot and ginger to the pan and stir-fry for approximately one minute.
11. Add the rest of the vegetables and stir-fry for about 3 minutes until the vegetables are soft but still crisp.
12. Return the chicken and almonds to the pan with the sauce and stir over a moderate heat for a few minutes until heated through.

ANISE CHICKEN

Yield: 4 Servings

Ingredients:

- 1 clove garlic, chopped
- 15 ml/1 tbsp plain (all-purpose) flour
- 15 ml/1 tbsp sugar
- 2 cloves star anise
- 2 onions, chopped
- 2 slices ginger root, chopped
- 225 g/8 oz potatoes, diced
- 30 ml/2 tbsp curry powder
- 30 ml/2 tbsp soy sauce
- 450 g/1 lb chicken, cubed
- 450 ml/¾ pt/2 cups chicken stock
- 75 ml/5 tbsp groundnut (peanut) oil

Directions:

1. Heat half the oil and fry the onions until slightly browned then remove them from the pan.
2. Heat the rest of the oil and fry the garlic and ginger for 30 seconds.
3. Mix in the flour and curry powder and cook for approximately two minutes.

4. Return the onions to the pan, add the chicken and stir-fry for approximately three minutes.
5. Put in the sugar, soy sauce, stock and anise, bring to the boil, cover and simmer for approximately fifteen minutes.
6. Put in the potatoes, return to the boil, cover and simmer for another 20 minutes until soft.

BACON-WRAPPED CHICKEN

Yield: 4 Servings

Ingredients:

- 1 eggs, slightly beaten
- 100 g/4 oz plain (all-purpose) flour
- 15 ml/1 tbsp rice wine or dry sherry
- 225 g/8 oz bacon rashers
- 225 g/8 oz chicken, cubed
- 30 ml/2 tbsp soy sauce
- 4 tomatoes, sliced
- 5 ml/1 tsp sesame oil
- 5 ml/1 tsp sugar
- oil for deep-frying
- salt and freshly ground pepper

Directions:

1. Combine the chicken with the soy sauce, wine or sherry, sugar, sesame oil, salt and pepper.
2. Cover and allow to marinate for one hour, stirring intermittently, then remove the chicken and discard the marinade.
3. Chop the bacon into pieces and wrap it around the chicken cubes.
4. Beat the eggs with the flour to make a thick batter, adding a little milk if needed.
5. Immerse the cubes in the batter.
6. Heat the oil and deep-fry the cubes until a golden-brown colour is achieved and cooked through.
7. Serve garnished with tomatoes.

BARBECUED CHICKEN DRUMSTICKS

Yield: 4 Servings

Ingredients:

- 120 ml/4 fl oz/½ cup chilli sauce
- 120 ml/4 fl oz/½ cup orange juice
- 15 ml/1 tbsp lemon juice
- 16 chicken drumsticks
- 2 slices ginger root, minced
- 30 ml/2 tbsp honey
- 30 ml/2 tbsp olive oil
- 30 ml/2 tbsp rice wine or dry sherry
- 30 ml/2 tbsp soy sauce
- 30 ml/2 tbsp wine vinegar
- salt and freshly ground pepper

Directions:

1. Combine all the ingredients except the chilli sauce, cover and allow to marinate in the refrigerator overnight.
2. Remove the chicken from the marinade and barbecue or grill (broil) for about 25 minutes, turning and basting with the chilli sauce as you cook.

BRAISED CHICKEN

Yield: 4 Servings

Ingredients:

- 1 chicken
- 120 ml/4 fl oz/½ cup soy sauce
- 3 slices ginger root
- 3 spring onions (scallions), sliced
- 30 ml/2 tbsp rice wine or dry sherry
- 5 ml/1 tsp sugar
- 75 ml/5 tbsp groundnut (peanut) oil

Directions:

1. Heat the oil and fry the chicken until browned.
2. Put in the spring onions, ginger, soy sauce and wine or sherry, and bring to the boil.
3. Cover and simmer for half an hour, turning intermittently.
4. Put in the sugar, cover and simmer for another 30 minutes until the chicken is cooked.

BRAISED CHICKEN WITH EGGS

Yield: 4 Servings

Ingredients:

- 1 green pepper, chopped into strips
- 1 red pepper, chopped into strips
- 100 g/4 oz iceberg lettuce, shredded
- 15 ml/1 tbsp cornflour (cornstarch)
- 250 ml/8 fl oz/1 cup chicken stock
- 30 ml/2 tbsp groundnut (peanut) oil
- 30 ml/2 tbsp hoisin sauce
- 30 ml/2 tbsp sherry
- 30 ml/2 tbsp water
- 4 chicken breast fillets, chopped into strips
- 4 eggs
- 45 ml/3 tbsp rice wine or dry sherry
- 45 ml/3 tbsp soy sauce
- 5 ml/1 tsp brown sugar
- salt and pepper

Directions:

1. Heat the oil and fry the chicken and peppers until a golden-brown colour is achieved.
2. Put in the soy sauce, wine or sherry and stock, bring to the boil, cover and simmer for half an hour.
3. Put in the lettuce, sugar and hoisin sauce and season with salt and pepper.
4. Combine the cornflour and water, mix it into the sauce and bring to the boil, stirring.
5. Beat the eggs with the sherry and fry as thin omelettes.
6. Drizzle with salt and pepper and tear into strips.
7. Lay out in a heated serving dish and spoon over the chicken.

BRAISED CHICKEN WITH POTATOES

Yield: 4 Servings

Ingredients:

- 1 clove garlic, crushed
- 1 onion, sliced
- 15 ml/1 tbsp brown sugar
- 2 potatoes, cubed
- 2 slices ginger root, minced
- 4 chicken pieces
- 45 ml/3 tbsp groundnut (peanut) oil
- 45 ml/3 tbsp soy sauce
- 450 ml/¾ pt/2 cups water

Directions:

1. Chop the chicken into 5 cm/2 in pieces.
2. Heat the oil and fry the onion, garlic and ginger until slightly browned.
3. Put in the chicken and fry until slightly browned.
4. Put in the water and soy sauce and bring to the boil.
5. Mix in the sugar, cover and simmer for about 30 minutes.
6. Put in the potatoes to the pan, cover and simmer for another 10 minutes until the chicken is soft and the potatoes are cooked.

BRAISED DUCK

Yield: 4 Servings

Ingredients:

- 1 duck
- 1 slice ginger root, minced
- 120 ml/4 fl oz/½ cup groundnut (peanut) oil
- 120 ml/4 fl oz/½ cup soy sauce
- 15 ml/1 tbsp brown sugar
- 30 ml/2 tbsp rice wine or dry sherry
- 4 spring onions (scallions), chopped
- 600 ml/1 pt/2½ cups water

Directions:

1. Combine the spring onions, ginger, soy sauce and wine or sherry and rub it over the duck inside and out.
2. Heat the oil and fry the duck until slightly browned on all sides.
3. Drain off the oil.
4. Put in the water and the rest of the soy sauce mixture, bring to the boil then cover and simmer for one hour.
5. Put in the sugar then cover and simmer for another 40 minutes until the duck is soft.

BRAISED DUCK WITH CHINESE LEAVES

Yield: 4 Servings

Ingredients:

- 1 duck
- 1 slice ginger root, minced
- 15 ml/1 tbsp cornflour (cornstarch)
- 2 cloves garlic, crushed
- 225 g/8 oz Chinese leaves, shredded
- 30 ml/2 tbsp hoisin sauce
- 30 ml/2 tbsp rice wine or dry sherry
- 4 spring onions (scallions), chopped
- 5 ml/1 tsp salt
- 5 ml/1 tsp sugar
- 60 ml/4 tbsp groundnut (peanut) oil
- 600 ml/1 pt/2½ cups water
- 75 ml/5 tbsp soy sauce

Directions:

1. Chop the duck into about 6 pieces.
2. Combine the wine or sherry, hoisin sauce, cornflour, salt and sugar and rub over the duck.
3. Allow to stand for one hour.
4. Heat the oil and fry the spring onions, garlic and ginger for a few seconds.
5. Put in the duck and fry until slightly browned on all sides.
6. Drain off any excess fat.

7. Pour in the soy sauce and water, bring to the boil, cover and simmer for about 30 minutes.
8. Put in the Chinese leaves, cover again and simmer for another 30 minutes until the duck is soft.

BRAISED DUCK WITH ONIONS

Yield: 4 Servings

Ingredients:

- 1 duck
- 1 slice ginger root, minced
- 1 spring onion (scallion), chopped
- 100 g/4 oz bamboo shoots, sliced
- 15 ml/1 tbsp brown sugar
- 15 ml/1 tbsp cornflour (cornstarch)
- 4 dried Chinese mushrooms
- 45 ml/3 tbsp rice wine or dry sherry
- 45 ml/3 tbsp water
- 450 g/1 lb onions, sliced
- 60 ml/4 tbsp groundnut (peanut) oil
- 90 ml/6 tbsp soy sauce

Directions:

1. Soak the mushrooms in warm water for half an hour then drain.
2. Discard the stalks and slice the caps.
3. Rub 15 ml/1 tbsp of soy sauce into the duck.
4. Reserve 15 ml/1 tbsp of oil, heat the rest of the oil and fry the spring onion and ginger until slightly browned.
5. Put in the duck and fry until slightly browned on all sides.
6. Pour off any excess fat.
7. Put in the wine or sherry, rest of the soy sauce to the pan and just enough water almost to cover the duck.
8. Bring to the boil, cover and simmer for one hour, turning intermittently.
9. Heat the reserved oil and fry the onions until softened.
10. Turn off the heat and mix in the bamboo shoots and mushrooms then put them into the duck, cover and simmer for another 30 minutes until the duck is soft.

11. Remove the duck from the pan, chopped into serving pieces and lay out on a warmed serving plate.
12. Bring the liquids in the pan to the boil, add the sugar and cornflour and simmer, stirring, until the mixture boils and becomes thick.
13. Pour over the duck to serve.

BRAISED DUCK WITH PINEAPPLE

Yield: 4 Servings

Ingredients:

- 1 duck
- 400 g/14 oz canned pineapple chunks in syrup
- 45 ml/3 tbsp soy sauce
- 5 ml/1 tsp salt
- pinch of freshly ground pepper

Directions:

1. Put the duck in a heavy-based pan, just cover with water, bring to the boil then cover and simmer for one hour.
2. Eliminate the excess liquid from the pineapple syrup into the pan with the soy sauce, salt and pepper, cover and simmer for another 30 minutes.
3. Put in the pineapple pieces and simmer for another 15 minutes until the duck is soft.

CHICKEN AND MUSHROOM STIR-FRY

Yield: 4 Servings

Ingredients:

- 1 clove garlic, crushed
- 1 slice ginger root, minced
- 1 spring onion (scallion), chopped
- 15 ml/1 tbsp rice wine or dry sherry
- 225 g/8 oz button mushrooms
- 225 g/8 oz chicken breast, chopped into slivers

- 45 ml/3 tbsp groundnut (peanut) oil
- 45 ml/3 tbsp soy sauce
- 5 ml/1 tsp cornflour (cornstarch)

Directions:

1. Heat the oil and fry the garlic, spring onion and ginger until slightly browned.
2. Put in the chicken and stir-fry for approximately five minutes.
3. Put in the mushrooms and stir-fry for approximately three minutes.
4. Put in the soy sauce, wine or sherry and cornflour and stir-fry for approximately five minutes until the chicken is cooked through.

CHICKEN AND PINEAPPLE

Yield: 4 Servings

Ingredients:

- 100 g/4 oz pineapple chunks
- 100 g/4 oz water chestnuts, sliced
- 2 cloves garlic, crushed
- 2 onions, sliced
- 30 ml/2 tbsp cornflour (cornstarch)
- 30 ml/2 tbsp groundnut (peanut) oil
- 30 ml/2 tbsp pineapple juice
- 30 ml/2 tbsp rice wine or dry sherry
- 30 ml/2 tbsp soy sauce
- 450 g/1 lb boned chicken, finely sliced
- 450 ml/¾ pt/2 cups chicken stock
- 5 ml/1 tsp salt
- 5 ml/1 tsp sugar
- freshly ground pepper

Directions:

1. Heat the oil, salt and garlic until the garlic turns light golden.
2. Put in the chicken and stir-fry for approximately two minutes.
3. Put in the onions, water chestnuts and pineapple and stir-fry for approximately two minutes.
4. Put in the wine or sherry, stock and sugar and season with pepper.

5. Bring to the boil, cover and simmer for approximately five minutes.
6. Combine the pineapple juice, soy sauce and cornflour.
7. Stir into the pan and simmer, stirring until the sauce becomes thick and clears.

CHICKEN AND TOMATOES WITH BLACK BEAN SAUCE

Yield: 4 Servings

Ingredients:

- 1 clove garlic, crushed
- 10 ml/2 tsp cornflour (cornstarch)
- 15 ml/1 tbsp rice wine or dry sherry
- 15 ml/1 tbsp soy sauce
- 225 g/8 oz chicken, diced
- 3 tomatoes, skinned and quartered
- 45 ml/3 tbsp black bean sauce
- 45 ml/3 tbsp groundnut (peanut) oil
- 45 ml/3 tbsp water
- 5 ml/1 tsp sugar
- 90 ml/6 tbsp chicken stock

Directions:

1. Heat the oil and fry the garlic for 30 seconds.
2. Put in the black bean sauce and fry for 30 seconds then add the chicken and stir until well coated in oil.
3. Put in the wine or sherry, sugar, soy sauce and stock, bring to the boil, cover and simmer for approximately five minutes until the chicken is cooked.
4. Combine the cornflour and water to a paste, mix it into the pan and simmer, stirring, until the sauce clears and becomes thick.

CHICKEN CHOP SUEY

Yield: 4 Servings

Ingredients:

- 1 slice ginger root, chopped
- 100 g/4 oz bamboo shoots, chopped into strips
- 100 g/4 oz Chinese leaves, shredded
- 15 ml/1 tbsp cornflour (cornstarch)
- 15 ml/1 tbsp rice wine or dry sherry
- 2 cloves garlic, crushed
- 2½ ml/½ tsp sugar
- 225 g/8 oz chicken breast, chopped into strips
- 3 spring onions (scallions), sliced
- 45 ml/3 tbsp soy sauce
- 5 ml/1 tsp salt
- 60 ml/4 tbsp groundnut (peanut) oil
- freshly ground pepper

Directions:

1. Briefly boil the Chinese leaves and bamboo shoots in boiling water for approximately two minutes.
2. Drain and pat dry.
3. Heat 45 ml/3 tbsp of oil and fry the onions, garlic and ginger until slightly browned.
4. Put in the chicken and stir-fry for 4 minutes.
5. Take out of the pan.
6. Heat the rest of the oil and stir-fry the vegetables for approximately three minutes.
7. Put in the chicken, soy sauce, wine or sherry, salt, sugar and a pinch of pepper and stir-fry for approximately one minute.
8. Combine the cornflour with a little water, mix it into the sauce and simmer, stirring, until the sauce clears and becomes thick.

CHICKEN CHOW MEIN

Yield: 4 Servings

Ingredients:

- 100 g/4 oz celery, sliced
- 2 cloves garlic, crushed
- 225 g/8 oz bamboo shoots, sliced
- 225 g/8 oz bean sprouts
- 225 g/8 oz dried Chinese noodles

- 225 g/8 oz mushrooms, sliced
- 30 ml/2 tbsp cornflour (cornstarch)
- 30 ml/2 tbsp groundnut (peanut) oil
- 30 ml/2 tbsp soy sauce
- 4 onions, chopped into wedges
- 450 g/1 lb chicken, sliced
- 450 ml/¾ pt/2 cups chicken stock

Directions:

1. Heat the oil with the garlic until slightly golden then add the chicken and stir-fry for approximately two minutes until slightly browned.
2. Put in the bamboo shoots, celery and mushrooms and stir-fry for approximately three minutes.
3. Add most of the stock, bring to the boil, cover and simmer for 8 minutes.
4. Put in the bean sprouts and onions and simmer for approximately two minutes, stirring, until there is just a little stock rest of the.
5. Combine the rest of the stock with the soy sauce and cornflour.
6. Stir it into the pan and simmer, stirring, until the sauce clears and becomes thick.
7. In the meantime, cook the noodles in boiling salted water for a few minutes, according to the instructions on the packet.
8. Drain thoroughly then toss with the chicken mixture and serve instantly.

CHICKEN EGG ROLLS

Yield: 4 Servings

Ingredients:

- 1 egg, beaten
- 100 g/4 oz chicken, chopped into strips
- 100 g/4 oz spinach
- 12 egg roll skins
- 15 ml/1 tbsp soy sauce
- 2½ ml/½ tsp salt
- 2½ ml/½ tsp sugar
- 225 g/8 oz bean sprouts
- 3 spring onions (scallions), chopped
- 4 dried Chinese mushrooms

- 5 ml/1 tsp cornflour (cornstarch)
- 60 ml/4 tbsp groundnut (peanut) oil
- oil for deep-frying

Directions:

1. Soak the mushrooms in warm water for half an hour then drain.
2. Discard the stalks and chop the caps.
3. Put the chicken into a container.
4. Combine the cornflour with 5 ml/1 tsp of soy sauce, the salt and sugar and stir into the chicken.
5. Allow to stand for approximately fifteen minutes.
6. Heat half the oil and stir-fry the chicken until slightly browned.
7. Briefly boil the bean sprouts in boiling water for approximately three minutes then drain.
8. Heat the rest of the oil and fry the spring onions until slightly browned.
9. Mix in the mushrooms, bean sprouts, spinach and rest of the soy sauce.
10. Add in the chicken and stir-fry for approximately two minutes.
11. Allow it to cool.
12. Put a little filling on the centre of each skin and brush the edges with beaten egg.
13. Fold in the sides then roll up the egg rolls, sealing the edges with egg.
14. Heat the oil and deep-fry the egg rolls until crisp and golden.

CHICKEN FOO YUNG

Yield: 4 Servings

Ingredients:

- 1 onion, finely chopped
- 100 g/4 oz mushrooms, roughly chopped
- 225 g/8 oz chicken breast, diced
- 45 ml/3 tbsp cornflour (cornstarch)
- 45 ml/3 tbsp groundnut (peanut) oil
- 5 ml/1 tsp salt
- 6 eggs, beaten

Directions:

1. Beat the eggs then beat in the cornflour.

2. Mix in all the rest of the ingredients except the oil.
3. Heat the oil.
4. Pour the mixture into the pan a little at a time to make small pancakes about 7.5 cm/3 in across.
5. Cook until the bottom is golden-brown then turn and cook the other side.

CHICKEN IN SESAME OIL

Yield: 4 Servings

Ingredients:

- 4 chicken pieces
- 5 ml/1 tsp sugar
- 5 slices ginger root
- 60 ml/4 tbsp sesame oil
- 600 ml/1 pt/2½ cups rice wine or dry sherry
- 90 ml/6 tbsp groundnut (peanut) oil
- salt and freshly ground pepper

Directions:

1. Heat the oils and fry the ginger and chicken until slightly browned.
2. Put in the wine or sherry and season with sugar, salt and pepper.
3. Bring to the boil and simmer gently, uncovered, until the chicken is soft and the sauce has reduced.
4. Serve in bowls.

CHICKEN IN SOY SAUCE

Yield: 4 Servings

Ingredients:

- 1 chicken
- 1 cucumber, peeled and sliced
- 1 onion, chopped
- 15 ml/1 tbsp cornflour (cornstarch)

- 3 slices root ginger, minced
- 30 ml/2 tbsp chopped fresh parsley
- 300 ml/½ pt/1¼ cups rice wine or dry sherry
- 300 ml/½ pt/1¼ cups soy sauce
- 50 g/2 oz/¼ cup sugar
- 60 ml/4 tbsp water

Directions:

1. Combine the soy sauce, wine or sherry, onion, ginger and sugar in a pan and bring to the boil.
2. Put in the chicken, return to the boil, cover and simmer gently for one hour, turning the chicken intermittently, until the chicken is cooked.
3. Transfer the chicken to a warmed serving plate and carve.
4. Pour out all but 250 ml/8 fl oz/1 cup of the cooking liquid and bring it back to the boil.
5. Blend the cornflour and water to a paste, mix it into the pan and simmer, stirring, until the sauce clears and becomes thick.
6. Brush a little of the sauce over the chicken and garnish the chicken with cucumber and parsley.
7. Serve the rest of the sauce separately.

CHICKEN IN TOMATO SAUCE

Yield: 4 Servings

Ingredients:

- 120 ml/4 fl oz/½ cup tomato ketchup (catsup)
- 15 ml/1 tbsp cornflour (cornstarch)
- 2 cloves garlic, crushed
- 30 ml/2 tbsp groundnut (peanut) oil
- 300 ml/½ pt/1¼ cups chicken stock
- 4 spring onions (scallions), sliced
- 450 g/1 lb chicken, cubed
- 5 ml/1 tsp salt

Directions:

1. Heat the oil with the salt and garlic until the garlic is slightly golden.
2. Put in the chicken and stir-fry until slightly browned.

3. Add most of the stock, bring to the boil, cover and simmer for about 15 minutes until the chicken is soft.
4. Stir the rest of the stock with the ketchup and cornflour and mix it into the pan.
5. Simmer, stirring, until the sauce becomes thick and clears.
6. If the sauce is too thin, leave it simmering for a while until it has reduced.
7. Put in the spring onions and simmer for approximately two minutes and serve.

CHICKEN LIVERS WITH BAMBOO SHOOTS

Yield: 4 Servings

Ingredients:

- 100 g/4 oz bamboo shoots, sliced
- 100 g/4 oz water chestnuts, sliced
- 15 ml/1 tbsp soy sauce
- 225 g/8 oz chicken livers, thickly sliced
- 45 ml/3 tbsp groundnut (peanut) oil
- 45 ml/3 tbsp rice wine or dry sherry
- 60 ml/4 tbsp chicken stock
- salt and freshly ground pepper

Directions:

1. Combine the chicken livers with the wine or sherry and allow to stand for half an hour.
2. Heat the oil and fry the chicken livers until slightly browned.
3. Put in the marinade, soy sauce, bamboo shoots, water chestnuts and stock.
4. Bring to the boil and season with salt and pepper.
5. Cover and simmer for approximately ten minutes until soft.

CHICKEN LIVERS WITH MANGETOUT

Yield: 4 Servings

Ingredients:

- 10 ml/2 tsp cornflour (cornstarch)
- 10 ml/2 tsp cornflour (cornstarch)

- 10 ml/2 tsp rice wine or dry sherry
- 100 g/4 oz mangetout (snow peas)
- 15 ml/1 tbsp soy sauce
- 2 slices ginger root, minced
- 2½ ml/½ tsp salt
- 225 g/8 oz chicken livers, thickly sliced
- 45 ml/3 tbsp groundnut (peanut) oil
- 60 ml/4 tbsp water

Directions:

1. Put the chicken livers into a container.
2. Put in the cornflour, wine or sherry and soy sauce and toss comprehensively. to coat.
3. Heat half the oil and fry the salt and ginger until slightly browned.
4. Put in the mangetout and stir-fry until well coated with oil then remove from the pan.
5. Heat the rest of the oil and fry the chicken livers for approximately five minutes until cooked through.
6. Combine the cornflour and water to a paste, mix it into the pan and simmer, stirring, until the sauce clears and becomes thick.
7. Return the mangetout to the pan and simmer until heated through.

CHICKEN LIVERS WITH NOODLE PANCAKE

Yield: 4 Servings

Ingredients:

- 1 onion, sliced
- 120 ml/4 fl oz/½ cup chicken stock
- 15 ml/1 tbsp cornflour (cornstarch)
- 15 ml/1 tbsp soy sauce
- 2 stalks celery, sliced
- 30 ml/2 tbsp groundnut (peanut) oil
- 30 ml/2 tbsp water
- 450 g/1 lb chicken livers, halved
- noodle pancake

Directions:

1. Heat the oil and fry the onion until softened.

2. Put in the chicken livers and stir-fry until coloured.
3. Put in the celery and stir-fry for approximately one minute.
4. Put in the stock, bring to the boil, cover and simmer for approximately five minutes.
5. Combine the cornflour, soy sauce and water to a paste, mix it into the pan and simmer, stirring, until the sauce clears and becomes thick.
6. Pour the mixture over the noodle pancake and serve.

CHICKEN LIVERS WITH OYSTER SAUCE

Yield: 4 Servings

Ingredients:

- 1 onion, chopped
- 100 g/4 oz mushrooms, sliced
- 120 ml/4 fl oz/½ cup chicken stock
- 15 ml/1 tbsp cornflour (cornstarch)
- 15 ml/1 tbsp rice wine or dry sherry
- 15 ml/1 tbsp soy sauce
- 225 g/8 oz chicken livers, halved
- 30 ml/2 tbsp oyster sauce
- 45 ml/3 tbsp groundnut (peanut) oil
- 45 ml/3 tbsp water
- 5 ml/1 tsp sugar

Directions:

1. Heat half the oil and fry the onion until softened.
2. Put in the chicken livers and fry until just coloured.
3. Put in the mushrooms and fry for approximately two minutes.
4. Combine the oyster sauce, soy sauce, wine or sherry, stock and sugar, pour it into the pan and bring to the boil, stirring.
5. Combine the cornflour and water to a paste, put it into the pan and simmer, stirring until the sauce clears and becomes thick and the livers are soft.

CHICKEN LIVERS WITH PINEAPPLE

Yield: 4 Servings

Ingredients:

- 100 g/4 oz pineapple chunks
- 15 ml/1 tbsp cornflour (cornstarch)
- 15 ml/1 tbsp sugar
- 15 ml/1 tbsp wine vinegar
- 225 g/8 oz chicken livers, halved
- 30 ml/2 tbsp soy sauce
- 45 ml/3 tbsp groundnut (peanut) oil
- 60 ml/4 tbsp chicken stock
- salt and freshly ground pepper

Directions:

1. Briefly boil the chicken livers in boiling water for 30 seconds then drain.
2. Heat the oil and stir-fry the chicken livers for 30 seconds.
3. Combine the soy sauce, cornflour, sugar, wine vinegar, salt and pepper, pour into the pan and stir thoroughly to coat the chicken livers.
4. Put in the pineapple chunks and stock and stir-fry for about 3 minutes until the livers are cooked.

CHICKEN PARCELS

Yield: 4 Servings

Ingredients:

- 225 g/8 oz chicken
- 30 ml/2 tbsp groundnut (peanut) oil
- 30 ml/2 tbsp rice wine or dry sherry
- 30 ml/2 tbsp soy sauce
- oil for deep-frying
- waxed paper or baking parchment

Directions:

1. Chop the chicken into 5 cm/2 in cubes.
2. Combine the wine or sherry and soy sauce, pour over the chicken and stir thoroughly.
3. Cover and allow to stand for one hour, stirring intermittently.
4. Chop the paper into 10 cm/4 in squares and brush with oil.

5. Eliminate the excess liquid from the chicken well.
6. Put a piece of paper on the work surface with one corner pointing towards you.
7. Put a piece of chicken on the square just below the centre, fold up the bottom corner and fold up again to encase the chicken.
8. Fold in the sides then fold down the top corner to secure the parcel.
9. Heat the oil and deep-fry the chicken parcels for approximately five minutes until cooked.
10. Serve hot in the parcels for the guests to open themselves.

CHICKEN RISSOLES

Yield: 4 Servings

Ingredients:

- 1 slice ginger root, minced
- 1 spring onion (scallion), chopped
- 120 ml/4 fl oz/½ cup groundnut (peanut) oil
- 2 egg whites
- 225 g/8 oz chicken meat, minced (ground)
- 3 water chestnuts, minced
- 5 ml/1 tsp chopped ham
- 5 ml/1 tsp freshly ground pepper
- 5 ml/2 tsp salt

Directions:

1. Combine the chicken, chestnuts, half the spring onion, the ginger, egg whites, salt and pepper.
2. mould into small balls and press flat.
3. Heat the oil and fry the rissoles until a golden-brown colour is achieved, turning once.
4. Serve sprinkled with the rest of the spring onion and the ham.

CHICKEN SPRING ROLLS

Yield: 4 Servings

Ingredients:

- 1 clove garlic, crushed
- 100 g/4 oz bamboo shoots, shredded
- 100 g/4 oz bean sprouts
- 100 g/4 oz mushrooms, sliced
- 15 ml/1 tbsp groundnut (peanut) oil
- 175 g/6 oz cabbage, shredded
- 225 g/8 oz chicken, chopped into strips
- 5 ml/1 tsp rice wine or dry sherry
- 5 ml/1 tsp soy sauce
- 5 ml/1 tsp sugar
- 50 g/2 oz water chestnuts, shredded
- 8 spring roll skins
- oil for deep-frying
- pinch of salt

Directions:

1. Heat the oil, salt and garlic and fry gently until the garlic begins to turn golden.
2. Put in the chicken and mushrooms and stir-fry for a few minutes until the chicken turns white.
3. Put in the cabbage, bamboo shoots, water chestnuts and bean sprouts and stir-fry for approximately three minutes.
4. Put in the sugar, wine or sherry and soy sauce, stir thoroughly, cover and stir-fry for a final 2 minutes.
5. Turn into a colander and leave to drain.
6. Put a few spoonfuls of the filling mixture in the centre of each spring roll skin, fold up the bottom, fold in the sides, then roll upwards, enclosing the filling.
7. Seal the edge with a little flour and water mixture then leave to dry for half an hour.
8. Heat the oil and deep-fry the spring rolls for approximately ten minutes until crisp and golden brown.
9. Drain thoroughly and serve.

CHICKEN WITH ALMONDS AND VEGETABLES

Yield: 4 Servings

Ingredients:

- 10 ml/2 tsp cornflour (cornstarch)

- 100 g/4 oz Chinese cabbage, shredded
- 100 g/4 oz flaked almonds, toasted
- 120 ml/4 fl oz/½ cup chicken stock
- 15 ml/1 tbsp rice wine or dry sherry
- 15 ml/1 tbsp water
- 2 stalks celery, diced
- 225 g/8 oz chicken breast, diced
- 3 water chestnuts, diced
- 4 slices ginger root, minced
- 5 ml/1 tsp salt
- 50 g/2 oz bamboo shoots, diced
- 50 g/2 oz mangetout (snow peas)
- 50 g/2 oz mushrooms, diced
- 75 ml/5 tbsp groundnut (peanut) oil

Directions:

1. Heat half the oil and stir-fry the ginger and salt for 30 seconds.
2. Put in the cabbage, bamboo shoots, mushrooms, celery and water chestnuts and stir-fry for approximately two minutes.
3. Put in the stock, bring to the boil, cover and simmer for approximately two minutes.
4. Remove the vegetables and sauce from the pan.
5. Heat the rest of the oil and fry the chicken for approximately one minute.
6. Put in the wine or sherry and fry for approximately one minute.
7. Put the vegetables back into the pan with the mangetout and almonds and simmer for 30 seconds.
8. Blend the cornflour and water to a paste, mix it into the sauce and simmer, stirring, until the sauce becomes thick.

CHICKEN WITH ALMONDS AND WATER CHESTNUTS

Yield: 4 Servings

Ingredients:

- 100 g/4 oz ground almonds
- 100 g/4 oz water chestnuts, sliced
- 30 ml/2 tbsp soy sauce
- 4 chicken pieces, boned

- 6 dried Chinese mushrooms
- 60 ml/4 tbsp groundnut (peanut) oil
- 75 ml/5 tbsp chicken stock
- salt and freshly ground pepper

Directions:

1. Soak the mushrooms in warm water for half an hour then drain.
2. Discard the stalks and slice the caps.
3. Thinly slice the chicken.
4. Season the almonds generously with salt and pepper and coat the chicken slices in the almonds.
5. Heat the oil and fry the chicken until slightly browned.
6. Put in the mushrooms, water chestnuts, stock and soy sauce, bring to the boil, cover and simmer for a few minutes until the chicken is cooked.

CHICKEN WITH APRICOTS

Yield: 4 Servings

Ingredients:

- 225 g/8 oz canned apricots, halved
- 30 ml/2 tbsp flaked almonds, toasted
- 300 ml/½ pt/1¼ cups Sweet and Sour Sauce
- 4 chicken pieces
- 60 ml/4 tbsp groundnut (peanut) oil
- pinch of ground ginger
- salt and freshly ground pepper

Directions:

1. Season the chicken with salt, pepper and ginger.
2. Heat the oil and fry the chicken until slightly browned.
3. Cover and cook for approximately twenty minutes until soft, turning intermittently.
4. Drain off the oil.
5. Put in the apricots and sauce to the pan, bring to the boil, cover and simmer gently for approximately five minutes or until heated through.
6. Garnish with flaked almonds.

CHICKEN WITH ASPARAGUS

Yield: 4 Servings

Ingredients:

- 1 chicken breast, sliced
- 1 clove garlic, crushed
- 1 spring onion (scallion), chopped
- 120 ml/4 fl oz/½ cup chicken stock
- 15 ml/1 tbsp cornflour (cornstarch)
- 30 ml/2 tbsp black bean sauce
- 350 g/12 oz asparagus, chopped into 2½ cm/1 in pieces
- 45 ml/3 tbsp groundnut (peanut) oil
- 45 ml/3 tbsp water
- 5 ml/1 tsp salt
- 5 ml/1 tsp sugar

Directions:

1. Heat half the oil and fry the salt, garlic and spring onion until slightly browned.
2. Put in the chicken and fry until slightly coloured.
3. Put in the black bean sauce and stir to coat the chicken.
4. Put in the asparagus, stock and sugar, bring to the boil, cover and simmer for approximately five minutes until the chicken is soft.
5. Combine the cornflour and water to a paste, mix it into the pan and simmer, stirring, until the sauce clears and becomes thick.

CHICKEN WITH AUBERGINE

Yield: 4 Servings

Ingredients:

- 1 aubergine (eggplant), peeled and chop into strips
- 15 ml/1 tbsp cornflour (cornstarch)
- 15 ml/1 tbsp rice wine or dry sherry
- 15 ml/1 tbsp soy sauce

- 2 cloves garlic, crushed
- 2 dried red chilli peppers
- 225 g/8 oz chicken, sliced
- 30 ml/2 tbsp groundnut (peanut) oil
- 75 ml/5 tbsp chicken stock

Directions:

1. Put the chicken into a container.
2. Combine the soy sauce, wine or sherry and cornflour, stir into the chicken and allow to stand for half an hour.
3. Briefly boil the aubergine in boiling water for approximately three minutes then eliminate the excess liquid well.
4. Heat the oil and fry the peppers until they darken then remove and discard them.
5. Put in the garlic and chicken and stir-fry until slightly coloured.
6. Put in the stock and aubergine, bring to the boil, cover and simmer for approximately three minutes, stirring intermittently.

CHICKEN WITH BAMBOO SHOOTS

Yield: 4 Servings

Ingredients:

- 1 clove garlic, crushed
- 1 slice ginger root, chopped
- 1 spring onion (scallion), chopped
- 15 ml/1 tbsp rice wine or dry sherry
- 225 g/8 oz bamboo shoots, chopped into slivers
- 225 g/8 oz chicken breast, chopped into slivers
- 45 ml/3 tbsp groundnut (peanut) oil
- 45 ml/3 tbsp soy sauce
- 5 ml/1 tsp cornflour (cornstarch)

Directions:

1. Heat the oil and fry the garlic, spring onion and ginger until slightly browned.
2. Put in the chicken and stir-fry for approximately five minutes.
3. Put in the bamboo shoots and stir-fry for approximately two minutes.

4. Mix in the soy sauce, wine or sherry and cornflour and stir-fry for about 3 minutes until the chicken is cooked through.

CHICKEN WITH BEAN SPROUTS

Yield: 4 Servings

Ingredients:

- 1 clove garlic, crushed
- 1 slice ginger root, chopped
- 1 spring onion (scallion), chopped
- 15 ml/1 tbsp rice wine or dry sherry
- 225 g/8 oz bean sprouts
- 225 g/8 oz chicken breast, chopped into slivers
- 45 ml/3 tbsp groundnut (peanut) oil
- 45 ml/3 tbsp soy sauce
- 5 ml/1 tsp cornflour (cornstarch)

Directions:

1. Heat the oil and fry the garlic, spring onion and ginger until slightly browned.
2. Put in the chicken and stir-fry for approximately five minutes.
3. Put in the bean sprouts and stir-fry for approximately two minutes.
4. Mix in the soy sauce, wine or sherry and cornflour and stir-fry for about 3 minutes until the chicken is cooked through.

CHICKEN WITH BLACK BEAN SAUCE

Yield: 4 Servings

Ingredients:

- 1 green pepper, diced
- 1 onion, chopped
- 15 ml/1 tbsp cornflour (cornstarch)
- 15 ml/1 tbsp soy sauce
- 2 cloves garlic, crushed

- 250 ml/8 fl oz/1 cup stock
- 30 ml/2 tbsp black bean sauce
- 30 ml/2 tbsp groundnut (peanut) oil
- 45 ml/3 tbsp water
- 450 g/1 lb chicken, diced
- 5 ml/1 tsp salt
- freshly ground pepper

Directions:

1. Heat the oil and fry the salt, black beans and garlic for 30 seconds.
2. Put in the chicken and fry until slightly browned.
3. Mix in the stock, bring to the boil, cover and simmer for 10 minutes.
4. Put in the pepper, onion, soy sauce and pepper, cover and simmer for another 10 minutes.
5. Blend the cornflour and water to a paste, stir into the sauce and simmer, stirring, until the sauce becomes thick and the chicken is soft.

CHICKEN WITH BROCCOLI

Yield: 4 Servings

Ingredients:

- 1 green pepper, diced
- 1 onion, diced
- 1 red pepper, diced
- 10 ml/2 tsp sesame oil
- 225 g/8 oz broccoli florets
- 225 g/8 oz chicken livers
- 30 ml/2 tbsp hoisin sauce
- 30 ml/2 tbsp honey
- 30 ml/2 tbsp soy sauce
- 30 ml/2 tbsp tomato purée (paste)
- 300 ml/½ pt/1¼ cups chicken stock
- 4 slices pineapple, diced
- 45 ml/3 tbsp groundnut (peanut) oil
- 45 ml/3 tbsp plain (all-purpose) flour
- 450 g/1 lb chicken meat, diced

Directions:

1. Toss the chicken and chicken livers in the flour.
2. Heat the oil and stir-fry the liver for approximately five minutes then remove from the pan.
3. Put in the chicken, cover and fry over a moderate heat for approximately fifteen minutes, stirring intermittently.
4. Put in the vegetables and pineapple and stir-fry for 8 minutes.
5. Return the livers to the wok, add the rest of the ingredients and bring to the boil.
6. Simmer, stirring, until the sauce becomes thick.

CHICKEN WITH CABBAGE AND PEANUTS

Yield: 4 Servings

Ingredients:

- ½ cabbage, chopped into squares
- 15 ml/1 tbsp black bean sauce
- 2 red chilli peppers, minced
- 30 ml/2 tbsp peanuts
- 45 ml/3 tbsp groundnut (peanut) oil
- 450 g/1 lb chicken, diced
- 5 ml/1 tsp salt

Directions:

1. Heat some oil and fry the peanuts for a few minutes, stirring constantly.
2. Remove, eliminate the excess liquid then crush.
3. Heat the rest of the oil and fry the chicken and cabbage until slightly browned.
4. Take out of the pan.
5. Put in the black bean sauce and chilli peppers and stir-fry for approximately two minutes.
6. Return the chicken and cabbage to the pan with the crushed peanuts and season with salt.
7. Stir-fry until heated through then serve instantly.

CHICKEN WITH CASHEWS

Yield: 4 Servings

Ingredients:

- 100 g/4 oz bamboo shoots
- 100 g/4 oz water chestnuts, sliced
- 15 ml/1 tbsp rice wine or dry sherry
- 2 cloves garlic, crushed
- 2½ ml/½ tsp salt
- 225 g/8 oz mushrooms, sliced
- 225 g/8 oz/2 cups cashew nuts
- 30 ml/2 tbsp cornflour (cornstarch)
- 30 ml/2 tbsp soy sauce
- 300 ml/½ pt/1¼ cups chicken stock
- 350 g/12 oz chicken, cubed
- 45 ml/3 tbsp groundnut (peanut) oil
- 50 g/2 oz mangetout (snow peas)

Directions:

1. Combine the soy sauce, cornflour and wine or sherry, pour over the chicken, cover and allow to marinate for at least 1 hour.
2. Heat 30 ml/2 tbsp of oil with the salt and garlic and fry until the garlic is slightly browned.
3. Put in the chicken with the marinade and stir-fry for approximately two minutes until the chicken is slightly browned.
4. Put in the mushrooms, water chestnuts, bamboo shoots and mangetout and stir-fry for approximately two minutes.
5. In the meantime, heat the rest of the oil in a separate pan and fry the cashew nuts over low heat for a few minutes until a golden-brown colour is achieved.
6. Add them to the pan with the stock, bring to the boil, cover and simmer for approximately five minutes.
7. If the sauce has not thickened sufficiently, mix in a little cornflour blended with a spoonful of water and stir until the sauce becomes thick and clears.

CHICKEN WITH CHESTNUTS

Yield: 4 Servings

Ingredients:

- 15 ml/1 tbsp chopped fresh parsley
- 15 ml/1 tbsp soy sauce
- 200 g/7 oz water chestnuts, chopped
- 225 g/8 oz chestnuts, chopped
- 225 g/8 oz chicken, sliced
- 225 g/8 oz mushrooms, quartered
- 250 ml/8 fl oz/1 cup chicken stock
- 5 ml/1 tsp salt
- oil for deep-frying

Directions:

1. Drizzle the chicken with salt and soy sauce and rub it well into the chicken.
2. Heat the oil and deep-fry the chicken until a golden-brown colour is achieved then remove and drain.
3. Put the chicken in a pan with the stock, bring to the boil and simmer for approximately five minutes.
4. Put in the water chestnuts, chestnuts and mushrooms, cover and simmer for approximately twenty minutes until everything is soft.
5. Serve garnished with parsley.

CHICKEN WITH GREEN BEANS

Yield: 4 Servings

Ingredients:

- 1 stalk celery, diagonally sliced
- 10 ml/2 tsp soy sauce
- 2½ ml/½ tsp freshly ground pepper
- 225 g/8 oz green beans, chopped into pieces
- 225 g/8 oz mushrooms, sliced
- 250 ml/8 fl oz/1 cup chicken stock
- 30 ml/2 tbsp cornflour (cornstarch)
- 45 ml/3 tbsp groundnut (peanut) oil
- 450 g/1 lb cooked chicken, shredded

- 5 ml/1 tsp salt
- 60 ml/4 tbsp water

Directions:

1. Heat the oil and fry the chicken, salt and pepper until slightly browned.
2. Put in the beans, celery and mushrooms and mix well.
3. Put in the stock, bring to the boil, cover and simmer for approximately fifteen minutes.
4. Combine the cornflour, water and soy sauce to a paste, mix it into the pan and simmer, stirring, until the sauce clears and becomes thick.

CHICKEN WITH HOISIN SAUCE

Yield: 4 Servings

Ingredients:

- 1 red pepper, chopped
- 10 ml/2 tsp grated ginger root
- 2 onions, chopped
- 20 ml/4 tsp soy sauce
- 225 g/8 oz broccoli florets
- 225 g/8 oz button mushrooms
- 250 ml/8 fl oz/1 cup chicken stock
- 4 chicken portions, halved
- 45 ml/3 tbsp cider vinegar
- 45 ml/3 tbsp hoisin sauce
- 45 ml/3 tbsp rice wine or dry sherry
- 50 g/2 oz/½ cup cornflour (cornstarch)
- oil for deep-frying

Directions:

1. Coat the chicken pieces in half the cornflour.
2. Heat the oil and fry the chicken pieces a few at a time for approximately eight minutes until a golden-brown colour is achieved and cooked through.
3. Take out of the pan and eliminate the excess liquid on kitchen paper.
4. Remove all but 30 ml/2 tbsp of oil from the pan and stir-fry the ginger for approximately one minute.
5. Put in the onions and stir-fry for approximately one minute.

6. Put in the broccoli, pepper and mushrooms and stir-fry for approximately two minutes.
7. Combine the stock with the reserved cornflour and rest of the ingredients and add to the pan.
8. Bring to the boil, stirring, and cook until the sauce clears.
9. Return the chicken to the wok and cook, stirring, for about 3 minutes until heated through.

CHICKEN WITH LEEKS

Yield: 4 Servings

Ingredients:

- 1 slice ginger root, chopped
- 15 ml/1 tbsp rice wine or dry sherry
- 15 ml/1 tbsp soy sauce
- 225 g/8 oz chicken, finely sliced
- 225 g/8 oz leeks, sliced
- 30 ml/2 tbsp groundnut (peanut) oil
- 5 ml/1 tsp salt

Directions:

1. Heat half the oil and fry the salt and leeks until slightly browned then remove them from the pan.
2. Heat the rest of the oil and fry the ginger and chicken until slightly browned.
3. Put in the wine or sherry and soy sauce and fry for another 2 minutes until the chicken is cooked.
4. Return the leeks to the pan and stir together until heated through.
5. Serve Immediately.

CHICKEN WITH LYCHEE SAUCE

Yield: 4 Servings

Ingredients:

- 1 spring onion (scallion)

- 2 egg whites
- 225 g/8 oz chicken
- 30 ml/2 tbsp cornflour (cornstarch)
- 30 ml/2 tbsp rice wine or dry sherry
- 4 water chestnuts
- 400 g/14 oz canned lychees in syrup
- 45 ml/3 tbsp soy sauce
- 5 tbsp chicken stock
- oil for deep-frying

Directions:

1. Mince (grind) the chicken with the spring onion and water chestnuts.
2. Mix in half the cornflour, 30 ml/2 tbsp of soy sauce, the wine or sherry and the egg whites.
3. Shape the mixture into walnut-sized balls.
4. Heat the oil and deep-fry the chicken until a golden-brown colour is achieved.
5. Drain on kitchen paper.
6. In the meantime, heat the lychee syrup gently with the stock and reserved soy sauce.
7. Mix the rest of the cornflour with a little water, mix it into the pan and simmer, stirring, until the sauce clears and becomes thick.
8. Mix in the lychees and simmer gently to heat through.
9. Put the chicken on a warmed serving plate, pour over the lychees and sauce and serve instantly.

CHICKEN WITH LYCHEES

Yield: 4 Servings

Ingredients:

- 1 red pepper, chopped into chunks
- 120 ml/4 fl oz/½ cup chicken stock
- 120 ml/4 fl oz/½ cup tomato sauce
- 275 g/10 oz peeled lychees
- 3 chicken breasts
- 45 ml/3 tbsp groundnut (peanut) oil
- 5 ml/1 tsp sugar
- 5 spring onions (scallions), sliced

- 60 ml/4 tbsp cornflour (cornstarch)

Directions:

1. Chop the chicken breasts in half and remove and discard the bones and skin.
2. Cut each breast into 6.
3. Reserve 5 ml/1 tsp of cornflour and toss the chicken in the remainder until it is well coated.
4. Heat the oil and stir-fry the chicken for approximately eight minutes until a golden-brown colour is achieved.
5. Put in the spring onions and pepper and stir-fry for approximately one minute.
6. Combine the tomato sauce, half the stock and the sugar and mix it into the wok with the lychees.
7. Bring to the boil, cover and simmer for approximately ten minutes until the chicken is cooked through.
8. Combine the reserved cornflour and stock then mix it into the pan.
9. Simmer, stirring, until the sauce clears and becomes thick.

CHICKEN WITH MANGETOUT

Yield: 4 Servings

Ingredients:

- 1 clove garlic, crushed
- 1 egg white, slightly beaten
- 1 slice ginger root, minced
- 100 g/4 oz mangetout (snow peas)
- 120 ml/4 fl oz/½ cup chicken stock
- 225 g/8 oz chicken, finely sliced
- 45 ml/3 tbsp groundnut (peanut) oil
- 5 ml/1 tsp cornflour (cornstarch)
- 5 ml/1 tsp rice wine or dry sherry
- 5 ml/1 tsp sesame oil
- salt and freshly ground pepper

Directions:

1. Combine the chicken with the cornflour, wine or sherry, sesame oil and egg white.
2. Heat half the oil and fry the garlic and ginger until slightly browned.

3. Put in the chicken and fry until golden then remove from the pan.
4. Heat the rest of the oil and fry the mangetout for approximately two minutes.
5. Put in the stock, bring to the boil, cover and simmer for approximately two minutes.
6. Return the chicken to the pan and season with salt and pepper.
7. Simmer gently until heated through.

CHICKEN WITH MANGOES

Yield: 4 Servings

Ingredients:

- 1 slice ginger root, minced
- 10 ml/2 tsp cornflour (cornstarch)
- 10 ml/2 tsp sugar
- 100 g/4 oz/1 cup plain (all-purpose) flour
- 150 ml/¼ pt/generous ½ cup chicken stock
- 20 ml/4 tsp soy sauce
- 2½ ml/½ tsp salt
- 250 ml/8 fl oz/1 cup water
- 3 chicken breasts
- 400 g/11 oz canned mangoes, drained and chopped into strips
- 45 ml/3 tbsp rice wine or dry sherry
- 45 ml/3 tbsp wine vinegar
- 5 ml/1 tsp sesame oil
- 5 spring onions (scallions), sliced
- oil for deep-frying
- pinch of baking powder

Directions:

1. Whisk together the flour, water, salt and baking powder.
2. Allow to stand for approximately fifteen minutes.
3. Remove and discard the skin and bones from the chicken.
4. Chop the chicken into thin strips.
5. Mix these into the flour mixture.
6. Heat the oil and fry the chicken for approximately five minutes until a golden-brown colour is achieved.
7. Take out of the pan and eliminate the excess liquid on kitchen paper.

8. Remove all but 15 ml/1 tbsp of oil from the wok and stir-fry the ginger until slightly browned.
9. Combine the stock with the wine vinegar, wine or sherry, soy sauce, sugar, cornflour and sesame oil.
10. Put into the pan and bring to the boil, stirring.
11. Put in the spring onions and simmer for approximately three minutes.
12. Put in the chicken and mangoes and simmer, stirring, for approximately two minutes.

CHICKEN WITH MUSHROOMS AND PEANUTS

Yield: 4 Servings

Ingredients:

- 1 green pepper, cubed
- 1 red pepper, cubed
- 1 slice ginger root, minced
- 100 g/4 oz bamboo shoots, chopped into strips
- 15 ml/1 tbsp soy sauce
- 15 ml/1 tbsp tabasco sauce
- 2 cloves garlic, crushed
- 225 g/8 oz button mushrooms
- 250 ml/8 fl oz/1 cup chicken stock
- 30 ml/2 tbsp cornflour (cornstarch)
- 30 ml/2 tbsp groundnut (peanut) oil
- 30 ml/2 tbsp rice wine or dry sherry
- 30 ml/2 tbsp water
- 450 g/1 lb boned chicken, cubed

Directions:

1. Heat the oil, garlic and ginger until the garlic is slightly golden.
2. Put in the chicken and stir-fry until it is slightly browned.
3. Put in the mushrooms, bamboo shoots and peppers and stir-fry for approximately three minutes.
4. Put in the stock, wine or sherry, soy sauce and tabasco sauce and bring to the boil, stirring.
5. Cover and simmer for approximately ten minutes until the chicken is comprehensively cooked.

6. Combine the cornflour and water and stir them into the sauce.
7. Simmer, stirring, until the sauce clears and becomes thick, adding a little more stock or water if the sauce is too thick.

CHICKEN WITH ONIONS

Yield: 4 Servings

Ingredients:

- 2 onions, chopped
- 250 ml/8 fl oz/1 cup chicken stock
- 30 ml/2 tbsp cornflour (cornstarch)
- 30 ml/2 tbsp rice wine or dry sherry
- 45 ml/3 tbsp soy sauce
- 45 ml/3 tbsp water
- 450 g/1 lb chicken, sliced
- 60 ml/4 tbsp groundnut (peanut) oil

Directions:

1. Heat the oil and fry the onions until slightly browned.
2. Put in the chicken and fry until slightly browned.
3. Put in the wine or sherry, stock and soy sauce, bring to the boil, cover and simmer for 25 minutes until the chicken is soft.
4. Blend the cornflour and water to a paste, mix it into the pan and simmer, stirring, until the sauce clears and becomes thick.

CHICKEN WITH OYSTER SAUCE

Yield: 4 Servings

Ingredients:

- 1 clove garlic, crushed
- 1 slice ginger, finely chopped
- 15 ml/1 tbsp rice wine or sherry
- 250 ml/8 fl oz/1 cup chicken stock

- 30 ml/2 tbsp groundnut (peanut) oil
- 30 ml/2 tbsp oyster sauce
- 450 g/1 lb chicken, sliced
- 5 ml/1 tsp sugar

Directions:

1. Heat the oil with the garlic and ginger and fry until slightly browned.
2. Put in the chicken and stir-fry for about 3 minutes until slightly browned.
3. Put in the stock, oyster sauce, wine or sherry and sugar, bring to the boil, stirring, then cover and simmer for about 15 minutes, stirring intermittently, until the chicken is cooked through.
4. Take the lid off and continue to cook, stirring, for about 4 minutes until the sauce has reduced and thickened.

CHICKEN WITH PEANUT BUTTER

Yield: 4 Servings

Ingredients:

- 1 onion, diced
- 1 stick celery, diced
- 10 ml/2 tsp cornflour (cornstarch)
- 10 ml/2 tsp tomato purée (paste)
- 100 g/4 oz peanut butter
- 15 ml/1 tbsp chopped chives
- 15 ml/1 tbsp soy sauce
- 2 carrots, diced
- 300 ml/½ pt/1¼ cups chicken stock
- 4 chicken breasts, diced
- 45 ml/3 tbsp groundnut (peanut) oil
- 5 ml/1 tsp five-spice powder
- pinch of brown sugar
- salt and freshly ground pepper

Directions:

1. Season the chicken with salt, pepper and five-spice powder.
2. Heat the oil and stir-fry the chicken until soft.

3. Take out of the pan.
4. Put in the vegetables and fry until soft but still crisp.
5. Combine the stock with the rest of the ingredients except the chives, stir into the pan and bring to the boil.
6. Return the chicken to the pan and reheat, stirring.
7. Serve sprinkled with sugar.

CHICKEN WITH PEANUTS

Yield: 4 Servings

Ingredients:

- 1 clove garlic, crushed
- 1 egg white, slightly beaten
- 1 slice ginger root, minced
- 10 ml/2 tsp cornflour (cornstarch)
- 100 g/4 oz roasted peanuts
- 15 ml/1 tbsp rice wine or dry sherry
- 2 leeks, chopped
- 225 g/8 oz chicken, finely sliced
- 30 ml/2 tbsp soy sauce
- 45 ml/3 tbsp groundnut (peanut) oil

Directions:

1. Combine the chicken with the egg white and cornflour until well coated.
2. Heat half the oil and stir-fry the chicken until a golden-brown colour is achieved then remove from the pan.
3. Heat the rest of the oil and fry and garlic and ginger until softened.
4. Put in the leeks and fry until slightly browned.
5. Mix in the soy sauce and wine or sherry and simmer for approximately three minutes.
6. Return the chicken to the pan with the peanuts and simmer gently until heated through.

CHICKEN WITH PEAS

Yield: 4 Servings

Ingredients:

- 1 onion, chopped
- 100 g/4 oz mushrooms, chopped
- 100 g/4 oz peas
- 15 ml/1 tbsp cornflour (cornstarch)
- 15 ml/1 tbsp soy sauce
- 2 stalks celery, chopped
- 250 ml/8 fl oz/1 cup chicken stock
- 450 g/1 lb chicken, diced
- 60 ml/4 tbsp groundnut (peanut) oil
- 60 ml/4 tbsp water
- salt and freshly ground pepper

Directions:

1. Heat the oil and fry the onion until slightly browned.
2. Put in the chicken and fry until coloured.
3. Season with salt and pepper and add the peas, celery and mushrooms and stir thoroughly.
4. Put in the stock, bring to the boil, cover and simmer for approximately fifteen minutes.
5. Blend the cornflour, soy sauce and water to a paste, mix it into the pan and simmer, stirring, until the sauce clears and becomes thick.

CHICKEN WITH PEPPERS

Yield: 4 Servings

Ingredients:

- 1 green pepper, cubed
- 2 cloves garlic, crushed
- 2 red peppers, cubed
- 2½ ml/½ tsp salt
- 300 ml/½ pt/1¼ cups chicken stock
- 45 ml/3 tbsp cornflour (cornstarch)
- 45 ml/3 tbsp rice wine or dry sherry
- 450 g/1 lb chicken, minced (ground)
- 5 ml/1 tsp sugar

- 60 ml/4 tbsp groundnut (peanut) oil
- 60 ml/4 tbsp soy sauce

Directions:

1. Combine half the soy sauce, half the wine or sherry and half the cornflour.
2. Pour over the chicken, stir thoroughly, and allow to marinate for at least 1 hour.
3. Heat half the oil with the salt and garlic until the garlic is slightly browned.
4. Put in the chicken and marinade and stir-fry for about 4 minutes until the chicken turns white then remove from the pan.
5. Add the rest of the oil to the pan and stir-fry the peppers for approximately two minutes.
6. Put in the sugar to the pan with the rest of the soy sauce, wine or sherry and cornflour and mix well.
7. Put in the stock, bring to the boil then simmer, stirring, until the sauce becomes thick.
8. Return the chicken to the pan, cover and simmer for 4 minutes until the chicken is cooked through.

CHICKEN WITH PEPPERS AND TOMATOES

Yield: 4 Servings

Ingredients:

- 1 green pepper, chopped into chunks
- 10 ml/2 tsp salt
- 120 ml/4 fl oz/½ cup water
- 15 ml/1 tbsp soy sauce
- 250 ml/8 fl oz/1 cup chicken stock
- 30 ml/2 tbsp cornflour (cornstarch)
- 4 large tomatoes, skinned and chop into wedges
- 45 ml/3 tbsp groundnut (peanut) oil
- 450 g/1 lb cooked chicken, sliced
- 5 ml/1 tsp freshly ground pepper

Directions:

1. Heat the oil and fry the chicken, salt and pepper until browned.
2. Put in the peppers and tomatoes.

3. Pour in the stock, bring to the boil, cover and simmer for approximately fifteen minutes.
4. Blend the cornflour, soy sauce and water to a paste, mix it into the pan and simmer, stirring, until the sauce clears and becomes thick.

CHICKEN WITH PINEAPPLE AND LYCHEES

Yield: 4 Servings

Ingredients:

- 1 slice ginger root, minced
- 15 ml/1 tbsp cornflour (cornstarch)
- 15 ml/1 tbsp rice wine or dry sherry
- 15 ml/1 tbsp soy sauce
- 200 g/7 oz canned lychees in syrup
- 200 g/7 oz canned pineapple chunks in syrup
- 225 g/8 oz chicken, finely sliced
- 30 ml/2 tbsp groundnut (peanut) oil

Directions:

1. Heat the oil and fry the chicken until slightly coloured.
2. Put in the soy sauce and wine or sherry and stir thoroughly.
3. Measure 250 ml/8 fl oz/1 cup of the mixed pineapple and lychee syrup and reserve 30 ml/2 tbsp.
4. Put in the rest to the pan, bring to the boil and simmer for a few minutes until the chicken is soft.
5. Put in the pineapple chunks and lychees.
6. Combine the cornflour with the reserved syrup, stir into the pan and simmer, stirring, until the sauce clears and becomes thick.

CHICKEN WITH PORK

Yield: 4 Servings

Ingredients:

- 1 chicken breast, finely sliced
- 1 egg white
- 100 g/4 oz lean pork, finely sliced
- 120 ml/4 fl oz/½ cup chicken stock
- 15 ml/1 tbsp cornflour (cornstarch)
- 225 g/8 oz Chinese leaves, shredded
- 225 g/8 oz mushrooms, sliced
- 3 slices ginger root, chopped
- 30 ml/2 tbsp water
- 45 ml/3 tbsp groundnut (peanut) oil
- 50 g/2 oz bamboo shoots, sliced
- 60 ml/4 tbsp soy sauce

Directions:

1. Combine the chicken and pork.
2. Combine the soy sauce, 5 ml/1 tsp of cornflour and the egg white and stir into the chicken and pork.
3. Allow to stand for half an hour.
4. Heat half the oil and fry the chicken and pork until slightly browned then remove them from the pan.
5. Heat the rest of the oil and fry the ginger, bamboo shoots, mushrooms and Chinese leaves until well coated in oil.
6. Put in the stock and bring to the boil.
7. Return the chicken mixture to the pan, cover and simmer for about 3 minutes until the meats are soft.
8. Blend the rest of the cornflour to a paste with the water, stir into the sauce and simmer, stirring, until the sauce becomes thick.
9. Serve Immediately.

CHICKEN WITH SOY SAUCE

Yield: 4 Servings

Ingredients:

- 15 ml/1 tbsp cornflour (cornstarch)
- 2 spring onions (scallions), chopped
- 3 slices ginger root, minced

- 30 ml/2 tbsp rice wine or dry sherry
- 30 ml/2 tbsp water
- 350 g/12 oz chicken, diced
- 45 ml/3 tbsp groundnut (peanut) oil
- 5 ml/1 tsp sugar
- 60 ml/4 tbsp thick soy sauce

Directions:

1. Combine the chicken, spring onions, ginger, cornflour, wine or sherry and water and allow to stand for half an hour, stirring intermittently.
2. Heat the oil and stir-fry the chicken for about 3 minutes until slightly browned.
3. Put in the soy sauce and sugar and stir-fry for about 1 minute until the chicken is cooked through and soft.

CHICKEN WITH SPINACH

Yield: 4 Servings

Ingredients:

- 100 g/4 oz chicken, minced
- 15 ml/1 tbsp ham fat, minced
- 175 ml/6 fl oz/¾ cup chicken stock
- 3 egg whites, slightly beaten
- 45 ml/3 tbsp groundnut (peanut) oil
- 450 g/1 lb spinach, finely chopped
- 5 ml/1 tsp cornflour (cornstarch)
- 5 ml/1 tsp water
- salt

Directions:

1. Combine the chicken, ham fat, 150 ml/¼ pt/generous ½ cup of chicken stock, the egg whites, 5 ml/1 tsp of salt and the water.
2. Combine the spinach with the rest of the stock, a pinch of salt and the cornflour mixed with a little water.
3. Heat half the oil, add the spinach mixture to the pan and stir constantly over a low heat until heated through.
4. Move to a warmed serving plate and keep warm.

5. Heat the rest of the oil and fry spoonfuls of the chicken mixture until set and white.
6. Lay out on top of the spinach and serve instantly.

CHICKEN WITH TOMATOES

Yield: 4 Servings

Ingredients:

- 1 onion, diced
- 15 ml/1 tbsp cornflour (cornstarch)
- 15 ml/1 tbsp rice wine or dry sherry
- 15 ml/1 tbsp soy sauce
- 2 tomatoes, skinned and diced
- 225 g/8 oz chicken, diced
- 45 ml/3 tbsp groundnut (peanut) oil
- 5 ml/1 tsp salt
- 5 ml/1 tsp sugar
- 60 ml/4 tbsp chicken stock

Directions:

1. Combine the chicken with the cornflour, soy sauce and wine or sherry and allow to stand for half an hour.
2. Heat the oil and fry the chicken until slightly coloured.
3. Put in the onion and stir-fry until softened.
4. Put in the stock, salt and sugar, bring to the boil and stir gently over a low heat until the chicken is cooked.
5. Put in the tomatoes and stir until heated through.

CHICKEN WITH WALNUTS

Yield: 4 Servings

Ingredients:

- 100 g/4 oz/1 cup shelled walnuts, halved
- oil for deep-frying

- 45 ml/3 tbsp groundnut (peanut) oil
- 2 slices ginger root, minced
- 225 g/8 oz chicken, diced
- 100 g/4 oz bamboo shoots, sliced
- 75 ml/5 tbsp chicken stock

Directions:

1. Prepare the walnuts, heat the oil and deep-fry the walnuts until a golden-brown colour is achieved then eliminate the excess liquid well.
2. Heat the groundnut oil and fry the ginger for 30 seconds.
3. Put in the chicken and stir-fry until slightly browned.
4. Add the rest of the ingredients, bring to the boil and simmer, stirring, until the chicken is cooked.

CHICKEN WITH WATER CHESTNUTS

Yield: 4 Servings

Ingredients:

- 1 slice ginger root, chopped
- 100 g/4 oz water chestnuts, chopped into slivers
- 15 ml/1 tbsp rice wine or dry sherry
- 2 cloves garlic, crushed
- 2 spring onions (scallions), chopped
- 225 g/8 oz chicken breast, chopped into slivers
- 45 ml/3 tbsp groundnut (peanut) oil
- 45 ml/3 tbsp soy sauce
- 5 ml/1 tsp cornflour (cornstarch)

Directions:

1. Heat the oil and fry the garlic, spring onions and ginger until slightly browned.
2. Put in the chicken and stir-fry for approximately five minutes.
3. Put in the water chestnuts and stir-fry for approximately three minutes.
4. Put in the soy sauce, wine or sherry and cornflour and stir-fry for approximately five minutes until the chicken is cooked through.

CHICKEN WONTONS

Yield: 4 Servings

Ingredients:

- 1 egg, beaten
- 1 spring onion (scallion), chopped
- 15 ml/1 tbsp soy sauce
- 2½ ml/½ tsp salt
- 225 g/8 oz mixed vegetables, chopped
- 4 dried Chinese mushrooms
- 40 wonton skins
- 450 g/1 lb chicken breast, shredded

Directions:

1. Soak the mushrooms in warm water for half an hour then drain.
2. Discard the stalks and chop the caps.
3. Mix with the chicken, vegetables, soy sauce and salt.
4. To fold the wontons, hold the skin in the palm of your left hand and spoon a little filling into the centre.
5. Moisten the edges with egg and fold the skin into a triangle, sealing the edges.
6. Moisten the corners with egg and twist them together.
7. Bring a saucepan of water to the boil.
8. Drop in the wontons and simmer for approximately ten minutes until they float to the top.

CHICKEN-STUFFED MELON

Yield: 4 Servings

Ingredients:

- 15 ml/1 tbsp soy sauce
- 2 shelled scallops
- 350 g/12 oz chicken meat
- 4 slices ginger root
- 5 ml/1 tsp salt
- 6 water chestnuts

- 600 ml/1 pt/2½ cups chicken stock
- 8 small or 4 medium cantaloupe melons

Directions:

1. Finely chop the chicken, chestnuts, scallops and ginger and mix with the salt, soy sauce and stock.
2. Chop the tops off the melons and scoop out the seeds.
3. Serrate the top edges.
4. Fill the melons with the chicken mixture and stand on a rack in a steamer.
5. Steam over boiling water for about forty minutes until the chicken is cooked.

CHILLI-CHICKEN CURRY

Yield: 4 Servings

Ingredients:

- 1 onion, chopped
- 120 ml/4 fl oz/½ cup groundnut (peanut) oil
- 15 ml/1 tbsp cornflour (cornstarch)
- 15 ml/1 tbsp rice wine or dry sherry
- 2½ ml/½ tsp salt
- 4 chicken pieces
- 45 ml/3 tbsp water
- 5 ml/1 tsp chilli sauce
- 5 ml/1 tsp curry powder
- 5 ml/1 tsp sesame oil
- 600 ml/1 pt/2½ cups chicken stock

Directions:

1. Heat the oil and fry the chicken pieces until a golden-brown colour is achieved on both sides then remove them from the pan.
2. Put in the onion, curry powder and chilli sauce and stir-fry for approximately one minute.
3. Put in the wine or sherry and salt, stir thoroughly, then return the chicken to the pan and stir again.
4. Put in the stock, bring to the boil and simmer gently for about 30 minutes until the chicken is soft.

5. If the sauce has not reduced sufficiently, blend the cornflour and water to a paste, stir a little into the sauce and simmer, stirring, until the sauce becomes thick.
6. Serve sprinkled with sesame oil.

CHINESE CHICKEN CURRY

Yield: 4 Servings

Ingredients:

- 1 onion, sliced
- 10 ml/2 tsp cornflour (cornstarch)
- 15 ml/1 tbsp water
- 150 ml/¼ pt/generous ½ cup chicken stock
- 350 g/12 oz chicken, diced
- 45 ml/3 tbsp curry powder
- 5 ml/1 tsp salt

Directions:

1. Heat the curry powder and onion using a dry pan for approximately two minutes, shaking the pan to coat the onion.
2. Put in the chicken and stir until well coated in curry powder.
3. Put in the stock and salt, bring to the boil, cover and simmer for approximately five minutes until the chicken is soft.
4. Combine the cornflour and water to a paste, stir into the pan and simmer, stirring, until the sauce becomes thick.

CHINESE ROAST TURKEY

Yield: 8 Servings

Ingredients:

- 1 small turkey
- 10 ml/2 tsp allspice
- 10 ml/2 tsp salt
- 45 ml/3 tbsp butter

- 5 ml/1 tsp sesame oil
- 500 ml/16 fl oz/2 cups soy sauce
- 600 ml/1 pt/2½ cups hot water

Directions:

1. Put the turkey in a pan and pour over the hot water.
2. Add the rest of the ingredients except the butter and allow to stand for one hour, turning several times.
3. Remove the turkey from the liquid and brush with butter.
4. Put in a roasting tin, cover loosely with kitchen foil and roast in a preheated oven at 160°C/325°F/gas mark 3 for about 4 hours, basting intermittently with the soy sauce liquid.
5. Remove the foil and allow the skin to crisp for the last 30 minutes of cooking.

COOKED CHICKEN WITH PINEAPPLE

Yield: 4 Servings

Ingredients:

- 10 ml/2 tbsp cornflour (cornstarch)
- 120 ml/4 fl oz/½ cup chicken stock
- 15 ml/1 tbsp soy sauce
- 2 stalks celery, diagonally sliced
- 225 g/8 oz cooked chicken, diced
- 3 slices pineapple, chopped into chunks
- 30 ml/2 tbsp water
- 45 ml/3 tbsp groundnut (peanut) oil
- salt and freshly ground pepper

Directions:

1. Heat the oil and fry the chicken until slightly browned.
2. Season with salt and pepper, add the celery and stir-fry for approximately two minutes.
3. Put in the pineapple, stock and soy sauce and stir for a few minutes until heated through.
4. Combine the cornflour and water to a paste, stir into the pan and simmer, stirring, until the sauce clears and becomes thick.

CRISPY CHICKEN CHUNKS

Yield: 4 Servings

Ingredients:

- 1 egg
- 100 g/4 oz plain (all -purpose) flour
- 15 ml/1 tbsp water
- 350 g/12 oz cooked chicken, cubed
- oil for deep-frying
- pinch of salt

Directions:

1. Combine the flour, salt, water and egg to a fairly stiff batter, adding a little more water if needed.
2. Immerse the chicken pieces into the batter until they are well covered.
3. Heat the oil until very hot and deep-fry the chicken for a few minutes until crispy and golden brown.

CRISPY CHICKEN WINGS

Yield: 4 Servings

Ingredients:

- 50 g/2 oz/½ cup cornflour (cornstarch)
- 60 ml/4 tbsp rice wine or dry sherry
- 60 ml/4 tbsp soy sauce
- 900 g/2 lb chicken wings
- groundnut (peanut) oil for deep-frying

Directions:

1. Put the chicken wings into a container.
2. Combine the rest of the ingredients and pour over the chicken wings, stirring well so that they are coated in the sauce.

3. Cover and allow to stand for half an hour.
4. Heat the oil and deep-fry the chicken a few at a time until cooked through and dark brown.
5. Drain thoroughly using kitchen paper and keep warm while you fry the rest of the chicken.

CRISPY-FRIED CHICKEN

Yield: 4 Servings

Ingredients:

- ½ cucumber, sliced
- 1 chicken
- 1 lettuce, shredded
- 1 slice ginger root
- 150 ml/¼ pt/generous ½ cup chicken stock
- 3 spring onions (scallions), diced
- 30 ml/2 tbsp rice wine or dry sherry
- 30 ml/2 tbsp soy sauce
- 30 ml/2 tbsp sugar
- 4 tomatoes, sliced
- 5 ml/1 tsp peppercorns
- 5 ml/1 tsp salt
- 5 ml/1 tsp whole cloves
- oil for deep-frying
- salt

Directions:

1. Rub the chicken with salt and allow to stand for approximately three hours.
2. Rinse and place into a container.
3. Put in the wine or sherry, ginger, soy sauce, sugar, cloves, salt, peppercorns and stock and baste well.
4. Stand the bowl in a steamer, cover and steam for about 2¼ hours until the chicken is comprehensively cooked.
5. Drain.
6. Heat the oil until smoking, then add the chicken and deep-fry until browned.
7. Fry for another 5 minutes then remove from the oil and drain.

8. Cut into pieces and lay out on a warmed serving plate.
9. Garnish with the lettuce, tomatoes and cucumber and serve with a pepper and salt immerse.

CRISPY-FRIED SPICED CHICKEN

Yield: 4 Servings

Ingredients:

- 1 clove garlic, crushed
- 1 green pepper, diced
- 1 red pepper, diced
- 100 g/4 oz/1 cup dried breadcrumbs
- 2 eggs, beaten
- 2½ ml/½ tsp ground ginger
- 30 ml/2 tbsp cornflour (cornstarch)
- 30 ml/2 tbsp groundnut (peanut) oil
- 30 ml/2 tbsp honey
- 30 ml/2 tbsp plum sauce
- 30 ml/2 tbsp soy sauce
- 30 ml/2 tbsp soy sauce
- 30 ml/2 tbsp wine vinegar
- 45 ml/3 tbsp mango chutney
- 450 g/1 lb chicken meat, chopped into chunks
- 6 spring onions (scallions), chopped
- few drops of brandy

Directions:

1. Put the chicken into a container.
2. Combine the sauces, chutney, garlic, ginger and brandy, pour over the chicken, cover and allow to marinate for 2 hours.
3. Eliminate the excess liquid from the chicken then dust it with cornflour.
4. Coat in eggs then breadcrumbs.
5. Heat the oil then fry the chicken until a golden-brown colour is achieved.
6. Take out of the pan.
7. Put in the vegetables and stir-fry for 4 minutes then remove.

8. Eliminate the excess liquid from the oil from the pan then return the chicken and vegetables to the pan with the rest of the ingredients.
9. Bring to the boil and heat through and serve.

CURRIED CHICKEN WITH POTATOES

Yield: 4 Servings

Ingredients:

- 1 clove garlic, crushed
- 15 ml/1 tbsp curry powder
- 2½ ml/½ tsp salt
- 225 g/8 oz mushrooms, sliced
- 225 g/8 oz potatoes, cubed
- 4 onions, chopped into wedges
- 45 ml/3 tbsp groundnut (peanut) oil
- 450 ml/¾ pt/2 cups chicken stock
- 750 g/1½ lb chicken, cubed

Directions:

1. Heat the oil with the salt and garlic, add the chicken and fry until slightly browned.
2. Put in the potatoes, onions and curry powder and stir-fry for approximately two minutes.
3. Put in the stock, bring to the boil, cover and simmer for approximately twenty minutes until the chicken is cooked, stirring intermittently.
4. Put in the mushrooms, remove the lid and simmer for another 10 minutes until the liquid has reduced.

DEEP-FRIED CHICKEN LEGS

Yield: 4 Servings

Ingredients:

- 1 slice ginger, beaten flat
- 120 ml/4 fl oz/½ cup soy sauce

- 2 large chicken legs, boned
- 2 spring onions (scallions)
- 5 ml/1 tsp rice wine or dry sherry
- 5 ml/1 tsp sesame oil
- freshly ground pepper
- oil for deep-frying

Directions:

1. Spread out the chicken flesh and score it all over.
2. Beat 1 spring onion flat and chop the other.
3. Mix tine flattened spring onion with the ginger, soy sauce and wine or sherry.
4. Pour over the chicken and allow to marinate for half an hour.
5. Remove and drain.
6. Put on a plate on a steamer rack and steam for approximately 20 minutes.
7. Heat the oil and deep-fry the chicken for approximately five minutes until a golden-brown colour is achieved.
8. Take out of the pan, eliminate the excess liquid well and slice thickly, then arrange the slices on a warmed serving plate.
9. Heat the sesame oil, add the chopped spring onion and pepper, pour over the chicken and serve.

DEEP-FRIED CHICKEN LIVERS

Yield: 4 Servings

Ingredients:

- 450 g/1 lb chicken livers, halved
- 50 g/2 oz/½ cup cornflour (cornstarch)
- oil for deep-frying

Directions:

1. Pat the chicken livers dry then dust with cornflour, shaking off any excess.
2. Heat the oil and deep-fry the chicken livers for a few minutes until a golden-brown colour is achieved and cooked through.
3. Drain using kitchen paper and serve.

DEEP-FRIED CHICKEN WITH CURRY SAUCE

Yield: 4 Servings

Ingredients:

- 1 egg, slightly beaten
- 2½ ml/½ tsp salt
- 225 g/8 oz chicken, cubed
- 25 g/1 oz/¼ cup plain (all-purpose) flour
- 30 ml/2 tbsp cornflour (cornstarch)
- 30 ml/2 tbsp curry powder
- 30 ml/2 tbsp groundnut (peanut) oil
- 60 ml/4 tbsp rice wine or dry sherry
- oil for deep-frying

Directions:

1. Beat the egg with the cornflour, flour and salt to a thick batter.
2. Pour over the chicken and stir thoroughly to coat.
3. Heat the oil and deep-fry the chicken until a golden-brown colour is achieved and cooked through.
4. In the meantime, heat the oil and fry the curry powder for approximately one minute.
5. Mix in the wine or sherry and bring to the boil.
6. Put the chicken on a warmed plate and pour over the curry sauce.

DEEP-FRIED CHICKEN WITH GINGER

Yield: 4 Servings

Ingredients:

- 1 chicken, halved
- 30 ml/2 tbsp rice wine or dry sherry
- 30 ml/2 tbsp soy sauce
- 4 slices ginger root, crushed
- 5 ml/1 tsp sugar
- oil for deep-frying

Directions:

1. Put the chicken in a shallow bowl.
2. Combine the ginger, wine or sherry, soy sauce and sugar, pour over the chicken and rub into the skin.
3. Allow to marinate for one hour.
4. Heat the oil and deep-fry the chicken, one half at a time, until slightly coloured.
5. Take out of the oil and allow to cool slightly while you reheat the oil.
6. Return the chicken to the pan and deep-fry until a golden-brown colour is achieved and cooked through.
7. Drain thoroughly and serve.

DEEP-FRIED STEAMED DUCK

Yield: 4 Servings

Ingredients:

- 1 duck
- hoisin sauce
- oil for deep-frying
- salt and freshly ground pepper

Directions:

1. Season the duck with salt and pepper and place in a heatproof bowl.
2. Stand in a pan filled with water to come two-thirds of the way up the bowl, bring to the boil, cover and simmer for about 1½ hours until the duck is soft.
3. Drain and allow to cool.
4. Heat the oil and deep-fry the duck until crispy and golden brown.
5. Remove and eliminate the excess liquid well.
6. Chop into bite-sized pieces and serve with hoisin sauce.

DEEP-FRIED WHOLE CHICKEN

Yield: 5 Servings

Ingredients:

- 1 chicken

- 10 ml/2 tsp salt
- 15 ml/1 tbsp rice wine or dry sherry
- 2 spring onions (scallions), halved
- 3 slices ginger root, chopped into strips
- oil for deep-frying

Directions:

1. Pat the chicken dry and rub the skin with salt and wine or sherry.
2. Put the spring onions and ginger inside the cavity.
3. Hang the chicken to dry in a cool place for approximately three hours.
4. Heat the oil and place the chicken in a frying basket.
5. Lower gently into the oil and baste constantly inside and out until the chicken is slightly coloured.
6. Take out of the oil and allow to cool slightly while you reheat the oil.
7. Fry again until a golden-brown colour is achieved.
8. Drain thoroughly then chop into pieces.

DRUNKEN CHICKEN

Yield: 4 Servings

Ingredients:

- 2 cloves garlic, crushed
- 2 egg whites
- 200 ml/½ pt/1¼ cups rice wine or dry sherry
- 30 ml/2 tbsp hoisin sauce
- 30 ml/2 tbsp plum sauce
- 30 ml/2 tbsp wine vinegar
- 450 g/1 lb chicken fillet, chopped into chunks
- 60 ml/4 tbsp cornflour (cornstarch)
- 60 ml/4 tbsp soy sauce
- few drops of chilli oil
- oil for deep-frying
- pinch of salt

Directions:

1. Put the chicken into a container.

2. Combine the sauces and wine vinegar, garlic, salt and chilli oil, pour over the chicken and marinate in the refrigerator for 4 hours.
3. Beat the egg whites until stiff and fold in the cornflour.
4. Remove the chicken from the marinade and coat with the egg white mixture.
5. Heat the oil and deep-fry the chicken until cooked through and golden brown.
6. Drain thoroughly using kitchen paper and place into a container.
7. Pour over the wine or sherry, cover and allow to marinate in the refrigerator for 12 hours.
8. Remove the chicken from the wine and serve cold.

DRUNKEN DUCK

Yield: 4 Servings

Ingredients:

- 1 duck
- 1.5 l/2½ pts/6 cups water
- 2 cloves garlic, chopped
- 2 spring onions (scallions), chopped
- 450 ml/¾ pt/2 cups rice wine or dry sherry

Directions:

1. Put the spring onions, garlic and water in a large pan and bring to the boil.
2. Put in the duck, return to the boil, cover and simmer for 45 minutes.
3. Drain well, reserving the liquid for stock.
4. Leave the duck to cool then refrigerate overnight.
5. Chop the duck into pieces and place them in a large screw-top jar.
6. Pour over the wine or sherry and chill for about 1 week before draining and serving cold.

DUCK WITH BAMBOO SHOOTS

Yield: 4 Servings

Ingredients:

- 1 duck
- 100 g/4 oz bamboo shoots, chopped into strips
- 2 slices ginger root, chopped into strips
- 2 spring onions (scallions), chopped into strips
- 5 ml/1 tsp salt
- 50 g/2 oz smoked ham, chopped into strips
- 6 dried Chinese mushrooms

Directions:

1. Soak the mushrooms in warm water for half an hour then drain.
2. Discard the stalks and chop the caps into strips.
3. Put all the ingredients in a heatproof bowl and stand in a pan filled with water to come two-thirds of the way up the bowl.
4. Bring to the boil, cover and simmer for about 2 hours until the duck is cooked, topping up with boiling water as necessary.

DUCK WITH BEAN SPROUTS

Yield: 4 Servings

Ingredients:

- 15 ml/1 tbsp oyster sauce
- 15 ml/1 tbsp rice wine or dry sherry
- 2½ ml/½ tsp salt
- 225 g/8 oz bean sprouts
- 30 ml/2 tbsp water
- 45 ml/3 tbsp groundnut (peanut) oil
- 450 g/1 lb cooked duck meat

Directions:

1. Briefly boil the bean sprouts in boiling water for approximately two minutes then drain.
2. Heat the oil, stir-fry the bean sprouts for 30 seconds.
3. Put in the duck, stir-fry until heated through.
4. Add the rest of the ingredients and stir-fry for approximately two minutes to blend the flavours.
5. Serve Immediately.

DUCK WITH EXOTIC FRUITS

Yield: 4 Servings

Ingredients:

- 10 ml/2 tsp wine vinegar
- 100 g/4 oz lychees, halved
- 100 g/4 oz melon, diced
- 130 ml/4 fl oz/½ cup chicken stock
- 15 ml/1 tbsp groundnut (peanut) oil
- 15 ml/1 tbsp sesame oil
- 2 slices pineapple, diced
- 2½ ml/½ tsp five-spice powder
- 3 stalks celery, diced
- 30 ml/2 tbsp hoisin sauce
- 30 ml/2 tbsp soy sauce
- 30 ml/2 tbsp tomato purée (paste)
- 4 duck breast fillets, chopped into strips
- pinch of brown sugar

Directions:

1. Put the duck into a container.
2. Combine the five-spice powder, soy sauce and sesame oil, pour over the duck and marinate for 2 hours, stirring intermittently.
3. Heat the oil and stir-fry the duck for 8 minutes.
4. Take out of the pan.
5. Put in the celery and fruits and stir-fry for approximately five minutes.
6. Return the duck to the pan with the rest of the ingredients, bring to the boil and simmer, stirring, for approximately two minutes and serve.

DUCK WITH GINGER

Yield: 4 Servings

Ingredients:

- 1 egg, slightly beaten
- 15 ml/1 tbsp water
- 2 slices ginger root, chopped
- 2½ ml/½ tsp rice wine or dry sherry
- 2½ ml/½ tsp sesame oil
- 2½ ml/½ tsp sugar
- 350 g/12 oz duck breast, finely sliced
- 5 ml/1 tsp cornflour (cornstarch)
- 5 ml/1 tsp groundnut (peanut) oil
- 5 ml/1 tsp soy sauce
- 50 g/2 oz bamboo shoots
- 50 g/2 oz mangetout (snow peas)
- oil for deep-frying

Directions:

1. Combine the duck with the egg, soy sauce, cornflour and oil and allow to stand for 10 minutes.
2. Heat the oil and deep-fry the duck and bamboo shoots until cooked and golden brown.
3. Take out of the pan and eliminate the excess liquid well.
4. Pour out all but 15 ml/1 tbsp of oil from the pan and stir-fry the duck, bamboo shoots, mangetout, ginger, water, sugar and wine or sherry for approximately two minutes.
5. Serve sprinkled with sesame oil.

DUCK WITH GREEN BEANS

Yield: 4 Servings

Ingredients:

- 1 duck
- 1 onion, chopped
- 120 ml/4 fl oz/½ cup rice wine or dry sherry
- 15 ml/1 tbsp cornflour (cornstarch)
- 15 ml/1 tbsp grated root ginger
- 2 cloves garlic, crushed
- 2½ ml/½ tsp salt
- 30 ml/2 tbsp water
- 300 ml/½ pt/1¼ cups chicken stock

- 45 ml/3 tbsp soy sauce
- 45 ml/3 tbsp wine vinegar
- 450 g/1 lb green beans, sliced
- 5 drops chilli oil
- 60 ml/4 tbsp groundnut (peanut) oil
- 60 ml/4 tbsp tomato ketchup (catsup)
- pinch of freshly ground pepper

Directions:

1. Chop the duck into 8 or 10 pieces.
2. Heat the oil and fry the duck until a golden-brown colour is achieved.
3. Move to a bowl.
4. Put in the garlic, salt, onion, ginger, soy sauce, wine or sherry, tomato ketchup and wine vinegar.
5. Mix, cover and marinate in the refrigerator for approximately three hours.
6. Reheat the oil, add the duck, stock and marinade, bring to the boil, cover and simmer for one hour.
7. Put in the beans, cover and simmer for approximately fifteen minutes.
8. Put in the pepper and chilli oil.
9. Combine the cornflour with the water, mix it into the pan and simmer, stirring, until the sauce becomes thick.

DUCK WITH HAM AND LEEKS

Yield: 4 Servings

Ingredients:

- 1 duck
- 2 leeks
- 2 slices ginger root, minced
- 2½ ml/½ tsp salt
- 45 ml/3 tbsp rice wine or dry sherry
- 45 ml/3 tbsp soy sauce
- 450 g/1 lb smoked ham

Directions:

1. Put the duck in a pan and just cover with cold water.

2. Bring to the boil, cover and simmer for about 20 minutes.
3. Drain and reserve 450 ml/¾ pts/2 cups of stock.
4. Let the duck cool slightly then chop the meat from the bones and chop it into 5 cm/2 in squares.
5. Chop the ham into similar pieces.
6. Cut off long pieces of leek and roll a slice of duck and ham inside the leaf and tie with string.
7. Put in a heatproof bowl.
8. Put in the ginger, wine or sherry, soy sauce and salt to the reserved stock and pour it over the duck rolls.
9. Put the bowl in a pan filled with water to come two-thirds of the way up the sides of the bowl.
10. Bring to the boil, cover and simmer for about 1 hour until the duck is soft.

DUCK WITH ORANGE

Yield: 4 Servings

Ingredients:

- 1 duck
- 1 slice orange rind
- 2 slices ginger root, chopped into strips
- 3 spring onions (scallions), chopped into chunks
- salt and freshly ground pepper

Directions:

1. Put the duck in a large pan, just cover with water and bring to the boil.
2. Put in the spring onions, ginger and orange rind, cover and simmer for about 1½ hours until the duck is soft.
3. Season with salt and pepper, eliminate the excess liquid and serve.

DUCK WITH PEARS AND CHESTNUTS

Yield: 4 Servings

Ingredients:

- 1 duck
- 1 large pear, peeled and thickly sliced
- 1 slice ginger root, minced
- 15 ml/1 tbsp rice wine or dry sherry
- 15 ml/1 tbsp sugar
- 225 g/8 oz chestnuts, shelled
- 250 ml/8 fl oz/1 cup chicken stock
- 45 ml/3 tbsp groundnut (peanut) oil
- 45 ml/3 tbsp soy sauce
- 5 ml/1 tsp salt

Directions:

1. Boil the chestnuts for approximately fifteen minutes then drain.
2. Chop the duck into 5 cm/2 in pieces.
3. Heat the oil and fry the duck until slightly browned on all sides.
4. Drain off any excess oil then add the stock, soy sauce, wine or sherry, salt and ginger.
5. Bring to the boil, cover and simmer for 25 minutes, stirring intermittently.
6. Put in the chestnuts, cover and simmer for another 15 minutes.
7. Drizzle the pear with sugar, add to the pan and simmer for approximately five minutes until heated through.

DUCK WITH PINEAPPLE AND LYCHEES

Yield: 4 Servings

Ingredients:

- 1 clove star anise
- 1 slice ginger root
- 100 g/4 oz/½ cup brown sugar
- 15 ml/1 tbsp cornflour (cornstarch)
- 15 ml/1 tbsp soy sauce
- 15 ml/1 tbsp tomato ketchup (catsup)
- 200 g/7 oz canned pineapple chunks in syrup
- 250 ml/8 fl oz/½ cup chicken stock
- 4 duck breasts
- 6 canned lychees
- 6 maraschino cherries

- 90 ml/6 tbsp wine vinegar
- groundnut (peanut) oil for deep-frying

Directions:

1. Put the ducks, soy sauce, anise and ginger in a saucepan and just cover with cold water.
2. Bring to the boil, skim, then cover and simmer for about 45 minutes until the duck is cooked.
3. Drain and pat dry.
4. Deep-fry in hot oil until crispy.
5. In the meantime, mix the wine vinegar, sugar, stock, tomato ketchup and 30 ml/2 tbsp of the pineapple syrup in a pan, bring to the boil and simmer for approximately five minutes until thick.
6. Mix in the fruit and heat through before pouring over the duck to serve.

DUCK WITH PORK AND CHESTNUTS

Yield: 4 Servings

Ingredients:

- 1 duck
- 1 slice ginger root, minced
- 225 g/8 oz chestnuts, shelled
- 225 g/8 oz lean pork, cubed
- 250 ml/8 fl oz/1 cup soy sauce
- 3 spring onions (scallions), chopped
- 6 dried Chinese mushrooms
- 900 ml/1½ pts/3¾ cups water

Directions:

1. Soak the mushrooms in warm water for half an hour then drain.
2. Discard the stalks and slice the caps.
3. Put in a large pan with all the rest of the ingredients, bring to the boil, cover and simmer for about 1½ hours until the duck is cooked.

DUCK WITH POTATOES

Yield: 4 Servings

Ingredients:

- ½ head Chinese leaves
- 1 clove star anise
- 1 duck
- 1.2 l/2 pts/5 cups water
- 10 ml/2 tsp salt
- 15 ml/1 tbsp cornflour (cornstarch)
- 15 ml/1 tbsp sugar
- 2 leeks, thickly sliced
- 3 cloves garlic, crushed
- 30 ml/2 tbsp black bean sauce
- 30 ml/2 tbsp water
- 45 ml/3 tbsp soy sauce
- 60 ml/4 tbsp rice wine or dry sherry
- 75 ml/5 tbsp groundnut (peanut) oil
- 900 g/2 lb potatoes, thickly sliced
- sprigs flat-leaf parsley

Directions:

1. Heat 60 ml/4 tbsp of oil and fry the duck until browned on all sides.
2. Tie or sew up the neck end and stand the duck, neck down, in a deep bowl.
3. Heat the rest of the oil and fry the garlic until slightly browned.
4. Put in the black bean sauce and salt and fry for approximately one minute.
5. Put in the water, leeks, sugar, soy sauce, wine or sherry and star anise and bring to the boil.
6. Pour 120 ml/8 fl oz/1 cup of the mixture into the duck cavity and tie or sew up to secure.
7. Bring the rest of the mixture in the pan to the boil.
8. Put in the duck and potatoes, cover and simmer for 40 minutes, turning the duck once.
9. Put the Chinese leaves on a serving plate.
10. Remove the duck from the pan, chop into 5 cm/2 in pieces and arrange on the serving plate with the potatoes.
11. Combine the cornflour to a paste with the water, mix it into the pan and simmer, stirring, until the sauce becomes thick.
12. Pour over the duck and serve garnished with parsley.

DUCK WITH SWEET POTATOES

Yield: 4 Servings

Ingredients:

- 1 duck
- 1 slice ginger root, minced
- 15 ml/1 tbsp cornflour (cornstarch)
- 15 ml/1 tbsp soy sauce
- 2 cloves garlic, crushed
- 2½ ml/½ tsp cinnamon
- 2½ ml/½ tsp ground cloves
- 225 g/8 oz sweet potatoes, peeled and cubed
- 250 ml/8 fl oz/1 cup chicken stock
- 250 ml/8 fl oz/1 cup groundnut (peanut) oil
- 30 ml/2 tbsp water
- 5 ml/1 tsp sugar
- Chop the duck into 5 cm/2 in pieces.
- pinch of ground anise

Directions:

1. Heat the oil and deep-fry the potatoes until a golden-brown colour is achieved.
2. Remove them from the pan and eliminate the excess liquid off all but 30 ml/2 tbsp of oil.
3. Put in the garlic and ginger and stir-fry for 30 seconds.
4. Put in the duck and fry until slightly browned on all sides.
5. Put in the spices, sugar, soy sauce and stock and bring to the boil.
6. Put in the potatoes, cover and simmer for approximately twenty minutes until the duck is soft.
7. Blend the cornflour to a paste with the water then mix it into the pan and simmer, stirring, until the sauce becomes thick.

DUCK WITH TWO MUSHROOMS

Yield: 4 Servings

Ingredients:

- 1 duck
- 100 g/4 oz bamboo shoots, chopped into strips
- 100 g/4 oz button mushrooms
- 45 ml/3 tbsp rice wine or dry sherry
- 5 ml/1 tsp salt
- 6 dried Chinese mushrooms
- 750 ml/1¼ pts/3 cups chicken stock

Directions:

1. Soak the mushrooms in warm water for half an hour then drain.
2. Discard the stalks and halve the caps.
3. Put the duck in a large heatproof bowl with the stock, wine or sherry and salt and stand in a pan filled with water to come two-thirds up the sides of the bowl.
4. Bring to the boil, cover and simmer for about 2 hours until the duck is soft.
5. Take out of the pan and chop the meat from the bone.
6. Transfer the cooking liquid to a separate pan.
7. Put the bamboo shoots and both types of mushrooms in the bottom of the steamer bowl, replace the duck meat, cover and steam for another 30 minutes.
8. Bring the cooking liquid to the boil and pour over the duck to serve.

DUCK WITH VEGETABLES

Yield: 4 Servings

Ingredients:

- 1 large duck, chopped into 16 pieces
- 120 ml/4 fl oz/½ cup wine vinegar
- 2 carrots, chopped
- 30 ml/2 tbsp hoisin sauce
- 30 ml/2 tbsp plum sauce
- 300 ml/½ pt/1¼ cups dry white wine
- 300 ml/½ pt/1¼ cups water
- 45 ml/3 tbsp soy sauce
- 5 cm/2 in white radish, chopped
- 5 ml/1 tsp five-spice powder
- 5 ml/1 tsp sugar
- 50 g/2 oz Chinese cabbage, diced

- 6 spring onions (scallions), chopped
- freshly ground pepper
- salt

Directions:

1. Put the duck pieces into a container, drizzle with salt and add the water and wine.
2. Put in the wine vinegar, soy sauce, plum sauce, hoisin sauce and five-spice powder, bring to the boil, cover and simmer for about 1 hour.
3. Put in the vegetables to the pan, remove the lid and simmer for another 10 minutes.
4. Season with salt, pepper and sugar then allow to cool.
5. Cover and place in the refrigerator overnight.
6. Remove all excess fat then reheat the duck in the sauce for approximately 20 minutes.

DUCK WITH WINE

Yield: 4 Servings

Ingredients:

- 1 bottle dry white wine
- 1 duck
- 1 onion, sliced
- 15 ml/1 tbsp yellow bean sauce

Directions:

1. Rub the duck inside and out with the yellow bean sauce.
2. Put the onion inside the cavity.
3. Bring the wine to the boil in a large pan, add the duck, return to the boil, cover and simmer as gently as possible for approximately three hours until the duck is soft.
4. Drain and slice to serve.

FAR EASTERN CHICKEN

Yield: 4 Servings

Ingredients:

- 15 ml/1 tbsp cornflour (cornstarch)
- 15 ml/1 tbsp water
- 2 cloves garlic, crushed
- 2 onions, chopped
- 2 pieces stem ginger, chopped
- 2½ ml/½ tsp salt
- 30 ml/2 tbsp hoisin sauce
- 300 ml/½ pt/1¼ cups chicken stock
- 45 ml/3 tbsp rice wine or dry sherry
- 45 ml/3 tbsp soy sauce
- 450 g/1 lb chicken meat, chopped into chunks
- 5 ml/1 tsp freshly ground pepper
- 6 hard-boiled (hard-cooked) eggs, chopped
- 60 ml/4 tbsp groundnut (peanut) oil

Directions:

1. Heat the oil and fry the chicken until a golden-brown colour is achieved.
2. Put in the garlic, salt, onions and ginger and fry for approximately two minutes.
3. Put in the soy sauce, hoisin sauce, wine or sherry, stock and pepper.
4. Bring to the boil, cover and simmer for half an hour.
5. Put in the eggs.
6. Combine the cornflour and water and mix it into the sauce.
7. Bring to the boil and simmer, stirring, until the sauce becomes thick.

FIVE-SPICE CHICKEN

Yield: 4 Servings

Ingredients:

- 1 chicken
- 1 clove garlic, crushed
- 120 ml/4 fl oz/½ cup soy sauce
- 15 ml/1 tbsp five-spice powder
- 2½ cm/1 in piece ginger root, minced
- 2½ ml/½ tsp sesame oil
- 30 ml/2 tbsp honey
- 30 ml/2 tbsp rice wine or dry sherry

- 30 ml/2 tbsp salt
- 5 ml/1 tsp freshly ground pepper
- oil for deep-frying

Directions:

1. Put the chicken in a large saucepan and fill with water to come half way up the thigh.
2. Reserve 15 ml/1 tbsp of the soy sauce and add the remainder to the pan with the ginger, garlic and half the five-spice powder.
3. Bring to the boil, cover and simmer for approximately five minutes.
4. Turn off the heat and leave the chicken to stand in the water until the water is lukewarm.
5. Drain.
6. Chop the chicken in half lengthways and place chop side down in a roasting tin.
7. Combine the rest of the soy sauce and five-spice powder with the wine or sherry, honey and sesame oil.
8. Rub the mixture over the chicken and allow to stand for 2 hours, brushing intermittently with the mixture.
9. Heat the oil and deep-fry the chicken halves for about 15 minutes until a golden-brown colour is achieved and cooked through.
10. Drain using kitchen paper and chop into serving sized pieces.
11. In the meantime, mix the salt and pepper and heat using a dry pan for about 2 minutes.
12. Serve as a immerse with the chicken.

FIVE-SPICE CHICKEN WINGS

Yield: 4 Servings

Ingredients:

- 2 cloves garlic, crushed
- 250 ml/8 fl oz/1 cup chicken stock
- 30 ml/2 tbsp groundnut (peanut) oil
- 30 ml/2 tbsp soy sauce
- 450 g/1 lb chicken wings
- 5 ml/1 tsp five-spice powder
- 5 ml/1 tsp sugar

Directions:

1. Heat the oil and garlic until the garlic is slightly browned.
2. Put in the chicken and fry until slightly browned.
3. Add the rest of the ingredients, stirring well, and bring to the boil.
4. Cover and simmer for about 15 minutes until the chicken is cooked through.
5. Take the lid off and continue to simmer, stirring intermittently, until almost all the liquid has evaporated.
6. Serve hot or cold.

FIVE-SPICE CHICKEN WITH POTATOES

Yield: 4 Servings

Ingredients:

- 1 potato, diced
- 45 ml/3 tbsp groundnut (peanut) oil
- 45 ml/3 tbsp soy sauce
- 45 ml/3 tbsp yellow bean paste
- 450 g/1 lb chicken, chopped into chunks
- 450 ml/¾ pt/2 cups chicken stock
- 5 ml/1 tsp five-spice powder
- 5 ml/1 tsp sugar
- salt

Directions:

1. Heat the oil and stir-fry the chicken until slightly browned.
2. Drizzle with salt then mix in the bean paste, soy sauce, sugar and five-spice powder and stir-fry for approximately one minute.
3. Put in the potato and mix in well then add the stock, bring to the boil, cover and simmer for about 30 minutes until soft.

FIVE-SPICE DUCK

Yield: 4 Servings

Ingredients:

- 1 duck
- 10 ml/2 tsp five-spice powder
- 150 ml/¼ pt/generous ½ cup rice wine or dry sherry
- 150 ml/¼ pt/generous ½ cup soy sauce

Directions:

1. Bring the wine or sherry and soy sauce to the boil.
2. Put in the duck and simmer, turning for about 5 minutes.
3. Remove the duck from the pan and rub the five-spice powder into the skin.
4. Return the bird to the pan and add enough water to half cover the duck.
5. Bring to the boil, cover and simmer for about 1½ hours until the duck is soft, turning and basting often.
6. Chop the duck into 5 cm/2 in pieces and serve hot or cold.

FRIED CHICKEN WITH CUCUMBER

Yield: 4 Servings

Ingredients:

- ½ cucumber
- 1 egg white
- 100 g/4 oz button mushrooms
- 15 ml/1 tbsp water
- 2½ ml/½ tsp cornflour (cornstarch)
- 2½ ml/½ tsp rice wine or dry sherry
- 2½ ml/½ tsp salt
- 2½ ml/½ tsp sesame oil
- 225 g/8 oz chicken meat
- 30 ml/2 tbsp groundnut (peanut) oil
- 50 g/2 oz bamboo shoots, chopped into strips
- 50 g/2 oz ham, diced
- salt

Directions:

1. Slice the chicken and chop it into chunks.
2. Mix with the egg white, cornflour and salt and leave to stand.
3. Halve the cucumber lengthways and chop diagonally into thick slices.

4. Heat the oil and stir-fry the chicken until slightly browned then remove from the pan.
5. Put in the cucumber and bamboo shoots and stir-fry for approximately one minute.
6. Return the chicken to the pan with the ham, water, salt and wine or sherry.
7. Bring to the boil and simmer until the chicken is soft.
8. Serve sprinkled with sesame oil.

FRIED PHEASANT

Yield: 4 Servings

Ingredients:

- 120 ml/4 fl oz/½ cup groundnut (peanut) oil
- 30 ml/2 tbsp soy sauce
- 4 eggs, beaten
- 900 g/2 lb pheasant

Directions:

1. Bone the pheasant and slice the meat.
2. Mix with the soy sauce and allow to stand for half an hour.
3. Eliminate the excess liquid from the pheasant then immerse it in the eggs.
4. Heat the oil and fry the pheasant quickly until a golden-brown colour is achieved.
5. Drain thoroughly and serve.

FRIED POUSSINS

Yield: 4 Servings

Ingredients:

- 1 spring onion (scallion), finely chopped
- 10 ml/2 tsp sugar
- 120 ml/4 fl oz/½ cup groundnut (peanut) oil
- 2 poussins, halved
- 30 ml/2 tbsp chicken stock
- 45 ml/3 tbsp rice wine or dry sherry
- 45 ml/3 tbsp soy sauce

- 5 ml/1 tsp chilli oil
- 5 ml/1 tsp garlic paste
- salt and pepper

Directions:

1. Put the poussins into a container.
2. Combine the soy sauce and wine or sherry, pour over the poussins, cover and marinate for 2 hours, basting often.
3. Heat the oil and fry the poussins for approximately twenty minutes until cooked through.
4. Remove them from the pan and reheat the oil.
5. Return them to the pan and fry until a golden-brown colour is achieved.
6. Drain off most of the oil.
7. Combine the rest of the ingredients, add to the pan and heat through quickly.
8. Pour over the poussins and serve.

GINGER AND SPRING ONION CHICKEN

Yield: 4 Servings

Ingredients:

- 1 chicken
- 10 ml/2 tsp white wine vinegar
- 2 slices ginger root, chopped into strips
- 5 ml/1 tsp soy sauce
- 8 spring onions (scallions), finely chopped
- 90 ml/4 tbsp groundnut (peanut) oil
- salt and freshly ground pepper

Directions:

1. Put the chicken in a large saucepan, add half the ginger and pour in enough water almost to cover the chicken.
2. Season with salt and pepper.
3. Bring to the boil, cover and simmer for about 1¼ hours until soft.
4. Leave the chicken to stand in the stock until cool.
5. Eliminate the excess liquid from the chicken and refrigerate until cold.
6. Cut into portions.

7. Grate the rest of the ginger and mix with the oil, spring onions, wine vinegar and soy sauce and salt and pepper.
8. Refrigerate for one hour.
9. Put the chicken pieces in a serving bowl and pour over the ginger dressing.
10. Serve with steamed rice.

GINGER CHICKEN

Yield: 4 Servings

Ingredients:

- 1 carrot, sliced
- 1 egg white
- 10 slices ginger root
- 15 ml/1 tbsp groundnut (peanut) oil
- 2 spring onions (scallions), sliced
- 2½ ml/½ tsp cornflour (cornstarch)
- 2½ ml/½ tsp sesame oil
- 225 g/8 oz chicken, finely sliced
- 5 ml/1 tsp rice wine or dry sherry
- 5 ml/1 tsp water
- 6 mushrooms, halved
- pinch of salt

Directions:

1. Combine the chicken with the egg white, salt and cornflour.
2. Heat half the oil and fry the chicken until slightly browned then remove it from the pan.
3. Heat the rest of the oil and fry the ginger, mushrooms, carrot and spring onions for approximately three minutes.
4. Return the chicken to the pan with the wine or sherry and water and simmer until the chicken is soft.
5. Serve sprinkled with sesame oil.

GINGER CHICKEN WITH MUSHROOMS AND CHESTNUTS

Yield: 4 Servings

Ingredients:

- 10 ml/2 tsp sugar
- 100 g/4 oz mushrooms, sliced
- 2 slices ginger root, chopped
- 225 g/8 oz onions, sliced
- 30 ml/2 tbsp plain (all-purpose) flour
- 450 g/1 lb chicken meat, diced
- 450 g/1 lb water chestnuts
- 60 ml/4 tbsp groundnut (peanut) oil
- 60 ml/4 tbsp soy sauce
- 900 ml/1½ pt/3¾ cups hot water
- salt and freshly ground pepper

Directions:

1. Heat the half oil and fry the onions for approximately three minutes then remove them from the pan.
2. Heat the rest of the oil and fry the chicken until slightly browned.
3. Put in the mushrooms and cook for approximately two minutes.
4. Drizzle the mixture with flour then mix in the soy sauce, sugar, salt and pepper.
5. Pour in the water and ginger, onions and chestnuts.
6. Bring to the boil, cover and simmer gently for approximately 20 minutes.
7. Take the lid off and carry on simmering gently until the sauce has reduced.

GOLDEN CHICKEN

Yield: 4 Servings

Ingredients:

- 1 sliced ginger root, minced
- 15 ml/1 tbsp rice wine or dry sherry
- 300 ml/½ pt/1¼ cups chicken stock

- 45 ml/3 tbsp soy sauce
- 5 ml/1 tsp sugar
- 8 small chicken pieces

Directions:

1. Put all the ingredients in a large pan, bring to the boil, cover and simmer for about 30 minutes until the chicken is comprehensively cooked.
2. Take the lid off and carry on simmering until the sauce has reduced.

GOLDEN COINS

Yield: 4 Servings

Ingredients:

- 100 g/4 oz/1 cup dried breadcrumbs
- 2 cloves garlic, crushed
- 2 eggs, beaten
- 30 ml/2 tbsp honey
- 30 ml/2 tbsp soy sauce
- 30 ml/2 tbsp tomato ketchup (catsup)
- 30 ml/2 tbsp wine vinegar
- 4 chicken breast fillets
- 45 ml/3 tbsp plain (all-purpose) flour
- 5 ml/1 tsp five-spice powder
- 5 ml/1 tsp grated lemon rind
- 5 ml/1 tsp grated root ginger
- oil for deep-frying
- pinch of salt
- Put the chicken into a bowl.

Directions:

1. Combine the honey, wine vinegar, tomato ketchup, soy sauce, salt, garlic and five-spice powder.
2. Pour over the chicken, stir thoroughly, cover and marinate in the refrigerator for 12 hours.
3. Remove the chicken from the marinade and chop into finger thick strips.
4. Dust with flour.

5. Beat the eggs, ginger and lemon rind.
6. Coat the chicken in the mixture then in the breadcrumbs until evenly coated.
7. Heat the oil and deep-fry the chicken until a golden-brown colour is achieved.

HAM AND CHICKEN FOO YUNG

Yield: 4 Servings

Ingredients:

- 100 g/4 oz ham, diced
- 225 g/8 oz chicken breast, diced
- 3 spring onions (scallions), finely chopped
- 45 ml/3 tbsp cornflour (cornstarch)
- 45 ml/3 tbsp groundnut (peanut) oil
- 5 ml/1 tsp salt
- 6 eggs, beaten

Directions:

1. Beat the eggs then beat in the cornflour.
2. Mix in all the rest of the ingredients except the oil.
3. Heat the oil.
4. Pour the mixture into the pan a little at a time to make small pancakes about 7.5 cm/3 in across.
5. Cook until the bottom is golden-brown then turn and cook the other side.

HOISIN CHICKEN DRUMSTICKS

Yield: 4 Servings

Ingredients:

- 100 g/4 oz/1 cup breadcrumbs
- 2 eggs, beaten
- 250 ml/8 fl oz/1 cup hoisin sauce
- 30 ml/2 tbsp plain (all-purpose) flour
- 600 ml/1 pt/2½ cups chicken stock

- 8 chicken drumsticks
- oil for deep-frying
- salt and freshly ground pepper

Directions:

1. Put the drumsticks and stock in a pan, bring to the boil, cover and simmer for approximately 20 minutes until cooked.
2. Remove the chicken from the pan and pat dry on kitchen paper.
3. Put the chicken into a container and season with salt and pepper.
4. Pour over the hoisin sauce and allow to marinate for one hour.
5. Drain.
6. Toss the chicken in the flour then cover with the eggs and breadcrumbs, then in egg and breadcrumbs again.
7. Heat the oil and fry the chicken for approximately five minutes until a golden-brown colour is achieved.
8. Drain using kitchen paper and serve hot or cold.

HONEY CHICKEN

Yield: 4 Servings

Ingredients:

- 1 slice ginger root, finely chopped
- 1 spring onion (scallion), chopped
- 120 ml/4 fl oz/½ cup rice wine or dry sherry
- 30 ml/2 tbsp groundnut (peanut) oil
- 30 ml/2 tbsp honey
- 30 ml/2 tbsp soy sauce
- 4 chicken pieces
- 5 ml/1 tsp salt

Directions:

1. Heat the oil and fry the chicken until browned on all sides.
2. Drain off excess oil.
3. Combine the rest of the ingredients and pour them into the pan.
4. Bring to the boil, cover and simmer for about 40 minutes until the chicken is cooked through.

HONEY-ROAST DUCK

Yield: 4 Servings

Ingredients:

- 1 duck
- 200 ml/7 fl oz/scant 1 cup boiling water
- 3 cloves garlic, crushed
- 3 spring onions (scallions), minced
- 45 ml/3 tbsp honey
- 45 ml/3 tbsp rice wine or dry sherry
- 45 ml/3 tbsp soy sauce
- salt

Directions:

1. Pat the duck dry and rub with salt inside and out.
2. Combine the garlic, spring onions, soy sauce and wine or sherry then divide the mixture in half.
3. Combine the honey into one half and rub over the duck then leave it to dry.
4. Put in the water to the rest of the honey mixture.
5. Pour the soy sauce mixture into the cavity of the duck and stand it on a rack in a roasting tin with a little water in the bottom.
6. Roast in a preheated oven at 180°C/350°F/gas mark 4 for about 2 hours until the duck is soft, basting throughout cooking with the rest of the honey mixture.

HOT CHILLI-CHICKEN

Yield: 4 Servings

Ingredients:

- 1 egg, slightly beaten
- 1 green pepper, diced
- 10 ml/2 tsp soy sauce
- 2 red chilli peppers, shredded
- 2½ ml/½ tsp chilli oil

- 2½ ml/½ tsp cornflour (cornstarch)
- 2½ ml/½ tsp sesame oil
- 2½ ml/½ tsp sugar
- 350 g/1 lb chicken meat, cubed
- 4 cloves garlic, crushed
- 5 ml/1 tsp freshly ground pepper
- 5 ml/1 tsp water
- 5 ml/1 tsp wine vinegar
- oil for deep-frying

Directions:

1. Combine the chicken with the egg, half the soy sauce and the cornflour and allow to stand for half an hour.
2. Heat the oil and deep-fry the chicken until a golden-brown colour is achieved then eliminate the excess liquid well.
3. Pour off all but 15 ml/1 tbsp of oil from the pan, add the pepper, garlic and chilli peppers and fry for 30 seconds.
4. Put in the pepper, wine vinegar, water and sugar and fry for 30 seconds.
5. Return the chicken to the pan and stir-fry for a few minutes until cooked through.
6. Serve sprinkled with chilli and sesame oils.

KUNG PAO CHICKEN

Yield: 4 Servings

Ingredients:

- 1 egg white
- 15 ml/1 tbsp rice wine or dry sherry 5 ml/1 tsp sugar
- 15 ml/1 tbsp soy sauce
- 25 g/1 oz dried red chilli peppers, trimmed
- 30 ml/2 tbsp cornflour (cornstarch)
- 30 ml/2 tbsp water
- 450 g/1 lb chicken, cubed
- 5 ml/1 tsp minced garlic
- 5 ml/1 tsp salt
- 5 ml/1 tsp sesame oil
- 5 ml/1 tsp wine vinegar

- 60 ml/4 tbsp groundnut (peanut) oil

Directions:

1. Put the chicken into a container with the egg white, salt and half the cornflour and allow to marinate for half an hour.
2. Heat the oil and fry the chicken until slightly browned then remove it from the pan.
3. Reheat the oil and fry the chilli peppers and garlic for approximately two minutes.
4. Return the chicken to the pan with the soy sauce, wine or sherry, sugar, wine vinegar and sesame oil and stir-fry for approximately two minutes.
5. Mix the rest of the cornflour with the water, mix it into the pan and simmer, stirring, until the sauce clears and becomes thick.

LEMON CHICKEN

Yield: 4 Servings

Ingredients:

- 1 head lettuce
- 150 ml/¼ pt/generous ½ cup water
- 2 eggs
- 250 ml/8 fl oz/1 cup chicken stock
- 30 ml/2 tbsp cornflour (cornstarch)
- 30 ml/2 tbsp rice wine or dry sherry
- 30 ml/2 tbsp tomato purée (paste)
- 4 boned chicken breasts
- 50 g/2 oz/½ cup cornflour (cornstarch)
- 50 g/2 oz/½ cup plain (all-purpose) flour
- 60 ml/5 tbsp lemon juice
- groundnut (peanut) oil for deep-frying

Directions:

1. Cut each chicken breast into 4 pieces.
2. Beat the eggs, cornflour and plain flour, adding just enough water to make a thick batter.
3. Put the chicken pieces in the batter and stir until comprehensively.
4. coated.

5. Heat the oil and deep-fry the chicken until a golden-brown colour is achieved and cooked through.
6. In the meantime, mix the stock, lemon juice, wine or sherry, cornflour and tomato purée and heat gently, stirring, until the mixture comes to the boil.
7. Simmer gently, stirring constantly, until the sauce becomes thick and clears.
8. Put the chicken on a warmed serving plate on a bed of lettuce leaves and either pour over the sauce or serve it separately.

LEMON CHICKEN STIR-FRY

Yield: 4 Servings

Ingredients:

- 15 ml/1 tbsp lemon juice
- 15 ml/1 tbsp rice wine or dry sherry
- 15 ml/1 tbsp soy sauce
- 15 ml/1 tbsp sugar
- 15 ml/1 tbsp tomato purée (paste)
- 2 cloves garlic, crushed
- 2½ ml/½ tsp salt
- 30 ml/2 tbsp cornflour (cornstarch)
- 30 ml/2 tbsp groundnut (peanut) oil
- 30 ml/2 tbsp lemon juice
- 450 g/1 lb boned chicken, sliced
- 50 g/2 oz bamboo shoots, chopped into strips
- 50 g/2 oz water chestnuts, chopped into strips
- 60 ml/4 tbsp chicken stock
- a few Chinese leaves, chopped into strips

Directions:

1. Put the chicken into a container.
2. Combine the lemon juice, soy sauce, wine or sherry and 15 ml/1 tbsp cornflour, pour over the chicken and allow to marinate for one hour, turning intermittently.
3. Heat the oil, salt and garlic until the garlic is slightly browned then add the chicken and marinade and stir-fry for approximately five minutes until the chicken is slightly browned.

4. Put in the water chestnuts, bamboo shoots and Chinese leaves and stir-fry for another 3 minutes or until the chicken is just cooked.
5. Add the rest of the ingredients and stir-fry for about 3 minutes until the sauce clears and becomes thick.

MARINATED CHICKEN WINGS

Yield: 4 Servings

Ingredients:

- 175 ml/6 fl oz/¾ cup chicken stock
- 2 cloves garlic, crushed
- 20 ml/4 tsp cornflour (cornstarch)
- 225 g/8 oz bamboo shoots, sliced
- 30 ml/2 tbsp brown sugar
- 30 ml/2 tbsp groundnut (peanut) oil
- 45 ml/3 tbsp rice wine or dry sherry
- 45 ml/3 tbsp soy sauce
- 450 g/1 lb chicken wings
- 5 ml/1 tsp grated ginger root
- 6 spring onions (scallions), sliced

Directions:

1. Combine the soy sauce, wine or sherry, sugar, ginger, garlic and spring onions.
2. Put in the chicken wings and stir to coat completely.
3. Cover and allow to stand for one hour, stirring intermittently.
4. Heat the oil and stir-fry the bamboo shoots for approximately two minutes.
5. Remove them from the pan.
6. Eliminate the excess liquid from the chicken and onions, reserving the marinade.
7. Reheat the oil and stir-fry the chicken until browned on all sides.
8. Cover and cook for another 20 minutes until the chicken is soft.
9. Blend the cornflour with the stock and the reserved marinade.
10. Pour over the chicken and bring to the boil, stirring, until the sauce becomes thick.
11. Mix in the bamboo shoots and simmer, stirring, for another 2 minutes.

MARINATED GOLDEN CHICKEN STEW

Yield: 4 Servings

Ingredients:

- 1 slice ginger root, minced
- 150 ml/1½ pt/generous ½ cup chicken stock
- 2 red chilli peppers, sliced
- 3 cloves star anise
- 30 ml/2 tbsp cornflour (cornstarch)
- 300 ml/½ pt/1¼ cups soy sauce
- 4 chicken pieces
- 4 spring onions (scallions), thickly sliced
- 5 ml/1 tsp sesame oil
- 50 g/2 oz bamboo shoots, sliced
- 60 ml/4 tbsp water
- oil for deep-frying

Directions:

1. Chop the chicken into large chunks and marinate in the soy sauce for 10 minutes.
2. Remove and drain, reserving the soy sauce.
3. Heat the oil and deep-fry the chicken for about 2 minutes until slightly browned.
4. Remove and drain.
5. Pour off all but 30 ml/2 tbsp of the oil then add the spring onions, ginger, chilli peppers and star anise and fry for approximately one minute.
6. Return the chicken to the pan with the bamboo shoots and reserved soy sauce and add just enough stock to cover the chicken.
7. Bring to the boil and simmer for approximately ten minutes until the chicken is soft.
8. Remove the chicken from the sauce using a slotted spoon and lay out on a heated serving dish.
9. Strain the sauce then return it to the pan.
10. Blend the cornflour and water to a paste, stir into the sauce and simmer, stirring, until the sauce becomes thick.
11. Pour over the chicken and serve sprinkled with a little sesame oil.

MOIST ROAST DUCK

Yield: 4 Servings

Ingredients:

- 1 duck
- 15 ml/1 tbsp sugar
- 2 slices ginger root, minced
- 2½ ml/½ tsp ground anise
- 250 ml/8 fl oz/1 cup water
- 45 ml/3 tbsp rice wine or dry sherry
- 6 spring onions (scallions), chopped
- 60 ml/4 tbsp soy sauce

Directions:

1. Put half the spring onions and ginger in a large heavy-based pan.
2. Put the remainder in the cavity of the duck and put it into the pan.
3. Add all the rest of the ingredients except the hoisin sauce, bring to the boil, cover and simmer for about 1½ hours, turning intermittently.
4. Remove the duck from the pan and leave it to dry for about 4 hours.
5. Put the duck on a rack in a roasting tin filled with a little cold water.
6. Roast in a preheated oven at 230°C/450°F/gas mark 8 for approximately fifteen minutes then turn it over and roast for another 10 minutes until crispy.
7. In the meantime, reheat the reserved liquid and pour over the duck to serve.

ORANGE AND LEMON CHICKEN

Yield: 4 Servings

Ingredients:

- 15 ml/1 tbsp cornflour (cornstarch)
- 15 ml/1 tbsp soy sauce
- 2 cloves garlic, crushed
- 2 slices ginger root, minced
- 3 spring onions (scallions), chopped
- 30 ml/2 tbsp groundnut (peanut) oil
- 350 g/1 lb chicken meat, chopped into strips
- 45 ml/1 tbsp water
- 45 ml/3 tbsp lemon juice

- 45 ml/3 tbsp orange juice
- grated rind of ½ lemon
- grated rind of ½ orange

Directions:

1. Briefly boil the chicken in boiling water for 30 seconds then drain.
2. Heat the oil and stir-fry the garlic and ginger for 30 seconds.
3. Put in the orange and lemon rind and juice, soy sauce and spring onions and stir-fry for approximately two minutes.
4. Put in the chicken and simmer for a few minutes until the chicken is soft.
5. Blend the cornflour and water to a paste, stir into the pan and simmer, stirring, until the sauce becomes thick.

ORANGE-ROAST DUCK

Yield: 4 Servings

Ingredients:

- 1 duck
- 1 onion
- 1 orange
- 120 ml/4 fl oz/½ cup rice wine or dry sherry
- 2 cloves garlic, halved
- 2 slices ginger root, minced
- 45 ml/3 tbsp groundnut (peanut) oil
- 5 ml/1 tsp salt

Directions:

1. Rub the garlic over the duck inside and out then brush it with oil.
2. Pierce the peeled onion using a fork, place it and the unpeeled orange inside the duck cavity and seal with a skewer.
3. Stand the duck on a rack over a roasting tin filled with a little hot water and roast in a preheated oven at 160°C/325°F/gas mark 3 for about 2 hours.
4. Discard the liquids and return the duck to the roasting tin.
5. Pour over the wine or sherry and drizzle with the ginger and salt.
6. Return to the oven for another 30 minutes.
7. Discard the onion and orange and chop the duck into serving pieces.

8. Pour the pan juices over the duck to serve.

PEKING CHICKEN

Yield: 4 Servings

Ingredients:

- 1 slice ginger root, minced
- 1 spring onion (scallion), chopped
- 15 ml/1 tbsp cornflour (cornstarch)
- 15 ml/1 tbsp rice wine or dry sherry
- 15 ml/1 tbsp soy sauce
- 4 chicken portions
- 5 ml/1 tsp sugar
- oil for deep-frying
- salt and freshly ground pepper

Directions:

1. Put the chicken portions in a shallow bowl and drizzle with salt and pepper.
2. Combine the sugar, spring onion, ginger, soy sauce and wine or sherry, rub into the chicken, cover and allow to marinate for approximately three hours.
3. Eliminate the excess liquid from the chicken and dust it with cornflour.
4. Heat the oil and deep-fry the chicken until a golden-brown colour is achieved and cooked through.
5. Drain thoroughly and serve.

PEKING DUCK

Yield: 6 Servings

Ingredients:

- 1 cucumber, chopped into strips
- 1 duck
- 120 ml/4 fl oz/½ cup hoisin sauce
- 120 ml/4 fl oz/½ cup honey

- 120 ml/4 fl oz/½ cup sesame oil
- 225 g/8 oz/2 cups plain (all-purpose) flour
- 250 ml/8 fl oz/1 cup water
- 250 ml/8 fl oz/1 cup water
- 30 ml/2 tbsp brown sugar
- 30 ml/2 tbsp soy sauce
- 5 ml/1 tsp sesame oil
- 6 spring onions (scallions), sliced lengthways
- For the dips:
- For the pancakes:
- groundnut (peanut) oil for frying

Directions:

1. The duck should be whole with the skin intact.
2. Tie the neck tightly with string and sew up or skewer the bottom opening.
3. Cut a small slit in the side of the neck, insert a straw and blow air under the skin until it is inflated.
4. Suspend the duck over a basin and leave to hang for one hour.
5. Bring a pan of water to the boil, insert the duck and boil for approximately one minute then remove and dry well.
6. Bring the water to the boil and mix in the honey.
7. Rub the mixture over the duck skin until it is saturated.
8. Hang the duck over a basin in a cool, airy place for about 8 hours until the skin is hard.
9. Suspend the duck or place on a rack over a roasting tin and roast in a preheated oven at 180°C/350°F/gas mark 4 for about 1½ hours, basting regularly with sesame oil.
10. To make the pancakes, boil the water then progressively add the flour.
11. Knead slightly until the dough is soft, cover with a damp cloth and allow to stand for approximately fifteen minutes.
12. Roll out on a floured surface and mould into a long cylinder.
13. Cut into 2½ cm/1 in slices then flatten until about 5 mm/¼ in thick and brush the tops with oil.
14. Stack in pairs with the oiled surfaces touching and dust the outsides slightly with flour.
15. Roll out the pairs to about 10 cm/4 in across and cook in pairs for about 1 minute on each side until slightly browned.
16. Separate and stack until ready to serve.
17. Prepare the dips by mixing half the hoisin sauce with the sugar and mixing the rest of the hoisin sauce with the soy sauce and sesame oil.
18. Remove the duck from the oven, chop off the skin and chop it into squares, and cube the meat.
19. Lay out on separate plates and serve with the pancakes, dips and accompaniments.

PHEASANT WITH ALMONDS

Yield: 4 Servings

Ingredients:

- 1 slice ginger root, minced
- 100 g/4 oz/1 cup flaked almonds
- 2 spring onions (scallions), chopped
- 2½ ml/½ tsp salt
- 225 g/8 oz pheasant, very finely sliced
- 30 ml/2 tbsp rice wine or dry sherry
- 30 ml/2 tbsp soy sauce
- 45 ml/3 tbsp groundnut (peanut) oil
- 5 ml/1 tsp freshly ground pepper
- 5 ml/1 tsp sugar
- 50 g/2 oz ham, shredded

Directions:

1. Heat the oil and fry the spring onions and ginger until slightly browned.
2. Put in the pheasant and ham and stir-fry for approximately five minutes until almost cooked.
3. Put in the soy sauce, wine or sherry, sugar, pepper and salt and stir-fry for approximately two minutes.
4. Put in the almonds and stir-fry for approximately one minute until the ingredients are comprehensively.
5. blended.

PINEAPPLE AND GINGER DUCK

Yield: 4 Servings

Ingredients:

- 1 duck
- 100 g/4 oz preserved ginger in syrup
- 15 ml/1 tbsp cornflour (cornstarch)

- 200 g/7 oz canned pineapple chunks in syrup
- 30 ml/2 tbsp water
- 5 ml/1 tsp salt

Directions:

1. Put the duck in a heatproof bowl and stand it in a pan filled with water to come two-thirds of the way up the sides of the bowl.
2. Bring to the boil, cover and simmer for about 2 hours until the duck is soft.
3. Remove the duck and allow to cool slightly.
4. Remove the skin and bone and chop the duck into pieces.
5. Lay out on a serving plate and keep them warm.
6. Eliminate the excess liquid from the syrup from the ginger and pineapple into a pan, add the salt, cornflour and water.
7. Bring to the boil, stirring and simmer for a few minutes, stirring, until the sauce clears and becomes thick.
8. Put in the ginger and pineapple, stir through then pour over the duck to serve.

POACHED CHICKEN

Yield: 4 Servings

Ingredients:

- 1 chicken
- 1 slice ginger root
- 1.2 l/2 pts/5 cups chicken stock or water
- 30 ml/2 tbsp rice wine or dry sherry
- 4 spring onions (scallions), chopped
- 5 ml/1 tsp salt

Directions:

1. Put the chicken in a large saucepan with all the rest of the ingredients.
2. The stock or water should come half way up the thigh.
3. Bring to the boil, cover and simmer gently for about 1 hour until the chicken is comprehensively cooked.
4. Drain, reserving the stock for soups.

POACHED CHICKEN WITH TOMATOES

Yield: 4 Servings

Ingredients:

- 15 ml/1 tbsp groundnut (peanut) oil
- 15 ml/1 tbsp rice wine or dry sherry
- 4 chicken portions
- 4 tomatoes, skinned and quartered
- salt

Directions:

1. Put the chicken in a pan and just cover with cold water.
2. Bring to the boil, cover and simmer for approximately 20 minutes.
3. Put in the tomatoes, wine or sherry, oil and salt, cover and simmer for another 10 minutes until the chicken is cooked.
4. Put the chicken on a warmed serving plate and chop into serving pieces.
5. Reheat the sauce and pour over the chicken to serve.

QUICK CURRIED CHICKEN

Yield: 4 Servings

Ingredients:

- 1 egg white
- 10 ml/2 tsp brown sugar
- 15 ml/1 tbsp curry powder
- 150 ml/¼ pt/generous ½ cup chicken stock
- 150 ml/¼ pt/generous ½ cup groundnut (peanut) oil
- 45 ml/3 tbsp rice wine or dry sherry
- 450 g/1 lb chicken breasts, cubed
- 50 g/2 oz cornflour (cornstarch)
- salt

Directions:

1. Combine the chicken cubes and sherry.

2. Reserve 10 ml/2 tsp of the cornflour.
3. Beat the egg white with the rest of the cornflour and a pinch of salt then mix it into the chicken until it is well coated.
4. Heat the oil and fry the chicken until cooked and golden.
5. Take out of the pan and eliminate the excess liquid off all but 15 ml/1 tbsp of the oil.
6. Mix in the reserved cornflour, curry powder and sugar and fry for approximately one minute.
7. Mix in the stock, bring to the boil and simmer, stirring constantly, until the sauce becomes thick.
8. Return the chicken to the pan, stir together and reheat and serve.

QUICK-COOKED CHICKEN WITH VEGETABLES

Yield: 4 Servings

Ingredients:

- 1 clove garlic, minced
- 1 egg white
- 1 green pepper, chopped into strips
- 1 slice ginger root, minced
- 15 ml/1 tbsp rice wine or dry sherry
- 200 g/7 oz bamboo shoots, chopped into strips
- 225 g/8 oz chicken breasts, chopped into strips
- 3 spring onions (scallions), sliced
- 50 g/2 oz bean sprouts
- 50 g/2 oz cornflour (cornstarch)
- 75 ml/5 tbsp groundnut (peanut) oil

Directions:

1. Beat the egg white and cornflour then immerse the chicken strips in the mixture.
2. Heat the oil to moderately hot and fry the chicken for a few minutes until just cooked.
3. Take out of the pan and eliminate the excess liquid well.
4. Put in the bamboo shoots, bean sprouts, pepper, onions, ginger and garlic to the pan and stir-fry for approximately three minutes.
5. Put in the wine or sherry and return the chicken to the pan.
6. Stir together well and heat through and serve.

RED-COOKED CHICKEN

Yield: 4 Servings

Ingredients:

- 120 ml/4 fl oz/½ cup soy sauce
- 15 ml/1 tbsp sugar
- 2 slices ginger root, finely chopped
- 30 ml/2 tbsp rice wine or dry sherry
- 4 spring onions (scallions), sliced
- 450 g/1 lb chicken, sliced
- 90 ml/6 tbsp chicken stock

Directions:

1. Put all the ingredients in a pan and bring to the boil.
2. Cover and simmer for about 15 minutes until the chicken is cooked through.
3. Take the lid off and carry on simmering for about 5 minutes, stirring intermittently, until the sauce has thickened.
4. Serve sprinkled with spring onions.

RED-COOKED CHICKEN

Yield: 4 Servings

Ingredients:

- 1 chicken
- 250 ml/8 fl oz/1 cup soy sauce

Directions:

1. Put the chicken in a pan, pour over the soy sauce and top up with water almost to cover the chicken.
2. Bring to the boil, cover and simmer for about 1 hour until the chicken is cooked, turning intermittently.

RED-COOKED DUCK

Yield: 4 Servings

Ingredients:

- 1 duck
- 10 ml/2 tsp salt
- 10 ml/2 tsp sugar
- 2 slices ginger root, chopped into strips
- 4 spring onions (scallions), chopped into chunks
- 45 ml/3 tbsp rice wine or dry sherry
- 90 ml/6 tbsp soy sauce

Directions:

1. Put the duck in a heavy pan, just cover with water and bring to the boil.
2. Put in the spring onions, ginger, wine or sherry and salt, cover and simmer for about 1 hour.
3. Put in the sugar and simmer for another 45 minutes until the duck is soft.
4. Slice the duck on to a serving plate and serve hot or cold, with or without the sauce.

RED-COOKED SPICED CHICKEN

Yield: 4 Servings

Ingredients:

- ½ cinnamon stick
- 1 chicken
- 15 ml/1 tbsp sugar
- 15 ml/1 tbsp Szechuan peppercorns
- 2 slices ginger root
- 2 spring onions (scallions)
- 3 cloves star anise
- 75 ml/5 tbsp rice wine or dry sherry
- 75 ml/5 tbsp sesame oil
- 75 ml/5 tbsp soy sauce

Directions:

1. Put the ginger and spring onions inside the chicken cavity and place the chicken in a pan.
2. Tie the star anise, cinnamon and peppercorns in a piece of muslin and put it into the pan.
3. Pour over the soy sauce, wine or sherry and sesame oil.
4. Bring to the boil, cover and simmer for about 45 minutes.
5. Put in the sugar, cover and simmer for another 10 minutes until the chicken is cooked through.

RICE WINE ROAST DUCK

Yield: 4 Servings

Ingredients:

- 1 duck
- 45 ml/3 tbsp soy sauce
- 5 ml/1 tsp salt
- 500 ml/14 fl oz/1¾ cups rice wine or dry sherry

Directions:

1. Put the duck in a heavy-based pan with the sherry and salt, bring to the boil, cover and simmer for approximately 20 minutes.
2. Eliminate the excess liquid from the duck, reserving the liquid, and rub it with soy sauce.
3. Put on a rack in a roasting tin filled with a little hot water and roast in a preheated oven at 180°C/350°F/gas mark 4 for about 1 hour, basting regularly with the reserved wine liquid.

ROYAL CHICKEN WINGS

Yield: 4 Servings

Ingredients:

- 10 slices bamboo shoots
- 12 chicken wings

- 15 ml/1 tbsp cornflour (cornstarch)
- 15 ml/1 tbsp granulated sugar
- 15 ml/1 tbsp water
- 2 spring onions (scallions), chopped into chunks
- 2½ ml/½ tsp sesame oil
- 250 ml/8 fl oz/1 cup chicken stock
- 250 ml/8 fl oz/1 cup groundnut (peanut) oil
- 250 ml/8 fl oz/1 cup rice wine or dry sherry
- 45 ml/3 tbsp soy sauce
- 5 ml/1 tsp salt
- 5 slices root ginger

Directions:

1. Briefly boil the chicken wings in boiling water for approximately five minutes then eliminate the excess liquid well.
2. Heat the oil, add the sugar and stir until melted and golden brown.
3. Put in the chicken, spring onions, ginger, salt, soy sauce, wine and stock, bring to the boil and simmer gently for approximately 20 minutes.
4. Put in the bamboo shoots and simmer for approximately two minutes or until the liquid has almost all evaporated.
5. Blend the cornflour with the water, mix it into the pan and stir until thick.
6. Transfer the chicken wings to a warmed serving plate and serve sprinkled with sesame oil.

SAVOURY CHICKEN

Yield: 4 Servings

Ingredients:

- 1 slice ginger root, chopped
- 120 ml/4 fl oz/½ cup soy sauce
- 15 ml/1 tbsp cornflour (cornstarch)
- 2 cloves garlic, crushed
- 3 spring onions (scallions), chopped
- 30 ml/2 tbsp brown sugar
- 30 ml/2 tbsp groundnut (peanut) oil
- 30 ml/2 tbsp rice wine or dry sherry

- 375 ml/13 fl oz/1½ cups water
- 4 chicken pieces
- 5 ml/1 tsp salt

Directions:

1. Heat the oil and fry the chicken pieces until a golden-brown colour is achieved.
2. Put in the spring onions, garlic and ginger and fry for approximately two minutes.
3. Put in the soy sauce, wine or sherry, sugar and salt and stir together well.
4. Put in the water and bring to the boil, cover and simmer for 40 minutes.
5. Combine the cornflour with a little water, mix it into the sauce and simmer, stirring, until the sauce clears and becomes thick.

SAVOURY CHICKEN WITH EGGS

Yield: 4 Servings

Ingredients:

- 1 clove garlic, crushed
- 1 slice ginger root, chopped
- 15 ml/1 tbsp cornflour (cornstarch)
- 175 ml/6 fl oz/¾ cup soy sauce
- 2 spring onions (scallions), chopped
- 30 ml/2 tbsp brown sugar
- 30 ml/2 tbsp groundnut (peanut) oil
- 30 ml/2 tbsp rice wine or dry sherry
- 375 ml/13 fl oz/1½ cups water
- 4 chicken pieces
- 4 hard-boiled (hard-cooked) eggs
- 5 ml/1 tsp salt

Directions:

1. Heat the oil and fry the chicken pieces until a golden-brown colour is achieved.
2. Put in the spring onions, garlic and ginger and fry for approximately two minutes.
3. Put in the soy sauce, wine or sherry, sugar and salt and stir together well.
4. Put in the water and bring to the boil, cover and simmer for approximately 20 minutes.
5. Put in the hard-boiled eggs, cover and cook for another 15 minutes.

6. Combine the cornflour with a little water, mix it into the sauce and simmer, stirring, until the sauce clears and becomes thick.

SAVOURY CHICKEN WITH WATER CHESTNUTS

Yield: 4 Servings

Ingredients:

- 1 slice ginger root, chopped
- 15 ml/1 tbsp cornflour (cornstarch)
- 2 cloves garlic, crushed
- 225 g/8 oz water chestnuts, sliced
- 250 ml/8 fl oz/1 cup soy sauce
- 3 spring onions (scallions), chopped
- 30 ml/2 tbsp brown sugar
- 30 ml/2 tbsp groundnut (peanut) oil
- 30 ml/2 tbsp rice wine or dry sherry
- 375 ml/13 fl oz/1¼ cups water
- 4 chicken pieces
- 5 ml/1 tsp salt

Directions:

1. Heat the oil and fry the chicken pieces until a golden-brown colour is achieved.
2. Put in the spring onions, garlic and ginger and fry for approximately two minutes.
3. Put in the soy sauce, wine or sherry, sugar and salt and stir together well.
4. Put in the water and bring to the boil, cover and simmer for approximately 20 minutes.
5. Put in the water chestnuts, cover and cook for another 20 minutes.
6. Combine the cornflour with a little water, mix it into the sauce and simmer, stirring, until the sauce clears and becomes thick.

SAVOURY DUCK

Yield: 4 Servings

Ingredients:

- 1 slice ginger root, chopped
- 15 ml/1 tbsp cornflour (cornstarch)
- 2 cloves garlic, crushed
- 250 ml/8 fl oz/1 cup soy sauce
- 3 spring onions (scallions), sliced
- 30 ml/2 tbsp brown sugar
- 30 ml/2 tbsp rice wine or dry sherry
- 4 duck breasts
- 45 ml/3 tbsp groundnut (peanut) oil
- 450 ml/¾ pt/2 cups water
- 5 ml/1 tsp salt

Directions:

1. Heat the oil and fry the duck breasts until a golden-brown colour is achieved.
2. Put in the spring onions, garlic and ginger and fry for approximately two minutes.
3. Put in the soy sauce, wine or sherry, sugar and salt and mix well.
4. Put in the water, bring to the boil, cover and simmer for about 1½ hours until the meat is very soft.
5. Combine the cornflour with a little water then mix it into the pan and simmer, stirring, until the sauce becomes thick.

SAVOURY DUCK WITH GREEN BEANS

Yield: 4 Servings

Ingredients:

- 1 slice ginger root, chopped
- 15 ml/1 tbsp cornflour (cornstarch)
- 2 cloves garlic, crushed
- 225 g/8 oz green beans
- 250 ml/8 fl oz/1 cup soy sauce
- 3 spring onions (scallions), sliced
- 30 ml/2 tbsp brown sugar
- 30 ml/2 tbsp rice wine or dry sherry
- 4 duck breasts
- 45 ml/3 tbsp groundnut (peanut) oil
- 450 ml/¾ pt/2 cups water

- 5 ml/1 tsp salt

Directions:

1. Heat the oil and fry the duck breasts until a golden-brown colour is achieved.
2. Put in the spring onions, garlic and ginger and fry for approximately two minutes.
3. Put in the soy sauce, wine or sherry, sugar and salt and mix well.
4. Put in the water, bring to the boil, cover and simmer for about 45 minutes.
5. Put in the beans, cover and simmer for another 20 minutes.
6. Combine the cornflour with a little water then mix it into the pan and simmer, stirring, until the sauce becomes thick.

SESAME CHICKEN

Yield: 4 Servings

Ingredients:

- 1 spring onion (scallion), finely chopped
- 10 ml/2 tsp sugar
- 150 ml/¼ pt/generous ½ cup soy sauce
- 2 slices ginger, finely chopped
- 450 g/1 lb cooked chicken, chopped into strips
- 5 ml/1 tsp wine vinegar
- 60 ml/4 tbsp rice wine or dry sherry
- 60 ml/4 tbsp sesame oil
- salt and freshly ground pepper

Directions:

1. Put the chicken on a serving plate and drizzle with ginger, spring onion, salt and pepper.
2. Combine the wine or sherry, sesame oil, sugar, wine vinegar and soy sauce.
3. Pour over the chicken.

SESAME ROAST CHICKEN

Yield: 4 Servings

Ingredients:

- 1 chicken
- 1 dried red chilli pepper, crushed
- 1 onion, finely chopped
- 10 ml/2 tsp salt
- 2 cloves garlic, minced
- 2½ ml/½ tsp ground cardamom
- 2½ ml/½ tsp ground ginger
- 50 g/2 oz sesame seeds
- 75 ml/5 tbsp groundnut (peanut) oil
- pinch of ground cloves

Directions:

1. Combine all the seasonings and oil and brush over the chicken.
2. Stand it in a roasting tin and add 30 ml/2 tbsp of water to the tin.
3. Roast in a preheated oven at 180°C/350°F/gas mark 4 for about 2 hours, basting and turning the chicken intermittently, until the chicken is golden and cooked through.
4. Add a little more water, if needed, to prevent burning.

SHERRY CHICKEN

Yield: 4 Servings

Ingredients:

- 1 slice ginger root, chopped
- 120 ml/4 fl oz/½ cup soy sauce
- 2 cloves garlic, crushed
- 30 ml/2 tbsp groundnut (peanut) oil
- 30 ml/2 tbsp sugar
- 4 chicken pieces
- 5 ml/1 tsp salt
- 500 ml/17 fl oz/2¼ cups rice wine or dry sherry

Directions:

1. Heat the oil and fry the chicken until browned on all sides.
2. Drain off excess oil and add all the rest of the ingredients.

3. Bring to the boil, cover and simmer over a fairly high heat for 25 minutes.
4. Reduce the heat and simmer for another 15 minutes until the chicken is cooked through and the sauce has reduced.

SIMPLE CHICKEN STIR-FRY

Yield: 4 Servings

Ingredients:

- 1 chicken breast, finely sliced
- 100 g/4 oz bamboo shoots, sliced
- 100 g/4 oz bean sprouts
- 100 g/4 oz mushrooms, sliced
- 120 ml/4 fl oz/½ cup chicken stock
- 15 ml/1 tbsp cornflour (cornstarch)
- 15 ml/1 tbsp rice wine or dry sherry
- 15 ml/1 tbsp soy sauce
- 2 slices ginger root, minced
- 2 spring onions (scallions), minced
- 2½ ml/½ tsp salt
- 30 ml/2 tbsp water
- 45 ml/3 tbsp groundnut (peanut) oil
- 5 ml/1 tsp sugar

Directions:

1. Put the chicken into a container.
2. Combine the ginger, spring onions, cornflour, wine or sherry, water and salt, stir into the chicken and allow to stand for one hour.
3. Heat half the oil and stir-fry the chicken until slightly browned then remove it from the pan.
4. Heat the rest of the oil and stir-fry the bamboo shoots, mushrooms and bean sprouts for 4 minutes.
5. Put in the soy sauce, sugar and stock, bring to the boil, cover and simmer for approximately five minutes until the vegetables are just soft.
6. Return the chicken to the pan, stir thoroughly and reheat gently and serve.

SLOW-COOKED DUCK

Yield: 4 Servings

Ingredients:

- 1 duck
- 10 ml/2 tsp sugar
- 2 cloves garlic, crushed
- 225 g/8 oz bamboo shoots, sliced
- 225 g/8 oz water chestnuts, sliced
- 30 ml/2 tbsp rice wine or dry sherry
- 30 ml/2 tbsp soy sauce
- 4 dried Chinese mushrooms
- 5 ml/1 tsp grated ginger root
- 5 spring onions (scallions), sliced
- 50 g/2 oz/½ cup cornflour (cornstarch)
- 750 ml/1¼ pts/3 cups chicken stock
- oil for deep-frying
- pinch of pepper

Directions:

1. Chop the duck into serving-size pieces.
2. Reserve 30 ml/2 tbsp of cornflour and coat the duck in the rest of the cornflour.
3. Dust off the excess.
4. Heat the oil and fry the garlic and duck until slightly browned.
5. Take out of the pan and eliminate the excess liquid on kitchen paper.
6. Put the duck in a large pan.
7. Combine the wine or sherry, 15 ml/1 tbsp of soy sauce and the ginger.
8. Put into the pan and cook over a high heat for approximately two minutes.
9. Add half the stock, bring to the boil, cover and simmer for about 1 hour until the duck is soft.
10. In the meantime, soak the mushrooms in warm water for half an hour then drain.
11. Discard the stalks and slice the caps.
12. Put in the mushrooms, bamboo shoots and water chestnuts to the duck and cook, stirring often, for approximately five minutes.
13. Remove all excess fat from the liquid.
14. Blend the rest of the stock, cornflour and soy sauce with the sugar and pepper and stir into the pan.

15. Bring to the boil, stirring, then simmer for approximately five minutes until the sauce becomes thick.
16. Move to a warmed serving bowl and serve garnished with spring onions.

SPICED CHICKEN WINGS

Yield: 4 Servings

Ingredients:

- 15 ml/1 tbsp Worcestershire sauce
- 2 cloves garlic, crushed
- 30 ml/2 tbsp groundnut (peanut) oil
- 30 ml/2 tbsp rice wine or dry sherry
- 30 ml/2 tbsp soy sauce
- 30 ml/2 tbsp tomato purée (paste)
- 5 ml/1 tsp salt
- 900 g/2 lb chicken wings

Directions:

1. Heat the oil, salt and garlic and fry until the garlic turns light golden.
2. Put in the chicken wings and fry, stirring often, for approximately ten minutes until a golden-brown colour is achieved and almost cooked through.
3. Add the rest of the ingredients and stir-fry for approximately five minutes until the chicken is crispy and comprehensively cooked.

SPICY BAKED CHICKEN

Yield: 4 Servings

Ingredients:

- 1 onion, finely chopped
- 1 slice ginger root, minced
- 1 slice lemon, chopped
- 150 ml/¼ pt/generous ½ cup soy sauce
- 2 cloves garlic, crushed

- 30 ml/2 tbsp tomato purée (paste)
- 4 large chicken pieces
- 45 ml/3 tbsp rice wine or dry sherry
- 50 g/2 oz/¼ cup brown sugar

Directions:

1. Combine all the ingredients except the chicken.
2. Put the chicken in an ovenproof dish, pour over the mixture, cover and marinate overnight, basting intermittently.
3. Bake the chicken in a preheated oven at 180°C/350°F/gas mark 4 for 40 minutes, turning and basting intermittently.
4. Remove the lid, raise the oven temperature to 200°C/400°F/gas mark 6 and continue to cook for another 15 minutes until the chicken is cooked through.

STEAMED CHICKEN

Yield: 4 Servings

Ingredients:

- 1 chicken
- 2 slices ginger root
- 2 spring onions (scallions)
- 250 ml/8 fl oz/1 cup chicken stock
- 45 ml/3 tbsp rice wine or dry sherry
- salt

Directions:

1. Put the chicken in an ovenproof bowl and rub with wine or sherry and salt and place the ginger and spring onions inside the cavity.
2. Put the bowl on a rack in a steamer, cover and steam over boiling water for about 1 hour until cooked through.
3. Serve hot or cold.

STEAMED CHICKEN WITH ANISE

Yield: 4 Servings

Ingredients:

- 1 chicken
- 15 ml/1 tbsp brown sugar
- 250 ml/8 fl oz/1 cup soy sauce
- 250 ml/8 fl oz/1 cup water
- 4 cloves star anise

Directions:

1. Combine the soy sauce, water, sugar and anise in a saucepan and bring to the boil over a gentle heat.
2. Put the chicken into a container and baste comprehensively.
3. with the mixture inside and out.
4. Reheat the mixture and repeat.
5. Put the chicken in an ovenproof bowl.
6. Put the bowl on a rack in a steamer, cover and steam over boiling water for about 1 hour until cooked through.

STEAMED CHICKEN WITH HAM

Yield: 4 Servings

Ingredients:

- 100 g/4 oz smoked ham, chopped
- 15 ml/1 tbsp flat-leaved parsley
- 15 ml/1 tbsp groundnut (peanut) oil
- 3 spring onions (scallions), chopped
- 4 chicken portions
- salt and freshly ground pepper

Directions:

1. Chop the chicken portions into 5 cm/1 in chunks and place in an ovenproof bowl with the ham and spring onions.
2. Drizzle with oil and season with salt and pepper then toss the ingredients together gently.

3. Put the bowl on a rack in a steamer, cover and steam over boiling water for about 40 minutes until the chicken is soft.
4. Serve garnished with parsley.

STEAMED CHICKEN WITH MUSHROOMS

Yield: 4 Servings

Ingredients:

- 100 g/4 oz mushrooms, sliced
- 2 slices root ginger, chopped
- 2½ ml/½ tsp salt
- 3 spring onions (scallions), chopped
- 30 ml/2 tbsp cornflour (cornstarch)
- 30 ml/2 tbsp soy sauce
- 4 chicken pieces

Directions:

1. Chop the chicken pieces into 5 cm/2 in chunks and place them in an ovenproof bowl.
2. Combine the cornflour and soy sauce to a paste, mix in the spring onions, ginger and salt and mix well with the chicken.
3. Gently mix in the mushrooms.
4. Put the bowl on a rack in a steamer, cover and steam over boiling water for about 35 minutes until the chicken is soft.

STEAMED DUCK WITH CELERY

Yield: 4 Servings

Ingredients:

- 1 head celery
- 1 tomato, chopped into wedges
- 2½ ml/½ tsp salt
- 250 ml/8 fl oz/1 cup chicken stock
- 350 g/12 oz cooked duck, sliced

- 5 ml/1 tsp sesame oil

Directions:

1. Put the duck on a steamer rack.
2. Trim the celery into 7.5 cm/3 in lengths and place in a pan.
3. Pour in the stock, season with salt and place the steamer over the pan.
4. Bring the stock to the boil then simmer gently for about 15 minutes until the celery is soft and the duck heated through.
5. Put the duck and celery on a warmed serving plate, drizzle the celery with sesame oil and serve garnished with tomato wedges.

STEAMED DUCK WITH RICE WINE

Yield: 4 Servings

Ingredients:

- 1 duck
- 1 slice ginger root, chopped
- 250 ml/8 fl oz/1 cup rice wine or dry sherry
- 30 ml/2 tbsp soy sauce
- 4 spring onions (scallions), halved
- pinch of salt

Directions:

1. Briefly boil the duck in boiling water for approximately five minutes then drain.
2. Put in a heatproof bowl with the rest of the ingredients.
3. Stand the bowl in a pan filled with water to come two-thirds of the way up the sides of the bowl.
4. Bring to the boil, cover and simmer for about 2 hours until the duck is soft.
5. Discard the spring onions and ginger and serve.

STIR-FRIED CHICKEN WITH CHILLI

Yield: 4 Servings

Ingredients:

- 1 tomato, sliced
- 100 g/4 oz spinach
- 15 ml/1 tbsp water
- 2½ ml/½ tsp chilli powder
- 2½ ml/½ tsp rice wine or dry sherry
- 2½ ml/½ tsp sesame oil
- 2½ ml/½ tsp soy sauce
- 225 g/8 oz chicken, sliced
- 4 spring onions (scallions), chopped
- 45 ml/3 tbsp groundnut (peanut) oil
- 5 ml/1 tsp cornflour (cornstarch)
- salt

Directions:

1. Combine the chicken with the soy sauce, sesame oil, wine or sherry, half the cornflour and a pinch of salt.
2. Allow to stand for half an hour.
3. Heat 15 ml/ 1 tbsp of oil and fry the chicken until slightly browned.
4. Take out of the wok.
5. Heat 15 ml/1 tbsp of oil and stir-fry the spinach until wilted then remove it from the wok.
6. Heat the rest of the oil and fry the spring onions, chilli powder, water and rest of the cornflour for approximately two minutes.
7. Mix in the chicken and stir-fry quickly.
8. Put the spinach around a warmed serving plate, top with the chicken and serve garnished with tomatoes.

STIR-FRIED CHICKEN WITH MUSHROOMS

Yield: 4 Servings

Ingredients:

- 1 chicken breast, finely sliced
- 1 slice ginger root, minced
- 100 g/4 oz bean sprouts
- 120 ml/4 fl oz/½ cup chicken stock
- 15 ml/1 tbsp cornflour (cornstarch)

- 15 ml/1 tbsp rice wine or dry sherry
- 15 ml/1 tbsp soy sauce
- 2 spring onions (scallions), minced
- 2½ ml/½ tsp salt
- 225 g/8 oz mushrooms, sliced
- 30 ml/2 tbsp water
- 45 ml/3 tbsp groundnut (peanut) oil
- 5 ml/1 tsp sugar
- 6 dried Chinese mushrooms

Directions:

1. Soak the mushrooms in warm water for half an hour then drain.
2. Discard the stalks and slice the caps.
3. Put the chicken into a container.
4. Combine the ginger, spring onions, cornflour, wine or sherry, water and salt, stir into the chicken and allow to stand for one hour.
5. Heat half the oil and stir-fry the chicken until slightly browned then remove it from the pan.
6. Heat the rest of the oil and stir-fry the dried and fresh mushrooms and the bean sprouts for approximately three minutes.
7. Put in the soy sauce, sugar and stock, bring to the boil, cover and simmer for 4 minutes until the vegetables are just soft.
8. Return the chicken to the pan, stir thoroughly and reheat gently and serve.

STIR-FRIED CHICKEN WITH PEPPERS

Yield: 4 Servings

Ingredients:

- 1 chicken breast, finely sliced
- 1 green pepper, chopped into strips
- 1 red pepper, chopped into strips
- 1 yellow pepper, chopped into strips
- 100 g/4 oz water chestnuts, sliced
- 120 ml/4 fl oz/½ cup chicken stock
- 15 ml/1 tbsp cornflour (cornstarch)
- 2 slices ginger root, minced

- 2 spring onions (scallions), minced
- 2½ ml/½ tsp salt
- 30 ml/2 tbsp rice wine or dry sherry
- 30 ml/2 tbsp soy sauce
- 30 ml/2 tbsp water
- 45 ml/3 tbsp groundnut (peanut) oil

Directions:

1. Put the chicken into a container.
2. Combine the ginger, spring onions, cornflour, wine or sherry, water and salt, stir into the chicken and allow to stand for one hour.
3. Heat half the oil and stir-fry the chicken until slightly browned then remove it from the pan.
4. Heat the rest of the oil and stir-fry the water chestnuts and peppers for approximately two minutes.
5. Put in the soy sauce and stock, bring to the boil, cover and simmer for approximately five minutes until the vegetables are just soft.
6. Return the chicken to the pan, stir thoroughly and reheat gently and serve.

STIR-FRIED DUCK

Yield: 4 Servings

Ingredients:

- 1 egg white, slightly beaten
- 1 green pepper, chopped into strips
- 2 spring onions (scallions), chopped into strips
- 20 ml/1½ tbsp cornflour (cornstarch)
- 2½ ml/½ tsp sugar
- 45 ml/3 tbsp groundnut (peanut) oil
- 450 g/1 lb duck breasts, finely sliced
- 5 ml/1 tsp rice wine or dry sherry
- 75 ml/5 tbsp chicken stock
- salt

Directions:

1. Beat the egg white with 15 ml/1 tbsp of cornflour and a pinch of salt.

2. Put in the sliced duck and mix until the duck is coated.
3. Heat the oil and fry the duck until cooked through and golden.
4. Remove the duck from the pan and eliminate the excess liquid off all but 30 ml/2 tbsp of the oil.
5. Put in the spring onions and pepper and stir-fry for approximately three minutes.
6. Put in the wine or sherry, stock and sugar and bring to the boil.
7. Mix the rest of the cornflour with a little water, mix it into the sauce and simmer, stirring, until the sauce becomes thick.
8. Mix in the duck, heat through and serve.

STIR-FRIED DUCK WITH GINGER

Yield: 4 Servings

Ingredients:

- 1 duck
- 15 ml/1 tbsp cornflour (cornstarch)
- 2 slices ginger root, shredded
- 2 spring onions (scallions), chopped
- 2½ ml/½ tsp salt
- 30 ml/2 tbsp rice wine or dry sherry
- 30 ml/2 tbsp soy sauce
- 45 ml/3 tbsp groundnut (peanut) oil

Directions:

1. Remove the meat from the bones and chop into pieces.
2. Combine the meat with all the rest of the ingredients except the oil.
3. Allow to stand for one hour.
4. Heat the oil and stir-fry the duck with the marinade for about 15 minutes until the duck is soft.

STIR-FRIED DUCK WITH MUSHROOMS

Yield: 4 Servings

Ingredients:

- 1 duck
- 15 ml/1 tbsp cornflour (cornstarch)
- 15 ml/1 tbsp soy sauce
- 15 ml/1 tbsp sugar
- 2 cloves garlic, crushed
- 225 g/8 oz mushrooms, halved
- 30 ml/2 tbsp water
- 45 ml/3 tbsp rice wine or dry sherry
- 5 ml/1 tsp salt
- 5 ml/1 tsp sesame oil
- 600 ml/1 pt/2½ cups chicken stock
- 75 ml/5 tbsp groundnut (peanut) oil
- pinch of pepper

Directions:

1. Chop the duck into 5 cm/2 in pieces.
2. Heat 45 ml/3 tbsp of oil and fry the duck until slightly browned on all sides.
3. Put in the wine or sherry, soy sauce, sugar, salt and pepper and stir-fry for 4 minutes.
4. Take out of the pan.
5. Heat the rest of the oil and fry the garlic until slightly browned.
6. Put in the mushrooms and stir until coated in oil then return the duck mixture to the pan and add the stock.
7. Bring to the boil, cover and simmer for about 1 hour until the duck is soft.
8. Combine the cornflour and water to a paste then mix it into the mixture and simmer, stirring, until the sauce becomes thick.
9. Drizzle with sesame oil and serve.

STIR-FRIED DUCK WITH PINEAPPLE

Yield: 4 Servings

Ingredients:

- 1 duck
- 15 ml/1 tbsp rice wine or dry sherry
- 2 slices ginger root, chopped into strips
- 225 g/8 oz canned pineapple in syrup
- 45 ml/3 tbsp cornflour (cornstarch)

- 45 ml/3 tbsp groundnut (peanut) oil
- 45 ml/3 tbsp soy sauce
- 5 ml/1 tsp salt

Directions:

1. Chop the meat from the bone and chop it into pieces.
2. Combine the soy sauce with 30 ml/2 tbsp of cornflour and mix into the duck until well coated.
3. Allow to stand for one hour, stirring intermittently.
4. Crush the pineapple and syrup and heat gently in a pan.
5. Mix the rest of the cornflour with a little water, stir into the pan and simmer, stirring, until the sauce becomes thick.
6. Keep warm.
7. Heat the oil and fry the ginger until slightly browned then discard the ginger.
8. Put in the duck and stir-fry until slightly browned on all sides.
9. Put in the wine or sherry and salt and stir-fry for another few minutes until the duck is cooked.
10. Put the duck on a warmed serving plate, pour over the sauce and serve instantly.

STIR-FRIED DUCK WITH VEGETABLES

Yield: 4 Servings

Ingredients:

- 1 duck
- 10 ml/2 tsp cornflour (cornstarch)
- 100 g/4 oz bamboo shoots, chopped into strips
- 120 ml/4 fl oz/½ cup chicken stock
- 15 ml/1 tbsp rice wine or dry sherry
- 15 ml/1 tbsp soy sauce
- 4 dried Chinese mushrooms
- 45 ml/3 tbsp groundnut (peanut) oil
- 5 ml/1 tsp salt
- 50 g/2 oz water chestnuts, chopped into strips

Directions:

1. Soak the mushrooms in warm water for half an hour then drain.

2. Discard the stalks and dice the caps.
3. Remove the meat from the bones and chop into pieces.
4. Combine the cornflour and soy sauce, add to the duck meat and allow to stand for one hour.
5. Heat the oil and fry the duck until slightly browned on all sides.
6. Take out of the pan.
7. Put in the mushrooms, bamboo shoots and water chestnuts to the pan and stir-fry for approximately three minutes.
8. Put in the stock, wine or sherry and salt, bring to the boil and simmer for approximately three minutes.
9. Return the duck to the pan, cover and simmer for another 10 minutes until the duck is soft.

STRANGE-FLAVOURED CHICKEN

Yield: 4 Servings

Ingredients:

- ½ lettuce, shredded
- 1 chicken
- 10 ml/2 tsp chilli oil
- 10 ml/2 tsp sesame sauce
- 15 ml/1 tbsp chopped fresh coriander
- 2½ ml/½ tsp wine vinegar
- 45 ml/3 tbsp thick soy sauce
- 5 ml/1 tsp freshly ground pepper
- 5 ml/1 tsp minced garlic
- 5 ml/1 tsp minced ginger root
- 5 ml/1 tsp sugar

Directions:

1. Put the chicken in a pan and fill with water to come half way up the chicken legs.
2. Bring to the boil, cover and simmer gently for about 1 hour until the chicken is soft.
3. Take out of the pan and eliminate the excess liquid well and soak in iced water until the meat cools completely.
4. Drain thoroughly and chop into 5 cm/2 in pieces.
5. Combine all the rest of the ingredients and pour over the chicken.

6. Serve garnished with lettuce and coriander.

SWEET AND SOUR CHICKEN LIVERS

Yield: 4 Servings

Ingredients:

- 10 ml/2 tsp soy sauce
- 100 g/4 oz/½ cup sugar
- 120 ml/4 fl oz/½ cup water
- 120 ml/4 fl oz/½ cup wine vinegar
- 2 green peppers, chopped into chunks
- 30 ml/2 tbsp cornflour (cornstarch)
- 30 ml/2 tbsp groundnut (peanut) oil
- 4 slices canned pineapple, chopped into chunks
- 450 g/1 lb chicken livers, quartered
- 60 ml/4 tbsp chicken stock

Directions:

1. Heat the oil and fry the livers until slightly browned then transfer them to a heated serving dish.
2. Put in the peppers to the pan and fry for approximately three minutes.
3. Put in the pineapple and stock, bring to the boil, cover and simmer for approximately fifteen minutes.
4. Blend the rest of the ingredients to a paste, stir into the pan and simmer, stirring, until the sauce becomes thick.
5. Pour over the chicken livers and serve.

SWEET AND SOUR DUCK

Yield: 4 Servings

Ingredients:

- 1 duck
- 1 mango, peeled and cubed

- 1.2 l/2 pts/5 cups chicken stock
- 10 ml/2 tsp groundnut (peanut) oil
- 10 ml/2 tsp salt
- 10 ml/2 tsp tomato purée (paste)
- 12 lychees, halved
- 15 ml/1 tbsp cornflour (cornstarch)
- 15 ml/1 tbsp pickling spice
- 15 ml/1 tbsp soy sauce
- 15 ml/1 tbsp wine vinegar
- 2 carrots
- 2 cloves garlic, sliced
- 2 onions
- 300 ml/½ pt/1¼ cups chicken stock
- 5 ml/1 tsp five-spice powder
- 6 spring onions (scallions), chopped

Directions:

1. Put the duck in a steam basket over a pan containing the stock, onions, carrots, garlic, pickling spice and salt.
2. Cover and steam for 2½ hours.
3. Cool the duck, cover and chill for 6 hours.
4. Remove the meat from the bones and chop it into cubes.
5. Heat the oil and fry the duck and spring onions until crisp.
6. Mix in the rest of the ingredients, bring to the boil and simmer for approximately two minutes, stirring, until the sauce becomes thick.

TANGERINE DUCK

Yield: 4 Servings

Ingredients:

- 1 duck
- 1 piece dried tangerine peel
- 5 ml/1 tsp salt
- 60 ml/4 tbsp groundnut (peanut) oil
- 900 ml/1½ pts/3¾ cups chicken stock

Directions:

1. Hang the duck to dry for 2 hours.
2. Heat half the oil and fry the duck until slightly browned.
3. Move to a large heatproof bowl.
4. Heat the rest of the oil and fry the tangerine peel for approximately two minutes then place it inside the duck.
5. Pour the stock over the duck and season with salt.
6. Put the bowl on a rack in a steamer, cover and steam for about 2 hours until the duck is soft.

TURKEY WITH MANGETOUT

Yield: 4 Servings

Ingredients:

- 1 slice ginger root, minced
- 100 g/4 oz bamboo shoots, chopped into strips
- 15 ml/1 tbsp cornflour (cornstarch)
- 15 ml/1 tbsp rice wine or dry sherry
- 2 cloves garlic, crushed
- 2 spring onions (scallions), chopped
- 225 g/8 oz mangetout (snow peas)
- 225 g/8 oz turkey breast, chopped into strips
- 45 ml/3 tbsp soy sauce
- 5 ml/1 tsp salt
- 5 ml/1 tsp sugar
- 50 g/2 oz water chestnuts, chopped into strips
- 60 ml/4 tbsp groundnut (peanut) oil

Directions:

1. Heat 45 ml/3 tbsp of oil and fry the spring onions, garlic and ginger until slightly browned.
2. Put in the turkey and stir-fry for approximately five minutes.
3. Take out of the pan and set aside.
4. Heat the rest of the oil and stir-fry the mangetout, bamboo shoots and water chestnuts for approximately three minutes.
5. Put in the soy sauce, wine or sherry, sugar and salt and return the turkey to the pan.

6. Stir-fry for approximately one minute.
7. Combine the cornflour with a little water, mix it into the pan and simmer, stirring, until the sauce clears and becomes thick.

TURKEY WITH PEPPERS

Yield: 4 Servings

Ingredients:

- 1 Chinese cabbage, chopped into strips
- 1 green pepper, chopped into strips
- 1 onion, sliced
- 1 red pepper, chopped into strips
- 10 ml/2 tsp cornflour (cornstarch)
- 120 ml/4 fl oz/½ cup chicken stock
- 15 ml/1 tbsp hoisin sauce
- 30 ml/2 tbsp groundnut (peanut) oil
- 30 ml/2 tbsp soy sauce
- 30 ml/2 tbsp tomato purée (paste)
- 350 g/12 oz smoked turkey, chopped into strips
- 4 dried Chinese mushrooms
- 45 ml/3 tbsp wine vinegar
- few drops of chilli oil

Directions:

1. Soak the mushrooms in warm water for half an hour then drain.
2. Discard the stalks and chop the caps into strips.
3. Heat half the oil and stir-fry the cabbage for approximately five minutes or until cooked down.
4. Take out of the pan.
5. Put in the turkey and stir-fry for approximately one minute.
6. Put in the vegetables and stir-fry for approximately three minutes.
7. Combine the stock with the tomato purée, wine vinegar and sauces and add to the pan with the cabbage.
8. Combine the cornflour with a little water, mix it into the pan and bring to the boil, stirring.
9. Drizzle with chilli oil and simmer for approximately two minutes, stirring constantly.

TURKEY WITH WALNUTS AND MUSHROOMS

Yield: 4 Servings

Ingredients:

- 10 ml/2 tsp soy sauce
- 12 pickled black walnuts with juice
- 15 ml/1 tbsp groundnut (peanut) oil
- 15 ml/1 tbsp plain (all-purpose) flour
- 2 spring onions (scallions), diced
- 225 g/8 oz button mushrooms
- 25 g/1 oz pine kernels
- 45 ml/3 tbsp rice wine or dry sherry
- 450 g/1 lb turkey breast fillet
- 5 ml/1 tsp cornflour (cornstarch)
- 50 g/2 oz/½ cup butter
- juice of 1 orange
- salt and pepper

Directions:

1. Chop the turkey into 1 cm/½ in thick slices.
2. Drizzle with salt, pepper and orange juice and dust with flour.
3. Drain and halve the walnuts, reserving the liquid, and mix the liquid with the cornflour.
4. Heat the oil and stir-fry the turkey until a golden-brown colour is achieved.
5. Put in the spring onions and mushrooms and stir-fry for approximately two minutes.
6. Mix in the wine or sherry and soy sauce and simmer for 30 seconds.
7. Put in the walnuts to the cornflour mixture then stir them into the pan and bring to the boil.
8. Put in the butter in small flakes but do not allow the mixture to boil.
9. Heat the pine kernels using a dry pan until golden.
10. Transfer the turkey mixture to a warmed serving plate and serve garnished with pine kernels.

VENISON WITH DRIED MUSHROOMS

Yield: 4 Servings

Ingredients:

- 15 ml/1 tbsp juniper berries, ground
- 15 ml/1 tbsp sesame oil
- 30 ml/2 tbsp groundnut (peanut) oil
- 30 ml/2 tbsp hoisin sauce
- 30 ml/2 tbsp honey
- 30 ml/2 tbsp soy sauce
- 30 ml/2 tbsp wine vinegar
- 450 g/1 lb venison fillet, chopped into strips
- 5 ml/1 tsp five-spice powder
- 6 spring onions (scallions), chopped
- 8 dried Chinese mushrooms

Directions:

1. Soak the mushrooms in warm water for half an hour then drain.
2. Discard the stalks and slice the caps.
3. Put the venison into a container.
4. Combine the juniper berries, sesame oil, soy sauce, hoisin sauce and five-spice powder, pour over the venison and marinate for at least 3 hours, stirring intermittently.
5. Heat the oil and stir-fry the meat for 8 minutes until cooked.
6. Take out of the pan.
7. Put in the spring onions and mushrooms to the pan and stir-fry for approximately three minutes.
8. Return the meat to the pan with the honey and wine vinegar and heat through, stirring.

WALNUT CHICKEN

Yield: 4 Servings

Ingredients:

- 1 slice ginger root, minced
- 100 g/4 oz/1 cup walnuts, chopped
- 2 spring onions (scallions), chopped
- 30 ml/2 tbsp rice wine or dry sherry
- 30 ml/2 tbsp soy sauce
- 45 ml/3 tbsp groundnut (peanut) oil
- 450 g/1 lb chicken breast, very finely sliced
- 5 ml/1 tsp salt
- 5 ml/1 tsp sugar
- 50 g/2 oz ham, shredded

Directions:

1. Heat the oil and stir-fry the onions and ginger for approximately one minute.
2. Put in the chicken and ham and stir-fry for approximately five minutes until almost cooked.
3. Put in the soy sauce, wine or sherry, sugar and salt and stir-fry for approximately three minutes.
4. Put in the walnuts and stir-fry for approximately one minute until the ingredients are comprehensively blended.

WHITE-COOKED DUCK

Yield: 4 Servings

Ingredients:

- 1 duck
- 1 slice ginger root, chopped
- 100 g/4 oz bamboo shoots, sliced
- 100 g/4 oz smoked ham, sliced
- 250 ml/8 fl oz/1 cup rice wine or dry sherry
- 3 spring onions (scallions), chopped
- 5 ml/1 tsp salt
- salt and freshly ground pepper

Directions:

1. Combine the ginger, 15 ml/1 tbsp wine or sherry, a little salt and pepper.
2. Rub over the duck and allow to stand for one hour.

3. Put the bird in a heavy-based pan with the marinade and add the spring onions and salt.
4. Add enough cold water just to cover the duck, bring to the boil, cover and simmer for about 2 hours until the duck is soft.
5. Put in the bamboo shoots and ham and simmer for another 10 minutes.

WINE-VAPOUR DUCK

Yield: 4 Servings

Ingredients:

- 1 duck
- 200 ml/7 fl oz/scant 1 cup rice wine or dry sherry
- 30 ml/2 tbsp chopped fresh parsley
- celery salt

Directions:

1. Rub the duck with celery salt inside and out then place it in a deep ovenproof dish.
2. Put an ovenproof cup containing the wine into the cavity of the duck.
3. Put the dish on a rack in a steamer, cover and steam over boiling water for about 2 hours until the duck is soft.

SEAFOOD

Seafood is a staple in the Chinese kitchen. The Chinese quick and easy cooking style makes absolutely mouth-watering seafood recipes! The wok is going to come in handy if you have one, or you can just improvise.

Also, depending on where in the world you are living, you might not be able to easily procure some of the seafood ingredients used in the recipes in this section. I do my best to mention alternatives for these ingredients, but if I haven't mentioned an alternative in a recipe, and you can't find the main ingredient, feel free to use your own imagination, and use a seafood ingredient you personally feel will go well in that recipe! Prawns, for example, will pretty much go with every recipe that follows.

Prawns are easily available all over the world, cooked and uncooked. If you get the cooked and peeled version, you only need to heat them and they are ready to eat. If you get them uncooked, you will need to briefly boil them using boiling water or hot oil until they turn pink then carry on with the recipe. All right! Let's dive right into the recipes!

ABALONE WITH ASPARAGUS

Yield: 4 Servings

Ingredients:

- ½ small carrot, sliced
- 10 dried Chinese mushrooms
- 15 ml/1 tbsp cornflour (cornstarch)
- 15 ml/1 tbsp water
- 2½ ml/ ½ tsp fish sauce
- 225 g/8 oz asparagus
- 225 g/8 oz canned abalone, sliced
- 30 ml/2 tbsp groundnut (peanut) oil
- 5 ml/1 tsp oyster sauce
- 5 ml/1 tsp rice wine or dry sherry
- 5 ml/1 tsp soy sauce
- 60 ml/4 tbsp stock

Directions:

1. Soak the mushrooms in warm water for half an hour then drain.
2. Discard the stalks.
3. Heat 15 ml/1 tbsp of oil with the water and fry the mushroom caps for 10 minutes.
4. In the meantime, cook the asparagus in boiling water with the fish sauce and 5 ml/1 tsp cornflour until soft.
5. Drain thoroughly and lay out on a warmed serving plate with the mushrooms.
6. Keep them warm.
7. Heat the rest of the oil and fry the abalone for a few seconds then add the stock, carrot, soy sauce, oyster sauce, wine or sherry and rest of the cornflour.
8. Cook for approximately five minutes until well done then spoon over the asparagus and serve.

ABALONE WITH CHICKEN

Yield: 4 Servings

Ingredients:

- 100 g/4 oz bamboo shoots, sliced
- 100 g/4 oz chicken breast, diced
- 15 ml/1 tbsp cornflour (cornstarch)
- 15 ml/1 tbsp rice wine or dry sherry
- 2½ ml/ ½ tsp salt
- 250 ml/8 fl oz/1 cup fish stock
- 30 ml/2 tbsp groundnut (peanut) oil
- 400 g/14 oz canned abalone
- 45 ml/3 tbsp water
- 5 ml/1 tsp sugar

Directions:

1. Drain and slice the abalone, reserving the juice.
2. Heat the oil and stir-fry the chicken until slightly coloured.
3. Put in the abalone and bamboo shoots and stir-fry for approximately one minute.
4. Put in the abalone liquid, stock, wine or sherry, sugar and salt, bring to the boil and simmer for approximately two minutes.
5. Combine the cornflour and water to a paste and simmer, stirring, until the sauce clears and becomes thick.
6. Serve Immediately.

ABALONE WITH MUSHROOMS

Yield: 4 Servings

Ingredients:

- 15 ml/1 tbsp rice wine or dry sherry
- 2½ ml/ ½ tsp salt
- 3 spring onions (scallions), thickly sliced
- 400 g/14 oz canned abalone
- 45 ml/3 tbsp groundnut (peanut) oil
- 6 dried Chinese mushrooms

Directions:

1. Soak the mushrooms in warm water for half an hour then drain.
2. Discard the stalks and slice the caps.
3. Drain and slice the abalone, reserving the juice.
4. Heat the oil and stir-fry the salt and mushrooms for approximately two minutes.
5. Put in the abalone liquid and sherry, bring to the boil, cover and simmer for approximately three minutes.
6. Put in the abalone and spring onions and simmer until heated through.
7. Serve Immediately.

ABALONE WITH OYSTER SAUCE

Yield: 4 Servings

Ingredients:

- 15 ml/1 tbsp cornflour (cornstarch)
- 15 ml/1 tbsp soy sauce
- 30 ml/2 tbsp groundnut (peanut) oil
- 400 g/14 oz canned abalone
- 45 ml/3 tbsp oyster sauce
- 50 g/2 oz smoked ham, minced

Directions:

1. Eliminate the excess liquid from the can of abalone and reserve 90 ml/6 tbsp of the liquid.
2. Mix this with the cornflour, soy sauce and oyster sauce.
3. Heat the oil and stir-fry the drained abalone for approximately one minute.
4. Mix in the sauce mixture and simmer, stirring, for about 1 minute until heated through.
5. Move to a warmed serving plate and serve garnished with ham.

ALMOND FISH ROLLS

Yield: 4 Servings

Ingredients:

- 1 egg, slightly beaten
- 1 lemon, chopped into wedges
- 1 slice ginger root, minced
- 1 spring onion (scallion), minced
- 100 g/4 oz/1 cup almonds
- 15 ml/1 tbsp rice wine or dry sherry
- 15 ml/1 tbsp soy sauce
- 2½ ml/ ½ tsp salt
- 4 slices smoked ham
- 450 g/1 lb cod fillets
- 5 ml/1 tsp cornflour (cornstarch)
- 5 ml/1 tsp sugar
- oil for deep-frying

Directions:

1. Briefly boil the almonds in boiling water for approximately five minutes then eliminate the excess liquid and mince.
2. Chop the fish into 9 cm/3 ½ in squares and the ham into 5 cm/2 in squares.
3. Combine the spring onion, ginger, cornflour, sugar, salt, soy sauce, wine or sherry and egg.
4. Immerse the fish in the mixture then lay the fish on a work surface.
5. Coat the top with almonds then lay a slice of ham on top.
6. Roll up the fish and tie with cooking string.
7. Heat the oil and fry the fish rolls for a few minutes until a golden-brown colour is achieved.

8. Drain using kitchen paper and serve with lemon.

ANISE PRAWNS

Yield: 4 Servings

Ingredients:

- 120 ml/4 fl oz/ ½ cup fish stock
- 15 ml/1 tbsp soy sauce
- 45 ml/3 tbsp groundnut (peanut) oil
- 450 g/1 lb peeled prawns
- 5 ml/1 tsp sugar
- pinch of ground anise

Directions:

1. Heat the oil, add the soy sauce, sugar, stock and anise and bring to the boil.
2. Put in the prawns and simmer for a few minutes until heated through and flavoured.

BAKED WHOLE FISH

Yield: 4 Servings

Ingredients:

- 1 large bass or similar fish
- 1 onion, chopped
- 100 g/4 oz peeled prawns
- 15 ml/1 tbsp rice wine or dry sherry
- 15 ml/1 tbsp soy sauce
- 2 cloves garlic, crushed
- 45 ml/3 tbsp cornflour (cornstarch)
- 45 ml/3 tbsp groundnut (peanut) oil
- 5 ml/1 tsp salt
- 5 ml/1 tsp sugar
- 50 g/2 oz ham, chopped into strips

Directions:

1. Coat the fish with cornflour.
2. Heat the oil and fry the onion and garlic until slightly browned.
3. Put in the fish and fry until a golden-brown colour is achieved on both sides.
4. Transfer the fish to a sheet of foil in a roasting tin and top with ham and prawns.
5. Put in the soy sauce, wine or sherry, sugar and salt to the pan and stir together well.
6. Pour over the fish, close the foil over the top and bake in a preheated oven at 150 degree C or gas mark 2 for approximately 20 minutes.

BARBECUED PRAWNS

Yield: 4 Servings

Ingredients:

- 1 clove garlic, crushed
- 100 g/4 oz bacon
- 120 ml/4 fl oz/ ½ cup soy sauce
- 2 slices ginger root, minced
- 225 g/8 oz chicken livers, sliced
- 30 ml/2 tbsp sugar
- 450 g/1 lb large peeled prawns
- salt and freshly ground pepper

Directions:

1. Chop the prawns lengthways down the back without cutting right through and flatten them slightly.
2. Chop the bacon into chunks and place into a container with the prawns and chicken livers.
3. Combine the rest of the ingredients, pour over the prawns and allow to stand for half an hour.
4. Thread the prawns, bacon and livers oh to skewers and grill or barbecue for about 5 minutes, turning often, until cooked through, basting occasionally with the marinade.

BRAISED FISH WITH MUSHROOMS

Yield: 4 Servings

Ingredients:

- 1 large carp or similar fish
- 1 slice ginger root, minced
- 100 g/4 oz bamboo shoots, chopped into strips
- 15 ml/1 tbsp rice wine or dry sherry
- 2 spring onions (scallions), minced
- 2½ ml/ ½ tsp sugar
- 250 ml/8 fl oz/1 cup fish stock
- 3 cloves garlic, crushed
- 30 ml/2 tbsp soy sauce
- 4 dried Chinese mushrooms
- 45 ml/3 tbsp groundnut (peanut) oil
- salt

Directions:

1. Soak the mushrooms in warm water for half an hour then drain.
2. Discard the stalks and slice the caps.
3. Score the fish diagonally a few times on both sides, drizzle with salt and allow to stand for 10 minutes.
4. Heat the oil and fry the fish until slightly browned on both sides.
5. Put in the spring onions, ginger and garlic and fry for approximately two minutes.
6. Add the rest of the ingredients, bring to the boil, cover and simmer for approximately fifteen minutes until the fish is cooked, turning once or twice and stirring intermittently.

BRAISED FISH WITH TOFU

Yield: 4 Servings

Ingredients:

- 1 clove garlic, crushed
- 120 ml/4 fl oz/ ½ cup water
- 15 ml/1 tbsp rice wine or dry sherry
- 15 ml/1 tbsp soy sauce
- 2 spring onions (scallions), minced

- 225 g/8 oz tofu, cubed
- 450 g/1 lb fish steaks
- 5 ml/1 tsp salt
- 60 ml/4 tbsp groundnut (peanut) oil

Directions:

1. Heat the oil and fry the fish until slightly browned on both sides.
2. Put in the spring onions and garlic and fry for 30 seconds.
3. Put in the soy sauce, wine or sherry, salt and water, bring to the boil, cover and simmer for 10 minutes.
4. Put in the tofu, cover again and simmer for another 10 minutes or until the fish is cooked.

BRAISED SOY FISH

Yield: 4 Servings

Ingredients:

- 1 large bass or similar fish
- 15 ml/1 tbsp rice wine or dry sherry
- 2½ ml/ ½ tsp sugar
- 250 ml/8 fl oz/1 cup water
- 3 slices ginger root, minced
- 3 spring onions (scallions), minced
- 45 ml/3 tbsp soy sauce
- 50 g/2 oz/ ½ cup plain (all-purpose) flour
- 60 ml/4 tbsp groundnut (peanut) oil
- salt

Directions:

1. Clean and scale the fish and score it diagonally on both sides.
2. Drizzle with salt and allow to stand for 10 minutes.
3. Heat the oil and fry the fish until browned on both sides, turning once and basting with oil as you cook.
4. Put in the ginger, spring onions, water, soy sauce, wine or sherry and sugar, bring to the boil, cover and simmer for approximately 20 minutes until the fish is cooked.
5. Serve hot or cold.

BRAISED SPICED CARP

Yield: 4 Servings

Ingredients:

- 1 large carp or similar fish
- 1 slice ginger root, chopped
- 100 g/4 oz bamboo shoots, sliced
- 15 ml/1 tbsp rice wine or dry sherry
- 15 ml/1 tbsp soy sauce
- 15 ml/1 tbsp sugar
- 15 ml/1 tbsp wine vinegar salt
- 150 ml groundnut (peanut) oil
- 150 ml cup fish stock
- 2 cloves garlic, finely chopped
- 2 spring onions (scallions), chopped

Directions:

1. Clean and scale the fish and soak it for several hours in cold water.
2. Drain and pat dry then score each side several times.
3. Heat the oil and fry the fish on both sides until firm.
4. Take out of the pan and pour off and reserve all but 30 ml/2 tbsp of the oil.
5. Put in the sugar to the pan and stir until it darkens.
6. Put in the garlic and bamboo shoots and stir well.
7. Add the rest of the ingredients, bring to the boil, then return the fish to the pan, cover and simmer gently for about 15 minutes until the fish is cooked.
8. Put the fish on a warmed serving plate and strain the sauce over the top.

CARP WITH TOFU

Yield: 4 Servings

Ingredients:

- 1 carp
- 1 clove garlic, finely chopped

- 15 ml/1 tbsp chilli sauce
- 15 ml/1 tbsp cornflour (cornstarch)
- 2 slices ginger root, finely chopped
- 2 spring onions (scallions), finely chopped
- 225 g/8 oz tofu, cubed
- 30 ml/2 tbsp rice wine or dry sherry
- 30 ml/2 tbsp soy sauce
- 30 ml/2 tbsp water
- 500 ml/16 fl oz/2 cups stock
- 60 ml/4 tbsp groundnut (peanut) oil

Directions:

1. Trim, scale and clean the fish and score 3 lines diagonally on each side.
2. Heat the oil and fry the tofu gently until a golden-brown colour is achieved.
3. Take out of the pan and eliminate the excess liquid well.
4. Put in the fish to the pan and fry until a golden-brown colour is achieved then remove from the pan.
5. Pour off all but 15 ml/1 tbsp of oil then stir-fry the spring onions, garlic and ginger for 30 seconds.
6. Put in the chilli sauce, soy sauce, stock and wine and bring to the boil.
7. Carefully add the fish to the pan with the tofu and simmer, uncovered, for approximately ten minutes until the fish is cooked and the sauce reduced.
8. Transfer the fish to a warmed serving plate and spoon the tofu on top.
9. Blend the cornflour and water to a paste, mix it into the sauce and simmer, stirring, until the sauce becomes thick slightly.
10. Spoon over the fish and serve instantly.

CHILLI PRAWNS

Yield: 4 Servings

Ingredients:

- 1 clove garlic, crushed
- 1 egg white
- 10 ml/2 tsp cornflour (cornstarch)
- 15 ml/1 tbsp soy sauce
- 2½ ml/ ½ tsp sesame oil

- 2½ ml/ ½ tsp sugar
- 2½ ml/ ½ tsp wine vinegar
- 25 g/1 oz dried red chilli peppers, trimmed
- 450 g/1 lb peeled prawns
- 5 ml/1 tsp freshly ground pepper
- 5 ml/1 tsp rice wine or dry sherry
- 5 ml/1 tsp salt
- 60 ml/4 tbsp groundnut (peanut) oil

Directions:

1. Put the prawns into a container with the egg white, cornflour and salt and allow to marinate for half an hour.
2. Heat the oil and fry the chilli peppers, garlic and pepper for approximately one minute.
3. Put in the prawns and rest of the ingredients and stir-fry for a few minutes until the prawns are heated through and the ingredients well mixed.

CHINESE FISH CAKES

Yield: 4 Servings

Ingredients:

- 1 clove garlic, crushed
- 15 ml/1 tbsp cornflour (cornstarch)
- 2 spring onions (scallions), finely chopped
- 45 ml/3 tbsp vegetable oil
- 450 g/1 lb minced (ground) cod
- 5 ml/1 tsp salt
- 5 ml/1 tsp soy sauce
- 5 ml/1 tsp sugar

Directions:

1. Combine the cod, spring onions, garlic, salt, sugar, soy sauce and 10 ml/2 tsp of oil.
2. Knead together comprehensively., sprinkling with a little cornflour from time to time until the mixture is soft and elastic.
3. mould into 4 fish cakes.
4. Heat the oil and fry the fish cakes for approximately ten minutes until golden, pressing them flat as they cook.

5. Serve hot or cold.

CHINESE TUNA

Yield: 4 Servings

Ingredients:

- 1 green pepper, chopped
- 1 onion, chopped
- 100 g/4 oz fine egg noodles
- 100 g/4 oz mushrooms, chopped
- 15 ml/1 tbsp cornflour (cornstarch)
- 2 stalks celery, chopped
- 200 g/7 oz canned tuna, drained and flaked
- 250 ml/8 fl oz/1 cup stock
- 30 ml/2 tbsp groundnut (peanut) oil
- 30 ml/2 tbsp soy sauce
- 45 ml/3 tbsp water
- salt

Directions:

1. Heat the oil and fry the onion until softened.
2. Put in the tuna and stir until well coated with oil.
3. Put in the celery, mushrooms and pepper and stir-fry for approximately two minutes.
4. Put in the stock and soy sauce, bring to the boil, cover and simmer for approximately fifteen minutes.
5. In the meantime, cook the noodles in boiling salt water for approximately five minutes until just soft then eliminate the excess liquid well and lay out on a warmed serving plate.
6. Combine the cornflour and water, stir the mixture into the tuna sauce and simmer, stirring, until the sauce clears and becomes thick.

CLAMS WITH BEAN SPROUTS

Yield: 4 Servings

Ingredients:

- 1 green pepper, chopped into strips
- 15 ml/1 tbsp groundnut (peanut) oil
- 15 ml/1 tbsp rice wine or dry sherry
- 150 g/5 oz bean sprouts
- 2 spring onions (scallions), chopped
- 2½ ml/ ½ tsp sesame oil
- 24 clams
- 50 g/2 oz smoked ham, chopped
- salt and freshly ground pepper

Directions:

1. Scrub the clams comprehensively.
2. then soak them in salted water for a few hours.
3. Rinse under running water.
4. Bring a pan of water to the boil, add the clams and simmer for a few minutes until they open.
5. Drain and discard any that remain closed.
6. Remove the clams from the shells.
7. Heat the oil and fry the bean sprouts for approximately one minute.
8. Put in the pepper and spring onions and stir-fry for approximately two minutes.
9. Put in the wine or sherry and season with salt and pepper.
10. Heat through then mix in the clams and stir until well mixed and heated through.
11. Move to a warmed serving plate and serve sprinkled with sesame oil and ham.

CLAMS WITH GINGER AND GARLIC

Yield: 4 Servings

Ingredients:

- 15 ml/1 tbsp groundnut (peanut) oil
- 15 ml/1 tbsp water
- 2 cloves garlic, crushed
- 2 slices ginger root, minced
- 24 clams
- 5 ml/1 tsp sesame oil
- salt and freshly ground pepper

Directions:

1. Scrub the clams comprehensively.
2. then soak them in salted water for a few hours.
3. Rinse under running water.
4. Heat the oil and fry the ginger and garlic for 30 seconds.
5. Put in the clams, water and sesame oil, cover and cook for approximately five minutes until the clams open.
6. Discard any that remain closed.
7. Season slightly with salt and pepper and serve instantly.

COD WITH BAMBOO SHOOTS

Yield: 4 Servings

Ingredients:

- 1 slice ginger root, minced
- 1 spring onion (scallion), sliced
- 100 g/4 oz bamboo shoots, sliced
- 120 ml/4 fl oz/ ½ cup fish stock
- 15 ml/1 tbsp soy sauce
- 30 ml/2 tbsp cornflour (cornstarch)
- 30 ml/2 tbsp groundnut (peanut) oil
- 4 dried Chinese mushrooms
- 45 ml/3 tbsp water
- 900 g/2 lb cod fillets, cubed
- oil for deep-frying
- salt

Directions:

1. Soak the mushrooms in warm water for half an hour then drain.
2. Discard the stalks and slice the caps.
3. Dust the fish with half the cornflour.
4. Heat the oil and deep-fry the fish until a golden-brown colour is achieved.
5. Drain using kitchen paper and keep warm.
6. In the meantime, heat the oil and fry the spring onion, ginger and salt until slightly browned.
7. Put in the bamboo shoots and stir-fry for approximately three minutes.

8. Put in the stock and soy sauce, bring to the boil and simmer for approximately three minutes.
9. Mix the rest of the cornflour to a paste with the water, stir into the pan and simmer, stirring, until the sauce becomes thick.
10. Pour over the fish and serve instantly.

COD WITH MANDARIN SAUCE

Yield: 4 Servings

Ingredients:

- 1 slice ginger root, minced
- 1 spring onion (scallion), chopped
- 100 g/4 oz mushrooms, sliced
- 120 ml/4 fl oz/ ½ cup soy sauce
- 15 ml/1 tbsp brown sugar
- 2 cloves garlic, crushed
- 250 ml/8 fl oz/1 cup chicken stock
- 30 ml/2 tbsp cornflour (cornstarch)
- 30 ml/2 tbsp rice wine or dry sherry
- 5 ml/1 tsp salt
- 50 g/2 oz bamboo shoots, chopped into strips
- 60 ml/4 tbsp groundnut (peanut) oil
- 675 g/1 ½ lb cod fillets, chopped into strips

Directions:

1. Immerse the fish in the cornflour until slightly coated.
2. Heat the oil and fry the fish until a golden-brown colour is achieved on both sides.
3. Remove it from the pan.
4. Put in the spring onion, garlic and ginger and stir-fry until slightly browned.
5. Put in the mushrooms and bamboo shoots and stir-fry for approximately two minutes.
6. Add the rest of the ingredients and bring to the boil, stirring.
7. Return the fish to the pan, cover and simmer for approximately 20 minutes.

CRAB CAKES

Yield: 4 Servings

Ingredients:

- 1 onion, chopped
- 15 ml/1 tbsp cornflour (cornstarch)
- 225 g/8 oz bean sprouts
- 225 g/8 oz crab meat, flaked
- 30 ml/2 tbsp soy sauce
- 4 eggs, slightly beaten
- 60 ml/4 tbsp groundnut (peanut) oil 100 g/4 oz bamboo shoots, chopped into strips
- salt and freshly ground pepper

Directions:

1. Briefly boil the bean sprouts in boiling water for 4 minutes then drain.
2. Heat half the oil and stir-fry the bean sprouts, bamboo shoots and onion until softened.
3. Turn off the heat and mix in the rest of the ingredients, except the oil.
4. Heat the rest of the oil in a clean pan and fry spoonfuls of the crab meat mixture to make small cakes.
5. Fry until slightly browned on both sides then serve instantly.

CRAB CUSTARD

Yield: 4 Servings

Ingredients:

- 1 spring onion (scallion) finely chopped
- 225 g/8 oz crab meat
- 250 ml/8 fl oz/1 cup water
- 5 eggs, beaten
- 5 ml/1 tsp salt
- 5 ml/1 tsp sesame oil

Directions:

1. Mix all the ingredients together well.
2. Put into a container, cover and stand in the top of the double boiler over hot water or on a steamer rack.

3. Steam for about 35 minutes until the consistency of custard, stirring intermittently.
4. Serve with rice.

CRAB FOO YUNG WITH BEAN SPROUTS

Yield: 4 Servings

Ingredients:

- 100 g/4 oz bean sprouts
- 2 spring onions (scallions), finely chopped
- 2½ ml/ ½ tsp salt
- 225 g/8 oz crab meat
- 45 ml/3 tbsp cornflour (cornstarch)
- 45 ml/3 tbsp groundnut (peanut) oil
- 6 eggs, beaten

Directions:

1. Beat the eggs then beat in the cornflour.
2. Mix in the rest of the ingredients except the oil.
3. Heat the oil and pour the mixture into the pan a little at a time to make small pancakes about 7.5 cm/3 in across.
4. Fry until browned on the bottom then turn and brown the other side.

CRAB LO MEIN

Yield: 4 Servings

Ingredients:

- 1 onion, sliced
- 100 g/4 oz bamboo shoots, sliced
- 100 g/4 oz bean sprouts
- 100 g/4 oz mushrooms, sliced
- 225 g/8 oz crab meat, flaked
- 30 ml/2 tbsp groundnut (peanut) oil
- 30 ml/2 tbsp soy sauce

- 5 ml/1 tsp salt
- 5 ml/1 tsp sesame oil
- 5 ml/1 tsp sugar
- salt and freshly ground pepper
- Tossed Noodles

Directions:

1. Briefly boil the bean sprouts in boiling water for approximately five minutes then drain.
2. Heat the oil and fry the salt and onion until softened.
3. Put in the mushrooms and stir-fry until softened.
4. Put in the crab meat and stir-fry for approximately two minutes.
5. Put in the bean sprouts and bamboo shoots and stir-fry for approximately one minute.
6. Put in the drained noodles to the pan and stir gently.
7. Combine the soy sauce, sugar and sesame oil and season with salt and pepper.
8. Stir into the pan until heated through.

CRAB MEAT WITH CHINESE LEAVES

Yield: 4 Servings

Ingredients:

- 15 ml/1 tbsp rice wine or dry sherry
- 15 ml/1 tbsp soy sauce
- 2 spring onions (scallions), chopped
- 225 g/8 oz crab meat
- 45 ml/3 tbsp vegetable oil
- 450 g/1 lb Chinese leaves, shredded
- 5 ml/1 tsp salt

Directions:

1. Briefly boil the Chinese leaves in boiling water for approximately two minutes then eliminate the excess liquid comprehensively.
2. and rinse in cold water.
3. Heat the oil and fry the spring onions until slightly browned.
4. Put in the crab meat and stir-fry for approximately two minutes.
5. Put in the Chinese leaves and stir-fry for 4 minutes.
6. Put in the soy sauce, wine or sherry and salt and mix well.

7. Put in the stock and cornflour, bring to the boil and simmer, stirring, for approximately two minutes until the sauce clears and becomes thick.

CRAB WITH GINGER

Yield: 4 Servings

Ingredients:

- 1 red chilli pepper, chopped
- 15 ml/1 tbsp groundnut (peanut) oil
- 15 ml/1 tbsp rice wine or dry sherry
- 15 ml/1 tbsp water
- 2 slices ginger root, chopped
- 2½ ml/ ½ tsp fish paste
- 2½ ml/ ½ tsp sesame oil
- 3 cloves garlic, crushed
- 350 g/12 oz crab meat, flaked
- 4 spring onions (scallions), chopped
- 5 ml/1 tsp cornflour (cornstarch)

Directions:

1. Heat the oil and fry the ginger, spring onions, garlic and chilli for approximately two minutes.
2. Put in the crab meat and stir until well coated with the spices.
3. Mix in the fish paste.
4. Mix the rest of the ingredients to a paste then stir them into the pan and stir-fry for approximately one minutes.
5. Serve Immediately.

CRISPY-FRIED FISH

Yield: 4 Servings

Ingredients:

- 1 egg white, slightly beaten

- 30 ml/2 tbsp rice wine or dry sherry
- 45 ml/3 tbsp cornflour (cornstarch)
- 450 g/1 lb fish fillets, chopped into strips
- oil for deep-frying
- salt and freshly ground pepper

Directions:

1. Toss the fish in the wine or sherry and season with salt and pepper.
2. Dust slightly with cornflour.
3. Beat the rest of the cornflour into the egg white until stiff then immerse the fish in the batter.
4. Heat the oil and deep-fry the fish strips for a few minutes until a golden-brown colour is achieved.

DEEP-FRIED BATTERED PRAWNS

Yield: 4 Servings

Ingredients:

- 1 egg, slightly beaten
- 2½ ml/ ½ tsp salt
- 30 ml/2 tbsp water
- 450 g/1 lb peeled prawns
- 50 g/2 oz/ ½ cup plain (all-purpose) flour
- oil for deep-frying

Directions:

1. Beat the flour, salt, egg and water to a batter, adding a little more water if needed.
2. Mix with the prawns until well coated.
3. Heat the oil and deep-fry the prawns for a few minutes until crispy and golden.

DEEP-FRIED COD

Yield: 4 Servings

Ingredients:

- 1 lemon, chopped into wedges
- 100 g/4 oz/1 cup plain (all-purpose) flour
- 2 eggs, beaten
- 900 g/2 lb cod fillets, cubed
- oil for deep-frying
- salt and freshly ground pepper

Directions:

1. Season the cod with salt and pepper.
2. Beat the eggs and flour to a batter and season with salt.
3. Immerse the fish in the batter.
4. Heat the oil and deep-fry the fish for a few minutes until a golden-brown colour is achieved and cooked through.
5. Drain using kitchen paper and serve with lemon wedges.

DEEP-FRIED CUTTLEFISH BALLS

Yield: 4 Servings

Ingredients:

- 1 egg white
- 2½ ml/ ½ tsp cornflour (cornstarch)
- 2½ ml/ ½ tsp sugar
- 450 g/1 lb cuttlefish
- 50 g/2 oz lard, mashed
- oil for deep-frying
- salt and freshly ground pepper

Directions:

1. Trim the cuttlefish and mash or purée it to a pulp.
2. Mix with the lard, egg white, sugar and cornflour and season with salt and pepper.
3. Press the mixture into small balls.
4. Heat the oil and fry the cuttlefish balls, in batches if needed, until they float to the top of the oil and turn golden brown.
5. Drain thoroughly and serve instantly.

DEEP-FRIED EEL

Yield: 4 Servings

Ingredients:

- 15 ml/1 tbsp brown sugar
- 250 ml/8 fl oz/1 cup groundnut (peanut) oil
- 30 ml/2 tbsp dark soy sauce
- 30 ml/2 tbsp rice wine or dry sherry
- 450 g/1 lb eel
- dash of sesame oil

Directions:

1. Skin the eel and chop it into chunks.
2. Heat the oil and fry the eel until golden.
3. Take out of the pan and drain.
4. Pour off all but 30 ml/2 tbsp of oil.
5. Reheat the oil and add the soy sauce, wine or sherry and sugar.
6. Heat through then add the eel and stir-fry until the eel is well coated and almost all the liquid has evaporated.
7. Drizzle with sesame oil and serve.

DEEP-FRIED FISH WITH VEGETABLES

Yield: 4 Servings

Ingredients:

- ½ head lettuce, shredded
- 100 g/4 oz bamboo shoots, chopped into strips
- 120 ml/4 fl oz/ ½ cup fish stock
- 15 ml/1 tbsp chopped flat-leaved parsley
- 15 ml/1 tbsp soy sauce
- 2 slices ginger root, minced
- 30 ml/2 tbsp cornflour (cornstarch)
- 30 ml/2 tbsp rice wine or dry sherry

- 30 ml/2 tbsp water
- 4 dried Chinese mushrooms
- 4 whole fish, cleaned and scaled
- 45 ml/3 tbsp groundnut (peanut) oil
- 5 ml/1 tsp sugar
- 50 g/2 oz Chinese cabbage, shredded
- 50 g/2 oz water chestnuts, chopped into strips
- oil for deep-frying
- salt and freshly ground pepper

Directions:

1. Soak the mushrooms in warm water for half an hour then drain.
2. Discard the stalks and slice the caps.
3. Dust the fish in half cornflour and shake off any excess.
4. Heat the oil and deep-fry the fish for about 12 minutes until cooked.
5. Drain using kitchen paper and keep warm.
6. Heat the oil and stir-fry the mushrooms, bamboo shoots, water chestnuts and cabbage for approximately three minutes.
7. Put in the ginger, wine or sherry, 15 ml/1 tbsp of water, the soy sauce and sugar and stir-fry for approximately one minute.
8. Put in the stock, salt and pepper, bring to the boil, cover and simmer for approximately three minutes.
9. Combine the cornflour with the rest of the water, mix it into the pan and simmer, stirring, until the sauce becomes thick.
10. Put the lettuce on a serving plate and place the fish on top.
11. Pour over the vegetables and sauce and serve garnished with parsley.

DEEP-FRIED LOBSTER

Yield: 4 Servings

Ingredients:

- 1 egg, beaten
- 30 ml/2 tbsp soy sauce
- 30 ml/3 tbsp plain (all-purpose) flour
- 450 g/1 lb lobster meat
- 5 ml/1 tsp sugar

- oil for deep-frying

Directions:

1. Chop the lobster meat into 2.5 cm/1 in cubes and toss with the soy sauce and sugar.
2. Leave to stand for approximately fifteen minutes then drain.
3. Beat the egg and flour then add the lobster and toss comprehensively. to coat.
4. Heat the oil and deep-fry the lobster until a golden-brown colour is achieved.
5. Drain using kitchen paper and serve.

DEEP-FRIED MARINATED FISH

Yield: 4 Servings

Ingredients:

- 1 clove star anise
- 120 ml/4 fl oz/ ½ cup soy sauce
- 15 ml/1 tbsp rice wine or dry sherry
- 15 ml/1 tbsp sesame oil
- 3 slices ginger root, minced
- 450 g/1 lb sprats or other small fish, cleaned
- oil for deep-frying

Directions:

1. Put the fish into a container.
2. Combine the ginger, soy sauce, wine or sherry and anise, pour over the fish and allow to stand for one hour, turning occasionally.
3. Eliminate the excess liquid from the fish, discarding the marinade.
4. Heat the oil and fry the fish in batches until crispy and golden brown.
5. Drain using kitchen paper and serve sprinkled with sesame oil.

DEEP-FRIED OYSTERS

Yield: 4 Servings

Ingredients:

- 1 egg, beaten
- 24 oysters, shelled
- 250 ml/8 fl oz/1 cup water
- 4 spring onions (scallions), chopped
- 50 g/2 oz/ ½ cup plain (all-purpose) flour
- oil for deep-frying
- salt and freshly ground pepper

Directions:

1. Drizzle the oysters with salt and pepper.
2. Beat the egg with the flour and water to a batter and use to coat the oysters.
3. Heat the oil and deep-fry the oysters until a golden-brown colour is achieved.
4. Drain using kitchen paper and serve garnished with spring onions.

DEEP-FRIED OYSTERS WITH GINGER

Yield: 4 Servings

Ingredients:

- 1 egg
- 1 lemon, chopped into wedges
- 100 g/4 oz bacon
- 15 ml/1 tbsp rice wine or dry sherry
- 2 slices ginger root, minced
- 24 oysters, shelled
- 30 ml/2 tbsp soy sauce
- 4 spring onions (scallions), chopped into strips
- 50 g/2 oz/ ½ cup plain (all-purpose) flour
- oil for deep-frying
- salt and freshly ground pepper

Directions:

1. Put the oysters into a container with the ginger, soy sauce and wine or sherry and toss comprehensively. to coat.
2. Leave to stand for half an hour.
3. Put a few strips of spring onion on top of each oyster.
4. Chop the bacon into pieces and wrap a piece around each oyster.

5. Beat the egg and flour to a batter and season with salt and pepper.
6. Immerse the oysters in the batter until well coated.
7. Heat the oil and deep-fry the oysters until a golden-brown colour is achieved.
8. Serve garnished with lemon wedges.

DEEP-FRIED PRAWNS

Yield: 4 Servings

Ingredients:

- 30 ml/2 tbsp rice wine or dry sherry
- 450 g/1 lb peeled prawns
- 5 ml/1 tsp salt
- oil for deep-frying
- soy sauce

Directions:

1. Toss the prawns in the wine or sherry and drizzle with salt.
2. Leave to stand for approximately fifteen minutes then eliminate the excess liquid and pat dry.
3. Heat the oil and deep-fry the prawns for a few seconds until crisp.
4. Serve sprinkled with soy sauce.

DEEP-FRIED PRAWNS WITH SHERRY SAUCE

Yield: 4 Servings

Ingredients:

- 1 egg, slightly beaten
- 1 onion, finely chopped
- 10 ml/2 tsp cornflour (cornstarch)
- 120 ml/4 fl oz/ ½ cup fish stock
- 15 ml/1 tbsp groundnut (peanut) oil
- 15 ml/1 tbsp soy sauce
- 2½ ml/ ½ tsp salt

- 30 ml/2 tbsp water
- 30 ml/2 tbsp water
- 45 ml/3 tbsp rice wine or dry sherry
- 450 g/1 lb peeled prawns
- 50 g/2 oz/ ½ cup plain (all-purpose) flour
- oil for deep-frying

Directions:

1. Beat together the flour, salt, egg and water to make a batter, adding a little more water if needed.
2. Mix with the prawns until they are well coated.
3. Heat the oil and deep-fry the prawns for a few minutes until crispy and golden.
4. Drain using kitchen paper and lay out on a heated serving dish.
5. In the meantime, heat the oil and fry the onion until softened.
6. Put in the wine or sherry, soy sauce and stock, bring to the boil and simmer for 4 minutes.
7. Combine the cornflour and water to a paste, stir into the pan and simmer, stirring, until the sauce clears and becomes thick.
8. Pour the sauce over the prawns and serve.

DEEP-FRIED PRAWNS WITH TOMATO SAUCE

Yield: 4 Servings

Ingredients:

- 1 egg, slightly beaten
- 1 onion, finely chopped
- 10 ml/2 tsp cornflour (cornstarch)
- 2 slices ginger root, minced
- 2½ ml/ ½ tsp salt
- 30 ml/2 tbsp groundnut (peanut) oil
- 30 ml/2 tbsp water
- 30 ml/2 tbsp water
- 450 g/1 lb peeled prawns
- 50 g/2 oz/ ½ cup plain (all-purpose) flour
- 75 ml/5 tbsp tomato ketchup (catsup)
- oil for deep-frying

Directions:

1. Beat together the flour, salt, egg and water to make a batter, adding a little more water if needed.
2. Mix with the prawns until they are well coated.
3. Heat the oil and deep-fry the prawns for a few minutes until crispy and golden.
4. Drain on kitchen paper.
5. In the meantime heat the oil and fry the onion and ginger until softened.
6. Put in the tomato ketchup and simmer for approximately three minutes.
7. Combine the cornflour and water to a paste, stir into the pan and simmer, stirring, until the sauce becomes thick.
8. Put in the prawns to the pan and simmer until heated through.
9. Serve Immediately.

DEEP-FRIED SESAME PRAWNS

Yield: 4 Servings

Ingredients:

- ½ egg white
- 450 g/1 lb peeled prawns
- 5 ml/1 tsp sesame oil
- 5 ml/1 tsp soy sauce
- 50 g/2 oz/ ½ cup cornflour (cornstarch)
- 60 ml/4 tbsp sesame seeds
- lettuce leaves
- oil for deep-frying
- salt and freshly ground white pepper

Directions:

1. Combine the prawns with the egg white, soy sauce, sesame oil, cornflour, salt and pepper.
2. Add a little water if the mixture is too thick.
3. Heat the oil and deep-fry the prawns for a few minutes until slightly golden.
4. In the meantime, toast the sesame seeds briefly using a dry pan until golden.
5. Eliminate the excess liquid from the prawns and mix with the sesame seeds.
6. Serve on a bed of lettuce.

DEEP-FRIED SQUID

Yield: 4 Servings

Ingredients:

- 1 egg
- 15 ml/1 tbsp groundnut (peanut) oil
- 2½ ml/ ½ tsp baking powder
- 2½ ml/ ½ tsp salt
- 25 g/1 oz cornflour (cornstarch)
- 450 g/1 lb squid, chopped into rings
- 50 g/2 oz plain (all-purpose) flour
- 75 ml/5 tbsp water
- oil for deep-frying

Directions:

1. Beat the flour, cornflour, baking powder, salt, egg, water and oil together to make a batter.
2. Immerse the squid in the batter until well coated.
3. Heat the oil and deep-fry the squid a few pieces at a time until a golden-brown colour is achieved.
4. Drain using kitchen paper and serve.

DEEP-FRIED TROUT

Yield: 4 Servings

Ingredients:

- 1 lemon, chopped into wedges
- 2 eggs, beaten
- 4 trout, cleaned and scaled
- 50 g/2 oz/ ½ cup plain (all-purpose) flour
- oil for deep-frying

Directions:

1. Slash the fish diagonally a few times on each side.
2. Immerse in the beaten eggs then toss in the flour to coat completely.
3. Shake off any excess.
4. Heat the oil and deep-fry the fish for about 10 to 15 minutes until cooked.
5. Drain using kitchen paper and serve with lemon.

DRY-COOKED EEL

Yield: 4 Servings

Ingredients:

- 10 water chestnuts
- 15 ml/1 tbsp brown sugar
- 15 ml/1 tbsp cornflour (cornstarch)
- 15 ml/1 tbsp rice wine or dry sherry
- 20 cloves garlic
- 3 spring onions (scallions)
- 30 ml/2 tbsp groundnut (peanut) oil
- 30 ml/2 tbsp soy sauce
- 45 ml/3 tbsp water
- 450 ml water
- 5 dried Chinese mushrooms
- 5 ml/1 tsp sesame oil
- 6 slices ginger root
- 900 g/2 lb eels

Directions:

1. Soak the mushrooms in warm water for half an hour then eliminate the excess liquid and discard the stalks.
2. Cut 1 spring onion into chunks and chop the other.
3. Heat the oil and fry the mushrooms, spring onion chunks, garlic, ginger and chestnuts for 30 seconds.
4. Put in the eels and stir-fry for approximately one minute.
5. Put in the soy sauce, sugar, wine or sherry and water, bring to the boil, cover and simmer gently for 1 ½ hours, adding a little water during cooking if needed.
6. Blend the cornflour and water to a paste, stir into the pan and simmer, stirring, until the sauce becomes thick.

7. Serve sprinkled with sesame oil and the chopped spring onions.

EEL WITH CELERY

Yield: 4 Servings

Ingredients:

- 1 slice ginger root, minced
- 2 spring onions (scallions), chopped
- 30 ml/2 tbsp chopped fresh parsley
- 30 ml/2 tbsp groundnut (peanut) oil
- 30 ml/2 tbsp water
- 350 g/12 oz eel
- 5 ml/1 tsp rice wine or dry sherry
- 5 ml/1 tsp soy sauce
- 5 ml/1 tsp sugar
- 6 stalks celery
- freshly ground pepper

Directions:

1. Skin and chop the eel into strips.
2. Chop the celery into strips.
3. Heat the oil and fry the spring onions and ginger for 30 seconds.
4. Put in the eel and stir-fry for 30 seconds.
5. Put in the celery and stir-fry for 30 seconds.
6. Add half the water, the sugar, wine or sherry, soy sauce and pepper.
7. Bring to the boil and simmer for a few minutes until the celery is just soft but still crisp and the liquid has reduced.
8. Serve sprinkled with parsley.

FAR EASTERN STYLE PRAWNS

Yield: 4 Servings

Ingredients:

- 1 clove garlic, chopped
- 120 ml/4 fl oz/ ½ cup dry white wine
- 15 ml/1 tbsp grated lemon rind
- 16-20 peeled king prawns
- 2 carrots, chopped into strips
- 30 ml/2 tbsp honey
- 30 ml/2 tbsp soy sauce
- 45 ml/3 tbsp groundnut (peanut) oil
- 5 ml/1 tsp cornflour (cornstarch)
- 5 ml/1 tsp five-spice powder
- 6 spring onions (scallions), chopped into strips
- juice of 1 lemon
- salt and pepper

Directions:

1. Combine the prawns with the lemon juice, wine, soy sauce, honey and lemon rind and season with salt and pepper.
2. Cover and marinate for one hour.
3. Heat the oil and fry the garlic until slightly browned.
4. Put in the vegetables and stir-fry until soft but still crisp.
5. Eliminate the excess liquid from the prawns, put them into the pan and stir-fry for approximately two minutes.
6. Strain the marinade and mix it with the five-spice powder and cornflour.
7. Put into the wok, stir well and bring to the boil.

FISH FILLETS IN BROWN SAUCE

Yield: 4 Servings

Ingredients:

- 1 slice ginger root, finely chopped
- 3 eggs, beaten
- 3 spring onions (scallions), finely chopped
- 30 ml/2 tbsp cornflour (cornstarch)
- 30 ml/2 tbsp rice wine or dry sherry
- 30 ml/2 tbsp soy sauce
- 450 g/1 lb cod fillets, thickly sliced

- 5 ml/1 tsp salt
- 5 ml/1 tsp sesame oil
- 90 ml/6 tbsp fish stock
- 90 ml/6 tbsp groundnut (peanut) oil

Directions:

1. Put the fish fillets into a container.
2. Combine the wine or sherry, soy sauce, spring onions, ginger, salt and sesame oil, pour over the fish, cover and allow to marinate for half an hour.
3. Remove the fish from the marinade and toss in the cornflour then immerse in the beaten egg.
4. Heat the oil and fry the fish until a golden-brown colour is achieved on the outside.
5. Pour off the oil and mix in the stock and any rest of the marinade.
6. Bring to the boil and simmer gently for approximately five minutes until the fish is cooked.

FISH IN BROWN SAUCE

Yield: 4 Servings

Ingredients:

- 2 slices ginger root, chopped
- 2 spring onions (scallions), chopped
- 2½ ml/ ½ tsp rice wine or dry sherry
- 2½ ml/ ½ tsp sesame oil
- 2½ ml/ ½ tsp sugar
- 2½ ml/ ½ tsp wine vinegar
- 4 haddock or similar fish
- 45 ml/3 tbsp groundnut (peanut) oil
- 5 ml/1 tsp soy sauce
- freshly ground pepper

Directions:

1. Trim the fish and chop into large chunks.
2. Heat the oil and fry the spring onions and ginger for 30 seconds.
3. Put in the fish and fry until slightly browned on both sides.

4. Put in the soy sauce, wine vinegar, wine or sherry, sugar and pepper and simmer for approximately five minutes until the sauce is thick.
5. Serve sprinkled with sesame oil.

FISH IN RICE WINE

Yield: 4 Servings

Ingredients:

- 10 ml/2 tsp cornflour (cornstarch)
- 120 ml/4 fl oz/ ½ cup water
- 15 ml/1 tbsp water
- 2 spring onions (scallions), chopped
- 30 ml/2 tbsp soy sauce
- 400 ml/14 fl oz/1¬æ cups rice wine or dry sherry
- 450 g/1 lb cod fillets
- 5 ml/1 tsp sesame oil
- 5 ml/1 tsp sugar
- salt and freshly ground pepper

Directions:

1. Bring the wine, water, soy sauce, sugar, salt and pepper to the boil and boil until reduced by half.
2. Combine the cornflour to a paste with the water, mix it into the pan and simmer, stirring, for approximately two minutes.
3. Season the fish with salt and drizzle with sesame oil.
4. Put into the pan and simmer very gently for approximately eight minutes until cooked.
5. Serve sprinkled with spring onions.

FISH ROLLS WITH PORK

Yield: 4 Servings

Ingredients:

- 1 slice ginger root, minced

- 100 g/4 oz cooked pork, minced (ground)
- 120 ml/4 fl oz/ ½ cup fish stock
- 15 ml/1 tbsp cornflour (cornstarch)
- 15 ml/1 tbsp soy sauce
- 15 ml/1 tbsp sugar
- 3 spring onions (scallions), minced
- 30 ml/2 tbsp rice wine or dry sherry
- 45 ml/3 tbsp water
- 450 g/1 lb fish fillets
- oil for deep-frying

Directions:

1. Chop the fish into 9 cm/3 ½ in squares.
2. Combine the pork with the wine or sherry and half the sugar, spread over the fish squares, roll them up and secure with string.
3. Heat the oil and deep-fry the fish until a golden-brown colour is achieved.
4. Drain on kitchen paper.
5. In the meantime, heat the stock and add the spring onions, ginger, soy sauce and rest of the sugar.
6. Bring to the boil and simmer for 4 minutes.
7. Combine the cornflour and water to a paste, stir into the pan and simmer, stirring, until the sauce clears and becomes thick.
8. Pour over the fish and serve instantly.

FISH WITH BEAN SPROUTS

Yield: 4 Servings

Ingredients:

- 10 ml/2 tsp cornflour (cornstarch)
- 15 ml/1 tbsp soy sauce
- 15 ml/1 tbsp water
- 3 slices ginger root, minced
- 4 spring onions (scallions), sliced
- 45 ml/3 tbsp groundnut (peanut) oil
- 450 g/1 lb bean sprouts
- 450 g/1 lb fish fillets, sliced

- 5 ml/1 tsp salt
- 60 ml/4 tbsp fish stock

Directions:

1. Briefly boil the bean sprouts in boiling water for 4 minutes then eliminate the excess liquid well.
2. Heat half the oil and fry the salt and ginger for approximately one minute.
3. Put in the fish and fry until slightly browned then remove it from the pan.
4. Heat the rest of the oil and fry the spring onions for approximately one minute.
5. Put in the soy sauce and stock and bring to the boil.
6. Return the fish to the pan, cover and simmer for approximately two minutes until the fish is cooked.
7. Combine the cornflour and water to a paste, stir into the pan and simmer, stirring, until the sauce clears and becomes thick.

FISH WITH GHERKINS

Yield: 4 Servings

Ingredients:

- 2 slices ginger root
- 2 spring onions (scallions)
- 2½ ml/ ½ tsp rice wine or dry sherry
- 2½ ml/ ½ tsp salt
- 30 ml/2 tbsp water
- 4 white fish fillets
- 5 ml/1 tsp groundnut (peanut) oil
- 75 g/3 oz small gherkins

Directions:

1. Put the fish on a heatproof plate and drizzle with the rest of the ingredients.
2. Put on a rack in a steamer, cover and steam for about 15 minutes over boiling water until the fish is soft.
3. Move to a warmed serving plate, discard the ginger and spring onions and serve.

FISH WITH PINEAPPLE

Yield: 4 Servings

Ingredients:

- 15 ml/1 tbsp cornflour (cornstarch)
- 15 ml/1 tbsp rice wine or dry sherry
- 2 eggs, slightly beaten
- 2 spring onions (scallions), minced
- 2½ ml/ ½ tsp salt
- 225 g/8 oz canned pineapple chunks in juice
- 30 ml/2 tbsp soy sauce
- 45 ml/3 tbsp groundnut (peanut) oil
- 450 g/1 lb fish fillets

Directions:

1. Chop the fish into 2.5 cm/1 in strips against the grain and place into a container.
2. Put in the spring onions, soy sauce, wine or sherry and salt, toss comprehensively. and allow to stand for half an hour.
3. Eliminate the excess liquid from the fish, discarding the marinade.
4. Beat the eggs and cornflour to a batter and immerse the fish in the batter to coat, draining off any excess.
5. Heat the oil and fry the fish until slightly browned on both sides.
6. Reduce the heat and continue to cook until soft.
7. In the meantime, mix 60 ml/4 tbsp of the pineapple juice with any rest of the batter and the pineapple chunks.
8. Pur inside the pan over a gentle heat and simmer until heated through, stirring constantly.
9. Put the cooked fish on a warmed serving plate and pour over the sauce to serve.

FISH WITH VINEGAR SAUCE

Yield: 4 Servings

Ingredients:

- 1 egg white, slightly beaten
- 15 ml/1 tbsp brown sugar

- 15 ml/1 tbsp rice wine or dry sherry
- 15 ml/1 tbsp wine vinegar
- 2 slices root ginger, minced
- 2 spring onions (scallions), minced
- 250 ml/8 fl oz/1 cup fish stock
- 45 ml/3 tbsp cornflour (cornstarch)
- 450 g/1 lb fish fillets, chopped into strips
- oil for deep-frying
- salt and freshly ground pepper

Directions:

1. Season the fish with a little salt and pepper.
2. Beat the egg white with 30 ml/2 tbsp of cornflour and the wine or sherry.
3. Toss the fish in the batter until coated.
4. Heat the oil and deep-fry the fish for a few minutes until a golden-brown colour is achieved.
5. Drain on kitchen paper.
6. In the meantime, bring the stock, sugar and wine vinegar to the boil.
7. Put in the ginger and spring onion and simmer for approximately three minutes.
8. Blend the rest of the cornflour to a paste with a little water, mix it into the pan and simmer, stirring, until the sauce clears and becomes thick.
9. Pour over the fish to serve.

FIVE-SPICE FISH

Yield: 4 Servings

Ingredients:

- 15 ml/1 tbsp soy sauce
- 2 cloves garlic, crushed
- 2½ ml/1 in root ginger, minced
- 30 ml/2 tbsp groundnut (peanut) oil
- 30 ml/2 tbsp rice wine or dry sherry
- 4 cod fillets
- 5 ml/1 tsp five-spice powder
- 5 ml/1 tsp salt
- few drops of sesame oil

Directions:

1. Rub the fish with the five-spice powder and salt.
2. Heat the oil and fry the fish until slightly browned on both sides.
3. Take out of the pan and add the rest of the ingredients.
4. Heat through, stirring, then return the fish to the pan and reheat gently and serve.

FIVE-SPICE FISH

Yield: 4 Servings

Ingredients:

- 10 ml/2 tsp sesame oil
- 15 ml/1 tbsp soy sauce
- 2 cloves garlic, crushed
- 2 slices ginger root, minced
- 30 ml/2 tbsp groundnut (peanut) oil
- 30 ml/2 tbsp rice wine or dry sherry
- 450 g/1 lb haddock fillets
- 5 ml/1 tsp five-spice powder
- 5 ml/1 tsp salt

Directions:

1. Rub the haddock fillets with the five-spice powder and salt.
2. Heat the oil and fry the fish until slightly browned on both sides then remove it from the pan.
3. Put in the garlic, ginger, wine or sherry, soy sauce and sesame oil and fry for approximately one minute.
4. Return the fish to the pan and simmer gently until the fish is soft.

FRAGRANT FISH STICKS

Yield: 4 Servings

Ingredients:

- 1 spring onion (scallion), finely chopped
- 10 ml/2 tsp curry powder
- 100 g/4 oz breadcrumbs
- 2 eggs, beaten
- 30 ml/2 tbsp rice wine or dry sherry
- 450 g/1 lb white fish fillets, chopped into strips
- 5 ml/1 tsp salt
- oil for deep-frying

Directions:

1. Combine the wine or sherry, spring onion, eggs, curry powder and salt.
2. Immerse the fish into the mixture so that the pieces are evenly coated then press them into the breadcrumbs.
3. Heat the oil and deep-fry the fish for a few minutes until crisp and golden brown.
4. Drain thoroughly and serve immediately.

FRIED PLAICE

Yield: 4 Servings

Ingredients:

- 1 clove garlic, crushed
- 1 slice ginger root, minced
- 30 ml/2 tbsp groundnut (peanut) oil
- 4 plaice fillets
- lettuce leaves
- salt and freshly ground pepper

Directions:

1. Season the plaice generously with salt and pepper.
2. Heat the oil and fry the ginger and garlic for 20 seconds.
3. Put in the fish and fry until cooked through and golden brown.
4. Drain thoroughly and serve on a bed of lettuce.

FRIED PRAWN BALLS WITH ONION SAUCE

Yield: 4 Servings

Ingredients:

- 15 ml/1 tbsp cornflour (cornstarch)
- 15 ml/1 tbsp groundnut (peanut) oil
- 175 ml water
- 2 onions, chopped
- 3 eggs, slightly beaten
- 30 ml/2 tbsp soy sauce
- 45 ml/3 tbsp plain (all-purpose) flour
- 450 g/1 lb peeled prawns
- oil for deep-frying
- salt and freshly ground pepper

Directions:

1. Combine the eggs, flour, salt and pepper.
2. Toss the prawns in the batter.
3. Heat the oil and deep-fry the prawns until a golden-brown colour is achieved.
4. In the meantime, heat the oil and fry the onions for approximately one minute.
5. Blend the rest of the ingredients to a paste, stir into the onions and cook, stirring, until the sauce becomes thick.
6. Eliminate the excess liquid from the prawns and lay out on a warmed serving plate.
7. Pour over the sauce and serve instantly.

FRIED PRAWNS IN SAUCE

Yield: 4 Servings

Ingredients:

- ½ egg, beaten
- 1 clove garlic, crushed
- 1 slice ginger root, minced
- 15 ml/1 tbsp fish stock
- 3 spring onions (scallions), sliced
- 45 ml/3 tbsp groundnut (peanut) oil

- 450 g/1 lb peeled prawns
- 5 ml/1 tsp rice wine or dry sherry
- 5 ml/1 tsp sesame oil
- 5 ml/1 tsp sugar
- 5 ml/1 tsp wine vinegar
- 75 g/3 oz cornflour (cornstarch)
- salt

Directions:

1. Combine the cornflour, egg, wine or sherry and a pinch of salt to make a batter.
2. Immerse the prawns in the batter so that they are slightly coated.
3. Heat the oil and fry the prawns until they are crisp outside.
4. Remove them from the pan and eliminate the excess oil.
5. Heat the sesame oil in the pan, add the prawns, garlic, ginger and spring onions and stir-fry for approximately three minutes.
6. Mix in the stock, wine vinegar and sugar, stir well and heat through and serve.

FRIED SQUID ROLLS

Yield: 4 Servings

Ingredients:

- 1 large green pepper, chopped into chunks
- 1 slice ginger root, finely chopped
- 100 g/4 oz bamboo shoots, sliced
- 15 ml/1 tbsp cornflour (cornstarch)
- 15 ml/1 tbsp fish stock or water
- 2 spring onions (scallions), finely chopped
- 225 g/8 oz squid rings
- 30 ml/2 tbsp rice wine or dry sherry
- 45 ml/2 tbsp soy sauce
- 45 ml/3 tbsp groundnut (peanut) oil
- 5 ml/1 tsp sesame oil
- 5 ml/1 tsp sugar
- 5 ml/1 tsp wine vinegar
- salt and freshly ground pepper

Directions:

1. Heat 15 ml/1 tbsp oil and fry the squid rings quickly until just sealed.
2. In the meantime, heat the rest of the oil in a separate pan and stir-fry the pepper, bamboo shoots, spring onions and ginger for approximately two minutes.
3. Put in the squid and stir-fry for approximately one minute.
4. Mix in the soy sauce, wine or sherry, cornflour, stock, sugar, wine vinegar and sesame oil and season with salt and pepper.
5. Stir-fry until the sauce clears and becomes thick.

GINGER HADDOCK WITH PAK SOI

Yield: 4 Servings

Ingredients:

- 1 onion, chopped
- 1 slice ginger root, chopped
- 10 ml/2 tsp fish sauce
- 10 ml/2 tsp malt vinegar
- 10 ml/2 tsp oyster sauce
- 10 ml/2 tsp soy sauce
- 10 ml/2 tsp tomato ketchup (catsup)
- 2 dried red chilli peppers
- 225 g/8 oz pak soi
- 30 ml/2 tbsp dry white wine
- 30 ml/2 tbsp groundnut (peanut) oil
- 450 g/1 lb haddock fillet
- 5 ml/1 tsp honey
- 5 ml/1 tsp shrimp paste
- salt and pepper

Directions:

1. Skin the haddock then chop into 2 cm in pieces.
2. Drizzle with salt and pepper.
3. Chop the cabbage into small pieces.
4. Heat the oil and fry the ginger and onion for approximately one minute.
5. Put in the cabbage and chilli peppers and fry for 30 seconds.
6. Put in the honey, tomato ketchup, vinegar and wine.

7. Put in the haddock and simmer for approximately two minutes.
8. Mix in the soy, fish and oyster sauces and the shrimp paste and simmer gently until the haddock is cooked.

GINGER-SPICED COD

Yield: 4 Servings

Ingredients:

- 1 egg white
- 10 ml/2 tsp sugar
- 100 g/4 oz/1 cup plain (all-purpose) flour
- 15 ml/1 tbsp chilli sauce
- 15 ml/1 tbsp grated ginger root
- 15 ml/1 tbsp soy sauce
- 15 ml/1 tbsp water
- 175 ml/6 fl oz/¬æ cup water
- 2½ ml/ ½ tsp salt
- 225 g/8 oz tomato purée (paste)
- 3 cloves garlic, crushed
- 30 ml/2 tbsp rice wine or dry sherry
- 450 g/1 lb cod fillets, skinned and cubed
- 75 ml/5 tbsp cornflour (cornstarch)
- oil for deep-frying

Directions:

1. To make the sauce, mix together the tomato purée, wine or sherry, ginger, chilli sauce, water, soy sauce, sugar and garlic.
2. Bring to the boil then simmer, stirring, for 4 minutes.
3. Beat together the flour, cornflour, water, egg white and salt until smooth.
4. Heat the oil.
5. Immerse the fish pieces in the batter and fry for approximately five minutes until cooked through and golden brown.
6. Drain on kitchen paper.
7. Drain off all the oil and return the fish and sauce to the pan.
8. Reheat gently for about 3 minutes until the fish is completely coated in sauce.

HADDOCK IN BLACK BEAN SAUCE

Yield: 4 Servings

Ingredients:

- 1 slice ginger root, minced
- 1 stick celery, sliced
- 15 ml/1 tbsp black bean sauce
- 15 ml/1 tbsp groundnut (peanut) oil
- 15 ml/1 tbsp rice wine or dry sherry
- 15 ml/1 tbsp soy sauce
- 2 cloves garlic, crushed
- 2 onions, chopped into wedges
- 250 ml/8 fl oz/1 cup chicken stock
- 450 g/1 lb haddock fillets

Directions:

1. Heat the oil and fry the garlic, ginger and black bean sauce until slightly browned.
2. Put in the onions and celery and stir-fry for approximately two minutes.
3. Put in the haddock and fry for about 4 minutes each side or until the fish is cooked.
4. Put in the soy sauce, wine or sherry and chicken stock, bring to the boil, cover and simmer for approximately three minutes.

HADDOCK PLAITS

Yield: 4 Servings

Ingredients:

- 15 ml/1 tbsp honey
- 30 ml/2 tbsp oyster sauce
- 30 ml/2 tbsp soy sauce
- 45 ml/3 tbsp wine vinegar
- 450 g/1 lb haddock fillets, skinned
- 5 ml/1 tsp aniseed, ground
- 5 ml/1 tsp five-spice powder
- 5 ml/1 tsp freshly ground pepper
- 60 ml/4 tbsp chopped chives

- 8-10 spinach leaves
- juice of 2 lemons
- salt

Directions:

1. Chop the fish into long thin strips and mould into plaits, drizzle with salt, five-spice powder and lemon juice and transfer to a bowl.
2. Combine the aniseed, pepper, soy sauce, oyster sauce, honey and chives, pour over the fish and allow to marinate for at least 30 minutes.
3. Line the steam basket with the spinach leaves, place the plaits on top, cover and steam over gently boiling water with the vinegar for about 25 minutes.

HADDOCK WITH GARLIC

Yield: 4 Servings

Ingredients:

- 15 ml/1 tbsp brown sugar
- 15 ml/1 tbsp rice wine or dry sherry
- 15 ml/1 tbsp yellow bean sauce
- 2 slices ginger root, crushed
- 30 ml/2 tbsp cornflour (cornstarch)
- 30 ml/2 tbsp soy sauce
- 45 ml/3 tbsp water
- 450 g/1 lb haddock fillets
- 5 ml/1 tsp salt
- 6 cloves garlic
- 60 ml/4 tbsp groundnut (peanut) oil

Directions:

1. Drizzle the haddock with salt and dust with cornflour.
2. Heat the oil and fry the fish until a golden-brown colour is achieved on both sides then remove it from the pan.
3. Put in the garlic and ginger and fry for approximately one minute.
4. Add the rest of the ingredients, bring to the boil, cover and simmer for approximately five minutes.
5. Return the fish to the pan, cover and simmer until soft.

HADDOCK-STUFFED PEPPERS

Yield: 4 Servings

Ingredients:

- 1 spring onion (scallion), chopped
- 10 ml/2 tsp cornflour (cornstarch)
- 100 g/4 oz peeled prawns, minced (ground)
- 120 ml/4 fl oz/ ½ cup chicken stock
- 2½ ml/ ½ tsp salt
- 225 g/8 oz haddock fillets, minced (ground)
- 4 green peppers
- 45 ml/3 tbsp groundnut (peanut) oil
- 5 ml/1 tsp soy sauce
- pepper

Directions:

1. Combine the haddock, prawns, spring onion, salt and pepper.
2. Cut off the stem of the peppers and lift out the centre.
3. Stuff the peppers with the seafood mixture.
4. Heat the oil and add the peppers and stock.
5. Bring to the boil, cover and simmer for approximately fifteen minutes.
6. Transfer the peppers to a warmed serving plate.
7. Combine the cornflour, soy sauce and a little water and mix it into the pan.
8. Bring to the boil and simmer, stirring, until the sauce clears and becomes thick.

HALIBUT WITH TOMATO SAUCE

Yield: 4 Servings

Ingredients:

- 1 clove garlic, crushed
- 15 ml/1 tbsp black bean sauce
- 15 ml/1 tbsp rice wine or dry sherry
- 15 ml/1 tbsp soy sauce

- 2 slices ginger root, minced
- 2 spring onions (scallions), chopped
- 200 g/7 oz canned tomatoes, drained
- 30 ml/2 tbsp groundnut (peanut) oil
- 450 g/1 lb halibut fillets
- salt

Directions:

1. Drizzle the halibut generously with salt and allow to stand for one hour.
2. Rinse off the salt and pat dry.
3. Put the fish in an ovenproof bowl and drizzle with the black bean sauce, garlic, spring onions, ginger, wine or sherry, soy sauce and tomatoes.
4. Put the bowl on a rack in a steamer, cover and steam for approximately 20 minutes over boiling water until the fish is cooked.
5. Heat the oil until almost smoking and drizzle over the fish and serve.

HOT-FRIED PRAWNS WITH

Yield: 4 Servings

Ingredients:

- 1 slice ginger root, chopped
- 15 ml/1 tbsp rice wine or dry sherry
- 15 ml/1 tbsp soy sauce
- 15 ml/1 tbsp water
- 2 cloves garlic, crushed
- 225 g/8 oz peeled prawns, chopped
- 5 ml/1 tsp cornflour (cornstarch)
- 5 ml/1 tsp salt
- 8 slices stale bread, cubed
- oil for deep-frying

Directions:

1. Heat the oil and fry the bread until a golden-brown colour is achieved.
2. Take out of the pan and eliminate the excess liquid well.
3. Pour off and reserve all but 30 ml/2 tbsp of oil.
4. Reheat the oil and fry the garlic and ginger until slightly browned.

5. Put in the prawns and all the rest of the ingredients and stir-fry for approximately two minutes.
6. Return the bread to the pan and stir together well and serve.

HOT-SPICED FISH

Yield: 4 Servings

Ingredients:

- 1 stick celery, chopped into strips
- 100 g/4 oz bamboo shoots, chopped into strips
- 15 ml/1 tbsp grated lemon rind
- 2 egg whites
- 250 ml/8 fl oz/1 cup chicken stock
- 30 ml/2 tbsp oyster sauce
- 30 ml/2 tbsp soy sauce
- 45 ml/3 tbsp cornflour (cornstarch)
- 450 g/1 lb haddock fillets, diced
- 5 ml/1 tsp five-spice powder
- 5 spring onions (scallions), chopped into strips
- 6 dried Chinese mushrooms
- juice of 1 lemon
- oil for deep-frying
- pinch of ground ginger
- salt and pepper

Directions:

1. Put the fish into a container and drizzle with lemon juice.
2. Combine the soy sauce, oyster sauce, lemon rind, ginger, salt, pepper, egg whites and all but 5 ml/1 tsp of the cornflour.
3. Allow to marinate for 2 hours, stirring intermittently.
4. Soak the mushrooms in warm water for half an hour then drain.
5. Discard the stalks and slice the caps.
6. Heat the oil and fry the fish for a few minutes until golden.
7. Take out of the pan.
8. Put in the vegetables and fry until soft but still crisp.
9. Pour off the oil.

10. Combine the chicken stock with the rest of the cornflour, put it into the vegetables and bring to the boil.
11. Return the fish to the pan, season with five-spice powder and heat through and serve.

LOBSTER CANTONESE

Yield: 4 Servings

Ingredients:

- 1 clove garlic, crushed
- 1 egg, beaten
- 1 onion, chopped
- 15 ml/1 tbsp black bean sauce
- 15 ml/1 tbsp cornflour (cornstarch)
- 2 lobsters
- 225 g/8 oz minced (ground) pork
- 30 ml/2 tbsp oil
- 45 ml/3 tbsp soy sauce
- 5 ml/1 tsp sugar
- 75 ml/5 tbsp water
- salt and freshly ground pepper

Directions:

1. Break open the lobsters, take out the meat and chop it into 2.5 cm/1 in cubes.
2. Heat the oil and fry the black bean sauce, garlic and onion until slightly browned.
3. Put in the pork and fry until browned.
4. Put in the soy sauce, sugar, salt, pepper and lobster, cover and simmer for approximately ten minutes.
5. Blend the cornflour and water to a paste, mix it into the pan and simmer, stirring, until the sauce clears and becomes thick.
6. Turn off the heat and mix in the egg and serve.

LOBSTER NESTS

Yield: 4 Servings

Ingredients:

- 1 onion, finely sliced
- 10 ml/2 tsp cornflour (cornstarch)
- 100 g/4 oz bamboo shoots, sliced 225 g/8 oz cooked lobster meat
- 100 g/4 oz mushrooms, sliced
- 120 ml/4 fl oz/ ½ cup chicken stock
- 15 ml/1 tbsp rice wine or dry sherry
- 15 ml/1 tbsp water
- 30 ml/2 tbsp groundnut (peanut) oil
- 4 noodle baskets
- 5 ml/1 tsp salt
- pinch of freshly ground pepper

Directions:

1. Heat the oil and fry the salt and onion until softened.
2. Put in the mushrooms and bamboo shoots and stir-fry for approximately two minutes.
3. Put in the lobster meat, wine or sherry and stock, bring to the boil, cover and simmer for approximately two minutes.
4. Season with pepper.
5. Combine the cornflour and water to a paste, stir into the pan and simmer, stirring, until the sauce becomes thick.
6. Put the noodle nests on a warmed serving plate and top with the lobster stir-fry.

LOBSTER TAILS WITH PORK

Yield: 4 Servings

Ingredients:

- 10 ml/2 tbsp cornflour (cornstarch)
- 100 g/4 oz minced (ground) pork
- 120 ml/4 fl oz/ ½ cup water
- 2 cloves garlic, crushed
- 3 dried Chinese mushrooms
- 30 ml/2 tbsp black bean sauce
- 30 ml/2 tbsp rice wine or dry sherry
- 4 lobster tails

- 45 ml/3 tbsp soy sauce
- 50 g/2 oz water chestnuts, finely chopped
- 60 ml/4 tbsp groundnut (peanut) oil
- salt and freshly ground pepper

Directions:

1. Soak the mushrooms in warm water for half an hour then drain.
2. Discard the stalks and chop the caps.
3. Chop the lobster tails in half lengthways.
4. Remove the meat from the lobster tails, reserving the shells.
5. Heat half the oil and fry the pork until slightly coloured.
6. Turn off the heat and mix in the mushrooms, lobster meat, water chestnuts, salt and pepper.
7. Press the meat back into the lobster shells and arrange on an ovenproof plate.
8. Put on a rack in a steamer, cover and steam for about 20 minutes until cooked.
9. In the meantime, heat the rest of the oil and fry the garlic, soy sauce, wine or sherry and black bean sauce for approximately two minutes.
10. Combine the cornflour and water to a paste, mix it into the pan and simmer, stirring, until the sauce becomes thick.
11. Put the lobster on a warmed serving plate, pour over the sauce and serve instantly.

LOBSTER WITH MUSHROOMS

Yield: 4 Servings

Ingredients:

- 1 clove garlic, crushed
- 100 g/4 oz mushrooms, sliced
- 15 ml/1 tbsp cornflour (cornstarch)
- 15 ml/1 tbsp rice wine or dry sherry
- 2½ ml/ ½ tsp salt
- 30 ml/2 tbsp groundnut (peanut) oil
- 30 ml/2 tbsp soy sauce
- 4 spring onions (scallions), thickly sliced
- 450 g/1 lb lobster meat
- 60 ml/4 tbsp water

Directions:

1. Chop the lobster meat into 2.5 cm/1 in cubes.
2. Combine the cornflour and water to a paste and toss the lobster cubes in the mixture to coat.
3. Heat half the oil and fry the lobster cubes until slightly browned them remove them from the pan.
4. Heat the rest of the oil and fry the spring onions until slightly browned.
5. Put in the mushrooms and stir-fry for approximately three minutes.
6. Put in the salt, garlic, soy sauce and wine or sherry and stir-fry for approximately two minutes.
7. Return the lobster to the pan and stir-fry until heated through.

MANDARIN FRIED PRAWNS

Yield: 4 Servings

Ingredients:

- 1 clove garlic, crushed
- 1 slice ginger root, minced
- 15 ml/1 tbsp cornflour (cornstarch)
- 30 ml/2 tbsp rice wine or dry sherry 30 ml/2 tbsp soy sauce
- 45 ml/3 tbsp water
- 450 g/1 lb peeled prawns
- 60 ml/4 tbsp groundnut (peanut) oil

Directions:

1. Heat the oil and fry the garlic and ginger until slightly browned.
2. Put in the prawns and stir-fry for approximately one minute.
3. Put in the wine or sherry and stir together well.
4. Put in the soy sauce, cornflour and water and stir-fry for approximately two minutes.

MANDARIN PRAWNS WITH PEAS

Yield: 4 Servings

Ingredients:

- 1 clove garlic, minced
- 1 slice ginger root, minced
- 15 ml/1 tbsp cornflour (cornstarch)
- 225 g/8 oz frozen peas, thawed
- 30 ml/2 tbsp rice wine or dry sherry
- 30 ml/2 tbsp soy sauce
- 45 ml/3 tbsp water
- 450 g/1 lb peeled prawns
- 60 ml/4 tbsp groundnut (peanut) oil

Directions:

1. Heat the oil and fry the garlic and ginger until slightly browned.
2. Put in the prawns and stir-fry for approximately one minute.
3. Put in the wine or sherry and stir together well.
4. Put in the peas and stir-fry for approximately five minutes.
5. Add the rest of the ingredients and stir-fry for approximately two minutes.

MARINATED FISH STEAKS

Yield: 4 Servings

Ingredients:

- 15 ml/1 tbsp rice wine or dry sherry
- 15 ml/1 tbsp wine vinegar
- 2 cloves garlic, crushed
- 2 slices ginger root, crushed
- 3 spring onions (scallions), chopped
- 4 whiting or haddock steaks
- 45 ml/3 tbsp groundnut (peanut) oil
- salt and freshly ground pepper

Directions:

1. Put the fish into a container.
2. Combine the garlic, ginger, spring onions, wine or sherry, wine vinegar, salt and pepper, pour over the fish, cover and allow to marinate for several hours.
3. Remove the fish from the marinade.
4. Heat the oil and fry the fish until browned on both sides then remove from the pan.

5. Put in the marinade to the pan, bring to the boil then return the fish to the pan and simmer gently until cooked through.

MARINATED SWEET AND SOUR FISH

Yield: 4 Servings

Ingredients:

- 1 onion, chopped
- 3 slices ginger root, minced
- 30 ml/2 tbsp cornflour (cornstarch)
- 450 g/1 lb fish fillets, chopped into chunks
- 5 ml/1 tsp soy sauce
- oil for deep-frying
- salt and freshly ground pepper
- sweet and sour sauce

Directions:

1. Put the fish into a container.
2. Combine the onion, ginger, soy sauce, salt and pepper, add to the fish, cover and allow to stand for one hour, turning occasionally.
3. Remove the fish from the marinade and dust with cornflour.
4. Heat the oil and deep-fry the fish until crisp and golden brown.
5. Drain using kitchen paper and lay out on a warmed serving plate.
6. In the meantime, prepare the sauce and pour over the fish to serve.

MONKFISH WITH BROCCOLI

Yield: 4 Servings

Ingredients:

- 1 clove garlic, crushed
- 1 small carrot, chopped into strips
- 2 slices ginger root, minced
- 275 g/10 oz broccoli florets

- 45 ml/3 tbsp groundnut (peanut) oil
- 45 ml/3 tbsp water
- 45 ml/3 tbsp water
- 450 g/1 lb monkfish tail, cubed
- 5 ml/1 tsp cornflour (cornstarch)
- 5 ml/1 tsp sugar
- 50 g/2 oz mushrooms, sliced
- salt and pepper

Directions:

1. Season the monkfish well with salt and pepper.
2. Heat 30 ml/2 tbsp of oil and fry the monkfish, mushrooms, carrot, garlic and ginger until slightly browned.
3. Put in the water and continue to simmer, uncovered, over a low heat.
4. In the meantime, briefly boil the broccoli in boiling water until just soft then eliminate the excess liquid well.
5. Heat the rest of the oil and stir-fry the broccoli and sugar with a pinch of salt until the broccoli is well coated in the oil.
6. Lay out round a warmed serving plate.
7. Combine the cornflour and water to a paste, stir into the fish and simmer, stirring, until the sauce becomes thick.
8. Pour over the broccoli and serve instantly.

MULLET WITH THICK SOY SAUCE

Yield: 4 Servings

Ingredients:

- 1 red chilli pepper, shredded
- 1 red mullet
- 15 ml/1 tbsp freshly ground white
- 15 ml/1 tbsp rice wine or dry sherry
- 15 ml/1 tbsp thick soy sauce
- 2 slices ginger root, shredded
- 2 spring onions (scallions), sliced
- 250 ml/8 fl oz/1 cup fish stock
- 30 ml/2 tbsp groundnut (peanut) oil

- oil for deep-frying
- pepper

Directions:

1. Trim the fish and score it diagonally on each side.
2. Heat the oil and deep-fry the fish until half cooked.
3. Take out of the oil and eliminate the excess liquid well.
4. Heat the oil and fry the spring onions, ginger and chilli pepper for approximately one minute.
5. Add the rest of the ingredients, stir together well and bring to the boil.
6. Put in the fish and simmer gently, uncovered, until the fish is cooked and the liquid has almost evaporated.

MUSSELS IN BLACK BEAN SAUCE

Yield: 4 Servings

Ingredients:

- 1.5 kg/3 lb mussels, scrubbed and bearded
- 15 ml/1 tbsp soy sauce
- 2 cloves garlic, crushed
- 2 slices ginger root, minced
- 2 spring onions (scallions), chopped
- 30 ml/2 tbsp black bean sauce
- 45 ml/3 tbsp groundnut (peanut) oil

Directions:

1. Heat the oil and fry the garlic and ginger for 30 seconds.
2. Put in the black bean sauce and soy sauce and fry for 10 seconds.
3. Put in the mussels, cover and cook for about 6 minutes until the mussels have opened.
4. Discard any that remain closed.
5. Move to a heated serving dish and serve sprinkled with spring onions.

MUSSELS WITH GINGER

Yield: 4 Servings

Ingredients:

- 1.5 kg/3 lb mussels, scrubbed and bearded
- 15 ml/1 tbsp oyster sauce
- 2 cloves garlic, crushed
- 4 slices ginger root, minced
- 45 ml/3 tbsp groundnut (peanut) oil
- 45 ml/3 tbsp water

Directions:

1. Heat the oil and fry the garlic and ginger for 30 seconds.
2. Put in the mussels and water, cover and cook for about 6 minutes until the mussels have opened.
3. Discard any that remain closed.
4. Move to a heated serving dish and serve sprinkled with oyster sauce.

OYSTERS WITH BACON

Yield: 4 Servings

Ingredients:

- 1 egg, slightly beaten
- 15 ml/1 tbsp cornflour (cornstarch)
- 15 ml/1 tbsp soy sauce
- 15 ml/1 tbsp water
- 175 g/6 oz bacon
- 2 onions, chopped
- 24 oysters, shelled
- 45 ml/3 tbsp groundnut (peanut) oil
- 90 ml/6 tbsp chicken stock

Directions:

1. Chop the bacon into pieces and wrap one piece around each oyster.
2. Beat the egg with the water then immerse in the oysters to coat.

3. Heat half the oil and fry the oysters until slightly browned on both sides then remove them from the pan and eliminate the excess liquid off the fat.
4. Heat the rest of the oil and fry the onions until softened.
5. Combine the cornflour, soy sauce and stock to a paste, pour into the pan and simmer, stirring, until the sauce clears and becomes thick.
6. Pour over the oysters and serve instantly.

OYSTERS WITH BLACK BEAN SAUCE

Yield: 4 Servings

Ingredients:

- 120 ml/4 fl oz/ ½ cup groundnut (peanut) oil
- 15 ml/1 tbsp black bean sauce
- 15 ml/1 tbsp sesame oil
- 2 cloves garlic, crushed
- 3 spring onions (scallions), sliced
- 30 ml/2 tbsp dark soy sauce
- 350 g/12 oz shelled oysters
- pinch chilli powder

Directions:

1. Briefly boil the oysters in boiling water for 30 seconds then drain.
2. Heat the oil and stir-fry the garlic and spring onions for 30 seconds.
3. Put in the black bean sauce, soy sauce, sesame oil and oysters and season to taste with chilli powder.
4. Stir-fry until heated through and serve instantly.

PEKING PRAWNS

Yield: 4 Servings

Ingredients:

- 1 slice ginger root, finely chopped
- 120 ml/4 fl oz/ ½ cup chicken stock

- 2 cloves garlic, crushed
- 225 g/8 oz peeled prawns
- 30 ml/2 tbsp groundnut (peanut) oil
- 4 spring onions (scallions), thickly sliced
- 5 ml/1 tsp brown sugar
- 5 ml/1 tsp hoisin sauce
- 5 ml/1 tsp soy sauce
- 5 ml/1 tsp tabasco sauce

Directions:

1. Heat the oil with the garlic and ginger and fry until the garlic is slightly browned.
2. Put in the prawns and stir-fry for approximately one minute.
3. Put in the spring onions and stir-fry for approximately one minute.
4. Add the rest of the ingredients, bring to the boil, cover and simmer for 4 minutes, stirring intermittently.
5. Check the seasoning and add a little more tabasco sauce if you prefer.

PLAICE WITH GARLIC

Yield: 4 Servings

Ingredients:

- 1 egg, beaten
- 15 ml/1 tbsp rice wine or dry sherry
- 3 cloves garlic, chopped
- 350 g/12 oz plaice fillets
- 4 spring onions (scallions), chopped
- 45 ml/3 tbsp cornflour (cornstarch)
- 5 ml/1 tsp sesame oil
- 60 ml/4 tbsp groundnut (peanut) oil
- salt

Directions:

1. Skin the plaice and chop it into strips.
2. Drizzle with salt and allow to stand for approximately 20 minutes.
3. Dust the fish with cornflour then immerse in the egg.

4. Heat the oil and fry the fish strips for about 4 minutes until a golden-brown colour is achieved.
5. Take out of the pan and eliminate the excess liquid on kitchen paper.
6. Pour off all but 5 ml/1 tsp of oil from the pan and add the rest of the ingredients.
7. Bring to the boil, stirring, then simmer for approximately three minutes.
8. Pour over the fish and serve immediately.

PLAICE WITH PINEAPPLE SAUCE

Yield: 4 Servings

Ingredients:

- 100 g/4 oz/ ½ cup cornflour (cornstarch)
- 2 eggs, beaten
- 200 g/7 oz canned pineapple chunks
- 30 ml/2 tbsp soy sauce
- 30 ml/2 tbsp water
- 450 g/1 lb plaice fillets
- 5 ml/1 tsp salt
- 5 ml/1 tsp sesame oil
- oil for deep-frying

Directions:

1. Chop the plaice into strips and place into a container.
2. Drizzle with salt, soy sauce and 30 ml/2 tbsp of the pineapple juice and allow to stand for 10 minutes.
3. Beat the eggs with 45 ml/3 tbsp of cornflour to a batter and immerse the fish in the batter.
4. Heat the oil and deep-fry the fish until a golden-brown colour is achieved.
5. Drain on kitchen pepper.
6. Put the rest of the pineapple juice in a small saucepan.
7. Blend 30 ml/2 tbsp of cornflour with the water and mix it into the pan.
8. Bring to the boil and simmer, stirring, until thickened.
9. Add half the pineapple pieces and heat through.
10. Just before serving, mix in the sesame oil.
11. Put the cooked fish on a warmed serving plate and garnish with the reserved pineapple.
12. Pour over the hot sauce and serve instantly.

POACHED PRAWNS WITH HAM AND TOFU

Yield: 4 Servings

Ingredients:

- 100 g/4 oz smoked ham, cubed
- 225 g/8 oz peeled prawns
- 225 g/8 oz tofu, cubed
- 30 ml/2 tbsp groundnut (peanut) oil
- 600 ml/1 pt/2 ½ cups chicken stock

Directions:

1. Heat the oil and fry the tofu until slightly browned.
2. Take out of the pan and drain.
3. Heat the stock, add the tofu and ham and simmer gently for approximately ten minutes until the tofu is cooked.
4. Put in the prawns and simmer for another 5 minutes until heated through.
5. Serve in deep bowls.

PORK-STUFFED CLAMS

Yield: 4 Servings

Ingredients:

- 1 spring onion (scallion), minced
- 15 ml/1 tbsp rice wine or dry sherry
- 15 ml/1 tbsp soy sauce
- 175 g/6 oz lean minced (ground) pork
- 2 slices ginger root, minced
- 2½ ml/ ½ tsp salt
- 2½ ml/ ½ tsp sugar
- 24 clams

Directions:

1. Scrub the clams comprehensively.
2. then soak them in salted water for a few hours.
3. Rinse under running water and lay out on a shallow ovenproof plate.
4. Put on a rack in a steamer, cover and steam over gently simmering water for approximately ten minutes until all the clams have opened.
5. Discard any that remain closed.
6. Remove the clams from their shells and mix the clams with the rest of the ingredients.
7. Stuff the mixture back into the half shells and arrange on an ovenproof plate.
8. Stand the plate on a rack in a steamer, cover and steam over simmering water for about 15 minutes until the pork mixture is cooked.

PORK-STUFFED FISH

Yield: 4 Servings

Ingredients:

- 1 large carp or similar fish
- 1 onion, sliced
- 1 spring onion (scallion), minced
- 100 g/4 oz minced (ground) pork
- 15 ml/1 tbsp cornflour (cornstarch)
- 15 ml/1 tbsp rice wine or dry sherry
- 2 cloves garlic, crushed
- 300 ml/ ½ pt/1¬º cups water
- 4 slices ginger root, minced
- 5 ml/1 tsp sugar
- 60 ml/4 tbsp soy sauce
- 75 ml/5 tbsp groundnut (peanut) oil
- salt

Directions:

1. Clean and scale the fish and drizzle with salt.
2. Combine the pork, spring onion, a little of the ginger, the cornflour, 15 ml/1 tbsp of soy sauce, the wine or sherry and sugar and use to stuff the fish.
3. Heat the oil and fry the fish until slightly browned on both sides then remove it from the pan and eliminate the excess liquid off most of the oil.
4. Put in the garlic and rest of the ginger and stir-fry until slightly browned.

5. Add the rest of the soy sauce and the water, bring to the boil and simmer for approximately two minutes.
6. Return the fish to the pan, cover and simmer for about 30 minutes until the fish is cooked, turning once or twice.

PRAWN AND EGG CUPS

Yield: 4 Servings

Ingredients:

- 1 red chilli pepper, chopped
- 15 ml/1 tbsp sesame oil
- 15 ml/1 tbsp soy sauce
- 2 spring onions (scallions), chopped
- 30 ml/2 tbsp chopped abalone (optional)
- 8 eggs
- 8 peeled king prawns
- few sprigs of flat-leaved parsley
- salt and freshly ground pepper

Directions:

1. Use the sesame oil to grease 8 ramekin dishes.
2. Put one prawn in each dish with a little of the chilli pepper, spring onions and abalone, if using.
3. Break an egg into each bowl and season with soy sauce, salt and pepper.
4. Stand the ramekins on a baking sheet and bake in a preheated oven at 200 degrees C/gas mark 6 for about 15 minutes until the eggs are set and slightly crisp around the outside.
5. Lift them carefully on to a warmed serving plate and garnish with parsley.

PRAWN AND MUSHROOM CURRY

Yield: 4 Servings

Ingredients:

- 1 onion, chopped into wedges
- 1 slice ginger root, finely chopped
- 100 g/4 oz button mushrooms
- 100 g/4 oz fresh or frozen peas
- 15 ml/1 tbsp cornflour (cornstarch)
- 15 ml/1 tbsp curry powder
- 150 ml chicken stock
- 2 cloves garlic, crushed
- 225 g/8 oz peeled prawns
- 30 ml/2 tbsp groundnut (peanut) oil
- 5 ml/1 tsp rice wine or dry sherry
- 5 ml/1 tsp soy sauce

Directions:

1. Combine the soy sauce, wine or sherry and prawns.
2. Heat the oil with the garlic and ginger and fry until slightly browned.
3. Put in the onion, mushrooms and peas and stir-fry for approximately two minutes.
4. Put in the curry powder and cornflour and stir-fry for approximately two minutes.
5. Progressively mix in the stock, bring to the boil, cover and simmer for approximately five minutes, stirring intermittently.
6. Put in the prawns and marinade, cover and simmer for approximately two minutes.

PRAWN AND PEA STIR-FRY

Yield: 4 Servings

Ingredients:

- 1 clove garlic, crushed
- 1 slice ginger root, minced
- 225 g/8 oz briefly boiled or frozen peas, thawed
- 30 ml/2 tbsp groundnut (peanut) oil
- 30 ml/2 tbsp water
- 4 spring onions (scallions), chopped
- 450 g/1 lb peeled prawns
- 5 ml/1 tsp salt
- 5 ml/1 tsp sesame oil
- salt and pepper

Directions:

1. Combine the prawns with the sesame oil and salt.
2. Heat the oil and stir-fry the garlic and ginger for approximately one minute.
3. Put in the prawns and stir-fry for approximately two minutes.
4. Put in the peas and stir-fry for approximately one minute.
5. Put in the spring onions and water and season with salt and pepper and a little more sesame oil, if liked.
6. Heat through, stirring carefully, and serve.

PRAWN BALLS

Yield: 4 Servings

Ingredients:

- 1 slice ginger root, finely minced
- 1 spring onion (scallion), finely minced
- 15 ml/1 tbsp cornflour (cornstarch)
- 2 eggs, beaten
- 3 dried Chinese mushrooms
- 450 g/1 lb prawns, finely minced
- 50 g/2 oz/ ½ cup plain (all-purpose) flour
- 6 water chestnuts, finely minced
- groundnut (peanut) oil for deep-frying
- salt and freshly ground pepper

Directions:

1. Soak the mushrooms in warm water for half an hour then drain.
2. Discard the stems and finely chop the caps.
3. Mix with the prawns, water chestnuts, spring onion and ginger and season with salt and pepper.
4. Mix in 1 egg and 5 ml/1 tsp cornflour roll into balls about the size of a heaped teaspoon.
5. Beat together the rest of the egg, cornflour and flour and add enough water to make a thick, smooth batter.
6. Roll the balls in the batter.
7. Heat the oil and deep-fry for a few minutes until light golden brown.

PRAWN CHOP SUEY

Yield: 4 Servings

Ingredients:

- 1 slice ginger root, chopped
- 100 g/4 oz button mushrooms, halved
- 100 g/4 oz frozen peas
- 15 ml/1 tbsp cornflour (cornstarch)
- 15 ml/1 tbsp rice wine or dry sherry
- 2 cloves garlic, crushed
- 2 spring onions (scallions), chopped
- 225 g/8 oz peeled prawns
- 30 ml/2 tbsp soy sauce
- 5 ml/1 tsp salt
- 5 ml/1 tsp sugar
- 60 ml/4 tbsp groundnut (peanut) oil

Directions:

1. Heat 45 ml/3 tbsp of oil and fry the spring onions, garlic and ginger until slightly browned.
2. Put in the prawns and stir-fry for approximately one minute.
3. Take out of the pan.
4. Heat the rest of the oil and stir-fry the peas and mushrooms for approximately three minutes.
5. Put in the prawns, soy sauce, wine or sherry, sugar and salt and stir-fry for approximately two minutes.
6. Combine the cornflour with a little water, mix it into the pan and simmer, stirring, until the sauce clears and becomes thick.

PRAWN CHOW MEIN

Yield: 4 Servings

Ingredients:

- 1 slice ginger root, minced
- 100 g/4 oz bamboo shoots, sliced
- 100 g/4 oz Chinese cabbage, sliced
- 15 ml/1 tbsp cornflour (cornstarch)
- 15 ml/1 tbsp rice wine or dry sherry
- 15 ml/1 tbsp soy sauce
- 30 ml/2 tbsp groundnut (peanut) oil
- 4 dried Chinese mushrooms
- 450 g/1 lb peeled prawns
- 5 ml/1 tsp salt
- Soft-Fried Noodles

Directions:

1. Combine the prawns with the cornflour, soy sauce and wine or sherry and leave to stand, stirring intermittently.
2. Soak the mushrooms in warm water for half an hour then drain.
3. Discard the stalks and slice the caps.
4. Heat the oil and fry the salt and ginger for approximately one minute.
5. Put in the cabbage and bamboo shoots and stir until coated with oil.
6. Cover and simmer for approximately two minutes.
7. Mix in the prawns and marinade and stir-fry for approximately three minutes.
8. Mix in the drained noodles and heat through and serve.

PRAWN CURRY

Yield: 4 Servings

Ingredients:

- 120 ml/4 fl oz/ ½ cup chicken stock
- 2½ ml/ ½ tsp salt
- 30 ml/2 tbsp curry powder
- 4 spring onions (scallions), sliced
- 45 ml/3 tbsp groundnut (peanut) oil
- 450 g/1 lb peeled prawns

Directions:

1. Heat the oil and fry the spring onions for 30 seconds.

2. Put in the curry powder and salt and stir-fry for approximately one minute.
3. Put in the stock, bring to the boil and simmer, stirring, for approximately two minutes.
4. Put in the prawns and heat through gently.

PRAWN DUMPLINGS WITH TOMATO SAUCE

Yield: 4 Servings

Ingredients:

- 100 g/4 oz ham, chopped
- 100 g/4 oz mushrooms, chopped
- 100 g/4 oz spring onions (scallions), chopped
- 15 ml/1 tbsp cornflour (cornstarch)
- 15 ml/1 tbsp groundnut (peanut) oil
- 15 ml/1 tbsp sugar
- 2 cloves garlic, crushed
- 2 stalks celery, chopped
- 200 g/7 oz tomatoes, skinned and chopped
- 30 ml/2 tbsp groundnut (peanut) oil
- 30 ml/2 tbsp soy sauce
- 300 ml water
- 4 eggs, beaten
- 450 g/1 lb minced (ground) cod
- 50 g/2 oz/ ½ cup cornflour (cornstarch)
- 900 g/2 lb peeled prawns
- For the sauce:
- salt and freshly ground pepper

Directions:

1. Finely chop the prawns and mix with the cod.
2. Mix in the eggs, cornflour, garlic, soy sauce, sugar and oil.
3. Bring a large saucepan of water to the boil and drop spoonfuls of the mixture into the saucepan.
4. Return to the boil and simmer for a few minutes until the dumplings float to the surface.
5. Drain well.
6. To make the sauce, heat the oil and fry the spring onions until soft but not browned.

7. Put in the mushrooms and fry for approximately one minute then add the ham, celery and tomatoes and fry for approximately one minute.
8. Put in the water, bring to the boil and season with salt and pepper.
9. Cover and simmer for 10 minutes, stirring intermittently.
10. Combine the cornflour with a little water and mix it into the sauce.
11. Simmer for a few minutes, stirring, until the sauce clears and becomes thick.
12. Serve with the dumplings.

PRAWN EGG ROLLS

Yield: 4 Servings

Ingredients:

- 1 egg, beaten
- 100 g/4 oz mushrooms, chopped
- 12 egg roll skins
- 15 ml/1 tbsp rice wine or dry sherry
- 2½ ml/ ½ tsp cornflour (cornstarch)
- 2½ ml/ ½ tsp salt
- 2½ ml/ ½ tsp sugar
- 225 g/8 oz bean sprouts
- 225 g/8 oz peeled prawns, chopped
- 30 ml/2 tbsp groundnut (peanut) oil
- 4 stalks celery, chopped
- oil for deep-frying

Directions:

1. Briefly boil the bean sprouts in boiling water for approximately two minutes then drain.
2. Heat the oil and stir-fry the celery for approximately one minute.
3. Put in the mushrooms and stir-fry for approximately one minute.
4. Put in the prawns, wine or sherry, cornflour, salt and sugar and stir-fry for approximately two minutes.
5. Allow it to cool.
6. Put a little of the filling on the centre of each skin and brush the edges with beaten egg.
7. Fold in the edges then roll the egg roll away from you, sealing the edges with egg.
8. Heat the oil and deep-fry until a golden-brown colour is achieved.

PRAWN FOO YUNG

Yield: 4 Servings

Ingredients:

- 100 g/4 oz mushrooms, sliced
- 2 spring onions (scallions), chopped
- 225 g/8 oz peeled prawns
- 45 ml/3 tbsp cornflour (cornstarch)
- 45 ml/3 tbsp groundnut (peanut) oil
- 5 ml/1 tsp salt
- 6 eggs, beaten

Directions:

1. Beat the eggs then beat in the cornflour.
2. Add all the rest of the ingredients except the oil.
3. Heat the oil and pour the mixture into the pan a little at a time to make pancakes about 7.5 cm/3 in across.
4. Fry until the bottom is golden-brown then turn and brown the other side.

PRAWN FRIES

Yield: 4 Servings

Ingredients:

- 1 egg, beaten
- 1 hard-boiled (hard-cooked) egg yolk, chopped
- 1 spring onion (scallion), chopped
- 12 large uncooked prawns
- 25 g/1 oz cooked ham, chopped
- 3 slices bread
- 30 ml/2 tbsp cornflour (cornstarch)
- oil for deep-frying
- pinch of pepper
- pinch of salt

Directions:

1. Remove the shells and back veins from the prawns, leaving the tails intact.
2. Cut down the back of the prawns with a sharp knife and gently press them flat.
3. Beat the egg, cornflour, salt and pepper.
4. Toss the prawns in the mixture until completely coated.
5. Remove the crusts from the bread and chop it into quarters.
6. Put one prawn, chop side down, on each piece and press down.
7. Brush a little egg mixture over each prawn then drizzle with the egg yolk, ham and spring onion.
8. Heat the oil and fry the prawn bread pieces in batches until golden.
9. Drain using kitchen paper and serve hot.

PRAWN TEMPURA

Yield: 4 Servings

Ingredients:

- 2 eggs, beaten
- 30 ml/2 tbsp cornflour (cornstarch)
- 30 ml/2 tbsp plain (all-purpose) flour
- 30 ml/2 tbsp water
- 450 g/1 lb peeled prawns
- oil for deep-frying

Directions:

1. Chop the prawns half way through on the inner curve and spread open to make a butterfly.
2. Combine the flour, cornflour and water to a batter then mix in the eggs.
3. Heat the oil and deep-fry the prawns until a golden-brown colour is achieved.

PRAWN WONTONS

Yield: 4 Servings

Ingredients:

- 15 ml/1 tbsp soy sauce

- 2½ ml/ ½ tsp salt
- 225 g/8 oz mixed vegetables, chopped
- 40 wonton skins
- 450 g/1 lb peeled prawns, chopped
- few drops of sesame oil
- oil for deep-frying

Directions:

1. Combine the prawns, vegetables, soy sauce, salt and sesame oil.
2. To fold the wontons, hold the skin in the palm of your left hand and spoon a little filling into the centre.
3. Moisten the edges with egg and fold the skin into a triangle, sealing the edges.
4. Moisten the corners with egg and twist them together.
5. Heat the oil and fry the wontons a few at a time until a golden-brown colour is achieved.
6. Drain thoroughly and serve.

PRAWNS IN LOBSTER SAUCE

Yield: 4 Servings

Ingredients:

- 100 g/4 oz minced (ground) pork
- 15 ml/1 tbsp rice wine or dry sherry
- 15 ml/1 tbsp soy sauce
- 2 cloves garlic, crushed
- 2 eggs, beaten
- 2 spring onions (scallions), chopped
- 2½ ml/ ½ tsp salt
- 2½ ml/ ½ tsp sugar
- 30 ml/2 tbsp cornflour (cornstarch)
- 300 ml/ ½ pt/1¬º cups chicken stock
- 45 ml/3 tbsp groundnut (peanut) oil
- 450 g/1 lb peeled prawns
- 5 ml/1 tsp minced black beans

Directions:

1. Heat the oil and fry the garlic and black beans until the garlic is until slightly browned.
2. Put in the pork and fry until browned.
3. Put in the prawns and stir-fry for approximately one minute.
4. Put in the sherry, cover and simmer for approximately one minute.
5. Put in the stock and cornflour, bring to the boil, stirring, cover and simmer for approximately five minutes.
6. Put in the eggs, stirring all the time so that they form into threads.
7. Put in the soy sauce, salt, sugar and spring onions and simmer for a few minutes and serve.

PRAWNS WITH ALMONDS

Yield: 4 Servings

Ingredients:

- 100 g/4 oz almonds
- 15 ml/1 tbsp cornflour (cornstarch)
- 2 cloves garlic
- 2 slices ginger root, minced
- 2 stalks celery, chopped
- 2½ ml/ ½ tsp salt
- 225 g/8 oz large unpeeled prawns
- 30 ml/2 tbsp groundnut (peanut) oil
- 30 ml/2 tbsp water
- 5 ml/1 tsp rice wine or dry sherry
- 5 ml/1 tsp soy sauce

Directions:

1. Heat the almonds using a dry pan until slightly browned then put to one side.
2. Peel the prawns, leaving on the tails, and chop in half lengthways to the tail.
3. Mix with the ginger, cornflour and salt.
4. Heat the oil and fry the garlic until slightly browned then discard the garlic.
5. Put in the celery, soy sauce, wine or sherry and water to the pan and bring to the boil.
6. Put in the prawns and stir-fry until heated through.
7. Serve sprinkled with toasted almonds.

PRAWNS WITH ASPARAGUS

Yield: 4 Servings

Ingredients:

- 15 ml/1 tbsp rice wine or dry sherry
- 15 ml/1 tbsp soy sauce
- 2 slices ginger root, minced
- 2½ ml/ ½ tsp salt
- 225 g/8 oz peeled prawns
- 45 ml/3 tbsp groundnut (peanut) oil
- 450 g/1 lb asparagus, chopped into chunks
- 5 ml/1 tsp sugar

Directions:

1. Briefly boil the asparagus in boiling water for approximately two minutes then eliminate the excess liquid well.
2. Heat the oil and fry the ginger for a few seconds.
3. Put in the asparagus and stir until well coated with oil.
4. Put in the soy sauce, wine or sherry, sugar and salt and heat through.
5. Put in the prawns and stir over a low heat until the asparagus is soft.

PRAWNS WITH BACON

Yield: 4 Servings

Ingredients:

- 1 egg, slightly beaten
- 100 g/4 oz bacon
- 15 ml/1 tbsp soy sauce
- 2½ ml/ ½ tsp salt
- 450 g/1 lb large unpeeled prawns
- 50 g/2 oz/ ½ cup cornflour (cornstarch)
- oil for deep-frying

Directions:

1. Peel the prawns, leaving the tails intact.
2. Cut in half lengthways to the tail.
3. Chop the bacon into small squares.
4. Press a piece of bacon in the centre of each prawn and press the two halves together.
5. Beat the egg with the salt and soy sauce.
6. Immerse the prawns in the egg then dust with cornflour.
7. Heat the oil and deep-fry the prawns until crispy and golden.

PRAWNS WITH BAMBOO SHOOTS

Yield: 4 Servings

Ingredients:

- 1 clove garlic, minced
- 1 slice ginger root, minced
- 15 ml/1 tbsp cornflour (cornstarch)
- 225 g/8 oz bamboo shoots
- 30 ml/2 tbsp rice wine or dry sherry
- 30 ml/2 tbsp soy sauce
- 45 ml/3 tbsp water
- 450 g/1 lb peeled prawns
- 60 ml/4 tbsp groundnut (peanut) oil

Directions:

1. Heat the oil and fry the garlic and ginger until slightly browned.
2. Put in the prawns and stir-fry for approximately one minute.
3. Put in the wine or sherry and stir together well.
4. Put in the bamboo shoots and stir-fry for approximately five minutes.
5. Add the rest of the ingredients and stir-fry for approximately two minutes.

PRAWNS WITH BEAN SPROUTS

Yield: 4 Servings

Ingredients:

- 1 clove garlic, crushed
- 120 ml/4 fl oz/ ½ cup chicken stock
- 15 ml/1 tbsp cornflour (cornstarch)
- 15 ml/1 tbsp rice wine or dry sherry
- 15 ml/1 tbsp soy sauce
- 2 spring onion (scallions), chopped
- 225 g/8 oz peeled prawns
- 30 ml/2 tbsp groundnut (peanut) oil
- 4 dried Chinese mushrooms
- 450 g/1 lb bean sprouts
- salt and freshly ground pepper

Directions:

1. Soak the mushrooms in warm water for half an hour then drain.
2. Discard the stems and slice the caps.
3. Heat the oil and fry the garlic until slightly browned.
4. Put in the prawns and stir-fry for approximately one minute.
5. Put in the wine or sherry and fry for approximately one minute.
6. Mix in the mushrooms and bean sprouts.
7. Combine the stock, soy sauce and cornflour and mix it into the pan.
8. Bring to the boil then simmer, stirring, until the sauce clears and becomes thick.
9. Season to taste with salt and pepper.
10. Serve sprinkled with spring onions.

PRAWNS WITH BLACK BEAN SAUCE

Yield: 4 Servings

Ingredients:

- 1 clove garlic, crushed
- 1 green pepper, chopped
- 1 onion, chopped
- 120 ml/4 fl oz/ ½ cup fish stock
- 15 ml/1 tbsp cornflour (cornstarch)
- 15 ml/1 tbsp soy sauce
- 225 g/8 oz peeled prawns
- 30 ml/2 tbsp groundnut (peanut) oil

- 45 ml/3 tbsp black bean sauce
- 45 ml/3 tbsp water
- 5 ml/1 tsp salt
- 5 ml/1 tsp sugar

Directions:

1. Heat the oil and stir-fry the salt, garlic and black bean sauce for approximately two minutes.
2. Put in the pepper and onion and stir-fry for approximately two minutes.
3. Put in the stock, sugar and soy sauce and bring to the boil.
4. Put in the prawns and simmer for approximately two minutes.
5. Combine the cornflour and water to a paste, put it into the pan and simmer, stirring, until the sauce clears and becomes thick.

PRAWNS WITH CELERY

Yield: 4 Servings

Ingredients:

- 100 g/4 oz almonds, chopped
- 15 ml/1 tbsp sherry
- 3 slices ginger root, minced
- 4 stalks celery, chopped
- 45 ml/3 tbsp groundnut (peanut) oil
- 450 g/1 lb peeled prawns
- 5 ml/1 tsp salt

Directions:

1. Heat half the oil and fry the ginger until slightly browned.
2. Put in the prawns, salt and sherry and stir-fry until well coated in oil then remove from the pan.
3. Heat the rest of the oil and stir-fry the celery and almonds for a few minutes until the celery is just soft but still crisp.
4. Return the prawns to the pan, mix well and heat through and serve.

PRAWNS WITH CHINESE MUSHROOMS

Yield: 4 Servings

Ingredients:

- 15 ml/1 tbsp soy sauce
- 3 slices ginger root, minced
- 45 ml/3 tbsp groundnut (peanut) oil
- 450 g/1 lb peeled prawns
- 5 ml/1 tsp salt
- 60 ml/4 tbsp fish stock
- 8 dried Chinese mushrooms

Directions:

1. Soak the mushrooms in warm water for half an hour then drain.
2. Discard the stalks and slice the caps.
3. Heat half the oil and fry the ginger until slightly browned.
4. Put in the prawns, soy sauce and salt and stir-fry until coated in oil then remove from the pan.
5. Heat the rest of the oil and stir-fry the mushrooms until coated with oil.
6. Put in the stock, bring to the boil, cover and simmer for approximately three minutes.
7. Return the prawns to the pan and stir until heated through.

PRAWNS WITH COURGETTES AND LYCHEES

Yield: 4 Servings

Ingredients:

- 10 ml/2 tsp cornflour (cornstarch)
- 10 ml/2 tsp mild curry powder
- 10 ml/2 tsp soy sauce
- 12 king prawns
- 12 lychees, stoned
- 120 ml/4 fl oz/ ½ cup coconut cream
- 15 ml/1 tbsp groundnut (peanut) oil
- 2 red chilli peppers, chopped
- 2 spring onions (scallions), chopped

- 225 g/8 oz courgettes (zucchini), diced
- 4 cloves garlic, crushed
- 5 ml/1 tsp fish sauce
- salt and pepper

Directions:

1. Peel the prawns, leaving on the tails.
2. Drizzle with salt, pepper and soy sauce then coat with cornflour.
3. Heat the oil and fry the garlic, chilli peppers and prawns for approximately one minute.
4. Put in the courgettes, spring onions and lychees and stir-fry for approximately one minute.
5. Take out of the pan.
6. Pour the coconut cream into the pan, bring to the boil and simmer for approximately two minutes until thick.
7. Mix in the curry powder and fish sauce and season with salt and pepper.
8. Return the prawns and vegetables to the sauce to heat through and serve.

PRAWNS WITH CRAB

Yield: 4 Servings

Ingredients:

- 1 sliced ginger root, minced
- 10 ml/2 tsp cornflour (cornstarch)
- 15 ml/1 tbsp rice wine or dry sherry
- 15 ml/1 tbsp soy sauce
- 225 g/8 oz crab meat
- 225 g/8 oz peeled prawns
- 3 spring onions (scallions), chopped
- 30 ml/2 tbsp chicken or fish stock
- 45 ml/3 tbsp groundnut (peanut) oil
- 5 ml/1 tsp brown sugar
- 5 ml/1 tsp wine vinegar
- freshly ground pepper

Directions:

1. Heat 30 ml/2 tbsp of oil and fry the spring onions and ginger until slightly browned.

2. Put in the crab meat and stir-fry for approximately two minutes.
3. Put in the wine or sherry, stock, soy sauce, sugar and vinegar and season to taste with pepper.
4. Stir-fry for approximately three minutes.
5. Combine the cornflour with a little water and mix it into the sauce.
6. Simmer, stirring, until the sauce becomes thick.
7. In the meantime, heat the rest of the oil in a separate pan and stir-fry the prawns for a few minutes until heated through.
8. Put the crab mixture on a warmed serving plate and top with the prawns.

PRAWNS WITH CUCUMBER

Yield: 4 Servings

Ingredients:

- 1 cucumber
- 1 onion, finely chopped
- 15 ml/1 tbsp cornflour (cornstarch)
- 15 ml/1 tbsp rice wine or dry sherry
- 2 cloves garlic, crushed
- 2 slices ginger root, minced
- 225 g/8 oz peeled prawns
- 45 ml/3 tbsp groundnut (peanut) oil
- salt and freshly ground pepper

Directions:

1. Season the prawns with salt and pepper and toss with the cornflour.
2. Peel and seed the cucumber and chop it into thick slices.
3. Heat half the oil and fry the garlic and onion until slightly browned.
4. Put in the prawns and sherry and stir-fry for approximately two minutes then remove the ingredients from the pan.
5. Heat the rest of the oil and fry the ginger for approximately one minute.
6. Put in the cucumber and stir-fry for approximately two minutes.
7. Return the prawn mixture to the pan and stir-fry until well mixed and heated through.

PRAWNS WITH LYCHEE SAUCE

Yield: 4 Servings

Ingredients:

- 1 egg, slightly beaten
- 15 ml/1 tbsp soy sauce
- 2 slices ginger root, minced
- 200 g/7 oz canned lychees, drained
- 2½ ml/ ½ tsp salt
- 2½ ml/ ½ tsp salt
- 30 ml/2 tbsp groundnut (peanut) oil
- 30 ml/2 tbsp water
- 30 ml/2 tbsp wine vinegar
- 450 g/1 lb peeled prawns
- 5 ml/1 tsp sugar
- 50 g/2 oz/ ½ cup plain (all-purpose)
- flour
- oil for deep-frying

Directions:

1. Beat together the flour, salt, egg and water to make a batter, adding a little more water if needed.
2. Mix with the prawns until they are well coated.
3. Heat the oil and deep-fry the prawns for a few minutes until crispy and golden.
4. Drain using kitchen paper and lay out on a warmed serving plate.
5. In the meantime, heat the oil and fry the ginger for approximately one minute.
6. Put in the wine vinegar, sugar, salt and soy sauce.
7. Put in the lychees and stir until warm and coated with sauce.
8. Pour over the prawns and serve instantly.

PRAWNS WITH MANGETOUT

Yield: 4 Servings

Ingredients:

- 15 ml/1 tbsp cornflour (cornstarch)

- 15 ml/1 tbsp rice wine or dry sherry
- 15 ml/1 tbsp soy sauce
- 2 cloves garlic, crushed
- 2 slices ginger root, minced
- 2 stalks celery, chopped
- 225 g/8 oz bean sprouts
- 225 g/8 oz mangetout (snow peas)
- 225 g/8 oz peeled prawns
- 4 spring onions (scallions), chopped
- 5 dried Chinese mushrooms
- 5 ml/1 tsp salt
- 60 ml/4 tbsp groundnut (peanut) oil
- 60 ml/4 tbsp water

Directions:

1. Soak the mushrooms in warm water for half an hour then drain.
2. Discard the stalks and slice the caps.
3. Briefly boil the bean sprouts in boiling water for approximately five minutes then eliminate the excess liquid well.
4. Heat half the oil and fry the salt, celery, spring onions and bean sprouts for approximately one minute then remove them from the pan.
5. Heat the rest of the oil and fry the garlic and ginger until slightly browned.
6. Add half the water, the soy sauce, wine or sherry, mangetout and prawns, bring to the boil and simmer for approximately three minutes.
7. Combine the cornflour and rest of the water to a paste, stir into the pan and simmer, stirring, until the sauce, becomes thick.
8. Return the vegetables to the pan, simmer until heated through.
9. Serve Immediately.

PRAWNS WITH MANGO CHUTNEY

Yield: 4 Servings

Ingredients:

- 1 fennel bulb, chopped
- 1 mango
- 100 g/4 oz mango chutney

- 12 king prawns
- 120 ml/4 fl oz/ ½ cup chicken stock
- 2 cloves garlic, chopped
- 2 spring onions (scallions), chopped
- 30 ml/2 tbsp coconut cream
- 30 ml/2 tbsp cornflour (cornstarch)
- 30 ml/2 tbsp mild curry powder
- 45 ml/3 tbsp groundnut (peanut) oil
- 5 ml/1 tsp honey
- 5 ml/1 tsp mustard powder
- juice of 1 lemon
- salt and pepper

Directions:

1. Peel the prawns, leaving the tails intact.
2. Drizzle with salt, pepper and lemon juice then coat with half the cornflour.
3. Peel the mango, chop the flesh away from the stone then dice the flesh.
4. Combine the mustard, honey, coconut cream, curry powder, the rest of the cornflour and the stock.
5. Heat half the oil and fry the garlic, spring onions and fennel for approximately two minutes.
6. Put in the stock mixture, bring to the boil and simmer for approximately one minute.
7. Put in the mango cubes and chutney and heat through gently then transfer to a warmed serving plate.
8. Heat the rest of the oil and stir-fry the prawns for approximately two minutes.
9. Lay out them on the vegetables and serve instantly.

PRAWNS WITH PEPPERS

Yield: 4 Servings

Ingredients:

- 1 green pepper, chopped into chunks
- 10 ml/2 tsp cornflour (cornstarch)
- 2½ ml/ ½ tsp salt
- 30 ml/2 tbsp groundnut (peanut) oil
- 45 ml/2 tbsp tomato purée (paste)

- 450 g/1 lb peeled prawns
- 5 ml/1 tsp rice wine or dry sherry
- 60 ml/4 tbsp water

Directions:

1. Heat the oil and stir-fry the pepper for approximately two minutes.
2. Put in the prawns and tomato purée and stir well.
3. Blend the cornflour water, wine or sherry and salt to a paste, mix it into the pan and simmer, stirring, until the sauce clears and becomes thick.

PRAWNS WITH TOFU

Yield: 4 Servings

Ingredients:

- 1 clove garlic, crushed
- 1 spring onion (scallion), minced
- 15 ml/1 tbsp cornflour (cornstarch)
- 15 ml/1 tbsp soy sauce
- 225 g/8 oz peeled prawns
- 225 g/8 oz tofu, cubed
- 45 ml/3 tbsp groundnut (peanut) oil
- 45 ml/3 tbsp water
- 5 ml/1 tsp sugar
- 90 ml/6 tbsp fish stock

Directions:

1. Heat half the oil and fry the tofu until slightly browned then remove it from the pan.
2. Heat the rest of the oil and stir-fry the spring onions and garlic until slightly browned.
3. Put in the soy sauce, sugar and stock and bring to the boil.
4. Put in the prawns and stir over a low heat for approximately three minutes.
5. Blend the cornflour and water to a paste, stir into the pan and simmer, stirring, until the sauce becomes thick.
6. Return the tofu to the pan and simmer gently until heated through.

PRAWNS WITH TOMATO AND CHILLI SAUCE

Yield: 4 Servings

Ingredients:

- 15 ml/1 tbsp chilli sauce
- 15 ml/1 tbsp cornflour (cornstarch)
- 15 ml/1 tbsp minced garlic
- 15 ml/1 tbsp minced ginger
- 15 ml/1 tbsp minced spring onion
- 15 ml/1 tbsp water
- 450 g/1 lb peeled prawns
- 60 ml/4 tbsp groundnut (peanut) oil
- 60 ml/4 tbsp tomato purée (paste)

Directions:

1. Heat the oil and stir-fry the ginger, garlic and spring onion for approximately one minute.
2. Put in the tomato purée and chilli sauce and mix well.
3. Put in the prawns and stir-fry for approximately two minutes.
4. Blend the cornflour and water to a paste, mix it into the pan and simmer until the sauce becomes thick.
5. Serve Immediately.

PRAWNS WITH TOMATO SAUCE

Yield: 4 Servings

Ingredients:

- 1 clove garlic, crushed
- 10 ml/2 tsp cornflour (cornstarch)
- 120 ml/4 fl oz/ ½ cup fish stock
- 15 ml/1 tbsp rice wine or dry sherry
- 15 ml/1 tbsp soy sauce
- 2 slices ginger root, minced
- 2½ ml/ ½ tsp salt
- 30 ml/2 tbsp groundnut (peanut) oil

- 30 ml/2 tbsp water
- 350 g/12 oz peeled prawns
- 6 ml/4 tbsp tomato ketchup (catsup)

Directions:

1. Heat the oil and stir-fry the garlic, ginger and salt for approximately two minutes.
2. Put in the wine or sherry, soy sauce, tomato ketchup and stock and bring to the boil.
3. Put in the prawns, cover and simmer for approximately two minutes.
4. Combine the cornflour and water to a paste, mix it into the pan and simmer, stirring, until the sauce clears and becomes thick.

PRAWNS WITH TOMATOES

Yield: 4 Servings

Ingredients:

- 2 egg whites
- 225 g/8 oz tomatoes, skinned, seeded and chopped
- 30 ml/2 tbsp cornflour (cornstarch)
- 30 ml/2 tbsp rice wine or dry sherry
- 450 g/1 lb peeled prawns
- 5 ml/1 tsp salt
- oil for deep-frying

Directions:

1. Combine the egg whites, cornflour and salt.
2. Mix in the prawns until they are well coated.
3. Heat the oil and deep-fry the prawns until cooked.
4. Pour off all but 15 ml/1 tbsp of the oil and reheat.
5. Put in the wine or sherry and tomatoes and bring to the boil.
6. Mix in the prawns and heat through quickly and serve.

PRAWNS WITH VEGETABLES

Yield: 4 Servings

Ingredients:

- 120 ml/4 fl oz/ ½ cup chicken stock
- 15 ml/1 tbsp groundnut (peanut) oil
- 2½ ml/ ½ tsp grated ginger root
- 2½ ml/ ½ tsp sugar
- 225 g/8 oz bamboo shoots, sliced
- 225 g/8 oz broccoli florets
- 225 g/8 oz button mushrooms
- 450 g/1 lb peeled prawns
- 5 ml/1 tsp cornflour (cornstarch)
- 5 ml/1 tsp oyster sauce
- pinch of freshly ground pepper

Directions:

1. Heat the oil and stir-fry the broccoli for approximately one minute.
2. Put in the mushrooms and bamboo shoots and stir-fry for approximately two minutes.
3. Put in the prawns and stir-fry for approximately two minutes.
4. Combine the rest of the ingredients and stir into the prawn mixture.
5. Bring to the boil, stirring, then simmer for approximately one minute, stirring constantly.

PRAWNS WITH WATER CHESTNUTS

Yield: 4 Servings

Ingredients:

- 1 clove garlic, minced
- 1 slice ginger root, minced
- 15 ml/1 tbsp cornflour (cornstarch)
- 30 ml/2 tbsp rice wine or dry sherry 225 g/8 oz water chestnuts, sliced
- 30 ml/2 tbsp soy sauce
- 45 ml/3 tbsp water
- 450 g/1 lb peeled prawns
- 60 ml/4 tbsp groundnut (peanut) oil

Directions:

1. Heat the oil and fry the garlic and ginger until slightly browned.
2. Put in the prawns and stir-fry for approximately one minute.
3. Put in the wine or sherry and stir together well.
4. Put in the water chestnuts and stir-fry for approximately five minutes.
5. Add the rest of the ingredients and stir-fry for approximately two minutes.

QUICK-FRIED FISH

Yield: 4 Servings

Ingredients:

- 450 g/1 lb cod fillets, chopped into strips
- oil for deep-frying
- salt
- soy sauce

Directions:

1. Drizzle the fish with salt and soy sauce and allow to stand for 10 minutes.
2. Heat the oil and deep-fry the fish for a few minutes until slightly golden.
3. Drain using kitchen paper and drizzle generously with soy sauce and serve.

SALMON WITH TOFU

Yield: 4 Servings

Ingredients:

- 100 g/4 oz salmon fillet, chopped
- 120 ml/4 fl oz/ ½ cup groundnut (peanut) oil
- 15 ml/1 tbsp cornflour (cornstarch)
- 2 spring onions (scallions), chopped
- 2½ ml/ ½ tsp sesame oil
- 250 ml/8 fl oz/1 cup fish stock
- 45 ml/3 tbsp water
- 450 g/1 lb tofu, cubed
- dash of chilli sauce

Directions:

1. Heat the oil and fry the tofu until slightly browned.
2. Take out of the pan.
3. Reheat the oil and sesame oil and fry the salmon and chilli sauce for approximately one minute.
4. Put in the stock, bring to the boil, then return the tofu to the pan.
5. Simmer gently, uncovered, until the ingredients are cooked through and the liquid has reduced.
6. Blend the cornflour and water to a paste.
7. Mix in a little at a time and simmer, stirring, until the mixture becomes thick.
8. You may not need all the cornflour paste if you have allowed the liquid to reduce.
9. Move to a warmed serving plate and drizzle with the spring onions.

SAUTÉED CRAB MEAT

Yield: 4 Servings

Ingredients:

- 1 clove garlic, crushed
- 1 slice ginger root, minced
- 10 ml/2 tsp cornflour (cornstarch)
- 15 ml/1 tbsp rice wine or dry sherry
- 15 ml/1 tbsp wine vinegar
- 225 g/8 oz crab meat
- 4 spring onions (scallions), finely chopped
- 45 ml/3 tbsp groundnut (peanut) oil
- 45 ml/3 tbsp soy sauce

Directions:

1. Heat the oil and fry the garlic, spring onions and ginger until slightly browned.
2. Put in the crab meat and stir-fry for approximately one minute.
3. Mix the rest of the ingredients and stir them into the pan.
4. Simmer, stirring, until the sauce clears and becomes thick.

SAUTÉED PRAWNS

Yield: 4 Servings

Ingredients:

- 1 slice ginger root, minced
- 15 ml/1 tbsp fish stock or water
- 15 ml/1 tbsp sugar
- 30 ml/2 tbsp rice wine or dry sherry
- 4 spring onions (scallions), chopped
- 450 g/1 lb uncooked prawns
- 5 ml/1 tsp salt
- 5 ml/1 tsp sesame oil
- 90 ml/6 tbsp groundnut (peanut) oil

Directions:

1. Clean the prawns and chop away the tentacles and feet.
2. Heat the oil and fry the prawns until pink.
3. Take out of the pan and pour off all but 30 ml/2 tbsp of oil.
4. Put in the spring onions and ginger and stir-fry for 30 seconds.
5. Add all the rest of the ingredients except the sesame oil and bring to the boil.
6. Simmer, uncovered, for approximately two minutes then return the prawns to the pan and simmer, stirring, for approximately five minutes.
7. Serve sprinkled with sesame oil.

SAUTÉED SWORDFISH

Yield: 4 Servings

Ingredients:

- 1 clove garlic, crushed
- 1 spring onion, chopped
- 2 slices ginger root, minced
- 2½ ml/ ½ tsp freshly ground pepper
- 30 ml/2 tbsp groundnut (peanut) oil
- 30 ml/2 tbsp soy sauce
- 450 g/1 lb swordfish steaks

- 5 ml/1 tsp sugar
- salt

Directions:

1. Drizzle the swordfish steaks on both sides with salt and allow to stand for half an hour.
2. Rinse and pat dry.
3. Heat the oil and add the swordfish.
4. Drizzle with ginger, garlic, salt, pepper, sugar and soy sauce and sauté gently for approximately ten minutes each side.
5. Put in the spring onions and fry for another 1 minute and serve.

SCALLOP AND ONION STIR-FRY

Yield: 4 Servings

Ingredients:

- 1 onion, sliced
- 15 ml/1 tbsp rice wine or dry sherry
- 45 ml/3 tbsp groundnut (peanut) oil
- 450 g/1 lb shelled scallops, quartered
- salt and freshly ground pepper

Directions:

1. Heat the oil and fry the onion until softened.
2. Put in the scallops and stir-fry until slightly browned.
3. Season with salt and pepper, drizzle with wine or sherry and serve instantly.

SCALLOP SCRAMBLE WITH HERBS

Yield: 4 Servings

Ingredients:

- 15 ml/1 tbsp groundnut (peanut) oil
- 15 ml/1 tbsp rice wine or dry sherry
- 225 g/8 oz shelled scallops

- 30 ml/2 tbsp chopped fresh coriander
- 4 eggs, beaten
- salt and freshly ground pepper

Directions:

1. Put the scallops in a steamer and steam for about 3 minutes until cooked, depending on the size.
2. Take out of the steamer and drizzle with coriander.
3. Beat the eggs with the wine or sherry and season to taste with salt and pepper.
4. Mix in the scallops and coriander.
5. Heat the oil and fry the egg and scallop mixture, stirring repetitively, until the eggs are just set.
6. Serve as soon as possible.

SCALLOPS WITH BAMBOO SHOOTS

Yield: 4 Servings

Ingredients:

- 15 ml/1 tbsp sugar
- 150 ml cup water
- 2 slices ginger root, chopped
- 225 g/8 oz bamboo shoots, sliced
- 225 g/8 oz mushrooms, quartered
- 30 ml/2 tbsp cornflour (cornstarch)
- 30 ml/2 tbsp wine vinegar
- 300 ml water
- 45 ml/3 tbsp soy sauce
- 450 g/1 lb shelled scallops
- 6 spring onions (scallions), chopped
- 60 ml/4 tbsp groundnut (peanut) oil
- salt and freshly ground pepper

Directions:

1. Heat the oil and fry the spring onions and mushrooms for approximately two minutes.
2. Put in the sugar, scallops, ginger, bamboo shoots, salt and pepper, cover and cook for approximately five minutes.

3. Put in the water and wine vinegar, bring to the boil, cover and simmer for approximately five minutes.
4. Blend the cornflour and water to a paste, stir into the pan and simmer, stirring, until the sauce becomes thick.
5. Season with soy sauce and serve.

SCALLOPS WITH BROCCOLI

Yield: 4 Servings

Ingredients:

- ½ small carrot, sliced
- 1 banana, sliced
- 1 clove garlic, crushed
- 15 ml/1 tbsp water
- 2½ ml/ ½ tsp bicarbonate of soda (baking soda)
- 2½ ml/ ½ tsp chilli sauce
- 2½ ml/ ½ tsp tomato purée (paste)
- 2½ ml/ ½ tsp wine vinegar
- 275 g/10 oz broccoli
- 3 slices ginger root, minced
- 30 ml/2 tbsp groundnut (peanut) oil
- 350 g/12 oz scallops, sliced
- 45 ml/3 tbsp plain (all-purpose) flour
- 5 ml/1 tsp sesame oil
- oil for deep-frying
- salt

Directions:

1. Combine the scallops with the ginger, carrot and garlic and leave to stand.
2. Combine the flour, bicarbonate of soda, 15 ml/ 1 tbsp of oil and the water to a paste and use to coat the banana slices.
3. Heat the oil and deep-fry the banana until a golden-brown colour is achieved then eliminate the excess liquid and arrange around a warmed serving plate.
4. In the meantime, cook the broccoli in boiling, salted water until just soft then drain.
5. Heat the rest of the oil with the sesame oil and stir-fry the broccoli briefly then arrange it round the plate with the bananas.

6. Put in the chilli sauce, wine vinegar and tomato purée to the pan and stir-fry the scallops until just cooked.
7. Spoon on to the serving plate and serve instantly.

SCALLOPS WITH EGG

Yield: 4 Servings

Ingredients:

- 15 ml/1 tbsp soy sauce
- 2 eggs, slightly beaten
- 2½ ml/ ½ tsp salt
- 25 g/1 oz smoked ham, chopped
- 30 ml/2 tbsp rice wine or dry sherry
- 350 g/12 oz shelled scallops
- 45 ml/3 tbsp groundnut (peanut) oil
- 5 ml/1 tsp sugar
- pinch of freshly ground pepper

Directions:

1. Heat the oil and stir-fry the scallops for 30 seconds.
2. Put in the ham and stir-fry for approximately one minute.
3. Put in the wine or sherry, sugar, salt and pepper and stir-fry for approximately one minute.
4. Put in the eggs and stir gently over a high heat until the ingredients are well coated in egg.
5. Serve sprinkled with soy sauce.

SCALLOPS WITH GINGER

Yield: 4 Servings

Ingredients:

- 15 ml/1 tbsp cornflour (cornstarch)
- 2 spring onions (scallions), thickly sliced

- 2½ ml/ ½ tsp salt
- 3 slices ginger root, minced
- 45 ml/3 tbsp groundnut (peanut) oil
- 450 g/1 lb shelled scallops, halved
- 60 ml/4 tbsp water

Directions:

1. Heat the oil and fry the salt and ginger for 30 seconds.
2. Put in the spring onions and stir-fry until slightly browned.
3. Put in the scallops and stir-fry for approximately three minutes.
4. Combine the cornflour and water to a paste, add to the pan and simmer, stirring, until thickened.
5. Serve Immediately.

SCALLOPS WITH HAM

Yield: 4 Servings

Ingredients:

- 1 onion, finely chopped
- 100 g/4 oz smoked ham, chopped
- 2 slices ginger root, minced
- 2½ ml/ ½ tsp salt
- 250 ml/8 fl oz/1 cup rice wine or dry sherry
- 450 g/1 lb shelled scallops, halved

Directions:

1. Put the scallops into a container and add the wine or sherry.
2. Cover and allow to marinate for half an hour, turning occasionally, then eliminate the excess liquid the scallops and discard the marinade.
3. Put the scallops in an ovenproof dish with the rest of the ingredients.
4. Put the dish on a rack in a steamer, cover and steam over boiling water for about 6 minutes until the scallops are soft.

SCALLOPS WITH PEPPERS

Yield: 4 Servings

Ingredients:

- 1 clove garlic, crushed
- 15 ml/1 tbsp soy sauce
- 15 ml/1 tbsp yellow bean sauce
- 2 red peppers, diced
- 2 slices ginger root, chopped
- 3 spring onions (scallions), chopped
- 30 ml/2 tbsp groundnut (peanut) oil
- 30 ml/2 tbsp rice wine or dry sherry
- 450 g/1 lb shelled scallops
- 5 ml/1 tsp sesame oil
- 5 ml/1 tsp sugar

Directions:

1. Heat the oil and stir-fry the spring onions, garlic and ginger for 30 seconds.
2. Put in the peppers and stir-fry for approximately one minute.
3. Put in the scallops and stir-fry for 30 seconds then add the rest of the ingredients and cook for about 3 minutes until the scallops are soft.

SCALLOPS WITH VEGETABLES

Yield: 4 Servings

Ingredients:

- 1 clove garlic, crushed
- 10 ml/2 tsp grated ginger root
- 2 onions
- 20 ml/4 tsp cornflour (cornstarch)
- 225 g/8 oz green beans, diagonally sliced
- 250 ml/8 fl oz/1 cup chicken stock
- 3 stalks celery, diagonally sliced
- 30 ml/2 tbsp groundnut (peanut) oil
- 30 ml/2 tbsp rice wine or dry sherry
- 30 ml/2 tbsp soy sauce
- 4 dried Chinese mushrooms

- 425 g/15 oz canned baby corn cobs
- 450 g/1 lb shelled scallops, quartered
- 6 spring onions (scallions), sliced

Directions:

1. Soak the mushrooms in warm water for half an hour then drain.
2. Discard the stalks and slice the caps.
3. Chop the onions into wedges and separate the layers.
4. Heat the oil and stir-fry the onions, celery, beans, ginger and garlic for approximately three minutes.
5. Blend the cornflour with a little of the stock then mix in the rest of the stock, wine or sherry and soy sauce.
6. Put into the wok and bring to the boil, stirring.
7. Put in the mushrooms, scallops, spring onions and corn and stir-fry for approximately five minutes until the scallops are soft.

SESAME SEED FISH

Yield: 4 Servings

Ingredients:

- 1 egg, slightly beaten
- 1 onion, chopped
- 10 ml/2 tsp brown sugar
- 120 ml/4 fl oz/ ½ cup rice wine or dry sherry
- 15 ml/1 tbsp cornflour (cornstarch)
- 2 slices ginger root, minced
- 2½ ml/ ½ tsp salt
- 45 ml/3 tbsp plain (all-purpose) flour
- 450 g/1 lb fish fillets, chopped into strips
- 60 ml/6 tbsp sesame seeds
- oil for deep-frying

Directions:

1. Put the fish into a container.
2. Combine the onion, ginger, wine or sherry, sugar and salt, add to the fish and allow to marinate for half an hour, turning occasionally.

3. Beat the egg, cornflour and flour to make a batter.
4. Immerse the fish in the batter then press into the sesame seeds.
5. Heat the oil and deep-fry the fish strips for about 1 minute until golden and crispy.

SOFT-FRIED PRAWNS

Yield: 4 Servings

Ingredients:

- 1 egg white
- 350 g/12 oz peeled prawns
- 5 ml/1 tsp rice wine or dry sherry
- 75 g/3 oz/ cornflour (cornstarch)
- oil for deep-frying
- salt

Directions:

1. Beat together the cornflour, egg white, wine or sherry and a pinch of salt to make a thick batter.
2. Immerse the prawns in the batter until they are well coated.
3. Heat the oil until moderately hot and fry the prawns for a few minutes until a golden-brown colour is achieved.
4. Remove from the oil, reheat it until hot then fry the prawns again until crisp and brown.

SOY FISH WITH OYSTER SAUCE

Yield: 4 Servings

Ingredients:

- 1 clove garlic, crushed
- 1 large bass or similar fish
- 2 slices ginger root, minced
- 250 ml/8 fl oz/1 cup fish stock
- 3 spring onions (scallions), minced
- 30 ml/2 tbsp soy sauce

- 45 ml/3 tbsp oyster sauce
- 5 ml/1 tsp sugar
- 60 ml/4 tbsp groundnut (peanut) oil
- salt

Directions:

1. Clean and scale the fish and score diagonally a few times on each side.
2.
3. Drizzle with salt and allow to stand for 10 minutes.
4. Heat most of the oil and fry the fish until browned on both sides, turning once.
5. In the meantime, heat the rest of the oil in a separate pan and fry the spring onions, ginger and garlic until slightly browned.
6. Put in the oyster sauce, soy sauce and sugar and stir-fry for approximately one minute.
7. Put in the stock and bring to the boil.
8. Pour the mixture into the browned fish, return to the boil, cover and simmer for about 15 minutes until the fish is cooked, turning once or twice during cooking.

SQUID PARCELS

Yield: 4 Servings

Ingredients:

- 1 egg, beaten
- 100 g/4 oz smoked ham
- 100 g/4 oz tofu
- 15 ml/1 tbsp plain (all-purpose) flour
- 2½ ml/ ½ tsp sesame oil
- 2½ ml/ ½ tsp sugar
- 450 g/1 lb squid
- 8 dried Chinese mushrooms
- 8 wonton skins
- oil for deep-frying
- salt and freshly ground pepper

Directions:

1. Soak the mushrooms in warm water for half an hour then drain.
2. Discard the stalks.

3. Trim the squid and chop into 8 pieces.
4. Chop the ham and tofu into 8 pieces.
5. Put them all into a container.
6. Combine the egg with the flour, sugar, sesame oil, salt and pepper.
7. Pour over the ingredients in the bowl and mix together gently.
8. Lay out a mushroom cap and a piece each of squid, ham and tofu just below the centre of each wonton skin.
9. Fold up the bottom corner, fold in the sides then roll up, moistening the edges with water to seal.
10. Heat the oil and deep-fry the parcels for approximately eight minutes until a golden-brown colour is achieved.
11. Drain thoroughly and serve.

SQUID STIR-FRY

Yield: 4 Servings

Ingredients:

- 15 ml/1 tbsp rice wine or dry sherry
- 15 ml/1 tbsp soy sauce
- 15 ml/1 tbsp water
- 2 slices ginger root, minced
- 3 spring onions (scallions), thickly sliced
- 45 ml/3 tbsp groundnut (peanut) oil
- 450 g/1 lb squid, chopped into chunks
- 5 ml/1 tsp cornflour (cornstarch)

Directions:

1. Heat the oil and fry the spring onions and ginger until softened.
2. Put in the squid and stir-fry until coated in oil.
3. Put in the soy sauce and wine or sherry, cover and simmer for approximately two minutes.
4. Combine the cornflour and water to a paste, put it into the pan and simmer, stirring, until the sauce becomes thick and the squid is soft.

SQUID WITH BEAN SPROUTS

Yield: 4 Servings

Ingredients:

- 1 red chilli pepper, shredded
- 100 g/4 oz bean sprouts
- 15 ml/1 tbsp rice wine or dry sherry
- 15 ml/1 tbsp soy sauce
- 2 slices ginger root, shredded
- 2 spring onions (scallions), shredded
- 30 ml/2 tbsp groundnut (peanut) oil
- 450 g/1 lb squid
- salt

Directions:

1. Remove the head, guts and membrane from the squid and chop into large pieces.
2. Cut a criss-cross pattern on each piece.
3. Bring a pan of water to the boil, add the squid and simmer until the pieces roll up then remove and drain.
4. Heat half the oil and stir-fry the squid quickly.
5. Drizzle with wine or sherry.
6. In the meantime, heat the rest of the oil and stir-fry the bean sprouts until just soft.
7. Season with soy sauce and salt.
8. Put the chilli pepper, ginger and spring onions around a serving plate.
9. Pile the bean sprouts in the centre and top with the squid.
10. Serve Immediately.

SQUID WITH DRIED MUSHROOMS

Yield: 4 Servings

Ingredients:

- 1 slice ginger root, minced
- 150 ml fish stock
- 2 spring onions (scallions), finely chopped
- 225 g/8 oz bamboo shoots, chopped into strips

- 30 ml/2 tbsp cornflour (cornstarch)
- 45 ml/3 tbsp groundnut (peanut) oil
- 45 ml/3 tbsp soy sauce
- 450 g/1 lb squid rings
- 50 g/2 oz dried Chinese mushrooms

Directions:

1. Soak the mushrooms in warm water for half an hour then drain.
2. Discard the stems and slice the caps.
3. Briefly boil the squid rings for a few seconds in boiling water.
4. Heat the oil then mix in the mushrooms, soy sauce, spring onions and ginger and stir-fry for approximately two minutes.
5. Put in the squid and bamboo shoots and stir-fry for approximately two minutes.
6. Combine the cornflour and stock and mix it into the pan.
7. Simmer, stirring, until the sauce clears and becomes thick.

SQUID WITH VEGETABLES

Yield: 4 Servings

Ingredients:

- 1 onion, sliced
- 100 g/4 oz bamboo shoots, sliced
- 100 g/4 oz mangetout (snow peas)
- 15 ml/1 tbsp water
- 2 stalks celery, diagonally sliced
- 45 ml/3 tbsp groundnut (peanut) oil
- 450 g/1 lb squid, chopped into chunks
- 5 ml/ 1 tsp cornflour (cornstarch)
- 5 ml/1 tsp salt
- 5 ml/1 tsp sugar
- 60 ml/4 tbsp chicken stock

Directions:

1. Heat the oil and fry the onion and salt until slightly browned.
2. Put in the squid and fry until coated in oil.
3. Put in the bamboo shoots and celery and stir-fry for approximately three minutes.

4. Put in the stock and sugar, bring to the boil, cover and simmer for approximately three minutes until the vegetables are just soft.
5. Mix in the mangetout.
6. Combine the cornflour and water to a paste, stir into the pan and simmer, stirring, until the sauce becomes thick.

STEAMED BASS

Yield: 4 Servings

Ingredients:

- 1 large bass or similar fish
- 15 ml/1 tbsp rice wine or dry sherry
- 15 ml/1 tbsp salt
- 2.25 l/4 pts/10 cups water
- 3 slices ginger root, minced
- 30 ml/2 tbsp groundnut (peanut) oil

Directions:

1. Clean and scale the fish and score both sides diagonally several times.
2. Bring the water to a rolling boil in a large pan and add the rest of the ingredients.
3. Lower the fish into the water, cover tightly, turn off the heat and allow to stand for half an hour until the fish is cooked.

STEAMED CLAMS

Yield: 4 Servings

Ingredients:

- 24 clams

Directions:

1. Scrub the clams comprehensively.
2. then soak them in salted water for a few hours.
3. Rinse under running water and lay out on a shallow ovenproof plate.
4. Put on a rack in a steamer, cover and steam over gently simmering water for approximately ten minutes until all the clams have opened.

5. Discard any that remain closed.
6. Serve with dips.

STEAMED FISH BALLS

Yield: 4 Servings

Ingredients:

- 1 egg, slightly beaten
- 1 slice ginger root, minced
- 15 ml/1 tbsp cornflour (cornstarch) 15 ml/1 tbsp rice wine or dry sherry
- 2½ ml/ ½ tsp salt
- 450 g/1 lb minced (ground) cod
- pinch of freshly ground pepper

Directions:

1. Mix all the ingredients together well and mould into walnut-sized balls.
2. Dust with a little flour if needed.
3. Lay out in a shallow ovenproof dish.
4. Stand the dish on a rack in a steamer, cover and steam over gently simmering water for approximately ten minutes until cooked.

STEAMED FISH ROULADES

Yield: 4 Servings

Ingredients:

- 1 egg, beaten
- 100 g/4 oz bean sprouts
- 100 g/4 oz green peas
- 225 g/8 oz Chinese cabbage, briefly boiled
- 30 ml/2 tbsp cornflour (cornstarch)
- 30 ml/2 tbsp oyster sauce
- 30 ml/2 tbsp plum sauce
- 30 ml/2 tbsp soy sauce

- 450 g/1 lb haddock fillets, skinned and diced
- 5 ml/1 tsp rice wine or dry sherry
- 50 g/2 oz/ ½ cup walnuts, chopped
- 6 dried Chinese mushrooms
- juice of 1 lemon
- salt and pepper

Directions:

1. Put the fish into a container.
2. Combine the lemon juice, soy, oyster and plum sauces, wine or sherry and salt and pepper.
3. Pour over the fish and allow to marinate for half an hour.
4. Put in the vegetables, nuts, egg and cornflour and mix together well.
5. Lay 3 Chinese leaves on top of each other, spoon on some of the fish mixture and roll up.
6. Continue until all the ingredients have been used up.
7. Put the rolls in a steam basket, cover and cook over gently simmering water for half an hour.

STEAMED LOBSTER WITH HAM

Yield: 4 Servings

Ingredients:

- 15 ml/1 tbsp chopped fresh parsley
- 15 ml/1 tbsp chopped smoked ham
- 15 ml/1 tbsp soy sauce
- 4 eggs, slightly beaten
- 450 g/1 lb lobster meat, flaked
- 5 ml/1 tsp salt
- 60 ml/4 tbsp water

Directions:

1. Beat the eggs with the water, salt and soy sauce.
2. Pour into an ovenproof bowl and drizzle with lobster meat.
3. Put the bowl on a rack in a steamer, cover and steam for approximately 20 minutes until the eggs are set.

4. Serve garnished with ham and parsley.

STEAMED MUSSELS

Yield: 4 Servings

Ingredients:

- 1.5 kg/3 lb mussels, scrubbed and bearded
- 3 spring onions (scallions), finely chopped
- 45 ml/3 tbsp soy sauce

Directions:

1. Put the mussels on a rack in a steamer, cover and steam over boiling water for approximately ten minutes until all the mussels have opened.
2. Discard any that remain closed.
3. Move to a heated serving dish and serve sprinkled with soy sauce and spring onions.

STEAMED PLAICE WITH CHINESE MUSHROOMS

Yield: 4 Servings

Ingredients:

- 1 clove garlic, crushed
- 1 slice ginger root, minced
- 15 ml/1 tbsp rice wine or dry sherry
- 15 ml/1 tbsp soy sauce
- 350 g/12 oz cooked long-grain rice
- 4 dried Chinese mushrooms
- 450 g/1 lb plaice fillets, cubed
- 5 ml/1 tsp brown sugar

Directions:

1. Soak the mushrooms in warm water for half an hour then drain.
2. Discard the stems and chop the caps.

3. Mix with the plaice, garlic, ginger, soy sauce, wine or sherry and sugar, cover and allow to marinate for one hour.
4. Put the rice in a steamer and arrange the fish on top.
5. Steam for about 30 minutes until the fish is cooked.

STIR-FRIED CLAMS

Yield: 4 Servings

Ingredients:

- 1 onion, minced
- 2½ ml/ ½ tsp salt
- 24 clams
- 4 cloves garlic, minced
- 60 ml/4 tbsp groundnut (peanut) oil

Directions:

1. Scrub the clams comprehensively.
2. then soak them in salted water for a few hours.
3. Rinse under running water then pat dry.
4. Heat the oil and fry the garlic, onion and salt until softened.
5. Put in the clams, cover and cook over a low heat for approximately five minutes until all the shells have opened.
6. Discard any that remain closed.
7. Stir-fry gently for another 1 minute, basting with oil.

STIR-FRIED CRAB MEAT

Yield: 4 Servings

Ingredients:

- 15 ml/1 tbsp cornflour (cornstarch)
- 2 slices ginger root, minced
- 2 spring onions (scallions), minced
- 2½ ml/ ½ tsp salt

- 30 ml/2 tbsp groundnut (peanut) oil
- 30 ml/2 tbsp rice wine or dry sherry
- 30 ml/2 tbsp soy sauce
- 450 g/1 lb crab meat, flaked
- 60 ml/4 tbsp water

Directions:

1. Heat the oil and stir-fry the crab meat, spring onions and ginger for approximately one minute.
2. Put in the soy sauce, wine or sherry and salt, cover and simmer for approximately three minutes.
3. Combine the cornflour and water to a paste, stir into the pan and simmer, stirring, until the sauce clears and becomes thick.

STIR-FRIED CRAB WITH PORK

Yield: 4 Servings

Ingredients:

- 100 g/4 oz minced (ground) pork
- 15 ml/1 tbsp rice wine or dry sherry
- 15 ml/1 tbsp soy sauce
- 2 eggs, slightly beaten
- 2 slices ginger root, minced
- 30 ml/2 tbsp groundnut (peanut) oil
- 30 ml/2 tbsp water
- 350 g/12 oz crab meat, flaked
- 4 spring onions (scallions), chopped into strips
- salt and freshly ground pepper

Directions:

1. Heat the oil and stir-fry the pork until slightly coloured.
2. Put in the crab meat and ginger and stir-fry for approximately one minute.
3. Mix in the eggs.
4. Put in the soy sauce, wine or sherry, water, salt and pepper and simmer for about 4 minutes, stirring.
5. Serve garnished with spring onions.

STIR-FRIED LOBSTER

Yield: 4 Servings

Ingredients:

- 1 clove garlic, crushed
- 15 ml/1 tbsp cornflour (cornstarch)
- 150 ml chicken stock
- 2½ ml/ ½ tsp salt
- 30 ml/2 tbsp groundnut (peanut) oil
- 350 g/12 oz bean sprouts
- 4 spring onions (scallions), thickly sliced
- 450 g/1 lb lobster tails
- 50 g/2 oz button mushrooms

Directions:

1. Bring a pan of water to the boil, add the lobster tails and boil for approximately one minute.
2. Drain, cool, remove the shell and chop into thick slices.
3. Heat the oil with the garlic and salt and fry until the garlic is slightly browned.
4. Put in the lobster and stir-fry for approximately one minute.
5. Put in the bean sprouts and mushrooms and stir-fry for approximately one minute.
6. Mix in the spring onions.
7. Add most of the stock, bring to the boil, cover and simmer for approximately three minutes.
8. Combine the cornflour with the rest of the stock, mix it into the pan and simmer, stirring, until the sauce clears and becomes thick.

STIR-FRIED PRAWNS IN THEIR SHELLS

Yield: 4 Servings

Ingredients:

- 120 ml/4 fl oz/ ½ cup tomato ketchup (catsup)
- 15 ml/1 tbsp cornflour (cornstarch)

- 15 ml/1 tbsp rice wine or dry sherry
- 15 ml/1 tbsp soy sauce
- 15 ml/1 tbsp sugar
- 2½ ml/ ½ tsp salt
- 3 slices ginger root, minced
- 3 spring onions (scallions), chopped
- 60 ml/4 tbsp groundnut (peanut) oil
- 60 ml/4 tbsp water
- 750 g/1 ½ lb unpeeled prawns

Directions:

1. Heat the oil and fry the prawns for approximately one minute if cooked or until they turn pink if they are uncooked.
2. Put in the spring onions, ginger, salt and wine or sherry and stir-fry for approximately one minute.
3. Put in the tomato ketchup, soy sauce and sugar and stir-fry for approximately one minute.
4. Combine the cornflour and water, mix it into the pan and simmer, stirring, until the sauce clears and becomes thick.

STIR-FRIED PRAWNS WITH CHICKEN

Yield: 4 Servings

Ingredients:

- 100 g/4 oz bamboo shoots, sliced
- 100 g/4 oz mushrooms, sliced
- 15 ml/1 tbsp cornflour (cornstarch)
- 2 cloves garlic, crushed
- 225 g/8 oz cooked chicken, finely sliced
- 225 g/8 oz mangetout (snow peas)
- 225 g/8 oz peeled prawns
- 30 ml/2 tbsp groundnut (peanut) oil
- 45 ml/3 tbsp water
- 75 ml/5 tbsp fish stock

Directions:

1. Heat the oil and fry the garlic until slightly browned.
2. Put in the chicken, bamboo shoots and mushrooms and stir-fry until well coated in oil.
3. Put in the stock and bring to the boil.
4. Put in the prawns and mangetout, cover and simmer for approximately five minutes.
5. Combine the cornflour and water to a paste, stir into the pan and simmer, stirring, until the sauce clears and becomes thick.
6. Serve Immediately.

STIR-FRIED PRAWNS WITH PORK

Yield: 4 Servings

Ingredients:

- 1 egg white
- 100 g/4 oz lean pork, shredded
- 15 ml/1 tbsp water (optional)
- 225 g/8 oz peeled prawns
- 45 ml/3 tbsp cornflour (cornstarch)
- 45 ml/3 tbsp fish stock
- 5 ml/1 tsp salt
- 5 ml/1 tsp sesame oil
- 60 ml/4 tbsp rice wine or dry sherry
- 90 ml/6 tbsp groundnut (peanut) oil

Directions:

1. Put the prawns and pork in separate bowls.
2. Combine 45 ml/ 3 tbsp of wine or sherry, the egg white, 30 ml/2 tbsp of cornflour and the salt to make a loose batter, adding the water if needed.
3. Divide the mixture between the pork and prawns and stir well to coat them evenly.
4. Heat the oil and fry the pork and prawns for a few minutes until a golden-brown colour is achieved.
5. Take out of the pan and pour off all but 15 ml/1 tbsp of oil.
6. Put in the stock to the pan with the rest of the wine or sherry and cornflour.
7. Bring to the boil and simmer, stirring, until the sauce becomes thick.
8. Pour over the prawns and pork and serve sprinkled with sesame oil.

SUB GUM

Yield: 4 Servings

Ingredients:

- 1 clove garlic, crushed
- 1 slice ginger root, chopped
- 100 g/4 oz bamboo shoots, chopped into strips
- 100 g/4 oz chicken breast, chopped into strips
- 100 g/4 oz ham, chopped into strips
- 100 g/4 oz water chestnuts, chopped into strips
- 2 spring onions (scallions), chopped
- 225 g/8 oz peeled prawns
- 30 ml/2 tbsp groundnut (peanut) oil
- 30 ml/2 tbsp rice wine or dry sherry
- 30 ml/2 tbsp soy sauce
- 5 ml/1 tsp cornflour (cornstarch)
- 5 ml/1 tsp salt
- 5 ml/1 tsp sugar

Directions:

1. Heat the oil and fry the spring onions, garlic and ginger until slightly browned.
2. Put in the chicken and stir-fry for approximately one minute.
3. Put in the ham, bamboo shoots and water chestnuts and stir-fry for approximately three minutes.
4. Put in the prawns and stir-fry for approximately one minute.
5. Put in the soy sauce, wine or sherry, salt and sugar and stir-fry for approximately two minutes.
6. Combine the cornflour with a little water, mix it into the pan and simmer, stirring for approximately two minutes.

SWEET AND SOUR CARP

Yield: 4 Servings

Ingredients:

- 1 large carp or similar fish

- 1 slice ginger root, finely chopped
- 15 ml/1 tbsp rice wine or dry sherry
- 150 g sugar
- 250 ml/8 fl oz/1 cup boiling water
- 250 ml/8 fl oz/1 cup vegetable oil
- 3 spring onions (scallions), finely chopped
- 30 ml/2 tbsp soy sauce
- 300 g cornflour (cornstarch)
- 5 ml/1 tsp salt
- 75 ml/5 tbsp wine vinegar

Directions:

1. Clean and scale the fish and soak it for several hours in cold water.
2. Drain and pat dry then score each side several times.
3. Reserve 30 ml/2 tbsp of cornflour then progressively mix enough water into the rest of the cornflour to make a stiff batter.
4. Coat the fish in the batter.
5. Heat the oil until very hot and deep-fry the fish until crisp on the outside then turn down the heat and carry on frying until the fish is soft.
6. In the meantime, mix together the rest of the cornflour, the soy sauce, salt, sugar, wine vinegar, wine or sherry, spring onions and ginger.
7. When the fish is cooked, transfer it to a warm serving plate.
8. Put in the sauce mixture and the water to the oil and bring to the boil, stirring well until the sauce becomes thick.
9. Pour over the fish and serve immediately.

SWEET AND SOUR FISH

Yield: 4 Servings

Ingredients:

- 1 egg, beaten
- 1 green pepper, chopped into strips
- 1 large bass or similar fish
- 1 onion, chopped into wedges
- 100 g/4 oz canned pineapple chunks in syrup
- 100 g/4 oz/ ½ cup brown sugar

- 15 ml/1 tbsp cornflour (cornstarch)
- 15 ml/1 tbsp groundnut (peanut) oil
- 15 ml/1 tbsp soy sauce
- 15 ml/1 tbsp tomato purée (paste)
- 3 spring onions (scallions), chopped
- 50 g/2 oz cornflour (cornstarch)
- 60 ml/4 tbsp chicken stock
- 60 ml/4 tbsp wine vinegar
- For the sauce:
- oil for frying

Directions:

1. Clean the fish and remove the fins and head if you prefer.
2.
3. Coat it in beaten egg then in cornflour.
4. Heat the oil and fry the fish until cooked through.
5. Drain thoroughly and keep warm.
6. To make the sauce, heat the oil and fry the pepper, drained pineapple and onion for 4 minutes.
7. Add 30 ml/2 tbsp of the pineapple syrup, the sugar, stock, wine vinegar, tomato purée, cornflour and soy sauce and bring to the boil, stirring.
8. Simmer, stirring, until the sauce clears and becomes thick.
9. Pour over the fish and serve sprinkled with spring onions.

SWEET AND SOUR PRAWNS

Yield: 4 Servings

Ingredients:

- 1 clove garlic, crushed
- 1 slice ginger root, chopped
- 1 spring onion (scallion), chopped
- 10 ml/2 tsp soy sauce
- 15 ml/1 tbsp cornflour (cornstarch)
- 30 ml/2 tbsp water
- 350 g/12 oz peeled prawns
- 5 ml/1 tsp rice wine or dry sherry

- 75 ml/5 tbsp brown sugar
- 75 ml/5 tbsp wine vinegar
- 8 slices stale bread, cubed
- oil for deep-frying

Directions:

1. Heat the oil and fry the bread cubes until a golden-brown colour is achieved.
2. Take out of the pan and eliminate the excess liquid well.
3. Pour off all but 30 ml/2 tbsp of the oil.
4. Reheat the oil and fry the onion, garlic and ginger until slightly browned.
5. Put in the prawns, sugar and wine vinegar and stir-fry for approximately two minutes.
6. Put in the cornflour, water, soy sauce and wine or sherry and stir-fry for approximately three minutes.
7. Return the croutons to the pan and stir together well and serve.

TROUT WITH CARROTS

Yield: 4 Servings

Ingredients:

- 1 clove garlic, crushed
- 1 slice ginger root, minced
- 15 ml/1 tbsp groundnut (peanut) oil
- 15 ml/1 tbsp rice wine or dry sherry
- 15 ml/1 tbsp soy sauce
- 2 carrots, chopped into strips
- 25 g/1 oz bamboo shoots, chopped into strips
- 25 g/1 oz water chestnuts, chopped into strips
- 4 trout

Directions:

1. Heat the oil and fry the garlic and ginger until slightly browned.
2. Put in the fish, cover and fry until the fish turns opaque.
3. Put in the carrots, bamboo shoots, chestnuts, soy sauce and wine or sherry, stir carefully, cover and simmer for about 5 minutes.

TROUT WITH LEMON SAUCE

Yield: 4 Servings

Ingredients:

- 150 ml/¬º pt/generous ½ cup lemon juice
- 175 ml water
- 2 egg whites
- 2 slices ginger root, chopped into strips
- 30 ml/2 tbsp cornflour (cornstarch)
- 375 g/12 oz/3 cups plain (all-purpose) flour
- 4 trout
- 450 ml/2 cups chicken stock
- 5 cm/2 in square piece lemon rind
- 8 spring onions (scallions), finely sliced
- 90 ml/6 tbsp brown sugar
- oil for deep-frying

Directions:

1. To make the sauce, mix together the stock, lemon rind and juice, sugar and for approximately five minutes.
2. Turn off the heat, strain and return to the pan.
3. Combine the cornflour with a little water then mix it into the pan.
4. Simmer for approximately five minutes, stirring often.
5. Turn off the heat and keep the sauce warm.
6. Lightly coat the fish on both sides with a little of the flour.
7. Beat the rest of the flour with the water and 10 ml/2 tsp of oil until smooth.
8. Beat the egg whites until stiff but not dry and fold them into the batter.
9. Heat the rest of the oil.
10. Immerse the fish in the batter to coat it completely.
11. Cook the fish for approximately ten minutes, turning once, until cooked through and golden.
12. Drain on kitchen paper.
13. Put the fish on a warmed serving plate.
14. Stir the spring onions into the warm sauce, pour over the fish and serve immediately.

WEST LAKE FISH

Yield: 4 Servings

Ingredients:

- 1 mullet
- 1 red chilli pepper, chopped
- 30 ml/2 tbsp groundnut (peanut) oil
- 30 ml/2 tbsp red wine vinegar
- 30 ml/2 tbsp soy sauce
- 30 ml/2 tbsp water
- 4 slices ginger root, shredded
- 4 spring onions (scallions), shredded
- 45 ml/3 tbsp brown sugar
- freshly ground pepper

Directions:

1. Clean and trim the fish and make 2 or 3 diagonal cuts on each side.
2. Heat the oil and stir-fry half the spring onions, the chilli pepper and ginger for 30 seconds.
3. Put in the fish and fry until slightly browned on both sides.
4. Put in the sugar, wine vinegar, water, soy sauce and pepper, bring to the boil, cover and simmer for about 20 minutes until the fish is cooked and the sauce has reduced.
5. Serve garnished with the rest of the spring onions.

BEEF

The Chinese way of cooking beef is quick and easy, and hence calls for the costlier and softer cuts of meat for the recipe to turn out tender. If you're on a budget, feel free to mix small quantities of the costly beef with cheaper vegetables to increase the serving size.

BAKED BEEF CURRY

Yield: 4 Servings

Ingredients:

- 1 hard-boiled (hard-cooked) egg, sliced
- 100 g/4 oz peas
- 15 ml/1 tbsp curry powder
- 15 ml/1 tbsp soy sauce
- 2 carrots, chopped
- 2 onions, chopped
- 225 g/8 oz cooked long-grain rice, hot
- 375 ml/13 fl oz/1 ½ cups milk
- 45 ml/3 tbsp butter
- 45 ml/3 tbsp plain (all-purpose) flour
- 450 g/1 lb cooked beef, chopped
- salt and freshly ground pepper

Directions:

1. Melt the butter, mix in the curry powder and flour and cook for approximately one minute.
2. Mix in the milk and soy sauce, bring to the boil and simmer, stirring, for approximately two minutes.
3. Season with salt and pepper.
4. Put in the beef, peas, carrots and onions and stir thoroughly to coat with the sauce.
5. Mix in the rice then transfer the mixture to an ovenproof dish and bake in a preheated over at 200¬∞C/ 400¬∞F/gas mark 6 for approximately 20 minutes until the vegetables are soft.
6. Serve garnished with slices of hard-boiled egg.

BARBECUED BEEF

Yield: 4 Servings

Ingredients:

- 10 ml/2 tsp sugar
- 2 cloves garlic, crushed
- 2½ ml/ ½ tsp freshly ground pepper
- 450 g/1 lb lean steak, sliced
- 5 ml/1 tsp salt
- 60 ml/4 tbsp soy sauce

Directions:

1. Combine all the ingredients and allow to marinate for approximately three hours.
2. Barbecue or grill (broil) over a hot grill for approximately five minutes each side.

BEEF AND PEAS

Yield: 4 Servings

Ingredients:

- 100 g/4 oz fresh or frozen peas, thawed
- 15 ml/1 tbsp cornflour (cornstarch)
- 15 ml/1 tbsp soy sauce
- 2 onions, sliced
- 2 stalks celery, sliced
- 250 ml/8 fl oz/1 cup chicken stock
- 30 ml/2 tbsp groundnut (peanut) oil
- 450 g/1 lb lean beef, cubed

Directions:

1. Heat the oil and stir-fry the beef until slightly browned.
2. Put in the onions, celery and peas and stir-fry for approximately two minutes.
3. Put in the stock and soy sauce, bring to the boil, cover and simmer for 10 minutes.
4. Combine the cornflour with a little water and mix it into the sauce.
5. Simmer, stirring, until the sauce clears and becomes thick.

BEEF AND SPINACH BALLS

Yield: 4 Servings

Ingredients:

- 1 egg
- 100 g/4 oz breadcrumbs
- 120 ml/4 fl oz/ ½ cup beef stock
- 15 ml/1 tbsp cornflour (cornstarch)
- 15 ml/1 tbsp rice wine or dry sherry
- 2½ ml/ ½ tsp salt
- 30 ml/2 tbsp groundnut (peanut) oil
- 350 g/12 oz spinach, shredded
- 45 ml/3 tbsp soy sauce
- 450 g/1 lb minced (ground) beef
- 60 ml/4 tbsp water

Directions:

1. Combine the beef, egg, breadcrumbs, water, cornflour, salt and wine or sherry.
2. mould into walnut-sized balls.
3. Heat the oil and fry the meatballs until browned on all sides.
4. Take out of the pan and eliminate the excess liquid off any excess oil.
5. Put in the soy sauce and stock to the pan and return the meatballs.
6. Bring to the boil, cover and simmer for half an hour, turning intermittently.
7. Steam the spinach in a separate pan until just softened then stir into the beef and heat through.

BEEF AND SPRING ONIONS WITH FISH SAUCE

Yield: 4 Servings

Ingredients:

- 15 ml/1 tbsp cornflour (cornstarch)
- 15 ml/1 tbsp water
- 2 cloves garlic, crushed

- 2 slices ginger, minced
- 2½ ml/ ½ tsp oyster sauce
- 2½ ml/ ½ tsp rice wine or dry sherry
- 350 g/12 oz lean beef, finely sliced
- 45 ml/3 tbsp groundnut (peanut) oil
- 5 ml/1 tsp fish sauce
- 6 spring onions (scallions), chopped into 5 cm/2 in pieces
- pinch of bicarbonate of soda (baking soda)
- pinch of salt

Directions:

1. Marinate the beef with the cornflour, water, wine or sherry, bicarbonate of soda and salt for one hour.
2. Heat 30 ml/ 2 tbsp of oil and stir-fry the beef with half the spring onions, half the garlic and the ginger until well browned.
3. In the meantime, heat the rest of the oil and fry the rest of the spring onions, garlic and ginger with the fish sauce and oyster sauce until softened.
4. Combine the two together and heat through and serve.

BEEF BALLS WITH GLUTINOUS RICE

Yield: 4 Servings

Ingredients:

- 1 egg, slightly beaten
- 1 slice ginger root, minced
- 1 small onion, minced
- 15 ml/1 tbsp soy sauce
- 2½ ml/ ½ tsp cornflour (cornstarch)
- 2½ ml/ ½ tsp salt
- 2½ ml/ ½ tsp sugar
- 225 g/8 oz glutinous rice
- 450 g/1 lb lean beef, minced (ground)
- 5 ml/1 tsp rice wine or dry sherry

Directions:

1. Soak the rice for half an hour then eliminate the excess liquid and spread on a plate.

2. Combine the beef, ginger, onion, egg, soy sauce, cornflour, sugar, salt and wine or sherry.
3. Form into walnut-sized balls.
4. Roll the meatballs in the rice to coat them completely then arrange them on a shallow ovenproof dish with spaces between.
5. Steam on a rack above gently simmering water for half an hour.
6. Serve with dips of soy sauce and Chinese mustard.

BEEF CHOP SUEY

Yield: 4 Servings

Ingredients:

- 1 slice ginger root, chopped
- 100 g/4 oz bean sprouts
- 100 g/4 oz broccoli florets
- 15 ml/1 tbsp cornflour (cornstarch)
- 15 ml/1 tbsp rice wine or dry sherry
- 2 cloves garlic, crushed
- 2½ ml/ ½ tsp sugar
- 225 g/8 oz lean beef, chopped into strips
- 3 spring onions (scallions), chopped
- 3 stalks celery, sliced
- 45 ml/3 tbsp soy sauce
- 5 ml/1 tsp salt
- 60 ml/4 tbsp groundnut (peanut) oil
- freshly ground pepper

Directions:

1. Briefly boil the celery, bean sprouts and broccoli in boiling water for approximately two minutes then eliminate the excess liquid and pat dry.
2. Heat 45 ml/3 tbsp of oil and fry the spring onions, garlic and ginger until slightly browned.
3. Put in the beef and stir-fry for 4 minutes.
4. Take out of the pan.
5. Heat the rest of the oil and stir-fry the vegetables for approximately three minutes.

6. Put in the beef, soy sauce, wine or sherry, salt, sugar and a pinch of pepper and stir-fry for approximately two minutes.
7. Combine the cornflour with a little water, mix it into the pan and simmer, stirring, until the sauce clears and becomes thick.

BEEF CHOW MEIN

Yield: 4 Servings

Ingredients:

- 1 green pepper, chopped into strips
- 100 g/4 oz bean sprouts
- 100 g/4 oz mushrooms, sliced
- 15 ml/1 tbsp cornflour (cornstarch)
- 15 ml/1 tbsp peanut butter
- 175 ml/6 fl oz chicken stock
- 2 onions
- 3 stalks celery, sliced
- 30 ml/2 tbsp oyster sauce
- 350 g/12 oz egg noodles
- 4 spring onions (scallions), chopped
- 45 ml/3 tbsp rice wine or dry sherry
- 45 ml/3 tbsp soy sauce
- 5 ml/1 tsp lemon juice
- 60 ml/4 tbsp groundnut (peanut) oil
- 750 g/1 ½ lb rump steak

Directions:

1. Remove and discard the fat from the meat.
2. Cut across the grain into thin slices.
3. Chop the onions into wedges and separate the layers.
4. Combine 15 ml/1 tbsp of soy sauce with 15 ml/1 tbsp of wine or sherry, the peanut butter and lemon juice.
5. Mix in the meat, cover and allow to stand for one hour.
6. Cook the noodles in boiling water for approximately five minutes or until soft.
7. Drain well.

8. Heat 15 ml/1 tbsp of oil, add 15 ml/1 tbsp of soy sauce and the noodles and fry for approximately two minutes until slightly browned.
9. Move to a warmed serving plate.
10. Combine the rest of the soy sauce and wine or sherry with the stock, cornflour and oyster sauce.
11. Heat 15 ml/1 tbsp of oil and stir-fry the onions for approximately one minute.
12. Put in the celery, mushrooms, pepper and bean sprouts and stir-fry for approximately two minutes.
13. Take out of the wok.
14. Heat the rest of the oil and stir-fry the beef until browned.
15. Put in the stock mixture, bring to the boil, cover and simmer for approximately three minutes.
16. Put the vegetables back into the wok and simmer, stirring, for about 4 minutes until hot.
17. Spoon the mixture over the noodles and serve.

BEEF DUMPLINGS

Yield: 4 Servings

Ingredients:

- 1 onion, chopped
- 1 sachet easy-mix yeast
- 10 ml/2 tsp caster sugar
- 15 ml/1 tbsp cornflour (cornstarch)
- 15 ml/1 tbsp soy sauce
- 2 pieces stem ginger, chopped
- 2½ ml/ ½ tsp five-spice powder
- 2½ ml/ ½ tsp wine vinegar
- 225 g/8 oz minced (ground) beef
- 30 ml/2 tbsp groundnut (peanut) oil
- 30 ml/2 tbsp hoisin sauce
- 300 ml/ ½ pt warm milk or water
- 45 ml/3 tbsp water
- 450 g/1 lb plain (all-purpose) flour
- 5 ml/1 tsp salt
- 50 g/2 oz cashews, chopped

Directions:

1. Combine the flour, yeast, sugar, salt and warm milk or water and knead to a smooth dough.
2. Cover and leave to rise in a warm place for 45 minutes.
3. Heat the oil and fry the beef until slightly browned.
4. Put in the onion, ginger, cashews, five-spice powder, soy sauce, hoisin sauce and wine vinegar and bring to the boil.
5. Combine the cornflour and water, stir into the sauce and simmer for approximately two minutes.
6. Allow it to cool.
7. Shape the dough into 16 balls.
8. Press flat, spoon some filling into each and close the dough around the filling.
9. Put in a steam basket in a wok or pan, cover and steam over salted water for about 30 minutes.

BEEF IN RED SAUCE

Yield: 4 Servings

Ingredients:

- 1 green pepper, chopped
- 1 onion, chopped
- 1 red pepper, chopped
- 2 slices pineapple, chopped
- 30 ml/2 tbsp honey
- 30 ml/2 tbsp wine vinegar
- 300 ml/ ½ pt beef stock
- 45 ml/3 tbsp dry white wine
- 45 ml/3 tbsp soy sauce
- 450 g/1 lb minced (ground) beef
- 60 ml/4 tbsp groundnut (peanut) oil
- few drops of chilli oil
- salt and freshly ground pepper

Directions:

1. Heat the oil and fry the beef until slightly browned.
2. Put in the vegetables and pineapple and stir-fry for approximately three minutes.

3. Put in the soy sauce, wine, wine vinegar, honey and stock.
4. Bring to the boil, cover and simmer for half an hour until cooked.
5. Season to taste with salt, pepper and chilli oil.

BEEF ROLLS

Yield: 4 Servings

Ingredients:

- 1 egg, beaten
- 350 g/12 oz minced (ground) beef
- 4 spring onions (scallions), chopped
- 5 ml/1 tsp cornflour (cornstarch)
- 5 ml/1 tsp groundnut (peanut) oil
- 8 spring roll wrappers oil for deep-frying
- salt and freshly ground pepper

Directions:

1. Combine the beef, egg, cornflour, oil, salt, pepper and spring onions.
2. Leave to stand for one hour.
3. Put spoonfuls of the mixture in each spring roll wrapper, fold up the base, fold in the sides then roll up the wrappers, sealing the edges with a little water.
4. Heat the oil and deep-fry the rolls until a golden-brown colour is achieved and cooked through.
5. Drain thoroughly and serve.

BEEF STEW

Yield: 4 Servings

Ingredients:

- 1 clove garlic, crushed
- 1 slice ginger root, chopped
- 100 g/4 oz cabbage, shredded
- 15 ml/1 tbsp brown sugar

- 15 ml/1 tbsp groundnut (peanut) oil
- 2 carrots, thickly sliced
- 2 onions, chopped into wedges
- 30 ml/2 tbsp rice wine or dry sherry
- 300 ml/ ½ pt chicken stock
- 45 ml/3 tbsp soy sauce
- 450 g/1 lb braising steak, cubed

Directions:

1. Heat the oil with the garlic and ginger and fry until the garlic is slightly browned.
2. Put in the steak and fry for approximately five minutes until browned.
3. Put in the soy sauce, wine or sherry and sugar, cover and simmer for 10 minutes.
4. Put in the stock, bring to the boil, cover and simmer for about 30 minutes.
5. Put in the onions, carrots and cabbage, cover and simmer for another 15 minutes.

BEEF STIR-FRY

Yield: 4 Servings

Ingredients:

- 1 red pepper, sliced
- 1 slice ginger root, chopped
- 120 ml/4 fl oz/ ½ cup beef stock
- 15 ml/1 tbsp cornflour (cornstarch)
- 15 ml/1 tbsp rice wine or dry sherry
- 2 cloves garlic, crushed
- 2 spring onions (scallions), chopped
- 225 g/8 oz cauliflower florets
- 225 g/8 oz lean beef
- 30 ml/2 tbsp soy sauce
- 45 ml/3 tbsp groundnut (peanut) oil
- 50 g/2 oz mangetout (snow peas)
- 50 g/2 oz mushrooms, sliced

Directions:

1. Slice the beef finely against the grain.
2. Heat half the oil and stir-fry the ginger, garlic and spring onions until slightly browned.

3. Put in the beef and stir-fry until just browned then remove from the pan.
4. Heat the rest of the oil and stir-fry the vegetables until coated with oil.
5. Mix in the stock, bring to the boil, cover and simmer until the vegetables are soft but still crisp.
6. Combine the soy sauce, cornflour and wine or sherry and mix it into the pan.
7. Simmer, stirring, until the sauce becomes thick.

BEEF TENDERLOIN

Yield: 4 Servings

Ingredients:

- 1 clove garlic, crushed
- 10 ml/2 tsp oyster sauce
- 15 ml/1 tbsp soy sauce
- 2 onions, finely sliced
- 2½ ml/ ½ tsp bicarbonate of soda (baking soda)
- 30 ml/2 tbsp groundnut (peanut) oil
- 45 ml/3 tbsp rice wine or dry sherry
- 450 g/1 lb lean beef
- 5 ml/1 tsp cornflour (cornstarch)
- 5 ml/1 tsp sugar
- pinch of salt

Directions:

1. Chop the meat across the grain into thin slices.
2. Combine the wine or sherry, soy sauce, oyster sauce, sugar, cornflour, bicarbonate of soda, salt and garlic.
3. Mix in the meat, cover and refrigerate for at least 3 hours.
4. Heat the oil and stir-fry the onions for approximately five minutes until a golden-brown colour is achieved.
5. Move to a warmed serving plate and keep warm.
6. Add some of the meat to the wok, spreading the slices so they do not overlap.
7. Fry for about 3 minutes on each side until browned then arrange on top of the onions and carry on frying the rest of the meat.

BEEF TOASTS

Yield: 4 Servings

Ingredients:

- 1 egg, beaten
- 4 slices bread
- 4 slices lean beef
- 50 g/2 oz/ ½ cup walnuts, ,chopped
- oil for deep-frying

Directions:

1. Flatten the beef slices then brush them well with egg.
2. Drizzle with walnuts and top with a slice of bread.
3. Heat the oil and fry the beef and bread slices for about 2 minutes.
4. Take out of the oil and allow to cool.
5. Reheat the oil and fry again until well browned.

BEEF WITH ASPARAGUS

Yield: 4 Servings

Ingredients:

- 1 clove garlic, crushed
- 120 ml/4 fl oz/ ½ cup chicken stock
- 15 ml/1 tbsp soy sauce
- 30 ml/2 tbsp rice wine or dry sherry
- 30 ml/2 tbsp soy sauce
- 350 g/12 oz asparagus tips
- 45 ml/3 tbsp cornflour (cornstarch)
- 45 ml/3 tbsp groundnut (peanut) oil
- 450 g/1 lb rump steak, cubed
- 5 ml/1 tsp salt

Directions:

1. Put the steak into a container.

2. Combine the soy sauce, wine or sherry and 30 ml/2 tbsp of cornflour, pour over the steak and stir thoroughly.
3. Allow to marinate for half an hour.
4. Heat the oil with the salt and garlic and fry until the garlic is slightly browned.
5. Put in the meat and marinade and stir-fry for 4 minutes.
6. Put in the asparagus and stir-fry gently for approximately two minutes.
7. Put in the stock and soy sauce, bring to the boil and simmer, stirring for approximately three minutes until the meat is cooked.
8. Mix the rest of the cornflour with a little more water or stock and mix it into the sauce.
9. Simmer, stirring, for a few minutes until the sauce clears and becomes thick.

BEEF WITH BAMBOO SHOOTS

Yield: 4 Servings

Ingredients:

- 1 clove garlic, crushed
- 1 slice ginger root, minced
- 1 spring onion (scallion), chopped
- 100 g/4 oz bamboo shoots
- 15 ml/1 tbsp rice wine or dry sherry
- 225 g/8 oz lean beef, chopped into strips
- 45 ml/3 tbsp groundnut (peanut) oil
- 45 ml/3 tbsp soy sauce
- 5 ml/1 tsp cornflour (cornstarch)

Directions:

1. Heat the oil and fry the garlic, spring onion and ginger until slightly browned.
2. Put in the beef and stir-fry for 4 minutes until slightly browned.
3. Put in the bamboo shoots and stir-fry for approximately three minutes.
4. Put in the soy sauce, wine or sherry and cornflour and stir-fry for 4 minutes.

BEEF WITH BAMBOO SHOOTS AND MUSHROOMS

Yield: 4 Servings

Ingredients:

- 1 slice ginger root, minced
- 10 ml/2 tsp soy sauce
- 100 g/4 oz bamboo shoots, sliced
- 100 g/4 oz mushrooms, sliced
- 120 ml/4 fl oz/ ½ cup beef stock
- 15 ml/1 tbsp cornflour (cornstarch)
- 225 g/8 oz lean beef
- 30 ml/2 tbsp water
- 45 ml/3 tbsp groundnut (peanut) oil
- 45 ml/3 tbsp rice wine or dry sherry
- 5 ml/1 tsp sugar
- salt and pepper

Directions:

1. Slice the beef finely against the grain.
2. Heat the oil and stir-fry the ginger for a few seconds.
3. Put in the beef and stir-fry until just browned.
4. Put in the bamboo shoots and mushrooms and stir-fry for approximately one minute.
5. Put in the wine or sherry, sugar and soy sauce and season with salt and pepper.
6. Mix in the stock, bring to the boil, cover and simmer for approximately three minutes.
7. Combine the cornflour and water, mix it into the pan and simmer, stirring, until the sauce becomes thick.

BEEF WITH BEAN SPROUTS

Yield: 4 Servings

Ingredients:

- 1 egg white
- 1 red chilli pepper, shredded
- 100 g/4 oz bean sprouts
- 15 ml/1 tbsp cornflour (cornstarch)
- 15 ml/1 tbsp soy sauce
- 2 slices ginger root, shredded
- 2 spring onions (scallions), shredded

- 25 g/1 oz pickled cabbage, shredded
- 30 ml/2 tbsp groundnut (peanut) oil
- 450 g/1 lb lean beef, sliced
- 5 ml/1 tsp oyster sauce
- 5 ml/1 tsp sesame oil
- salt

Directions:

1. Combine the beef with the egg white, half the oil, the cornflour and soy sauce and allow to stand for half an hour.
2. Briefly boil the bean sprouts in boiling water for approximately eight minutes until almost soft then drain.
3. Heat the rest of the oil and stir-fry the beef until slightly browned then remove from the pan.
4. Put in the pickled cabbage, chilli pepper, ginger, salt, oyster sauce and sesame oil and stir-fry for approximately two minutes.
5. Put in the bean sprouts and stir-fry for approximately two minutes.
6. Return the beef to the pan and stir-fry until well mixed and heated through.
7. Serve Immediately.

BEEF WITH BROCCOLI

Yield: 4 Servings

Ingredients:

- 1 clove garlic, crushed
- 15 ml/1 tbsp rice wine or dry sherry
- 15 ml/1 tbsp soy sauce
- 150 ml/generous ½ cup beef stock
- 225 g/8 oz broccoli florets
- 30 ml/2 tbsp cornflour (cornstarch)
- 30 ml/2 tbsp groundnut (peanut) oil
- 450 g/1 lb rump steak, finely sliced
- 5 ml/1 tsp salt

Directions:

1. Put the steak into a container.

2. Combine 15 ml/1 tbsp of cornflour with the wine or sherry and soy sauce, stir into the meat and allow to marinate for half an hour.
3. Heat the oil with the salt and garlic and fry until the garlic is slightly browned.
4. Put in the steak and marinade and stir-fry for 4 minutes.
5. Put in the broccoli and stir-fry for approximately three minutes.
6. Put in the stock, bring to the boil, cover and simmer for approximately five minutes until the broccoli is just soft but still crisp.
7. Mix the rest of the cornflour with a little water and mix it into the sauce.
8. Simmer, stirring until the sauce clears and becomes thick.

BEEF WITH CARROTS

Yield: 4 Servings

Ingredients:

- 1 slice ginger root, minced
- 2 cloves garlic, crushed
- 2 spring onions (scallions), sliced
- 250 ml/8 fl oz/1 cup soy sauce
- 30 ml/2 tbsp brown sugar
- 30 ml/2 tbsp groundnut (peanut) oil
- 30 ml/2 tbsp rice wine or dry sherry
- 4 carrots, diagonally sliced
- 450 g/1 lb lean beef, cubed
- 5 ml/1 tsp salt
- 600 ml/1 pt/2 ½ cups water

Directions:

1. Heat the oil and fry the beef until slightly browned.
2. Drain off the excess oil and add the spring onions, garlic, ginger and anise fry for approximately two minutes.
3. Put in the soy sauce, wine or sherry, sugar and salt and mix together well.
4. Put in the water, bring to the boil, cover and simmer for one hour.
5. Put in the carrots, cover and simmer for another 30 minutes.
6. Take the lid off and simmer until the sauce has reduced.

BEEF WITH CASHEWS

Yield: 4 Servings

Ingredients:

- 1 slice ginger root, chopped
- 120 ml/4 fl oz/ ½ cup water
- 2 cloves garlic, crushed
- 20 ml/4 tsp cornflour (cornstarch)
- 20 ml/4 tsp soy sauce
- 450 g/1 lb rump steak, finely sliced
- 5 ml/1 tsp chilli sauce
- 5 ml/1 tsp oyster sauce
- 5 ml/1 tsp sesame oil
- 60 ml/4 tbsp groundnut (peanut) oil
- 75 g/3 oz roasted cashews
- 8 spring onions (scallions), chopped into chunks

Directions:

1. Heat half the oil and stir-fry the meat until slightly browned.
2. Take out of the pan.
3. Heat the rest of the oil and stir-fry the spring onions, garlic, ginger and cashews for approximately one minute.
4. Return the meat to the pan.
5. Combine the rest of the ingredients and stir the mixture into the pan.
6. Bring to the boil and simmer, stirring, until the mixture becomes thick.

BEEF WITH CAULIFLOWER

Yield: 4 Servings

Ingredients:

- 10 water chestnuts, chopped into strips
- 120 ml/4 fl oz/ ½ cup chicken stock
- 15 ml/1 tbsp cornflour (cornstarch)
- 15 ml/1 tbsp oyster sauce
- 15 ml/1 tbsp soy sauce

- 15 ml/1 tbsp tomato purée (paste)
- 2½ ml/ ½ tsp sesame oil
- 225 g/8 oz beef, chopped into strips
- 225 g/8 oz cauliflower florets
- 50 g/2 oz bamboo shoots, chopped into strips
- oil for deep-frying

Directions:

1. Parboil the cauliflower for approximately two minutes in boiling water then drain.
2. Heat the oil and deep-fry the cauliflower until slightly browned.
3. Remove and eliminate the excess liquid using kitchen paper.
4. Reheat the oil and deep-fry the beef until slightly browned then remove and drain.
5. Pour off all but 15 ml/1 tbsp of oil and stir-fry the bamboo shoots and water chestnuts for approximately two minutes.
6. Add the rest of the ingredients, bring to the boil and simmer, stirring, until the sauce becomes thick.
7. Return the beef and cauliflower to the pan and reheat gently.
8. Serve Immediately.

BEEF WITH CELERY

Yield: 4 Servings

Ingredients:

- 1 slice ginger root, minced
- 100 g/4 oz celery, chopped into strips
- 2 spring onions (scallions), chopped
- 2½ ml/ ½ tsp salt
- 2½ ml/ ½ tsp sugar
- 225 g/8 oz lean beef, chopped into strips
- 30 ml/2 tbsp rice wine or dry sherry
- 30 ml/2 tbsp soy sauce
- 45 ml/3 tbsp groundnut (peanut) oil

Directions:

1. Briefly boil the celery in boiling water for approximately one minute then eliminate the excess liquid comprehensively..

2. Heat the oil and fry the spring onions and ginger until slightly browned.
3. Put in the beef and stir-fry for 4 minutes.
4. Put in the celery and stir-fry for approximately two minutes.
5. Put in the soy sauce, wine or sherry, sugar and salt and stir-fry for approximately three minutes.

BEEF WITH CHINESE CABBAGE

Yield: 4 Servings

Ingredients:

- 10 ml/2 tsp cornflour (cornstarch)
- 120 ml/4 fl oz/ ½ cup beef stock
- 225 g/8 oz lean beef
- 30 ml/2 tbsp groundnut (peanut) oil
- 30 ml/2 tbsp water
- 350 g/12 oz Chinese cabbage, shredded
- salt and freshly ground pepper

Directions:

1. Slice the beef finely against the grain.
2. Heat the oil and stir-fry the beef until just browned.
3. Put in the Chinese cabbage and stir-fry until slightly softened.
4. Put in the stock, bring to the boil and season with salt and pepper.
5. Cover and simmer for 4 minutes until the beef is soft.
6. Combine the cornflour and water, mix it into the pan and simmer, stirring, until the sauce becomes thick.

BEEF WITH CHINESE PICKLES

Yield: 4 Servings

Ingredients:

- 100 g/4 oz Chinese pickles, shredded
- 15 ml/1 tbsp cornflour (cornstarch)

- 2½ ml/ ½ tsp freshly ground pepper
- 30 ml/2 tbsp soy sauce
- 450 g/1 lb lean steak, sliced against the grain
- 5 ml/1 tsp salt
- 60 ml/4 tbsp groundnut (peanut) oil

Directions:

1. Mix all the ingredients comprehensively and place in an ovenproof bowl.
2. Stand the bowl on a rack in a steamer, cover and steam over boiling water for about forty minutes until the beef is cooked.

BEEF WITH CUCUMBER

Yield: 4 Servings

Ingredients:

- 2 cucumbers, peeled, seeded and sliced
- 30 ml/2 tbsp cornflour (cornstarch)
- 30 ml/2 tbsp rice wine or dry sherry
- 45 ml/3 tbsp soy sauce
- 450 g/1 lb rump steak, finely sliced
- 60 ml/4 tbsp chicken stock
- 60 ml/4 tbsp groundnut (peanut) oil
- salt and freshly ground pepper

Directions:

1. Put the steak into a container.
2. Combine the soy sauce and cornflour and stir into the steak.
3. Allow to marinate for half an hour.
4. Heat half the oil and stir-fry the cucumbers for approximately three minutes until opaque then remove them from the pan.
5. Heat the rest of the oil and stir-fry the steak until browned.
6. Put in the cucumbers and stir-fry for approximately two minutes.
7. Put in the stock, wine or sherry and season with salt and pepper.
8. Bring to the boil, cover and simmer for approximately three minutes.

BEEF WITH DRIED ORANGE RIND

Yield: 4 Servings

Ingredients:

- 100 g/4 oz dried orange rind
- 15 ml/1 tbsp rice wine or dry sherry
- 2 dried chilli peppers, finely chopped
- 2½ ml/ ½ tsp sesame oil
- 2½ ml/ ½ tsp sugar
- 30 ml/2 tbsp groundnut (peanut) oil
- 45 ml/3 tbsp beef stock
- 450 g/1 lb lean beef, finely sliced
- 5 ml/1 tsp freshly ground pepper
- 5 ml/1 tsp salt
- 5 ml/1 tsp wine vinegar
- oil for deep-frying

Directions:

1. Drizzle the beef with salt and allow to stand for half an hour.
2. Heat the oil and deep-fry the beef until half cooked.
3. Remove and eliminate the excess liquid well.
4. Heat the oil and stir-fry the orange rind, chilli peppers and pepper for approximately one minute.
5. Put in the beef and stock and bring to the boil.
6. Put in the sugar and wine vinegar and simmer until there is not much liquid left.
7. Mix in the wine vinegar and sesame oil and mix well.
8. Serve on a bed of lettuce leaves.

BEEF WITH GARLIC

Yield: 4 Servings

Ingredients:

- 1 red chilli pepper, sliced
- 15 ml/1 tbsp water
- 350 g/12 oz lean beef, sliced

- 4 cloves garlic, sliced
- 45 ml/3 tbsp groundnut (peanut) oil
- 45 ml/3 tbsp soy sauce
- 5 ml/1 tsp cornflour (cornstarch)

Directions:

1. Combine the beef with the garlic, chilli pepper and 30 ml/2 tbsp of soy sauce and allow to stand for half an hour, stirring intermittently.
2. Heat the oil and fry the beef mixture for a few minutes until almost cooked.
3. Mix the rest of the ingredients to a paste, mix in to the pan and continue to stir-fry until the beef is cooked.

BEEF WITH GINGER

Yield: 4 Servings

Ingredients:

- 1 onion, finely sliced
- 15 ml/1 tbsp groundnut (peanut) oil
- 15 ml/1 tbsp soy sauce
- 150 ml/generous ½ cup water
- 2 cloves garlic, crushed
- 2 pieces crystallised ginger, finely sliced
- 2 stalks celery, diagonally sliced
- 450 g/1 lb lean beef, sliced
- 5 ml/1 tsp salt

Directions:

1. Heat the oil and fry the beef, onion and garlic until slightly browned.
2. Put in the ginger, soy sauce and water, bring to the boil, cover and simmer for 25 minutes.
3. Put in the celery, cover and simmer for another 5 minutes.
4. Drizzle with salt and serve.

BEEF WITH GREEN BEANS

Yield: 4 Servings

Ingredients:

- 15 ml/1 tbsp rice wine or dry sherry
- 15 ml/1 tbsp soy sauce
- 150 ml/generous ½ cup chicken stock
- 2 cloves garlic, crushed
- 2½ ml/ ½ tsp salt
- 225 g/8 oz bamboo shoots, sliced
- 225 g/8 oz green beans
- 225 g/8 oz rump steak, finely sliced
- 30 ml/2 tbsp cornflour (cornstarch)
- 30 ml/2 tbsp groundnut (peanut) oil
- 50 g/2 oz mushrooms, sliced
- 50 g/2 oz water chestnuts, sliced

Directions:

1. Put the steak into a container.
2. Combine 15 ml/1 tbsp of the cornflour, the wine or sherry and soy sauce, stir into the meat and marinate for half an hour.
3. Heat the oil with the salt and garlic and fry until the garlic is slightly browned.
4. Put in the meat and marinade and stir-fry for 4 minutes.
5. Put in the beans and stir-fry for approximately two minutes.
6. Add the rest of the ingredients, bring to the boil and simmer for 4 minutes.
7. Mix the rest of the cornflour with a little water and mix it into the sauce.
8. Simmer, stirring, until the sauce clears and becomes thick.

BEEF WITH MANGETOUT

Yield: 4 Servings

Ingredients:

- 10 ml/2 tsp rice wine or dry sherry
- 10 ml/2 tsp water
- 2 slices ginger root, minced

- 2½ ml/ ½ tsp salt
- 225 g/8 oz lean beef
- 225 g/8 oz mangetout (snow peas)
- 30 ml/2 tbsp cornflour (cornstarch)
- 30 ml/2 tbsp groundnut (peanut) oil
- 5 ml/1 tsp soy sauce
- 5 ml/1 tsp sugar
- 60 ml/4 tbsp beef stock
- freshly ground pepper

Directions:

1. Slice the beef finely against the grain.
2. Mix half the cornflour, the sugar, soy sauce and wine or sherry, add to the beef and stir thoroughly to coat.
3. Heat half the oil and stir-fry the salt and ginger for a few seconds.
4. Add mangetout and stir to coat with oil.
5. Put in the stock, bring to the boil and stir thoroughly then remove the mangetout and liquid from the pan.
6. Heat the rest of the oil and stir-fry the beef until slightly browned.
7. Return the mangetout to the pan.
8. Mix the rest of the cornflour with the water, stir into the pan and season with pepper.
9. Simmer, stirring, until the sauce becomes thick.

BEEF WITH ONIONS

Yield: 4 Servings

Ingredients:

- 100 g/4 oz onions, chopped into strips
- 15 ml/1 tbsp chicken stock
- 300 g/11 oz lean beef, chopped into strips
- 5 ml/1 tsp rice wine or dry sherry
- 5 ml/1 tsp soy sauce
- 5 ml/1 tsp sugar
- 60 ml/4 tbsp groundnut (peanut) oil
- salt
- sesame oil

Directions:

1. Heat the oil and fry the beef and onions over a high heat until slightly browned.
2. Mix in the stock, wine or sherry, sugar and soy sauce and stir-fry quickly until well mixed.
3. Season to taste with salt and sesame oil and serve.

BEEF WITH OYSTER SAUCE

Yield: 4 Servings

Ingredients:

- 100 g/4 oz button mushrooms
- 15 ml/1 tbsp cornflour (cornstarch)
- 15 ml/1 tbsp groundnut (peanut) oil
- 15 ml/1 tbsp rice wine or dry sherry
- 150 ml/generous ½ cup chicken stock
- 2 cloves garlic, crushed
- 30 ml/2 tbsp oyster sauce
- 4 spring onions (scallions), sliced
- 450 g/1 lb rump steak, sliced
- 5 ml/1 tsp brown sugar
- salt and freshly ground pepper

Directions:

1. Heat the oil and fry the garlic until slightly browned.
2. Put in the steak and mushrooms and stir-fry until slightly browned.
3. Put in the wine or sherry and stir-fry for approximately two minutes.
4. Put in the stock, oyster sauce and sugar and season with salt and pepper.
5. Bring to the boil and simmer, stirring intermittently, for 4 minutes.
6. Put in the spring onions.
7. Combine the cornflour with a little water and mix it into the pan.
8. Simmer, stirring, until the sauce clears and becomes thick.

BEEF WITH PEPPER

Yield: 4 Servings

Ingredients:

- 2 onions, sliced
- 350 g/12 oz lean beef, chopped into strips
- 5 ml/1 tsp cornflour (cornstarch)
- 5 ml/1 tsp oyster sauce
- 75 ml/5 tbsp groundnut (peanut) oil
- 75 ml/5 tbsp soy sauce
- 75 ml/5 tbsp water
- freshly ground pepper
- noodles baskets

Directions:

1. Marinate the beef with the soy sauce, 15 ml/1 tbsp of oil, the cornflour and water for one hour.
2. Remove the meat from the marinade and eliminate the excess liquid well.
3. Heat the rest of the oil stir-fry the beef and onions until slightly browned.
4. Put in the marinade and the oyster sauce and season generously with pepper.
5. Bring to the boil, cover and simmer for approximately five minutes, stirring intermittently.
6. Serve with noodle baskets.

BEEF WITH PEPPERS

Yield: 4 Servings

Ingredients:

- 1 carrot, sliced
- 15 ml/1 tbsp black bean sauce
- 15 ml/1 tbsp groundnut (peanut) oil
- 2 cloves garlic, crushed
- 3 green peppers, chopped into chunks
- 3 red chilli peppers, seeded and chopped
- 3 spring onions (scallions), chopped into chunks
- 350 g/12 oz lean beef, finely sliced
- 45 ml/3 tbsp water

- 5 ml/1 tsp cornflour (cornstarch)
- 5 ml/1 tsp rice wine or dry sherry
- 5 ml/1 tsp soy sauce
- salt

Directions:

1. Marinate the beef with the chilli peppers, spring onions, garlic, black bean sauce and carrot for one hour.
2. Briefly boil the peppers in boiling salted water for approximately three minutes then eliminate the excess liquid well.
3. Heat the oil and stir-fry the beef mixture for approximately two minutes.
4. Put in the peppers and stir-fry for approximately three minutes.
5. Put in the soy sauce, water and wine or sherry.
6. Combine the cornflour with a little water, mix it into the pan and simmer, stirring, until the sauce becomes thick.

BEEF WITH RICE NOODLES

Yield: 4 Servings

Ingredients:

- 1 onion, sliced
- 10 ml/2 tsp cornflour (cornstarch)
- 100 g/4 oz bamboo shoots, sliced
- 100 g/4 oz celery, sliced
- 100 g/4 oz rice noodles
- 120 ml/4 fl oz/ ½ cup beef stock
- 15 ml/1 tbsp water
- 2½ ml/ ½ tsp salt
- 2½ ml/ ½ tsp sugar
- 225 g/8 oz lean beef, sliced
- 30 ml/2 tbsp groundnut (peanut) oil
- 4 dried Chinese mushrooms
- 5 ml/1 tsp soy sauce
- oil for deep-frying

Directions:

1. Soak the mushrooms in warm water for half an hour then drain.
2. Discard the stalks and slice the caps.
3. Heat half the oil and fry the salt and beef until slightly browned then remove from the pan.
4. Heat the rest of the oil and stir-fry the vegetables until softened.
5. Mix in the stock and sugar and bring to the boil.
6. Return the beef to the pan, cover and simmer for approximately three minutes.
7. Combine the cornflour, soy sauce and water, stir into the pan and simmer, stirring, until the mixture becomes thick.
8. In the meantime, deep-fry the rice noodles in hot oil for a few seconds until puffed and crisp and serve on top of the beef.

BEEF WITH TOMATOES

Yield: 4 Servings

Ingredients:

- 15 ml/1 tbsp cornflour (cornstarch)
- 225 g/8 oz lean beef, chopped into strips
- 3 spring onions (scallions), chopped into chunks
- 30 ml/2 tbsp groundnut (peanut) oil
- 4 tomatoes, skinned and quartered
- 45 ml/3 tbsp water
- 60 ml/4 tbsp beef stock
- Heat the oil and stir-fry the spring onions until softened.

Directions:

1. Put in the beef and stir-fry until just browned.
2. Mix in the stock, bring to the boil, cover and simmer for approximately two minutes.
3. Combine the cornflour and water, stir into the pan and simmer, stirring, until the sauce becomes thick.
4. Mix in the tomatoes and simmer just until they are heated through.

BEEF WITH VEGETABLES

Yield: 4 Servings

Ingredients:

- 1 red pepper, sliced
- 1 slice ginger root, chopped
- 100 g/4 oz bamboo shoots, sliced
- 100 g/4 oz carrots, sliced
- 100 g/4 oz onion, sliced
- 120 ml/4 fl oz/ ½ cup beef stock
- 15 ml/1 tbsp cornflour (cornstarch)
- 15 ml/1 tbsp rice wine or dry sherry
- 15 ml/1 tbsp soy sauce
- 2 stalks celery, sliced
- 2½ ml/ ½ tsp salt
- 2½ ml/ ½ tsp sugar
- 225 g/8 oz lean beef
- 45 ml/3 tbsp groundnut (peanut) oil

Directions:

1. Slice the beef finely against the grain and place it into a container.
2. Combine the cornflour, soy sauce, wine or sherry and sugar, pour over the beef and toss to coat.
3. Leave to stand for half an hour, turning intermittently.
4. Heat half the oil and stir-fry the beef until just browned then remove it from the pan.
5. Heat the rest of the oil, mix in the ginger and salt then add the vegetables and stir-fry until coated with oil.
6. Mix in the stock, bring to the boil, cover and simmer until the vegetables are soft but still crisp.
7. Return the beef to the pan and stir over a gentle heat for about 1 minute to heat through.

BLACK BEAN BEEF WITH SPRING ONIONS

Yield: 4 Servings

Ingredients:

- 1 egg, slightly beaten
- 15 ml/1 tbsp water
- 2 cloves garlic, crushed

- 2 slices ginger root, shredded
- 2½ ml/ ½ tsp cornflour (cornstarch)
- 2½ ml/ ½ tsp rice wine or dry sherry
- 225 g/8 oz lean beef, finely sliced
- 250 ml/8 fl oz/1 cup groundnut (peanut) oil
- 30 ml/2 tbsp black bean sauce
- 5 ml/1 tsp light soy sauce
- 6 spring onions (scallions), diagonally sliced

Directions:

1. Combine the beef with the egg, soy sauce, wine or sherry and cornflour.
2. Leave to stand for 10 minutes.
3. Heat the oil and fry the beef until almost cooked.
4. Take out of the pan and eliminate the excess liquid well.
5. Pour off all but 15 ml/1 tbsp of oil, reheat then fry the garlic and black bean sauce for 30 seconds.
6. Put in the beef, and water and fry for about 4 minutes until the beef is soft.
7. In the meantime, heat a further 15 ml/ 1 tbsp of the oil and briefly stir-fry the spring onions and ginger.
8. Spoon the beef on to a warmed serving plate, top with the spring onions and serve.

BRAISED ANISE BEEF

Yield: 4 Servings

Ingredients:

- 1 clove garlic, crushed
- 15 ml/1 tbsp rice wine or dry sherry
- 15 ml/1 tbsp water
- 2 cloves star anise
- 30 ml/2 tbsp groundnut (peanut) oil
- 45 ml/3 tbsp soy sauce
- 450 g/1 lb chuck steak
- 5 ml/1 tsp salt
- 5 ml/1 tsp sugar

Directions:

1. Heat the oil and fry the beef until browned on all sides.
2. Add the rest of the ingredients, bring to a simmer, cover and simmer gently for about 45 minutes then turn the meat over, adding a little more water and soy sauce if the meat is drying.
3. Simmer for another 45 minutes until the meat is soft.
4. Discard the star anise and serve.

BRAISED BEEF WITH MUSHROOMS

Yield: 4 Servings

Ingredients:

- 1 kg/2 lb topside of beef
- 15 ml/1 tbsp water
- 2 carrots, grated
- 30 ml/2 tbsp hoisin sauce
- 30 ml/2 tbsp honey
- 30 ml/2 tbsp plum sauce
- 30 ml/2 tbsp wine vinegar
- 400 g/14 oz canned tomatoes
- 5 ml/1 tsp aniseed, ground
- 5 ml/1 tsp freshly ground pepper
- 5 ml/1 tsp ground coriander
- 5 ml/2 tsp cornflour (cornstarch)
- 6 dried Chinese mushrooms
- 6 spring onions (scallions), chopped into strips
- 60 ml/4 tbsp chopped chives
- 60 ml/4 tbsp groundnut (peanut) oil
- 60 ml/4 tbsp soy sauce
- salt and freshly ground pepper

Directions:

1. Pierce the beef multiple times using a fork.
2. Season with salt and pepper and place into a container.
3. Combine the sauces, honey, wine vinegar, pepper and spices, pour over the meat, cover and allow to marinate in the refrigerator overnight.
4. Soak the mushrooms in warm water for half an hour then drain.

5. Discard the stalks and slice the caps.
6. Heat the oil and fry the meat until well browned, turning often.
7. Combine the cornflour and water and put it into the pan with the tomatoes.
8. Bring to the boil, cover and simmer gently for about 1 ½ hours until soft.
9. Put in the spring onions and carrots and carry on simmering for approximately ten minutes until the carrots are soft.
10. Mix in the plum sauce and simmer for approximately two minutes.
11. Remove the meat from the sauce and chop it into thick slices.
12. Return it to the sauce to heat through then serve sprinkled with chives.

BRAISED CURRIED BEEF

Yield: 4 Servings

Ingredients:

- 1 clove garlic, crushed
- 1 slice ginger root, minced
- 15 ml/1 tbsp cornflour (cornstarch)
- 15 ml/1 tbsp rice wine or dry sherry
- 15 ml/1 tbsp sugar
- 30 ml/2 tbsp curry powder
- 4 spring onions (scallions), sliced
- 400 ml/14 fl oz beef stock
- 45 ml/3 tbsp groundnut (peanut) oil
- 45 ml/3 tbsp water
- 450 g/1 lb chuck steak, cubed
- 5 ml/1 tsp salt

Directions:

1. Heat the oil and fry the salt and garlic until slightly browned.
2. Put in the steak and toss in the oil then add the spring onions and ginger and fry until the meat is browned on all sides.
3. Put in the curry powder and stir-fry for approximately one minute.
4. Mix in the wine or sherry and sugar then add the stock, bring to the boil, cover and simmer for about 35 minutes until the beef is soft.
5. Blend the cornflour and water to a paste, stir into the sauce and simmer, stirring, until the sauce becomes thick.

CANTONESE BEEF

Yield: 4 Servings

Ingredients:

- 2 egg whites, beaten
- 2 onions, sliced
- 20 ml/4 tsp salt
- 30 ml/2 tbsp cornflour (cornstarch)
- 30 ml/2 tbsp sugar
- 4 stalks celery, sliced
- 450 g/1 lb steak, chopped into strips
- 60 ml/4 tbsp rice wine or dry sherry
- 60 ml/4 tbsp water
- 75 ml/5 tbsp soy sauce
- freshly ground pepper
- oil for deep-frying

Directions:

1. Mix half the cornflour with the egg whites.
2. Put in the steak and mix to coat the beef in the batter.
3. Heat the oil and deep-fry the steak until browned.
4. Take out of the pan and eliminate the excess liquid on kitchen paper.
5. Heat 15 ml/1 tbsp of oil and stir-fry the celery and onions for approximately three minutes.
6. Put in the meat, water, salt, soy sauce, wine or sherry and sugar and season with pepper.
7. Bring to the boil and simmer, stirring, until the sauce becomes thick.

CHILLI BEEF

Yield: 4 Servings

Ingredients:

- 1 onion, chopped into strips

- 1 stick celery, chopped into matchsticks
- 120 ml/4 fl oz/ ½ cup chicken stock
- 15 ml/1 tbsp brown sugar
- 15 ml/1 tbsp cornflour (cornstarch)
- 15 ml/1 tbsp finely chopped ginger root
- 15 ml/1 tbsp rice wine or dry sherry
- 2 red chilli peppers, seeded and chop into strips
- 30 ml/2 tbsp groundnut (peanut) oil
- 45 ml/3 tbsp soy sauce
- 450 g/1 lb rump steak, chopped into strips
- 50 g/2 oz bamboo shoots, chopped into matchsticks

Directions:

1. Put the steak into a container.
2. Combine the soy sauce, wine or sherry, sugar and ginger and mix it into the steak.
3. Allow to marinate for one hour.
4. Remove the steak from the marinade.
5. Heat half the oil and stir-fry the bamboo shoots, onion, celery and chilli for approximately three minutes then remove them from the pan.
6. Heat the rest of the oil and stir-fry the steak for approximately three minutes.
7. Mix in the marinade, bring to the boil and add the fried vegetables.
8. Simmer, stirring, for approximately two minutes.
9. Combine the stock and cornflour and put it into the pan.
10. Bring to the boil and simmer, stirring, until the sauce clears and becomes thick.

CHINESE BRAISED BEEF

Yield: 4 Servings

Ingredients:

- 1 clove garlic, minced
- 1 slice ginger root, minced
- 1 spring onion (scallion), sliced
- 30 ml/2 tbsp rice wine or dry sherry
- 45 ml/3 tbsp groundnut (peanut) oil
- 5 ml/1 tsp salt
- 5 ml/1 tsp sugar

- 60 ml/4 tbsp soy sauce
- 750 ml/3 cups boiling water
- 900 g/2 lb chuck steak
- pinch of pepper

Directions:

1. Heat the oil and brown the beef quickly on all sides.
2. Put in the spring onion, garlic, ginger, soy sauce, wine or sherry, sugar, salt and pepper.
3. Bring to the boil, stirring.
4. Put in the boiling water, bring back to the boil, stirring, then cover and simmer for about 2 hours until the beef is soft.

CRISPY BEEF WITH CURRY SAUCE

Yield: 4 Servings

Ingredients:

- 1 egg, beaten
- 100 g/4 oz curry paste
- 15 ml/1 tbsp cornflour (cornstarch)
- 15 ml/1 tbsp rice wine or dry sherry
- 15 ml/1 tbsp soy sauce
- 225 g/8 oz lean beef, sliced
- 5 ml/1 tsp bicarbonate of soda (baking soda)
- 90 ml/6 tbsp oil

Directions:

1. Combine the egg, cornflour, bicarbonate of soda, wine or sherry and soy sauce.
2. Mix in the beef and 15 ml/1 tbsp of oil.
3. Heat the rest of the oil and stir-fry the beef and egg mixture for approximately two minutes.
4. Remove the beef and eliminate the excess oil.
5. Put in the curry paste to the pan and bring to the boil then return the beef to the pan, stir thoroughly and serve.

CRISPY MEATBALLS

Yield: 4 Servings

Ingredients:

- 100 g/4 oz water chestnuts, minced
- 15 ml/1 tbsp cornflour (cornstarch)
- 15 ml/1 tbsp groundnut (peanut) oil
- 2 eggs, beaten
- 225 g/8 oz minced (ground) beef
- 225 g/8 oz/2 cups plain (all-purpose) flour
- 300 ml/ ½ pt/1 ½ cups water
- 5 ml/1 tsp baking powder
- 5 ml/1 tsp grated orange rind
- 5 ml/1 tsp minced ginger root
- 5 ml/1 tsp salt
- oil for deep-frying

Directions:

1. Combine the beef, water chestnuts, 1 egg, orange rind, ginger, salt and cornflour.
2. Form into small balls.
3. Lay out into a container in a steamer over boiling water and steam for approximately twenty minutes until cooked.
4. Allow it to cool.
5. Combine the flour, baking powder, rest of the egg, water and groundnut (peanut) oil to a thick batter.
6. Immerse the meatballs in the batter.
7. Heat the oil and fry the meatballs until a golden-brown colour is achieved.

CUCUMBER STEAK

Yield: 4 Servings

Ingredients:

- 1 cucumber, peeled and sliced
- 1 onion, finely chopped
- 10 ml/2 tsp cornflour (cornstarch)

- 10 ml/2 tsp salt
- 120 ml/4 fl oz/ ½ cup beef stock
- 2½ ml/ ½ tsp freshly ground pepper
- 450 g/1 lb rump steak
- 90 ml/6 tbsp groundnut (peanut) oil

Directions:

1. Chop the steak into strips then into thin slices against the grain.
2. Put into a container and mix in the cornflour, salt, pepper and half the oil.
3. Allow to marinate for half an hour.
4. Heat the rest of the oil and fry the beef and onion until slightly browned.
5. Put in the cucumbers and stock, bring to the boil, cover and simmer for approximately five minutes.

DEEP-FRIED BEEF SLIVERS WITH CELERY

Yield: 4 Servings

Ingredients:

- 1 onion, shredded
- 1 slice ginger root, minced
- 1 spring onion (scallion), sliced
- 10 ml/2 tsp cornflour (cornstarch)
- 15 ml/1 tbsp rice wine or dry sherry
- 2½ ml/ ½ tsp salt
- 2½ ml/ ½ tsp sugar
- 3 stalks celery, shredded
- 30 ml/2 tbsp groundnut (peanut) oil
- 30 ml/2 tbsp soy sauce
- 30 ml/2 tbsp water
- 450 g/1 lb lean beef, chopped into slivers

Directions:

1. Heat half the oil until very hot and fry the beef for approximately one minute until just browned.
2. Take out of the pan.

3. Heat the rest of the oil and fry the celery, onion, spring onion and ginger until slightly softened.
4. Return the beef to the pan with the soy sauce, wine or sherry, sugar and salt, bring to the boil and stir-fry to heat through.
5. Combine the cornflour and water, stir into the pan and simmer until the sauce is thickened.
6. Serve Immediately.

FAMILY-STYLE SHREDDED BEEF

Yield: 4 Servings

Ingredients:

- 1 red chilli pepper, chopped
- 1 slice ginger root, minced
- 15 ml/1 tbsp hot bean sauce
- 15 ml/1 tbsp oyster sauce
- 15 ml/1 tbsp rice wine or dry sherry
- 15 ml/1 tbsp soy sauce
- 225 g/8 oz beef, shredded
- 4 stalks celery, diagonally sliced
- 45 ml/3 tbsp groundnut (peanut) oil
- 5 ml/1 tsp salt
- 5 ml/1 tsp sesame oil
- 5 ml/1 tsp wine vinegar
- freshly ground pepper

Directions:

1. Put the beef into a container with the soy sauce and oyster sauce and allow to marinate for half an hour.
2. Heat the oil and fry the beef until slightly browned then remove them from the pan.
3. Put in the ginger and chilli pepper and stir-fry for a few seconds.
4. Put in the celery and stir-fry until half cooked.
5. Put in the beef, hot bean sauce and salt and mix well.
6. Put in the wine or sherry, sesame oil and vinegar and stir-fry until the beef is soft and the ingredients well mixed.
7. Serve sprinkled with pepper.

HOT BEEF

Yield: 4 Servings

Ingredients:

- 1 clove star anise
- 10 peppercorns
- 15 ml/1 tbsp rice wine or dry sherry
- 15 ml/1 tbsp soy sauce
- 2½ ml/ ½ tsp chilli oil
- 300 ml/ ½ pt water
- 4 dried red chilli peppers, chopped
- 4 slices ginger root
- 450 g/1 lb lean beef
- 6 spring onions (scallions), sliced

Directions:

1. Put the beef into a container with 2 spring onions, 1 slice of ginger and half the wine and allow to marinate for half an hour.
2. Bring a large pan of water to the boil, add the beef and boil until sealed on all sides then remove and drain.
3. Put the rest of the spring onions, ginger and wine or sherry in a pan with the chilli peppers, peppercorns and star anise and add the water.
4. Bring to the boil, add the beef, cover and simmer for about 40 minutes until the beef is soft.
5. Remove the beef from the liquid and eliminate the excess liquid well.
6. Slice it finely and lay out on a warmed serving plate.
7. Serve sprinkled with chilli oil.

HOT BEEF SHREDS

Yield: 4 Servings

Ingredients:

- 1 dried red chilli pepper, chopped

- 1 slice ginger root, minced
- 10 ml/2 tsp salt
- 15 ml/1 tbsp rice wine or dry sherry
- 150 ml/generous ½ cup groundnut (peanut) oil
- 2 carrots, shredded
- 2 stalks celery, diagonally sliced
- 225 g/8 oz/1 cup long-grain rice
- 45 ml/3 tbsp soy sauce
- 450 g/1 lb lean beef, sliced against the grain

Directions:

1. Heat two-thirds of the oil and stir-fry the beef, soy sauce and wine or sherry for 10 minutes.
2. Remove the beef and reserve the sauce.
3. Heat the rest of the oil and stir-fry the ginger, pepper and carrots for approximately one minute.
4. Put in the celery and stir-fry for approximately one minute.
5. Put in the beef and salt and stir-fry for approximately one minute.
6. In the meantime, cook the rice in boiling water for approximately twenty minutes until just soft.
7. Drain thoroughly and lay out on a serving dish.
8. Pour over the beef mixture and the hot sauce.

MARINATED BEEF WITH SPINACH

Yield: 4 Servings

Ingredients:

- 15 ml/1 tbsp soy sauce
- 2 slices ginger root, minced
- 2½ ml/ ½ tsp sesame oil
- 30 ml/2 tbsp beef stock
- 45 ml/3 tbsp groundnut (peanut) oil
- 45 ml/3 tbsp rice wine or dry sherry
- 450 g/1 lb lean beef, finely sliced
- 450 g/1 lb spinach
- 5 ml/1 tsp cornflour (cornstarch)

- 5 ml/1 tsp sugar

Directions:

1. Flatten the meat slightly by pressing with the fingers.
2. Combine the wine or sherry, soy sauce, sherry and sesame oil.
3. Put in the meat, cover and refrigerate for 2 hours, stirring intermittently.
4. Chop the spinach leaves into large pieces and the stems into thick slices.
5. Heat 30 ml/2 tbsp of oil and stir-fry the spinach stems and ginger for approximately two minutes.
6. Take out of the pan.
7. Heat the rest of the oil.
8. Eliminate the excess liquid from the meat, reserving the marinade.
9. Add half the meat to the pan, spreading out the slices so they do not overlap.
10. Cook for about 3 minutes until slightly browned on both sides.
11. Take out of the pan and fry the rest of the meat, then remove it from the pan.
12. Blend the stock and cornflour into the marinade.
13. Put in the mixture to the pan and bring to the boil.
14. Put in the spinach leaves, stems and ginger.
15. Simmer for about 3 minutes until the spinach wilts then mix in the meat.
16. Cook for another 1 minute then serve instantly.

MARINATED BRAISED BEEF

Yield: 4 Servings

Ingredients:

- 15 ml/1 tbsp brown sugar
- 15 ml/1 tbsp cornflour (cornstarch)
- 15 ml/1 tbsp wine vinegar
- 45 ml/3 tbsp groundnut (peanut) oil
- 450 g/1 lb chuck steak
- 5 ml/1 tsp salt
- 60 ml/4 tbsp rice wine or dry sherry
- 75 ml/5 tbsp soy sauce

Directions:

1. Pierce the steak in several places and place into a container.

2. Combine the soy sauce, wine or sherry and salt, pour over the meat and allow to stand for approximately three hours, turning intermittently.
3. Eliminate the excess liquid from the beef and discard the marinade.
4. Pat the beef dry and dust with cornflour.
5. Heat the oil and fry the beef until browned on all sides.
6. Put in the sugar and wine vinegar and enough water just to cover the beef.
7. Bring to the boil, cover and simmer for about 1 hour until the meat is soft.

MARINATED STIR-FRIED BEEF

Yield: 4 Servings

Ingredients:

- 15 ml/1 tbsp brown sugar
- 2 cloves garlic, crushed
- 30 ml/2 tbsp groundnut (peanut) oil
- 450 g/1 lb lean beef, sliced
- 5 ml/1 tsp salt
- 60 ml/4 tbsp soy sauce

Directions:

1. Put the beef into a container and add the garlic, soy sauce, sugar and salt.
2. Combine well, cover and allow to marinate for about 2 hours, turning intermittently.
3. Drain, discarding the marinade.
4. Heat the oil and stir-fry the beef until browned on all sides then serve instantly.

MEATBALLS WITH SWEET AND SOUR SAUCE

Yield: 4 Servings

Ingredients:

- 1 egg, beaten
- 1 green pepper, cubed
- 1 onion, finely chopped
- 100 g/4 oz mixed Chinese sweet pickles

- 100 g/4 oz pineapple chunks in syrup
- 100 g/4 oz/ ½ cup brown sugar
- 100 g/4 oz/ ½ cup cornflour (cornstarch)
- 120 ml/4 fl oz/ ½ cup chicken stock
- 15 ml/1 tbsp cornflour (cornstarch)
- 15 ml/1 tbsp groundnut (peanut) oil
- 15 ml/1 tbsp rice wine or dry sherry
- 15 ml/1 tbsp soy sauce
- 15 ml/1 tbsp soy sauce
- 15 ml/1 tbsp tomato purée (paste)
- 25 g/1 oz water chestnuts, finely chopped
- 45 ml/3 tbsp shredded coconut
- 450 g/1 lb minced (ground) beef
- 60 ml/4 tbsp wine vinegar
- For the sauce:
- oil for deep-frying
- salt and freshly ground pepper

Directions:

1. Combine the beef, onion, water chestnuts, soy sauce and wine or sherry.
2. mould into small balls and roll in beaten egg then in cornflour.
3. Deep-fry in hot oil for a few minutes until browned.
4. Move to a warmed serving plate and keep them warm.
5. In the meantime, heat the oil and stir-fry the pepper for approximately two minutes.
6. Add 30 ml/2 tbsp of the pineapple syrup, 15 ml/1 tbsp of the pickle vinegar, the sugar, stock, wine vinegar, tomato purée, cornflour and soy sauce.
7. Stir well, bring to the boil and simmer, stirring, until the mixture clears and becomes thick.
8. Eliminate the excess liquid from the rest of the pineapple and pickles and put them into the pan.
9. Simmer, stirring, for approximately two minutes.
10. Pour over the meatballs and serve sprinkled with coconut.

MINCED BEEF WITH CASHEW NUTS

Yield: 4 Servings

Ingredients:

- ½ egg white
- 15 ml/1 tbsp beef stock
- 25 g/1 oz cashew nuts, chopped
- 25 g/1 oz fresh parsley, chopped
- 4 large lettuce leaves
- 45 ml/3 tbsp groundnut (peanut) oil
- 450 g/1 lb minced (ground) beef
- 5 ml/1 tsp light soy sauce
- 5 ml/1 tsp oyster sauce
- few drops of sesame oil

Directions:

1. Combine the beef with the egg white, oyster sauce, soy sauce, sesame oil and parsley and leave to stand.
2. Heat half the oil and fry the cashew nuts until slightly browned then remove them from the pan.
3. Heat the rest of the oil and stir-fry the meat mixture until browned.
4. Put in the stock and carry on frying until almost all the liquid has evaporated.
5. Put the lettuce leaves on a warmed serving plate and spoon in the meat.
6. Serve sprinkled with the fried cashew nuts

PEPPER STEAK

Yield: 4 Servings

Ingredients:

- 1 onion, chopped into wedges
- 120 ml/4 fl oz/ ½ cup beef stock
- 2 cloves garlic, crushed
- 2 green peppers, roughly chopped
- 30 ml/2 tbsp cornflour (cornstarch)
- 30 ml/2 tbsp soy sauce
- 45 ml/3 tbsp groundnut (peanut) oil
- 450 g/1 lb sirloin steak, finely sliced
- 5 ml/1 tsp brown sugar
- 5 ml/1 tsp rice wine or dry sherry
- 5 ml/1 tsp salt

- salt and freshly ground pepper

Directions:

1. Heat the oil with the salt and garlic until the garlic is slightly browned then add the steak and stir-fry until just browned on all sides.
2. Put in the onion and peppers and stir-fry for approximately two minutes.
3. Put in the stock, sugar, wine or sherry and season with salt and pepper.
4. Bring to the boil, cover and simmer for approximately five minutes.
5. Combine the cornflour and soy sauce and stir then into the sauce.
6. Simmer, stirring, until the sauce clears and becomes thick, adding a little extra water if needed to make the sauce the consistency you prefer.

RED-COOKED BEEF

Yield: 4 Servings

Ingredients:

- 120 ml/4 fl oz/ ½ cup soy sauce
- 15 ml/1 tbsp brown sugar
- 375 ml/13 fl oz/1 ½ cups water
- 450 g/1 lb lean beef
- 60 ml/4 tbsp rice wine or dry sherry

Directions:

1. Put the beef, soy sauce, wine or sherry and sugar in a heavy-based pan and bring to a simmer.
2. Cover and simmer for 10 minutes, turning once or twice.
3. Mix in the water and bring to the boil.
4. Cover and simmer for about 1 hour until the meat is soft, adding a little boiling water if needed during cooking if the meat becomes too dry.
5. Serve hot or cold.

RED-COOKED BEEF WITH GINGER

Yield: 4 Servings

Ingredients:

- 120 ml/4 fl oz/ ½ cup soy sauce
- 15 ml/1 tbsp brown sugar
- 2 slices ginger root, minced
- 4 spring onions (scallions) chopped
- 400 ml/14 fl oz water
- 450 g/1 lb lean beef
- 60 ml/4 tbsp rice wine or dry sherry

Directions:

1. Put all the ingredients in a heavy pan, bring to the boil, cover and simmer, turning intermittently, for about 1 hour until the beef is soft.
2. Serve!

RED-COOKED BEEF WITH TURNIPS

Yield: 4 Servings

Ingredients:

- 1 slice ginger root, minced
- 1 small turnip, diced
- 1 spring onion (scallion), chopped 120 ml/4 fl oz/ ½ cup rice wine or dry sherry
- 120 ml/4 fl oz/ ½ cup soy sauce
- 15 ml/1 tbsp sugar
- 2 cloves star anise
- 250 ml/8 fl oz/1 cup water
- 450 g/1 lb lean beef

Directions:

1. Put the beef, ginger, spring onion, wine or sherry, water and anise in a heavy-based pan, bring to the boil, cover and simmer for 45 minutes.
2. Put in the turnip, soy sauce and sugar and a little more water if needed, bring back to the boil, cover and simmer for another 45 minutes until the beef is soft.
3. Allow it to cool.
4. Remove the beef and turnip from the sauce.
5. Slice the beef and lay out on a serving plate with the turnip.

6. Strain over the sauce and serve cold.

SAVOURY BEEF

Yield: 4 Servings

Ingredients:

- 1 slice ginger root, minced
- 2 cloves garlic, crushed
- 2 cloves star anise, crushed
- 2 spring onions (scallions), sliced
- 250 ml/8 fl oz/1 cup soy sauce
- 30 ml/2 tbsp brown sugar
- 30 ml/2 tbsp groundnut (peanut) oil
- 30 ml/2 tbsp rice wine or dry sherry
- 450 g/1 lb lean beef, cubed
- 5 ml/1 tsp salt
- 600 ml/1 pt/2 ½ cups water

Directions:

1. Heat the oil and fry the beef until slightly browned.
2. Drain off the excess oil and add the spring onions, garlic, ginger and anise and fry for approximately two minutes.
3. Put in the soy sauce, wine or sherry, sugar and salt and mix together well.
4. Put in the water, bring to the boil, cover and simmer for one hour.
5. Take the lid off and simmer until the sauce has reduced.

SESAME BEEF WITH BROCCOLI

Yield: 4 Servings

Ingredients:

- 100 g/4 oz broccoli florets
- 150 g/5 oz lean beef, finely sliced
- 2½ ml/ ½ tsp oyster sauce

- 2½ ml/ ½ tsp soy sauce
- 250 ml/8 fl oz/1 cup beef stock
- 30 ml/2 tbsp sesame seeds
- 5 ml/1 tsp cornflour (cornstarch)
- 5 ml/1 tsp fish sauce
- 5 ml/1 tsp white wine vinegar
- 60 ml/4 tbsp groundnut (peanut) oil

Directions:

1. Marinate the beef with the oyster sauce, 2½ ml/ ½ tsp of cornflour, 2½ ml/ ½ tsp of wine vinegar and 15 ml/ 1 tbsp of oil for one hour.
2. In the meantime, heat 15 ml/1 tbsp of oil, add the broccoli, 2½ ml/ ½ tsp of fish sauce, the soy sauce and rest of the wine vinegar and just cover with boiling water.
3. Simmer for approximately ten minutes until just soft.
4. Heat 30 ml/2 tbsp of oil in a separate pan and stir-fry the beef briefly until sealed.
5. Put in the stock, the rest of the cornflour and fish sauce, bring to the boil, cover and simmer for approximately ten minutes until the meat is soft.
6. Eliminate the excess liquid from the broccoli and lay out on a warmed serving plate.
7. Top with the meat and drizzle generously with sesame seeds.

SHREDDED BEEF

Yield: 4 Servings

Ingredients:

- 120 ml/4 fl oz/ ½ cup soy sauce
- 250 ml/8 fl oz/1 cup beef stock
- 45 ml/3 tbsp groundnut (peanut) oil
- 60 ml/4 tbsp rice wine or dry sherry
- 750 g/1 ½ lb lean beef, cubed

Directions:

1. Put the beef, stock, soy sauce and wine or sherry in a heavy-based pan.
2. Bring to the boil and boil, stirring, until the liquid evaporated.
3. Allow it to cool then chill.
4. Shred the beef with two forks.
5. Heat the oil then add the beef and stir-fry quickly until coated with oil.

6. Continue to cook over a medium heat until the beef dries out completely.
7. Allow it to cool and serve with noodles or rice.

SHREDDED BEEF WITH CHICKEN AND CELERY

Yield: 4 Servings

Ingredients:

- 1 sliced ginger root, minced
- 100 g/4 oz chicken, chopped into strips
- 100 g/4 oz lean beef, chopped into strips
- 2 carrots, chopped into strips
- 2 cloves garlic, crushed
- 2 stalks celery, chopped into strips
- 4 dried Chinese mushrooms
- 4 spring onions (scallions), chopped into strips
- 45 ml/3 tbsp groundnut (peanut) oil
- 45 ml/3 tbsp water
- 5 ml/1 tsp cornflour (cornstarch)
- 5 ml/1 tsp rice wine or dry sherry
- 5 ml/1 tsp salt
- 5 ml/1 tsp soy sauce
- 5 ml/1 tsp sugar

Directions:

1. Soak the mushrooms in warm water for half an hour then drain.
2. Discard the stalks and chop the caps.
3. Heat the oil and fry the garlic, ginger and salt until slightly browned.
4. Put in the beef and chicken and fry until just beginning to brown.
5. Put in the celery, spring onions, sugar, soy sauce, wine or sherry and water and bring to the boil.
6. Cover and simmer for about 15 minutes until the meat is soft.
7. Combine the cornflour with a little water, mix it into the sauce and simmer, stirring, until the sauce becomes thick.

SHREDDED SPICED BEEF

Yield: 4 Servings

Ingredients:

- 15 ml/1 tbsp minced ginger root
- 225 g/8 oz celery, chopped into chunks
- 30 ml/2 tbsp rice wine or dry sherry
- 30 ml/2 tbsp soy sauce
- 450 g/1 lb lean beef, chopped into strips
- 5 ml/1 tsp sugar
- 5 ml/1 tsp wine vinegar
- 50 g/2 oz chilli bean paste
- 90 ml/6 tbsp groundnut (peanut) oil
- freshly ground pepper

Directions:

1. Heat the oil and fry the beef until browned.
2. Put in the chilli bean paste and pepper and stir-fry for approximately three minutes.
3. Put in the ginger, wine or sherry and celery and stir thoroughly together.
4. Put in the soy sauce, sugar and vinegar and stir-fry for approximately two minutes.

SHREDDED TOFU-CHILLI BEEF

Yield: 4 Servings

Ingredients:

- 1 egg white
- 1 slice ginger root, chopped
- 10 ml/2 tsp soy sauce
- 100 g/4 oz dried tofu, chopped into strips
- 15 ml/1 tbsp water
- 2½ ml/ ½ tsp sesame oil
- 225 g/8 oz lean beef, chopped
- 250 ml/8 fl oz/1 cup groundnut (peanut) oil
- 5 ml/1 tsp cornflour (cornstarch)
- 5 red chilli peppers, chopped into strips

- pinch of salt

Directions:

1. Combine the beef with the egg white, half the sesame oil, the cornflour and salt.
2. Heat the oil and stir-fry the beef until almost cooked.
3. Take out of the pan.
4. Put in the tofu to the pan and stir-fry for approximately two minutes then remove from the pan.
5. Put in the chilli peppers and stir-fry for approximately one minute.
6. Return the tofu to the pan with the water, ginger and soy sauce and stir thoroughly.
7. Put in the beef and stir-fry until well blended.
8. Serve sprinkled with the rest of the sesame oil.

SLOW BEEF CASSEROLE

Yield: 4 Servings

Ingredients:

- 1 turnip, cubed
- 10 ml/2 tbsp salt
- 15 ml/1 tbsp black dates, stoned
- 15 ml/1 tbsp lotus seeds
- 250 ml/8 fl oz/1 cup rice wine or dry sherry
- 3 carrots, sliced
- 3 slices ginger root, minced
- 30 ml/2 tbsp groundnut (peanut) oil
- 30 ml/2 tbsp tomato purée (paste)
- 450 g/1 lb stewing beef, cubed
- 900 ml beef stock

Directions:

1. Heat the oil in a large flameproof casserole or pan and fry the beef until sealed on all sides.
2. Add the rest of the ingredients, bring to the boil, cover tightly and simmer on the lowest heat for about 5 hours.
3. Serve from the pot.

STEAK STRIPS

Yield: 4 Servings

Ingredients:

- 1 cm/ ½ in slice ginger root
- 120 ml/4 fl oz/ ½ cup chicken stock
- 120 ml/4 fl oz/ ½ cup soy sauce
- 15 ml/1 tbsp brown sugar
- 15 ml/1 tbsp groundnut (peanut) oil
- 2 cloves garlic, crushed
- 30 ml/2 tbsp rice wine or dry sherry
- 450 g/1 lb rump steak

Directions:

1. Firm the steak in the freezer then chop it into long thin slices.
2. Combine all the rest of the ingredients and marinate the steak in the mixture for about 6 hours.
3. Weave the steak on to soaked wooden skewers and grill for a few minutes until cooked to your liking, brushing occasionally with the marinade.

STEAK WITH POTATOES

Yield: 4 Servings

Ingredients:

- 1 clove garlic, crushed
- 1 onion, chopped
- 15 ml/1 tbsp soy sauce
- 175 ml/6 fl oz beef stock
- 2½ ml/ ½ tsp freshly ground pepper
- 225 g/8 oz potatoes, cubed
- 250 ml/8 fl oz/1 cup chopped celery leaves
- 30 ml/2 tbsp cornflour (cornstarch)
- 450 g/1 lb steak

- 5 ml/1 tsp salt
- 60 ml/4 tbsp groundnut (peanut) oil
- 60 ml/4 tbsp water

Directions:

1. Chop the steak into strips then into thin slivers against the grain.
2. Heat the oil and fry the steak, salt, pepper, onion and garlic until slightly browned.
3. Put in the potatoes and stock, bring to the boil, cover and simmer for 10 minutes.
4. Put in the celery leaves and simmer for about 4 minutes until just soft.
5. Blend the cornflour, soy sauce and water to a paste, add to the pan and simmer, stirring, until the sauce clears and becomes thick.

STEAMED BEEF

Yield: 4 Servings

Ingredients:

- 15 ml/1 tbsp chopped flat-leaved parsley
- 15 ml/1 tbsp groundnut (peanut) oil
- 15 ml/1 tbsp rice wine or dry sherry
- 15 ml/1 tbsp soy sauce
- 2 slices ginger root, minced
- 2 spring onions (scallions), minced
- 2½ ml/ ½ tsp salt
- 2½ ml/ ½ tsp sugar
- 450 g/1 lb lean beef, sliced
- 5 ml/1 tsp cornflour (cornstarch)

Directions:

1. Put the beef into a container.
2. Combine the cornflour, ginger, soy sauce, wine or sherry, salt and sugar then stir into the beef.
3. Leave to stand for half an hour, stirring intermittently.
4. Put the beef slices in a shallow heatproof dish and drizzle with the oil and spring onions.
5. Steam on a rack over boiling water for about 40 minutes until the beef is cooked.
6. Serve sprinkled with parsley.

STEAMED BEEF WITH SWEET POTATOES

Yield: 4 Servings

Ingredients:

- 100 g/4 oz breadcrumbs
- 15 ml/1 tbsp black bean sauce
- 15 ml/1 tbsp sesame oil
- 15 ml/1 tbsp soy sauce
- 15 ml/1 tbsp sweet bean sauce
- 2 slices ginger root, minced
- 2 sweet potatoes, cubed
- 3 spring onions (scallions), finely chopped
- 30 ml/2 tbsp groundnut (peanut) oil
- 450 g/1 lb lean beef, finely sliced
- 5 ml/1 tsp sugar

Directions:

1. Put the beef into a container with the bean sauces, soy sauce, sugar and ginger and allow to marinate for half an hour.
2. Remove the beef from the marinade and add the sweet potatoes.
3. Leave to stand for approximately 20 minutes.
4. Put the potatoes on the base of a small bamboo steamer.
5. Coat the beef in the breadcrumbs and arrange on top of the potatoes.
6. Cover and steam over boiling water for 40 minutes.
7. Heat the sesame oil and stir-fry the spring onions for a few seconds.
8. Spoon over the beef and serve.

STEAMED MEAT PUDDING

Yield: 4 Servings

Ingredients:

- 1 clove garlic, crushed
- 1 egg, beaten

- 1 onion, diced
- 10 cabbage leaves
- 20 ml/2 tbsp mango chutney
- 225 g/8 oz minced (ground) beef
- 225 g/8 oz minced (ground) pork
- 30 ml/2 tbsp hoisin sauce
- 30 ml/2 tbsp soy sauce
- 300 ml/ ½ pt beef stock
- 45 ml/3 tbsp cornflour (cornstarch)
- 5 ml/1 tsp five-spice powder
- 5 ml/1 tsp salt
- 6 dried Chinese mushrooms
- 60 ml/4 tbsp chopped chives

Directions:

1. Soak the mushrooms in warm water for half an hour then drain.
2. Discard the caps and chop the caps.
3. Mix with the minced meats, onion, chutney, hoisin sauce, soy sauce, five-spice powder and garlic and season with salt.
4. Put in the egg and cornflour and mix in the chives.
5. Line the steam basket with the cabbage leaves.
6. Shape the mince into a cake shape and place on the leaves.
7. Cover and steam over gently simmering meat stock for half an hour.

STEAMED MINCED BEEF

Yield: 4 Servings

Ingredients:

- 100 g/4 oz water chestnuts, finely
- 2 onions, finely chopped
- 450 g/1 lb minced (ground) beef
- 60 ml/4 tbsp rice wine or dry sherry
- 60 ml/4 tbsp soy sauce
- chopped
- salt and freshly ground pepper

Directions:

1. Combine all the ingredients, seasoning to taste with salt and pepper.
2. Press into a small heatproof bowl and stand in a steamer over simmering water.
3. Cover and steam for approximately twenty minutes until the meat is cooked and the dish has created its own tasty sauce.

STEWED BEEF

Yield: 4 Servings

Ingredients:

- 1 slice ginger root, chopped
- 2 spring onions (scallions), chopped
- 30 ml/2 tbsp rice wine or dry sherry
- 30 ml/2 tbsp soy sauce
- 30 ml/2 tbsp sugar
- 350 g/12 oz rolled joint of beef
- 45 ml/3 tbsp sesame oil
- 5 ml/1 tsp cinnamon

Directions:

1. Bring a saucepan of water to a rolling boil, add the meat, return the water to the boil and boil rapidly to seal the meat.
2. Take out of the pan.
3. Put the meat in a clean pan and add all the rest of the ingredients, reserving 15 ml/1 tbsp of sesame oil.
4. Fill the pan with just enough water to cover the meat, bring to the boil, cover and simmer gently for about 1 hour until the meat is soft.
5. Drizzle with the rest of the sesame oil and serve.

STEWED BEEF BRISKET

Yield: 4 Servings

Ingredients:

- 1 clove garlic, crushed
- 120 ml/4 fl oz/ ½ cup soy sauce
- 15 ml/1 tbsp cornflour (cornstarch)
- 2 slices ginger root, chopped
- 225 g/8 oz Chinese cabbage
- 3 cloves star anise
- 3 spring onions (scallions), sliced
- 4 carrots, cubed
- 45 ml/3 tbsp groundnut (peanut) oil
- 45 ml/3 tbsp rice wine or dry sherry
- 45 ml/3 tbsp water
- 450 g/1 lb beef brisket
- 5 ml/1 tsp sugar

Directions:

1. Put the beef in a pan and just cover with water.
2. Bring to the boil, cover and simmer gently for about 1 ½ hours until the meat is soft.
3. Take out of the pan and eliminate the excess liquid well.
4. Cut into 2.5 cm/1 in cubes and reserve 250 ml/ 8 fl oz/1 cup of stock.
5. Heat the oil and fry the spring onions, ginger and garlic for a few seconds.
6. Put in the soy sauce, sugar, wine or sherry and star anise and stir thoroughly.
7. Put in the beef and reserved stock.
8. Bring to the boil, cover and simmer for approximately 20 minutes.
9. In the meantime, cook the Chinese cabbage in boiling water until soft.
10. Transfer the meat and vegetables to a warmed serving plate.
11. Blend the cornflour and water to a paste, mix it into the sauce and simmer, stirring, until the sauce clears and becomes thick.
12. Pour over the beef and serve with the Chinese cabbage.

STIR-FRIED BEEF AND MUSHROOMS

Yield: 4 Servings

Ingredients:

- 1 slice ginger root, minced
- 120 ml/4 fl oz/ ½ cup beef stock
- 15 ml/1 tbsp cornflour (cornstarch)

- 15 ml/1 tbsp rice wine or dry sherry
- 15 ml/1 tbsp soy sauce
- 2½ ml/ ½ tsp salt
- 2½ ml/ ½ tsp sugar
- 225 g/8 oz lean beef
- 225 g/8 oz mushrooms, sliced
- 45 ml/3 tbsp groundnut (peanut) oil

Directions:

1. Slice the beef finely against the grain.
2. Combine the cornflour, wine or sherry, soy sauce and sugar, stir into the beef and toss comprehensively. to coat.
3. Heat the oil and stir-fry the ginger for approximately one minute.
4. Put in the beef and stir-fry until just browned.
5. Put in the salt and mushrooms and stir thoroughly.
6. Put in the stock, bring to the boil and simmer, stirring, until the sauce becomes thick.

STIR-FRIED BEEF SHREDS WITH GREEN PEPPERS

Yield: 4 Servings

Ingredients:

- 1 egg white
- 15 ml/1 tbsp cornflour (cornstarch)
- 15 ml/1 tbsp soy sauce
- 2 large green peppers, diced
- 2 red chilli peppers, diced
- 2 slices ginger root, shredded
- 2½ ml/ ½ tsp salt
- 2½ ml/ ½ tsp sugar
- 225 g/8 oz lean beef, shredded
- 30 ml/2 tbsp groundnut (peanut) oil
- 5 ml/1 tsp rice wine or dry sherry
- oil for deep-frying

Directions:

1. Put the beef into a container with the egg white, cornflour, salt, wine or sherry and sugar and allow to marinate for half an hour.
2. Heat the oil and deep-fry the beef until slightly browned.
3. Take out of the pan and eliminate the excess liquid well.
4. Heat the oil and stir-fry the chilli peppers and ginger for a few seconds.
5. Put in the beef and soy sauce and stir-fry until just soft.
6. Put in the green peppers, mix well and stir-fry for approximately two minutes.
7. Serve Immediately.

STIR-FRIED BEEF WITH NOODLES

Yield: 4 Servings

Ingredients:

- 100 g/4 oz thin egg noodles
- 120 ml/4 fl oz/ ½ cup water
- 15 ml/1 tbsp rice wine or dry sherry
- 2½ ml/ ½ tsp salt
- 2½ ml/ ½ tsp sugar
- 225 g/8 oz lean beef, shredded
- 30 ml/2 tbsp groundnut (peanut) oil
- 30 ml/2 tbsp soy sauce

Directions:

1. Soak the noodles until slightly softened then eliminate the excess liquid and chop them into 7.5 cm/3 in lengths.
2. Heat half the oil and stir-fry the beef until just browned.
3. Put in the soy sauce, wine or sherry, salt and sugar and stir-fry for approximately two minutes then remove from the pan.
4. Heat the rest of the oil and stir-fry the noodles until coated with oil.
5. Return the beef mixture to the pan, add the water and bring to the boil.
6. Cook and simmer for approximately five minutes until the liquid is absorbed.

STIR-FRIED BEEF WITH SPRING ONIONS

Yield: 4 Servings

Ingredients:

- 15 ml/1 tbsp rice wine or dry sherry
- 225 g/8 oz lean beef, finely sliced
- 30 ml/2 tbsp sesame oil
- 45 ml/3 tbsp groundnut (peanut) oil
- 75 ml/5 tbsp soy sauce
- 8 spring onions (scallions), sliced

Directions:

1. Heat the oil and stir-fry the beef and onions until slightly browned.
2. Put in the soy sauce and wine or sherry and stir-fry until the meat is cooked to your liking.
3. Mix in the sesame oil and serve.

STIR-FRIED BEEF WITH TOFU

Yield: 4 Servings

Ingredients:

- 1 clove garlic, crushed
- 10 ml/2 tsp rice wine or dry sherry
- 10 ml/2 tsp soy sauce
- 120 ml/4 fl oz/ ½ cup beef stock
- 2 spring onions (scallions), chopped
- 20 ml/4 tsp cornflour (cornstarch)
- 2½ ml/ ½ tsp salt
- 2½ ml/ ½ tsp sugar
- 225 g/8 oz minced (ground) beef
- 225 g/8 oz tofu, cubed
- 30 ml/2 tbsp groundnut (peanut) oil
- pinch of freshly ground pepper

Directions:

1. Mix half the cornflour, half the soy sauce and half the wine or sherry.
2. Put into the beef and mix well.
3. Heat the oil and stir-fry the salt and garlic for a few seconds.

4. Put in the beef and stir-fry until just browned.
5. Mix in the stock and bring to the boil.
6. Put in the tofu, cover and simmer for approximately two minutes.
7. Mix the rest of the cornflour, soy sauce and wine or sherry, put them into the pan and simmer, stirring, until the sauce becomes thick.

STIR-FRIED CURRIED BEEF

Yield: 4 Servings

Ingredients:

- 1 large onion, sliced
- 1 slice ginger root, minced
- 120 ml/4 fl oz/ ½ cup beef stock
- 15 ml/1 tbsp cornflour (cornstarch)
- 15 ml/1 tbsp rice wine or dry sherry
- 225 g/8 oz lean beef
- 30 ml/2 tbsp curry powder
- 30 ml/2 tbsp groundnut (peanut) oil
- 45 ml/3 tbsp water
- 5 ml/1 tsp sugar

Directions:

1. Slice the beef finely against the grain.
2. Heat the oil and fry the onion until translucent.
3. Put in the curry and ginger and stir-fry for a few seconds.
4. Put in the beef and stir-fry until just browned.
5. Put in the wine or sherry and stock, bring to the boil, cover and simmer for approximately five minutes until the beef is cooked.
6. Combine the sugar, cornflour and water, stir into the pan and simmer, stirring, until the sauce becomes thick.

STIR-FRIED MINCE WITH OYSTER SAUCE

Yield: 4 Servings

Ingredients:

- 1 onion, chopped
- 15 ml/1 tbsp oyster sauce
- 15 ml/1 tbsp soy sauce
- 2 cloves garlic, crushed
- 225 g/8 oz minced (ground) beef
- 30 ml/2 tbsp groundnut (peanut) oil
- 30 ml/2 tbsp rice wine or dry sherry
- 50 g/2 oz bamboo shoots, chopped
- 50 g/2 oz water chestnuts, chopped

Directions:

1. Heat the oil and fry the garlic until slightly browned.
2. Put in the meat and stir until browned on all sides.
3. Put in the onion, water chestnuts and bamboo shoots and stir-fry for approximately two minutes.
4. Mix in the soy sauce and wine or sherry, cover and simmer for 4 minutes.

STIR-FRIED ONION CRACKLE BEEF

Yield: 4 Servings

Ingredients:

- 1 clove garlic, crushed
- 2 spring onions (scallions), minced
- 225 g/8 oz lean beef
- 30 ml/2 tbsp groundnut (peanut) oil
- 30 ml/2 tbsp rice wine or dry sherry
- 30 ml/2 tbsp soy sauce
- 5 ml/1 tsp wine vinegar
- few drops of sesame oil

Directions:

1. Chop the beef into thin slices against the grain.
2. Combine the spring onions, soy sauce and wine or sherry, stir into the beef and allow to stand for half an hour.
3. Drain, discarding the marinade.
4. Heat the oil and fry the garlic until slightly browned.
5. Put in the beef and stir-fry until just browned.
6. Put in the vinegar and sesame oil, cover and simmer for approximately two minutes.

STUFFED STEAK

Yield: 4 Servings

Ingredients:

- 1 bay leaf, crushed
- 1 onion, sliced
- 10 ml/2 tsp soy sauce
- 2½ ml/ ½ tsp freshly ground pepper
- 2½ ml/ ½ tsp whole cloves
- 225 g/8 oz cooked long-grain rice
- 30 ml/2 tbsp groundnut (peanut) oil
- 30 ml/2 tbsp lard
- 30 ml/2 tbsp sugar
- 5 ml/1 tsp chopped fresh parsley
- 5 ml/1 tsp ground cinnamon
- 60 ml/4 tbsp wine vinegar
- 675 g/1 ½ lb rump steak in one piece
- pinch of salt

Directions:

1. Put the steak into a large bowl.
2. Bring the wine vinegar, sugar, soy sauce, pepper, cloves, cinnamon and bay leaf to the boil in a pan then allow to cool.
3. Pour over the steak, cover and allow to marinate in the refrigerator overnight, turning intermittently.
4. Combine the rice, parsley, salt and oil.
5. Eliminate the excess liquid from the beef and spread the mixture over the steak, roll up and tie securely with string.

6. Melt the lard, add the onion and steak and fry until browned on all sides.
7. Pour in enough water almost to cover the steak, cover and simmer for 1 ½ hours or until the meat is soft.

PORK AND HAM

Pork is very popular in china, and Chinese porn dishes are famous for being sweet and sour. Chinese pork recipes have wide ranging flavours and combinaitons.

BACON WITH CABBAGE

Yield: 4 Servings

Ingredients:

- ½ cabbage, shredded
- 1 slice ginger root, minced
- 15 ml/1 tbsp oyster sauce
- 2½ ml/½ tsp salt
- 4 rashers streaky bacon, rinded and chopped
- 75 ml/5 tbsp chicken stock

Directions:

1. Fry the bacon until crisp then remove it from the pan.
2. Put in the salt and ginger and stir-fry for approximately two minutes.
3. Put in the cabbage and stir thoroughly then mix in the bacon and add the stock, cover and simmer for approximately five minutes until the cabbage is soft but still slightly crisp.
4. Mix in the oyster sauce, cover and simmer for approximately one minute and serve.

BARBECUED MAPLE SPARE RIBS

Yield: 4 Servings

Ingredients:

- 1 clove garlic, crushed

- 15 ml/1 tbsp rice wine or dry sherry
- 45 ml/3 tbsp soy sauce
- 5 ml/1 tsp salt
- 5 ml/1 tsp sugar
- 60 ml/4 tbsp maple syrup
- 900 g/2 lb pork spare ribs

Directions:

1. Chop the spare ribs into 5 cm/2 in pieces and place into a container.
2. Combine all the ingredients, add the spare ribs and stir thoroughly.
3. Cover and allow to marinate overnight.
4. Grill (broil) or barbecue over a medium heat for about 30 minutes.

BARBECUED PORK

Yield: 4 Servings

Ingredients:

- 1 clove garlic, crushed
- 1 spring onion (scallion), chopped into chunks
- 10 ml/2 tsp red food colour (optional)
- 15 ml/1 tbsp brown sugar
- 15 ml/1 tbsp honey
- 2 pork fillets
- 2½ ml/½ tsp cinnamon
- 30 ml/2 tbsp red wine
- 60 ml/4 tbsp soy sauce

Directions:

1. Put the meat into a container.
2. Combine all the rest of the ingredients, pour over the pork and allow to marinate for 2 hours, turning intermittently.
3. Eliminate the excess liquid from the meat and place it on a wire rack in a roasting tin.
4. Cook in a preheated oven at 180°C/350°'F/gas mark 4 for about 45 minutes, turning and basting with the marinade during cooking.
5. Serve chop into thin slices.

BARBECUED SPARE RIBS

Yield: 4 Servings

Ingredients:

- 15 ml/1 tbsp honey
- 3 cloves garlic, crushed
- 30 ml/2 tbsp tomato purée (paste)
- 45 ml/3 tbsp brown sugar
- 60 ml/4 tbsp hoisin sauce
- 60 ml/4 tbsp rice wine or dry sherry
- 75 ml/5 tbsp soy sauce
- 900 g/2 lb pork spare ribs

Directions:

1. Combine the garlic, soy sauce, hoisin sauce, wine or sherry, brown sugar and tomato purée, pour over the ribs, cover and allow to marinate overnight.
2. Eliminate the excess liquid from the ribs and arrange them on a rack in a roasting tin with a little water underneath.
3. Roast in a preheated oven at 180°C/350°F/gas mark 4 for 45 minutes, basting intermittently with the marinade, reserving 30 ml/2 tbsp of the marinade.
4. Combine the reserved marinade with the honey and brush over the ribs.
5. Barbecue or grill (broil) using a hot grill for approximately ten minutes.

BARBECUE-ROAST PORK

Yield: 4 Servings

Ingredients:

- 1.25 kg/3 lb boned pork shoulder
- 100 g/4 oz/½ cup brown sugar
- 120 ml/4 fl oz/½ cup rice wine or dry sherry
- 2 cloves garlic, crushed
- 2 spring onions (scallions), chopped
- 250 ml/8 fl oz/1 cup soy sauce

- 5 ml/1 tsp salt

Directions:

1. Put the pork into a container.
2. Combine the rest of the ingredients, pour over the pork, cover and allow to marinate for approximately three hours.
3. Transfer the pork and marinade to a roasting tin and roast in a preheated oven at 200°C/400°F/gas mark 6 for 10 minutes.
4. Reduce the temperature to 160°C/325°F/gas mark 3 for 1¾ hours until the pork is cooked.

BRAISED FRAGRANT PORK

Yield: 6-8 Servings

Ingredients:

- ½ cinnamon stick
- 1 piece tangerine peel
- 1 slice ginger root, chopped
- 120 ml/4 fl oz/½ cup soy sauce
- 2 spring onions (scallions), sliced
- 2½ ml/½ tsp anise powder
- 250 ml/8 fl oz/1 cup rice wine or dry sherry
- 250 ml/8 fl oz/1 cup water
- 4 cloves
- 45 ml/3 tbsp groundnut (peanut) oil
- 5 ml/1 tsp salt
- 900 g/2 lb lean pork, cubed

Directions:

1. Soak the tangerine peel in water while you prepare the dish.
2. Heat the oil and fry the pork until slightly browned.
3. Put in the wine or sherry, soy sauce, anise powder, cinnamon, cloves, salt and water.
4. Bring to the boil, add the tangerine peel, spring onion and ginger.
5. Cover and simmer for about 1½ hours until soft, stirring intermittently and adding a little extra boiling water if needed.
6. Remove the spices and serve.

BRAISED PORK KNUCKLE IN RED SAUCE

Yield: 4 Servings

Ingredients:

- 1 clove garlic, crushed
- 1 l/1½ pts/4¼ cups boiling water
- 1 large knuckle of pork
- 1 stick celery, sliced
- 120 ml/4 fl oz/½ cup soy sauce
- 120 ml/4 fl oz/½ cup wine vinegar
- 2 carrots, finely sliced
- 30 ml/2 tbsp mango chutney
- 45 ml/3 tbsp hoisin sauce
- 45 ml/3 tbsp honey
- 5 ml/1 tsp aniseed
- 5 ml/1 tsp coriander
- 5 ml/1 tsp juniper berries
- 5 ml/1 tsp salt
- 6 spring onions (scallions), sliced
- 60 ml/4 tbsp chopped chives
- 60 ml/4 tbsp groundnut (peanut) oil
- 75 ml/5 tbsp tomato purée (paste)

Directions:

1. Bring the knuckle of pork to the boil with the water, salt, wine vinegar, 45 ml/3 tbsp of soy sauce, the honey and spices.
2. Put in the vegetables, bring back to the boil, cover and simmer for about 1½ hours until the meat is soft.
3. Remove the meat and vegetables from the pan, chop the meat off the bone and dice it.
4. Heat the oil and fry the meat until a golden-brown colour is achieved.
5. Put in the vegetables and stir-fry for approximately five minutes.
6. Add the rest of the soy sauce, the hoisin sauce, chutney, tomato purée and garlic.
7. Bring to the boil, stirring, then simmer for approximately three minutes.
8. Serve sprinkled with chives.

BRAISED PORK WITH EGGS

Yield: 4 Servings

Ingredients:

- 1 onion, chopped
- 15 ml/1 tbsp brown sugar
- 3 hard-boiled (hard-cooked) eggs
- 30 ml/2 tbsp groundnut (peanut) oil
- 45 ml/3 tbsp rice wine or dry sherry
- 450 g/1 lb lean pork
- 90 ml/6 tbsp soy sauce

Directions:

1. Bring a saucepan of water to the boil, add the pork, return to the boil and boil until sealed.
2. Take out of the pan, eliminate the excess liquid well then chop into cubes.
3. Heat the oil and fry the onion until softened.
4. Put in the pork and stir-fry until slightly browned.
5. Mix in the soy sauce, wine or sherry and sugar, cover and simmer for half an hour, stirring intermittently.
6. Score the outside of the eggs slightly then put them into the pan, cover and simmer for another 30 minutes.

CHINESE ROAST PORK

Yield: 6 Servings

Ingredients:

- 1.25 kg/3 lb joint of pork, thickly sliced
- 15 ml/1 tbsp brown sugar
- 15 ml/1 tbsp honey
- 2 cloves garlic, finely chopped
- 2½ ml/½ tsp five-spice powder
- 30 ml/2 tbsp rice wine or dry sherry
- 90 ml/6 tbsp soy sauce

Directions:

1. Put the pork in a shallow dish.
2. Combine the rest of the ingredients, pour over the pork, cover and marinate in the refrigerator overnight, turning and basting intermittently.
3. Put the pork slices on a rack in a roasting tin filled with a little water and baste well with the marinade.
4. Roast in a preheated oven at 180°C/350°F/gas mark 5 for about 1 hour, basting intermittently, until the pork is cooked.

COLD PORK WITH MUSTARD

Yield: 4 Servings

Ingredients:

- 1 kg/2 lb boned roasting pork
- 100 g/4 oz/½ cup brown sugar
- 120 ml/4 fl oz/½ cup rice wine or dry sherry
- 250 ml/8 fl oz/1 cup soy sauce
- 3 spring onions (scallions), chopped
- 30 ml/2 tbsp mustard powder
- 5 ml/1 tsp salt

Directions:

1. Put the pork into a container.
2. Combine all the rest of the ingredients except the mustard and pour over the pork.
3. Allow to marinate for at least 2 hours, basting often.
4. Line a roasting tin with foil and stand the pork on a rack in the tin.
5. Roast in a preheated oven at 200°C/400°F/gas mark 6 for approximately ten minutes then reduce the temperature to 160°C/325°F/gas mark 3 for another 1¾ hours until the pork is soft.
6. Allow it to cool then chill in the refrigerator.
7. Slice very finely.
8. Combine the mustard powder with just enough water to make a creamy paste to serve with the pork.

CRISPY PORK PARCELS

Yield: 4 Servings

Ingredients:

- 100 g/4 oz/1 cup cornflour (cornstarch)
- 15 ml/1 tbsp cornflour (cornstarch)
- 15 ml/1 tbsp soy sauce
- 225 g/8 oz pork fillet, minced (ground)
- 30 ml/2 tbsp groundnut (peanut) oil
- 30 ml/2 tbsp water
- 4 dried Chinese mushrooms
- 50 g/2 oz peeled prawns, chopped
- 8 spring roll wrappers
- oil for deep-frying

Directions:

1. Soak the mushrooms in warm water for half an hour then drain.
2. Discard the stalks and finely chop the caps.
3. Heat the oil and fry the mushrooms, pork, prawns and soy sauce for approximately two minutes.
4. Blend the cornflour and water to a paste and stir into the mixture to make the filling.
5. Chop the wrappers into strips, place a little filling on the end of each one and roll up into triangles, sealing with a little flour and water mixture.
6. Dust generously with cornflour.
7. Heat the oil and deep-fry the triangles until crisp and golden brown.
8. Drain thoroughly and serve.

CRISPY PRAWN SPARE RIBS

Yield: 4 Servings

Ingredients:

- 1 egg, slightly beaten
- 100 g/4 oz breadcrumbs
- 30 ml/2 tbsp plain (all-purpose) flour
- 450 g/1 lb peeled prawns

- 5 ml/1 tsp sugar
- 900 g/2 lb pork spare ribs
- oil for deep-frying
- salt and freshly ground pepper

Directions:

1. Chop the spare ribs into 5 cm/2 in chunks.
2. Trim off a little of the meat and mince it with the prawns, sugar, salt and pepper.
3. Mix in the flour and enough egg to make the mixture sticky.
4. Press round the pieces of spare rib then drizzle them with breadcrumbs.
5. Heat the oil and deep-fry the spare ribs until they come to the surface.
6. Drain thoroughly and serve hot.

DEEP-FRIED HAM AND EGG BALLS

Yield: 4 Servings

Ingredients:

- 10 ml/2 tbsp plain (all-purpose) flour
- 2 spring onions (scallions), minced
- 2½ ml/½ tsp salt
- 225 g/8 oz smoked ham, minced
- 3 eggs, beaten
- 4 slices stale bread
- oil for deep-frying

Directions:

1. Combine the ham, spring onions and eggs.
2. Make the bread into crumbs and mix it into the ham with the flour and salt.
3. mould into walnut-sized balls.
4. Heat the oil and deep-fry the meat balls until a golden-brown colour is achieved.
5. Drain thoroughly on kitchen paper.

DEEP-FRIED PORK BALLS

Yield: 4 Servings

Ingredients:

- 1 slice ginger root, minced
- 10 ml/2 tsp soy sauce
- 15 ml/1 tbsp cornflour (cornstarch)
- 15 ml/1 tbsp water
- 2½ ml/½ tsp salt
- 450 g/1 lb minced (ground) pork
- oil for deep-frying

Directions:

1. Combine the pork and ginger.
2. Combine the cornflour, water, salt and soy sauce then stir the mixture into the pork and mix well.
3. mould into walnut-sized balls.
4. Heat the oil and fry the pork balls until they rise to the top of the oil.
5. Take out of the oil and reheat.
6. Return the pork to the pan and fry for approximately one minute.
7. Drain well.

DEEP-FRIED PORK FILLET

Yield: 4 Servings

Ingredients:

- 15 ml/1 tbsp rice wine or dry sherry
- 15 ml/1 tbsp soy sauce
- 30 ml/2 tbsp cornflour (cornstarch)
- 350 g/12 oz pork fillet, cubed
- 5 ml/1 tsp sesame oil
- oil for deep-frying

Directions:

1. Combine the pork, wine or sherry, soy sauce, sesame oil and cornflour so that the pork is coated with a thick batter.
2. Heat the oil and deep-fry the pork for about 3 minutes until crisp.

3. Remove the pork from the pan, reheat the oil and deep-fry again for about 3 minutes.

DEEP-FRIED PORK WITH CRAB MEAT

Yield: 4 Servings

Ingredients:

- 1 egg white, slightly beaten
- 100 g/4 oz bamboo shoots, chopped
- 100 g/4 oz mushrooms, chopped
- 15 ml/1 tbsp chopped fresh flat-leaved parsley
- 2½ ml/½ tsp salt
- 225 g/8 oz cooked pork, sliced
- 225 g/8 oz crab meat, flaked
- 5 ml/1 tsp cornflour (cornstarch)
- oil for deep-frying

Directions:

1. Combine the crab meat, mushrooms, bamboo shoots, most of the cornflour and the salt.
2. Chop the meat into 5 cm/2 in squares.
3. Make into sandwiches with the crab meat mixture.
4. Coat in the egg white.
5. Heat the oil and deep-fry the sandwiches a few at a time until a golden-brown colour is achieved.
6. Drain well.
7. Serve sprinkled with parsley.

DEEP-FRIED SPARE RIBS

Yield: 4 Servings

Ingredients:

- 120 ml/4 fl oz/½ cup tomato ketchup (catsup)
- 120 ml/4 fl oz/½ cup wine vinegar

- 15 ml/1 tbsp mild curry powder
- 15 ml/1 tbsp paprika
- 2 cloves garlic, chopped
- 30 ml/2 tbsp honey
- 45 ml/3 tbsp rice wine or dry sherry
- 45 ml/3 tbsp soy sauce
- 5 ml/1 tsp salt
- 60 ml/4 tbsp chopped chives
- 60 ml/4 tbsp mango chutney
- 900 g/2 lb pork spare ribs
- oil for deep-frying

Directions:

1. Put the spare ribs into a container.
2. Combine all the ingredients except the oil and chives, pour over the ribs, cover and allow to marinate for at least 1 hour.
3. Heat the oil and deep-fry the ribs until crisp.
4. Serve sprinkled with chives.

DRUNKEN PORK

Yield: 6 Servings

Ingredients:

- 1 bottle dry white wine
- 1 spring onion (scallion), chopped
- 1.25 kg/3 lb boneless rolled pork joint
- 2 cloves garlic, chopped
- 30 ml/2 tbsp salt
- freshly ground pepper

Directions:

1. Put the pork in a pan and add the salt, pepper, spring onion and garlic.
2. Cover with boiling water, return to the boil, cover and simmer for half an hour.
3. Remove the pork from the pan, allow to cool and dry for 6 hours or overnight in the refrigerator.
4. Chop the pork into large pieces and place in a large screw-top jar.

5. Cover with the wine, seal and store in the refrigerator for at least 1 week.

FIERY PORK

Yield: 4 Servings

Ingredients:

- 1 green pepper, chopped into chunks
- 15 ml/1 tbsp brown sugar
- 15 ml/1 tbsp pepper
- 15 ml/1 tbsp sesame oil
- 150 ml/¼ pt/generous ½ cup chicken stock
- 2 slices pineapple, diced
- 200 g/7 oz bean sprouts
- 30 ml/2 tbsp groundnut (peanut) oil
- 30 ml/2 tbsp hoisin sauce
- 30 ml/2 tbsp soy sauce
- 45 ml/3 tbsp tomato ketchup (catsup)
- 450 g/1 lb pork fillet, chopped into strips
- 5 ml/1 tsp five-spice powder
- 6 spring onions (scallions), chopped

Directions:

1. Put the meat into a container.
2. Combine the soy sauce, hoisin sauce, five-spice powder, pepper and sugar, pour over the meat and allow to marinate for one hour.
3. Heat the oils and stir-fry the meat until a golden-brown colour is achieved.
4. Take out of the pan.
5. Put in the vegetables and fry for approximately two minutes.
6. Put in the pineapple, tomato ketchup and stock and bring to the boil.
7. Return the meat to the pan and heat through and serve.

FIVE-SPICE PORK

Yield: 4 Servings

Ingredients:

- 120 ml/4 fl oz/½ cup chicken stock
- 15 ml/1 tbsp rice wine or dry sherry
- 20 ml/2 tbsp groundnut (peanut) oil
- 2½ ml/½ tsp five-spice powder
- 2½ ml/½ tsp salt
- 225 g/8 oz lean pork
- 5 ml/1 tsp cornflour (cornstarch)
- Slice the pork finely against the grain.

Directions:

1. Combine the pork with the cornflour, five-spice powder, salt and wine or sherry and stir thoroughly to coat the pork.
2. Allow to stand for half an hour, stirring intermittently.
3. Heat the oil, add the pork and stir-fry for about 3 minutes.
4. Put in the stock, bring to the boil, cover and simmer for approximately three minutes.
5. Serve as soon as possible.

FRIED PORK KEBABS

Yield: 4 Servings

Ingredients:

- 100 g/4 oz cooked ham, finely sliced
- 15 ml/1 tbsp brown sugar
- 15 ml/1 tbsp oyster sauce
- 2 eggs, beaten
- 30 ml/2 tbsp rice wine or dry sherry
- 30 ml/2 tbsp soy sauce
- 30 ml/2 tbsp wine vinegar
- 45 ml/3 tbsp cornflour (cornstarch)
- 450 g/1 lb pork fillet, finely sliced
- 6 water chestnuts, finely sliced
- few drops of chilli oil
- oil for deep-frying

Directions:

1. Thread the pork, ham and water chestnuts alternately on to small skewers.
2. Combine the soy sauce, wine vinegar, sugar, oyster sauce and chilli oil.
3. Pour over the kebabs, cover and allow to marinate in the refrigerator for approximately three hours.
4. Combine the cornflour, wine or sherry and eggs to a smooth, thickish batter.
5. Twist the kebabs in the batter to coat them.
6. Heat the oil and deep-fry the kebabs until light golden brown.

HAM AND PINEAPPLE

Yield: 4 Servings

Ingredients:

- 1 clove garlic, crushed
- 120 ml/4 fl oz/½ cup chicken stock
- 15 ml/1 tbsp cornflour (cornstarch)
- 15 ml/1 tbsp groundnut (peanut) oil
- 15 ml/1 tbsp soy sauce
- 225 g/8 oz canned pineapple chunks in fruit juice
- 225 g/8 oz ham, chopped
- 4 dried Chinese mushrooms
- 50 g/2 oz bamboo shoots
- 50 g/2 oz water chestnuts, sliced

Directions:

1. Soak the mushrooms in warm water for half an hour then drain.
2. Discard the stems and slice the caps.
3. Heat the oil and fry the garlic until slightly browned.
4. Put in the mushrooms, water chestnuts and bamboo shoots and stir-fry for approximately two minutes.
5. Put in the ham and drained pineapple chunks and stir-fry for approximately one minute.
6. Add 30 ml/2 tbsp of the juice from the pineapple, most of the chicken stock and the soy sauce.
7. Bring to the boil, cover and simmer for approximately five minutes.
8. Combine the cornflour with the rest of the stock and mix it into the sauce.
9. Simmer, stirring, until the sauce clears and becomes thick.

HAM AND SPINACH STIR-FRY

Yield: 4 Servings

Ingredients:

- 1 clove garlic, minced
- 15 ml/1 tbsp cornflour (cornstarch)
- 15 ml/1 tbsp soy sauce
- 2 spring onions (scallions), chopped
- 2½ ml/½ tsp salt
- 225 g/8 oz ham, diced
- 30 ml/2 tbsp groundnut (peanut) oil
- 45 ml/3 tbsp water
- 450 g/1 lb spinach, shredded
- 5 ml/1 tsp sugar
- 60 ml/4 tbsp chicken stock

Directions:

1. Heat the oil and fry the salt, garlic and spring onions until slightly browned.
2. Put in the ham and stir-fry for approximately one minute.
3. Put in the spinach and stir until coated in oil.
4. Put in the stock, bring to the boil, cover and simmer for approximately two minutes until the spinach begins to wilt.
5. Combine the cornflour, soy sauce, water and sugar then mix it into the pan.
6. Simmer, stirring, until the sauce becomes thick.

MARINATED PORK

Yield: 4 Servings

Ingredients:

- 1 clove garlic, crushed
- 1 slice ginger root, minced
- 1 spring onion (scallion), sliced
- 15 ml/1 tbsp brown sugar

- 15 ml/1 tbsp rice wine or dry sherry
- 45 ml/3 tbsp groundnut (peanut) oil
- 450 g/1 lb lean pork
- 90 ml/6 tbsp soy sauce
- freshly ground pepper

Directions:

1. Combine the pork with the ginger, garlic, 30 ml/2 tbsp soy sauce and wine or sherry.
2. Allow to stand for half an hour, stirring intermittently, then lift the meat from the marinade.
3. Heat the oil and fry the pork until slightly browned.
4. Put in the spring onion, sugar, rest of the soy sauce and a pinch of pepper, cover and simmer for about 45 minutes until the pork is cooked.
5. Chop the pork into cubes then serve.

MARINATED PORK CHOPS

Yield: 6 Servings

Ingredients:

- 1 clove garlic, crushed
- 1 slice ginger root, minced
- 15 ml/1 tbsp brown sugar
- 2 spring onions (scallions), chopped
- 30 ml/2 tbsp rice wine or dry sherry
- 45 ml/3 tbsp groundnut (peanut) oil
- 6 pork chops
- 90 ml/6 tbsp soy sauce
- freshly ground pepper

Directions:

1. Chop the bone from the pork chops and chop the meat into cubes.
2. Combine the ginger, garlic, 30 ml/2 tbsp of soy sauce and the wine or sherry, pour over the pork and allow to marinate for half an hour, stirring intermittently.
3. Remove the meat from the marinade.
4. Heat the oil and fry the pork until slightly browned.
5. Put in the spring onions and stir-fry for approximately one minute.

6. Mix the rest of the soy sauce with the sugar and a pinch of pepper.
7. Stir into the sauce, bring to the boil, cover and simmer for about 30 minutes until the pork is soft.

MARINATED PORK WITH CABBAGE

Yield: 4 Servings

Ingredients:

- 1 slice ginger root, minced
- 1 stick cinnamon
- 100 g/4 oz Chinese cabbage hearts
- 100 g/4 oz pak choi
- 15 ml/1 tbsp groundnut (peanut) oil
- 15 ml/1 tbsp soy sauce
- 2 spring onions (scallions), chopped
- 3 cloves star anise
- 350 g/12 oz belly pork
- 45 ml/3 tbsp brown sugar
- 5 ml/1 tsp oyster sauce
- 5 ml/1 tsp tomato purée (paste)
- 600 ml/1 pt/2½ cups water

Directions:

1. Chop the pork into 10 cm/4 in chunks and place into a container.
2. Put in the spring onions, ginger, cinnamon, star anise, sugar and water and allow to stand for 40 minutes.
3. Heat the oil, lift the pork from the marinade and put it into the pan.
4. Fry until slightly browned then add the soy sauce, tomato purée and oyster sauce.
5. Bring to the boil and simmer for about 30 minutes until the pork is soft and the liquid has reduced, adding a little more water during cooking, if needed.
6. In the meantime, steam the cabbage hearts and pak choi over boiling water for approximately ten minutes until soft.
7. Lay out them on a warmed serving plate, top with the pork and spoon over the sauce.

PINEAPPLE SPARE RIBS

Yield: 4 Servings

Ingredients:

- 120 ml/4 fl oz/½ cup chicken stock
- 15 ml/1 tbsp cornflour (cornstarch)
- 15 ml/1 tbsp soy sauce
- 2 cloves garlic, finely chopped
- 200 g/7 oz canned pineapple chunks in fruit juice
- 3 spring onions (scallions), chopped
- 30 ml/2 tbsp groundnut (peanut) oil
- 50 g/2 oz/¼ cup brown sugar
- 60 ml/4 tbsp wine vinegar
- 600 ml/1 pt/2½ cups water
- 900 g/2 lb pork spare ribs

Directions:

1. Put the pork and water in a pan, bring to the boil, cover and simmer for approximately 20 minutes.
2. Drain well.
3. Heat the oil and fry the garlic until slightly browned.
4. Put in the ribs and stir-fry until well coated in the oil.
5. Eliminate the excess liquid from the pineapple chunks and add 120 ml/4 fl oz/½ cup of juice to the pan with the stock, wine vinegar, sugar and soy sauce.
6. Bring to the boil, cover and simmer for 10 minutes.
7. Put in the drained pineapple.
8. Combine the cornflour with a little water, mix it into the sauce and simmer, stirring, until the sauce clears and becomes thick.
9. Serve sprinkled with spring onions.

PORK AND BEAN SPROUTS

Yield: 4 Servings

Ingredients:

- 1 slice ginger root, minced

- 15 ml/1 tbsp rice wine or dry sherry
- 2½ ml/½ tsp salt
- 2½ ml/½ tsp sugar
- 225 g/8 oz lean pork, chopped into strips
- 30 ml/2 tbsp soy sauce
- 45 ml/3 tbsp groundnut (peanut) oil
- 450 g/1 lb bean sprouts

Directions:

1. Combine the pork, ginger, 15 ml/ 1 tbsp of soy sauce, the wine or sherry and sugar.
2. Briefly boil the bean sprouts in boiling water for approximately two minutes then drain.
3. Heat half the oil and stir-fry the pork for approximately three minutes until slightly browned.
4. Take out of the pan.
5. Heat the rest of the oil and stir-fry the bean sprouts with the salt for approximately one minute.
6. Drizzle with the rest of the soy sauce and stir-fry for another 1 minute.
7. Return the pork to the pan and stir-fry until heated through.

PORK AND PRAWN EGG ROLLS

Yield: 4 Servings

Ingredients:

- 1 egg, beaten
- 100 g/4 oz peeled prawns, chopped
- 12 egg roll skins
- 15 ml/1 tbsp soy sauce
- 2½ ml/½ tsp salt
- 225 g/8 oz bean sprouts
- 225 g/8 oz lean pork, shredded
- 30 ml/2 tbsp groundnut (peanut) oil
- 6 spring onions (scallions), chopped
- oil for deep-frying

Directions:

1. Heat the oil and fry the pork and spring onions until slightly browned.

2. In the meantime briefly boil the bean sprouts in boiling water for approximately two minutes then drain.
3. Put in the bean sprouts to the pan and stir-fry for approximately one minute.
4. Put in the prawns, soy sauce and salt and stir-fry for approximately two minutes.
5. Allow it to cool.
6. Put a little filling on the centre of each skin and brush the edges with beaten egg.
7. Fold in the sides then roll up the egg rolls, sealing the edges with egg.
8. Heat the oil and deep-fry the egg rolls until crisp and golden.

PORK AND PRAWN EGG ROLLS

Yield: 4 Servings

Ingredients:

- 10 ml/2 tsp soy sauce
- 100 g/4 oz bamboo shoots, chopped into strips
- 100 g/4 oz Chinese leaves, shredded
- 100 g/4 oz water chestnuts, chopped into strips
- 225 g/8 oz minced (ground) pork
- 225 g/8 oz prawns
- 3 spring onions (scallions), finely chopped
- 30 ml/2 tbsp groundnut (peanut) oil
- 5 ml/1 tsp salt
- 5 ml/1 tsp sugar
- 8 egg roll skins
- oil for deep-frying

Directions:

1. Heat the oil and fry the pork until sealed.
2. Put in the prawns and stir-fry for approximately one minute.
3. Put in the Chinese leaves, bamboo shoots, water chestnuts, soy sauce, salt and sugar and stir-fry for approximately one minute then cover and simmer for approximately five minutes.
4. Mix in the spring onions, turn into a colander and leave to drain.
5. Put a few spoonfuls of the filling mixture in the centre of each egg roll skin, fold up the bottom, fold in the sides, then roll upwards, enclosing the filling.
6. Seal the edge with a little flour and water mixture then leave to dry for half an hour.

7. Heat the oil and fry the egg rolls for approximately ten minutes until crisp and golden brown.
8. Drain thoroughly and serve.

PORK AND PRAWN WONTONS

Yield: 4 Servings

Ingredients:

- 100 g/4 oz mixed vegetables, chopped
- 100 g/4 oz mushrooms, chopped
- 15 ml/1 tbsp soy sauce
- 2 spring onions (scallions), chopped
- 2½ ml/½ tsp salt
- 225 g/8 oz minced (ground) pork
- 225 g/8 oz peeled prawns, chopped
- 40 wonton skins
- oil for deep-frying

Directions:

1. Heat a pan and fry the pork and spring onions until slightly browned.
2. Mix in the rest of the ingredients.
3. To fold the wontons, hold the skin in the palm of your left hand and spoon a little filling into the centre.
4. Moisten the edges with egg and fold the skin into a triangle, sealing the edges.
5. Moisten the corners with egg and twist them together.
6. Heat the oil and fry the wontons a few at a time until a golden-brown colour is achieved.
7. Drain thoroughly and serve.

PORK AND PRAWNS WITH NOODLE PANCAKE

Yield: 4 Servings

Ingredients:

- 1 clove garlic, crushed
- 10 ml/1 tsp cornflour (cornstarch)
- 100 g/4 oz mushrooms, sliced
- 225 g/8 oz lean pork, chopped into strips
- 225 g/8 oz peeled prawns
- 30 ml/2 tbsp groundnut (peanut) oil
- 30 ml/2 tbsp soy sauce
- 4 spring onions (scallions), chopped
- 4 stalks celery, sliced
- 45 ml/3 tbsp water
- 5 ml/1 tsp salt
- noodle pancake

Directions:

1. Heat the oil and salt and fry the spring onions and garlic until softened.
2. Put in the pork and stir-fry until slightly browned.
3. Put in the mushrooms and celery and stir-fry for approximately two minutes.
4. Put in the prawns, drizzle with soy sauce and stir until heated through.
5. Combine the cornflour and water to a paste, stir into the pan and simmer, stirring, until hot.
6. Pour over the noodle pancake to serve.

PORK CHOP SUEY

Yield: 4 Servings

Ingredients:

- 1 slice ginger root, chopped
- 100 g/4 oz bamboo shoots, chopped into strips
- 100 g/4 oz water chestnuts, finely sliced
- 15 ml/1 tbsp cornflour (cornstarch)
- 15 ml/1 tbsp rice wine or dry sherry
- 2 cloves garlic, crushed
- 225 g/8 oz lean pork, chopped into strips
- 3 spring onions (scallions), chopped
- 45 ml/3 tbsp soy sauce
- 5 ml/1 tsp salt

- 5 ml/1 tsp sugar
- 60 ml/4 tbsp groundnut (peanut) oil
- freshly ground pepper

Directions:

1. Briefly boil the bamboo shoots and water chestnuts in boiling water for approximately two minutes then eliminate the excess liquid and pat dry.
2. Heat 45 ml/3 tbsp of oil and fry the spring onions, garlic and ginger until slightly browned.
3. Put in the pork and stir-fry for 4 minutes.
4. Take out of the pan.
5. Heat the rest of the oil and stir-fry the vegetables for approximately three minutes.
6. Put in the pork, soy sauce, wine or sherry, salt, sugar and a pinch of pepper and stir-fry for 4 minutes.
7. Combine the cornflour with a little water, mix it into the pan and simmer, stirring, until the sauce clears and becomes thick.

PORK CHOW MEIN

Yield: 4 Servings

Ingredients:

- 1 onion, chopped into wedges
- 100 g/4 oz mushrooms, halved
- 120 ml/4 fl oz/½ cup chicken stock
- 15 ml/1 tbsp soy sauce
- 2½ ml/½ tsp salt
- 225 g/8 oz lean pork, chopped into strips
- 3 stalks celery, chopped
- 30 ml/2 tbsp groundnut (peanut) oil
- 4 dried Chinese mushrooms
- 4 spring onions (scallions), chopped
- 5 ml/1 tsp sugar
- soft-fried noodles

Directions:

1. Soak the mushrooms in warm water for half an hour then drain.

2. Discard the stalks and slice the caps.
3. Heat the oil and salt and fry the spring onions until softened.
4. Put in the pork and fry until slightly browned.
5. Mix in the soy sauce, sugar, celery, onion and both fresh and dried mushrooms and stir-fry for about 4 minutes until the ingredients are well blended.
6. Put in the stock and simmer for approximately three minutes.
7. Add half the noodles to the pan and stir gently, then add the rest of the noodles and stir until heated through.

PORK EGG ROLLS

Yield: 4 Servings

Ingredients:

- 1 egg, beaten
- 1 slice ginger root, minced
- 1 spring onion, chopped
- 12 egg roll skins
- 15 ml/1 tbsp soy sauce
- 15 ml/1 tbsp water
- 225 g/8 oz lean pork, shredded
- oil for deep-frying

Directions:

1. Combine the pork, ginger, onion, soy sauce and water.
2. Put a little of the filling on the centre of each skin and brush the edges with beaten egg.
3. Fold in the sides then roll the egg roll away from you, sealing the edges with egg.
4. Steam on a rack in a steamer for half an hour until the pork is cooked.
5. Heat the oil and deep-fry for a few minutes until crisp and golden.

PORK IN RED SAUCE

Yield: 4 Servings

Ingredients:

- 1 onion, sliced
- 1 red pepper, chopped into strips
- 1 stick celery, chopped into strips
- 15 ml/1 tbsp cornflour (cornstarch)
- 15 ml/1 tbsp water
- 2 carrots, chopped into strips
- 225 g/8 oz pork kidneys, chopped into strips
- 30 ml/2 tbsp groundnut (peanut) oil
- 30 ml/2 tbsp plum sauce
- 30 ml/2 tbsp wine vinegar
- 300 ml/½ pt/1¼ cups chicken stock
- 4 spring onions (scallions), chopped into strips
- 45 ml/3 tbsp dry white wine
- 45 ml/3 tbsp soy sauce
- 450 g/1 lb pork, chopped into strips
- 5 ml/1 tsp brown sugar
- 5 ml/1 tsp five-spice powder

Directions:

1. Heat the oil and fry the kidneys for approximately two minutes then remove them from the pan.
2. Reheat the oil and fry the pork until slightly browned.
3. Put in the vegetables and stir-fry for approximately three minutes.
4. Put in the soy sauce, wine, stock, plum sauce, wine vinegar, five-spice powder and sugar, bring to the boil, cover and simmer for half an hour until cooked.
5. Put in the kidneys.
6. Combine the cornflour and water and stir into the pan.
7. Bring to the boil then simmer, stirring, until the sauce becomes thick.

PORK KIDNEYS WITH MANGETOUT

Yield: 4 Servings

Ingredients:

- 1 onion, chopped
- 1 slice ginger root, minced
- 15 ml/1 tbsp cornflour (cornstarch)

- 15 ml/1 tbsp rice wine or dry sherry
- 2½ ml/½ tsp salt
- 225 g/8 oz mangetout (snow peas)
- 3 stalks celery, chopped
- 30 ml/2 tbsp groundnut (peanut) oil
- 30 ml/2 tbsp soy sauce
- 4 pork kidneys, halved and cored
- 45 ml/3 tbsp water
- 5 ml/1 tsp sugar
- 60 ml/4 tbsp chicken stock

Directions:

1. Parboil the kidneys for 10 minute then eliminate the excess liquid and rinse in cold water.
2. Heat the oil and fry the salt and ginger for a few seconds.
3. Put in the kidneys and stir-fry for 30 seconds until coated with oil.
4. Put in the celery and onion and stir-fry for approximately two minutes.
5. Put in the soy sauce, wine or sherry and sugar and stir-fry for approximately one minute.
6. Put in the stock, bring to the boil, cover and simmer for approximately one minute.
7. Mix in the mangetout, cover and simmer for approximately one minute.
8. Combine the cornflour and water then mix it into the sauce and simmer until the sauce clears and becomes thick.
9. Serve Immediately.

PORK WITH ALMONDS

Yield: 4 Servings

Ingredients:

- 100 g/4 oz bamboo shoots, diced
- 100 g/4 oz mushrooms, diced
- 250 ml/8 fl oz/1 cup stock
- 3 stalks celery, diced
- 350 g/12 oz pork, diced
- 4 water chestnuts, diced
- 45 ml/3 tbsp soy sauce

- 50 g/2 oz peas
- 50 g/2 oz/½ cup flaked almonds
- 60 ml/4 tbsp groundnut (peanut) oil
- salt and freshly ground pepper

Directions:

1. Heat the oil and fry the almonds until slightly browned.
2. Pour off most of the oil, add the pork and stir-fry for approximately one minute.
3. Put in the bamboo shoots, celery, peas, water chestnuts and mushrooms and stir-fry for approximately one minute.
4. Put in the stock, soy sauce, salt and pepper, bring to the boil, cover and simmer for 10 minutes.

PORK WITH BAMBOO SHOOTS

Yield: 4 Servings

Ingredients:

- 1 slice ginger root, minced
- 100 g/4 oz bamboo shoots, sliced
- 2 cloves garlic, crushed
- 250 ml/8 fl oz/1 cup soy sauce
- 3 spring onions (scallions), sliced
- 30 ml/2 tbsp brown sugar
- 30 ml/2 tbsp groundnut (peanut) oil
- 30 ml/2 tbsp rice wine or dry sherry
- 450 g/1 lb lean pork, cubed
- 5 ml/1 tsp salt
- 600 ml/1 pt/2½ cups water

Directions:

1. Heat the oil and fry the pork until a golden-brown colour is achieved.
2. Drain off any excess oil, add the spring onions, garlic and ginger and fry for approximately two minutes.
3. Put in the soy sauce, wine or sherry, sugar and salt and stir thoroughly.
4. Put in the water, bring to the boil, cover and simmer for 45 minutes.
5. Put in the bamboo shoots, cover and simmer for another 20 minutes.

PORK WITH BEAN SPROUTS

Yield: 4 Servings

Ingredients:

- 120 ml/4 fl oz/½ cup chicken stock
- 15 ml/1 tbsp cornflour (cornstarch)
- 15 ml/1 tbsp rice wine or dry sherry
- 15 ml/1 tbsp soy sauce
- 2 cloves garlic, crushed
- 2½ ml/½ tsp salt
- 2½ ml/½ tsp sesame oil
- 225 g/8 oz cooked pork, cubed
- 3 spring onions (scallions), chopped
- 30 ml/2 tbsp groundnut (peanut) oil
- 450 g/1 lb bean sprouts
- 5 ml/1 tsp sugar

Directions:

1. Heat the oil and fry the salt and garlic until slightly browned.
2. Put in the bean sprouts and pork and stir-fry for approximately two minutes.
3. Add half the stock, bring to the boil, cover and simmer for approximately three minutes.
4. Mix the rest of the stock with the rest of the ingredients, stir into the pan, return to the boil and simmer for 4 minutes, stirring.
5. Serve sprinkled with spring onion.

PORK WITH CABBAGE

Yield: 4 Servings

Ingredients:

- 10 ml/2 tsp cornflour (cornstarch)
- 120 ml/4 fl oz/½ cup dry white wine
- 15 ml/1 tbsp water

- 2 cloves garlic, chopped
- 2 onions, sliced
- 2 pieces stem ginger, chopped
- 2 red peppers, chopped into strips
- 30 ml/2 tbsp groundnut (peanut) oil
- 30 ml/2 tbsp honey
- 350 g/12 oz white cabbage, shredded
- 45 ml/3 tbsp soy sauce
- 450 g/1 lb pork, chopped into strips
- 6 dried Chinese mushrooms
- salt and pepper

Directions:

1. Soak the mushrooms in warm water for half an hour then drain.
2. Discard the stalks and slice the caps.
3. Heat the oil and fry the pork until slightly browned.
4. Put in the vegetables, garlic and ginger and stir-fry for approximately one minute.
5. Put in the honey, soy sauce and wine, bring to the boil, cover and simmer for about forty minutes until the meat is cooked.
6. Season with salt and pepper.
7. Combine the cornflour and water and mix it into the pan.
8. Bring just up to the boil, stirring constantly, then simmer for approximately one minute.

PORK WITH CABBAGE AND TOMATOES

Yield: 4 Servings

Ingredients:

- ½ cabbage, shredded
- 1 clove garlic, crushed
- 1 onion, finely chopped
- 15 ml/1 tbsp soy sauce
- 250 ml/8 fl oz/1 cup stock
- 30 ml/2 tbsp cornflour (cornstarch)
- 30 ml/2 tbsp groundnut (peanut) oil
- 450 g/1 lb lean pork, chopped into slivers
- 450 g/1 lb tomatoes, skinned and quartered

- 60 ml/4 tbsp water
- salt and freshly ground pepper

Directions:

1. Heat the oil and fry the pork, salt, pepper, garlic and onion until slightly browned.
2. Put in the cabbage, tomatoes and stock, bring to the boil, cover and simmer for approximately ten minutes until the cabbage is just soft.
3. Blend the cornflour, soy sauce and water to a paste, stir into the pan and simmer, stirring, until the sauce clears and becomes thick.

PORK WITH CELERY

Yield: 4 Servings

Ingredients:

- 1 clove garlic, crushed
- 1 slice ginger root, minced
- 1 spring onion (scallion), chopped
- 100 g/4 oz celery, finely sliced
- 15 ml/1 tbsp rice wine or dry sherry
- 225 g/8 oz lean pork, chopped into strips
- 45 ml/3 tbsp groundnut (peanut) oil
- 45 ml/3 tbsp soy sauce
- 5 ml/1 tsp cornflour (cornstarch)

Directions:

1. Heat the oil and fry the garlic, spring onion and ginger until slightly browned.
2. Put in the pork and stir-fry for approximately ten minutes until a golden-brown colour is achieved.
3. Put in the celery and stir-fry for approximately three minutes.
4. Add the rest of the ingredients and stir-fry for approximately three minutes.

PORK WITH CHESTNUTS AND MUSHROOMS

Yield: 4 Servings

Ingredients:

- 100 g/4 oz water chestnuts, sliced
- 100 g/4 oz/1 cup chestnuts
- 15 ml/1 tbsp soy sauce
- 2½ ml/½ tsp salt
- 30 ml/2 tbsp groundnut (peanut) oil
- 375 ml/13 fl oz/1½ cups chicken stock
- 4 dried Chinese mushrooms
- 450 g/1 lb lean pork, cubed

Directions:

1. Soak the mushrooms in warm water for half an hour then drain.
2. Discard the stalks and halve the caps.
3. Briefly boil the chestnuts in boiling water for approximately one minute then drain.
4. Heat the oil and salt then fry the pork until slightly browned.
5. Put in the soy sauce and stir-fry for approximately one minute.
6. Put in the stock and bring to the boil.
7. Put in the chestnuts and water chestnuts, bring back to the boil, cover and simmer for about 1½ hours until the meat is soft.

PORK WITH CHUTNEY

Yield: 4 Servings

Ingredients:

- 1 stick celery, chopped into strips
- 1 x 200 g/7 oz jar Chinese sweet pickles, diced
- 10 ml/2 tsp cornflour (cornstarch)
- 100 g/4 oz bean sprouts
- 150 ml/¼ pt/generous ½ cup chicken stock
- 30 ml/2 tbsp groundnut (peanut) oil
- 30 ml/2 tbsp soy sauce
- 30 ml/2 tbsp tomato purée (paste)
- 45 ml/3 tbsp mango chutney
- 450 g/1 lb pork, chopped into strips
- 5 ml/1 tsp curry powder

- 5 ml/1 tsp five-spice powder
- 6 spring onions (scallions), chopped into strips
- Rub the spices well into the pork.

Directions:

1. Heat the oil and stir-fry the meat for 8 minutes or until cooked.
2. Take out of the pan.
3. Put in the vegetables to the pan and stir-fry for approximately five minutes.
4. Return the pork to the pan with all the rest of the ingredients except the cornflour.
5. Stir until heated through.
6. Combine the cornflour with a little water, mix it into the pan and simmer, stirring, until the sauce becomes thick.

PORK WITH CUCUMBER

Yield: 4 Servings

Ingredients:

- 225 g/8 oz cucumber, peeled and sliced
- 225 g/8 oz lean pork, chopped into strips
- 30 ml/2 tbsp plain (all-purpose) flour
- 30 ml/2 tbsp soy sauce
- 60 ml/4 tbsp groundnut (peanut) oil
- salt and freshly ground pepper

Directions:

1. Toss the pork in the flour and season with salt and pepper.
2. Heat the oil and stir-fry the pork for approximately five minutes until cooked.
3. Put in the cucumber and soy sauce and stir-fry for another 4 minutes.
4. Check and adjust the seasoning and serve with fried rice.

PORK WITH GREEN BEANS

Yield: 4 Servings

Ingredients:

- 1 slice ginger root, minced
- 120 ml/4 fl oz/½ cup chicken stock
- 15 ml/1 tbsp cornflour (cornstarch)
- 2 eggs
- 2½ ml/½ tsp salt
- 225 g/8 oz lean pork, minced (ground)
- 30 ml/2 tbsp groundnut (peanut) oil
- 450 g/1 lb green beans, chopped into chunks
- 75 ml/5 tbsp water

Directions:

1. Parboil the beans for about 2 minutes then drain.
2. Heat the oil and stir-fry the salt and ginger for a few seconds.
3. Put in the pork and stir-fry until slightly browned.
4. Put in the beans and stir-fry for 30 seconds, coating with the oil.
5. Mix in the stock, bring to the boil, cover and simmer for approximately two minutes.
6. Beat 30 ml/2 tbsp of water with the eggs and stir them into the pan.
7. Mix the rest of the water with the cornflour.
8. When the eggs begin to set, mix in the cornflour and cook until the mixture becomes thick.
9. Serve as soon as possible.

PORK WITH HAM AND TOFU

Yield: 4 Servings

Ingredients:

- 1 slice ginger root, chopped
- 1 spring onion (scallion), chopped
- 10 ml/2 tsp cornflour (cornstarch)
- 100 g/4 oz smoked ham, sliced
- 15 ml/1 tbsp rice wine or dry sherry
- 225 g/8 oz lean pork, sliced
- 225 g/8 oz tofu, sliced
- 30 ml/2 tbsp water

- 4 dried Chinese mushrooms
- 5 ml/1 tsp groundnut (peanut) oil
- salt and freshly ground pepper

Directions:

1. Soak the mushrooms in warm water for half an hour then drain.
2. Discard the stalks and halve the caps.
3. Rub a heatproof bowl with the groundnut (peanut) oil.
4. Put the mushrooms, ham, tofu and pork in layers in the dish, with pork on top.
5. Drizzle with wine or sherry, salt and pepper, ginger and spring onion.
6. Cover and steam on a rack over boiling water for about 45 minutes until cooked.
7. Eliminate the excess liquid from the gravy from the bowl without disturbing the ingredients.
8. Add enough water to make up 250 ml/8 fl oz/1 cup.
9. Combine the cornflour and water and mix it into the sauce.
10. Bring to the bowl and simmer, stirring, until the sauce clears and becomes thick.
11. Turn the pork mixture on to a warmed serving plate, pour over the sauce and serve.

PORK WITH MINCED GARLIC

Yield: 4 Servings

Ingredients:

- 15 ml/1 tbsp chicken stock
- 2 spring onions (scallions), chopped
- 2½ ml/½ tsp chilli oil
- 3 slices ginger root
- 30 ml/2 tbsp minced garlic
- 30 ml/2 tbsp soy sauce
- 4 sprigs coriander
- 450 g/1 lb belly of pork, skinned
- 5 ml/1 tsp salt

Directions:

1. Put the pork in a pan with the ginger and spring onions, cover with water, bring to the boil and simmer for half an hour until cooked through.

2. Remove and eliminate the excess liquid well, then chop into thin slices about 5 cm/2 in square.
3. Put the slices in a metal strainer.
4. Bring a pan of water to the boil, add the pork slices and cook for approximately three minutes until heated through.
5. Lay out on a warmed serving plate.
6. Combine the garlic, soy sauce, salt, stock and chilli oil and spoon over the pork.
7. Serve garnished with coriander.

PORK WITH MUSHROOMS

Yield: 4 Servings

Ingredients:

- 1 clove garlic, chopped
- 15 ml/1 tbsp rice wine or dry sherry
- 15 ml/1 tbsp soy sauce
- 225 g/8 oz lean pork, chopped into slivers
- 25 g/1 oz dried Chinese mushrooms
- 30 ml/2 tbsp groundnut (peanut) oil
- 4 spring onions (scallions), chopped
- 5 ml/1 tsp sesame oil

Directions:

1. Soak the mushrooms in warm water for half an hour then drain.
2. Discard the stems and slice the caps.
3. Heat the oil and fry the garlic until slightly browned.
4. Put in the pork and stir-fry until browned.
5. Mix in the spring onions, mushrooms, soy sauce and wine or sherry and stir-fry for approximately three minutes.
6. Mix in the sesame oil and serve immediately.

PORK WITH NOODLE PANCAKE

Yield: 4 Servings

Ingredients:

- 10 ml/2 tsp cornflour (cornstarch)
- 100 g/4 oz bamboo shoots, shredded
- 100 g/4 oz mushrooms, finely sliced
- 15 ml/1 tbsp rice wine or dry sherry
- 15 ml/1 tbsp water
- 150 ml/¼ pt/generous ½ cup chicken stock
- 225 g/8 oz Chinese cabbage, shredded
- 225 g/8 oz lean pork, chopped into strips
- 30 ml/2 tbsp groundnut (peanut) oil
- 5 ml/2 tsp salt
- noodle pancake

Directions:

1. Heat the oil and fry the salt and pork until slightly coloured.
2. Put in the cabbage, bamboo shoots and mushrooms and stir-fry for approximately one minute.
3. Put in the stock, bring to the boil, cover and simmer for 4 minutes until the pork is cooked.
4. Combine the cornflour to a paste with the wine or sherry and water, mix it into the pan and simmer, stirring, until the sauce clears and becomes thick.
5. Pour over the noodle pancake to serve.

PORK WITH OYSTER SAUCE

Yield: 4 Servings

Ingredients:

- 1 slice ginger root, minced
- 10 ml/2 tsp rice wine or dry sherry
- 10 ml/2 tsp water
- 15 ml/1 tbsp cornflour (cornstarch)
- 30 ml/2 tbsp oyster sauce
- 45 ml/3 tbsp groundnut (peanut) oil
- 450 g/1 lb lean pork
- 60 ml/4 tbsp chicken stock

- freshly ground pepper
- pinch of sugar

Directions:

1. Slice the pork finely against the grain.
2. Mix 5 ml/1 tsp of cornflour with the wine or sherry, sugar and 5 ml/1 tsp of oil, add to the pork and stir thoroughly to coat.
3. Blend the rest of the cornflour with the water, oyster sauce and a pinch of pepper.
4. Heat the rest of the oil and fry the ginger for approximately one minute.
5. Put in the pork and stir-fry until slightly browned.
6. Put in the stock and the water and oyster sauce mixture, bring to the boil, cover and simmer for approximately three minutes.

PORK WITH PEANUTS

Yield: 4 Servings

Ingredients:

- ½ cucumber, cubed
- 1 clove garlic, chopped
- 1 egg white
- 1 slice ginger root, chopped
- 10 ml/2 tsp black treacle
- 15 ml/1 tbsp cornflour (cornstarch)
- 15 ml/1 tbsp rice wine or dry sherry
- 15 ml/1 tbsp soy sauce
- 25 g/1 oz/¼ cup shelled peanuts
- 3 spring onions (scallions), chopped
- 45 ml/3 tbsp chicken stock
- 45 ml/3 tbsp groundnut (peanut) oil
- 450 g/1 lb lean pork, cubed
- 5 ml/1 tsp chilli oil
- 5 ml/1 tsp salt

Directions:

1. Combine the pork with half the cornflour, the salt and egg white and stir thoroughly to coat the pork.

2. Mix the rest of the cornflour with the spring onions, garlic, ginger, stock, wine or sherry, soy sauce and treacle.
3. Heat the oil and stir-fry the pork until slightly browned then remove it from the pan.
4. Put in the cucumber to the pan and stir-fry for a few minutes.
5. Return the pork to the pan and stir lightly.
6. Mix in the seasoning mixture, bring to the boil and simmer, stirring, until the sauce clears and becomes thick.
7. Mix in the peanuts and chilli oil and heat through and serve.

PORK WITH PEPPERS

Yield: 4 Servings

Ingredients:

- ½ head Chinese leaves, diced
- 1 onion, diced
- 1 slice ginger root, minced
- 15 ml/1 tbsp soy sauce
- 15 ml/1 tbsp sugar
- 2 green peppers, diced
- 2½ ml/½ tsp salt
- 225 g/8 oz lean pork, cubed
- 45 ml/3 tbsp groundnut (peanut) oil

Directions:

1. Heat the oil and stir-fry the pork for about 4 minutes until a golden-brown colour is achieved.
2. Put in the onion and stir-fry for about 1 minute.
3. Put in the peppers and stir-fry for approximately one minute.
4. Put in the Chinese leaves and stir-fry for approximately one minute.
5. Combine the rest of the ingredients, stir them into the pan and stir-fry for another 2 minutes.

PORK WITH PLUM SAUCE

Yield: 4 Servings

Ingredients:

- 2 cloves garlic, crushed
- 2½ ml/½ tsp freshly ground pepper
- 30 ml/2 tbsp soy sauce
- 4 carrots, chopped into strips
- 45 ml/3 tbsp groundnut (peanut) oil
- 45 ml/3 tbsp plum sauce
- 450 g/1 lb stewing pork, diced
- 5 ml/1 tsp curry powder
- 5 ml/1 tsp paprika
- 6 spring onions (scallions), chopped into strips
- 60 ml/4 tbsp tomato ketchup (catsup)
- salt

Directions:

1. Marinate the meat with the garlic, salt, tomato ketchup, soy sauce, plum sauce, curry powder, paprika and pepper for half an hour.
2. Heat the oil and fry the meat until slightly browned.
3. Take out of the wok.
4. Put in the vegetables to the oil and fry until just soft.
5. Return the meat to the pan and reheat gently and serve.

PORK WITH PRAWNS

Yield: 6-8 Servings

Ingredients:

- (ground)
- 1 onion, sliced
- 1 spring onion (scallion), chopped
- 15 ml/1 tbsp sugar
- 2 cloves garlic, crushed
- 30 ml/2 tbsp groundnut (peanut) oil
- 30 ml/2 tbsp soy sauce
- 50 g/2 oz peeled prawns, minced
- 600 ml/1 pt/2½ cups boiling water

- 900 g/2 lb lean pork

Directions:

1. Bring a saucepan of water to the boil, add the pork, cover and simmer for 10 minutes.
2. Take out of the pan and eliminate the excess liquid well then chop into cubes.
3. Heat the oil and fry the onion, spring onion and garlic until slightly browned.
4. Put in the pork and fry until slightly browned.
5. Put in the soy sauce and prawns and stir-fry for approximately one minute.
6. Put in the boiling water and sugar, cover and simmer for about 40 minutes until the pork is soft.

PORK WITH RICE NOODLES

Yield: 4 Servings

Ingredients:

- 1 slice ginger root, minced
- 100 g/4 oz rice noodles
- 120 ml/4 fl oz/½ cup chicken stock
- 15 ml/1 tbsp cornflour (cornstarch)
- 15 ml/1 tbsp rice wine or dry sherry
- 15 ml/1 tbsp soy sauce
- 2 spring onions (scallions), sliced
- 2 stalks celery, chopped
- 2½ ml/½ tsp salt
- 225 g/8 oz lean pork, chopped into strips
- 4 dried Chinese mushrooms
- 45 ml/3 tbsp groundnut (peanut) oil

Directions:

1. Soak the mushrooms in warm water for half an hour then drain.
2. Discard and stalks and slice the caps.
3. Soak the noodles in warm water for half an hour then eliminate the excess liquid and chop into 5 cm/2 in pieces.
4. Put the pork into a container.
5. Combine the cornflour, soy sauce and wine or sherry, pour over the pork and toss to coat.

6. Heat the oil and fry the salt and ginger for a few seconds.
7. Put in the pork and stir-fry until slightly browned.
8. Put in the mushrooms and celery and stir-fry for approximately one minute.
9. Put in the stock, bring to the boil, cover and simmer for approximately two minutes.
10. Add and noodles and heat through for approximately two minutes.
11. Mix in the spring onions and serve instantly.

PORK WITH SPINACH

Yield: 6-8 Servings

Ingredients:

- 1.25 kg/3 lb loin of pork
- 15 ml/1 tbsp brown sugar
- 250 ml/8 fl oz/1 cup chicken stock
- 30 ml/2 tbsp groundnut (peanut) oil
- 60 ml/4 tbsp soy sauce
- 900 g/2 lb spinach
- Heat the oil and brown the pork on all sides.
- Pour off most of the fat.

Directions:

1. Put in the stock, sugar and soy sauce, bring to the boil, cover and simmer for about 2 hours until the pork is cooked.
2. Remove the meat from the pan and leave it to cool slightly, then slice it.
3. Put in the spinach to the pan and simmer, stirring gently, until softened.
4. Eliminate the excess liquid from the spinach and lay out on a warmed serving plate.
5. Top with the pork slices and serve.

PORK WITH SPINACH AND CARROTS

Yield: 4 Servings

Ingredients:

- 1 spring onion (scallion), finely chopped

- 10 ml/2 tsp cornflour (cornstarch)
- 15 ml/1 tbsp soy sauce
- 2 carrots, chopped into strips
- 2½ ml/½ tsp salt
- 225 g/8 oz lean pork
- 225 g/8 oz spinach
- 30 ml/2 tbsp water
- 45 ml/3 tbsp groundnut (peanut) oil

Directions:

1. Slice the pork finely against the grain then chop it into strips.
2. Parboil the carrots for about 3 minutes then drain.
3. Halve the spinach leaves.
4. Heat the oil and fry the spring onion until translucent.
5. Put in the pork and stir-fry until slightly browned.
6. Put in the carrots and soy sauce and stir-fry for approximately one minute.
7. Put in the salt and spinach and stir-fry for about 30 seconds until it begins to soften.
8. Combine the cornflour and water to a paste, mix it into the sauce and stir-fry until it clears then serve instantly.

PORK WITH SWEET POTATOES

Yield: 4 Servings

Ingredients:

- 1 onion, sliced
- 1 slice ginger root, sliced
- 15 ml/1 tbsp soy sauce
- 2 large sweet potatoes, sliced
- 2½ ml/½ tsp salt
- 250 ml/8 fl oz/1 cup chicken stock
- 30 ml/2 tbsp curry powder
- 30 ml/2 tbsp groundnut (peanut) oil
- 450 g/1 lb lean pork, cubed
- freshly ground pepper
- oil for deep-frying

Directions:

1. Heat the oil and deep-fry the sweet potatoes until golden.
2. Take out of the pan and eliminate the excess liquid well.
3. Heat the groundnut (peanut) oil and fry the ginger and onion until slightly browned.
4. Put in the pork and stir-fry until slightly browned.
5. Put in the soy sauce, salt and a pinch of pepper then mix in the stock and curry powder, bring to the boil and simmer, stirring for approximately one minute.
6. Put in the fried potatoes, cover and simmer for half an hour until the pork is cooked.

PORK WITH TOFU

Yield: 4 Servings

Ingredients:

- 1 clove garlic, crushed
- 1 onion, sliced
- 15 ml/1 tbsp brown sugar
- 2½ ml/½ tsp salt
- 225 g/8 oz tofu, cubed
- 375 ml/13 fl oz/1½ cups chicken stock
- 45 ml/3 tbsp groundnut (peanut) oil
- 450 g/1 lb lean pork
- 60 ml/4 tbsp soy sauce

Directions:

1. Put the pork in a saucepan and cover with water.
2. Bring to the boil then simmer for approximately five minutes.
3. Drain and allow to cool then chop into cubes.
4. Heat the oil and fry the onion and garlic until slightly browned.
5. Put in the pork and fry until slightly browned.
6. Put in the tofu and stir gently until coated with oil.
7. Put in the stock, sugar, soy sauce and salt, bring to the boil, cover and simmer for about 40 minutes until the pork is soft.

PORK WITH VEGETABLES

Yield: 4 Servings

Ingredients:

- 1 onion, chopped
- 1 piece stem ginger, chopped
- 1 red pepper, diced
- 15 ml/1 tbsp honey
- 2 cloves garlic, crushed
- 2 oranges, peeled and diced
- 20 ml/2 tbsp wine vinegar
- 200 g/7 oz cauliflower florets
- 2½ ml/½ tsp cumin
- 2½ ml/½ tsp freshly ground pepper
- 225 g/8 oz broccoli florets
- 30 ml/2 tbsp cornflour (cornstarch)
- 30 ml/2 tbsp groundnut (peanut) oil
- 30 ml/2 tbsp soy sauce
- 300 ml/½ pt/1¼ cups water
- 5 ml/1 tsp salt
- pinch of ground ginger

Directions:

1. Crush the garlic, salt and pepper into the meat.
2. Heat the oil and stir-fry meat until slightly browned.
3. Take out of the pan.
4. Put in the soy sauce and vegetables to the pan and stir-fry until soft but still crisp.
5. Put in the oranges and ginger.
6. Combine the cornflour and water and mix it into the pan with the wine vinegar, honey, ginger and cumin.
7. Bring to the boil and simmer, stirring, for approximately two minutes.
8. Return the pork to the pan and heat through and serve.

PORK WITH WALNUTS

Yield: 4 Servings

Ingredients:

- 15 ml/1 tbsp groundnut (peanut) oil
- 225 g/8 oz lean pork, chopped into strips
- 30 ml/2 tbsp brown sugar
- 30 ml/2 tbsp plain (all-purpose) flour
- 30 ml/2 tbsp soy sauce
- 50 g/2 oz/½ cup walnuts
- oil for deep-frying

Directions:

1. Briefly boil the walnuts in boiling water for approximately two minutes then drain.
2. Combine the pork with the flour, sugar and 15 ml/ 1 tbsp of soy sauce until well coated.
3. Heat the oil and deep-fry the pork until crispy and golden.
4. Drain on kitchen paper.
5. Heat the groundnut (peanut) oil and stir-fry the walnuts until golden.
6. Put in the pork to the pan, drizzle with the rest of the soy sauce and stir-fry until heated through.

PORK WITH WATER CHESTNUTS

Yield: 4 Servings

Ingredients:

- 1 clove garlic, crushed
- 1 slice ginger root, minced
- 1 spring onion (scallion), chopped
- 100 g/4 oz water chestnuts, finely sliced
- 15 ml/1 tbsp rice wine or dry sherry
- 225 g/8 oz lean pork, chopped into strips
- 45 ml/3 tbsp groundnut (peanut) oil
- 45 ml/3 tbsp soy sauce
- 5 ml/1 tsp cornflour (cornstarch)

Directions:

1. Heat the oil and fry the garlic, spring onion and ginger until slightly browned.

2. Put in the pork and stir-fry for approximately ten minutes until a golden-brown colour is achieved.
3. Put in the water chestnuts and stir-fry for approximately three minutes.
4. Add the rest of the ingredients and stir-fry for approximately three minutes.

PORK WONTONS

Yield: 4 Servings

Ingredients:

- 1 spring onion (scallion), chopped
- 225 g/8 oz mixed vegetables, chopped
- 30 ml/2 tbsp soy sauce
- 40 wonton skins
- 450 g/1 lb minced (ground) pork
- 5 ml/1 tsp salt
- oil for deep-frying

Directions:

1. Heat a pan and fry the pork and spring onion until slightly browned.
2. Turn off the heat and mix in the vegetables, soy sauce and salt.
3. To fold the wontons, hold the skin in the palm of your left hand and spoon a little filling into the centre.
4. Moisten the edges with egg and fold the skin into a triangle, sealing the edges.
5. Moisten the corners with egg and twist them together.
6. Heat the oil and fry the wontons a few at a time until a golden-brown colour is achieved.
7. Drain thoroughly and serve.

RED-COOKED HAM WITH CHESTNUTS

Yield: 4 Servings

Ingredients:

- 1.25 kg/3 lb ham

- 2 cloves garlic, crushed
- 2 spring onions (scallions), halved
- 30 ml/2 tbsp rice wine or dry sherry
- 350 g/12 oz chestnuts
- 45 ml/3 tbsp brown sugar
- 450 ml/¾ pt/2 cups water
- 60 ml/4 tbsp soy sauce

Directions:

1. Put the ham in a pan with the spring onions, garlic, sugar, wine or sherry, soy sauce and water.
2. Bring to the boil, cover and simmer for about 1½ hours, turning the ham intermittently.
3. Briefly boil the chestnuts in boiling water for approximately five minutes then drain.
4. Put into the ham, cover and simmer for another 1 hour, turning the ham once or twice.

RED-COOKED PORK

Yield: 4 Servings

Ingredients:

- 1 slice ginger root, crushed
- 10 ml/2 tsp brown sugar
- 15 ml/1 tbsp rice wine or dry sherry
- 250 ml/8 fl oz/1 cup water
- 5 ml/1 tsp salt
- 60 ml/4 tbsp soy sauce
- 675 g/1½ lb lean pork, cubed

Directions:

1. Put the pork and water in a pan and bring the water to the boil.
2. Put in the ginger, soy sauce, sherry and salt, cover and simmer for 45 minutes.
3. Put in the sugar, turn the meat over, cover and simmer for another 45 minutes until the pork is soft.

RED-COOKED PORK WITH MUSHROOMS

Yield: 4 Servings

Ingredients:

- 15 ml/1 tbsp rice wine or dry sherry
- 15 ml/1 tbsp soy sauce
- 225 g/8 oz button mushrooms
- 250 ml/8 fl oz/1 cup water
- 450 g/1 lb lean pork, cubed
- 5 ml/1 tsp salt
- 5 ml/1 tsp sugar

Directions:

1. Put the pork and water in a pan and bring the water to the boil.
2. Cover and simmer for half an hour then drain, reserving the stock.
3. Return the pork to the pan and add the soy sauce.
4. Simmer over a low heat, stirring, until the soy sauce is absorbed.
5. Mix in the wine or sherry, sugar and salt.
6. Pour in the reserved stock, bring to the boil, cover and simmer for about 30 minutes, turning the meat intermittently.
7. Put in the mushrooms and simmer for another 20 minutes.

RICH PORK BALLS

Yield: 4 Servings

Ingredients:

- 1 slice ginger root, minced
- 100 g/4 oz tofu, mashed
- 120 ml/4 fl oz/½ cup groundnut (peanut) oil
- 15 ml/1 tbsp soy sauce
- 4 water chestnuts, finely chopped
- 450 g/1 lb minced (ground) pork
- 5 ml/1 tsp brown sugar
- 5 ml/1 tsp rice wine or dry sherry
- 600 ml/1 pt/2½ cups chicken stock

- salt and freshly ground pepper

Directions:

1. Combine the pork, tofu and chestnuts and season with salt and pepper.
2. mould into large balls.
3. Heat the oil and fry the pork balls until a golden-brown colour is achieved on all sides then remove from the pan.
4. Drain off all but 15 ml/1 tbsp of the oil and add the ginger, stock, soy sauce, sugar and wine or sherry.
5. Return the pork balls to the pan, bring to the boil and simmer gently for approximately 20 minutes until cooked through.

ROAST PORK CHOPS

Yield: 4 Servings

Ingredients:

- 1 slice ginger root, chopped
- 100 g/4 oz celery sticks
- 120 ml/4 fl oz/½ cup chicken stock
- 15 ml/1 tbsp rice wine or dry sherry
- 3 spring onions (scallions), chopped
- 4 pork chops
- 5 ml/1 tsp sesame oil
- 75 ml/5 tbsp soy sauce
- oil for deep-frying
- salt and freshly ground pepper

Directions:

1. Immerse the pork chops in the soy sauce until they are well coated.
2. Heat the oil and deep-fry the chops until a golden-brown colour is achieved.
3. Remove and eliminate the excess liquid well.
4. Put the celery in the base of a shallow ovenproof dish.
5. Drizzle with the spring onions and ginger and arrange the pork chops on top.
6. Pour over the wine or sherry and stock and season with salt and pepper.
7. Drizzle with sesame oil.

8. Roast in a preheated oven at 200°C/400°C/gas mark 6 for approximately fifteen minutes.

ROAST PORK CHOW MEIN

Yield: 4 Servings

Ingredients:

- 100 g/4 oz bean sprouts
- 100 g/4 oz Chinese cabbage, shredded
- 15 ml/1 tbsp rice wine or dry sherry
- 225 g/8 oz roast pork, sliced
- 45 ml/3 tbsp groundnut (peanut) oil
- 5 ml/1 tsp salt

Directions:

1. Briefly boil the bean sprouts in boiling water for 4 minutes then drain.
2. Heat the oil and stir-fry the bean sprouts and cabbage until just softened.
3. Put in the pork, salt and sherry and stir-fry until heated through.
4. Add half the drained noodles to the pan and stir gently until heated through.
5. Add the rest of the noodles and stir until heated through.

SAUTÉED SPARE RIBS

Yield: 4 Servings

Ingredients:

- 1 egg, beaten
- 10 ml/2 tsp cornflour (cornstarch)
- 10 ml/2 tsp sugar
- 250 ml/8 fl oz/1 cup rice wine or dry sherry
- 250 ml/8 fl oz/1 cup water
- 250 ml/8 fl oz/1 cup wine vinegar
- 5 ml/1 tsp salt
- 5 ml/1 tsp soy sauce

- 60 ml/4 tbsp groundnut (peanut) oil
- 900 g/2 lb pork spare ribs

Directions:

1. Put the spare ribs into a container.
2. Combine the egg with the soy sauce, salt, half the cornflour and half the sugar, add to the spare ribs and stir thoroughly.
3. Heat the oil and fry the spare ribs until browned.
4. Add the rest of the ingredients, bring to the boil and simmer until the liquid has almost evaporated.

SAVOURY PORK

Yield: 4 Servings

Ingredients:

- 1 slice ginger root, minced
- 2 cloves garlic, crushed
- 250 ml/8 fl oz/1 cup soy sauce
- 3 spring onions (scallions), sliced
- 30 ml/2 tbsp brown sugar
- 30 ml/2 tbsp groundnut (peanut) oil
- 30 ml/2 tbsp rice wine or dry sherry
- 450 g/1 lb lean pork, cubed
- 5 ml/1 tsp salt
- 600 ml/1 pt/2½ cups water

Directions:

1. Heat the oil and fry the pork until a golden-brown colour is achieved.
2. Drain off any excess oil, add the spring onions, garlic and ginger and fry for approximately two minutes.
3. Put in the soy sauce, wine or sherry, sugar and salt and stir thoroughly.
4. Put in the water, bring to the boil, cover and simmer for one hour.

SLIPPERY PORK SLICES

Yield: 4 Servings

Ingredients:

- 15 ml/1 tbsp cornflour (cornstarch)
- 15 ml/1 tbsp rice wine or dry sherry
- 150 ml/¼ pt/generous ½ cup chicken stock
- 2 egg whites
- 2½ ml/½ tsp salt
- 225 g/8 oz lean pork, sliced
- 45 ml/3 tbsp groundnut (peanut) oil
- 50 g/2 oz bamboo shoots, sliced
- 6 spring onions (scallions), chopped

Directions:

1. Toss the pork with the egg whites and cornflour until well coated.
2. Heat the oil and stir-fry the pork until slightly browned then remove it from the pan.
3. Put in the bamboo shoots and spring onions and stir-fry for approximately two minutes.
4. Return the pork to the pan with the salt, wine or sherry and chicken stock.
5. Bring to the boil and simmer, stirring for 4 minutes until the pork is cooked.

SOFT-FRIED PORK

Yield: 4 Servings

Ingredients:

- 1 egg white
- 225 g/8 oz cornflour (cornstarch)
- 225 g/8 oz pork fillet, cubed
- 30 ml/2 tbsp rice wine or dry sherry
- oil for deep-frying
- salt

Directions:

1. Combine the pork with the egg white, wine or sherry and a little salt.
2. Progressively work in enough cornflour to make a thick batter.

3. Heat the oil and fry the pork until a golden-brown colour is achieved and crisp outside and soft inside.

SPARE RIBS WITH BLACK BEAN SAUCE

Yield: 4 Servings

Ingredients:

- 120 ml/4 fl oz/½ cup chicken stock
- 120 ml/4 fl oz½ cup water
- 15 ml/1 tbsp cornflour (cornstarch)
- 15 ml/1 tbsp water
- 2 cloves garlic, crushed
- 2 spring onions (scallions), chopped
- 2½ ml/½ tsp salt
- 30 ml/2 tbsp black bean sauce
- 30 ml/2 tbsp oil
- 30 ml/2 tbsp rice wine or dry sherry
- 30 ml/2 tbsp soy sauce
- 5 ml/1 tsp sugar
- 900 g/2 lb pork spare ribs

Directions:

1. Chop the spare ribs into 2½ cm/1 in pieces.
2. Combine the garlic, spring onions, black bean sauce, wine or sherry, water and 15 ml/1 tbsp of soy sauce.
3. Mix the rest of the soy sauce with the cornflour, sugar and water.
4. Heat the oil and salt and fry the spare ribs until a golden-brown colour is achieved.
5. Drain off the oil.
6. Put in the garlic mixture and stir-fry for approximately two minutes.
7. Put in the stock, bring to the boil, cover and simmer for 4 minutes.
8. Mix in the cornflour mixture and simmer, stirring, until the sauce clears and becomes thick.

SPARE RIBS WITH LEEKS

Yield: 4 Servings

Ingredients:

- 2 leeks, chopped into chunks
- 2½ ml/½ tsp salt
- 2½ ml/½ tsp sugar
- 250 ml/8 fl oz/1 cup stock
- 30 ml/2 tbsp tomato ketchup (catsup)
- 450 g/1 lb pork spare ribs
- 5 ml/1 tsp sesame oil
- 50 g/2 oz broccoli florets
- 6 spring onions (scallions), chopped into chunks
- oil for deep-frying

Directions:

1. Chop the spare ribs into 5 cm/2 in chunks.
2. Heat the oil and deep-fry the spare ribs until just beginning to brown.
3. Remove them from the pan and pour off all but 30 ml/2 tbsp of oil.
4. Put in the stock, tomato ketchup, salt and sugar, bring to the boil and simmer for approximately one minute.
5. Return the spare ribs to the pan and simmer for approximately twenty minutes until soft.
6. In the meantime, heat a further 30 ml/ 2 tbsp of oil and fry the leeks, spring onions and broccoli for about 5 minutes.
7. Drizzle with sesame oil and arrange round a warmed serving plate.
8. Spoon the spare ribs and sauce into the centre and serve.

SPARE RIBS WITH MUSHROOMS

Yield: 4 Servings

Ingredients:

- 15 ml/1 tbsp cornflour (cornstarch)
- 2 cloves star anise
- 45 ml/3 tbsp soy sauce
- 5 ml/1 tsp salt
- 6 dried Chinese mushrooms

- 900 g/2 lb pork spare ribs

Directions:

1. Soak the mushrooms in warm water for half an hour then drain.
2. Discard and stalks and slice the caps.
3. Chop the spare ribs into 5 cm/2 in pieces.
4. Bring a pan of water to the boil, add the spare ribs and simmer for approximately fifteen minutes.
5. Drain well.
6. Return the ribs to the pan and cover with cold water.
7. Put in the mushrooms, star anise, soy sauce and salt.
8. Bring to the boil, cover and simmer for about 45 minutes until the meat is soft.
9. Combine the cornflour with a little cold water, mix it into the pan and simmer, stirring, until the sauce clears and becomes thick.

SPARE RIBS WITH ORANGE

Yield: 4 Servings

Ingredients:

- 1 orange, sliced
- 15 ml/1 tbsp tomato purée (paste)
- 15 ml/1 tbsp water
- 2½ ml/½ tsp chilli sauce
- 2½ ml/½ tsp sugar
- 45 ml/3 tbsp rice wine or dry sherry
- 5 ml/1 tsp cornflour (cornstarch)
- 5 ml/1 tsp grated cheese
- 900 g/2 lb pork spare ribs
- grated rind of 1 orange
- oil for deep-frying
- salt

Directions:

1. Chop the spare ribs into chunks and mix with the cheese, cornflour, 5 ml/ 1 tsp wine or sherry and a pinch of salt.
2. Allow to marinate for half an hour.

3. Heat the oil and deep-fry the ribs for about 3 minutes until a golden-brown colour is achieved.
4. Heat 15 ml/1 tbsp of oil in a wok, add the water, sugar, tomato purée, chilli sauce, orange rind and rest of the wine or sherry and stir over a gently heat for approximately two minutes.
5. Put in the pork and stir together until well coated.
6. Move to a warmed serving plate and serve garnished with orange slices.

SPARE RIBS WITH RICE WINE

Yield: 4 Servings

Ingredients:

- 30 ml/2 tbsp rice wine
- 450 ml/¾ pt/2 cups water
- 5 ml/1 tsp salt
- 5 ml/1 tsp sugar
- 60 ml/4 tbsp soy sauce
- 900 g/2 lb pork spare ribs

Directions:

1. Chop the ribs into 2½ cm/1 in pieces.
2. Pur inside the pan with the water, soy sauce and salt, bring to the boil, cover and simmer for one hour.
3. Drain well.
4. Heat a pan and add the spare ribs, rice wine and sugar.
5. Stir-fry over a high heat until the liquid evaporates.

SPARE RIBS WITH SESAME SEEDS

Yield: 4 Servings

Ingredients:

- 1 egg
- 10 ml/2 tsp wine vinegar

- 30 ml/2 tbsp brown sugar
- 30 ml/2 tbsp groundnut (peanut) oil
- 30 ml/2 tbsp plain (all-purpose) flour
- 30 ml/2 tbsp tomato ketchup (catsup)
- 4 lettuce leaves
- 45 ml/3 tbsp sesame seeds
- 45 ml/3 tbsp water
- 5 ml/1 tsp potato flour
- 900 g/2 lb pork spare ribs
- oil for deep-frying

Directions:

1. Chop the spare ribs into 10 cm/4 in pieces and place into a container.
2. Combine the egg with the flour, potato flour and water, stir into the spare ribs and allow to stand for 4 hours.
3. Heat the oil and deep-fry the spare ribs until golden then remove and drain.
4. Heat the oil and fry the tomato ketchup, brown sugar, wine vinegar for a few minutes.
5. Put in the spare ribs and stir-fry until comprehensively.
6. coated.
7. Drizzle with sesame seeds and stir-fry for approximately one minutes.
8. Put the lettuce leaves on a warmed serving plate, top with the spare ribs and serve.

SPARE RIBS WITH TOMATO

Yield: 4 Servings

Ingredients:

- 1 onion, finely sliced
- 10 ml/2 tsp brown sugar
- 2 eggs, beaten
- 250 ml/8 fl oz/1 cup chicken stock
- 30 ml/2 tbsp rice wine or dry sherry
- 45 ml/3 tbsp cornflour (cornstarch)
- 45 ml/3 tbsp groundnut (peanut) oil
- 60 ml/4 tbsp tomato ketchup (catsup)
- 75 ml/5 tbsp soy sauce
- 900 g/2 lb pork spare ribs

- oil for deep-frying

Directions:

1. Chop the spare ribs into 2½ cm/1 in pieces.
2. Mix with 60 ml/4 tbsp of soy sauce and the wine or sherry and allow to marinate for one hour, stirring intermittently.
3. Drain, discarding marinade.
4. Coat the spare ribs in egg then in cornflour.
5. Heat the oil and deep-fry the ribs, a few at a time, until golden.
6. Drain well.
7. Heat the groundnut (peanut) oil and fry the onion until translucent.
8. Put in the stock, rest of the soy sauce, ketchup and brown sugar and simmer for approximately one minute, stirring.
9. Put in the ribs and simmer for 10 minutes.

SPICED PORK

Yield: 4 Servings

Ingredients:

- 1 clove garlic, chopped
- 1 cucumber, cubed
- 1 red chilli pepper, seeded and chopped
- 1 slice ginger root, chopped
- 15 ml/1 tbsp brown sugar
- 30 ml/2 tbsp cornflour (cornstarch)
- 30 ml/2 tbsp rice wine or dry sherry
- 45 ml/3 tbsp soy sauce
- 450 g/1 lb lean pork, cubed
- 5 ml/1 tsp salt
- 60 ml/4 tbsp chicken stock
- 60 ml/4 tbsp groundnut (peanut) oil
- salt

Directions:

1. Drizzle the cucumber with salt and leave to one side.

2. Combine the pork, salt, 15 ml/1 tbsp of soy sauce, 15 ml/1 tbsp of wine or sherry, 15 ml/ 1 tbsp of cornflour, the brown sugar and 15 ml/1 tbsp of oil.
3. Allow to stand for half an hour then lift the meat from the marinade.
4. Heat the rest of the oil and stir-fry the pork until slightly browned.
5. Put in the ginger, garlic and chilli and stir-fry for approximately two minutes.
6. Put in the cucumber and stir-fry for approximately two minutes.
7. Combine the stock and rest of the soy sauce, wine or sherry and cornflour into the marinade.
8. Stir this into the pan and bring to the boil, stirring.
9. Simmer, stirring, until the sauce clears and becomes thick and carry on simmering until the meat is cooked through.

SPICY BRAISED PORK

Yield: 4 Servings

Ingredients:

- 120 ml/4 fl oz/½ cup rice wine or dry sherry
- 15 ml/1 tbsp cornflour (cornstarch)
- 225 g/8 oz oyster mushrooms, sliced
- 30 ml/2 tbsp hoisin sauce
- 30 ml/2 tbsp soy sauce
- 300 ml/½ pt/1¼ cups chicken stock
- 45 ml/3 tbsp groundnut (peanut) oil
- 450 g/1 lb pork, diced
- 5 ml/1 tsp five-spice powder
- 6 spring onions (scallions), chopped
- salt and pepper

Directions:

1. Season the meat with salt and pepper.
2. Put in a dish and mix in the soy sauce and hoisin sauce.
3. Cover and allow to marinate for one hour.
4. Heat the oil and stir-fry the meat until a golden-brown colour is achieved.
5. Put in the wine or sherry, stock and five-spice powder, bring to the boil, cover and simmer for one hour.

6. Put in the spring onions and mushrooms, remove the lid and simmer for another 4 minutes.
7. Blend the cornflour with a little water, bring back to the boil and simmer, stirring, for approximately three minutes until the sauce becomes thick.

SPICY PORK WITH PICKLES

Yield: 4 Servings

Ingredients:

- 2½ ml/½ tsp five-spice powder
- 30 ml/2 tbsp cornflour (cornstarch)
- 30 ml/2 tbsp sweet sherry
- 45 ml/3 tbsp soy sauce
- 5 ml/1 tsp grated ginger root
- 60 ml/4 tbsp chicken stock
- 900 g/2 lb pork chops
- Chinese pickled vegetables
- oil for deep-frying
- pinch of freshly ground pepper

Directions:

1. Trim the chops, discarding all the fat and bones.
2. Combine the cornflour, 30 ml/2 tbsp of soy sauce, the sherry, ginger, five-spice powder and pepper.
3. Pour over the pork and stir to coat it completely.
4. Cover and allow to marinate for 2 hours, turning intermittently.
5. Heat the oil and deep-fry the pork until a golden-brown colour is achieved and cooked through.
6. Drain on kitchen paper.
7. Chop the pork into thick slices, transfer to a heated serving dish and keep warm.
8. Combine the stock and rest of the soy sauce in a small pan.
9. Bring to the boil and pour over the sliced pork.
10. Serve garnished with mixed pickles.

STEAMED HAM

Yield: 6-8 Servings

Ingredients:

- 30 ml/2 tbsp brown sugar
- 60 ml/4 tbsp rice wine or dry sherry
- 900 g/2 lb fresh ham

Directions:

1. Put the ham in a heatproof dish on a rack, cover and steam over boiling water for about 1 hour.
2. Put in the sugar and wine or sherry to the dish, cover and steam for another 1 hour or until the ham is cooked.
3. Allow it to cool in the bowl before slicing.

STEAMED LEG OF PORK

Yield: 6-8 Servings

Ingredients:

- 1 small leg of pork
- 15 ml/1 tbsp rice wine or dry sherry
- 2½ ml/½ tsp salt
- 3 cloves garlic, crushed
- 30 ml/2 tbsp cornflour (cornstarch)
- 30 ml/2 tbsp groundnut (peanut) oil
- 45 ml/3 tbsp brown sugar
- 450 g/1 lb spinach
- 450 ml/¾ pt/2 cups water
- 90 ml/6 tbsp soy sauce

Directions:

1. Pierce the pork skin all over with a pointed knife then rub in 30 ml/2 tbsp of soy sauce.
2. Put in a heavy saucepan with the water, bring to the boil, cover and simmer for 40 minutes.

3. Drain, reserving the liquid, and leave the pork to cool then place it in a heatproof bowl.
4. Combine 15 ml/1 tbsp of sugar, the wine or sherry and 30 ml/2 tbsp of soy sauce then rub over the pork.
5. Heat the oil and fry the garlic until slightly browned.
6. Add the rest of the sugar and soy sauce, pour the mixture over the pork and cover the bowl.
7. Stand the bowl in a wok and fill with water to come half way up the sides.
8. Cover and steam for about 1½ hours, topping up with boiling water as necessary.
9. Chop the spinach into 5 cm/2 in pieces then drizzle with salt.
10. Bring a pan of water to the boil then pour over the spinach.
11. Allow to stand for approximately two minutes until the spinach begins to soften then eliminate the excess liquid and lay out on a warmed serving plate.
12. Put the pork on top.
13. Bring the pork stock to the boil.
14. Blend the cornflour with a little water, mix it into the stock and simmer, stirring, until sauce clears and becomes thick.
15. Pour over pork and serve.

STEAMED MEAT CAKE

Yield: 4 Servings

Ingredients:

- 1 egg, slightly beaten
- 225 g/8 oz mushrooms, finely chopped
- 4 water chestnuts, finely chopped
- 450 g/1 lb minced (ground) pork
- 5 ml/1 tsp soy sauce
- salt and freshly ground pepper

Directions:

1. Combine all the ingredients together well and shape the mixture into a flat pie on an ovenproof plate.
2. Put the plate on a rack in a steamer, cover and steam for approximately an hour and a half.

STEAMED MINCED MEATBALLS

Yield: 4 Servings

Ingredients:

- 1 egg, beaten
- 1 green pepper, chopped
- 1 onion, chopped
- 1 red pepper, chopped
- 2 cloves garlic, crushed
- 2 pieces stem ginger, chopped
- 2½ ml/½ tsp salt
- 45 ml/3 tbsp cornflour (cornstarch)
- 450 g/1 lb minced (ground) pork
- 5 ml/1 tsp curry powder
- 5 ml/1 tsp paprika
- 50 g/2 oz short-grain rice
- 60 ml/4 tbsp chopped chives
- salt and freshly ground pepper

Directions:

1. Combine the garlic, salt, pork, onion, peppers, ginger, curry powder and paprika.
2. Work the egg into the mixture with the cornflour and rice.
3. Season with salt and pepper then mix in the chives.
4. With wet hands, shape the mixture into small balls.
5. Put these in a steam basket, cover and cook over gently boiling water for approximately 20 minutes until cooked.

STEAMED MINCED PORK

Yield: 4 Servings

Ingredients:

- 10 ml/2 tsp soy sauce
- 2½ ml/½ tsp salt
- 450 g/1 lb minced (ground) pork
- 5 ml/1 tsp cornflour (cornstarch)

Directions:

1. Combine the pork with the rest of the ingredients and spread the mixture flat in a shallow ovenproof dish.
2. Put in a steamer over boiling water and steam for about 30 minutes until cooked.
3. Serve hot.

STEAMED PORK

Yield: 4 Servings

Ingredients:

- 120 ml/4 fl oz/½ cup rice wine or dry sherry
- 120 ml/4 fl oz/½ cup soy sauce
- 15 ml/1 tbsp brown sugar
- 450 g/1 lb lean pork, cubed

Directions:

1. Combine all the ingredients and place in a heatproof bowl.
2. Steam on a rack over boiling water for about 1½ hours until cooked through.

STEAMED PORK BUNS

Yield: 12

Ingredients:

- 1 clove garlic, crushed
- 10 ml/2 tsp grated ginger root
- 12 x 13 cm/5 in greaseproof paper squares
- 15 ml/1 tbsp baking powder
- 15 ml/1 tbsp cornflour (cornstarch)
- 15 ml/1 tbsp oyster sauce
- 15 ml/1 tbsp soy sauce
- 2½ ml/½ tsp salt
- 2½ ml/½ tsp sesame oil

- 225 g/8 oz cooked pork, finely chopped
- 30 ml/2 tbsp groundnut (peanut) oil
- 30 ml/2 tbsp hoisin sauce
- 300 ml/½ pt/1¼ cups water
- 350 g/12 oz/3 cups plain (all-purpose) flour
- 4 spring onions (scallions), finely chopped
- 5 ml/1 tsp wine vinegar
- 50 g/2 oz/½ cup lard

Directions:

1. Combine the hoisin, oyster and soy sauces and the sesame oil.
2. Heat the oil and fry the ginger and garlic until slightly browned.
3. Put in the sauce mixture and fry for approximately two minutes.
4. Blend 120 ml/4 fl oz/½ cup of the water with the cornflour and mix it into the pan.
5. Bring to the boil, stirring, then simmer until the mixture becomes thick.
6. Mix in the pork and onions then allow to cool.
7. Combine the flour, baking powder and salt.
8. Rub in the lard until the mixture resembles fine breadcrumbs.
9. Combine the wine vinegar and rest of the water then mix this into the flour to form a firm dough.
10. Knead slightly on a floured surface then cover and allow to stand for approximately 20 minutes.
11. Knead the dough again then divide it into 12 and shape each one into a ball.
12. Roll out to 15 cm/6 in circles on a floured surface.
13. Put spoonfuls of the filling in the centre of each circle, brush the edges with water and pinch the edges together to seal around the filling.
14. Brush one side of each greaseproof paper square with oil.
15. Put each bun on a square of paper, seam side down.
16. Put the buns in a single layer on a steamer rack over boiling water.
17. Cover and steam the buns for approximately twenty minutes until cooked.

STIR-FRIED PORK

Yield: 4 Servings

Ingredients:

- 1 green pepper, diced
- 15 ml/1 tbsp groundnut (peanut) oil

- 15 ml/1 tbsp rice wine or dry sherry
- 15 ml/1 tbsp soy sauce
- 25 g/1 oz dried Chinese mushrooms
- 450 g/1 lb lean pork, sliced
- 5 ml/1 tsp salt
- 5 ml/1 tsp sesame oil

Directions:

1. Soak the mushrooms in warm water for half an hour then drain.
2. Discard the stems and slice the caps.
3. Heat the oil and stir-fry the pork until slightly browned.
4. Put in the pepper and stir-fry for approximately one minute.
5. Put in the mushrooms, soy sauce, wine or sherry and salt and stir-fry for a few minutes until the meat is cooked.
6. Mix in the sesame oil and serve.

STIR-FRIED PORK WITH GINGER

Yield: 4 Servings

Ingredients:

- 1 slice ginger root, minced
- 1 spring onion (scallion), sliced
- 225 g/8 oz lean pork
- 30 ml/2 tbsp groundnut (peanut) oil
- 30 ml/2 tbsp soy sauce
- 45 ml/3 tbsp water
- 5 ml/1 tsp brown sugar
- 5 ml/1 tsp cornflour (cornstarch)

Directions:

1. Slice the pork finely against the grain.
2. Toss in cornflour then drizzle with soy sauce and toss again.
3. Heat the oil and stir-fry the pork for approximately two minutes until sealed.
4. Put in the ginger and spring onion and stir-fry for approximately one minute.
5. Put in the water and sugar, cover and simmer for approximately five minutes until cooked through.

STIR-FRIED ROAST PORK WITH VEGETABLES

Yield: 4 Servings

Ingredients:

- 1 onion, diced
- 1 spring onion (scallion), chopped
- 100 g/4 oz bamboo shoots, diced
- 100 g/4 oz mangetout (snow peas), diced
- 100 g/4 oz mushrooms, diced
- 15 ml/1 tbsp cornflour (cornstarch)
- 2 stalks celery, diced
- 20 ml/4 fl oz/½ cup chicken stock
- 2½ ml/½ tsp sugar
- 225 g/8 oz Barbecue-Roast Pork , cubed
- 30 ml/2 tbsp groundnut (peanut) oil
- 4 water chestnuts, diced
- 45 ml/3 tbsp water
- 50 g/2 oz/½ cup briefly boiled almonds
- freshly ground pepper
- salt

Directions:

1. Heat the almonds until slightly browned.
2. Heat the oil and salt then add the vegetables and stir-fry for approximately two minutes until coated with oil.
3. Put in the stock, bring to the boil, cover and simmer for approximately two minutes until the vegetables are almost cooked but still crisp.
4. Put in the pork and heat through.
5. Combine the cornflour, water, sugar and pepper and stir into the sauce.
6. Simmer, stirring, until the sauce clears and becomes thick.

SWEET AND SOUR PORK

Yield: 4 Servings

Ingredients:

- 1 clove garlic, crushed
- 1 egg, beaten
- 100 g/4 oz cornflour (cornstarch)
- 15 ml/1 tbsp groundnut (peanut) oil
- 15 ml/1 tbsp rice wine or dry sherry
- 450 g/1 lb lean pork, cubed
- 5 ml/1 tsp curry powder
- 5 ml/1 tsp sesame oil
- 5 ml/1 tsp wine vinegar
- 50 g/2 oz tomato ketchup (catsup)
- 75 g/3 oz/½ cup sugar
- oil for deep-frying
- salt

Directions:

1. Combine the pork with the wine or sherry, oil, curry powder, egg and a little salt.
2. Mix in the cornflour until the pork is covered with the batter.
3. Heat the oil until smoking then add the pork cubes a few a time.
4. Fry for about 3 minutes then eliminate the excess liquid and set aside.
5. Reheat the oil and fry the cubes again for about 2 minutes.
6. Remove and drain.
7. Heat the garlic, sugar, tomato ketchup and wine vinegar, stirring until the sugar dissolves.
8. Bring to the boil then add the pork cubes and stir thoroughly.
9. Mix in the sesame oil and serve.

SWEET AND SOUR SPARE RIBS

Yield: 4 Servings

Ingredients:

- 100 g/4 oz canned pineapple chunks in syrup
- 100 g/4 oz/½ cup brown sugar
- 15 ml/1 tbsp cornflour (cornstarch)
- 15 ml/1 tbsp soy sauce

- 15 ml/1 tbsp tomato purée (paste)
- 2 cloves garlic, crushed
- 30 ml/2 tbsp desiccated coconut
- 30 ml/2 tbsp groundnut (peanut) oil
- 5 ml/1 tsp salt
- 60 ml/4 tbsp wine vinegar
- 600 ml/1 pt/2½ cups water
- 75 ml/5 tbsp chicken stock
- 900 g/2 lb pork spare ribs

Directions:

1. Put the pork and water in a pan, bring to the boil, cover and simmer for approximately 20 minutes.
2. Drain well.
3. Heat the oil and fry the ribs with the garlic and salt until browned.
4. Put in the sugar, stock and wine vinegar and bring to the boil.
5. Eliminate the excess liquid from the pineapple and add 30 ml/2 tbsp of the syrup to the pan with the tomato purée, soy sauce and cornflour.
6. Stir thoroughly and simmer, stirring, until the sauce clears and becomes thick.
7. Put in the pineapple, simmer for approximately three minutes and serve sprinkled with coconut.

TWICE-COOKED PORK

Yield: 4 Servings

Ingredients:

- 15 ml/1 tbsp chicken stock
- 15 ml/1 tbsp hot bean sauce
- 2 cloves garlic, chopped
- 2 green peppers, chopped into chunks
- 2 spring onions (scallions), sliced
- 225 g/8 oz lean pork
- 45 ml/3 tbsp groundnut (peanut) oil
- 5 ml/1 tsp sugar

Directions:

1. Put the piece of pork in a pan, cover with water, bring to the boil and simmer for approximately 20 minutes until cooked through.
2. Remove and eliminate the excess liquid then allow to cool.
3. Slice finely.
4. Heat the oil and stir-fry the pork until slightly browned.
5. Put in the peppers, garlic and spring onions and stir-fry for approximately two minutes.
6. Take out of the pan.
7. Put in the bean sauce, stock and sugar to the pan and simmer, stirring, for approximately two minutes.
8. Return the pork and peppers and stir-fry until heated through.
9. Serve Immediately.

TWICE-COOKED PORK

Yield: 4 Servings

Ingredients:

- 1 clove garlic, crushed
- 1 slice ginger root, chopped
- 15 ml/1 tbsp rice wine or dry sherry
- 15 ml/1 tbsp soy sauce
- 2½ ml/½ tsp salt
- 225 g/8 oz cooked pork, cubed
- 30 ml/2 tbsp chilli bean paste
- 45 ml/3 tbsp groundnut (peanut) oil
- 6 spring onions (scallions), chopped

Directions:

1. Heat the oil and fry the spring onions, garlic, ginger and salt until slightly browned.
2. Put in the pork and stir-fry for approximately two minutes.
3. Put in the soy sauce, wine or sherry and chilli bean paste and stir-fry for approximately three minutes.

LAMB

Although chicken and beef are more popular, lamb has its fair share of recipes and tastes delicious.

BAKED LAMB

Yield: 4 Servings

Ingredients:

- 100 g/4 oz breadcrumbs
- 15 ml/1 tbsp cornflour (cornstarch)
- 15 ml/1 tbsp soy sauce
- 225 g/8 oz cooked lamb, chopped
- 30 ml/2 tbsp water
- 300 ml/ ½ pt stock
- 4 hard-boiled (hard-cooked) eggs, chopped

Directions:

1. Put the breadcrumbs, hard-boiled eggs and lamb in layers in an ovenproof dish.
2. Bring the stock and soy sauce to the boil in a saucepan.
3. Combine the cornflour and water to a paste, stir into the stock and simmer, stirring, until the sauce becomes thick.
4. Pour over the lamb mixture, cover and bake in a preheated oven at 180¬∞C/350¬∞C/gas mark 4 for about 25 minutes until a golden-brown colour is achieved.

BARBECUED LAMB

Yield: 4 Servings

Ingredients:

- 1 clove garlic, crushed
- 120 ml/4 fl oz/ ½ cup rice wine or dry sherry

- 120 ml/4 fl oz/ ½ cup soy sauce
- 3 spring onions (scallions), chopped
- 450 g/1 lb lean lamb, chopped into strips
- 5 ml/1 tsp sesame oil
- salt and freshly ground pepper

Directions:

1. Put the lamb into a container.
2. Combine the rest of the ingredients, pour over the lamb and allow to marinate for one hour.
3. Grill (broil) over hot coals until the lamb is cooked, basting with the sauce, as required.

BRAISED LAMB

Yield: 4 Servings

Ingredients:

- 10 ml/2 tsp grated ginger root
- 15 ml/1 tbsp groundnut (peanut) oil
- 15 ml/1 tbsp hoisin sauce
- 15 ml/1 tbsp rice wine or dry sherry
- 200 ml/ ½ pt chicken stock
- 30 ml/2 tbsp soy sauce
- 30 ml/2 tbsp sugar
- 4 spring onions (scallions), sliced
- 450 g/1 lb boned shoulder of lamb, cubed
- 5 ml/1 tsp sesame oil

Directions:

1. Briefly boil the lamb in boiling water for approximately five minutes then drain.
2. Heat the oil and stir-fry the lamb for approximately five minutes until browned.
3. Take out of the pan and eliminate the excess liquid on kitchen paper.
4. Remove all but 15 ml/1 tbsp of oil from the pan.
5. Reheat the oil and stir-fry the spring onions and ginger for approximately two minutes.
6. Return the meat to the pan with the rest of the ingredients.
7. Bring to the boil, cover and simmer gently for 1 ½ hours until the meat is soft.

FRAGRANT LAMB

Yield: 4 Servings

Ingredients:

- 1 clove garlic, crushed
- 1 slice ginger root, minced
- 120 ml/4 fl oz/ ½ cup soy sauce
- 15 ml/1 tbsp brown sugar
- 15 ml/1 tbsp rice wine or dry sherry
- 2 spring onions (scallions), chopped
- 2½ ml/ ½ tsp salt
- 30 ml/2 tbsp groundnut (peanut) oil
- 300 ml/ ½ pt water
- 450 g/1 lb lean lamb, cubed
- freshly ground pepper

Directions:

1. Heat the oil and fry the lamb until slightly browned.
2. Put in the spring onions, garlic and ginger and fry for approximately two minutes.
3. Put in the soy sauce, wine or sherry, sugar and salt and season to taste with pepper.
4. Stir the ingredients together well.
5. Put in the water, bring to the boil, cover and simmer for 2 hours.

GRILLED LAMB CUBES

Yield: 4 Servings

Ingredients:

- 120 ml/4 fl oz/ ½ cup groundnut (peanut) oil
- 15 ml/1 tbsp soy sauce
- 2 cloves garlic, crushed
- 2½ ml/ ½ tsp freshly ground pepper
- 2½ ml/ ½ tsp oregano
- 450 g/1 lb lean lamb, cubed

- 5 ml/1 tsp salt
- 60 ml/4 tbsp wine vinegar

Directions:

1. Combine all the ingredients, cover and allow to marinate overnight.
2. Drain.
3. Put the meat on a grill (broiler) rack and grill (broil) for about 15 minutes, turning several times, until the lamb is soft and slightly browned.

LAMB AND RICE

Yield: 4 Servings

Ingredients:

- 10 ml/2 tsp salt
- 10 ml/2 tsp soy sauce
- 15 ml/1 tbsp cornflour (cornstarch)
- 2 carrots, sliced
- 30 ml/2 tbsp groundnut (peanut) oil
- 30 ml/2 tbsp water
- 350 g/12 oz cooked lamb, cubed
- 350 g/12 oz cooked long-grain rice, hot
- 4 onions, quartered
- 50 g/2 oz peas
- 600 ml/1 pt/2 ½ cups stock

Directions:

1. Heat the oil and fry the lamb until slightly browned.
2. Put in the stock, salt and soy sauce, bring to the boil, cover and simmer for 10 minutes.
3. Put in the onions, carrots and peas, cover and simmer for approximately 20 minutes until the vegetables are soft.
4. Pour off the liquid into a saucepan.
5. Blend the cornflour and water to a paste, stir into the sauce and simmer, stirring, until the sauce clears and becomes thick.
6. Put the rice on a warmed serving plate and pile the lamb mixture on top.
7. Pour over the sauce and serve instantly.

LAMB AND VEGETABLES

Yield: 4 Servings

Ingredients:

- 100 g/4 oz bamboo shoots, sliced
- 100 g/4 oz mushrooms, sliced
- 100 g/4 oz water chestnuts, sliced
- 15 ml/1 tbsp cornflour (cornstarch)
- 15 ml/1 tbsp sesame oil
- 150 ml/generous ½ cup chicken stock
- 2 cloves garlic, crushed
- 225 g/8 oz lean lamb, sliced
- 30 ml/2 tbsp groundnut (peanut) oil
- 30 ml/2 tbsp rice wine or dry sherry
- 30 ml/2 tbsp soy sauce
- 4 spring onions (scallions), sliced

Directions:

1. Combine the lamb, bamboo shoots, water chestnuts and mushrooms.
2. Mix 15 ml/1 tbsp of oil, 15 ml/1 tbsp of soy sauce and 15 ml/1 tbsp of wine or sherry and pour over the lamb mixture.
3. Allow to marinate for one hour.
4. Heat the rest of the oil and fry the garlic until slightly browned.
5. Put in the meat mixture and stir-fry until browned.
6. Mix in the spring onions then add the rest of the soy sauce and wine or sherry, most of the stock and the sesame oil.
7. Bring to the boil, stirring, cover and simmer for 10 minutes.
8. Combine the cornflour with the rest of the stock, mix it into the sauce and simmer, stirring, until the sauce clears and becomes thick.

LAMB CHOW MEIN

Yield: 4 Servings

Ingredients:

- 1 celery heart, sliced
- 1 onion, sliced
- 100 g/4 oz bean sprouts
- 100 g/4 oz mushrooms
- 175 ml/6 fl oz water
- 20 ml/2 tsp cornflour (cornstarch)
- 45 ml/3 tbsp groundnut (peanut) oil
- 450 g/1 lb egg noodles
- 450 g/1 lb lamb, sliced
- salt and freshly ground pepper

Directions:

1. Cook the noodles in boiling water for approximately eight minutes then drain.
2. Heat the oil and stir-fry the lamb until slightly browned.
3. Put in the onion, celery, mushrooms and bean sprouts and
4. stir-fry for approximately five minutes.
5. Combine the cornflour and water, pour into the pan and bring to the boil.
6. Simmer, stirring, until the sauce becomes thick.
7. Pour over the noodles and serve instantly.

LAMB CURRY

Yield: 4 Servings

Ingredients:

- 1 green pepper, diced
- 1 slice ginger root, minced
- 100 g/4 oz mushrooms, sliced
- 100 g/4 oz potato, cubed
- 15 ml/1 tbsp curry powder
- 2 carrots, cubed
- 2 cloves garlic, crushed
- 250 ml/8 fl oz/1 cup chicken stock
- 30 ml/2 tbsp groundnut (peanut) oil
- 450 g/1 lb lean lamb, cubed

- 50 g/2 oz water chestnuts, sliced

Directions:

1. Heat the oil and fry the garlic and ginger until slightly browned.
2. Put in the lamb and stir-fry for approximately five minutes.
3. Put in the potato and carrots and stir-fry for approximately three minutes.
4. Put in the curry powder and stir-fry for approximately one minute.
5. Mix in the stock, bring to the boil, cover and simmer for about 25 minutes.
6. Put in the mushrooms, pepper and water chestnuts and simmer for approximately five minutes.
7. If you prefer a thicker sauce, boil for a few minutes to reduce the sauce or thicken it with 15 ml/1 tbsp cornflour mixed with a little water.

LAMB STEW

Yield: 4 Servings

Ingredients:

- 1 bay leaf
- 1 stalk celery, sliced
- 100 g/4 oz mushrooms, halved
- 15 ml/1 tbsp chopped fresh parsley
- 15 ml/1 tbsp rice wine or dry sherry
- 15 ml/1 tbsp sugar
- 15 ml/1 tbsp tomato purée (paste)
- 2 cloves garlic, crushed
- 3 carrots, quartered
- 3 potatoes, cubed
- 30 ml/2 tbsp plain (all-purpose) flour
- 300 ml/ ½ pt water
- 45 ml/3 tbsp groundnut (peanut) oil
- 450 g/1 lb lean lamb, cubed
- 5 ml/1 tsp soy sauce
- 50 g/2 oz peas
- 6 small onions, quartered
- freshly ground pepper

Directions:

1. Heat half the oil.
2. Toss the garlic and soy sauce with the lamb and season with pepper.
3. Fry the meat until slightly browned.
4. Drizzle with flour and cook, stirring, until the flour is absorbed.
5. Put in the water, tomato purée and bay leaf, bring to the boil, cover and simmer for half an hour.
6. Heat the rest of the oil and fry the mushrooms for approximately three minutes then remove them from the pan.
7. Put in the carrots and onions to the pan and fry for approximately two minutes.
8. Drizzle with sugar and heat until the vegetables glisten.
9. Put in the mushrooms, carrots, onions, celery and potatoes to the stew, cover again and simmer for another 1 hour.
10. Put in the wine or sherry, peas and parsley, cover and simmer for another 30 minutes.

LAMB WITH ASPARAGUS

Yield: 4 Servings

Ingredients:

- 1 tomato, skinned and chopped into wedges
- 15 ml/1 tbsp cornflour (cornstarch)
- 15 ml/1 tbsp soy sauce
- 2 cloves garlic, crushed
- 250 ml/8 fl oz/1 cup stock
- 350 g/12 oz asparagus
- 45 ml/3 tbsp groundnut (peanut) oil
- 45 ml/3 tbsp water
- 450 g/1 lb lean lamb
- salt and freshly ground pepper

Directions:

1. Chop the asparagus into diagonal chunks and place into a container.
2. Pour over boiling water and allow to stand for approximately two minutes then drain.
3. Slice the lamb finely against the grain.
4. Heat the oil and stir-fry the lamb until slightly coloured.
5. Put in the salt, pepper and garlic and stir-fry for approximately five minutes.

6. Put in the asparagus, stock and tomato, bring to the boil, cover and simmer for approximately two minutes.
7. Combine the cornflour, water and soy sauce to a paste, mix it into the pan and simmer, stirring, until the sauce clears and becomes thick.

LAMB WITH BROCCOLI

Yield: 4 Servings

Ingredients:

- 1 clove garlic, crushed
- 2½ ml/ ½ tsp freshly ground pepper
- 250 ml/8 fl oz/1 cup stock
- 30 ml/2 tbsp cornflour (cornstarch)
- 450 g/1 lb broccoli florets
- 450 g/1 lb lamb, chopped into strips
- 5 ml/1 tsp salt
- 5 ml/1 tsp soy sauce
- 75 ml/5 tbsp groundnut (peanut) oil
- 75 ml/5 tbsp water

Directions:

1. Heat the oil and fry the garlic and lamb until cooked through.
2. Put in the broccoli and stock, bring to the boil, cover and simmer for about 15 minutes until the broccoli is soft.
3. Season with salt and pepper.
4. Combine the cornflour, water and soy sauce to a paste, mix it into the pan and simmer, stirring, until the sauce clears and becomes thick.

LAMB WITH CABBAGE

Yield: 4 Servings

Ingredients:

- 1 clove garlic, crushed

- 120 ml/4 fl oz/ ½ cup stock
- 15 ml/1 tbsp cornflour (cornstarch)
- 15 ml/1 tbsp soy sauce
- 45 ml/3 tbsp groundnut (peanut) oil
- 450 g/1 lb Chinese cabbage, shredded
- 450 g/1 lb lamb, finely sliced
- 60 ml/4 tbsp water
- salt and freshly ground black pepper

Directions:

1. Heat the oil and fry the lamb, salt, pepper and garlic until slightly browned.
2. Put in the cabbage and stir until coated with oil.
3. Put in the stock, bring to the boil, cover and simmer for 10 minutes.
4. Combine the cornflour, soy sauce and water to a paste, stir into the pan and simmer, stirring, until the sauce clears and becomes thick.

LAMB WITH GREEN BEANS

Yield: 4 Servings

Ingredients:

- 15 ml/1 tbsp cornflour (cornstarch)
- 2½ ml/ ½ tsp freshly ground pepper
- 250 ml/8 fl oz/1 cup stock
- 45 ml/3 tbsp groundnut (peanut) oil
- 450 g/1 lb green beans, chopped into julienne strips
- 450 g/1 lb lean lamb, finely sliced
- 5 ml/1 tsp salt
- 5 ml/1 tsp soy sauce
- 75 ml/5 tbsp water

Directions:

- Briefly boil the beans in boiling water for approximately three minutes then eliminate the excess liquid well.
- Put in the beans, salt and pepper, cover and simmer for 4 minutes until the meat is cooked.
- Put in the stock, bring to the boil, cover and simmer for approximately five minutes.

- Blend the cornflour, soy sauce and water to a paste, stir into the pan and simmer, stirring, until the sauce clears and becomes thick.
- Heat the oil and fry the meat until slightly browned on all sides.

LAMB WITH MANGETOUT

Yield: 4 Servings

Ingredients:

- 10 ml/2 tsp grated lemon rind
- 2 cloves garlic, crushed
- 2½ ml/ ½ tsp salt
- 250 ml/8 fl oz/1 cup chicken stock
- 30 ml/ 2 tbsp cornflour (cornstarch)
- 30 ml/2 tbsp groundnut (peanut) oil
- 30 ml/2 tbsp honey
- 30 ml/2 tbsp soy sauce
- 30 ml/2 tbsp tomato purée (paste)
- 30 ml/2 tbsp wine vinegar
- 450 g/1 lb lamb, diced
- 450 g/1 lb mangetout (snow peas), chopped into 4
- 5 ml/1 tsp caraway seeds, ground
- 5 ml/1 tsp ground coriander

Directions:

1. Combine the garlic and salt and toss with the lamb.
2. Coat the lamb in cornflour.
3. Heat the oil and stir-fry the lamb until cooked.
4. Put in the mangetout and stir-fry for approximately two minutes.
5. Mix the rest of the cornflour with the stock and pour into the pan with the rest of the ingredients.
6. Bring to the boil, stirring, then simmer for approximately three minutes.

LAMB WITH MUSHROOMS

Yield: 4 Servings

Ingredients:

- 100 g/4 oz bamboo shoots, sliced
- 15 ml/1 tbsp cornflour (cornstarch)
- 15 ml/1 tbsp soy sauce
- 250 ml/8 fl oz/1 cup stock
- 3 slices ginger root, chopped
- 350 g/12 oz mushrooms, sliced
- 45 ml/3 tbsp groundnut (peanut) oil
- 450 g/1 lb lamb, finely sliced
- 60 ml/4 tbsp water

Directions:

1. Heat the oil and fry the mushrooms, bamboo shoots and ginger for approximately three minutes.
2. Put in the lamb and stir-fry until slightly browned.
3. Put in the stock, bring to the boil, cover and simmer for about 30 minutes until the lamb is cooked and the sauce has reduced by half.
4. Combine the cornflour, soy sauce and water, stir into the pan and simmer, stirring, until the sauce clears and becomes thick.

LAMB WITH OYSTER SAUCE

Yield: 4 Servings

Ingredients:

- 1 clove garlic, crushed
- 1 slice ginger, finely chopped
- 15 ml/1 tbsp rice wine or sherry
- 250 ml/8 fl oz/1 cup stock
- 30 ml/2 tbsp groundnut (peanut) oil
- 30 ml/2 tbsp oyster sauce
- 450 g/1 lb lean iamb, sliced
- 5 ml/1 tsp sugar

Directions:

1. Heat the oil with the garlic and ginger and fry until slightly browned.
2. Put in the lamb and stir-fry for about 3 minutes until slightly browned.
3. Put in the stock, oyster sauce, wine or sherry and sugar, bring to the boil, stirring, then cover and simmer for about 30 minutes, stirring intermittently, until the lamb is cooked through.
4. Take the lid off and continue to cook, stirring, for about 4 minutes until the sauce has reduced and thickened.

LAMB WITH SPRING ONIONS

Yield: 4 Servings

Ingredients:

- 2 cloves garlic, crushed
- 30 ml/2 tbsp groundnut (peanut) oil
- 30 ml/2 tbsp rice wine or dry sherry
- 30 ml/2 tbsp soy sauce
- 350 g/12 oz lean lamb, cubed
- 8 spring onions (scallions), thickly sliced

Directions:

1. Put the lamb into a container.
2. Mix 15 ml/ 1 tbsp of soy sauce, 15 ml/1 tbsp of wine or sherry and 15 ml/1 tbsp of oil and stir into the lamb.
3. Allow to marinate for half an hour.
4. Heat the rest of the oil and fry the garlic until slightly browned.
5. Eliminate the excess liquid from the meat, put it into the pan and stir-fry for approximately three minutes.
6. Put in the spring onions and stir-fry for approximately two minutes.
7. Put in the marinade and rest of the soy sauce and wine or sherry and stir-fry for approximately three minutes.

LAMB WITH TOFU

Yield: 4 Servings

Ingredients:

- 100 g/4 oz tofu, cubed
- 15 ml/1 tbsp soy sauce
- 2 spring onions (scallions), chopped
- 2½ ml/ ½ tsp oyster sauce
- 2½ ml/ ½ tsp sesame oil
- 3 cloves garlic, crushed
- 4 water chestnuts, diced
- 450 g/1 lb lean lamb, coarsely chopped
- 5 ml/1 tsp grated orange rind
- 60 ml/4 tbsp groundnut (peanut) oil
- pinch of salt

Directions:

1. Heat half the oil and stir-fry the lamb, garlic and onions until slightly browned.
2. Put in the water chestnuts, orange rind and soy sauce and enough boiling water just to cover the meat.
3. Bring back to the boil, cover and simmer for about 30 minutes until the lamb is very soft.
4. In the meantime, heat the rest of the oil and stir-fry the tofu until slightly browned.
5. Add it to the lamb with the oyster sauce and sesame oil and simmer, uncovered for approximately five minutes.

LAMB WITH WATER CHESTNUTS

Yield: 4 Servings

Ingredients:

- 1 carrot, diced
- 1 stick cinnamon
- 100 g/4 oz turnip, cubed
- 100 g/4 oz water chestnuts
- 15 ml/1 tbsp cornflour (cornstarch)
- 15 ml/1 tbsp groundnut (peanut) oil
- 15 ml/1 tbsp rice wine or dry sherry
- 15 ml/1 tbsp soy sauce

- 2 cloves star anise
- 2 red chilli peppers, chopped
- 2 slices ginger root, chopped
- 2 spring onions (scallions), sliced
- 2½ ml/ ½ tsp sugar
- 350 g/12 oz lean lamb, chopped into chunks
- 45 ml/3 tbsp water
- 600 ml/1 pt/2 ½ cups water

Directions:

1. Briefly boil the lamb in boiling water for approximately two minutes then drain.
2. Heat the oil and fry the spring onions, ginger and chilli peppers for 30 seconds.
3. Put in the lamb and stir-fry until well coated in the spices.
4. Add the rest of the ingredients except the water chestnuts, cornflour and water, bring to the boil, partially cover and simmer for about 1 hour until the lamb is soft.
5. Check intermittently and top up with boiling water if needed.
6. Remove the cinnamon and anise, add the water chestnuts and simmer, uncovered for about 5 minutes.
7. Blend the cornflour and water to a paste and stir a little into the sauce.
8. Simmer, stirring, until the sauce becomes thick.
9. You may not need all the cornflour paste if you have let the sauce reduce while cooking.

MARINATED LAMB

Yield: 4 Servings

Ingredients:

- 120 ml/4 fl oz/ ½ cup soy sauce
- 2 cloves garlic, crushed
- 450 g/1 lb lean lamb
- 5 ml/1 tsp celery salt
- 5 ml/1 tsp salt
- oil for deep-frying

Directions:

1. Put the lamb in a pot and just cover with cold water.

2. Put in the garlic and salt, bring to the boil, cover and simmer for one hour until the lamb is cooked.
3. Take out of the pan and drain.
4. Put the lamb into a container, add the soy sauce and drizzle with celery salt.
5. Cover and allow to marinate for 2 hours or overnight.
6. Chop the lamb into small pieces.
7. Heat the oil and deep-fry the lamb until brittle.
8. Drain thoroughly and serve.

MUSTARD-ROAST LAMB

Yield: 8 Servings

Ingredients:

- 1 clove garlic, crushed
- 1 slice ginger root, minced
- 1.25 kg/3 lb leg of lamb
- 15 ml/1 tbsp groundnut (peanut) oil
- 15 ml/1 tbsp soy sauce
- 5 ml/1 tsp chopped fresh thyme
- 75 ml/5 tbsp prepared mustard

Directions:

1. Combine all the seasoning ingredients until creamy.
2. Spread over the lamb and allow to stand for a few hours.
3. Roast in a preheated oven at 180 degrees C/gas mark 4 for about 1 ½ hours.

RED-COOKED LAMB

Yield: 4 Servings

Ingredients:

- 1 onion, chopped into wedges
- 1 slice ginger root, chopped
- 120 ml/4 fl oz/ ½ cup soy sauce

- 250 ml/8 fl oz/1 cup chicken stock
- 30 ml/2 tbsp groundnut (peanut) oil
- 450 g/1 lb lamb chops
- 5 ml/1 tsp salt

Directions:

1. Heat the oil and fry the chops until browned on both sides.
2. Add the rest of the ingredients, bring to the boil, cover and simmer for about 1 ½ hours until the lamb is soft and the sauce has reduced.

ROAST LAMB

Yield: 4 Servings

Ingredients:

- 1 onion, finely chopped
- 1 slice ginger root, chopped
- 120 ml/4 fl oz/ ½ cup soy sauce
- 15 ml/1 tbsp lemon juice
- 15 ml/1 tbsp wine vinegar
- 2 cloves garlic, crushed
- 2 kg/4 lb leg of lamb
- 30 ml/2 tbsp rice wine or dry sherry
- 30 ml/2 tbsp tomato purée (paste)
- 50 g/2 oz brown sugar

Directions:

1. Put the lamb in a dish.
2. Purée the rest of the ingredients then pour them over the lamb, cover and refrigerate overnight, turning and basting intermittently.
3. Roast the lamb in a preheated oven at 220¬∞C/425¬∞F/gas mark 7 for approximately ten minutes then reduce the heat to 190 degrees C/gas mark 5 and continue to cook for approximately 20 minutes per 450 g/1 lb plus 20 minutes, basting intermittently with the marinade.

STIR-FRIED LAMB

Yield: 4 Servings

Ingredients:

- 1 slice ginger root, finely chopped
- 2½ ml/ ½ tsp salt
- 3 eggs, beaten
- 350 g/12 oz lean lamb, chopped into strips
- 45 ml/3 tbsp groundnut (peanut) oil
- 5 ml/1 tsp rice wine or dry sherry

Directions:

1. Combine the lamb, ginger and eggs.
2. Heat the oil and stir-fry the lamb mixture for approximately two minutes.
3. Mix in the salt and wine or sherry and stir-fry for approximately two minutes.

STUFFED BREAST OF LAMB

Yield: 6-8 Servings

Ingredients:

- 1 breast of lamb
- 1 small green pepper, chopped
- 15 ml/1 tbsp cornflour (cornstarch)
- 15 ml/1 tbsp soy sauce
- 2 spring onions (scallions), chopped
- 225 g/8 oz cooked long-grain rice
- 375 ml/13 fl oz/1 ½ cups water
- 90 ml/6 tbsp groundnut (peanut) oil
- salt and freshly ground pepper

Directions:

1. Cut a pocket in the wide end of the breast of lamb.
2. Combine the rice, pepper, spring onions, 30 ml/2 tbsp of oil, salt and pepper and stuff the cavity with the mixture.

3. Secure the end with string.
4. Heat the rest of the oil and fry the lamb until slightly browned on all sides.
5. Season with salt and pepper, add 250 ml/8 fl oz/1 cup of water, bring to the boil, cover and simmer for 2 hours or until the meat is soft.
6. Blend the cornflour, soy sauce and rest of the water to a paste, stir into the pan and simmer, stirring, until the sauce clears and becomes thick.

TENDER LAMB STEAKS

Yield: 4 Servings

Ingredients:

- 1 small onion, chopped
- 10 ml/2 tsp rice wine or dry sherry
- 15 ml/1 tbsp soy sauce
- 2½ ml/ ½ tsp salt
- 45 ml/3 tbsp groundnut (peanut) oil
- 450 g/1 lb lean lamb

Directions:

1. Slice the lamb finely against the grain and arrange in a dish.
2. Combine the soy sauce, wine or sherry, salt and oil, pour over the lamb, cover and marinate for one hour.
3. Drain well.
4. Heat the oil and fry the lamb for about 2 minutes until just soft.

WILLOW LAMB

Yield: 3 Servings

Ingredients:

- 1 clove garlic, crushed
- 1 egg, slightly beaten
- 1 small carrot, shredded
- 2½ ml/ ½ tsp rice wine or dry sherry

- 2½ ml/ ½ tsp sugar
- 2½ ml/ ½ tsp wine vinegar
- 30 ml/2 tbsp soy sauce
- 450 g/1 lb lean lamb
- 5 ml/1 tsp cornflour (cornstarch)
- freshly ground pepper
- oil for deep-frying
- pinch of salt

Directions:

1. Slice the lamb into thin strips about 5 cm/2 in long.
2. Combine the egg, 15 ml/1 tbsp of soy sauce, the cornflour and salt, mix with the lamb and allow to marinate for another 30 minutes.
3. Heat the oil and deep-fry the lamb until half cooked.
4. Take out of the pan and drain.
5. Pour off all but 30 ml/2 tbsp of oil and fry the carrot and garlic for approximately one minute.
6. Put in the lamb and the rest of the ingredients and stir-fry for approximately three minutes.

EGGS

Eggs are easy to cook, high in nutrition, and absolutely delicious.

CAULIFLOWER OMELETTE

Yield: 4 Servings

Ingredients:

- 1 cauliflower, broken into florets
- 2½ ml/½ tsp celery salt
- 225 g/8 oz chicken meat, minced (ground)
- 3 egg whites, slightly beaten
- 45 ml/3 tbsp chicken stock
- 45 ml/3 tbsp groundnut (peanut) oil
- 5 ml/1 tsp salt

Directions:

1. Briefly boil the cauliflower florets in boiling water for approximately ten minutes then eliminate the excess liquid well.
2. Combine the chicken, salt, egg whites, celery salt and stock.
3. Beat with an electric whisk until the mixture forms soft peaks.
4. Heat the oil, add the chicken mixture and stir-fry for about 2 minutes.
5. Put in the cauliflower and stir-fry for another 2 minutes and serve.

CHICKEN SOUFFLÉ

Yield: 4 Servings

Ingredients:

- (ground)
- 100 g/4 oz chicken breast, minced
- 2½ ml/½ tsp salt
- 4 egg whites

- 45 ml/3 tbsp chicken stock
- 75 ml/5 tbsp groundnut (peanut) oil

Directions:

1. Combine the chicken, stock and salt together well.
2. Whisk the egg whites until firm and fold them into the mixture.
3. Heat the oil to smoking point, add the mixture and stir thoroughly then lower the heat and continue to cook, stirring gently, until the mixture is just firm.

CHINESE OMELETTE

Yield: 4 Servings

Ingredients:

- 30 ml/2 tbsp groundnut (peanut) oil
- 4 eggs
- salt and freshly ground pepper

Directions:

1. Beat the eggs slightly and season with salt and pepper.
2. Heat the oil then pour the eggs into the pan and tilt the pan so that the egg covers the surface.
3. Lift the edges of the omelette as the eggs set so that the uncooked egg can run underneath.
4. Cook until just set then fold in half and serve instantly.

CHINESE OMELETTE WITH BEAN SPROUTS

Yield: 4 Servings

Ingredients:

- ½ small green pepper, chopped
- 100 g/4 oz bean sprouts
- 2 spring onions (scallions), chopped
- 30 ml/2 tbsp groundnut (peanut) oil

- 4 eggs
- salt and freshly ground pepper

Directions:

1. Briefly boil the bean sprouts in boiling water for approximately two minutes then eliminate the excess liquid well.
2. Beat the eggs slightly and season with salt and pepper.
3. Heat the oil and stir-fry the pepper and spring onions for approximately one minute.
4. Put in the bean sprouts and stir until coated with oil.
5. Pour the eggs into the pan and tilt the pan so that the egg covers the surface.
6. Lift the edges of the omelette as the eggs set so that the uncooked egg can run underneath.
7. Cook until just set then fold in half and serve instantly.

CHINESE SCRAMBLED EGGS

Yield: 4 Servings

Ingredients:

- 2 spring onions (scallions), chopped
- 30 ml/2 tbsp groundnut (peanut) oil
- 4 eggs, beaten
- 5 ml/1 tsp soy sauce (optional)
- pinch of salt

Directions:

1. Beat the eggs with the spring onions, salt and soy sauce, if using.
2. Heat the oil then pour in the egg mixture.
3. Stir gently using a fork until the eggs are just set.
4. Serve Immediately.

CRAB AND GINGER SOUFFLÉ

Yield: 4 Servings

Ingredients:

- 1 spring onion (scallion), minced
- 100 g/4 oz crab meat, flaked
- 120 ml/4 ft oz/k cup milk
- 15 ml/1 tbsp rice wine or dry sherry
- 15 ml/2 tbsp cornflour (cornstarch)
- 2 slices ginger root, minced
- 4 egg whites
- 5 ml/1 tsp sesame oil
- 60 ml/4 tbsp chicken stock
- 75 ml/5 tbsp groundnut (peanut) oil
- salt

Directions:

1. Heat half the oil and stir-fry the ginger and onion until softened.
2. Mix in the crab meat and salt, remove from the heat and allow to cool slightly.
3. Combine the wine or sherry, milk, stock and cornflour then stir this into the crab meat mixture.
4. Whisk the egg whites until firm then fold them into the mixture.
5. Heat the rest of the oil to smoking point, add the mixture and stir thoroughly then lower the heat and continue to cook, stirring gently, until the mixture is just firm.

CRAB FOO YUNG WITH MUSHROOMS

Yield: 4 Servings

Ingredients:

- 100 g/4 oz crab meat
- 100 g/4 oz frozen peas
- 100 g/4 oz mushrooms, diced
- 2 spring onions (scallions), chopped
- 45 ml/3 tbsp cornflour (cornstarch)
- 45 ml/3 tbsp groundnut (peanut) oil
- 5 ml/1 tsp salt
- 6 eggs, beaten

Directions:

1. Beat the eggs then beat in the cornflour.

2. Add all the rest of the ingredients except the oil.
3. Heat some of the oil and pour the mixture into the pan a little at a time to make small pancakes about 7.5 cm/3 in across.
4. Fry until the bottom is slightly browned then turn and brown the other side.
5. Continue until you have used all the mixture.

CRAB OMELETTE WITH BROWN SAUCE

Yield: 4 Servings

Ingredients:

- 10 ml/2 tsp cornflour (cornstarch)
- 15 ml/1 tbsp groundnut (peanut) oil
- 15 ml/1 tbsp soy sauce
- 175 ml/6 fl oz/¾ cup chicken stock
- 200 g/7 oz crab meat, flaked
- 2½ ml/½ tsp salt
- 4 eggs, beaten
- 45 ml/3 tbsp cooked green peas
- Heat the oil.

Directions:

1. Beat the eggs and salt and mix in the crab meat.
2. Pour into the pan and cook, lifting the edges of the omelette as the eggs set so that the uncooked egg can run underneath.
3. Cook until just set then fold in half and transfer to a warmed serving plate.
4. In the meantime, heat the stock with the soy sauce and cornflour, stirring until the mixture boils and becomes thick.
5. Simmer for approximately two minutes then mix in the peas.
6. Pour over the omelette immediately before serving.

CRAB SOUFFLÉ

Yield: 4 Servings

Ingredients:

- 100 g/4 oz crab meat, flaked
- 120 ml/4 fl oz/½ cup milk
- 15 ml/1 tbsp cornflour (cornstarch)
- 4 egg whites
- 75 ml/5 tbsp groundnut (peanut) oil
- salt

Directions:

1. Combine the crab meat, salt, cornflour and mix together well.
2. Whisk the egg whites until firm then fold them into the mixture.
3. Heat the oil to smoking point, add the mixture and stir thoroughly then lower the heat and continue to cook, stirring gently, until the mixture is just firm.

DEEP-FRIED EGG FOO YUNG

Yield: 4 Servings

Ingredients:

- 100 g/4 oz mushrooms, chopped
- 100 g/4 oz smoked ham, chopped
- 15 ml/1 tbsp soy sauce
- 4 eggs, slightly beaten
- 5 ml/1 tsp salt
- oil for deep-frying

Directions:

1. Combine the eggs with the salt, ham, mushrooms and soy sauce.
2. Heat the oil and carefully drop spoonfuls of the mixture into the oil.
3. Cook until they rise to the surface turn them over until they are brown on both sides.
4. Take out of the oil and eliminate the excess liquid while you cook the rest of the pancakes.

DEEP-FRIED PORK EGGS

Yield: 4 Servings

Ingredients:

- ½ head lettuce, shredded
- 100 g/4 oz minced (ground) pork
- 15 ml/1 tbsp cornflour (cornstarch)
- 15 ml/1 tbsp rice wine or dry sherry
- 15 ml/1 tbsp soy sauce
- 2 spring onions (scallions) minced
- 2½ ml/½ tsp salt
- 4 hard-boiled (hard-cooked) eggs
- oil for deep-frying

Directions:

1. Combine the pork, spring onions, cornflour, wine or sherry, soy sauce and salt.
2. Shape around the eggs to coat them completely.
3. Heat the oil and deep-fry the eggs until the coating is golden-brown and cooked through.
4. Remove and eliminate the excess liquid well then serve on a bed of lettuce.

EGG CUSTARD

Yield: 4 Servings

Ingredients:

- 1 spring onion (scallion), minced
- 100 g/4 oz peeled prawns, roughly chopped
- 15 ml/1 tbsp groundnut (peanut) oil
- 15 ml/1 tbsp soy sauce
- 2½ ml/½ tsp salt
- 375 ml/13 fl oz/1½ cups chicken stock
- 4 eggs, beaten

Directions:

1. Combine all the ingredients except the oil in a deep bowl and stand the bowl in a roasting tin filled with 2½ cm/1 in of water.
2. Cover and steam for approximately fifteen minutes.
3. Heat the oil and pour it over the custard.

4. Cover and steam for another 15 minutes.

EGG FOO YUNG

Yield: 4 Servings

Ingredients:

- 1 onion, chopped
- 100 g/4 oz cooked chicken, chopped
- 2 stalks celery, chopped
- 30 ml/2 tbsp groundnut (peanut) oil
- 4 eggs, slightly beaten
- 50 g/2 oz mushrooms, chopped
- egg foo yung sauce
- salt

Directions:

1. Combine the eggs, salt, chicken, onion, celery and mushrooms.
2. Heat some of the oil and spoon one quarter of the mixture into the pan.
3. Fry until the underside is slightly browned then turn and brown the other side.
4. Serve with egg foo yung sauce.

FISH SOUFFLÉ

Yield: 4 Servings

Ingredients:

- 3 eggs, separated
- 45 ml/3 tbsp groundnut (peanut) oil
- 450 g/1 lb fish fillets
- 5 ml/1 tsp soy sauce
- 5 ml/1 tsp sugar
- salt and freshly ground pepper

Directions:

1. Combine the egg yolks with the soy sauce, sugar, salt and pepper.
2. Chop the fish into large pieces.
3. Immerse the fish into the mixture until well coated.
4. Heat the oil and fry the fish until slightly browned on the underside.
5. In the meantime, whisk the egg whites until firm.
6. Turn the fish over and spoon the egg white on to the top of the fish.
7. Cook for approximately two minutes until the underside is slightly browned then turn again and cook for another 1 minute until the egg white is set and golden brown.
8. Serve with tomato sauce.

FRIED EGGS WITH VEGETABLES

Yield: 4 Servings

Ingredients:

- ¼ head lettuce, shredded
- 10 ml/2 tsp cornflour (cornstarch)
- 15 ml/1 tbsp water
- 2½ ml/½ tsp salt
- 3 spring onions (scallions), chopped
- 30 ml/2 tbsp groundnut (peanut) oil
- 4 dried Chinese mushrooms
- 4 eggs
- 5 ml/1 tsp sugar
- 50 g/2 oz bamboo shoots, sliced
- 50 g/2 oz water chestnuts, sliced
- 90 ml/6 tbsp chicken stock
- oil for deep-frying

Directions:

1. Soak the mushrooms in warm water for half an hour then drain.
2. Discard the stalks and slice the caps.
3. Heat the oil and salt and stir-fry the spring onions for 30 seconds.
4. Put in the bamboo shoots and water chestnuts and stir-fry for approximately two minutes.
5. Put in the stock, bring to the boil, cover and simmer for approximately two minutes.
6. Blend the cornflour and water to a paste and mix it into the pan with the sugar.

7. Simmer, stirring, until the sauce becomes thick.
8. In the meantime, heat the oil and deep-fry the eggs for a few minutes until the edges begin to brown.
9. Put the lettuce on a serving plate, top with the eggs and pour over the hot sauce.

HALF-MOON EGGS

Yield: 4 Servings

Ingredients:

- 15 ml/1 tbsp chopped fresh flat-leaved parsley
- 15 ml/1 tbsp soy sauce
- 4 eggs
- 45 ml/3 tbsp groundnut (peanut) oil
- salt and freshly ground pepper

Directions:

1. Heat the oil until very hot and break the eggs into the pan.
2. Cook until the underside is slightly browned then drizzle with salt, pepper and soy sauce.
3. Fold the egg in half and press down gently so that it holds together.
4. Cook for another 2 minutes until a golden-brown colour is achieved on both sides then serve sprinkled with parsley.

HAM EGG FOO YUNG

Yield: 4 Servings

Ingredients:

- 15 ml/1 tbsp soy sauce
- 2 spring onions (scallions), chopped
- 2 stalks celery, diced
- 2½ ml/½ tsp salt
- 2½ ml/½ tsp sugar
- 4 eggs, slightly beaten

- 50 g/2 oz bamboo shoots, diced
- 50 g/2 oz smoked ham, diced
- 50 g/2 oz water chestnuts, diced
- 60 ml/4 tbsp groundnut (peanut) oil

Directions:

1. Heat half the oil and stir-fry the bamboo shoots, water chestnuts, spring onions and celery for about 2 minutes.
2. Mix in the ham, soy sauce, sugar and salt, remove from the pan and allow to cool slightly.
3. Stir the mixture into the beaten eggs.
4. Heat some of the rest of the oil and pour the mixture into the pan a little at a time to make small pancakes about 7.5 cm/3 in across.
5. Fry until the bottom is slightly browned then turn and brown the other side.
6. Continue until you have used all the mixture.

OMELETTE WITH HAM AND WATER CHESTNUTS

Yield: 2 Servings

Ingredients:

- 1 clove garlic, crushed
- 1 onion, chopped
- 15 ml/1 tbsp soy sauce
- 3 eggs, beaten
- 30 ml/2 tbsp groundnut (peanut) oil
- 50 g/2 oz Cheddar cheese
- 50 g/2 oz ham, chopped
- 50 g/2 oz water chestnuts, chopped

Directions:

1. Heat half the oil and fry the onion, garlic, ham, water chestnuts and soy sauce until slightly browned.
2. Remove them from the pan.
3. Heat the rest of the oil, add the eggs and draw the egg into the centre as it begins to set so that the uncooked egg can run underneath.

4. When the egg is just set, spoon the ham mixture onto half the omelette, top with the cheese and fold over the other half of the omelette.
5. Cover and cook for approximately two minutes then turn and cook for another 2 minutes until a golden-brown colour is achieved.

OMELETTE WITH LOBSTER

Yield: 4 Servings

Ingredients:

- 100 g/4 oz lobster meat, chopped
- 3 spring onions (scallions), chopped
- 30 ml/2 tbsp groundnut (peanut) oil
- 4 eggs
- salt and freshly ground pepper

Directions:

1. Beat the eggs slightly and season with salt and pepper.
2. Heat the oil and stir-fry the spring onions for approximately one minute.
3. Put in the lobster and stir until coated with oil.
4. Pour the eggs into the pan and tilt the pan so that the egg covers the surface.
5. Lift the edges of the omelette as the eggs set so that the uncooked egg can run underneath.
6. Cook until just set then fold in half and serve instantly.

OMELETTE WITH PRAWNS

Yield: 4 Servings

Ingredients:

- 1 slice ginger root, minced
- 15 ml/1 tbsp rice wine or dry sherry
- 225 g/8 oz peeled prawns
- 30 ml/2 tbsp groundnut (peanut) oil
- 4 eggs

- salt and freshly ground pepper

Directions:

1. Beat the eggs slightly with the wine or sherry and season with salt and pepper.
2. Heat the oil and stir-fry the ginger until slightly browned.
3. Put in the prawns and stir until coated with oil.
4. Pour the eggs into the pan and tilt the pan so that the egg covers the surface.
5. Lift the edges of the omelette as the eggs set so that the uncooked egg can run underneath.
6. Cook until just set then fold in half and serve instantly.

OMELETTE WITH SCALLOPS

Yield: 4 Servings

Ingredients:

- 225 g/8 oz scallops, halved
- 3 spring onions (scallions), chopped
- 30 ml/2 tbsp groundnut (peanut) oil
- 4 eggs
- 5 ml/1 tsp soy sauce
- salt and freshly ground pepper

Directions:

1. Beat the eggs slightly with the soy sauce and season with salt and pepper.
2. Heat the oil and stir-fry the spring onions until slightly browned.
3. Put in the scallops and stir-fry for approximately three minutes.
4. Pour the eggs into the pan and tilt the pan so that the egg covers the surface.
5. Lift the edges of the omelette as the eggs set so that the uncooked egg can run underneath.
6. Cook until just set then fold in half and serve instantly.

OMELETTE WITH TOFU

Yield: 4 Servings

Ingredients:

- 225 g/8 oz tofu, mashed
- 30 ml/2 tbsp groundnut (peanut) oil
- 4 eggs
- salt and freshly ground pepper

Directions:

1. Beat the eggs slightly and season with salt and pepper.
2. Heat the oil then add the tofu and stir-fry until heated through.
3. Pour the eggs into the pan and tilt the pan so that the egg covers the surface.
4. Lift the edges of the omelette as the eggs set so that the uncooked egg can run underneath.
5. Cook until just set then fold in half and serve instantly.

OYSTER OMELETTE

Yield: 4 Servings

Ingredients:

- 12 shelled oysters
- 120 ml/4 fl oz/½ cup milk
- 3 spring onions (scallions), chopped
- 30 ml/2 tbsp groundnut (peanut) oil
- 4 eggs
- 50 g/2 oz bamboo shoots, sliced
- 50 g/2 oz lean pork, shredded
- 50 g/2 oz mushrooms, sliced
- salt and freshly ground pepper

Directions:

1. Lightly beat the eggs with the milk, oysters, spring onions, salt and pepper.
2. Heat the oil and stir-fry the pork until slightly browned.
3. Put in the mushrooms and bamboo shoots and stir-fry for approximately two minutes.
4. Pour the egg mixture into the pan and cook, lifting the edges of the omelette as the eggs set so that the uncooked egg can run underneath.

5. Cook until just set then fold in half, turn the omelette over and cook until slightly browned on the other side.
6. Serve Immediately.

OYSTER PANCAKES

Yield: 4 Servings

Ingredients:

- 12 oysters
- 2½ ml/½ tsp baking powder
- 3 spring onions (scallions), sliced
- 4 eggs, slightly beaten
- 45 ml/3 tbsp groundnut (peanut) oil
- 6 ml/4 tbsp plain (all-purpose) flour
- salt and freshly ground pepper

Directions:

1. Shell the oysters, reserving 60 ml/4 tbsp of the liquor, and chop them coarsely.
2. Combine the eggs with the oysters, spring onions, salt and pepper.
3. Combine the flour and baking powder, blend it to a paste with the oyster liquor then stir the mixture into the eggs.
4. Heat some oil and fry spoonfuls of the batter to make small pancakes.
5. Cook until slightly browned on each side then add a little more oil to the pan and continue until all the mixture has been used.

PORK AND PRAWN EGG FOO YUNG

Yield: 4 Servings

Ingredients:

- 1 onion, chopped
- 100 g/4 oz lean pork, chopped into slivers
- 225 g/8 oz peeled prawns, chopped into slivers
- 4 eggs, slightly beaten

- 45 ml/3 tbsp groundnut (peanut) oil
- 50 g/2 oz Chinese cabbage, shredded
- salt and freshly ground pepper

Directions:

1. Heat 30 ml/2 tbsp of oil and stir-fry the pork and onion until slightly browned.
2. Put in the prawns and stir-fry until coated with oil then add the cabbage, stir thoroughly, cover and simmer for approximately three minutes.
3. Take out of the pan and allow to cool slightly.
4. Put in the meat mixture to the eggs and season with salt and pepper.
5. Heat some of the rest of the oil and pour the mixture into the pan a little at a time to make small pancakes about 7.5 cm/3 in across.
6. Fry until the bottom is slightly browned then turn and brown the other side.
7. Continue until you have used all the mixture.

PORK-STUFFED OMELETTE

Yield: 4 Servings

Ingredients:

- 1 stalk celery, chopped
- 15 ml/1 tbsp soy sauce
- 225 g/8 oz lean pork, diced
- 3 spring onions (scallions), chopped
- 4 eggs, slightly beaten
- 5 ml/1 tsp sugar
- 50 g/2 oz bean sprouts
- 60 ml/4 tbsp groundnut (peanut) oil
- salt

Directions:

1. Briefly boil the bean sprouts in boiling water for approximately three minutes then eliminate the excess liquid well.
2. Heat half the oil and stir-fry the pork until slightly browned.
3. Put in the spring onions and celery and stir-fry for approximately one minute.

4. Put in the soy sauce and sugar and stir-fry for approximately two minutes.
5. Take out of the pan.
6. Season the beaten eggs with salt.
7. Heat the rest of the oil and pour the eggs into the pan, tilting the pan so that the egg covers the surface.
8. Lift the edges of the omelette as the eggs set so that the uncooked egg can run underneath.
9. Spoon the filling on to half the omelette and fold in half.
10. Cook until just set then serve instantly.

PRAWN PANCAKES

Yield: 4 Servings

Ingredients:

- 120 ml/4 fl oz/½ cup chicken stock
- 2 spring onions (scallions), chopped
- 30 ml/2 tbsp groundnut (peanut) oil
- 4 eggs, slightly beaten
- 50 g/4 oz peeled prawns, minced
- 75 g/3 oz/heaped ½ cup plain (all-purpose) flour
- salt and freshly ground pepper

Directions:

1. Combine all the ingredients except the oil.
2. Heat some of the oil, pour in one quarter of the batter, tilting the pan to spread it over the base.
3. Cook until slightly browned on the underside then turn and brown the other side.
4. Take out of the pan and continue to cook the rest of the pancakes.

PRAWN SOUFFLÉ

Yield: 4 Servings

Ingredients:

- 1 slice ginger root, minced
- 15 ml/1 tbsp rice wine or dry sherry
- 15 ml/1 tbsp soy sauce
- 225 g/8 oz peeled prawns, chopped
- 4 egg whites
- 45 ml/3 tbsp groundnut (peanut) oil
- salt and freshly ground pepper

Directions:

1. Combine the prawns, ginger, wine or sherry, soy sauce, salt and pepper.
2. Whisk the egg whites until firm then fold them into the mixture.
3. Heat the oil to smoking point, add the mixture and stir thoroughly then lower the heat and continue to cook, stirring gently, until the mixture is just firm.

PRAWN SOUFFLÉ WITH BEAN SPROUTS

Yield: 4 Servings

Ingredients:

- 100 g/4 oz bean sprouts
- 100 g/4 oz peeled prawns, coarsely chopped
- 120 ml/4 fl oz/½ cup chicken stock
- 15 ml/1 tbsp rice wine or dry sherry
- 2 spring onions (scallions), chopped
- 4 egg whites
- 45 ml/3 tbsp groundnut (peanut) oil
- 5 ml/1 tsp cornflour (cornstarch)
- salt

Directions:

1. Briefly boil the bean sprouts in boiling water for approximately two minutes then eliminate the excess liquid and keep warm.
2. In the meantime, mix the prawns, onions, cornflour, wine or sherry and stock and season with salt.
3. Whisk the egg whites until firm then fold them into the mixture.
4. Heat the oil to smoking point, add the mixture and stir thoroughly then lower the heat and continue to cook, stirring gently, until the mixture is just firm.

5. Put on a heated serving dish and top with the bean sprouts.

PRAWN STUFFED OMELETTE

Yield: 4 Servings

Ingredients:

- 2 spring onions (scallions), chopped
- 2 stalks celery, chopped
- 225 g/8 oz peeled prawns, halved
- 30 ml/2 tbsp groundnut (peanut) oil
- 4 eggs, slightly beaten
- salt

Directions:

1. Heat half the oil and stir-fry the celery and onions until slightly browned.
2. Put in the prawns and stir-fry until heated through.
3. Take out of the pan.
4. Season the beaten eggs with salt.
5. Heat the rest of the oil and pour the eggs into the pan, tilting the pan so that the egg covers the surface.
6. Lift the edges of the omelette as the eggs set so that the uncooked egg can run underneath.
7. Spoon the filling on to half the omelette and fold in half.
8. Cook until just set then serve instantly.

ROAST PORK EGG FOO YUNG

Yield: 4 Servings

Ingredients:

- 100 g/4 oz Chinese cabbage, shredded
- 100 g/4 oz roast pork, shredded
- 4 dried Chinese mushrooms
- 4 eggs, slightly beaten

- 50 g/2 oz bamboo shoots, sliced
- 50 g/2 oz water chestnuts, sliced
- 60 ml/3 tbsp groundnut (peanut) oil
- salt and freshly ground pepper

Directions:

1. Soak the mushrooms in warm water for half an hour then drain.
2. Discard the stalks and slice the caps.
3. Heat 30 ml/2 tbsp of oil and stir-fry the mushrooms, pork, cabbage, bamboo shoots and water chestnuts for approximately three minutes.
4. Take out of the pan and allow to cool slightly then mix them into the eggs and season with salt and pepper.
5. Heat some of the rest of the oil and pour the mixture into the pan a little at a time to make small pancakes about 7.5 cm/3 in across.
6. Fry until the bottom is slightly browned then turn and brown the other side.
7. Continue until you have used all the mixture.

SALTED EGGS

Yield: 6

- 1.2 l/2 pts/5 cups water
- 100 g/4 oz rock salt
- 6 duck eggs

Directions:

1. Bring the water to the boil with the salt and stir until the salt has dissolved.
2. Allow it to cool.
3. Pour the salt water into a large jar, add the eggs, cover and allow to stand for 1 month.
4. Hard-boil the eggs before steaming with rice.

SCRAMBLED EGGS WITH FISH

Yield: 4 Servings

Ingredients:

- 1 slice ginger root, minced
- 2 spring onions (scallions), chopped
- 225 g/8 oz fish fillet
- 30 ml/2 tbsp groundnut (peanut) oil
- 4 eggs, slightly beaten
- salt and freshly ground pepper

Directions:

1. Put the fish in an ovenproof bowl and place on a rack in a steamer.
2. Cover and steam for approximately twenty minutes then remove the skin and flake the flesh.
3. Heat the oil and stir-fry the ginger and spring onions until slightly browned.
4. Put in the fish and stir until coated with oil.
5. Season the eggs with salt and pepper then pour them into the pan and stir gently using a fork until the eggs are just set.
6. Serve Immediately.

SCRAMBLED EGGS WITH MUSHROOMS

Yield: 4 Servings

Ingredients:

- 100 g/4 oz mushrooms, roughly chopped
- 3 spring onions (scallions), chopped
- 30 ml/2 tbsp groundnut (peanut) oil
- 4 eggs, beaten
- 5 ml/1 tsp soy sauce
- pinch of salt

Directions:

1. Heat half the oil and gently fry the mushrooms for a few minutes until heated through then remove them from the pan.
2. Beat the eggs with the spring onions, salt and soy sauce.
3. Heat the rest of the oil then pour in the egg mixture.
4. Stir gently using a fork until the eggs begin to set, then return the mushrooms to the pan and cook until the eggs are just set.
5. Serve Immediately.

SCRAMBLED EGGS WITH OYSTER SAUCE

Yield: 4 Servings

Ingredients:

- 100 g/4 oz cooked ham, shredded
- 15 ml/1 tbsp oyster sauce
- 2 sprigs flat-leaved parsley
- 3 spring onions (scallions), chopped
- 30 ml/2 tbsp groundnut (peanut) oil
- 4 eggs, beaten
- 5 ml/1 tsp soy sauce
- salt and freshly ground pepper

Directions:

1. Beat the eggs with the spring onions, salt, pepper and soy sauce.
2. Mix in half the oil.
3. Heat the rest of the oil then pour in the egg mixture.
4. Stir gently using a fork until the eggs begin to set, then mix in the oyster sauce and cook until the eggs are just set.
5. Serve garnished with the ham and parsley.

SCRAMBLED EGGS WITH PORK

Yield: 4 Servings

Ingredients:

- 2 spring onions (scallions), chopped
- 225 g/8 oz lean pork, chopped into slivers
- 30 ml/2 tbsp groundnut (peanut) oil
- 30 ml/2 tbsp soy sauce
- 4 eggs, beaten
- 5 ml/1 tsp soy sauce
- pinch of salt

Directions:

1. Combine the pork and soy sauce so that the pork is well coated.
2. Heat the oil and stir-fry the pork until slightly browned.
3. Put in the spring onions and stir-fry for approximately one minute.
4. Beat the eggs with the spring onions, salt and soy sauce then pour the egg mixture into the pan.
5. Stir gently using a fork until the eggs are just set.
6. Serve Immediately.

SCRAMBLED EGGS WITH PORK AND PRAWNS

Yield: 4 Servings

Ingredients:

- 1 slice ginger root, minced
- 100 g/4 oz minced (ground) pork
- 15 ml/1 tbsp rice wine or dry sherry
- 15 ml/1 tbsp soy sauce
- 2 spring onions (scallions), chopped
- 225 g/8 oz peeled prawns
- 4 eggs, slightly beaten
- 45 ml/3 tbsp groundnut (peanut) oil
- 5 ml/1 tsp cornflour (cornstarch)
- salt and freshly ground pepper

Directions:

1. Combine the pork, prawns, spring onions, ginger, cornflour, wine or sherry, soy sauce, salt and pepper.
2. Heat the oil and stir-fry the pork mixture until slightly browned.
3. Pour in the eggs and stir gently using a fork until the eggs are just set.
4. Serve Immediately.

SCRAMBLED EGGS WITH SPINACH

Yield: 4 Servings

Ingredients:

- 2 spring onions (scallions), chopped
- 225 g/8 oz spinach
- 4 eggs, beaten
- 45 ml/3 tbsp groundnut (peanut) oil
- pinch of salt

Directions:

1. Heat half the oil and stir-fry the spinach for a few minutes until it turns bright green but does not wilt.
2. Remove it from the pan and chop it finely.
3. Beat the eggs with the spring onions, salt and soy sauce, if using.
4. Mix in the spinach.
5. Heat the oil then pour in the egg mixture.
6. Stir gently using a fork until the eggs are just set.
7. Serve Immediately.

SCRAMBLED EGGS WITH SPRING ONIONS

Yield: 4 Servings

Ingredients:

- 30 ml/2 tbsp groundnut (peanut) oil
- 4 eggs, beaten
- 5 ml/1 tsp soy sauce
- 8 spring onions (scallions), chopped
- salt and freshly ground pepper

Directions:

1. Beat the eggs with the spring onions, salt, pepper and soy sauce.
2. Heat the oil then pour in the egg mixture.
3. Stir gently using a fork until the eggs are just set.
4. Serve Immediately.

SCRAMBLED EGGS WITH TOMATOES

Yield: 4 Servings

Ingredients:

- 2 spring onions (scallions), chopped
- 3 tomatoes, skinned and chopped
- 30 ml/2 tbsp groundnut (peanut) oil
- 4 eggs, beaten
- pinch of salt

Directions:

1. Beat the eggs with the spring onions and salt.
2. Heat the oil then pour in the egg mixture.
3. Stir gently until the eggs begin to set, then mix in the tomatoes and continue to cook, stirring, until just set.
4. Serve Immediately.

SCRAMBLED EGGS WITH VEGETABLES

Yield: 4 Servings

Ingredients:

- 1 clove garlic, chopped
- 1 green pepper, diced
- 100 g/4 oz mangetout (snow peas), halved
- 2 spring onions (scallions), chopped
- 30 ml/2 tbsp groundnut (peanut) oil
- 4 eggs, beaten
- 5 ml/1 tsp sesame oil
- 5 ml/1 tsp soy sauce
- pinch of salt

Directions:

1. Heat half the groundnut (peanut) oil with the sesame oil and stir-fry the pepper and garlic until slightly browned.

2. Put in the mangetout and stir-fry for approximately one minute.
3. Beat the eggs with the spring onions, salt and soy sauce then pour the mixture into the pan.
4. Stir gently using a fork until the eggs are just set.
5. Serve Immediately.

SOY EGGS

Yield: 4 Servings

Ingredients:

- ½ head lettuce, shredded
- 120 ml/4 fl oz/½ cup soy sauce
- 120 ml/4 fl oz/½ cup water
- 2 tomatoes, sliced
- 4 eggs
- 50 g/2 oz/¼ cup brown sugar

Directions:

1. Put the eggs in a saucepan, cover with cold water, bring to the boil and boil for 10 minutes.
2. Drain and cool under running water.
3. Return the eggs to the pan and add the soy sauce, water and sugar.
4. Bring to the boil, cover and simmer for one hour.
5. Put the lettuce on a serving plate.
6. Quarter the eggs and place on top of the lettuce.
7. Serve garnished with tomatoes.

SOY-SAUCE FRIED EGGS

Yield: 4 Servings

Ingredients:

- ¼ head lettuce, shredded
- 15 ml/1 tbsp soy sauce

- 4 eggs
- 45 ml/3 tbsp groundnut (peanut) oil

Directions:

1. Heat the oil until very hot and break the eggs into the pan.
2. Cook until the underside is slightly browned them drizzle generously with soy sauce and turn over without breaking the yolk.
3. Fry for another 1 minute.
4. Put the lettuce on a serving plate and place the eggs on top to serve.

STEAMED EGGS

Yield: 4 Servings

Ingredients:

- 15 ml/1 tbsp rice wine or dry sherry
- 15 ml/1 tbsp soy sauce
- 2 spring onions (scallions), chopped
- 2½ ml/½ tsp salt
- 2½ ml/½ tsp sugar
- 250 ml/8 fl oz/1 cup chicken stock
- 4 eggs, slightly beaten
- 5 ml/1 tsp groundnut (peanut) oil

Directions:

1. Beat the eggs slightly with the wine or sherry, oil, salt, sugar and spring onions.
2. Warm the stock then slowly mix it into the egg mixture and pour into a shallow ovenproof dish.
3. Put the dish on a rack in a steamer, cover and steam for about 30 minutes over gently simmering water until the mixture is the consistency of thick custard.
4. Drizzle with soy sauce and serve.

STEAMED EGGS WITH FISH

Yield: 4 Servings

Ingredients:

- ½ small green pepper, finely chopped
- 1 spring onion (scallion), finely chopped
- 120 ml/4 fl oz/½ cup chicken stock
- 225 g/8 oz sole fillets, chopped into strips
- 3 eggs, slightly beaten
- 30 ml/2 tbsp cornflour (cornstarch)
- 30 ml/2 tbsp groundnut (peanut) oil
- pinch of salt

Directions:

1. Dust the strips of fish slightly in cornflour then shake off any excess.
2. Lay out them in a shallow ovenproof dish.
3. Drizzle with the pepper, spring onion and oil.
4. Warm the chicken stock, mix it into the eggs and season with salt then pour the mixture over the fish.
5. Put the dish on a rack in a steamer, cover and steam for approximately forty minutes over gently simmering water until the fish is cooked and the eggs are just set.

STEAMED EGGS WITH HAM AND FISH

Yield: 4 Servings

Ingredients:

- 15 ml/1 tbsp groundnut (peanut) oil
- 225 g/8 oz minced (ground) cod
- 375 ml/13 fl oz/1½ cups warm water
- 50 g/2 oz smoked ham, chopped
- 6 eggs, separated
- pinch of salt
- sprigs flat-leaf parsley

Directions:

1. Combine the egg white with the fish, half the water and a little salt and pour the mixture into a shallow ovenproof dish.

2. Combine the egg yolks with the rest of the water, the ham and a little salt and pour it on top of the egg white mixture.
3. Put the dish on a rack in a steamer, cover and steam over gently simmering water for approximately twenty minutes until the eggs are set.
4. Heat the oil to smoking point, pour it over the eggs and serve garnished with parsley.

STEAMED EGGS WITH PORK

Yield: 4 Servings

Ingredients:

- 1 spring onion (scallion), chopped
- 100 g/4 oz water chestnuts, minced (ground)
- 120 ml/4 fl oz/½ cup chicken stock
- 225 g/8 oz lean pork, minced (ground)
- 30 ml/2 tbsp soy sauce
- 4 eggs, slightly beaten
- 45 ml/3 tbsp groundnut (peanut) oil
- 5 ml/1 tsp salt

Directions:

1. Heat the oil and fry the pork, water chestnuts and spring onions until slightly coloured.
2. Mix in the soy sauce and salt then eliminate the excess liquid off any excess oil and spoon into a shallow ovenproof dish.
3. Warm the stock then mix it into the eggs and pour over the meat mixture.
4. Put the dish on a rack in a steamer, cover and steam over gently simmering water for about 30 minutes until the eggs are just set.

STEAMED OMELETTE ROLLS WITH CHICKEN FILLING

Yield: 4 Servings

Ingredients:

- 1 onion, chopped
- 100 g/4 oz cooked chicken, minced

- 120 ml/4 fl oz/½ cup chicken stock
- 15 ml/1 tbsp groundnut (peanut) oil
- 15 ml/1 tbsp rice wine or dry sherry
- 2 slices ginger root, minced
- 4 eggs, slightly beaten
- salt

Directions:

1. Beat the eggs and season with salt.
2. Heat some oil and pour in one quarter of the eggs, tilting to spread the mixture over the pan.
3. Fry until slightly browned on one side and just set then turn upside down on to a plate.
4. Cook the rest of the 4 omelettes.
5. Combine the chicken, ginger and onion.
6. Spoon the mixture equally between the omelettes, roll them up, secure with cocktail sticks and arrange the rolls in a shallow ovenproof dish.
7. Put on a rack in a steamer, cover and steam for approximately fifteen minutes.
8. Move to a warmed serving plate and chop into thick slices.
9. In the meantime, heat the stock and sherry and season with salt.
10. Pour over the omelettes and serve.

TEA EGGS

Yield: 4 Servings

Ingredients:

- 1 clove star anise, broken apart
- 10 ml/2 tsp salt
- 3 China tea bags
- 45 ml/3 tbsp soy sauce
- 6 eggs

Directions:

1. Put the eggs in a pan, cover with cold water then bring to a slow boil and simmer for approximately fifteen minutes.
2. Turn off the heat and place the eggs in cold water until cool.
3. Allow to stand for approximately five minutes.

4. Remove the eggs from the pan and gently crack the shells but do not remove them.
5. Return the eggs to the pan and cover with cold water.
6. Add the rest of the ingredients, bring to the boil then simmer for approximately an hour and a half.
7. Cool and remove the shell.

VEGETABLE SOUFFLÉ

Yield: 4 Servings

Ingredients:

- 1 small onion, finely chopped
- 15 ml/1 tbsp chopped fresh parsley
- 3 potatoes, grated
- 5 eggs, separated
- 5 ml/1 tsp soy sauce
- salt and freshly ground pepper

Directions:

1. Beat the egg whites until firm.
2. Beat the egg yolks until pale and thick then add the potatoes, onion, parsley and soy sauce and thoroughly stir together.
3. Fold in the egg whites.
4. Pour into a greased soufflé dish and bake in a preheated oven at 180°C/350°F/gas mark 4 for approximately forty minutes.

RICE

Rice is an important Chinese staple. It is cheap, and goes great with the Chinese way of cooking. The best cooked rice are soft but not mushy.

ALMOND FRIED RICE

Yield: 4 Servings

Ingredients:

- 15 ml/1 tbsp soy sauce
- 2 shallots, finely chopped
- 250 ml/8 fl oz/1 cup groundnut (peanut) oil
- 3 slices cooked ham, chopped into strips
- 4 eggs, beaten
- 450 g/1 lb/3 cups cooked long-grain rice
- 5 ml/1 tsp salt
- 50 g/2 oz/½ cup flaked almonds

Directions:

1. Heat the oil and fry the almonds until a golden-brown colour is achieved.
2. Take out of the pan and eliminate the excess liquid on kitchen paper.
3. Pour most of the oil out of the pan then reheat and pour in the eggs, stirring constantly.
4. Put in the rice and salt and cook for approximately five minutes, lifting and stirring quickly so that the rice grains are coated with the egg.
5. Mix in the ham, shallots and soy sauce and cook for another 2 minutes.
6. Fold in most of the almonds and serve garnished with the rest of the almonds.

BEEF FRIED RICE

Yield: 4 Servings

Ingredients:

- 1 onion, chopped

- 15 ml/1 tbsp cornflour (cornstarch)
- 15 ml/1 tbsp rice wine or dry sherry
- 15 ml/1 tbsp soy sauce
- 225 g/8 oz lean beef, chopped into strips
- 45 ml/3 tbsp chicken stock
- 450 g/1 lb/3 cups cooked long-grain rice
- 5 ml/1 tsp sugar
- 75 ml/5 tbsp groundnut (peanut) oil

Directions:

1. Combine the beef with the cornflour, soy sauce, wine or sherry and sugar.
2. Heat half the oil and fry the onion until translucent.
3. Put in the beef and stir-fry for approximately two minutes.
4. Take out of the pan.
5. Heat the rest of the oil, add the rice and stir-fry for approximately two minutes.
6. Put in the stock and heat through.
7. Add half the beef and onion mixture and stir until hot then transfer to a warmed serving plate and top with the rest of the beef and onions.

BOILED BROWN RICE

Yield: 4 Servings

Ingredients:

- 225 g/8 oz/1 cup long-grain brown rice
- 5 ml/1 tsp salt
- 900 ml/1½ pts/3¾ cups water

Directions:

1. Rinse the rice then place it in a saucepan.
2. Put in the salt and water so that it comes about 3 cm/1¼ in above the rice.
3. Bring to the boil, cover with a tight-fitting lid, reduce the heat and simmer gently for half an hour, making sure that it does not boil dry.

CHICKEN AND MUSHROOM RICE

Yield: 4 Servings

Ingredients:

- 100 g/4 oz chicken meat, shredded
- 100 g/4 oz mushrooms, diced
- 15 ml/1 tbsp chopped spring onions (scallions)
- 15 ml/1 tbsp oyster sauce
- 225 g/8 oz/1 cup long-grain rice
- 5 ml/1 tsp cornflour (cornstarch)
- 5 ml/1 tsp rice wine or dry sherry
- 5 ml/1 tsp soy sauce
- pinch of salt

Directions:

1. Put the rice in a large pan and bring to the boil.
2. Cover and simmer for approximately ten minutes until most of the liquid has been absorbed.
3. Combine all the rest of the ingredients except the spring onions and oyster sauce, arrange on top of the rice, cover and cook for another 20 minutes over a low heat until cooked.
4. Stir the ingredients together and drizzle with spring onions and oyster sauce and serve.

CHICKEN FRIED RICE

Yield: 4 Servings

Ingredients:

- 1 onion, finely chopped
- 100 g/4 oz cooked chicken, shredded
- 15 ml/1 tbsp soy sauce
- 2 cloves garlic, crushed
- 225 g/8 oz/1 cup long-grain rice
- 3 spring onions (scallions), chopped
- 30 ml/2 tbsp groundnut (peanut) oil
- 750 ml/1¼ pts/3 cups water
- pinch of salt

Directions:

1. Put the rice and water in a saucepan, bring to the boil, cover and simmer for approximately twenty minutes until the rice is cooked.
2. Drain thoroughly.
3. Heat the oil and fry the garlic and salt until the garlic turns light golden.
4. Put in the onion and stir-fry for approximately one minute.
5. Put in the rice and stir-fry for approximately two minutes.
6. Put in the spring onions and chicken and stir-fry for approximately two minutes.
7. Mix in the soy sauce until the rice is covered.

CHICKEN LIVER RICE

Yield: 4 Servings

Ingredients:

- 2 cooked chicken livers, finely sliced
- 225 g/8 oz/1 cup long-grain rice
- 375 ml/13 fl oz/1½ cups chicken stock
- salt

Directions:

1. Put the rice and stock in a large pan and bring to the boil.
2. Cover and simmer for approximately ten minutes until the rice is almost soft.
3. Take the lid off and carry on simmering until most of the stock has been absorbed.
4. Season to taste with salt, mix in the chicken livers and heat through gently and serve.

COCONUT RICE

Yield: 4 Servings

Ingredients:

- 1 l/1¾ pts/4¼ cups coconut milk
- 1 sprig coriander, chopped
- 150 ml/¼ pt/generous ½ cup coconut cream
- 225 g/8 oz/1 cup Thai scented rice

- pinch of salt

Directions:

1. Bring all the ingredients to the boil in a pan, cover and leave the rice to swell over a low heat for about 25 minutes, stirring intermittently.

CRAB MEAT RICE

Yield: 4 Servings

Ingredients:

- 100 g/4 oz crab meat, flaked
- 15 ml/1 tbsp rice wine or dry sherry
- 15 ml/1 tbsp soy sauce
- 2 slices ginger root, minced
- 225 g/8 oz/1 cup long-grain rice
- 5 ml/1 tsp cornflour (cornstarch)
- 5 ml/1 tsp groundnut (peanut) oil
- salt and freshly ground pepper

Directions:

1. Put the rice in a large pan and bring to the boil.
2. Cover and simmer for approximately ten minutes until most of the liquid has been absorbed.
3. Combine the rest of the ingredients, arrange on top of the rice, cover and cook for another 20 minutes over a low heat until cooked.
4. Stir the ingredients together and serve.

DUCK FRIED RICE

Yield: 4 Servings

Ingredients:

- 100 g/4 oz cooked duck, shredded
- 15 ml/1 tbsp rice wine or dry sherry

- 2 spring onions (scallions), sliced
- 225 g/8 oz Chinese cabbage, shredded
- 350 g/12 oz cooked long-grain rice
- 4 dried Chinese mushrooms
- 45 ml/3 tbsp chicken stock
- 45 ml/3 tbsp groundnut (peanut) oil
- 45 ml/3 tbsp soy sauce

Directions:

1. Soak the mushrooms in warm water for half an hour then drain.
2. Discard the stalks and chop the caps.
3. Heat half the oil and fry the spring onions until translucent.
4. Put in the Chinese cabbage and stir-fry for approximately one minute.
5. Put in the duck, soy sauce and wine or sherry and stir-fry for approximately three minutes.
6. Take out of the pan.
7. Heat the rest of the oil and stir-fry the rice until coated with oil.
8. Put in the stock, bring to the boil and stir-fry for approximately two minutes.
9. Return the duck mixture to the pan and stir until heated through and serve.

FRIED RICE

Yield: 4 Servings

Ingredients:

- 1 egg, beaten
- 1 onion, finely chopped
- 2 cloves garlic, crushed
- 2½ ml/½ tsp black treacle
- 225 g/8 oz/1 cup long-grain rice
- 3 spring onions (scallions), chopped
- 30 ml/2 tbsp groundnut (peanut) oil
- 750 ml/1¼ pts/3 cups water
- pinch of salt

Directions:

1. Put the rice and water in a saucepan, bring to the boil, cover and simmer for approximately twenty minutes until the rice is cooked.
2. Drain thoroughly.
3. Heat 5 ml/1 tsp oil and pour in the egg.
4. Cook until it sets on the base then turn and continue to cook until set.
5. Take out of the pan and chop into strips.
6. Add the rest of the oil to the pan with the garlic and salt and fry until the garlic turns light golden.
7. Put in the onion and rice and stir-fry for approximately two minutes.
8. Put in the spring onions and stir-fry for approximately two minutes.
9. Mix in the black treacle until the rice is covered then mix in the egg strips and serve.

FRIED RICE AND PEAS

Yield: 4 Servings

Ingredients:

- 2 cloves garlic, crushed
- 225 g/8 oz briefly boiled or frozen peas, thawed
- 30 ml/2 tbsp finely chopped fresh parsley
- 30 ml/2 tbsp groundnut (peanut) oil
- 350 g/12 oz cooked long-grain rice
- 4 spring onions (scallions), finely chopped
- 5 ml/1 tsp salt

Directions:

1. Heat the oil and fry the garlic and salt until slightly browned.
2. Put in the rice and stir-fry for approximately two minutes.
3. Put in the peas, onions and parsley and stir-fry for a few minutes until heated through.
4. Serve hot or cold.

FRIED RICE WITH BACON AND EGG

Yield: 4 Servings

Ingredients:

- 1 onion, finely chopped
- 225 g/8 oz bacon, chopped
- 225 g/8 oz cooked long-grain rice
- 3 eggs, beaten
- 45 ml/3 tbsp groundnut (peanut) oil

Directions:

1. Heat the oil and fry the bacon and onion until slightly browned.
2. Put in the eggs and stir-fry until the eggs are almost cooked.
3. Put in the rice and stir-fry until the rice is heated through.

FRIED RICE WITH BEEF AND ONIONS

Yield: 4 Servings

Ingredients:

- 1 onion, chopped
- 15 ml/1 tbsp cornflour (cornstarch)
- 15 ml/1 tbsp rice wine or dry sherry
- 225 g/8 oz cooked long-grain rice
- 45 ml/3 tbsp groundnut (peanut) oil
- 45 ml/3 tbsp soy sauce
- 450 g/1 lb lean beef, finely sliced
- salt and freshly ground pepper

Directions:

1. Marinate the beef in the soy sauce, wine or sherry, salt, pepper and cornflour for approximately fifteen minutes.
2. Heat the oil and fry the onion until slightly browned.
3. Put in the beef and marinade and stir-fry for approximately three minutes.
4. Put in the rice and stir-fry until heated through.

FRIED RICE WITH MINCED BEEF

Yield: 4 Servings

Ingredients:

- 1 carrot, diced
- 1 clove garlic, crushed
- 1 leek, diced
- 1 onion, diced
- 30 ml/2 tbsp groundnut (peanut) oil
- 30 ml/2 tbsp hoisin sauce
- 30 ml/2 tbsp soy sauce
- 450 g/1 lb cooked long-grain rice
- 450 g/1 lb minced (ground) beef
- pinch of salt

Directions:

1. Heat the oil and fry the garlic and salt until slightly browned.
2. Put in the soy and hoisin sauces and stir until heated through.
3. Put in the beef and fry until brown and crumbly.
4. Put in the vegetables and fry until soft, stirring often.
5. Put in the rice and fry, stirring constantly, until heated through and coated in the sauces.

FRIED TUNA RICE

Yield: 4 Servings

Ingredients:

- 1 green pepper, chopped
- 2 onions, sliced
- 2 shallots, finely chopped
- 3 eggs, beaten
- 30 ml/2 tbsp groundnut (peanut) oil
- 30 ml/2 tbsp soy sauce
- 300 g/12 oz canned tuna, flaked
- 450 g/1 lb/3 cups cooked long-grain rice
- salt

Directions:

1. Heat the oil and fry the onions until soft.
2. Put in the pepper and fry for approximately one minute.
3. Push to one side of the pan.
4. Put in the rice, drizzle with salt and stir-fry for approximately two minutes, progressively mixing in the pepper and onions.
5. Make a well in the centre of the rice, pour in a little more oil and pour in the eggs.
6. Stir until almost scrambled and mix in with the rice.
7. Cook for another 3 minutes.
8. Put in the tuna and soy sauce and heat through comprehensively..
9. Serve sprinkled with the chopped shallots.

HAM FRIED RICE

Yield: 4 Servings

Ingredients:

- 1 clove garlic, crushed
- 1 egg, beaten
- 1 green pepper, chopped
- 1 onion, finely chopped
- 100 g/4 oz ham, chopped
- 15 ml/1 tbsp oyster sauce
- 15 ml/1 tbsp rice wine or dry sherry
- 15 ml/1 tbsp soy sauce
- 30 ml/2 tbsp groundnut (peanut) oil
- 350 g/12 oz cooked long-grain rice
- 50 g/2 oz bamboo shoots, chopped
- 50 g/2 oz water chestnuts, sliced

Directions:

1. Heat some of the oil in a pan and add the egg, tilting the pan so that it spreads across the pan.
2. Cook until the underside is slightly browned, then turn it and cook the other side.
3. Remove it from the pan and chop it in and fry the garlic until slightly browned.
4. Put in the rice, onion and pepper and stir-fry for approximately three minutes.

5. Put in the ham, water chestnuts and bamboo shoots and stir-fry for approximately five minutes.
6. Add the rest of the ingredients and stir-fry for about 4 minutes.
7. Serve sprinkled with the egg strips.

PEPPER RICE

Yield: 4 Servings

Ingredients:

- 1 red pepper, diced
- 2 spring onions (scallions), minced
- 225 g/8 oz/1 cup long-grain rice
- 30 ml/2 tbsp groundnut (peanut) oil
- 45 ml/3 tbsp soy sauce
- 5 ml/1 tsp sugar

Directions:

1. Put the rice in a pan, cover with cold water, bring to the boil, cover and simmer for approximately twenty minutes until soft.
2. Drain thoroughly then mix in the spring onions, pepper, soy sauce, oil and sugar.
3. Move to a warmed serving bowl and serve instantly.

POACHED EGG RICE

Yield: 4 Servings

Ingredients:

- 15 ml/1 tbsp oyster sauce
- 225 g/8 oz/1 cup long-grain rice
- 4 eggs

Directions:

1. Put the rice in a pan, cover with cold water, bring to the boil, cover and simmer for approximately ten minutes until soft.

2. Drain and lay out on a warmed serving plate.
3. In the meantime, bring a pan of water to the boil, carefully break in the eggs and poach for a few minutes until the whites are set but the eggs are still moist.
4. Lift out of the pan using a slotted spoon and arrange on top of the rice.
5. Serve sprinkled with oyster sauce.

PORK AND PRAWN FRIED RICE

Yield: 4 Servings

Ingredients:

- 100 g/4 oz roast pork
- 2 spring onions (scallions), chopped
- 2½ ml/½ tsp salt
- 225 g/8 oz peeled prawns
- 350 g/12 oz cooked long-grain rice
- 45 ml/3 tbsp groundnut (peanut) oil
- 45 ml/3 tbsp soy sauce
- 50 g/2 oz Chinese leaves, shredded

Directions:

1. Heat the oil and fry the salt and spring onions until slightly browned.
2. Put in the rice and stir-fry to break up the grains.
3. Put in the pork and stir-fry for approximately two minutes.
4. Put in the prawns, Chinese leaves and soy sauce and stir-fry until heated through.

PORK FRIED RICE

Yield: 4 Servings

Ingredients:

- 100 g/4 oz roast pork, diced
- 2 eggs, beaten
- 2½ ml/½ tsp salt
- 3 spring onions (scallions), chopped

- 30 ml/2 tbsp soy sauce
- 350 g/12 oz cooked long-grain rice
- 45 ml/3 tbsp groundnut (peanut) oil

Directions:

1. Heat the oil and stir-fry the spring onions until translucent.
2. Put in the pork and stir until coated with oil.
3. Put in the rice, soy sauce and salt and stir-fry for approximately three minutes.
4. Put in the eggs and fold in until they begin to set.

PRAWN FRIED RICE

Yield: 4 Servings

Ingredients:

- 1 onion, finely chopped
- 2 cloves garlic, crushed
- 225 g/8 oz peeled prawns
- 225 g/8 oz/1 cup long-grain rice
- 30 ml/2 tbsp groundnut (peanut) oil
- 5 ml/1 tsp soy sauce
- 750 ml/1¼ pts/3 cups water
- pinch of salt

Directions:

1. Put the rice and water in a saucepan, bring to the boil, cover and simmer for approximately twenty minutes until the rice is cooked.
2. Drain thoroughly.
3. Heat the oil with the garlic and salt and fry until the garlic turns light golden.
4. Put in the rice and onion and stir-fry for approximately two minutes.
5. Put in the prawns and stir-fry for approximately two minutes.
6. Mix in the soy sauce and serve.

RICE WITH BEEF

Yield: 4 Servings

Ingredients:

- 1 slice ginger root, minced
- 100 g/4 oz minced (ground) beef
- 15 ml/1 tbsp rice wine or dry sherry
- 15 ml/1 tbsp soy sauce
- 2½ ml/½ tsp salt
- 2½ ml/½ tsp sugar
- 225 g/8 oz/1 cup long-grain rice
- 5 ml/1 tsp groundnut (peanut) oil

Directions:

1. Put the rice in a large pan and bring to the boil.
2. Cover and simmer for approximately ten minutes until most of the liquid has been absorbed.
3. Combine the rest of the ingredients, arrange on top of the rice, cover and cook for another 20 minutes over a low heat until cooked.
4. Stir the ingredients together and serve.

RICE WITH PEAS

Yield: 4 Servings

Ingredients:

- 225 g/8 oz/1 cup long-grain rice
- 30 ml/2 tbsp soy sauce
- 350 g/12 oz peas

Directions:

1. Put the rice and stock in a large pan and bring to the boil.
2. Put in the peas, cover and simmer for approximately twenty minutes until the rice is almost soft.
3. Take the lid off and carry on simmering until most of the liquid has been absorbed.
4. Cover and allow to stand off the heat for approximately five minutes then serve sprinkled with soy sauce.

SALMON FRIED RICE

Yield: 4 Servings

Ingredients:

- 150 g/5 oz cooked long-grain rice
- 2 cloves garlic, chopped
- 2 spring onions (scallions), sliced
- 30 ml/2 tbsp groundnut (peanut) oil
- 50 g/2 oz salmon, chopped
- 75 g/3 oz spinach, chopped

Directions:

1. Heat the oil and fry the garlic and spring onions for 30 seconds.
2. Put in the salmon and fry for approximately one minute.
3. Put in the spinach and fry for approximately one minute.
4. Put in the rice and stir-fry until heated through and well mixed.

SINGAPORE-STYLE RICE

Yield: 4 Servings

Ingredients:

- 1.2 l/2 pts/5 cups water
- 225 g/8 oz/1 cup long-grain rice
- 5 ml/1 tsp salt

Directions:

1. Rinse the rice then place it in a saucepan with the salt and water.
2. Bring to the boil then reduce the heat and simmer for about 15 minutes until the rice is soft.
3. Drain in a colander and rinse with hot water and serve.

SLOW BOAT RICE

Yield: 4 Servings

Ingredients:

- 15 ml/1 tbsp oil
- 225 g/8 oz/1 cup long-grain rice
- 5 ml/1 tsp salt
- 750 ml/1¼ pts/3 cups water

Directions:

1. Rinse the rice then place it in an ovenproof dish with the salt, oil and water.
2. Cover and bake in a preheated oven at 120°C/250°F/gas mark ½ for about 1 hour until all the water has been absorbed.

SMOKED HAM RICE WITH STOCK

Yield: 4 Servings

Ingredients:

- 100 g/4 oz bamboo shoots, sliced
- 100 g/4 oz smoked ham, shredded
- 3 eggs, beaten
- 30 ml/2 tbsp groundnut (peanut) oil
- 350 g/12 oz cooked long-grain rice
- 600 ml/1 pt/2½ cups chicken stock

Directions:

1. Heat the oil then pour in the eggs.
2. When they begin to set, add the rice and stir-fry for approximately two minutes.
3. Put in the stock and ham and bring to the boil.
4. Simmer for approximately two minutes then add the bamboo shoots and serve.

SPECIAL FRIED RICE

Yield: 4 Servings

Ingredients:

- 1 onion, finely chopped
- 100 g/4 oz bacon, chopped
- 100 g/4 oz mushrooms, sliced
- 15 ml/1 tbsp cornflour (cornstarch)
- 2 eggs, beaten
- 225 g/8 oz cooked long-grain rice
- 30 ml/2 tbsp rice wine or dry sherry
- 50 g/2 oz cooked chicken, shredded
- 50 g/2 oz frozen peas
- 50 g/2 oz ham, chopped
- 50 g/2 oz peeled prawns
- 60 ml/4 tbsp groundnut (peanut) oil
- 60 ml/4 tbsp soy sauce
- salt and freshly ground pepper

Directions:

1. Heat the oil and fry the onion and bacon until slightly browned.
2. Put in the ham and chicken and stir-fry for approximately two minutes.
3. Put in the prawns, soy sauce, wine or sherry, salt, pepper and cornflour and stir-fry for approximately two minutes.
4. Put in the rice and stir-fry for approximately two minutes.
5. Put in the eggs, mushrooms and peas and stir-fry for approximately two minutes until hot.

STEAMED OVEN RICE

Yield: 4 Servings

Ingredients:

- 225 g/8 oz/1 cup long-grain rice
- 450 ml/¾ pt/2 cups water
- 5 ml/1 tsp salt

Directions:

1. Put the rice, salt and water in a casserole dish, cover and bake in a preheated oven at 180°C/350°F/gas mark 4 for about 30 minutes.
2. Reheating Rice
3. There are several ways of reheating rice successfully, so you can always prepare a large quantity then reheat it for subsequent meals.
4. Put the rice in a pan with 5 ml/1 tsp water, cover and simmer gently for approximately ten minutes until the rice has reheated.
5. Put the rice in a colander over a pan of hot water and cover.
6. Bring the water to the boil and steam for about 5 minutes.
7. Put the rice in the top of a double boiler and bring the water in the bottom to the boil.
8. Cover and simmer for about 15 minutes until the rice is heated through.
9. Put the rice in a saucepan with 1.2 l/2 pts/5 cups water, bring to the boil then simmer for approximately two minutes.
10. Strain comprehensively..

TEN PRECIOUS RICE

Yield: 6-8 Servings

Ingredients:

- 1 chicken breast, shredded
- 1 spring onion (scallion), chopped
- 100 g/4 oz bamboo shoots, chopped into strips
- 100 g/4 oz ham, shredded
- 100 g/4 oz lean pork, shredded
- 250 ml/8 fl oz/1 cup chicken stock
- 30 ml/2 tbsp rice wine or dry sherry
- 30 ml/2 tbsp soy sauce
- 350 g/12 oz cooked long-grain rice
- 45 ml/3 tbsp groundnut (peanut) oil
- 5 ml/1 tsp salt
- 50 g/2 oz water chestnuts, sliced

Directions:

1. Heat the oil and fry the spring onion until translucent.
2. Put in the pork and stir-fry for approximately two minutes.
3. Put in the chicken and ham and stir-fry for approximately two minutes.

4. Mix in the soy sauce, sherry and salt.
5. Mix in the rice and stock and bring to the boil.
6. Put in the bamboo shoots and water chestnuts, cover and simmer for half an hour.

WHITE RICE

Yield: 4 Servings

Ingredients:

- 15 ml/1 tbsp oil
- 225 g/8 oz/1 cup long-grain rice
- 750 ml/1¼ pts/3 cups water

Directions:

1. Rinse the rice then place it in a saucepan.
2. Put in the water to the oil then put it into the pan so that it comes about 2½ cm/1 in above the rice.
3. Bring to the boil, cover with a tight-fitting lid, reduce the heat and simmer gently for approximately 20 minutes.

NOODLES AND PASTRY

Noodles are the first things that come to mind when thinks of Chinese food. Noodles are an alternative to rice, and taste delicious.

BEEF NOODLES

Yield: 4 Servings

Ingredients:

- 1 clove garlic, crushed
- 1 green pepper, chopped
- 1 onion, finely chopped
- 100 g/4 oz mushrooms, sliced
- 15 ml/1 tbsp soy sauce
- 2 stalks celery, chopped
- 250 ml/8 fl oz/1 cup beef stock
- 30 ml/2 tbsp cornflour (cornstarch)
- 350 g/12 oz egg noodles
- 45 ml/3 tbsp groundnut (peanut) oil
- 450 g/1 lb minced (ground) beef
- 60 ml/4 tbsp water
- salt and freshly ground pepper

Directions:

1. Cook the noodles in boiling water for approximately eight minutes until just soft then drain.
2. In the meantime, heat the oil and fry the beef, salt, pepper, garlic and onion until slightly browned.
3. Put in the stock, mushrooms, celery and pepper, bring to the boil, cover and simmer for approximately five minutes.
4. Blend the cornflour, water and soy sauce to a paste, stir into the pan and simmer, stirring, until the sauce becomes thick.
5. Put the noodles on a warmed serving plate and pour over the beef and sauce.

BOILED EGG NOODLES

Yield: 4 Servings

Ingredients:

- 10 ml/2 tsp salt
- 30 ml/2 tbsp groundnut (peanut) oil
- 450 g/1 lb egg noodles

Directions:

1. Bring a pan of water to the boil, add the salt and toss in the noodles.
2. Return to the boil and boil for approximately ten minutes until soft but still firm.
3. Drain well, rinse in cold water, drain, then rinse in hot water.
4. Toss with the oil and serve.

BRAISED NOODLES

Yield: 4 Servings

Ingredients:

- 100 g/4 oz cauliflower florets
- 100 g/4 oz lean pork, chopped into strips
- 15 ml/1 tbsp cornflour (cornstarch)
- 15 ml/1 tbsp sesame oil
- 250 ml/8 fl oz/1 cup chicken stock
- 3 spring onions (scallions), chopped
- 30 ml/2 tbsp groundnut (peanut) oil
- 4 dried Chinese mushrooms
- 450 g/1 lb egg noodles
- 5 ml/1 tsp salt

Directions:

1. Soak the mushrooms in warm water for half an hour then drain.
2. Discard the stalks and slice the caps.
3. Bring a saucepan of water to the boil, add the noodles and boil for approximately five minutes then drain.

4. Heat the oil and fry the salt and spring onions for 30 seconds.
5. Put in the pork and stir-fry until slightly coloured.
6. Put in the cauliflower and mushrooms and stir-fry for approximately three minutes.
7. Combine the cornflour and stock, mix it into the pan, bring to the boil, cover and simmer for 10 minutes, stirring intermittently.
8. Heat the sesame oil in a separate pan, add the noodles and stir gently over a medium heat until slightly browned.
9. Move to a heated serving dish, pour over the pork mixture and serve.

CHINESE PANCAKES

Yield: 4 Servings

Ingredients:

- 225 g/8 oz/2 cups plain (all-purpose) flour
- 250 ml/8 fl oz/1 cup water
- groundnut (peanut) oil for frying

Directions:

1. Boil the water then progressively add the flour.
2. Knead slightly until the dough is soft, cover with a damp cloth and allow to stand for approximately fifteen minutes.
3. Roll out on a floured surface and mould into a long cylinder.
4. Cut into 2½ cm/ 1 in slices then flatten until about 5 mm/¬º in thick and brush the tops with oil.
5. Stack in pairs with the oiled surfaces touching and dust the outsides slightly with flour.
6. Roll out the pairs to about 10 cm/4 in across and cook in pairs for about 1 minute on each side until slightly browned.
7. Separate and stack until ready to serve.

COLD NOODLES

Yield: 4 Servings

Ingredients:

- 1 cucumber, chopped into strips
- 12 radishes, chopped into strips
- 15 ml/1 tbsp groundnut (peanut) oil
- 225 g/8 oz bean sprouts
- 225 g/8 oz roast pork, shredded
- 450 g/1 lb egg noodles
- 5 ml/1 tsp salt

Directions:

1. Bring a pan of water to the boil, add the salt and toss in the noodles.
2. Return to the boil and boil for approximately ten minutes until soft but still firm.
3. Drain well, rinse in cold water then eliminate the excess liquid again.
4. Toss with the oil then arrange in a serving dish.
5. Put the other ingredients in small dishes surrounding the noodles.
6. Guests serve a selection of ingredients into small bowls.

COOKED EGG ROLL SKINS

Yield: 12

Ingredients:

- 175 g/6 oz/1 ½ cups plain (all-purpose) flour
- 2 eggs, beaten
- 2½ ml/ ½ tsp salt
- 375 ml/13 fl oz/1 ½ cups water

Directions:

1. Combine the flour and salt then blend in the eggs.
2. Progressively add the water to make a smooth batter.
3. Lightly grease a small frying pan then pour in 30 ml/2 tbsp of batter and tilt the pan to spread it evenly over the surface.
4. When the dough shrinks from the sides of the pan, remove it and cover with a damp cloth while you cook the rest of the skins.

DAN-DAN NOODLES

Yield: 4 Servings

Ingredients:

- 100 g/4 oz egg noodles
- 20 ml/4 tsp salt
- 4 spring onions (scallions), minced
- 45 ml/3 tbsp mustard
- 60 ml/4 tbsp chicken stock
- 60 ml/4 tbsp groundnut (peanut) oil
- 60 ml/4 tbsp peanuts, ground
- 60 ml/4 tbsp sesame sauce
- 60 ml/4 tbsp soy sauce

Directions:

1. Cook the noodles in boiling water for approximately ten minutes until soft then eliminate the excess liquid well.
2. Combine the rest of the ingredients, pour over the noodles and toss together well and serve.

EGG ROLL SKINS

Yield: 12

Ingredients:

- 1 egg, beaten
- 120 ml/4 fl oz/ ½ cup iced water
- 2½ ml/ ½ tsp salt
- 225 g/8 oz/2 cups plain (all-purpose) flour

Directions:

1. Combine all the ingredients together then knead until smooth and elastic.
2. Cover with a damp cloth and chill for half an hour.
3. Roll out on a floured surface until paper thin then chop into squares.

FRIED NOODLES

Yield: 4 Servings

Ingredients:

- 225 g/8 oz thin egg noodles
- oil for deep-frying
- salt

Directions:

1. Cook the noodles in boiling salted water according to the instructions on the packet.
2. Drain thoroughly.
3. Lay out several layers of kitchen paper on a baking sheet, spread out the noodles and leave to dry for several hours.
4. Heat the oil and fry spoonfuls of the noodles at a time for about 30 seconds until golden.
5. Drain on kitchen paper.

GINGER AND SPRING ONION NOODLES

Yield: 4 Servings

Ingredients:

- 15 ml/1 tbsp groundnut (peanut) oil
- 15 ml/1 tbsp oyster sauce
- 2 slices ginger root, shredded
- 2½ ml/ ½ tsp sesame oil
- 225 g/8 oz egg noodles
- 4 spring onions (scallions), shredded
- 900 ml/1 ½ pts/4¬º cups chicken stock

Directions:

1. Bring the stock to the boil, add the oil and noodles and simmer, uncovered, for about 15 minutes until soft.
2. Transfer the noodles to a warmed serving plate and add the sesame oil, spring onions and ginger to the wok.

3. Simmer, uncovered, for approximately five minutes until the vegetables are slightly softened and the stock reduced.
4. Spoon the vegetables over the noodles with a little of the stock.
5. Drizzle with oyster sauce and serve instantly.

HOT AND SOUR NOODLES

Yield: 4 Servings

Ingredients:

- 1 clove garlic, crushed
- 15 ml/1 tbsp chilli oil
- 15 ml/1 tbsp red wine vinegar
- 15 ml/1 tbsp soy sauce
- 2 spring onions (scallions), minced
- 225 g/8 oz egg noodles
- 5 ml/1 tsp freshly ground pepper

Directions:

1. Cook the noodles in boiling water for approximately ten minutes until soft.
2. Drain thoroughly and transfer to a heated serving dish.
3. Combine the rest of the ingredients, pour over the noodles and toss together well and serve.

NOODLE BASKETS

Yield: 4 Servings

Ingredients:

- Drain thoroughly.
- 225 g/8 oz thin egg noodles
- Cook the noodles in boiling salted water according to the instructions on the packet.
- oil for deep-frying
- salt

Directions:

1. Lay out several layers of kitchen paper on a baking sheet, spread out the noodles and leave to dry for several hours.
2. Brush the inside of a medium-sized strainer with a little oil.
3. Spread an even layer of noodles about 1 cm/ ½ in thick in the strainer.
4. Brush the outside of a smaller strainer with oil and press slightly into the larger one.
5. Heat the oil, lower the two strainers into the oil and fry for about 1 minute until the noodles are golden.
6. Carefully remove the strainers, running a knife around the edges of the noodles if needed to loosen them.

NOODLE PANCAKE

Yield: 4 Servings

Ingredients:

- 225 g/8 oz egg noodles
- 5 ml/1 tsp salt
- 75 ml/5 tbsp groundnut (peanut) oil

Directions:

1. Bring a saucepan of water to the boil, add the salt and toss in the noodles.
2. Return to the boil and boil for approximately ten minutes until soft but still firm.
3. Drain well, rinse in cold water, drain, then rinse in hot water.
4. Toss with 15 ml/1 tbsp of oil.
5. Heat the rest of the oil.
6. Put in the noodles to the pan to make a thick pancake.
7. Fry until slightly browned on the underside then turn and fry until slightly browned but soft in the centre.

NOODLES IN CURRY SAUCE

Yield: 4 Servings

Ingredients:

- 1 onion, sliced
- 100 g/4 oz roast pork, shredded
- 120 ml/4 fl oz/ ½ cup tomato ketchup (catsup)
- 15 ml/1 tbsp hoisin sauce
- 30 ml/2 tbsp curry powder
- 450 g/1 lb egg noodles
- 5 ml/1 tsp salt
- 75 ml/5 tbsp chicken stock
- salt and freshly ground pepper

Directions:

1. Bring a pan of water to the boil, add the salt and toss in the noodles.
2. Return to the boil and boil for approximately ten minutes until soft but still firm.
3. Drain well, rinse in cold water, drain, then rinse in hot water.
4. In the meantime, cook the curry powder using a dry pan for approximately two minutes, shaking the pan.
5. Put in the onion and stir until well coated.
6. Mix in the stock then add the pork and bring to the boil.
7. Mix in the tomato ketchup, hoisin sauce, salt and pepper and simmer, stirring, until heated through.
8. Put the noodles in a heated serving dish, pour over the sauce and serve.

NOODLES IN MEAT SAUCE

Yield: 4 Servings

Ingredients:

- 100 g/4 oz mushrooms, sliced
- 15 ml/1 tbsp rice wine or dry sherry
- 15 ml/1 tbsp soy sauce
- 2 eggs, slightly beaten
- 225 g/8 oz lean pork, sliced
- 30 ml/2 tbsp cornflour (cornstarch)
- 30 ml/2 tbsp groundnut (peanut) oil
- 350 g/12 oz egg noodles
- 4 dried Chinese mushrooms
- 4 spring onions (scallions), sliced

- 600 ml/1 pt/2 ½ cups chicken stock
- salt and freshly ground pepper

Directions:

1. Soak the mushrooms in warm water for half an hour then drain.
2. Discard the stalks and slice the caps.
3. Heat the oil and fry the pork until slightly coloured.
4. Put in the dried and fresh mushrooms and spring onions and stir-fry for approximately two minutes.
5. Put in the soy sauce, wine or sherry and stock, bring to the boil, cover and simmer for half an hour.
6. In the meantime, bring a pan of water to the boil, add the noodles and boil for approximately ten minutes until the noodles are soft but still firm.
7. Drain, rinse in cold then hot water then eliminate the excess liquid again and arrange on in a heated serving dish.
8. Blend the cornflour with a little water, mix it into the pan and simmer, stirring, until the sauce clears and becomes thick.
9. Progressively mix in the eggs and season with salt and pepper.
10. Pour the sauce over the noodles to serve.

NOODLES WITH CHICKEN

Yield: 4 Servings

Ingredients:

- 100 g/4 oz bean sprouts
- 100 g/4 oz cooked chicken, diced
- 2 cloves garlic, minced
- 2 spring onions (scallions), chopped
- 2½ ml/ ½ tsp salt
- 350 g/12 oz egg noodles
- 45 ml/3 tbsp groundnut (peanut) oil
- 5 ml/1 tsp sesame oil

Directions:

1. Bring a saucepan of water to the boil, add the noodles and boil until they are just soft.

2. Briefly boil the bean sprouts in boiling water for approximately three minutes then drain.
3. Heat the oil and fry the salt, garlic and spring onions until softened.
4. Put in the chicken and stir-fry until heated through.
5. Put in the bean sprouts and heat through.
6. Eliminate the excess liquid from the noodles well, rinse in cold water then hot water.
7. Toss in sesame oil and lay out on a warmed serving plate.
8. Top with the chicken mixture and serve.

NOODLES WITH CRAB MEAT

Yield: 4 Servings

Ingredients:

- 15 ml/1 tbsp cornflour (cornstarch)
- 15 ml/1 tbsp rice wine or dry sherry
- 2 slices ginger root, chopped into strips
- 3 spring onions (scallions), chopped
- 30 ml/2 tbsp water
- 30 ml/2 tbsp wine vinegar
- 350 g/12 oz crab meat, flaked
- 350 g/12 oz egg noodles
- 45 ml/3 tbsp groundnut (peanut) oil
- 5 ml/1 tsp salt

Directions:

1. Bring a pan of water to the boil, add the noodles and boil for approximately ten minutes until just soft.
2. In the meantime, heat 30 ml/2 tbsp of the oil and fry the spring onions and ginger until slightly browned.
3. Put in the crab meat and salt, stir-fry for approximately two minutes.
4. Put in the wine or sherry stir-fry for approximately one minute.
5. Combine the cornflour and water to a paste, mix it into the pan and simmer, stirring, until thickened.
6. Eliminate the excess liquid from the noodles and rinse in cold water then hot water.
7. Toss in the rest of the oil and lay out on a warmed serving plate.
8. Top with the crab meat mixture and serve sprinkled with wine vinegar.

NOODLES WITH EGG SAUCE

Yield: 4 Servings

Ingredients:

- 15 ml/1 tbsp groundnut (peanut) oil
- 225 g/8 oz egg noodles
- 3 eggs, beaten
- 3 spring onions (scallions), chopped into strips
- 45 ml/3 tbsp rice wine or dry sherry
- 45 ml/3 tbsp soy sauce
- 750 ml/3 cups chicken stock

Directions:

1. Bring a pan of water to the boil, add the noodles, bring back to the boil and simmer for approximately ten minutes until just soft.
2. Drain and arrange in a warmed serving bowl.
3. In the meantime, bring the stock to the boil with the soy sauce and wine or sherry.
4. In a separate pan, heat the oil and fry the spring onions until softened.
5. Put in the eggs then mix in the hot stock and continue to stir over a medium heat until the mixture comes to the boil.
6. Pour the sauce over the noodles and serve.

NOODLES WITH POACHED EGGS

Yield: 4 Servings

Ingredients:

- 1 clove garlic, minced
- 100 g/4 oz cooked ham, finely chopped
- 120 ml/4 fl oz/ ½ cup water
- 30 ml/2 tbsp groundnut (peanut) oil
- 350 g/12 oz rice noodles
- 4 eggs
- 45 ml/3 tbsp tomato purée (paste)

- 5 ml/1 tsp salt
- 5 ml/1 tsp sugar
- soy sauce

Directions:

1. Bring a pan of water to the boil, add the noodles and simmer for approximately eight minutes until just cooked.
2. Drain and rinse in cold water.
3. Lay out in nest shapes on a warmed serving plate.
4. In the meantime, poach the eggs and place one on each nest.
5. Heat the oil and stir-fry the garlic for 30 seconds.
6. Put in the ham and stir-fry for approximately one minute.
7. Add all the rest of the ingredients except the soy sauce and stir-fry until heated through.
8. Pour over the eggs, drizzle with soy sauce and serve instantly.

NOODLES WITH PORK AND VEGETABLES

Yield: 4 Servings

Ingredients:

- 10 ml/2 tsp cornflour (cornstarch)
- 100 g/4 oz bamboo shoots, shredded
- 100 g/4 oz Chinese cabbage, shredded
- 225 g/8 oz lean pork, shredded
- 350 g/12 oz rice noodles
- 45 ml/3 tbsp water
- 450 ml/¬æ pt/2 cups chicken stock
- 75 ml/5 tbsp groundnut (peanut) oil

Directions:

1. Parboil the noodles for about 6 minutes until cooked but still firm then drain.
2. Heat 45 ml/3 tbsp of oil and stir-fry the pork for approximately two minutes.
3. Put in the bamboo shoots and cabbage and stir-fry for approximately one minute.
4. Put in the stock, bring to the boil, cover and simmer for 4 minutes.
5. Combine the cornflour and water, mix it into the pan and simmer, stirring, until the sauce becomes thick.

6. Heat the rest of the oil and fry the noodles until slightly browned.
7. Move to a warmed serving plate, top with the pork mixture and serve.

SOFT-FRIED NOODLES

Yield: 4 Servings

Ingredients:

- 350 g/12 oz egg noodles
- 75 ml/5 tbsp groundnut (peanut) oil
- salt

Directions:

1. Bring a pan of water to the boil, add the noodles and boil until the noodles are just soft.
2. Drain and rinse in cold water, then hot water then eliminate the excess liquid again.
3. Toss in 15 ml/1 tbsp of oil then allow to cool and chill in the refrigerator.
4. Heat the rest of the oil almost to smoking point.
5. Put in the noodles and stir gently until coated with oil.
6. Reduce the heat and continue to stir for a few minutes until the noodles are golden-brown on the outside but soft inside.

STEAMED EGG NOODLES

Yield: 4 Servings

Ingredients:

- 10 ml/2 tsp salt
- 450 g/1 lb thin egg noodles

Directions:

1. Bring a saucepan of water to the boil, add the salt and toss in the noodles.
2. Stir thoroughly then drain.
3. Put the noodles in a colander, place in a steamer and steam over boiling water for approximately twenty minutes until just soft.

STEWED NOODLES

Yield: 4 Servings

Ingredients:

- 1 clove garlic, crushed
- 100 g/4 oz ham, chopped into strips
- 100 g/4 oz lean pork, chopped into strips
- 100 g/4 oz peeled prawns
- 2 slices ginger root, minced
- 3 spring onions (scallions), chopped into strips
- 30 ml/2 tbsp groundnut (peanut) oil
- 30 ml/2 tbsp soy sauce
- 450 g/1 lb egg noodles
- 450 ml/2 cups chicken stock
- 5 ml/1 tsp salt

Directions:

1. Bring a pan of water to the boil, add the salt and toss in the noodles.
2. Return to the boil and boil for approximately five minutes then eliminate the excess liquid and rinse in cold water.
3. In the meantime, heat the oil and fry the spring onions, garlic and ginger until slightly browned.
4. Put in the pork and stir-fry until slightly coloured.
5. Put in the ham and prawns and mix in the stock, soy sauce and noodles.
6. Bring to the boil, cover and simmer for 10 minutes.

TOSSED NOODLES

Yield: 8 Servings

Ingredients:

- 10 ml/2 tsp salt
- 30 ml/2 tbsp groundnut (peanut) oil
- 450 g/1 lb egg noodles

- stir-fried dish

Directions:

1. Bring a saucepan of water to the boil, add the salt and toss in the noodles.
2. Return to the boil and boil for approximately ten minutes until soft but still firm.
3. Drain well, rinse in cold water, drain, then rinse in hot water.
4. Toss with the oil then toss gently with any stir-fried mixture and heat through gently to blend the flavours together.

TRANSPARENT NOODLES WITH MINCED PORK

Yield: 4 Servings

Ingredients:

- 1 clove garlic, chopped
- 1 slice ginger root, chopped
- 2 spring onions (scallions), chopped
- 200 g/7 oz transparent noodles
- 225 g/8 oz minced (ground) pork
- 25 g/1 oz chilli bean paste
- 250 ml/8 fl oz/1 cup chicken stock
- 30 ml/2 tbsp rice wine or dry sherry
- 30 ml/2 tbsp soy sauce
- 5 ml/1 tsp chilli powder
- 75 ml/5 tbsp groundnut (peanut) oil
- oil for deep-frying
- salt

Directions:

1. Heat the oil until boiling and deep-fry the noodles until they expand.
2. Remove and drain.
3. Heat the 75 ml/ 5 tbsp of oil and fry the pork until browned.
4. Mix in the bean paste, spring onions, garlic, ginger and chilli powder and fry for approximately two minutes.
5. Mix in the stock, wine or sherry, soy sauce and noodles and simmer until the sauce becomes thick.
6. Season to taste with salt and serve.

WONTON SKINS

Yield: about 40

- 1 egg, beaten
- 45 ml/3 tbsp water
- 450 g/1 lb/2 cups plain (all-purpose) flour
- 5 ml/1 tsp salt

Directions:

1. Sift the flour and salt then make a well in the centre.
2. Blend in the egg, drizzle with water and knead the mixture to a smooth dough.
3. Put into a container, cover with a damp cloth and chill for one hour.
4. Roll out the dough on a floured surface until it is wafer thin and even.
5. Cut into 7.5 cm/3 in strips, dust slightly with flour and stack then chop into squares.
6. Cover with a damp cloth until ready to use.

VEGETABLES

Many Chinese recipes include a range of vegetables in the main dish, but you can prepare simple vegetables in a Chinese style to make a side dish to accompany a meat course, or as attractive and delicious meals in their own right.

ASPARAGUS STIR-FRY

Yield: 4 Servings

Ingredients:

- 1 spring onion (scallion), chopped
- 120 ml/4 fl oz/½ cup chicken stock
- 30 ml/2 tbsp soy sauce
- 45 ml/3 tbsp groundnut (peanut) oil
- 450 g/1 lb asparagus
- 5 ml/1 tsp cornflour (cornstarch)
- 5 ml/1 tsp sugar

Directions:

1. Heat the oil and fry the spring onion until slightly browned.
2. Put in the asparagus and stir-fry for approximately three minutes.
3. Add the rest of the ingredients and stir-fry for 4 minutes.

ASPARAGUS WITH CLAMS

Yield: 4 Servings

Ingredients:

- 1 red chilli pepper, chopped into strips
- 120 ml/4 fl oz/½ cup groundnut (peanut) oil
- 2 slices ginger root, shredded
- 2 spring onions (scallions), chopped into strips
- 2½ ml/½ tsp sesame oil
- 225 g/8 oz asparagus, chopped into pieces
- 225 g/8 oz clams, soaked and scrubbed

- 30 ml/2 tbsp thick soy sauce

Directions:

1. Heat the oil and stir-fry the chilli pepper, spring onions and ginger for 30 seconds.
2. Put in the asparagus and soy sauce, cover and simmer until the asparagus is almost soft.
3. Put in the sesame oil and clams, cover and cook until the clams open.
4. Discard any clams that have not opened and serve instantly.

ASPARAGUS WITH EGG SAUCE

Yield: 4 Servings

Ingredients:

- 1 egg, slightly beaten
- 15 ml/1 tbsp cornflour (cornstarch)
- 250 ml/8 fl oz/1 cup chicken stock
- 30 ml/2 tbsp rice wine or dry sherry
- 45 ml/3 tbsp groundnut (peanut) oil
- 450 g/1 lb asparagus
- salt

Directions:

1. Trim the asparagus and chop into 5 cm/2 in pieces.
2. Heat the oil and stir-fry the asparagus for about 4 minutes until soft but still crisp.
3. Drizzle with wine or sherry and salt.
4. In the meantime, bring the stock and cornflour to the boil, stirring, and season with salt.
5. Mix a little of the warm stock into the egg, then mix the egg into the pan and simmer, stirring, until the sauce becomes thick.
6. Put the asparagus on a warmed serving plate, pour over the sauce and serve instantly.

ASPARAGUS WITH MUSHROOMS AND SPRING ONIONS

Yield: 4 Servings

Ingredients:

- 1 bunch spring onions (scallions), trimmed
- 10 dried Chinese mushrooms
- 15 ml/1 tbsp water
- 225 g/8 oz asparagus
- 5 ml/1 tsp cornflour (cornstarch)
- 5 ml/1 tsp salt
- 600 ml/1 pt/2½ cups chicken stock

Directions:

1. Soak the mushrooms in warm water for half an hour then drain.
2. Discard the stalks.
3. Put the mushrooms in the centre of a strainer then arrange the spring onions and asparagus in a circle radiating out from the centre.
4. Bring the stock to the boil then lower the strainer into the stock, cover and simmer gently for approximately ten minutes until the vegetables are just soft.
5. Remove the vegetables and invert them on to a warmed serving plate to maintain the pattern.
6. Bring the stock to the boil.
7. Blend the water, cornflour and salt to a paste, mix it into the stock and simmer, stirring, until the sauce becomes thick slightly.
8. Spoon over the vegetables and serve instantly.

AUBERGINE WITH BASIL

Yield: 4 Servings

Ingredients:

- 1 large bunch basil
- 1 red chilli pepper, diagonally sliced
- 2 aubergines (eggplants)
- 2 cloves garlic, crushed
- 45 ml/3 tbsp soy sauce
- 60 ml/4 tbsp groundnut (peanut) oil
- 60 ml/4 tbsp water

Directions:

1. Heat the oil and fry the aubergine until slightly browned.
2. Put in the water, garlic, chilli pepper and soy sauce and stir-fry until the aubergine changes colour.
3. Put in the basil and stir-fry until the leaves are wilted.
4. Serve Immediately.

BAKED ONIONS

Yield: 4 Servings

Ingredients:

- 120 ml/4 fl oz/½ cup water
- 15 ml/1 tbsp chopped fresh parsley
- 15 ml/1 tbsp cornflour (cornstarch)
- 30 ml/2 tbsp groundnut (peanut) oil
- 8 large onions
- salt and freshly ground pepper

Directions:

1. Put the onions in a pan and just cover with boiling salted water.
2. Cover and simmer for approximately five minutes then drain.
3. Put the onions in an ovenproof dish, season with salt and pepper and brush with oil.
4. Pour in the water, cover and bake in a preheated oven at 190°C/375°F/gas mark 5 for one hour.
5. Blend the cornflour with a little water and mix it into the onion liquid.
6. Bake for another 5 minutes, stirring intermittently, until the sauce becomes thick.
7. Serve garnished with parsley.

BAMBOO SHOOTS IN OYSTER SAUCE

Yield: 4 Servings

Ingredients:

- 15 ml/1 tbsp groundnut (peanut) oil
- 15 ml/1 tbsp oyster sauce

- 2½ ml/½ tsp brown sugar
- 2½ ml/½ tsp sesame oil
- 250 ml/8 fl oz/1 cup chicken stock
- 350 g/12 oz bamboo shoots, chopped into strips
- 5 ml/1 tsp soy sauce

Directions:

1. Heat the oil and stir-fry the bamboo shoots for approximately one minute.
2. Put in the stock, oyster sauce, soy sauce and sugar and bring to the boil.
3. Simmer for approximately ten minutes until the bamboo shoots are soft and the liquid has reduced.
4. Serve sprinkled with sesame oil.

BAMBOO SHOOTS WITH CHICKEN

Yield: 4 Servings

Ingredients:

- 15 ml/1 tbsp chopped flat-leaved parsley
- 15 ml/1 tbsp cornflour (cornstarch)
- 2 egg whites
- 225 g/8 oz bamboo shoots, chopped into thick strips
- 50 g/2 oz chicken meat, minced (ground)
- 50 g/2 oz smoked ham, minced (ground)
- 50 g/2 oz water chestnuts, minced (ground)

Directions:

1. Combine the chicken, ham and water chestnuts.
2. Combine the egg whites and cornflour then stir them into the minced ingredients.
3. Stir the bamboo shoots into the mixture until well coated then arrange in an ovenproof dish.
4. Put on a rack in a steamer, cover and steam over gently simmering water for approximately fifteen minutes.
5. Serve garnished with parsley.

BAMBOO SHOOTS WITH DRIED MUSHROOMS

Yield: 4 Servings

Ingredients:

- 15 ml/1 tbsp cornflour (cornstarch)
- 15 ml/1 tbsp groundnut (peanut) oil
- 15 ml/1 tbsp rice wine or dry sherry
- 15 ml/1 tbsp soy sauce
- 225 g/8 oz bamboo shoots, sliced
- 250 ml/8 fl oz/1 cup chicken stock
- 6 dried Chinese mushrooms

Directions:

1. Soak the mushrooms in warm water for half an hour then drain.
2. Discard the stems and slice the caps.
3. Put the mushroom caps in a pan with half the stock, the wine or sherry and soy sauce.
4. Bring to the boil, cover and simmer for approximately ten minutes until thick.
5. Put in the oil and stir over a medium heat for approximately two minutes.
6. Put in the bamboo shoots and stir-fry for approximately three minutes.
7. Combine the cornflour into the rest of the stock and mix it into the pan.
8. Bring to the boil, stirring, then simmer for about 4 minutes until the sauce becomes thick and clears.

BAMBOO SHOOTS WITH MUSHROOMS

Yield: 4 Servings

Ingredients:

- 15 ml/1 tbsp cornflour (cornstarch)
- 30 ml/2 tbsp soy sauce
- 350 g/12 oz bamboo shoots, chopped into strips
- 45 ml/3 tbsp groundnut (peanut) oil
- 45 ml/3 tbsp water
- 5 ml/1 tsp brown sugar
- 8 dried Chinese mushrooms

Directions:

1. Soak the mushrooms in warm water for half an hour then drain.
2. Discard the stalks and slice the caps.
3. Heat the oil and stir-fry the mushrooms for approximately two minutes.
4. Put in the bamboo shoots and stir-fry for approximately three minutes.
5. Put in the soy sauce and sugar and stir thoroughly until heated through.
6. Transfer the vegetables to a warmed serving plate using a slotted spoon.
7. Combine the cornflour and water to a paste and mix it into the pan.
8. Simmer, stirring, until the sauce clears and becomes thick then pour it over the vegetables and serve instantly.

BAMBOO SHOOTS WITH SESAME OIL

Yield: 4 Servings

Ingredients:

- 100 g/4 oz bean sprouts
- 225 g/8 oz bamboo shoots
- 45 ml/3 tbsp groundnut (peanut) oil
- 5 ml/1 tsp salt
- 5 ml/1 tsp sesame oil

Directions:

1. Cook the bean sprouts in boiling water for approximately ten minutes until soft but still crisp.
2. Drain thoroughly.
3. In the meantime, heat the oil and stir-fry the bamboo shoots for approximately five minutes until soft but still crisp.
4. Drizzle with salt, mix well then arrange with the bean sprouts on a warmed serving plate.
5. Drizzle with sesame oil and serve.

BAMBOO SHOOTS WITH SPINACH

Yield: 4 Servings

Ingredients:

- 100 g/4 oz spinach
- 120 ml/4 fl oz/½ cup chicken stock
- 2½ ml/½ tsp sesame oil
- 45 ml/3 tbsp groundnut (peanut) oil
- 450 g/1 lb bamboo shoots
- 5 ml/1 tsp rice wine or dry sherry
- pinch of salt

Directions:

1. Heat the oil and fry the bamboo shoots for about 1 minute.
2. Put in the wine or sherry, salt and stock, bring to the boil and simmer for approximately three minutes.
3. Put in the spinach and simmer until the spinach has wilted and the liquid reduced slightly.
4. Move to a warmed serving bowl and serve sprinkled with sesame oil.

BEAN SPROUT STIR-FRY

Yield: 4 Servings

Ingredients:

- 1 clove garlic, crushed
- 15 ml/1 tbsp groundnut (peanut) oil
- 2½ ml/½ tsp salt
- 3 spring onions (scallions), chopped
- 450 g/1 lb bean sprouts
- 5 ml/1 tsp soy sauce
- 5 ml/1 tsp sugar
- 60 ml/4 tbsp chicken stock

Directions:

1. Heat the oil, salt and garlic until the garlic turns light golden.
2. Put in the bean sprouts and spring onions and stir-fry for approximately two minutes.
3. Add the rest of the ingredients and stir-fry for a few minutes until all the liquid has evaporated.

BEAN SPROUTS AND CELERY

Yield: 4 Servings

Ingredients:

- 15 ml/1 tbsp soy sauce
- 4 stalks celery, chopped into strips
- 45 ml/3 tbsp groundnut (peanut) oil
- 450 g/1 lb bean sprouts
- 5 ml/1 tsp salt
- 90 ml/6 tbsp chicken stock

Directions:

1. Briefly boil the bean sprouts in boiling water for approximately three minutes then drain.
2. Heat the oil and stir-fry the celery for approximately one minute.
3. Put in the bean sprouts and stir-fry for approximately one minute.
4. Add the rest of the ingredients, bring to the boil, cover and simmer for approximately three minutes and serve.

BEAN SPROUTS AND PEPPERS

Yield: 4 Servings

Ingredients:

- 1 green pepper, chopped into strips
- 1 red pepper, chopped into strips
- 1 slice ginger root, minced
- 2 dried chilli peppers
- 225 g/8 oz bean sprouts
- 45 ml/3 tbsp groundnut (peanut) oil
- 90 ml/6 tbsp chicken stock

Directions:

1. Briefly boil the bean sprouts in boiling water for approximately three minutes then drain.
2. Heat the oil and fry the whole chilli peppers for about 3 minutes then discard the peppers.
3. Put in the ginger and peppers to the pan and stir-fry for approximately three minutes.
4. Put in the bean sprouts and stir-fry for approximately two minutes.
5. Put in the stock, bring to the boil, cover and simmer for approximately three minutes and serve.

BEAN SPROUTS WITH PORK

Yield: 4 Servings

Ingredients:

- 100 g/4 oz lean pork, chopped into strips
- 15 ml/1 tbsp cornflour (cornstarch)
- 15 ml/1 tbsp rice wine
- 15 ml/1 tbsp soy sauce
- 2½ ml/½ tsp salt
- 30 ml/2 tbsp groundnut (peanut) oil
- 450 g/1 lb bean sprouts
- 5 ml/1 tsp sugar
- 75 ml/5 tbsp chicken stock

Directions:

1. Briefly boil the bean sprouts in boiling water for approximately three minutes then drain.
2. Toss the pork with the cornflour, wine or sherry, soy sauce, sugar and salt then allow to stand for half an hour.
3. Heat half the oil and stir-fry the bean sprouts for approximately one minute.
4. Take out of the pan.
5. Heat the rest of the oil and stir-fry the pork until slightly browned.
6. Put in the stock, cover and simmer for approximately three minutes.
7. Return the bean sprouts to the pan and stir until heated through.
8. Serve Immediately.

BRAISED AUBERGINE

Yield: 4 Servings

Ingredients:

- 1 aubergine (eggplant)
- 1 slice ginger root, chopped
- 15 ml/1 tbsp black bean sauce
- 15 ml/1 tbsp brown sugar
- 15 ml/1 tbsp groundnut (peanut) oil
- 15 ml/1 tbsp rice wine or dry sherry
- 15 ml/1 tbsp soy sauce
- 3 spring onions (scallions), chopped
- 90 ml/6 tbsp chicken stock
- oil for deep-frying

Directions:

1. Peel the aubergine and chop it into large cubes.
2. Heat the oil and deep-fry the aubergine until soft and slightly browned.
3. Remove and eliminate the excess liquid well.
4. Heat the oil and fry the spring onions and ginger until slightly browned.
5. Put in the aubergine and stir thoroughly.
6. Put in the stock, wine or sherry, soy sauce, black bean sauce and sugar.
7. Stir-fry for approximately two minutes.

BRAISED AUBERGINE WITH TOMATOES

Yield: 4 Servings

Ingredients:

- 1 aubergine (eggplant), peeled and diced
- 2 cloves garlic, crushed
- 2 spring onions (scallions), chopped
- 4 tomatoes, skinned and quartered
- 6 slices bacon
- salt and freshly ground pepper

Directions:

1. Chop the rind off the bacon and chop into chunks.
2. Fry until slightly browned.
3. Put in the garlic and spring onions and stir-fry for approximately two minutes.
4. Put in the aubergine and stir-fry for approximately five minutes until slightly soft.
5. Carefully mix in the tomatoes and season with salt and pepper.
6. Stir gently over a low heat until heated through.

BRAISED LETTUCE

Yield: 4 Servings

Ingredients:

- 1 clove garlic, crushed
- 1 head crisp lettuce
- 15 ml/1 tbsp groundnut (peanut) oil
- 2½ ml/½ tsp salt
- 5 ml/1 tsp soy sauce
- 60 ml/4 tbsp chicken stock

Directions:

1. Separate the lettuce into leaves.
2. Heat the oil and fry the salt and garlic until slightly browned.
3. Put in the lettuce and simmer for approximately one minute, stirring to coat the lettuce in oil.
4. Put in the stock and simmer for approximately two minutes.
5. Serve sprinkled with soy sauce.

BROAD BEAN SAUTÉ

Yield: 4 Servings

Ingredients:

- 10 ml/2 tsp brown sugar
- 2 spring onions (scallions), chopped

- 450 g/1 lb shelled broad beans
- 5 ml/1 tsp salt
- 60 ml/4 tbsp groundnut (peanut) oil
- 75 ml/5 tbsp chicken stock
- salt

Directions:

1. Put the beans in a pan, just cover with water, bring to the boil and simmer until soft.
2. Drain thoroughly.
3. Heat the oil then add the beans and stir until well coated with oil.
4. Put in the sugar and stock and season to taste with salt.
5. Stir-fry for approximately three minutes.
6. Mix in the spring onions and serve.

BROCCOLI IN BROWN SAUCE

Yield: 4 Servings

Ingredients:

- 1 clove garlic, crushed
- 100 g/4 oz bamboo shoots, sliced
- 15 ml/1 tbsp cornflour (cornstarch)
- 15 ml/1 tbsp oyster sauce
- 15 ml/1 tbsp soy sauce
- 225 g/8 oz broccoli florets
- 250 ml/8 fl oz/1 cup chicken stock
- 30 ml/2 tbsp groundnut (peanut) oil
- 30 ml/2 tbsp rice wine or dry sherry

Directions:

1. Parboil the broccoli in boiling water for 4 minutes then eliminate the excess liquid well.
2. Heat the oil and fry the garlic until a golden-brown colour is achieved.
3. Put in the broccoli and bamboo shoots and stir-fry for approximately one minute.
4. Put in the stock, soy sauce and oyster sauce, bring to the boil, cover and simmer for 4 minutes.
5. Combine the cornflour and wine or sherry, mix it into the pan and simmer, stirring, until the sauce has thickened.

BROCCOLI STIR-FRY

Yield: 4 Servings

Ingredients:

- 1 spring onion (scallion), chopped
- 120 ml/4 fl oz/½ cup chicken stock
- 30 ml/2 tbsp soy sauce
- 45 ml/3 tbsp groundnut (peanut) oil
- 450 g/1 lb broccoli florets
- 5 ml/1 tsp cornflour (cornstarch)
- 5 ml/1 tsp sugar

Directions:

1. Heat the oil and fry the spring onion until slightly browned.
2. Put in the broccoli and stir-fry for approximately three minutes.
3. Add the rest of the ingredients and stir-fry for approximately two minutes.

CABBAGE WITH BACON SHREDS

Yield: 4 Servings

Ingredients:

- 120 ml/4 fl oz/½ cup chicken or vegetable stock
- 2 cloves garlic
- 3 slices streaky bacon, rinded and chop into strips
- 30 ml/2 tbsp groundnut (peanut) oil
- 350 g/12 oz cabbage, finely shredded
- 5 ml/1 tsp grated ginger root
- 5 ml/1 tsp sugar
- salt

Directions:

1. Drizzle the cabbage with salt and allow to stand for approximately fifteen minutes.

2. Fry the bacon until crisp.
3. Heat the oil and fry the garlic until slightly browned then discard.
4. Put in the cabbage to the pan with the ginger and sugar and stir-fry for approximately two minutes.
5. Put in the stock and bacon and stir-fry for another 2 minutes.
6. Serve with fried rice.

CARROT AND PEPPER STIR-FRY

Yield: 4 Servings

Ingredients:

- 1 green pepper, chopped into strips
- 15 ml/1 tbsp cornflour (cornstarch)
- 15 ml/1 tbsp wine vinegar
- 2½ ml/½ tsp salt
- 250 ml/8 fl oz/1 cup chicken tock
- 30 ml/2 tbsp groundnut (peanut) oil
- 30 ml/2 tbsp sugar
- 4 carrots, sliced

Directions:

1. Heat the oil and salt then add the carrots and pepper and stir-fry for approximately three minutes.
2. Put in the sugar, wine vinegar and half the stock, bring to the boil, cover and simmer for approximately five minutes.
3. Stir the cornflour into the rest of the stock, add to the pan and simmer, stirring, until the sauce becomes thick and clears.

CARROTS WITH HONEY

Yield: 4 Servings

Ingredients:

- 1 kg/2 lb small spring carrots

- 10 ml/2 tsp honey
- 100 g/4 oz pine kernels
- 15 ml/1 tbsp chopped fresh coriander
- 15 ml/1 tbsp water
- 20 ml/4 tsp groundnut (peanut) oil
- 20 ml/4 tsp unsalted butter
- salt and freshly ground pepper

Directions:

1. Wash the carrots and chop the green down to 5 mm/¼ in.
2. Heat the oil and butter, add the water and honey and bring to the boil.
3. Put in the carrots and cook for about 4 minutes.
4. Put in the coriander and pine kernels and season with salt and pepper.

CAULIFLOWER WITH MUSHROOMS

Yield: 4 Servings

Ingredients:

- 1 small cauliflower
- 100 g/4 oz water chestnuts, sliced
- 15 ml/1 tbsp rice wine or dry sherry
- 30 ml/2 tbsp water
- 45 ml/3 tbsp groundnut (peanut) oil
- 45 ml/3 tbsp soy sauce
- 5 ml/1 tsp cornflour (cornstarch)
- 6 dried Chinese mushrooms

Directions:

1. Soak the mushrooms in warm water for half an hour then drain, reserving 120 ml/4 fl oz/½ cup of liquid.
2. Discard the stalks and slice the caps.
3. Chop the cauliflower into small florets.
4. Heat the oil and stir-fry the mushrooms until coated with oil.
5. Put in the water chestnuts and stir-fry for approximately one minute.
6. Combine the soy sauce and wine or sherry with the mushroom liquid and put it into the pan with the cauliflower.

7. Bring to the boil, cover and simmer for approximately five minutes.
8. Blend the cornflour and water to a paste, stir into the sauce and simmer, stirring, until the sauce becomes thick.

CELERY AND MUSHROOMS

Yield: 4 Servings

Ingredients:

- 225 g/8 oz mushrooms, sliced
- 30 ml/2 tbsp rice wine or dry sherry
- 45 ml/3 tbsp groundnut (peanut) oil
- 6 stalks celery, diagonally sliced
- salt and freshly ground pepper

Directions:

1. Heat the oil and stir-fry the celery for approximately three minutes.
2. Put in the mushrooms and stir-fry for approximately two minutes.
3. Put in the wine or sherry and season with salt and pepper.
4. Stir-fry for a few minutes until heated through.

CELERY STIR-FRY

Yield: 4 Servings

Ingredients:

- ½ head celery, chopped into chunks
- 15 ml/1 tbsp soy sauce
- 30 ml/2 tbsp groundnut (peanut) oil
- 5 ml/1 tsp salt
- 6 spring onions (scallions), chopped

Directions:

1. Heat the oil and fry the spring onions until slightly browned.
2. Put in the celery and stir until well coated with oil.

3. Put in the soy sauce and salt, stir thoroughly, cover and simmer for approximately three minutes.

CHINESE CABBAGE WITH MUSHROOMS

Yield: 4 Servings

Ingredients:

- 1 Chinese cabbage, diced
- 1 green pepper, diced
- 1 red pepper, diced
- 120 ml/4 fl oz/½ cup chicken stock
- 20 ml/2 tbsp chopped chives
- 20 ml/4 tsp honey
- 20 ml/4 tsp soy sauce
- 225 g/8 oz garlic sausage, diced
- 45 ml/3 tbsp groundnut (peanut) oil
- 45 ml/3 tbsp wine vinegar
- 5 ml/1 tsp cornflour (cornstarch)
- 6 dried Chinese mushrooms
- salt and freshly ground pepper

Directions:

1. Soak the mushrooms in warm water for half an hour then drain.
2. Discard the stalks and chop the caps.
3. Heat the oil and stir-fry the mushrooms, cabbage and peppers for approximately five minutes.
4. Put in the garlic sausage and fry briefly.
5. Combine the stock with the wine vinegar, soy sauce, honey and cornflour.
6. Stir into the pan and bring to the boil.
7. Season with salt and pepper and simmer, stirring, until the sauce becomes thick.
8. Serve sprinkled with chives.

CHINESE LEAVES IN MILK

Yield: 4 Servings

Ingredients:

- 15 ml/1 tbsp cornflour (cornstarch)
- 15 ml/1 tbsp rice wine or dry sherry
- 3 spring onions (scallions), chopped
- 350 g/12 oz Chinese leaves, shredded
- 45 ml/3 tbsp groundnut (peanut) oil
- 5 ml/1 tsp sesame oil
- 90 ml/6 tbsp chicken stock
- 90 ml/6 tbsp milk
- salt

Directions:

1. Steam the Chinese leaves for approximately five minutes until just soft.
2. Heat the oil and fry the spring onions until slightly browned.
3. Put in the wine or sherry and chicken stock and season with salt.
4. Mix in the cabbage, cover and simmer gently for approximately five minutes.
5. Combine the milk and cornflour, stir into pan and simmer, stirring, for approximately two minutes.
6. Serve sprinkled with sesame oil.

CHINESE LEAVES WITH MUSHROOMS

Yield: 4 Servings

Ingredients:

- 10 ml/2 tsp sesame oil
- 120 ml/4 fl oz/½ cup chicken stock
- 15 ml/1 tbsp cornflour (cornstarch)
- 15 ml/1 tbsp soy sauce
- 45 ml/3 tbsp groundnut (peanut) oil
- 450 g/1 lb Chinese leaves
- 5 ml/1 tsp salt
- 5 ml/1 tsp sugar
- 50 g/2 oz dried Chinese mushrooms

Directions:

1. Soak the mushrooms in warm water for half an hour then drain.
2. Discard the stems and slice the caps.
3. Chop the head of Chinese leaves into thick slices.
4. Heat half the oil, add the Chinese leaves and stir-fry for approximately two minutes.
5. Put in the chicken stock, soy sauce, salt and sugar and stir-fry for about 4 minutes.
6. Put in the mushrooms and stir-fry until the vegetables are soft.
7. Combine the cornflour with a little water, mix it into the sauce and simmer, stirring until the sauce clears and becomes thick.
8. Serve sprinkled with sesame oil.

CHINESE LEAVES WITH SCALLOPS

Yield: 4 Servings

Ingredients:

- 100 g/4 oz shelled scallops, sliced
- 4 hearts Chinese leaves
- 5 ml/1 tsp cornflour (cornstarch)
- 600 ml/1 pt/2½ cups chicken stock

Directions:

1. Put the Chinese leaves and stock in a pan, bring to the boil and simmer for approximately ten minutes until just soft.
2. Transfer the Chinese leaves to a warmed serving plate and keep them warm.
3. Pour out all but 250 ml/8 fl oz/1 cup of the stock.
4. Put in the scallops and simmer for a few minutes until the scallops are soft.
5. Blend the cornflour with a little water, mix it into the pan and simmer, stirring, until the sauce becomes thick slightly.
6. Pour over the Chinese leaves and serve.

CHINESE LEAVES WITH WATER CHESTNUTS

Yield: 4 Servings

Ingredients:

- 100 g/4 oz water chestnuts, sliced
- 15 ml/1 tbsp cornflour (cornstarch)
- 15 ml/1 tbsp soy sauce
- 15 ml/1 tbsp water
- 250 ml/8 fl oz/1 cup chicken stock
- 45 ml/3 tbsp groundnut (peanut) oil
- 450 g/1 lb Chinese leaves, shredded

Directions:

1. Briefly boil the Chinese leaves in boiling water for approximately two minutes then drain.
2. Heat the oil and stir-fry the water chestnuts for approximately two minutes.
3. Put in the Chinese leaves and stir-fry for approximately three minutes.
4. Put in the chicken stock and soy sauce, bring to the boil, cover and simmer for approximately five minutes.
5. Combine the cornflour and water to a paste, stir into the pan and simmer, stirring, until the sauce clears and becomes thick.

CHINESE MARROW

Yield: 4 Servings

Ingredients:

- 10 ml/2 tsp salt
- 30 ml/2 tbsp soy sauce
- 450 g/1 lb marrow, finely sliced
- 60 ml/4 tbsp groundnut (peanut) oil
- freshly ground pepper

Directions:

1. Heat the oil and stir-fry the marrow slices for approximately two minutes.
2. Put in the soy sauce, salt and a pinch of pepper and stir-fry for another 4 minutes.

COURGETTE STIR-FRY

Yield: 4 Servings

Ingredients:

- 1 spring onion (scallion), chopped
- 120 ml/4 fl oz/½ cup chicken stock
- 30 ml/2 tbsp soy sauce
- 45 ml/3 tbsp groundnut (peanut) oil
- 450 g/1 lb courgettes (zucchini), thickly sliced
- 5 ml/1 tsp cornflour (cornstarch)
- 5 ml/1 tsp sugar

Directions:

1. Heat the oil and fry the spring onion until slightly browned.
2. Put in the courgettes and stir-fry for approximately three minutes.
3. Add the rest of the ingredients and stir-fry for 4 minutes.

COURGETTES IN BLACK BEAN SAUCE

Yield: 4 Servings

Ingredients:

- 1 clove garlic, crushed
- 15 ml/1 tbsp chilli bean sauce
- 15 ml/1 tbsp sesame oil
- 30 ml/2 tbsp groundnut (peanut) oil
- 30 ml/2 tbsp rice wine or dry sherry
- 45 ml/3 tbsp water
- 450 g/1 lb courgettes (zucchini), thickly sliced
- 5 ml/1 tsp salt

Directions:

1. Heat the oil and fry the garlic, salt and chilli bean sauce for a few seconds.
2. Put in the courgettes and stir-fry for approximately three minutes until slightly browned.

3. Add the rest of the ingredients, including sesame oil to taste, and stir-fry for approximately one minute.

CREAMED CABBAGE

Yield: 4 Servings

Ingredients:

- 15 ml/1 tbsp cornflour (cornstarch)
- 250 ml/8 fl oz/1 cup chicken stock
- 45 ml/3 tbsp groundnut (peanut) oil
- 450 g/1 lb Chinese cabbage
- 50 g/2 oz smoked ham, diced
- salt

Directions:

1. Chop the cabbage into 5 cm/2 in strips.
2. Heat the oil and stir-fry the cabbage for approximately three minutes.
3. Put in the stock and season with salt.
4. Bring to the boil, cover and simmer for 4 minutes.
5. Combine the cornflour with a little water, mix it into the pan and simmer, stirring, until the sauce becomes thick.
6. Move to a warmed serving plate and serve sprinkled with ham.

CRISPY SEAWEED

Yield: 4 Servings

Ingredients:

- 10 ml/2 tsp caster sugar
- 5 ml/1 tsp salt
- 750 g/1½ lb spring greens, very finely shredded
- oil for deep-frying

Directions:

1. Rinse the greens then dry comprehensively..
2. Heat the oil and deep-fry the greens in batches over a medium heat until they float to the surface.
3. Take out of the oil and eliminate the excess liquid well on kitchen paper.
4. Drizzle with salt and sugar and toss together gently.
5. Serve cold.

CUCUMBER WITH PRAWNS

Yield: 4 Servings

Ingredients:

- 1 cucumber, peeled and thickly sliced
- 100 g/4 oz peeled prawns
- 30 ml/2 tbsp soy sauce
- 45 ml/3 tbsp groundnut (peanut) oil
- 45 ml/3 tbsp water
- 5 ml/1 tsp brown sugar
- 5 ml/1 tsp rice wine or dry sherry
- salt

Directions:

1. Heat the oil and stir-fry the prawns for 30 seconds.
2. Put in the cucumber and stir-fry for approximately one minute.
3. Put in the soy sauce, wine or sherry and sugar and season with salt.
4. Stir-fry for approximately three minutes, adding a little water if needed.
5. Serve as soon as possible.

CUCUMBERS WITH SESAME OIL

Yield: 4 Servings

Ingredients:

- 1 large cucumber
- 2½ ml/½ tsp sugar

- 30 ml/2 tbsp sesame oil
- salt

Directions:

1. Peel the cucumber and chop in half lengthways.
2. Scoop out the seeds then chop into thick slices.
3. Put the cucumber slices in a colander and drizzle generously with salt.
4. Allow to stand for one hour then press out as much moisture as possible.
5. Heat the oil and stir-fry the cucumbers for approximately two minutes until softened.
6. Mix in the sugar and serve instantly.

CURRIED ONIONS WITH PEAS

Yield: 4 Servings

Ingredients:

- 10 ml/2 tsp curry powder
- 10 ml/2 tsp salt
- 225 g/8 oz peas
- 45 ml/3 tbsp groundnut (peanut) oil
- 450 g/1 lb pearl onions
- freshly ground pepper

Directions:

1. Put the onions in a pan and just cover with boiling water.
2. Season with 5 ml/1 tsp of salt and boil for approximately five minutes.
3. Cover and boil for another 10 minutes.
4. Put in the peas and cook for another 5 minutes then drain.
5. Heat the oil and fry the curry powder, rest of the salt and rest of the pepper for 30 seconds.
6. Put in the drained vegetables and stir-fry until hot and glazed with the curry oil.

DEEP-FRIED BAMBOO SHOOTS

Yield: 4 Servings

Ingredients:

- 10 ml/2 tsp cornflour (cornstarch)
- 15 ml/1 tbsp brown sugar
- 15 ml/1 tbsp groundnut (peanut) oil
- 15 ml/1 tbsp soy sauce
- 225 g/8 oz bamboo shoots, chopped into strips
- 90 ml/6 tbsp water
- oil for deep-frying

Directions:

1. Heat the oil and deep-fry the bamboo shoots until golden.
2. Drain thoroughly.
3. Heat the groundnut (peanut) oil and stir-fry the bamboo shoots until coated with oil.
4. Combine the sugar, soy sauce, cornflour and water, stir into the pan and stir-fry until heated through.

DEEP-FRIED POTATOES AND CARROTS

Yield: 4 Servings

Ingredients:

- 120 ml/4 fl oz/½ cup chicken stock
- 15 ml/1 tbsp cornflour (cornstarch)
- 15 ml/1 tbsp rice wine or dry sherry
- 2 carrots, diced
- 30 ml/2 tbsp groundnut (peanut) oil
- 450 g/1 lb potatoes
- 5 ml/1 tsp salt
- 5 ml/1 tsp soy sauce
- 5 ml/1 tsp sugar
- oil for deep-frying

Directions:

1. Briefly boil the carrots in boiling water for approximately three minutes then drain.
2. Chop the potatoes into chips and dust with a little cornflour.
3. Heat the oil and deep-fry until crisp then drain.

4. Heat the oil and salt and stir-fry the carrots until coated with oil.
5. Put in the wine or sherry and stock, bring to the boil, cover and simmer for approximately two minutes.
6. Blend the rest of the cornflour to a paste with the sugar and soy sauce.
7. Stir into the pan and simmer, stirring, until the sauce becomes thick.
8. Put in the potatoes and reheat.
9. Serve Immediately.

FISH-STUFFED PEPPERS

Yield: 4 Servings

Ingredients:

- 120 ml/4 fl oz/½ cup chicken stock
- 15 ml/1 tbsp groundnut (peanut) oil
- 2 spring onions (scallions), minced
- 2½ ml/½ tsp salt
- 225 g/8 oz fish fillets, flaked
- 30 ml/2 tbsp cornflour (cornstarch)
- 30 ml/2 tbsp water
- 4 green peppers
- 60 ml/4 tbsp water
- salt and freshly ground pepper

Directions:

1. Combine the fish, spring onions, half the cornflour, the oil and water and season with salt and pepper.
2. Chop the tops off the peppers and scoop out the seeds.
3. Fill with the stuffing mixture and replace the tops as lids.
4. Stand the peppers upright in a pan and add the stock.
5. Bring to the boil and season with salt and pepper.
6. Cover and simmer for one hour.
7. Transfer the peppers to a heated serving dish.
8. Blend the rest of the cornflour and water to a paste, stir into the pan and bring to the boil.
9. Simmer, stirring, until the sauce clears and becomes thick.
10. Pour over the peppers and serve instantly.

FRIED BAMBOO SHOOTS

Yield: 4 Servings

Ingredients:

- 1 clove garlic, crushed
- 1 red chilli pepper, chopped into strips
- 1 spring onion, chopped into strips
- 15 ml/1 tbsp thick soy sauce
- 2½ ml/½ tsp sesame oil
- 225 g/8 oz bamboo shoots
- 90 ml/6 tbsp groundnut (peanut) oil

Directions:

1. Heat the oil and stir-fry the spring onion, garlic and chilli pepper for 30 seconds.
2. Put in the bamboo shoots and stir-fry until just soft and well coated in the spices.
3. Put in the soy sauce and sesame oil and stir-fry for another 3 minutes.
4. Serve Immediately.

FRIED SPRING VEGETABLES

Yield: 4 Servings

Ingredients:

- 1 green pepper, chopped
- 1 red pepper, chopped
- 100 g/4 oz bean sprouts
- 120 ml/4 fl oz/½ cup chicken stock
- 2 cloves garlic, crushed
- 225 g/8 oz mangetout (snow peas), chopped into 4
- 30 ml/2 tbsp hoisin sauce
- 30 ml/2 tbsp soy sauce
- 45 ml/3 tbsp groundnut (peanut) oil
- 5 ml/1 tsp cornflour (cornstarch)
- 5 ml/1 tsp tomato purée (paste)

- 6 spring onions (scallions), chopped
- 60 ml/4 tbsp chopped chives
- few drops of lemon juice
- salt

Directions:

1. Heat the oil and fry the garlic and salt until slightly browned.
2. Put in the soy and hoisin sauces and stir-fry for approximately one minute.
3. Put in the peppers, bean sprouts and mangetout and cook, stirring, until they are just soft but still crisp.
4. Stir the tomato purée and cornflour into the stock then put it into the pan.
5. Bring to the boil and simmer, stirring, until the sauce becomes thick.
6. Drizzle with lemon juice, stir, then serve sprinkled with chives.

GREEN BEANS WITH CHILLI

Yield: 4 Servings

Ingredients:

- 2 dried red chilli peppers
- 2 onions, chopped
- 45 ml/3 tbsp groundnut (peanut) oil
- 450 g/1 lb green beans

Directions:

1. Heat the oil with the chilli peppers and fry until they change colour then remove them from the pan.
2. Put in the onions and stir-fry until slightly browned.
3. In the meantime, briefly boil the beans in boiling water for approximately two minutes then eliminate the excess liquid well.
4. Put into the onions and stir-fry for approximately ten minutes until soft but still crisp and well coated in the spiced oil.

MANGETOUT WITH BAMBOO SHOOTS

Yield: 4 Servings

Ingredients:

- 100 g/4 oz minced (ground) pork
- 100 g/4 oz mushrooms
- 120 ml/4 fl oz/½ cup chicken stock
- 15 ml/1 tbsp cornflour (cornstarch)
- 15 ml/1 tbsp soy sauce
- 225 g/8 oz bamboo shoots, sliced
- 225 g/8 oz mangetout (snow peas)
- 30 ml/2 tbsp groundnut (peanut) oil
- 5 ml/1 tsp sugar

Directions:

1. Heat the oil and fry the pork until slightly browned.
2. Mix in the mushrooms and bamboo shoots and stir-fry for approximately two minutes.
3. Put in the mangetout and stir-fry for approximately two minutes.
4. Drizzle with soy sauce.
5. Combine the cornflour, sugar and stock to a paste, stir into the pan and simmer, stirring, until the sauce becomes thick.

MANGETOUT WITH MUSHROOMS AND GINGER

Yield: 4 Servings

Ingredients:

- 1 slice ginger root, minced
- 10 ml/2 tsp cornflour (cornstarch)
- 15 ml/1 tbsp oyster sauce
- 15 ml/1 tbsp water
- 225 g/8 oz mangetout (snow peas)
- 225 g/8 oz mushrooms, halved
- 3 spring onions (scallions), sliced
- 300 ml/½ pt/1¼ cup chicken stock
- 45 ml/3 tbsp groundnut (peanut) oil

Directions:

1. Heat the oil and fry the spring onions and ginger until slightly browned.
2. Put in the mushrooms and stir-fry for approximately three minutes.
3. Put in the stock, bring to the boil, cover and simmer for approximately three minutes.
4. Blend the cornflour to a paste with the water and oyster sauce, mix it into the pan and simmer, stirring, until the sauce becomes thick.
5. Mix in the mangetout and heat through and serve.

MARINATED STEAMED VEGETABLES

Yield: 4 Servings

Ingredients:

- 1 stick celery, finely sliced
- 100 g/4 oz oyster mushrooms
- 120 ml/4 fl oz/½ cup dry white wine
- 2 carrots, finely sliced
- 225 g/8 oz broccoli florets
- 225 g/8 oz cauliflower florets
- 30 ml/2 tbsp groundnut (peanut) oil
- 30 ml/2 tbsp plum sauce
- 30 ml/2 tbsp soy sauce
- 30 ml/2 tbsp wine vinegar
- 5 ml/1 tsp freshly ground pepper
- juice of 1 orange

Directions:

1. Heat the oil and stir-fry the vegetables for approximately five minutes then transfer them to a bowl.
2. Put in the wine, plum sauce, soy sauce, orange juice and pepper and toss comprehensively. to mix.
3. Cover and place in the refrigerator overnight.
4. Put the marinated vegetables in a steamer, cover and cook over gently boiling water to which the wine vinegar has been added for about 15 minutes.

MIXED VEGETABLES

Yield: 4 Servings

Ingredients:

- 15 ml/1 tbsp grated ginger root
- 175 ml/6 fl oz/¾ cup vegetable stock
- 2 onions
- 225 g/8 oz broccoli florets
- 225 g/8 oz mangetout (snow peas)
- 225 g/8 oz spinach, chopped
- 30 ml/2 tbsp groundnut (peanut) oil
- 4 stalks celery, diagonally sliced
- 6 spring onions (scallions), diagonally sliced

Directions:

1. Chop the onions into wedges and separate the layers.
2. Heat the oil and stir-fry the onions, ginger and broccoli for approximately one minute.
3. Add the rest of the vegetables and toss lightly.
4. Put in the stock and toss until the vegetables are completely coated.
5. Bring to the boil, cover and simmer for approximately three minutes until the vegetables are soft but still crisp.

MIXED VEGETABLES WITH GINGER

Yield: 4 Servings

Ingredients:

- 1 spring onion (scallion), chopped
- 100 g/4 oz bamboo shoots, sliced
- 100 g/4 oz cauliflower florets
- 100 g/4 oz Chinese cabbage, shredded
- 100 g/4 oz mushrooms, sliced
- 120 ml/4 fl oz/½ cup chicken stock
- 2 slices ginger root, minced
- 30 ml/2 tbsp soy sauce
- 45 ml/3 tbsp groundnut (peanut) oil
- salt and freshly ground pepper

Directions:

1. Briefly boil the cauliflower in boiling water for approximately three minutes then drain.
2. Heat the oil and stir-fry the ginger for approximately one minute.
3. Put in the vegetables and stir-fry for approximately three minutes until coated with oil.
4. Put in the soy sauce and stock and season with salt and pepper.
5. Stir-fry for another 2 minutes until the vegetables are just soft but still crisp.

MUSHROOMS AND BAMBOO SHOOTS

Yield: 4 Servings

Ingredients:

- 1 clove garlic, crushed
- 15 ml/1 tbsp cornflour (cornstarch)
- 15 ml/1 tbsp rice wine or dry sherry
- 15 ml/1 tbsp sugar
- 225 g/8 oz bamboo shoots, sliced
- 225 g/8 oz mushrooms, sliced
- 45 ml/3 tbsp groundnut (peanut) oil
- 45 ml/3 tbsp soy sauce
- 5 ml/1 tsp salt
- 90 ml/6 tbsp chicken stock

Directions:

1. Heat the oil and fry the salt and garlic until the garlic turns light golden.
2. Put in the bamboo shoots and mushrooms and stir-fry for approximately three minutes.
3. Put in the soy sauce, wine or sherry and sugar and stir-fry for approximately three minutes.
4. Combine the cornflour and stock and mix it into the pan.
5. Bring to the boil, stirring, then simmer for a few minutes until the sauce becomes thick and clears.

MUSHROOMS WITH ANCHOVY SAUCE

Yield: 4 Servings

Ingredients:

- 1 large tomato, diced
- 1 stick lemon grass, chopped
- 15 ml/1 tbsp groundnut (peanut) oil
- 2 shallots, sliced
- 20 ml/4 tsp anchovy paste
- 4 slices bread
- 450 g/1 lb button mushrooms
- 50 g/2 oz/½ cup butter
- 60 ml/4 tbsp chopped flat-leaved parsley
- 8 anchovy fillets
- salt and freshly ground pepper

Directions:

1. Heat the oil and fry the mushrooms, shallots and lemon grass until slightly browned.
2. Put in the tomato and half the parsley and stir thoroughly.
3. Mix in the anchovy paste and the butter, chopped into flakes.
4. Season with salt and pepper.
5. Heat the bread then drizzle with the rest of the parsley.
6. Put the anchovy fillets on top and serve with the mushrooms.

MUSHROOMS WITH BAMBOO SHOOTS AND MANGETOUT

Yield: 4 Servings

Ingredients:

- 100 g/4 oz bamboo shoots, sliced
- 100 g/4 oz mangetout (snow peas)
- 30 ml/2 tbsp groundnut (peanut) oil
- 30 ml/2 tbsp soy sauce
- 5 ml/1 tsp sugar
- 60 ml/4 tbsp stock
- 8 dried Chinese mushrooms

Directions:

1. Soak the mushrooms in warm water for half an hour then drain.
2. Discard the stalks and slice the caps.
3. Heat the oil and fry the mangetout for about 30 seconds then remove from the pan.
4. Put in the mushrooms and bamboo shoots and stir-fry until well coated with oil.
5. Put in the stock, soy sauce and sugar, bring to the boil, cover and simmer gently for approximately three minutes.
6. Return the mangetout to the pan and simmer, uncovered, until heated through.
7. Serve Immediately.

MUSHROOMS WITH MANGETOUT

Yield: 4 Servings

Ingredients:

- 10 ml/2 tsp sesame oil
- 15 ml/1 tbsp soy sauce
- 225 g/8 oz button mushrooms
- 30 ml/2 tbsp groundnut (peanut) oil
- 450 g/1 lb mangetout (snow peas)
- 5 ml/1 tsp brown sugar

Directions:

1. Heat the oil and fry the mushrooms for approximately five minutes.
2. Put in the mangetout and stir-fry for approximately one minute.
3. Add the rest of the ingredients and stir-fry for 4 minutes.

ONION CUSTARD

Yield: 4 Servings

Ingredients:

- 10 ml/2 tsp salt
- 120 ml/4 fl oz/½ cup water
- 2 eggs, slightly beaten
- 4 rashers bacon

- 450 g/1 lb onions, sliced
- 50 g/2 oz/½ cup cornflour (cornstarch)
- pinch of grated nutmeg

Directions:

1. Fry the bacon until crisp then eliminate the excess liquid and chop.
2. Put in the onions to the pan and fry until softened.
3. Beat the cornflour with the eggs and water and season with nutmeg and salt.
4. Combine the bacon with the onions and place in a greased ovenproof dish.
5. Top with the egg mixture and stand the dish in a roasting tin half filled with water.
6. Bake in a preheated oven at 180°C/ 350°F/gas mark 4 for 45 minutes until the custard is set.

PAK CHOI

Yield: 4 Servings

Ingredients:

- 120 ml/4 fl oz/½ cup chicken stock
- 15 ml/1 tbsp soy sauce
- 2 spring onions (scallions), chopped
- 2½ ml/½ tsp sugar
- 45 ml/3 tbsp groundnut (peanut) oil
- 450 g/1 lb pak choi, shredded
- 5 ml/1 tsp cornflour (cornstarch)

Directions:

1. Heat the oil and fry the spring onions until slightly browned.
2. Put in the pak choi and stir-fry for approximately three minutes.
3. Add the rest of the ingredients and stir-fry for approximately two minutes.

PEARL ONIONS IN ORANGE-GINGER SAUCE

Yield: 4 Servings

Ingredients:

- 1 slice ginger root, chopped
- 10 ml/2 tsp cider vinegar
- 10 ml/2 tsp sugar
- 15 ml/1 tbsp red peppercorns
- 15 ml/1 tbsp walnut oil
- 2 red chilli peppers
- 3 oranges
- 450 g/1 lb pearl onions
- 5 ml/1 tsp grated lemon rind
- a few coriander leaves
- salt

Directions:

1. Using a zester, chop the orange peel into narrow slivers.
2. Halve the oranges and squeeze the juice.
3. Halve the chilli peppers and remove the seeds.
4. Heat the oil and stir-fry the onions, ginger and chilli peppers for approximately one minute.
5. Put in the sugar then simmer until the onions are translucent.
6. Mix in the orange juice, cider vinegar, peppercorns and orange rind and season with salt.
7. Mix in the lemon rind and most of the coriander leaves.
8. Lay out on a warmed serving plate and garnish with the rest of the coriander leaves.

PEAS WITH MUSHROOMS

Yield: 4 Servings

Ingredients:

- 1 spring onion (scallion), chopped
- 120 ml/4 fl oz/½ cup chicken stock
- 225 g/8 oz frozen peas
- 225 g/8 oz mushrooms, halved
- 30 ml/2 tbsp soy sauce
- 45 ml/3 tbsp groundnut (peanut) oil

- 5 ml/1 tsp cornflour (cornstarch)
- 5 ml/1 tsp sugar

Directions:

1. Heat the oil and fry the spring onion until slightly browned.
2. Put in the mushrooms and stir-fry for approximately three minutes.
3. Put in the peas and stir-fry for 4 minutes.
4. Add the rest of the ingredients and stir-fry for approximately two minutes.

PEPPER AND BEAN STIR-FRY

Yield: 4 Servings

Ingredients:

- 2 cloves garlic, crushed
- 2 red peppers, chopped into strips
- 225 g/8 oz French beans
- 30 ml/2 tbsp groundnut (peanut) oil
- 30 ml/2 tbsp water
- 5 ml/1 tsp salt
- 5 ml/1 tsp sugar

Directions:

1. Heat the oil and stir-fry the garlic, salt, peppers and beans for approximately three minutes.
2. Put in the sugar and water and stir-fry for approximately five minutes until the vegetables are soft but still crisp.

PORK-STUFFED PEPPERS

Yield: 4 Servings

Ingredients:

- 120 ml/4 fl oz/½ cup chicken stock
- 15 ml/1 tbsp cornflour (cornstarch)

- 2 spring onions (scallions), chopped
- 2½ ml/½ tsp salt
- 225 g/8 oz minced (ground) pork
- 30 ml/2 tbsp groundnut (peanut) oil
- 30 ml/2 tbsp soy sauce
- 4 green peppers
- 4 water chestnuts, chopped
- 60 ml/4 tbsp water
- salt and freshly ground pepper

Directions:

1. Heat the oil and fry the pork, spring onions and water chestnuts until slightly browned.
2. Turn off the heat, stir half the soy sauce and season with salt and pepper.
3. Chop the tops off the peppers and scoop out the seeds.
4. Fill with the stuffing mixture and replace the tops as lids.
5. Stand the peppers upright in a pan and add the stock.
6. Bring to the boil and season with salt and pepper.
7. Cover and simmer for one hour.
8. Transfer the peppers to a heated serving dish.
9. Blend the cornflour, rest of the soy sauce and water to a paste, stir into the pan and bring to the boil.
10. Simmer, stirring, until the sauce clears and becomes thick.
11. Pour over the peppers and serve instantly.

POTATO SAUTÉ

Yield: 4 Servings

Ingredients:

- 1 clove garlic, crushed
- 15 ml/1 tbsp soy sauce
- 3 spring onions (scallions), chopped
- 30 ml/2 tbsp groundnut (peanut) oil
- 350 g/12 oz potatoes, peeled and chop into matchsticks
- 5 ml/1 tsp wine vinegar
- salt and freshly ground pepper

Directions:

1. Briefly boil the potatoes in boiling water for 20 seconds then drain.
2. Heat the oil and fry the garlic and spring onions until slightly browned.
3. Put in the potatoes and stir-fry for approximately two minutes.
4. Put in the soy sauce and wine vinegar and season to taste with salt and pepper.
5. Fry for a few minutes until the potatoes are cooked and slightly browned.

PUMPKIN WITH RICE NOODLES

Yield: 4 Servings

Ingredients:

- 100 g/4 oz peeled prawns
- 15 ml/1 tbsp groundnut (peanut) oil
- 2 spring onions (scallions), sliced
- 2½ ml/½ tsp sugar
- 225 g/8 oz pumpkin, cubed
- 250 ml/8 fl oz/1 cup chicken stock
- 350 g/12 oz rice noodles
- salt and freshly ground pepper

Directions:

1. Briefly boil the noodles in boiling water for approximately two minutes then drain.
2. Heat the oil and stir-fry the spring onions for 30 seconds.
3. Put in the pumpkin and stir-fry for approximately one minute.
4. Put in the stock and noodles, bring to the boil and simmer, uncovered, for approximately five minutes until the pumpkin is almost cooked.
5. Put in the sugar and season with salt and pepper.
6. Simmer for approximately ten minutes until the noodles are just soft and the liquid has reduced slightly.
7. Put in the prawns and heat through and serve.

SAUTÉED BEAN SPROUTS

Yield: 4 Servings

Ingredients:

- 15 ml/1 tbsp groundnut (peanut) oil
- 15 ml/1 tbsp soy sauce
- 450 g/1 lb bean sprouts
- salt and freshly ground pepper

Directions:

1. Heat the oil and stir-fry the bean sprouts for about 3 minutes.
2. Put in the soy sauce, salt and pepper and thoroughly stir together.
3. Cover and simmer for approximately five minutes then remove the lid and simmer for another 1 minute.

SHALLOTS IN MALT BEER

Yield: 4 Servings

Ingredients:

- 1 lamb's lettuce
- 10 ml/2 tsp brown sugar
- 15 ml/1 tbsp walnut oil
- 2½ ml/½ tsp paprika
- 250 ml/8 fl oz/1 cup malt beer
- 45 ml/3 tbsp balsamic vinegar
- 450 g/1 lb shallots
- 5 ml/1 tsp red peppercorns
- salt and freshly ground pepper

Directions:

1. Heat the oil and fry the shallots until a golden-brown colour is achieved.
2. Put in the sugar and stir-fry until translucent.
3. Put in the peppercorns, beer and balsamic vinegar and simmer for approximately one minute.
4. Season with salt, pepper and paprika.
5. Put the lettuce leaves around the edge of a warmed serving plate and spoon the shallots into the centre.

SIMPLE STIR-FRIED VEGETABLES

Yield: 4 Servings

Ingredients:

- 120 ml/4 fl oz/½ cup chicken or vegetable stock
- 15 ml/1 tbsp soy sauce
- 2 slices ginger root, minced
- 45 ml/3 tbsp groundnut (peanut) oil
- 450 g/1 lb mixed vegetables such as sliced bamboo shoots, briefly boiled bean sprouts, broccoli florets, sliced carrots, cauliflower florets, diced peppers
- 5 ml/1 tsp salt
- 5 ml/1 tsp sugar

Directions:

1. Heat the oil and stir-fry the salt and ginger until slightly browned.
2. Put in the vegetables and stir-fry for approximately three minutes until well coated with oil.
3. Put in the stock, soy sauce and sugar and stir-fry for about 2 minutes until heated through.

SPICED GREEN BEANS

Yield: 4 Servings

Ingredients:

- 15 ml/1 tbsp salt
- 450 g/1 lb green beans
- 5 ml/1 tsp freshly ground red pepper
- 5 ml/1 tsp ground anise

Directions:

1. Put all the ingredients in a large pan and just cover with water.
2. Bring to the boil and simmer for approximately eight minutes until the beans are just soft.
3. Drain thoroughly and serve.

SPICED POTATOES

Yield: 4 Servings

Ingredients:

- 1 clove garlic, crushed
- 2 dried chilli peppers, seeded and chopped
- 2 spring onions (scallions), chopped
- 2½ ml/½ tsp salt
- 30 ml/2 tbsp groundnut (peanut) oil
- 350 g/12 oz potatoes, peeled and diced

Directions:

1. Heat the oil and fry the potatoes until slightly golden.
2. Remove them from the pan.
3. Reheat the oil and fry the garlic, salt, spring onions and chilli peppers until slightly browned.
4. Return the potatoes to the pan and stir-fry until the potatoes are cooked.

SPICY CABBAGE STIR-FRY

Yield: 4 Servings

Ingredients:

- 1 slice ginger root, minced
- 15 ml/1 tbsp chilli bean sauce
- 15 ml/1 tbsp oyster sauce
- 15 ml/1 tbsp soy sauce
- 2 cloves garlic, crushed
- 30 ml/2 tbsp groundnut (peanut) oil
- 450 g/1 lb cabbage, shredded
- 5 ml/1 tsp sesame oil

Directions:

1. Briefly boil the cabbage in boiling salted water for approximately two minutes.
2. Drain thoroughly.
3. Heat the oil and stir-fry the garlic and ginger for a few seconds until slightly browned.
4. Put in the cabbage and stir-fry for approximately two minutes.
5. Add the rest of the ingredients and stir-fry for another 2 minutes.

SPICY MUSHROOMS

Yield: 4 Servings

Ingredients:

- 1 clove garlic, finely chopped
- 1 slice ginger root, minced
- 15 ml/1 tbsp groundnut (peanut) oil
- 15 ml/1 tbsp hoisin sauce
- 15 ml/1 tbsp rice wine or dry sherry
- 2 spring onions (scallions), chopped
- 225 g/8 oz button mushrooms
- 45 ml/3 tbsp chicken stock
- 5 ml/1 tsp sesame oil

Directions:

1. Heat the oil and stir-fry the garlic, ginger and spring onions for approximately two minutes.
2. Put in the mushrooms and stir-fry for approximately two minutes.
3. Add the rest of the ingredients and stir-fry for approximately five minutes.

SPINACH WITH GARLIC

Yield: 4 Servings

Ingredients:

- 15 ml/1 tbsp soy sauce
- 2½ ml/½ tsp salt
- 3 cloves garlic, crushed

- 30 ml/2 tbsp groundnut (peanut) oil
- 450 g/1 lb spinach leaves

Directions:

1. Heat the oil, add the spinach and salt and stir-fry for approximately three minutes until the spinach begins to wilt.
2. Put in the garlic and soy sauce and stir-fry for approximately three minutes and serve.

SPINACH WITH GINGER

Yield: 4 Servings

Ingredients:

- 1 clove garlic, crushed
- 1 slice ginger root, minced
- 10 ml/2 tsp sesame oil
- 30 ml/2 tbsp groundnut (peanut) oil
- 450 g/1 lb spinach
- 5 ml/1 tsp salt
- 5 ml/1 tsp sugar

Directions:

1. Heat the oil and stir-fry the ginger, garlic and salt until slightly browned.
2. Put in the spinach and stir-fry for approximately three minutes until wilted.
3. Put in the sugar and sesame oil and stir-fry for approximately three minutes.
4. Serve hot or cold.

SPINACH WITH MUSHROOMS

Yield: 4 Servings

Ingredients:

- 15 ml/1 tbsp cornflour (cornstarch)
- 15 ml/1 tbsp rice wine or dry sherry
- 15 ml/1 tbsp water

- 450 g/1 lb spinach
- 5 ml/1 tsp sugar
- 60 ml/4 tbsp soy sauce
- 75 ml/5 tbsp groundnut (peanut) oil
- 8 dried Chinese mushrooms
- salt

Directions:

1. Soak the mushrooms in warm water for half an hour then drain, reserving 120 ml/4 fl oz/½ cup of soaking liquid.
2. Discard the stalks and chop the caps in half, if large.
3. Heat half the oil and fry the mushrooms for approximately two minutes.
4. Mix in the soy sauce, wine or sherry, sugar and a pinch of salt and mix well.
5. Put in the mushroom liquid, bring to the boil, cover and simmer for 10 minutes.
6. Blend the cornflour and water to a paste, mix it into the sauce and simmer, stirring, until the sauce becomes thick.
7. Leave over a very low heat to keep warm.
8. In the meantime, heat the rest of the oil in a separate pan, add the spinach and stir-fry for about 2 minutes until softened.
9. Move to a heated serving dish, pour over the mushrooms and serve.

SPINACH WITH PEANUTS

Yield: 4 Servings

Ingredients:

- 100 g/4 oz smoked ham, chopped
- 15 ml/1 tbsp groundnut (peanut) oil
- 2½ ml/½ tsp salt
- 30 ml/2 tbsp peanuts
- 450 g/1 lb spinach, shredded

Directions:

1. Heat the peanuts using a dry pan then chop coarsely.
2. Briefly boil the spinach in boiling water for approximately two minutes then eliminate the excess liquid well and chop.
3. Mix in the peanuts, salt, ham and oil and serve instantly.

STEAMED AUBERGINE

Yield: 4 Servings

Ingredients:

- 1 aubergine (eggplant)
- 30 ml/2 tbsp soy sauce
- 5 ml/1 tsp groundnut (peanut) oil

Directions:

1. Score the aubergine skin a few times and place it in an ovenproof dish.
2. Put on a rack in a steamer and steam over gently simmering water for about 25 minutes until soft.
3. Allow it to cool slightly then peel off the skin and tear the flesh into shreds.
4. Drizzle with soy sauce and oil and stir thoroughly.
5. Serve hot or cold.

STEAMED CHINESE LEAVES

Yield: 4 Servings

Ingredients:

- 15 ml/1 tbsp cornflour (cornstarch)
- 300 ml/½ pt/1¼ cups chicken stock
- 450 g/1 lb Chinese leaves, separated
- 5 ml/1 tsp salt

Directions:

1. Put the leaves in an ovenproof bowl, place it on a rack in a steamer and steam over gently boiling water for approximately fifteen minutes.
2. In the meantime, blend the cornflour, salt and stock over a gentle heat, bring to the boil and simmer, stirring, until the mixture becomes thick.
3. Put the Chinese leaves on a warmed serving plate, pour over the sauce and serve.

STEAMED MUSHROOMS

Yield: 4 Servings

Ingredients:

- 18 dried Chinese mushrooms
- 30 ml/2 tbsp groundnut (peanut) oil
- 450 ml/¾ pt/2 cups stock
- 5 ml/1 tsp sugar

Directions:

1. Soak the mushrooms in warm water for half an hour then drain, reserving 250 ml/8 fl oz/1 cup of soaking liquid.
2. Discard the stalks and arrange the caps in a heatproof bowl.
3. Add the rest of the ingredients, stand the bowl on a rack in a steamer, cover and steam over boiling water for about 1 hour.

STEAMED STUFFED MUSHROOMS

Yield: 4 Servings

Ingredients:

- 120 ml/4 fl oz/½ cup
- 15 ml/1 tbsp cornflour (cornstarch)
- 225 g/8 oz minced (ground) pork
- 225 g/8 oz peeled prawns, finely chopped
- 30 ml/2 tbsp soy sauce
- 4 water chestnuts, finely chopped
- 450 g/1 lb large mushrooms
- 5 ml/1 tsp salt
- 5 ml/1 tsp sugar

Directions:

1. Remove the stalks from the mushrooms.
2. Chop the stalks and mix them with the rest of the ingredients.

3. Put the mushroom caps on an ovenproof plate and top with the stuffing mixture, pressing it down into a dome shape.
4. Spoon a little stock over each one, reserving a little stock.
5. Put the plate on a rack in a steamer, cover and steam over gently simmering water for about 45 minutes until the mushrooms are cooked, basting with a little more stock during cooking if needed.

STIR-FRIED AUBERGINE

Yield: 4 Servings

Ingredients:

- 1 aubergine (eggplant), peeled and diced
- 30 ml/2 tbsp cornflour (cornstarch)
- 30 ml/2 tbsp rice wine or dry sherry
- 30 ml/2 tbsp soy sauce
- 4 dried Chinese mushrooms
- 45 ml/3 tbsp groundnut (peanut) oil
- 5 ml/1 tsp salt
- 5 ml/1 tsp sugar
- 50 g/2 oz bamboo shoots, chopped
- 50 g/2 oz cooked chicken, diced
- 50 g/2 oz smoked ham, diced
- 50 g/2 oz/½ cup chopped mixed nuts
- oil for deep-frying

Directions:

1. Soak the mushrooms in warm water for half an hour then drain.
2. Discard the stalks and slice the caps.
3. Toss the aubergine slightly in cornflour.
4. Heat the oil and deep-fry the aubergine until golden.
5. Take out of the pan and eliminate the excess liquid well.
6. Heat the oil and stir-fry the chicken, ham, bamboo shoots and nuts.
7. Add the rest of the ingredients and stir-fry for approximately three minutes.
8. Return the aubergine to the pan and stir-fry until heated through.

STIR-FRIED CAULIFLOWER

Yield: 4 Servings

Ingredients:

- 1 spring onion (scallion), chopped
- 120 ml/4 fl oz/½ cup chicken stock
- 45 ml/3 tbsp groundnut (peanut) oil
- 450 g/1 lb cauliflower florets
- 5 ml/1 tsp cornflour (cornstarch)

Directions:

1. Briefly boil the cauliflower in boiling water for approximately two minutes then eliminate the excess liquid well.
2. Heat the oil and fry the spring onion until slightly browned.
3. Put in the cauliflower and stir-fry for 4 minutes.
4. Add the rest of the ingredients and stir-fry for approximately two minutes.

STIR-FRIED CHINESE LEAVES

Yield: 4 Servings

Ingredients:

- 1 clove garlic, chopped
- 15 ml/1 tbsp groundnut (peanut) oil
- 2½ ml/½ tsp salt
- 3 spring onions (scallions), chopped
- 350 g/12 oz Chinese leaves, shredded
- 450 ml/¾ pt boiling water

Directions:

1. Heat the oil and fry the garlic and onion until slightly browned.
2. Put in the Chinese leaves and salt and stir thoroughly.
3. Put in the boiling water, return to the boil, cover arid simmer for approximately five minutes until the Chinese leaves are soft but still crisp.
4. Drain thoroughly.

STIR-FRIED DANDELION LEAVES

Yield: 4 Servings

Ingredients:

- 15 ml/1 tbsp sugar
- 30 ml/2 tbsp groundnut (peanut) oil
- 450 g/1 lb dandelion leaves
- 5 ml/1 tsp salt

Directions:

1. Heat the oil, add the dandelion leaves, salt and sugar and stir-fry over a moderate heat for approximately five minutes.
2. Serve Immediately.

STIR-FRIED GREEN BEANS

Yield: 4 Servings

Ingredients:

- 120 ml/4 fl oz/½ cup chicken stock
- 15 ml/1 tbsp soy sauce
- 45 ml/3 tbsp groundnut (peanut) oil
- 450 g/1 lb string beans, chopped into pieces
- 5 ml/1 tsp salt

Directions:

1. Heat the oil and salt then add the beans and stir-fry for approximately two minutes.
2. Put in the stock and soy sauce, bring to the boil, cover and simmer for approximately five minutes until the beans are soft but still slightly crisp.

STIR-FRIED LETTUCE WITH GINGER

Yield: 4 Servings

Ingredients:

- 1 cm/½ in slice ginger root, finely chopped
- 1 head lettuce, shredded
- 2 cloves garlic, crushed
- 45 ml/3 tbsp groundnut (peanut) oil

Directions:

1. Heat the oil and fry the garlic and ginger until light golden.
2. Put in the lettuce and stir-fry for about 2 minutes until glossy and slightly wilted.
3. Serve Immediately.

STIR-FRIED PEPPERS

Yield: 4 Servings

Ingredients:

- 15 ml/1 tbsp chicken stock or water
- 2 green peppers, cubed
- 2 red peppers, cubed
- 30 ml/2 tbsp groundnut (peanut) oil
- 5 ml/1 tsp brown sugar
- 5 ml/1 tsp salt

Directions:

1. Heat the oil until very hot, add the peppers and stir-fry until the skins wrinkle slightly.
2. Put in the stock or water, salt and sugar and stir-fry for approximately two minutes.

STRAW MUSHROOMS IN OYSTER SAUCE

Yield: 4 Servings

Ingredients:

- 120 ml/4 fl oz/½ cup chicken stock
- 15 ml/1 tbsp groundnut (peanut) oil
- 15 ml/1 tbsp water
- 2½ ml/½ tsp sugar
- 225 g/8 oz straw mushrooms
- 5 ml/1 tsp cornflour (cornstarch)
- 5 ml/1 tsp oyster sauce

Directions:

1. Heat the oil and fry the mushrooms gently until well coated.
2. Put in the stock, sugar and oyster sauce, bring to the boil then simmer gently until the mushrooms are soft.
3. Combine the cornflour and water to a paste, stir into the pan and simmer, stirring, until the sauce clears and becomes thick.

STUFFED AUBERGINE

Yield: 4 Servings

Ingredients:

- 1 aubergine (eggplant), halved lengthways
- 1 slice ginger root, minced
- 15 ml/1 tbsp rice wine or dry sherry
- 2 spring onions (scallions), minced
- 225 g/8 oz minced (ground) pork
- 30 ml/2 tbsp soy sauce
- 4 dried Chinese mushrooms
- 5 ml/1 tsp sugar

Directions:

1. Soak the mushrooms in warm water for half an hour then drain.
2. Discard the stalks and chop the caps.
3. Mix with the pork, spring onions, ginger, soy sauce, wine or sherry and sugar.
4. Scoop out the seeds of the aubergine to make a hollow shape.
5. Stuff with the pork mixture and arrange in an ovenproof dish.
6. Put on a rack in a steamer and steam over gently simmering water for half an hour until soft.

STUFFED COURGETTE BITES

Yield: 4 Servings

Ingredients:

- 2 eggs, beaten
- 225 g/8 oz crab meat, flaked
- 225 g/8 oz minced (ground) pork
- 30 ml/2 tbsp oyster sauce
- 30 ml/2 tbsp soy sauce
- 4 large courgettes (zucchini)
- 50 g/2 oz/½ cup breadcrumbs
- 75 ml/5 tbsp cornflour (cornstarch)
- oil for deep-frying
- pinch of ground ginger
- salt and freshly ground pepper

Directions:

1. Chop the courgettes in half lengthways and remove the seeds and cores with a spoon.
2. Combine the pork, crab meat, eggs, sauces, ginger, salt and pepper.
3. Bind with the cornflour and breadcrumbs.
4. Cover and chill for half an hour.
5. Fill the courgettes with the mixture then chop them into chunks.
6. Heat the oil and deep-fry the courgettes until golden.
7. Drain using kitchen paper and serve.

STUFFED CUCUMBERS

Yield: 4 Servings

Ingredients:

- 1 egg, beaten
- 15 ml/1 tbsp rice wine or dry sherry
- 150 ml/¼ pt/generous ½ cup chicken stock
- 2 large cucumbers

- 225 g/8 oz minced (ground) pork
- 30 ml/2 tbsp cornflour (cornstarch)
- 30 ml/2 tbsp plain (all-purpose) flour
- 30 ml/2 tbsp soy sauce
- 30 ml/2 tbsp water
- 45 ml/3 tbsp groundnut (peanut) oil
- salt and freshly ground pepper

Directions:

1. Combine the pork, egg, half the cornflour, the wine or sherry and half the soy sauce and season with salt and pepper.
2. Peel the cucumbers then chop into 5 cm/2 in chunks.
3. Scoop out some of the seeds to make hollows and fill with stuffing, pressing it down.
4. Dust with flour.
5. Heat the oil and fry the cucumber pieces, stuffing side down, until slightly browned.
6. Turn over and cook until the other side is browned.
7. Put in the stock and soy sauce, bring to the boil, cover and simmer for approximately 20 minutes until soft, turning intermittently.
8. Transfer the cucumbers to a warmed serving plate.
9. Mix the rest of the cornflour with the water, mix it into the pan and simmer, stirring, until the sauce clears and becomes thick.
10. Pour over the cucumbers and serve.

STUFFED MARROW

Yield: 4 Servings

Ingredients:

- 1 marrow, halved
- 100 g/4 oz smoked ham, chopped
- 15 ml/1 tbsp chopped flat-leaved parsley
- 15 ml/1 tbsp soy sauce
- 2 spring onions (scallions), chopped
- 250 ml/8 fl oz/1 cup chicken stock
- 30 ml/2 tbsp cornflour (cornstarch)
- 450 g/1 lb fish fillets, flaked
- 5 ml/1 tsp salt

- 5 ml/1 tsp sesame oil
- 5 ml/1 tsp sugar
- 50 g/2 oz/½ cup chopped almonds
- 60 ml/4 tbsp water
- oil for deep-frying

Directions:

1. Combine the fish, salt, spring onions, ham and almonds.
2. Scoop out the seeds of the marrow and some of the flesh to make a hollow.
3. Press the fish mixture into the marrow.
4. Heat the oil and deep-fry the marrow halves, one at a time if needed, until a golden-brown colour is achieved.
5. Move to a clean pan and add the stock.
6. Bring to the boil, cover and simmer for 40 minutes.
7. Blend the cornflour, soy sauce, sugar, water and sesame oil to a paste, stir into the pan and simmer, stirring, until the sauce clears and becomes thick.
8. Serve garnished with parsley.

SWEET AND SOUR ASPARAGUS

Yield: 4 Servings

Ingredients:

- 15 ml/1 tbsp cornflour (cornstarch)
- 15 ml/1 tbsp rice wine or dry sherry
- 15 ml/1 tbsp soy sauce
- 30 ml/2 tbsp groundnut (peanut) oil
- 450 g/1 lb asparagus, chop in diagonal pieces
- 5 ml/1 tsp salt
- 50 g/2 oz/¼ cup brown sugar
- 60 ml/4 tbsp wine vinegar

Directions:

1. Heat the oil and stir-fry the asparagus for 4 minutes.
2. Put in the wine vinegar, sugar, soy sauce, wine or sherry and salt and stir-fry for approximately two minutes.

3. Combine the cornflour with a little water, mix it into the pan and stir-fry for approximately one minute.

SWEET AND SOUR CABBAGE

Yield: 4 Servings

Ingredients:

- 1 head cabbage, shredded
- 15 ml/1 tbsp cornflour (cornstarch)
- 15 ml/1 tbsp groundnut (peanut) oil
- 15 ml/1 tbsp soy sauce
- 30 ml/2 tbsp sugar
- 30 ml/2 tbsp wine vinegar
- 45 ml/3 tbsp water
- 5 ml/1 tsp salt

Directions:

1. Heat the oil and stir-fry the cabbage for approximately three minutes.
2. Put in the salt and continue to stir-fry until the cabbage is just soft.
3. Blend the wine vinegar, sugar, soy sauce, cornflour and water to a paste, put it into the pan and simmer, stirring, until the sauce coats the cabbage.

SWEET AND SOUR MIXED VEGETABLES

Yield: 4 Servings

Ingredients:

- 1 green pepper, cubed
- 1 onion, chopped into wedges
- 100 g/4 oz bamboo shoots, chopped into strips
- 100 g/4 oz water chestnuts, chopped into strips
- 100 g/4 oz/½ cup sugar
- 15 ml/1 tbsp cornflour (cornstarch)
- 2 carrots, sliced

- 2 cloves garlic, crushed
- 2½ ml/½ tsp salt
- 30 ml/2 tbsp soy sauce
- 45 ml/3 tbsp groundnut (peanut) oil
- 60 ml/4 tbsp chicken stock
- 60 ml/4 tbsp wine vinegar

Directions:

1. Heat the oil, salt and garlic until the garlic turns light golden.
2. Put in the carrots, pepper, bamboo shoots and onions and stir-fry for approximately three minutes.
3. Put in the water chestnuts and stir-fry for approximately two minutes.
4. Combine the sugar, stock, wine vinegar, soy sauce and cornflour then mix it into the pan.
5. Cook, stirring, until the sauce becomes thick and clears.

SWEET AND SOUR RED CABBAGE

Yield: 4 Servings

Ingredients:

- 15 ml/1 tbsp cornflour (cornstarch)
- 15 ml/1 tbsp soy sauce
- 30 ml/2 tbsp groundnut (peanut) oil
- 45 ml/ 3 tbsp wine vinegar
- 450 g/1 lb red cabbage, shredded
- 5 ml/ 1 tsp salt
- 50 g/2 oz/¼ cup brown sugar

Directions:

1. Heat the oil and stir-fry the cabbage for 4 minutes.
2. Put in the sugar, wine vinegar, soy sauce and salt and stir-fry for approximately two minutes.
3. Combine the cornflour with a little water and stir-fry for approximately one minute.

VEGETABLE CHOW MEIN

Yield: 4 Servings

Ingredients:

- 100 g/4 oz bamboo shoots, sliced
- 2½ ml/½ tsp salt
- 30 ml/2 tbsp soy sauce
- 45 ml/3 tbsp groundnut (peanut) oil
- 450 g/1 lb spinach
- 6 dried Chinese mushrooms
- soft-fried noodles

Directions:

1. Soak the mushrooms in warm water for half an hour then drain.
2. Discard the stalks and slice the caps.
3. Halve the spinach leaves.
4. Heat the oil and stir-fry the mushrooms and bamboo shoots for 4 minutes.
5. Put in the spinach, salt and soy sauce and stir-fry for approximately one minute.
6. Put in the drained noodles and stir gently until heated through.

VEGETABLE SPRING ROLLS

Yield: 4 Servings

Ingredients:

- 1 green pepper, sliced
- 100 g/4 oz bean sprouts
- 100 g/4 oz Chinese leaves, shredded
- 15 ml/1 tbsp soy sauce
- 2 cloves garlic, finely chopped
- 2 stalks celery, chopped
- 2½ ml/½ tsp salt
- 3 spring onions (scallions), chopped
- 30 ml/2 tbsp groundnut (peanut) oil
- 4 water chestnuts, chopped into strips
- 5 ml/1 tsp sugar

- 50 g/2 oz bamboo shoots, sliced
- 6 dried Chinese mushrooms
- 8 spring roll skins
- groundnut (peanut) oil for frying

Directions:

1. Soak the mushrooms in warm water for half an hour then drain.
2. Discard the stems and chop the caps.
3. Heat the oil, salt and garlic until the garlic turns golden then add the mushrooms and stir-fry for approximately two minutes.
4. Put in the celery, pepper and bamboo shoots and stir-fry for approximately three minutes.
5. Put in the cabbage, bean sprouts, chestnuts and spring onions and stir-fry for approximately two minutes.
6. Mix in the soy sauce and sugar, remove from the heat and allow to stand for approximately two minutes.
7. Turn into a colander and leave to drain.
8. Put a few spoonfuls of the filling mixture in the centre of each spring roll skin, fold up the bottom, fold in the sides, then roll upwards, enclosing the filling.
9. Seal the edge with a little flour and water mixture then leave to dry for half an hour.
10. Heat the oil and fry the spring rolls for approximately ten minutes until crisp and golden brown.
11. Drain thoroughly and serve.

VEGETABLE SURPRISES

Yield: 4 Servings

Ingredients:

- 15 ml/1 tbsp grated lemon rind
- 2 eggs, separated
- 225 g/8 oz broccoli florets
- 225 g/8 oz brussels sprouts
- 225 g/8 oz cauliflower florets
- 225 g/8 oz/2 cups plain (all-purpose) flour
- 250 ml/8 fl oz/1 cup dry white wine
- 30 ml/2 tbsp honey

- 30 ml/2 tbsp soy sauce
- 30 ml/2 tbsp wine vinegar
- 5 ml/1 tsp five-spice powder
- oil for deep-frying
- salt and freshly ground pepper

Directions:

1. Briefly boil the vegetables for approximately one minute in boiling water then drain.
2. Combine the honey, soy sauce, wine vinegar, five-spice powder, salt and pepper.
3. Put the vegetables in the marinade, cover and chill for about two hours, stirring intermittently.
4. Combine the flour, wine and egg yolks until smooth.
5. Whisk the egg whites until firm then fold them into the batter.
6. Season with salt, pepper and lemon rind.
7. Eliminate the excess liquid from the vegetables and coat them in the batter.
8. Heat the oil and deep-fry until a golden-brown colour is achieved.
9. Drain using kitchen paper and serve.

VEGETABLES IN TOMATO SAUCE

Yield: 4 Servings

Ingredients:

- 1 green pepper, chopped into strips
- 1 red pepper, chopped into strips
- 1 stick celery, chopped into strips
- 10 ml/2 tsp wine vinegar
- 100 g/4 oz bean sprouts
- 100 g/4 oz green peas
- 100 g/4 oz smoked bacon, diced
- 2 cloves garlic, crushed
- 30 ml/2 tbsp groundnut (peanut) oil
- 30 ml/2 tbsp hoisin sauce
- 30 ml/2 tbsp honey
- 30 ml/2 tbsp soy sauce
- 30 ml/2 tbsp tomato purée (paste)
- 300 ml/½ pt/1¼ cups vegetable stock

- 5 ml/1 tsp salt

Directions:

1. Heat the oil and fry the garlic and salt until slightly browned.
2. Put in the bacon and fry until crisp.
3. Blend together the tomato purée, soy sauce, honey, hoisin sauce and stock.
4. Put in the vegetables to the pan and stir-fry for approximately two minutes until coated in oil.
5. Put in the stock mixture, bring to the boil, cover and simmer for approximately twenty minutes until cooked.

VEGETABLES WITH HONEY

Yield: 4 Servings

Ingredients:

- 1 green pepper, diced
- 1 red pepper, diced
- 1 slice ginger root, chopped
- 10 ml/2 tsp soy sauce
- 100 g/4 oz baby sweetcorn
- 100 g/4 oz mushrooms, halved
- 15 ml/1 tbsp fruit vinegar
- 15 ml/1 tbsp groundnut (peanut) oil
- 15 ml/1 tbsp honey
- 2 cloves garlic, chopped
- 2 spring onions (scallions), sliced
- salt and freshly ground pepper

Directions:

1. Heat the oil and fry the ginger and garlic until slightly browned.
2. Put in the vegetables and stir-fry for approximately one minute.
3. Put in the honey, fruit vinegar and soy sauce and season with salt and pepper.
4. thoroughly stir together and heat through and serve.

VEGETABLE-STUFFED PEPPERS

Yield: 4 Servings

Ingredients:

- 1 onion, grated
- 120 ml/4 fl oz/½ cup chicken stock
- 15 ml/1 tbsp cornflour (cornstarch)
- 15 ml/1 tbsp soy sauce
- 2 carrots, grated
- 2½ ml/½ tsp salt
- 30 ml/2 tbsp groundnut (peanut) oil
- 4 green peppers
- 45 ml/3 tbsp tomato ketchup (catsup)
- 5 ml/1 tsp sugar
- 60 ml/4 tbsp water
- salt and freshly ground pepper

Directions:

- Chop the tops off the peppers and scoop out the seeds.
- Turn off the heat and mix in the tomato ketchup and sugar.
- Blend the cornflour, soy sauce and water to a paste, stir into the pan and bring to the boil.
- Bring to the boil and season with salt and pepper.
- Cover and simmer for one hour.
- Fill with the stuffing mixture and replace the tops as lids.
- Heat the oil and fry the carrots and onions until slightly softened.
- Pour over the peppers and serve instantly.
- Season with salt and pepper.
- Simmer, stirring, until the sauce clears and becomes thick.
- Stand the peppers upright in a pan and add the stock.
- Transfer the peppers to a heated serving dish.

WATER CHESTNUT CAKES

Yield: 4 Servings

Ingredients:

- 100 g/4 oz sesame seeds
- 120 ml/4 fl oz/½ cup vegetable stock
- 15 ml/1 tbsp plain (all-purpose) flour
- 15 ml/1 tbsp sesame oil
- 225 g/8 oz red bean paste
- 5 ml/1 tsp cinnamon
- 5 ml/1 tsp salt
- 900 g/2 lb water chestnuts
- freshly ground pepper
- oil for deep-frying

Directions:

1. Heat the sesame seeds using a dry pan until slightly browned.
2. Mince the water chestnuts and eliminate the excess liquid off a little of the water.
3. Mix with the flour, salt and pepper and mould into small balls.
4. Press a little bean paste into the centre of each one.
5. Coat the cakes in sesame seeds.
6. Heat the oil and deep-fry the cakes for about 3 minutes then remove from the pan and drain.
7. Pour off all but 30 ml/2 tbsp of oil from the pan then return the cakes to the pan and fry over a low heat for 4 minutes.
8. Add the rest of the ingredients, bring to a simmer and simmer until most of the liquid has been absorbed.
9. Move to a warmed serving plate and serve instantly.

TOFU

Tofu is a great source of protein, and an important part of the Chinese diet, especially for the vegetarians and vegans.

BATTERED TOFU

Yield: 4 Servings

Ingredients:

- 1 egg
- 1 spring onion, chopped
- 175 ml/6 fl oz/¾ cup water
- 2 dried Chinese mushrooms
- 275 g/10 oz plain (all-purpose) flour
- 30 ml/2 tbsp cornflour (cornstarch)
- 450 g/1 lb tofu
- 5 ml/1 tsp baking powder
- 5 ml/1 tsp grated cheese
- 5 ml/1 tsp ground coriander
- oil for deep-frying
- salt and freshly ground pepper

Directions:

1. Soak the mushrooms in warm water for half an hour then drain.
2. Discard the stalks and mince the caps with the tofu, egg, spring onion, coriander, cheese, cornflour, salt and pepper.
3. The mixture should be sticky.
4. Press on to a plate and steam over gently simmering water for approximately ten minutes.
5. Chop the tofu into squares.
6. Combine the flour, baking powder and water to a sticky batter and use to coat the tofu.
7. Heat the oil and deep-fry the squares until slightly golden.
8. Drain thoroughly and serve.

CHINESE TOFU

Yield: 4 Servings

Ingredients:

- 120 ml/4 fl oz/½ cup chicken stock
- 30 ml/2 tbsp soy sauce
- 45 ml/3 tbsp groundnut (peanut) oil
- 450 g/1 lb tofu, cubed
- 5 ml/1 tsp salt
- 5 ml/1 tsp sugar

Directions:

1. Heat the oil and salt and fry the tofu for about 4 minutes until a golden-brown colour is achieved on all sides.
2. Put in the soy sauce, stock and sugar, bring to the boil and stir-fry for about 2 minutes.

DEEP-FRIED TOFU

Yield: 4 Servings

Ingredients:

- 350 g/12 oz tofu, cubed
- oil for deep-frying
- salt

Directions:

1. Heat the oil and deep-fry the tofu until puffed and golden brown.
2. Lay out on a warmed serving plate and drizzle generously with salt and serve.

FOUR-JEWELLED TOFU

Yield: 4 Servings

Ingredients:

- ½ small carrot, shredded
- 100 g/4 oz broccoli florets
- 100 g/4 oz chicken, shredded
- 100 g/4 oz peeled prawns
- 120 ml/4 fl oz/½ cup chicken stock
- 15 ml/1 tbsp oyster sauce
- 15 ml/1 tbsp soy sauce
- 2½ ml/½ tsp cornflour (cornstarch)
- 2½ ml/½ tsp fish sauce
- 2½ ml/½ tsp rice wine or dry sherry
- 45 ml/3 tbsp groundnut (peanut) oil
- 450 g/1 oz tofu, cubed
- 6 dried Chinese mushrooms

Directions:

1. Soak the mushrooms in warm water for half an hour then drain.
2. Discard the stalks and halve the caps.
3. Heat 15 ml/1 tbsp of oil and fry the mushroom caps until soft then remove from the pan.
4. In the meantime, briefly boil the broccoli in boiling water until almost soft then eliminate the excess liquid well.
5. Heat 15 ml/ 1 tbsp of oil in the wok and cook the broccoli with the fish sauce, wine or sherry, cornflour and chicken stock until just soft.
6. Take out of the wok.
7. Heat the rest of the oil and stir-fry the tofu until slightly browned.
8. Put in the prawns, chicken and carrot and stir-fry for approximately three minutes.
9. Return the broccoli mixture to the pan with the oyster and soy sauce and cook for a few minutes until soft.

PENG TOFU

Yield: 4 Servings

Ingredients:

- 1 red chilli pepper, shredded
- 120 ml/4 fl oz/½ cup oil
- 15 ml/1 tbsp black bean sauce

- 15 ml/1 tbsp shredded pork
- 2½ ml/½ tsp sugar
- 3 spring onions (scallions), shredded
- 450 g/1 lb tofu, thickly sliced
- 450 ml/¾ pt/2 cups stock
- 5 ml/1 tsp cornflour (cornstarch)
- 5 ml/1 tsp sesame oil
- 60 ml/4 tbsp soy sauce
- pinch of salt

Directions:

1. Heat the oil and fry the tofu until a golden-brown colour is achieved.
2. Take out of the pan and drain.
3. Pour off all but 30 ml/ 2 tbsp of oil and fry the pork, spring onions, chilli and black bean sauce for 30 seconds.
4. Return the tofu to the pan with the stock, soy sauce, sugar and salt.
5. Bring to the boil and simmer for 10 minutes.
6. Blend the cornflour to a paste with a little water, mix it into the pan and simmer, stirring, for approximately one minute.
7. Serve sprinkled with sesame oil.

PEPPERS WITH TOFU

Yield: 4 Servings

Ingredients:

- 1 bunch basil
- 1 bunch parsley
- 1 large green pepper
- 1 large red pepper
- 10 ml/2 tsp soy sauce
- 15 ml/1 tbsp olive oil
- 150 g/5 oz onions
- 2 beef tomatoes, skinned
- 225 g/8 oz tofu, cubed
- pinch of sambal oelek
- salt and freshly ground pepper

Directions:

1. Chop the peppers into strips and the onion into rings.
2. Reserve a few basil and parsley leaves for garnish and chop the rest finely.
3. Quarter the tomatoes, remove the seeds and purée the flesh with the salt, pepper sambal oelek and soy sauce.
4. Heat the oil and fry the tofu until a golden-brown colour is achieved.
5. Put in the peppers and onions and stir-fry for approximately three minutes.
6. Put in the tomato purée and simmer for approximately one minute.
7. Mix in the chopped herbs and serve garnished with the reserved herbs.

PORK-STUFFED TOFU

Yield: 4 Servings

Ingredients:

- 15 ml/1 tbsp rice wine or dry sherry
- 15 ml/1 tbsp soy sauce
- 2 spring onions (scallions), chopped
- 225 g/8 oz minced (ground) pork
- 450 g/1 lb tofu
- 5 ml/1 tsp sesame oil

Directions:

1. Combine the pork, spring onions, half the soy sauce, the wine or sherry and the sesame oil.
2. Chop the tofu into 8 large rectangles and scoop out a hollow in the top of each piece.
3. Stuff with the pork mixture and arrange in a shallow ovenproof dish.
4. Drizzle with the rest of the soy sauce.
5. Put on a rack in a steamer and steam over gently simmering water for about 30 minutes.

TOFU BALLS WITH VEGETABLES

Yield: 4 Servings

Ingredients:

- 100 g/4 oz mangetout (snow peas)
- 100 g/4 oz/1 cup plain (all-purpose) flour
- 2 carrots, chopped into strips
- 250 ml/8 fl oz/1 cup chicken stock
- 4 water chestnuts, minced
- 45 ml/3 tbsp cornflour (cornstarch)
- 45 ml/3 tbsp water
- 450 g/1 lb tofu
- 5 ml/1 tsp salt
- 75 g/3 oz minced (ground) chicken
- oil for deep-frying

Directions:

1. Mash the tofu and place it in a strainer or colander to drain.
2. Mix with the chicken, water chestnuts and 30 ml/2 tbsp of cornflour and mould into balls about the size of ping-pong balls.
3. Combine the flour with enough water to make a thick batter.
4. Immerse the tofu balls in the batter.
5. Heat the oil and deep-fry the tofu until a golden-brown colour is achieved.
6. Remove and drain.
7. Spoon 30 ml/2 tbsp of oil into a wok and fry the carrots and mangetout for approximately two minutes.
8. Put in the stock and salt and bring to the boil.
9. Put in the tofu balls and simmer until heated through.
10. Blend the rest of the cornflour to a paste with a little water, mix it into the pan and simmer, until the sauce becomes thick slightly.
11. Serve Immediately.

TOFU STIR-FRY

Yield: 4 Servings

Ingredients:

- 1 clove garlic, crushed

- 1 spring onion (scallion), chopped
- 15 ml/1 tbsp cornflour (cornstarch)
- 15 ml/1 tbsp rice wine or dry sherry
- 2½ ml/½ tsp salt
- 45 ml/3 tbsp groundnut (peanut) oil
- 45 ml/3 tbsp soy sauce
- 450 g/1 lb tofu, cubed

Directions:

1. Heat the oil and fry the spring onion and garlic until slightly browned.
2. Put in the tofu and fry until golden.
3. Add the rest of the ingredients, bring to the boil, cover and simmer for approximately five minutes.

TOFU WITH BLACK BEAN SAUCE

Yield: 4 Servings

Ingredients:

- 15 ml/1 tbsp chicken stock
- 15 ml/1 tbsp rice wine or dry sherry
- 15 ml/1 tbsp soy sauce
- 2 cloves garlic, crushed
- 30 ml/2 tbsp groundnut (peanut) oil
- 4 spring onions (scallions), sliced
- 450 g/1 lb tofu, cubed
- 60 ml/4 tbsp black bean sauce

Directions:

1. Heat the oil and fry the garlic until light golden.
2. Put in the spring onions and stir-fry for approximately one minute.
3. Put in the tofu and stir-fry carefully for approximately two minutes until golden.
4. Put in the stock, soy sauce and wine or sherry, bring to the boil and stir-fry for about 1 minute.

TOFU WITH CHILLI SAUCE

Yield: 4 Servings

Ingredients:

- 1 spring onion, finely chopped
- 100 g/4 oz minced (ground) pork
- 15 ml/1 tbsp rice wine or dry sherry
- 15 ml/1 tbsp soy sauce
- 15 ml/1 tbsp water
- 2½ ml/½ tsp sesame oil
- 30 ml/2 tbsp chilli sauce
- 30 ml/2 tbsp groundnut (peanut) oil
- 450 g/1 lb tofu, cubed
- 450 ml/¾ pt/2 cups chicken stock
- 5 ml/1 tsp cornflour (cornstarch)
- 5 ml/1 tsp minced ginger root
- freshly ground pepper

Directions:

1. Briefly boil the tofu in boiling water for approximately two minutes then drain.
2. Heat the oil and fry the pork, chilli sauce and ginger until the pork is well cooked.
3. Put in the stock, tofu, soy sauce and wine or sherry, bring to the boil and simmer gently until almost all the liquid has evaporated.
4. Blend the cornflour and water to a paste, mix it into the pan and simmer, stirring, until thickened.
5. Move to a heated serving dish and serve sprinkled with sesame oil, spring onions and pepper.

TOFU WITH CHINESE MUSHROOMS

Yield: 4 Servings

Ingredients:

- 100 g/4 oz peeled prawns
- 15 ml/1 tbsp rice wine or dry sherry
- 2 spring onions (scallions), thickly sliced

- 2½ ml/½ tsp salt
- 2½ ml/½ tsp sugar
- 250 ml/8 fl oz/1 cup chicken stock
- 3 slices ginger root, chopped
- 3 slices ham, shredded
- 4 dried Chinese mushrooms
- 45 ml/3 tbsp soy sauce
- 450 g/1 lb tofu, chopped into squares
- 60 ml/4 tbsp groundnut (peanut) oil

Directions:

1. Soak the mushrooms in warm water for half an hour then drain.
2. Discard the stalks and quarter the caps.
3. Heat the oil and fry the tofu until a golden-brown colour is achieved then remove from the pan.
4. Reheat the oil and fry the spring onions and ginger for 30 seconds.
5. Put in the tofu, ham, prawns, stock, soy sauce, wine or sherry, salt and sugar, bring to the boil, cover and simmer for approximately ten minutes.
6. Take the lid off and simmer until the sauce is reduced.
7. Move to a heated serving dish and serve instantly.

TOFU WITH CRAB MEAT

Yield: 4 Servings

Ingredients:

- 1 clove garlic, crushed
- 1 slice ginger root, chopped
- 15 ml/1 tbsp cornflour (cornstarch)
- 175 ml/6 fl oz/¾ cup chicken stock
- 2 spring onions (scallions), chopped
- 225 g/8 oz crab meat
- 225 g/8 oz tofu, cubed
- 45 ml/3 tbsp groundnut (peanut) oil
- 5 ml/1 tsp sugar

Directions:

1. Heat the oil and fry the garlic, spring onions and ginger until slightly browned.
2. Put in the tofu and stir-fry for 4 minutes.
3. Put in the crab meat, sugar and stock, bring to the boil then simmer for 4 minutes.
4. Combine the cornflour with a little water, mix it into the sauce and simmer, stirring, until the sauce clears and becomes thick.

TOFU WITH OYSTER SAUCE

Yield: 4 Servings

Ingredients:

- 1 red pepper, chopped into chunks
- 120 ml/4 fl oz/½ cup water
- 15 ml/1 tbsp cornflour (cornstarch)
- 15 ml/1 tbsp rice wine or dry sherry
- 15 ml/1 tbsp soy sauce
- 225 g/8 oz mushrooms, sliced
- 225 g/8 oz tofu, cubed
- 3 stalks celery, sliced
- 30 ml/2 tbsp groundnut (peanut) oil
- 30 ml/2 tbsp oyster sauce
- 6 spring onions (scallions), chopped into chunks

Directions:

1. Heat half the oil and fry the tofu until slightly browned.
2. Take out of the pan.
3. Heat the rest of the oil and fry the mushrooms, spring onions, celery and pepper for approximately two minutes.
4. Return the tofu to the pan and toss slightly to combine the ingredients.
5. Blend the water, cornflour, oyster sauce, wine or sherry and soy sauce.
6. Pour the mixture into the wok and bring to the boil, stirring constantly.
7. Simmer, stirring, for approximately two minutes and serve.

TOFU WITH PRAWNS

Yield: 4 Servings

Ingredients:

- 1 clove garlic, crushed
- 225 g/8 oz peeled prawns
- 225 g/8 oz tofu, cubed
- 250 ml/8 fl oz/1 cup chicken stock
- 30 ml/2 tbsp cornflour (cornstarch)
- 30 ml/2 tbsp rice wine or dry sherry
- 30 ml/2 tbsp soy sauce
- 45 ml/3 tbsp groundnut (peanut) oil
- 5 ml/1 tsp salt

Directions:

1. Heat the oil and fry the garlic and salt until slightly browned.
2. Put in the tofu and stir-fry for approximately two minutes.
3. Put in the prawns, wine or sherry and soy sauce and stir until the tofu and prawns are well coated in the flavoured oil.
4. Add most of the chicken stock, bring to the boil, cover and simmer for approximately three minutes.
5. Combine the cornflour with the rest of the stock, mix it into the pan and simmer, stirring, until the sauce clears and becomes thick.

TOFU WITH SPRING ONION

Yield: 4 Servings

Ingredients:

- 10 ml/½ tsp salt
- 45 ml/3 tbsp soy sauce
- 450 g/1 lb tofu, cubed
- 60 ml/4 tbsp groundnut (peanut) oil
- 8 spring onions (scallions), chopped into chunks

Directions:

1. Heat the oil and fry the spring onions for approximately two minutes.
2. Put in the tofu stir-fry for approximately two minutes.
3. Put in the soy sauce and salt stir-fry for another 1 minute.

DESSERTS, CAKES AND CONFECTIONERY

It is usually a good idea to finish with something sweet.

ALMOND BISCUITS

Yield: 12

- 100 g/4 oz self-raising flour
- 100 g/4 oz sugar
- 12 almonds
- 2 eggs, beaten
- 5 ml/1 tsp baking powder
- 50 g/2 oz lard

Directions:

1. Combine the flour and baking powder then rub in the large until the mixture resembles breadcrumbs.
2. Stir in the sugar and 1 egg to form a thick paste.
3. Divide into 12 balls and press into circles on a greased baking tray.
4. Press an almond on to the top of each one.
5. Glaze with the rest of the egg and bake in a preheated oven at 200°C/400°F/gas mark 6 for approximately 20 minutes until a golden-brown colour is achieved.
6. Cool on a wire rack.

ALMOND MILK JELLY WITH LYCHEES

Yield: 4 Servings

Ingredients:

- 15 g/½ oz gelatine
- 250 ml/8 fl oz/1 cup milk

- 400 g/14 oz canned lychees in syrup
- 5 ml/1 tsp almond essence (extract)
- 50 g/2 oz/¼ cup brown sugar
- 75 ml/5 tbsp water

Directions:

1. Combine the water and gelatine and heat gently over a bowl of warm water until the gelatine dissolves.
2. Bring the milk to the boil then mix in the sugar until it dissolves.
3. Mix in the gelatine mixture then the almond essence.
4. Turn off the heat and continue to stir until all the ingredients are well mixed.
5. Pour into a dish and cool then chill until set.
6. Cut into cubes and arrange in dessert bowls then top with the lychees and syrup.

CANDIED PEEL

Yield: 4 Servings

Ingredients:

- 250 ml/8 fl oz/1 cup water
- 450 g/1 lb sugar
- pinch of salt
- rind of 1 grapefruit
- rind of 1 lemon
- rind of 1 orange

Directions:

1. Chop the rinds into thin strips and place in a pan.
2. Cover with water, add the salt, bring to the boil and simmer for half an hour then drain.
3. Combine the sugar with the water, bring to the boil and simmer until a syrup is formed.
4. Put in the rinds and simmer until the rinds are soft and clear.
5. Remove from the pot and spread out on nonstick paper to dry.
6. Store the excess syrup for future use.

CANTON FRUIT CUP

Yield: 4 Servings

Ingredients:

- 1 piece preserved ginger in syrup, minced
- 2 bananas, sliced
- 2 oranges, peeled and chop into segments
- 200 g/7 oz pineapple chunks

Directions:

1. Combine all the ingredients together and chill.
2. Serve in glass sundae dishes.

CHAMPAGNE MELON

Yield: 4 Servings

Ingredients:

- 1 bottle Champagne or sparkling wine
- 1 egg white
- 1 small melon
- 100 g/4 oz/½ cup sugar
- 120 ml/4 fl oz/½ cup water
- 225 g/8 fl oz/1 cup caster sugar
- 450 g/1 lb seedless grapes
- 60 ml/4 tbsp ginger wine

Directions:

1. Chop the melon in half and remove the seeds.
2. mould into balls using a melon bailer or chop into cubes.
3. Put into a container, cover with clingfilm and refrigerate until cold.
4. Combine the water, sugar and ginger wine in a small saucepan and cook over a low heat, stirring until the sugar dissolves.
5. Bring to the boil and boil for approximately three minutes then remove from the heat.
6. Allow it to cool and refrigerate until cold.
7. Chill the Champagne or wine.
8. Chop the grapes into small bunches, leaving a large enough stem section on each to hook over the rim of the glass.

9. Beat the egg white until frothy.
10. Brush over the grapes then immerse them in caster sugar, turning to coat them completely.
11. Put on a large plate and leave to dry for about two hours.
12. Divide the melon balls between 6 large dessert glasses.
13. Spoon about 30 ml/2 tbsp of the ginger syrup into each glass and fill with Champagne or wine.
14. Hang a bunch of grapes over the outside edge of each glass and serve instantly.

CHINESE NUT MERINGUE

Yield: 4 Servings

Ingredients:

- 10 ml/2 tsp baking powder
- 100 g/4 oz/½ cup brown sugar
- 100 g/4 oz/½ cup butter
- 175 g/6 oz/1¼ cups mixed nuts
- 225 g/8 oz plain (all-purpose) flour
- 25 g/1 oz/2 tbsp caster sugar
- 3 eggs, separated
- 45 ml/3 tbsp milk
- few drops of vanilla essence (extract)
- pinch of salt

Directions:

1. Cream the butter and sugar then add the egg yolks and 1 egg white and beat well.
2. Put in the vanilla essence, flour, baking powder, salt and milk.
3. Spread the mixture into a greased rectangular baking tin and drizzle with the nuts.
4. Beat the rest of the egg whites until firm, add the caster sugar and beat again until firm.
5. Spread over the mixture and bake in a preheated oven at 180°C/350°F/gas mark 4 for 35 minutes, cool and chop into squares.

CHOCOLATE LYCHEES

Yield: 4 Servings

Ingredients:

- 15 ml/1 tbsp vegetable fat
- 175 g/6 oz plain chocolate
- 500 g/1 lb 2 oz canned lychees, drained

Directions:

1. Spread the lychees between several layers of kitchen paper and allow to stand for about 1 hour until dry.
2. Melt the chocolate and fat in the top of a double boiler over boiling water.
3. Turn off the heat and allow to cool slightly.
4. Immerse each lychee in chocolate to coat it completely.
5. Carefully lift the lychees out of the chocolate and place round side up on greased baking parchment or greaseproof paper.
6. Drizzle the rest of the chocolate over the lychees and refrigerate until cold.

EGG CUSTARDS

Yield: 4 Servings

Ingredients:

- 225 g/8 oz/1 cup lard
- 3 eggs
- 375 g/12 oz/ 3 cups plain (all-purpose) flour
- 375 ml/13 fl oz/1½ cups milk
- 5 ml/1 tsp salt
- 60–90 ml/4–6 tbsp hot water
- 75 g/3 oz/heaped ¼ cup sugar

Directions:

1. Combine the flour and half the salt then rub in the lard until the mixture resembles breadcrumbs.
2. Mix in enough water to form a soft dough.

3. Chop the dough in half and roll out each half on a floured surface to 5 mm thick.
4. Cut out 12 x 8 cm/3 in circles and press the circles into greased muffin tins.
5. Beat the eggs then mix in the sugar and rest of the salt.
6. Progressively blend in the milk.
7. Spoon the mixture into the pastry cases and bake in a preheated oven at 180°C/350°F/gas mark 4 for about 30 minutes until set.
8. Remove the tarts from the tin and cool on a wire rack.

FRUITS WITH ALMOND CREAM

Yield: 4 Servings

Ingredients:

- 1 sachet gelatine
- 100 g/4 oz/½ cup sugar
- 175 ml/6 fl oz/¾ cup boiling water
- 175 ml/6 fl oz/¾ cup water
- 2 kiwi fruits, peeled and sliced
- 2½ ml/½ tsp almond essence (extract)
- 2½ ml/½ tsp vanilla essence (extract)
- 300 ml/½ pt/1¼ cups evaporated milk
- 4 strawberries

Directions:

1. Drizzle the gelatine on to the cold water into a container and allow to stand for approximately one minute.
2. Put in the sugar and stir until the gelatine dissolves.
3. Stir the gelatine mixture into the boiling water.
4. Combine the evaporated milk, vanilla and almond essences and pour into the gelatine mixture.
5. Divide the mixture between 4 serving dishes and refrigerate for approximately three hours until set.
6. Serve garnished with kiwi fruits and strawberries.

GLAZED CHESTNUTS

Yield: 4 Servings

Ingredients:

- 250 g/9 oz/¾ cup honey
- 450 g/1 lb chestnuts
- 450 g/1 lb/2 cups sugar

Directions:

1. Soak the chestnuts in water to cover.
2. Drain, shell and pat dry.
3. Combine the sugar and honey and cook over a low heat, stirring constantly, until the mixture forms a syrup.
4. Put in the chestnuts, stir thoroughly, cover and simmer very gently for about 2 hours until soft, stirring often.
5. Put the chestnuts separately on a greased serving plate and allow to cool and serve.

HONEYED BANANAS

Yield: 4 Servings

Ingredients:

- 120 ml/4 fl oz/½ cup honey
- 120 ml/4 fl oz/½ cup water
- 30 ml/2 tbsp groundnut (peanut) oil
- 350 g/12 oz/1 cup brown sugar
- 4 firm bananas, halved lengthways
- 5 ml/1 tsp wine vinegar

Directions:

1. Heat the oil and fry the bananas until slightly browned.
2. Take out of the pan and chop into 2½ cm/1 in pieces.
3. Put the honey, sugar, water and wine vinegar in a pan and heat gently until the mixture starts to thicken.
4. When the mixture forms threads when a little is dropped into cold water, add the bananas and stir gently until they are completely coated.
5. Immerse the bananas into iced water to set them.

ICE CREAM PUFFS

Yield: 4 Servings

Ingredients:

- 1.2 l/2 pts/5 cups vanilla ice cream
- 2½ ml/½ tsp baking powder
- 25 g/1 oz/¼ cup plain (all-purpose) flour
- 4 eggs, beaten
- oil for deep-frying

Directions:

1. Divide the ice cream into scoops and freeze until very hard.
2. Beat the eggs, flour and baking powder, coat the ice cream with the mixture and freeze again until hard.
3. Heat the oil and immerse the ice cream again in the batter mixture.
4. Deep-fry for a few seconds until the pastry coverings puff up.
5. Serve as soon as possible.

LYCHEES WITH PAPAYA SAUCE

Yield: 4 Servings

Ingredients:

- 45 ml/3 tbsp sugar
- 450 g/1 lb lychees
- 450 g/1 lb papaya, peeled and seeded

Directions:

1. If you have fresh lychees, peel and stone them.
2. Canned lychees should be drained comprehensively..
3. Lay out them in a glass bowl.
4. Purée the papaya flesh then mix in the sugar.
5. Spoon the papaya over the lychees and chill and serve.

MANDARIN LIQUEUR SORBET WITH LYCHEES

Yield: 4 Servings

Ingredients:

- 100 g/4 oz/½ cup sugar
- 30 ml/2 tbsp orange liqueur
- 450 ml/¾ pt/2 cups water
- 500 g/1 lb 2 oz canned lychees in syrup
- 550 g/1¼ lb canned mandarin oranges in syrup
- 60 ml/4 tbsp lemon juice

Directions:

1. Put the water and sugar in a pan and cook over a low heat, stirring constantly, until the mixture boils.
2. Boil, without stirring, for approximately three minutes then remove from the heat and allow to cool.
3. Purée 1 can of mandarins with their syrup until smooth.
4. Strain.
5. Stir the purée, lemon juice and liqueur into the cooled syrup.
6. Pour into a large freezer dish and freeze for at least 3 hours until firm.
7. Refrigerate the rest of the mandarins and lychees until cold.
8. To serve, eliminate the excess liquid the mandarins and lychees, reserving the lychee syrup.
9. Spoon the fruit and lychee syrup into serving dishes.
10. Remove the sorbet from the freezer and flake it slightly using a fork.
11. Spoon over the fruit and serve.

MANGO FOOL

Yield: 4 Servings

Ingredients:

- 250 ml/8 fl oz/1 cup double cream
- 30 ml/2 tbsp sugar

- 450 g/ 1 lb mangoes, peeled and sliced

Directions:

1. Purée the mango flesh then mix in the sugar.
2. Whip the cream until firm, then mix it into the mango purée.

PEANUT CRISPS

Yield: 4 Servings

Ingredients:

- 20 ml/4 tsp water
- 225 g/8 oz/2 cups roast unsalted
- 450 g/1 lb/2 cups sugar
- 50 g/2 oz sesame seeds
- 75 ml/5 tbsp wine vinegar
- skinned peanuts

Directions:

1. Heat the sesame seeds using a dry pan until golden.
2. Combine the sugar, wine vinegar and water in a saucepan and cook over a low heat, stirring as the sugar dissolves.
3. Bring to the boil without stirring.
4. Boil, without stirring, for approximately ten minutes until the mixture is golden and reaches 149°C/300°F or hard-crack stage.
5. While the sugar is boiling, grease a large baking tin.
6. Drizzle half the sesame seeds and all the peanuts evenly into the tin.
7. Pour the sugar over the nuts and smooth the surface with the back of a greased wooden spoon.
8. Drizzle with the rest of the sesame seeds and allow to cool slightly.
9. While still warm, chopped into squares then allow to cool completely.

PEAR COMPOTE

Yield: 4 Servings

Ingredients:

- 50 g/2 oz/½ cup chopped walnuts
- 6 large pears, peeled
- 75 g/3 oz/½ cup chopped dates
- 90 ml/6 tbsp honey

Directions:

1. Core the pears from the top to form a cavity without cutting through to the base.
2. Stand the pears in a container on a rack in a wok or pan with water in the bottom to come immediately below the steaming rack.
3. Fill the pears with the dates and walnuts and cover with honey.
4. Bring the water to the boil, cover and steam for approximately twenty minutes, topping up with boiling water as needed, until the pears are cooked.
5. The length of time will vary with the size and ripeness of the pears.

PEARL BARLEY PUDDING

Yield: 4 Servings

Ingredients:

- 100 g/4 oz/1 cup pearl barley
- 100 g/4 oz/1 cup walnuts
- 2½ ml/½ tsp cinnamon
- 225 g/8 oz/2 cups brown sugar
- 450 ml/¾ pt/2 cups milk
- 450 ml/¾ pt/2 cups water
- 50 g/2 oz/heaped ¼ cup raisins
- salt

Directions:

1. Put the pearl barley, water and salt in a pan, bring to the boil, cover and simmer for one hour.
2. Transfer the barley to the top of a double boiler and mix in the sugar and milk.
3. Bring the water in the bottom to the boil and cook for approximately three hours over a low heat.

4. Briefly boil the walnuts in boiling water for approximately five minutes then eliminate the excess liquid and chop.
5. Put into the barley mixture with the raisins and simmer for another 15 minutes.

PEKING DUST

Yield: 6 Servings

Ingredients:

- ½ egg white
- 120 ml/4 fl oz/½ cup double (heavy) cream, whipped
- 15 ml/1 tbsp brandy
- 25 g/1 oz/2 tbsp butter
- 450 g/1 lb chestnuts
- 5 ml/1 tsp vanilla essence (extract)
- 50 g/2 oz maraschino cherries
- 50 g/2 oz/¼ cup icing sugar
- 50 g/2 oz/¼ cup sugar
- milk
- pinch of cream of tartar
- pinch of salt

Directions:

1. Shell the chestnuts, place in a pan of cold water and bring to the boil.
2. Simmer for approximately three minutes then drain.
3. Cover the chestnuts with milk and add half the vanilla essence.
4. Heat gently but do not boil.
5. Cover and simmer for approximately twenty minutes until the chestnuts are soft.
6. Drain, discarding the milk.
7. Mash the chestnuts with the butter, half the sugar and the brandy.
8. Beat the egg white with the cream of tartar then fold in the salt and the rest of the sugar and vanilla essence.
9. Spoon the mixture into a piping bag and squeeze into a nest shape on a foil-lined baking tray.
10. Bake in a preheated oven at 140°C/275°F/gas mark 1 for approximately forty minutes until golden.
11. Allow it to cool slightly then transfer to a serving plate.

12. Spoon the chestnut mixture into a clean piping bag and squeeze it out in thin threads over the egg nest to form a mound on top.
13. Whip the cream with the icing sugar and garnish the nest with cream and cherries.

PRECIOUS FRUIT

Yield: 4 Servings

Ingredients:

- 100 g/4 oz/½ cup brown sugar
- 30 ml/2 tbsp cornflour (cornstarch)
- 400 ml/14 fl oz/1¼ cups water
- 450 g/1 lb mixed fresh fruit (apples, satsumas, bananas), sliced
- 600 ml/1 pt/2½ cups fruit juice

Directions:

1. Bring the fruit juice to the boil.
2. Put in the fruit and sugar and stir until the sugar dissolves.
3. Mix the rest of the water and cornflour and mix it into the pan.
4. Bring almost to boiling, stirring constantly, but do not allow the mixture to boil.
5. Serve hot in soup bowls.

RASPBERRY FOOL

Yield: 4 Servings

Ingredients:

- 250 ml/8 fl oz/1 cup double cream
- 30 ml/2 tbsp sugar
- 350 g/12 oz raspberries

Directions:

1. Purée the raspberries then rub them through a sieve if you prefer not to have pips in the fool.
2. Mix in the sugar.

3. Whip the cream until firm then gently fold it into the raspberries.

RASPBERRY SORBET

Yield: 4 Servings

Ingredients:

- 175 g/6 oz/¾ cup sugar
- 2 egg whites
- 250 ml/8 fl oz/1 cup water
- 30 ml/2 tbsp lemon juice
- 30 ml/2 tbsp orange liqueur
- 375 g/12 oz raspberries
- pinch of cream of tartar

Directions:

1. Purée the raspberries with the water, half the sugar, the lemon juice and liqueur.
2. Rub through a sieve into a freezer dish and freeze for about 4 hours until firm.
3. Beat the egg whites and cream of tartar until frothy.
4. Progressively add the rest of the sugar and whisk until the whites are stiff but not dry.
5. Remove the raspberry mixture from the freezer and flake it using a fork.
6. Spoon the egg whites over the top and fold them into the raspberry sorbet gently but comprehensively..
7. Freeze for at least 2 hours until firm.

RICE PUDDING WITH CANDIED FRUITS

Yield: 4 Servings

Ingredients:

- 120 ml/4 fl oz/½ cup double cream
- 150 g/5 oz/ short-grain rice
- 150 ml/¼ pt/generous ½ cup milk
- 150 ml/¼ pt/generous ½ cup rice wine or dry sherry
- 150 ml/¼ pt/generous ½ cup water

- 25 g/1 oz candied ginger, chopped
- 25 g/1 oz candied pineapple, chopped
- 25 g/1 oz chopped mixed peel
- 25 g/1 oz glacé cherries, chopped
- 300 ml/½ pt/1¼ cups whipping cream, whipped
- 50 g/2 oz candied kumquats or other fruits, sliced
- 50 g/2 oz/¼ cup sugar

Directions:

Soak the rice in the water for about two hours.

Bring to the boil with the wine or sherry and milk and simmer for approximately twenty minutes until soft.

Put in the sugar, fruits and cream and allow to cool.

When cold, blend in the whipped cream and garnish with kumquats.

SESAME SEED BISCUITS

Yield: 4 Servings

Ingredients:

- 1 egg
- 120 ml/4 fl oz/½ cup groundnut (peanut) oil
- 225 g/8 oz/1 cup sugar
- 45 ml/3 tbsp sesame seeds
- 450 g/1 lb plain (all-purpose) flour
- 5 ml/1 tsp baking powder
- 5 ml/1 tsp grated nutmeg
- pinch of salt

Directions:

1. Heat a pan and gently toast the sesame seeds until slightly browned.
2. Beat together the oil and sugar then blend in the egg and most of the sesame seeds.
3. Combine the flour, baking powder, salt and nutmeg and progressively blend it into the mixture.

4. Knead well, adding a little water if needed to make a firm dough, then chill for about two hours.
5. Roll out the dough and use a pastry cutter to chop into about 35 biscuits.
6. Drizzle with the rest of the sesame seeds and press them in lightly.
7. Bake on a greased baking tray in a preheated oven at 180°C/350°F/gas mark 4 for about 15 minutes until a golden-brown colour is achieved.

SPLIT PEA PUDDING

Yield: 4 Servings

Ingredients:

- 100 g/4 oz maraschino cherries
- 100 g/4 oz/½ cup brown sugar
- 30 ml/2 tbsp cornflour (cornstarch)
- 500 ml/17 fl oz/2¼ cups water
- 60 ml/4 tbsp water
- 675 g/1½ lb split peas

Directions:

1. Soak the split peas overnight in the water.
2. Bring to the boil in the same water, cover and simmer for about 2 hours until soft.
3. Rub through a fine sieve then mix in the sugar and return to a very low heat.
4. Combine the cornflour with the water then stir into the pan.
5. Pour into a shallow rectangular cake tin and allow to cool then chill until set.
6. Cut into cubes, pile into a bowl and serve garnished with cherries.

STEAMED LEMON CAKE

Yield: 4 Servings

Ingredients:

- 175 g/6 oz/1½ cup plain (all-purpose) flour
- 2½ ml/½ tsp baking powder
- 2½ ml/½ tsp vanilla essence (extract)

- 225 g/8 oz/1 cup sugar
- 45 ml/3 tbsp water
- 5 ml/1 tsp lemon essence (extract)
- 6 eggs, separated

Directions:

1. Beat the egg yolks, sugar and water until pale and fluffy.
2. Progressively beat in the flour and baking powder then the vanilla and lemon essence.
3. Beat the egg whites until firm and fold them into the mixture using a metal spoon.
4. Pour the batter into a greased and lined 20 cm/8 in square cake tin and stand the tin on a steamer rack in a wok or pan over simmering water.
5. Cover and simmer for about 25 minutes until a skewer inserted in the centre comes out clean.
6. Allow it to cool slightly in the tin then turn out and serve hot, chopped into squares.

STEAMED PEARS

Yield: 4 Servings

Ingredients:

- 4 pears, peeled
- 60 ml/4 tbsp honey

Directions:

1. Chop off the tops of the pears about 2½ cm/1 in from the top and save the tops for later.
2. Core the pears from the top, shaping a deep hole without cutting through the base.
3. Fill with honey and replace the tops.
4. Lay out the pears in a container on a rack in a wok or a pan with water in the bottom to come immediately below the steaming rack.
5. Boil the water, cover and steam for approximately twenty minutes, topping up with boiling water as needed, until the pears are cooked.
6. The length of time will vary with the size and ripeness of the pears.

SUGARED NUTS

Yield: 4 Servings

Ingredients:

- 100 g/4 oz/½ cup sugar
- 120 ml/4 fl oz/½ cup groundnut (peanut) oil
- 225 g/8 oz shelled walnuts
- 300 ml/½ pt/1¼ cups boiling water

Directions:

1. Put the walnuts into a container and pour over the boiling water.
2. Allow to stand for half an hour then eliminate the excess liquid and dry well.
3. Combine the sugar and oil over a low heat, stirring until the sugar dissolves.
4. Put in the nuts and stir until well coated.

SWEET CHESTNUT BALLS

Yield: 4 Servings

Ingredients:

- 2½ ml/½ tsp cinnamon
- 450 g/1 lb chestnuts
- 75 g/3 oz/¼ cup honey
- 75 g/3 oz/heaped ¼ cup icing sugar

Directions:

1. Score the chestnuts, immerse into boiling water and cook for approximately twenty minutes until the shells burst.
2. Drain, cool and shell.
3. Mince the chestnuts, blend with the honey and shaped into balls.
4. Combine the sugar and cinnamon and roll the chestnut balls in to mixture until coated.

SWEET GINGER BALLS

Yield: 4 Servings

Ingredients:

- 1 sachet easy-mix yeast
- 15 ml/1 tbsp caster sugar
- 15 ml/1 tbsp rice wine or dry sherry
- 2½ ml/½ tsp salt
- 25 g/1 oz/¼ cup walnuts, chopped
- 30 ml/2 tbsp butter
- 300 ml/½ pt/1¼ cups warm milk or water
- 450 g/1 lb/4 cups strong plain (all-purpose) flour
- 50 g/2 oz/ ¼ cup glacé cherries
- 50 g/2 oz/heaped ¼ cup chopped mixed peel
- 50 g/2 oz/heaped ¼ cup dates, chopped
- pinch of ground ginger

Directions:

1. Sift the flour into a bowl.
2. Rub in the butter then add the sugar, salt and yeast.
3. Work in the warm milk or water and knead to a smooth dough.
4. Cover and leave in a warm place for 45 minutes.
5. Combine all the rest of the ingredients.
6. Knead the dough and shape it into 18 small balls.
7. Press them flat, spoon some of the mixture into each and close the dough around the filling.
8. Put the balls in a steamer basket, cover and leave to rise in a warm place for half an hour.
9. Simmer over slightly sweetened water for about 30 minutes.

SWEET PEANUT SOUP

Yield: 4 Servings

Ingredients:

- 1.5 l/2½ pts/6 cups water
- 10 ml/2 tsp bicarbonate of soda (baking soda)
- 225 g/8 oz peanuts
- 225 g/8 oz/1 cup brown sugar

Directions:

1. Heat the water to lukewarm then mix in the bicarbonate of soda.
2. Put in the peanuts and bring to the boil.
3. Cover and simmer for about 1½ hours until soft.
4. Put in the sugar and simmer gently, stirring, until the sugar has dissolved.
5. Serve hot in small bowls.

SWEET PURÉED WATER CHESTNUTS

Yield: 4 Servings

Ingredients:

- 2 glacé cherries, sliced
- 225 g/8 oz sugar
- 450 g/1 lb water chestnuts
- 600 ml/1 pt/2½ cups water

Directions:

1. Purée the water chestnuts in a food processor.
2. Dissolve the sugar in the water over a low heat then mix in the water chestnuts and simmer gently until heated through and thickened.
3. Serve Immediately.

TOFFEE APPLES

Yield: 4 Servings

Ingredients:

- 1 egg
- 175 g/6 oz sugar
- 3 firm dessert apples, peeled and chop into wedges
- 30 ml/2 tbsp sesame seeds
- 300 ml/½ pt/generous ½ cup groundnut (peanut) oil
- 5 ml/1 tsp sesame oil

- 50 g/2 oz plain (all-purpose) flour

Directions:

1. Combine the flour, egg and sesame oil to a smooth batter.
2. Put in the apples.
3. Heat the groundnut (peanut) oil and deep-fry a few pieces of fruit at a time for about 2 minutes until a golden-brown colour is achieved.
4. Drain using kitchen paper and keep them warm while you fry the rest of the fruit pieces.
5. Reheat the oil and deep-fry the fruit for another 2 minutes then eliminate the excess liquid on kitchen paper.
6. In the meantime, mix the sugar, sesame seeds and 30 ml/2 tbsp oil from the deep-frying pan and heat until the mixture begins to caramelise.
7. Stir the fruit into the caramel a few at a time then place then in iced water to harden.
8. Remove from the water and serve instantly.

WATER CHESTNUT PUDDING

Yield: 4 Servings

Ingredients:

- 100 g/4 oz/½ cup brown sugar
- 100 g/4 oz/1 cup water chestnut flour
- 120 ml/4 fl oz/½ cup water
- 600 ml/1 pt/ 2½ cups water

Directions:

1. Combine the chestnut flour with the first quantity of water and place in a heatproof bowl.
2. Blend in the sugar and rest of the water then cover the bowl.
3. Put on a steaming rack over boiling water and steam for one hour.
4. Serve hot or cold.

WATER MELON IN GINGER WINE

Yield: 4 Servings

Ingredients:

- ½ water melon
- 120 ml/4 fl oz/½ cup ginger wine
- 25 g/1 oz candied ginger, chopped into slivers
- 250 ml/8 fl oz/1 cup water
- 30 ml/2 tbsp sugar

Directions:

1. Shape the melon into balls, using a melon baller, removing the seeds as needed.
2. Combine the water, ginger wine and sugar in a small pan.
3. Cook over a medium heat, stirring until the sugar dissolves and the mixture is hot.
4. Turn off the heat.
5. Mix in the ginger, pour over the melon then cool and refrigerate for several hours, preferably overnight, and serve.

PICKLES, TEAS, & OTHER PRESERVES

If you're into canning and pickling, you will find a few gems here.

ALMOND CUSTARD TEA

Yield: 4 Servings

Ingredients:

- 1.5 l/2½ pts/6 cups water
- 100 g/4 oz ground almonds
- 100 g/4 oz/½ cup long-grain rice
- 100 g/4 oz/½ cup sugar
- 2½ ml/½ tsp salt
- 5 ml/1 tsp vanilla essence (extract)

Directions:

1. Soak the rice overnight in cold water to cover then eliminate the excess liquid well.
2. Put in the almonds and the water and soak for one hour then stir thoroughly.
3. Strain and squeeze the liquid into the top of a double boiler over gently simmering water.
4. Simmer gently, stirring, until the mixture becomes thick then mix in the sugar, salt and vanilla essence, bring to the boil and serve warm in small bowls.

CHINESE PICKLED VEGETABLES

Yield: 450 g/1 lb

Ingredients:

- 1 cucumber, cubed
- 1 green pepper, chopped into chunks
- 1 head celery, roughly chopped
- 1 head Chinese leaves, chopped into chunks
- 1 leek, sliced
- 1 red pepper, chopped into chunks
- 10 ml/2 tsp peppercorns

- 100 g/4 oz green beans, chopped into chunks
- 100 g/4 oz salt
- 100 g/4 oz shallots
- 2 l/3½ pts/8½ cups boiled water
- 30 ml/2 tbsp wine vinegar
- 50 g/2 oz dried red chilli peppers
- 50 g/2 oz ginger root, sliced
- 50 g/2 oz/¼ cup brown sugar

Directions:

1. Combine all the spice ingredients with the water in a large jar.
2. Put in the prepared vegetables, stir thoroughly, seal and store in a cool place for at least 5 days and serve.
3. Nibbles and Drinks
4. The Chinese have enjoyed tea as a refreshing drink since the end of the sixth century and tea is now the most common drink in Chinese homes.
5. There are two types – green and black – which differ because of the way the leaves are dried, and each has its own special flavour.
6. Many Chinese teas are available in supermarkets and delicatessens, some of the most popular being Lapsang Souchong, Jasmine and Oolong.
7. The Chinese also make some sweet teas which are served as a refreshing sweet dessert drink at the end of a meal.

CRISPY PINE NUTS

Yield: 4 Servings

Ingredients:

- 100 g/4 oz pine nuts
- 450 ml/¾ pt/2 cups water
- 50 g/2 oz brown sugar
- oil for deep-frying

Directions:

1. Dissolve the sugar in the water over a low heat, add the pine nuts and bring to the boil.
2. Simmer for approximately three minutes then remove from the heat and allow to stand for 6 hours.

3. Drain thoroughly and leave to dry.
4. Heat the oil until moderately hot and deep-fry the pine nuts until a golden-brown colour is achieved.
5. Drain thoroughly then spread out and allow to cool, stirring intermittently so that they do not stick together.

FRIED CASHEWS

Yield: 4 Servings

Ingredients:

- 2½ ml/½ tsp five-spice powder
- 225 g/8 oz cashew nuts
- groundnut (peanut) oil for deep-frying
- pinch of chilli powder
- salt and freshly ground pepper

Directions:

1. Heat the oil then fry the nuts until slightly browned.
2. Transfer the nuts to a hot frying pan, add the spices and toss over a medium heat for a few minutes until well coated.
3. Cool and serve.

GRAPEFRUIT TEA

Yield: 4 Servings

Ingredients:

- 1 l/1¾ pts/4 cups water
- 100 g/4 oz/½ cup brown sugar
- 30 ml/2 tbsp cornflour (cornstarch)
- 450 g/1 lb canned grapefruit segments in syrup

Directions:

1. Bring half the water to the boil, add the grapefruit and syrup and the sugar and stir until the sugar dissolves then add the rest of the water.
2. Blend the cornflour with a little cold water then mix it into the mixture and bring to the boil.
3. Simmer, stirring, until the mixture becomes thick.
4. Serve hot in small bowls.

HOT LOTUS TEA

Yield: 4 Servings

Ingredients:

- 1.2 l/2 pts/5 cups water
- 2 eggs, slightly beaten
- 2½ ml/½ tsp bicarbonate of soda (baking soda)
- 225 g/8 oz brown sugar
- 450 g/1 lb lotus seeds
- 900 ml/1½ pts/3¾ cups water

Directions:

1. Bring the water to the boil, mix in the bicarbonate of soda, pour over the lotus seeds and allow to stand for 10 minutes.
2. Rub the seeds with your fingers to remove the husks.
3. Rinse and drain.
4. Bring the second quantity of water to the boil, mix in the sugar until dissolved then add the lotus seeds, cover and simmer for one hour.
5. Progressively mix in the eggs, remove from the heat and serve instantly.

MANGO PICKLE

Yield: 450 g/1 lb

Ingredients:

- 10 ml/2 tsp salt
- 10 ml/2 tsp sugar

- 450 g/1 lb unripe mango, peeled and sliced
- 60 ml/4 tbsp wine vinegar
- pinch of freshly ground pepper

Directions:

1. Season the mango with salt and pepper and add the vinegar and sugar.
2. Stir thoroughly and allow to marinate for at least 2 hours before serving with fish or cold meats.

ORANGE TEA

Yield: 4 Servings

Ingredients:

- 100 g/4 oz/½ cup sugar
- 3 oranges
- 30 ml/2 tbsp cornflour (cornstarch)
- 750 ml/1¼ pts/3 cups water

Directions:

1. Peel and seed the oranges, removing the pith and membranes.
2. Catch the juice and chop the flesh roughly.
3. Combine the cornflour, sugar and water and bring to the boil, stirring constantly.
4. Put in the orange juice and flesh and heat through gently, stirring.
5. Serve hot in small bowls.

PICKLED CABBAGE

Yield: 450 g/1 lb

Ingredients:

- 15 ml/1 tbsp brown sugar
- 15 ml/1 tbsp soy sauce
- 2½ ml/½ tsp salt
- 30 ml/2 tbsp groundnut (peanut) oil

- 30 ml/2 tbsp wine vinegar
- 450 g/1 lb white cabbage, cubed

Directions:

1. Heat half the oil and stir-fry the cabbage for about 3 minutes until translucent but still crisp.
2. Move to a bowl.
3. Heat the rest of the oil and heat the sugar, sauce, wine vinegar and salt, stirring until the sugar dissolves.
4. Pour over the cabbage and toss.
5. Move to a screw-top jar and refrigerate overnight.

PICKLED CELERY

Yield: 225 g/8 oz

Ingredients:

- 15 ml/1 tbsp soy sauce
- 15 ml/1 tbsp wine vinegar
- 2½ ml/½ tsp salt
- 2½ ml/½ tsp sugar
- 6 stalks celery, chopped into chunks
- few drops of sesame oil

Directions:

1. Briefly boil the celery in boiling water for approximately two minutes then eliminate the excess liquid well.
2. Combine the rest of the ingredients, pour over the celery and toss.
3. Cover and chill for approximately twenty minutes.

PINEAPPLE TEA

Yield: 4 Servings

Ingredients:

- 100 g/4 oz/½ cup brown sugar
- 450 g/1 lb canned pineapple in syrup, crushed
- 75 g/3 oz/¼ cup honey
- 75 ml/1¼ pts/3 cups water

Directions:

1. Combine all the ingredients together in a pan, bring to the boil then simmer gently for approximately fifteen minutes, stirring often.
2. Serve hot in small bowls.

PRESERVED KUMQUATS

Yield: 900 g/2 lb

Ingredients:

- 225 g/8 oz/1 cup sugar
- 50 g/2 oz stem ginger, minced
- 600 ml/1 pt/2½ cups water
- 675 g/1½ lb kumquats
- juice of 1 lime

Directions:

1. Puncture each kumquat in 4 places with a large needle.
2. Put all the ingredients in a large pan, bring to the boil then simmer until the liquid becomes thick and translucent.
3. Seal in warmed jars.

ROASTED SPICED NUTS

Yield: 4 Servings

Ingredients:

- 10 ml/2 tsp salt
- 2½ ml/½ tsp five-spice powder
- 450 g/1 lb/4 cups shelled peanuts

- 60 ml/4 tbsp water

Directions:

1. Dissolve the salt in the water over a gentle heat, then mix in the five-spice powder.
2. Mix in the peanuts and thoroughly stir together.
3. Spread the peanuts out in a roasting tin and roast in a preheated oven at 140°C/275°F/gas mark 1 for about 1 hour until golden, stirring intermittently.

TURNIP PICKLE

Yield: 450 g/1 lb

- 10 ml/2 tsp minced ginger root
- 10 ml/2 tsp salt
- 25 g/1 oz/2 tbsp sugar
- 45 ml/3 tbsp rice wine or dry sherry
- 45 ml/3 tbsp soy sauce
- 450 g/1 lb turnips, sliced
- 90 ml/6 tbsp wine vinegar

Directions:

1. Combine all the ingredients together well and place in a screw-top jar.
2. Cover and store in the refrigerator for 3 days before serving with duck or pork.

WALNUT TEA

Yield: 4 Servings

Ingredients:

- 100 g/4 oz/½ cup sugar
- 30 ml/2 tbsp cornflour (cornstarch)
- 45 g/1 lb shelled walnuts
- 60 ml/4 tbsp vegetable oil
- 600 ml/1 pt/2½ cups water
- pinch of salt

Directions:

1. Put the walnuts in a pan, cover with water, bring to the boil and simmer for 10 minutes.
2. Turn off the heat and allow to cool.
3. Rub off the walnut skins then eliminate the excess liquid the walnuts on kitchen paper.
4. Heat the oil in a wok and fry the walnuts for a few minutes until a golden-brown colour is achieved.
5. Drain and allow to cool.
6. Grind them finely in a blender or crush with a rolling pin.
7. Bring the water, sugar to taste, and salt to the boil and mix in the walnuts.
8. Combine the cornflour with a little water then stir into the tea.
9. Simmer, stirring, until heated through and translucent.
10. Serve after a banquet.

ENDNOTE

Thank your for purchasing this book! Don't forget to leave a review on amazon so I can make any changes required to this book, and do better in my future publications.

Good luck, and happy cooking.... And Happy eating!!

Made in the USA
Middletown, DE
27 May 2021

40455004R00418